Quantitative Methods for Decision Making using Excel

Quantitative Methods for Decision Making using Excel

Glyn Davis | Branko Pecar

OXFORD
UNIVERSITY PRESS

Great Clarendon Street, Oxford, OX2 6DP,
United Kingdom

Oxford University Press is a department of the University of Oxford. It furthers the University's objective of excellence in research, scholarship, and education by publishing worldwide. Oxford is a registered trade mark of Oxford University Press in the UK and in certain other countries

Impression: 1

British Library Cataloguing in Publication Data
Data available

ISBN 978-0-19-969406-8

Printed in Italy by
L.E.G.O. S.p.A. — Lavis TN

Preface

Quantitative Methods for Decision Making using Excel is the perfect introduction to key quantitative method techniques that are used to solve problems in the real business world. The book and online support materials are designed to allow you to develop your key numeracy skills and develop your confidence in using quantitative methods in solving problems. Furthermore, the emphasis on the use of Excel will allow you to gain confidence in handling and analysing numerical data together with improving your skills in the use of a standard business software package. Detailed Excel screenshot graphics are employed within the text and online resources to enable students to understand the application of Excel in solving problems.

The textbook assumes no prior knowledge and starts with a refresher course in key numerical skills. Further chapters explore key quantitative methods techniques applied to the functional areas of business such as decision making in marketing and finance. Finally, the Online Resource Centre includes visual walkthrough flash movies that provide further reinforcement to the student of the use of Excel.

Unique features of the book

- Accurate map of the table of contents to a typical Quantitative Methods for Decision Making courses in the UK and Europe.
- Short and concise: many of the leading textbooks in this market, while excellent in their way, have become too big and unwieldy for students to use within a typical 15 week-programme. This book combines rigour, accuracy, shorter length, and practicality at a reasonable price.
- Selection of most frequently used methods in accordance with the major enterprise functions (marketing, sales, business development, manufacturing, quality, and finance).
- Flexibility: can be used either as a one-semester or two-semester course core textbook.
- Refresher chapter in key numerical skills.
- Full integration of Excel exercises and applications both within the textbook and through the website to allow real flexibility to lecturers for teaching through a variety of learning schemes: classroom-led or self-directed study.
- The use of Excel as the primary application tool for explaining the mechanics of the methods as well as for explaining how to solve real-life problems.
- Detailed use of graphics (screenshots) to illustrate the use of Excel in solving problems.
- Detailed online examples using real-life data with complete solutions.
- Visual walkthrough flash movies taking students step by step through the mechanics of the application process using Excel.

For students

- Data from exercises in the book.
- Visual walkthrough flash movies—a set of flash movies exploring the use of Excel in solving key examples from the textbook.
- Online glossary.
- Revision tips.
- Critical test statistics for Z, T, F, chi-square, and binomial distributions.

For lecturers

- A complete set of PowerPoint presentations for each chapter.
- Instructor's manual containing a complete set of exercise and techniques in practice solutions.
- Excel files containing: (a) exercise data, and (b) a complete set of Excel exercise and techniques in practice solutions.
- A complete set of test bank questions with answers.

Hints on using the book

The sequence of chapters has been arranged so that there is a progressive accumulation of knowledge. Each chapter guides students step by step through the theoretical and spreadsheet skills required. Chapters also contain exercises that give students the chance to check their progress.

To make the most effective use of this book:

- Be patient and work slowly and methodically, especially in the early stages when progress may be slow.
- Do not omit items or 'jump around' between chapters; each chapter builds upon knowledge and skills previously gained. You may also find that the Excel applications that you develop require earlier ones in order to be effective.
- Try not to compare your progress with others too much. Fastest is not always best!
- Do not try to achieve too much in one session. Time for rest and reflection is important.
- Mistakes are part of learning. Do not worry about them. The more you repeat something, the fewer mistakes you will make.
- Make time to complete the exercises, especially if you are learning on your own. They are your best route to progress.

The visual walkthrough flash movies have been developed to explore using Excel to solve a particular numerical problem. If you are not sure about the Excel solution then use the visual walkthrough flash movie as a reminder.

Brief Contents

Detailed Contents

4 Prediction and forecasting 150

How to use this Book

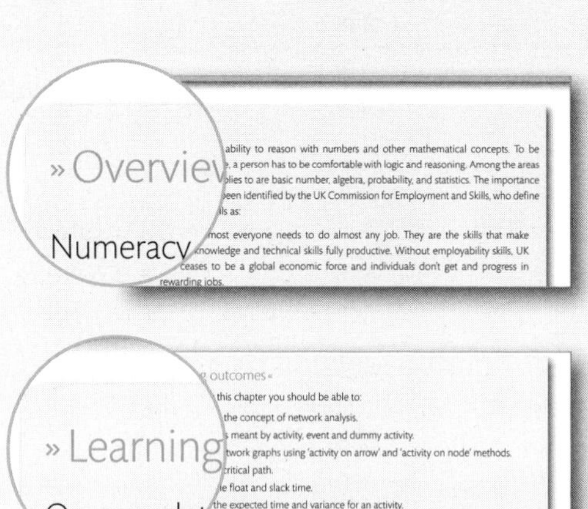

Chapter overview

A concise overview can be found at the beginning of each chapter to help guide you through the different topics you will encounter in this section of the book and enable you to quickly navigate your way around specific topics that will be addressed.

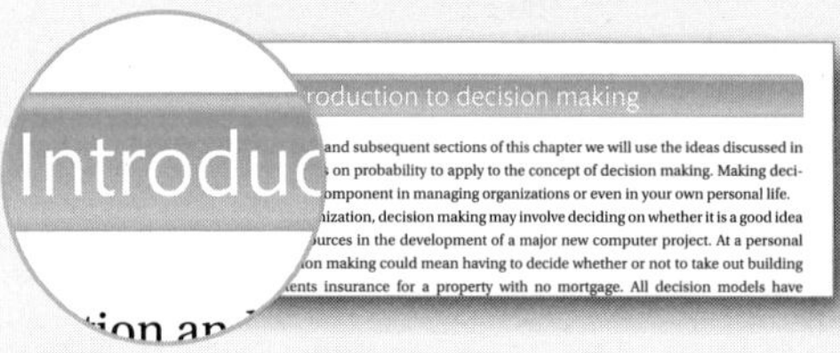

Learning objectives

Each chapter identifies the key learning objectives that you will be able to achieve having completed the unit. They also serve as helpful summaries of essential concepts during revision.

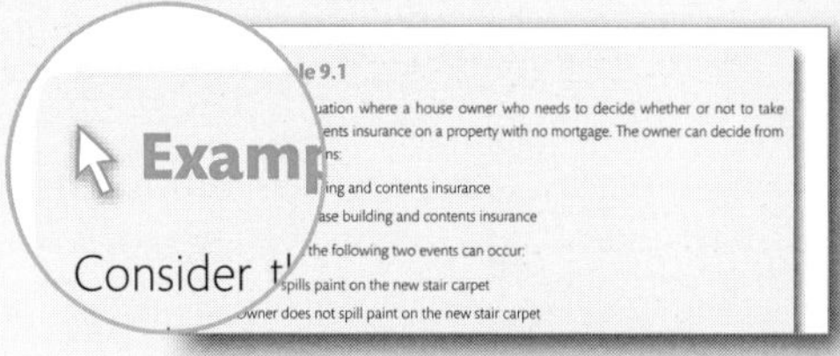

Introduction

Each chapter will begin with an introduction to set the scene for the unit and introduce topics, techniques, and skills that will be covered.

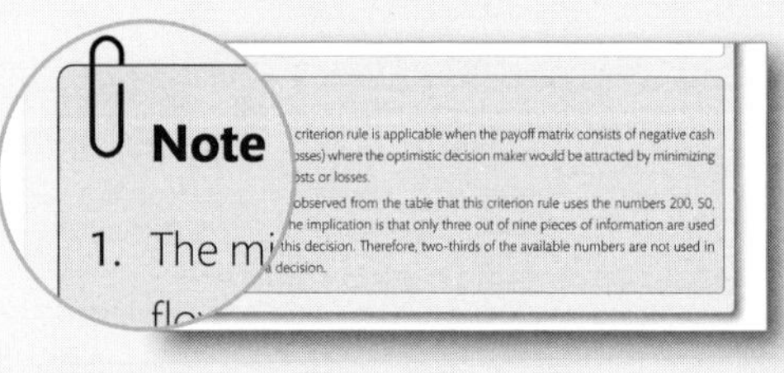

Example boxes

Detailed worked examples run throughout each chapter to demonstrate how the techniques translate from theory into practice. Concepts are broken down into clear and logical phases and frequently accompanied by step-by-step Excel screenshots to guide you through processes.

Note boxes

The note boxes feature throughout each chapter and present additional information, including crucial points to consider as well as areas where extra care should be taken, or particular exceptions to rules.

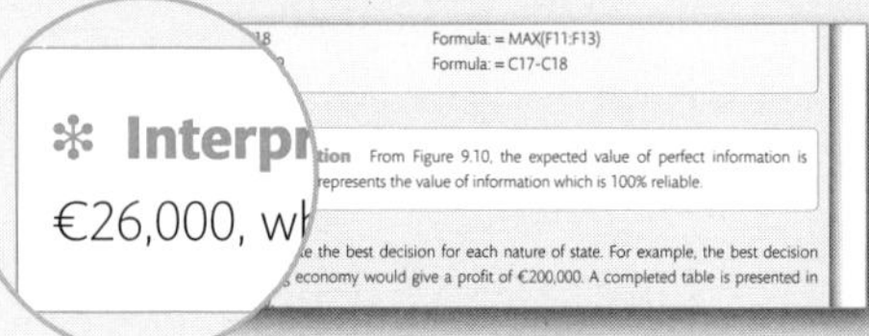

Interpretation boxes

Interpretation boxes appear throughout each chapter and provide you with further explanations to aid your understanding of the concepts and techniques being discussed.

Techniques in practice

These are a type of practice exercise which appear at the end of every chapter and offer questions that will test your knowledge of the skills learnt in that particular unit. These have been tailored to exemplify techniques that can be applied in the 'real' working environment.

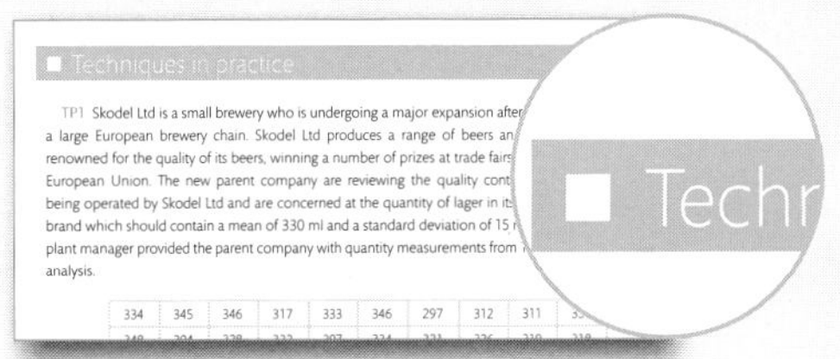
■ Techniques in practice

TP1 Skodel Ltd is a small brewery who is undergoing a major expansion after a large European brewery chain. Skodel Ltd produces a range of beers an renowned for the quality of its beers, winning a number of prizes at trade fairs European Union. The new parent company are reviewing the quality cont being operated by Skodel Ltd and are concerned at the quantity of lager in its brand which should contain a mean of 330 ml and a standard deviation of 15 plant manager provided the parent company with quantity measurements from analysis.

334	345	346	317	333	346	297	312	311

Step-by-step Excel guidance

Excel screenshots are fully integrated throughout the text to illustrate Excel formulas, functions, and solutions to provide you with logical step-by-step guidance on solving the statistical problems presented.

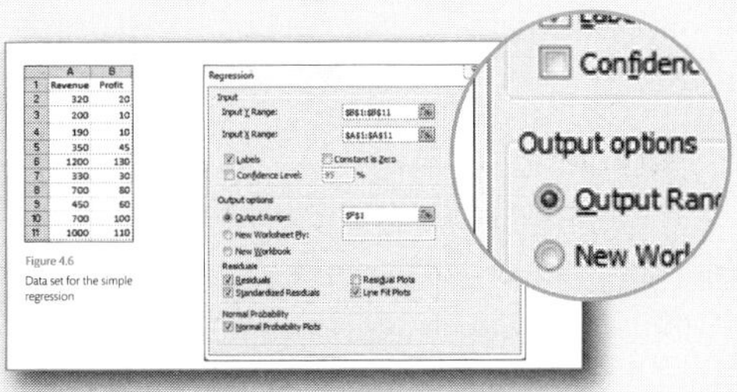

Figure 4.6
Data set for the simple regression

Student exercises

Each chapter will regularly present opportunities for you to test your knowledge and understanding of the topics covered through a range of student exercises. You can independently monitor your progress by checking the solutions which can be found on the accompanying Online Resource Centre for the textbook.

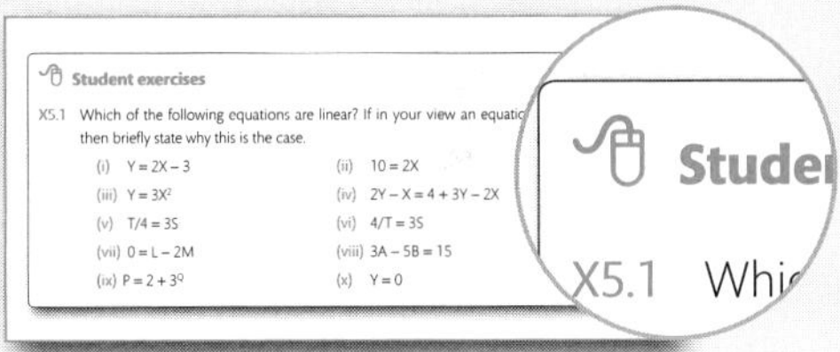
Student exercises

X5.1 Which of the following equations are linear? If in your view an equatio then briefly state why this is the case.

(i) Y = 2X − 3	(ii) 10 = 2X
(iii) Y = 3X²	(iv) 2Y − X = 4 + 3Y − 2X
(v) T/4 = 35	(vi) 4/T = 35
(vii) 0 = L − 2M	(viii) 3A − 5B = 15
(ix) P = 2 + 3²	(x) Y = 0

Glossary

Key terminology will be identified throughout each chapter and you can familiarize yourself with their corresponding definitions which will appear in the margin. A full glossary can also be located at the back of the book and on the Online Resource Centre.

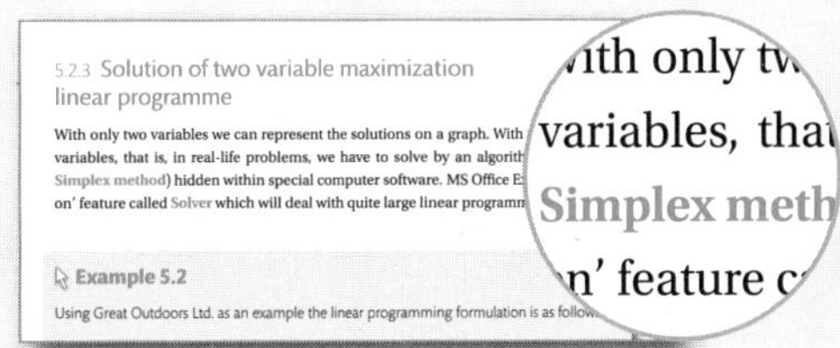
5.2.3 Solution of two variable maximization linear programme

With only two variables we can represent the solutions on a graph. With variables, that is, in real-life problems, we have to solve by an algorith Simplex method) hidden within special computer software. MS Office E on' feature called Solver which will deal with quite large linear programm

Example 5.2

Using Great Outdoors Ltd. as an example the linear programming formulation is as follow

Chapter summary

Each chapter ends with an overview of the techniques covered and is an ideal tool to help you check your understanding of core areas in that unit.

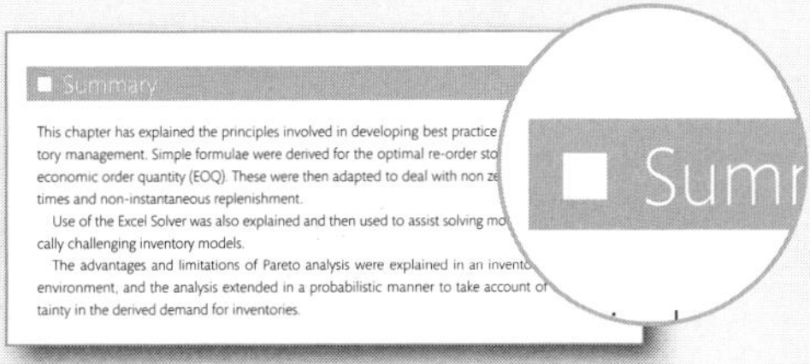
■ Summary

This chapter has explained the principles involved in developing best practice tory management. Simple formulae were derived for the optimal re-order sto economic order quantity (EOQ). These were then adapted to deal with non ze times and non-instantaneous replenishment.

Use of the Excel Solver was also explained and then used to assist solving mo cally challenging inventory models.

The advantages and limitations of Pareto analysis were explained in an invento environment, and the analysis extended in a probabilistic manner to take account o tainty in the derived demand for inventories.

Further reading

At the end of each chapter you will find a list of recommended reading to help direct you to further reliable sources which will explore a particular subject area in more depth. Annotated web links are also provided to help you locate additional statistical resources.

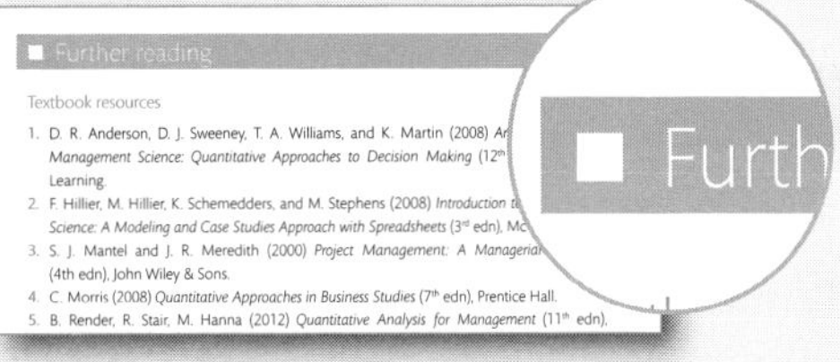
■ Further reading

Textbook resources

1. D. R. Anderson, D. J. Sweeney, T. A. Williams, and K. Martin (2008) *An Management Science: Quantitative Approaches to Decision Making* (12th Learning.
2. F. Hillier, M. Hillier, K. Schemedders, and M. Stephens (2008) *Introduction to Science: A Modeling and Case Studies Approach with Spreadsheets* (3rd edn), Mc
3. S. J. Mantel and J. R. Meredith (2000) *Project Management: A Manageria* (4th edn), John Wiley & Sons.
4. C. Morris (2008) *Quantitative Approaches in Business Studies* (7th edn), Prentice Hall.
5. B. Render, R. Stair, M. Hanna (2012) *Quantitative Analysis for Management* (11th edn).

How to use the Online Resource Centre

www.oxfordtextbooks.co.uk/orc/davis_pecar_qm/

Free resources available to students include:

Numerical skills workbook

The authors have provided a numerical skills refresher course which is packed with exercises and examples to help equip you with the essential skills you will need to confidently approach topics in the textbook.

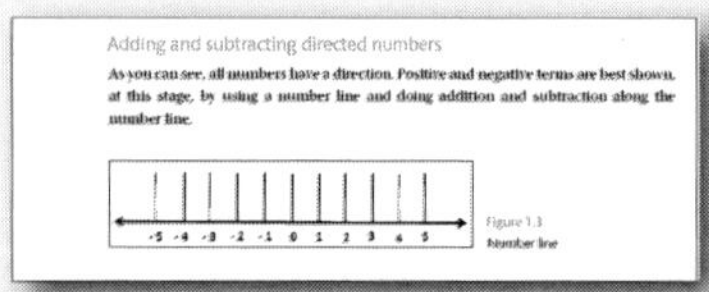

Adding and subtracting directed numbers

As you can see, all numbers have a direction. Positive and negative terms are best shown, at this stage, by using a number line and doing addition and subtraction along the number line.

Figure 1.3 Number line

Data from exercises in the book

Raw data from the textbook examples and exercises is available to assist you in self-study and revision.

Online glossary of terms

Key glossary terms from the textbook have been placed online along with their definitions for use as a quick revision and reference tool.

Revision tips

As experts in the field, the authors have offered a series of helpful revision tips that will help you consolidate your learning and assist you in your exam preparation.

Visual walkthroughs

An assortment of Flash movies cover a variety of quantitative methods applications to guide you through the processes you have seen in the book.

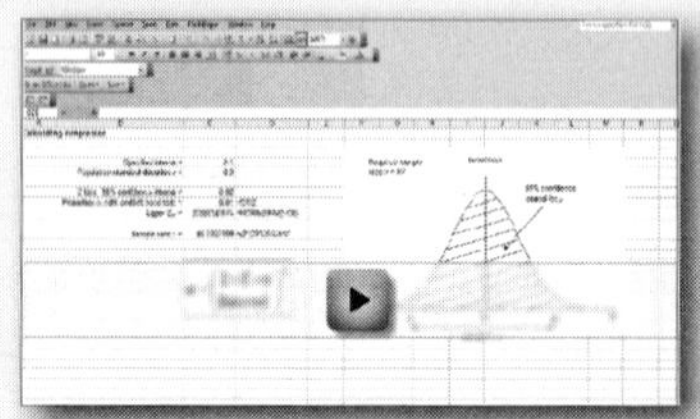

Resources for registered adopters of the textbook include:

Instructor's manual

This resource includes a chapter-by-chapter guide to structuring lectures and seminars as well as teaching tips and solutions from the techniques and exercises in the text.

Aims of the book

Qua tative Methods for Decision Making Using Excel is the perf
key quantitative method techniques that are used to solve problem
business world. The textbook and online support materials are de
to develop your key numeracy skills and develop your confidence
quantitative methods in solving problems. Furthermore, the empha
Excel will allow you to gain confidence in handling and analysing

PowerPoint presentations

A suite of fully customizable PowerPoint slides have been designed by the authors to assist you in your lectures and presentations.

Test bank

Each chapter of the book is accompanied by a bank of assorted questions, covering a variety of techniques for the topics covered, including multiple-choice questions, multiple-response, and true or false questions.

Test banks provide a ready-made electronic testing resource, which can be customis
to meet your teaching needs. Whilst every effort has been made to ensure that this
resource will be error free we suggest that you check that it meets your requirements
before using it for assessment or other purposes.

This test bank contains 116 questions. These are organised in groups to accompany t
11 chapters in the textbook.

Click on one of the options below:

Assignment and examination questions

This section of the site offers a comprehensive set of assignment and examination questions for you to set your students, enabling them to practise answering a range of in-depth and exam-style questions.

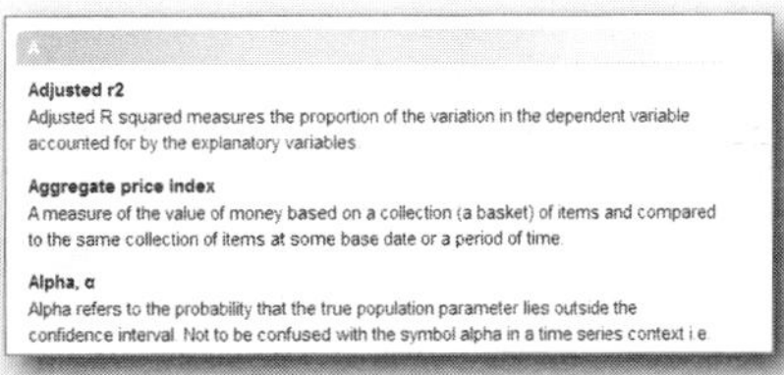

Adjusted r2
Adjusted R squared measures the proportion of the variation in the dependent variable accounted for by the explanatory variables

Aggregate price index
A measure of the value of money based on a collection (a basket) of items and compared to the same collection of items at some base date or a period of time

Alpha, α
Alpha refers to the probability that the true population parameter lies outside the confidence interval Not to be confused with the symbol alpha in a time series context i.e

Contributors

Glyn Davis, BSc, PGCE, MSc, MPhil, FHEA, Principal Lecturer in e-Business and Data Analysis, Teesside University.

Branko Pecar, Ph.D., Visiting Fellow, University of Gloucestershire.

Martyn Jarvis, BSc, MSc, Senior Lecturer in Quantitative Methods, Faculty of Business and Society, University of Glamorgan.

David Ward, PhD, Technical-Managerial consultant specialising in Innovation, Engineering Design, Strategy and Applied Quantitative methods.

David Whigham, M.A. M.Phil.

Part I

Refresher Course in Business Mathematics and Statistics

Refresher course in key numerical skills

1

» Overview «

Numeracy is the ability to reason with numbers and other mathematical concepts. To be numerically literate, a person has to be comfortable with logic and reasoning. Among the areas that numeracy applies to are basic number, algebra, probability, and statistics. The importance of numeracy has been identified by the UK Commission for Employment and Skills, who define employability skills as:

> the skills almost everyone needs to do almost any job. They are the skills that make specific knowledge and technical skills fully productive. Without employability skills, UK PLC ceases to be a global economic force and individuals don't get and progress in rewarding jobs.

Furthermore, the report identified literacy, language, numeracy and ICT skills underpin employability skills, as illustrated in Figure 1.1.

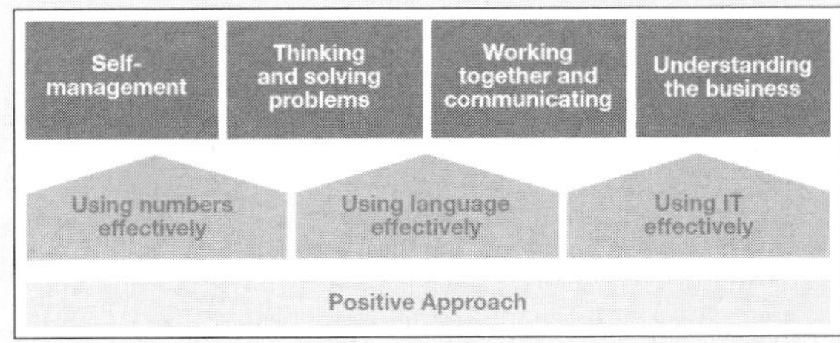

Figure 1.1

Source: UKCES (2009), p. 11.

So, what numerical skills matter most in solving business problems? In terms of quantitative methods, the core areas of arithmetic, algebra, mathematical modelling, and statistics are most often applied to solve real business problems. A real business problem requires formulating a multi-stepped plan for addressing the question(s), tracking down relevant information and making realistic assumptions, estimating the answer(s), performing required calculations (which often require the use of calculators or computer software), evaluating the outcomes, and communicating the findings. The aim of this chapter is to briefly outline the key numerical skills required to enable the reader to tackle the topics found in this textbook. The aim of the online workbook is to provide the reader with a set of tools that can be used to study the topics in this textbook, that will be useful to you throughout your studies, and will make you more employable.

» Learning objectives «

On completion of this chapter you should be able to:

- » Understand terms such as square and square root, indices, and standard form (or scientific notation).
- » Identify a simple equation and solve it.
- » Understand what a logarithm represents.
- » Identify both linear and non-linear equations.
- » Locate information on Excel 2010 mathematical functions.
- » Plot a graph of y against x where the relationship between y and x is linear or non-linear.
- » Describe change using calculus.

1.1 Basic algebra

1.1.1 Squares

The square of a number is that number multiplied by itself. For example, 'three squared' is written 3^2, which means $3 \times 3 = 9$, and 'four squared' is written 4^2, which means $4 \times 4 = 16$.

1.1.2 Square roots

The square root of a number is a value that can be multiplied by itself to give the original number. The sign $\sqrt{4}$ means the square root of the number 4. For example, $\sqrt{16} = \sqrt{4 \times 4} = 4$.

1.1.3 Indices

The index is the power of a number. The number 2^3 is said 'two to the power three' or 'two cubed' and means $2 * 2 * 2 = 8$. The number 3^2 is said 'three to the power two' or 'three squared' and means $3 * 3 = 9$. We could use the method described earlier to calculate 2^3 or we could use the Excel symbol ^ or Excel function POWER () to undertake the calculation.

1.1.4 To solve simple equations

Here are some examples of very simple equations: $2a = 8$, $a + 2 = 4$, $3a + 6 = a + 10$, $3(a + 2) = 9$. In all these examples, there are letters and numbers on both sides of the equals sign and the letters have no powers higher than 1. (i.e. there are no a^2 or a^3 or b^2 or b^3 terms). Your answer must have a letter, which must be positive, on one side of the = sign, and a number on the other side. It does not matter which side of the equals sign the letter is. To solve simple equations you must follow a set of rules. For example, solve the equation $3(a + 2) = 9$ for the unknown term.

X

standard form (or scientific notation) a number written in the form $A * 10^n$.

equation algebraic formula that shows the relationship between variables, saying that the value of one expression equals the value of the second expression.

logarithm the value of n when a number is represented in the logarithmic format $b^n = x$.

square of a number is that number multiplied by itself.

square root of a number the square root of n ($\sqrt{n}$) is the number that is multiplied by itself to give n.

index or index number a number that compares the value of a variable at any point in time with its value in a base period.

simple equations equations containing but one unknown quantity, and that quantity only in the first degree.

Step 1 Remove any brackets by multiplying them out: $3(a+2)=9$, $3a+6=9$.

Step 2 Put all the terms containing letters on one side and numbers on the other side: $3a+6=9$, $3a=9-6$, $3a=3$, $a=3/3=1$. Check by substituting $a=1$ into equation $3(a+2) = 3a+6=9=3(1)+6=3+6=9$.

1.1.5 Standard form (or scientific notation)

Very large and very small numbers must sometimes be expressed in standard form (also called scientific notation), $A * 10^n$, where $1 < A < 10$ and n is an integer. In other words, this means that A must be a number between 1 and 10 and n is a positive or negative number. Here is an example to clarify how we can write a number using standard form. For example, the number 87,000 can be written in standard form as 8.7×10^4.

1.1.6 Logarithms and exponential functions

The logarithm was invented by John Napier (*c*.1614) and developed by Napier and Professor Briggs (*c*.1624) to aid in the calculation process of index numbers. The term is an alternative word for an index or power of a given positive number base. For example, in $3^2 = 9$ we define the index (or exponent) 2 to be the logarithm of 9 to the base of 3 and write $2 = \log_3 9$. For example, consider calculating the value of 10^4. We can solve this problem by multiplying 10 by itself 4 times: $10^4 = 10 \times 10 \times 10 \times 10 = 10{,}000$. This can be written in index form as $10^4 = 10{,}000$. Then, $\log_{10} 10{,}000 = 4$. The logarithm of 10,000 to the base 10 is 4. The number 4 is the exponent to which 10 must be raised to produce 10,000.

Note In general, when $b^n = x$ then $\log_b x = n$.

1. $10^4 = 10{,}000$ is called the exponential form.
2. $\text{Log}_{10}\, 10{,}000 = 4$ is called the logarithmic form.

In practice, only two types of logarithm are used: (1) **common logarithms**, and (2) **natural logarithms**. The system of common logarithms has 10 as its base. When the base is not indicated, log 100 = 2, then the system of common logarithms (base 10) is implied. The natural logarithms use the base e, where e is named after the eighteenth-century Swiss mathematician Leonhard Euler. The numerical value of e = 2.71828182845904..... can be obtained from the following series involving factorials:

$$e = 1 + \frac{1}{1!} + \frac{1}{2!} + \frac{1}{3!} + \ldots\ldots\ldots\ldots + \frac{1}{n!}$$

To indicate a natural logarithm we use the symbol In (In x means $\log_e x$) and e is called an irrational number since it cannot be written in a fraction form e.g. c/d. A common example of natural logarithms in finance is calculating how long it will take a bank deposit at a set interest rate to reach a specified higher amount.

X

exponential form is a number with an exponent in it, e.g. $y = b^x$.

the logarithmic form is an exponent written with a logarithm in it, e.g. $y = \log_b x$.

common logarithms logarithm to the base 10.

natural logarithms logarithm to the base e.

1.1.7 Linear and non-linear equations

An equation is a mathematical expression that allows a relationship to be written between one variable and another variable (or variables). For example, the relationship between the cost of 10 tins of baked beans can be written as C = 10p, where p is a term that represents the cost of one tin of baked beans. In this case we notice that the term labelled C is dependent upon the linear term p. In this case the power of p is equal to 1 and the relationship between C and p is called a **linear relationship** (or simple equation). Any relationship between variables which is not linear is called a **non-linear relationship**. For example, the relationship between two variables (x, y) might be of the form $y = x^2$. In this example, we note that whatever the value of the variable x is equal to, the value of y is equal to x multiplied by x, and therefore $y = x^2$ is a non-linear equation. Another way of describing this is to say that y is a function of x^2.

1.1.8 Excel mathematical functions

Excel provides a range of mathematical and statistical functions that can be useful in undertaking the analysis of data, for example, the Excel function ABS returns the absolute value of a number. Consider calculating the absolute value of −4. From Excel this is equal to ABS(−4) = 4. For a detailed list of Excel mathematical functions then please see the online refresher course in key numerical skills or the Microsoft support site for Excel 2010 at http://office.microsoft.com/en-us/excel-help/CH010369014.aspx (accessed 12 April 2012).

1.2 Drawing graphs

In this section we will explore the concept of **coordinate geometry** and how Excel can be used to plot algebraic relationships between two variables. Before we do this we need to understand the concept of a **coordinate of a point** and the Excel method we can use to plot a series of points. This section concludes by looking at equations of the form y = mx + c and the Excel method to calculate the terms 'm' and 'c' in the equation.

1.2.1 The coordinates of a point

The coordinates of a point can be written as an ordered pair (x, y).

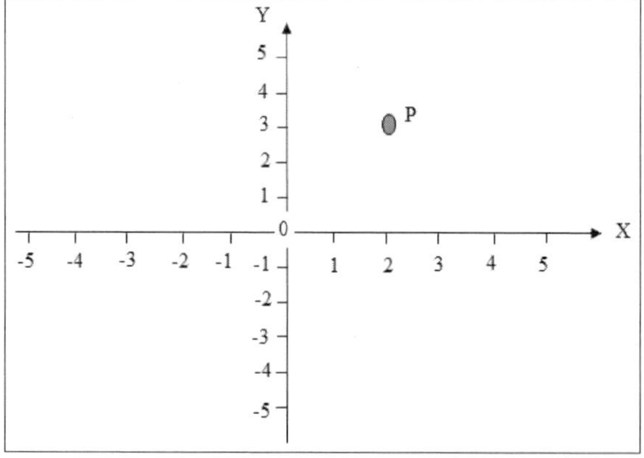

Figure 1.2

X

linear relationship a relationship between two variables of the form y = ax + c, giving a straight line graph.

non-linear relationship a relationship between y and x that is not of the form y = mx + c but depends upon the power of x, e.g. $y = x^2 + 4$.

coordinate geometry values of x and y that define a point on Cartesian axes.

coordinates of a point the coordinates of a point are a pair of numbers that define its exact location on a two-dimensional plane.

For example, point P in Figure 1.2 has coordinates (2, 3) on the axes y, x. Its horizontal distance along the x axis from the origin 0 is 2 units so the x coordinate is 2.

Its vertical distance along the y axis from the origin 0 is 3 units so the y coordinate is 3. Remember the x coordinate is always written first. Points often have one or both coordinates which are negative: (a) positive values of x are to the right of the origin, (b) negative values of x are to the left of the origin, (c) positive values of y are upwards from the origin, and (d) negative values of y are downwards from the origin.

1.2.2 Plotting straight line graphs

If we are given an equation of the form $y = mx + c$ (e.g. $y = 2x + 4$) and calculate the values of y for a range of x values, we will find if we plot the points onto a graph that a straight line will fit through every coordinate point (x, y). Any values of x can be chosen to draw the graph but it is best to choose x values that are neither too large nor too small. To illustrate this concept consider the equation $y = 2x + 4$. To plot a straight line on to a graph of y versus x we require three coordinate points only. In this example we will calculate the value of y when x equals 0, 2, and 4. Table 1.1 illustrates the calculation process:

Point	x	y = 2x + 4
A	0	4
D	2	8
B	4	12

Table 1.1

If we plot these coordinate points on to a graph of y against x we will create Figure 1.3.

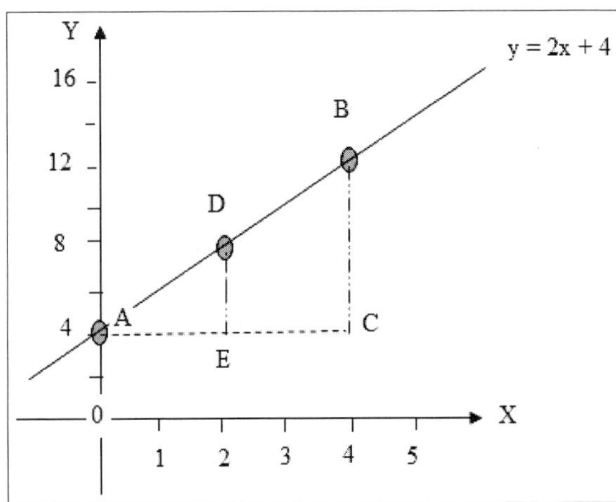

Figure 1.3

For the equation $y = 2x + 4$ the value of y depends upon x to the power 1 and is called a polynomial of order 1.

axes rectangular scales for drawing graphs.

origin the point where x and y Cartesian axes cross.

1.2.3 Linear equation parameters 'm' and 'c'

For the previous example, we calculated the coordinate points (x, y) for the equation $y = 2x + 4$. The general form of the equation for a **straight line graph** is given by Equation (1.1):

$$y = mx + c \tag{1.1}$$

Where the value 'c' is the value of y when $x = 0$ and is called the **y-intercept** and 'm' is called the **gradient** (or slope) of the line. In this example, $m = 2$ and $c = 4$. Figures 1.4–1.7 illustrate graphically the relationship between the slope of the line and the value of 'm'.

Figure 1.4 illustrates a line with a positive gradient ($m > 0$).

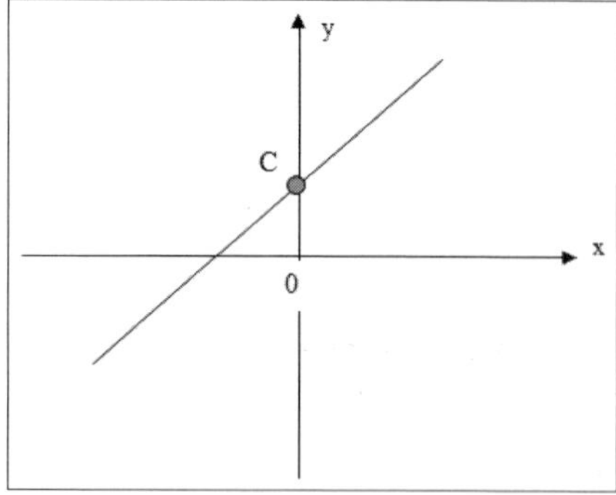

Figure 1.4

Figure 1.5 illustrates a line with a gradient of 0 ($m = 0$) and $y = c$.

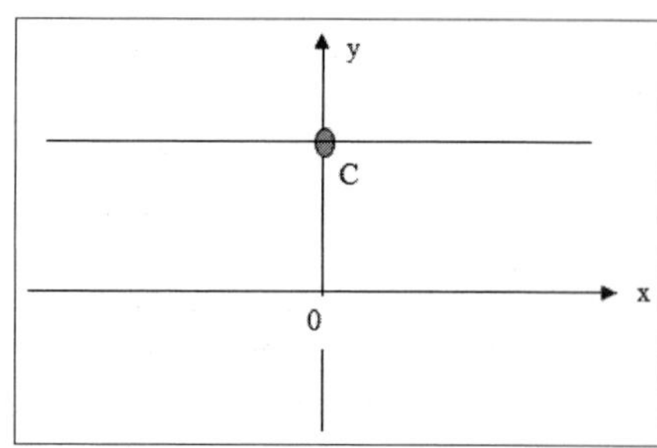

Figure 1.5

Figure 1.6 illustrates a line with a negative gradient ($m < 0$).

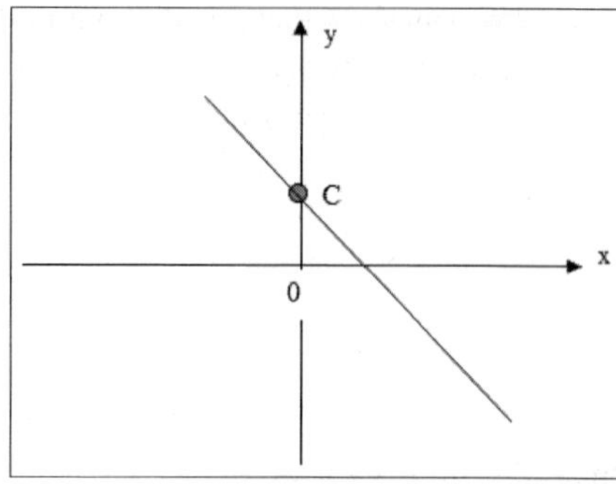

Figure 1.6

X

straight line graph a plot of y against x for $y = 2x + 3$ will result in a straight line when the line is plotted through the coordinate points (x, y).

y-intercept point on the y-axis that a linear equation ($y = mx + c$) crosses the $x = 0$ axis.

gradient a measure of how steeply a function is changing (dy/dx).

Figure 1.7 illustrates a line with an infinite gradient ($m = \infty$).

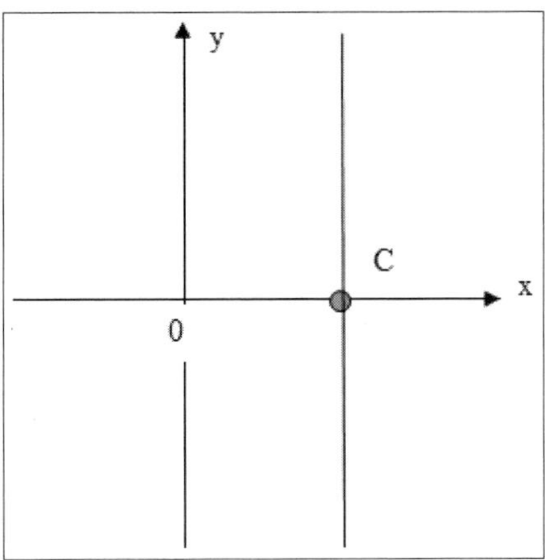

Figure 1.7

1.2.4 Plotting non-linear relationships when y is a polynomial of x

In certain situations you may find that the relationship between two variables (say y and x) is not a linear (or line) relationship but a non-linear relationship. Figure 1.8 illustrates a graph of y against x for the non-linear equation $y = 2x^2 - 4x + 2$.

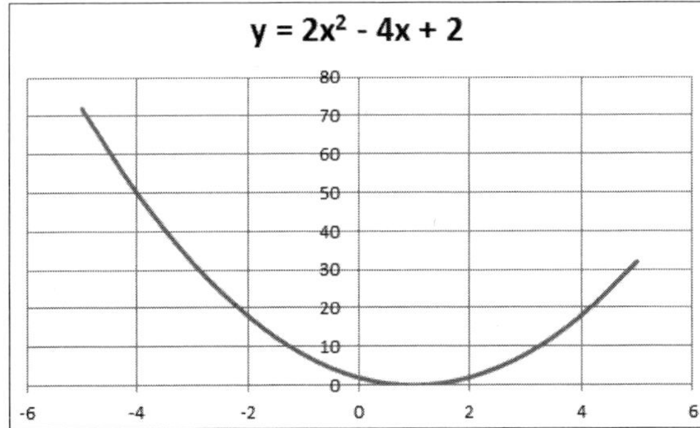

Figure 1.8

We observe that this curve as a minimum value of the variable y when x is approximately equal to 1. If we know the theoretical relationship between y and x then we can use the concept of calculus to identify the value of x (and y) from this relationship (e.g. for $y = 2x^2 - 4x + 2$ we can show that the minimum value of y is 0 when the value of x equals 1). The equation $y = 2x^2 - 4x + 2$ tells us that the relationship between y and x is a polynomial of order 2 (given the highest power of x is 2). This is also called a quadratic equation.

> X
>
> minimum value is the smallest possible value of y.
>
> polynomial of order 2 is any equation where a variable depends upon the second power of another variable e.g. $y = ax^2 + bx + c$.
>
> quadratic equation equation with the general form $y = ax^2 + bx + c$.
>
> differentiation algebraic process to calculate the instantaneous rate of change of one variable.

1.3 Describe change with calculus

1.3.1 Introducing the concept of differentiation

In Section 1.2.4, we observed from Figure 1.8 that the quadratic equation as a minimum at approximately x = 1. It is possible that for different quadratic equations to have a maximum value as illustrated in Figure 1.10. The general form of a quadratic equation is given by Equation (1.2):

$$y = ax^2 + bx + c \tag{1.2}$$

Whether a quadratic equation as a minimum or maximum depends upon the value of x (= –b/2a). In this section we expand on this by using differentiation to calculate the value of the minimum value, maximum value, and the corresponding (x, y) coordinates at the minimum/maximum. For example, reconsider $y = 2x^2 - 4x + 2$.

Figure 1.9 illustrates the shape of the curve in which we can observe that a minimum value of y occurs at x = –b/2a = –(–4)/(2(2)) = 1 with a minimum value of y = 0.

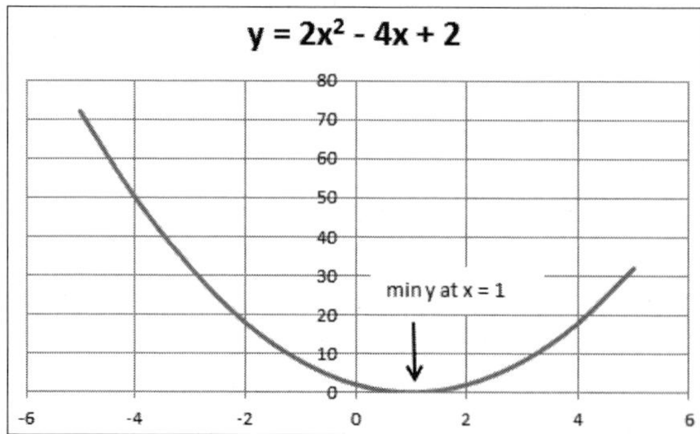

Figure 1.9

Min y = 2*(1)^2 – 4*1 + 2 = 0.

Furthermore, consider $y = -x^2 - 8x + 1$.

Figure 1.10 illustrates the shape of the curve in which we can observe that a maximum value of y occurs at x = –b/2a = –(–8)/(2(–1)) = –4 with a maximum value of y = 17.

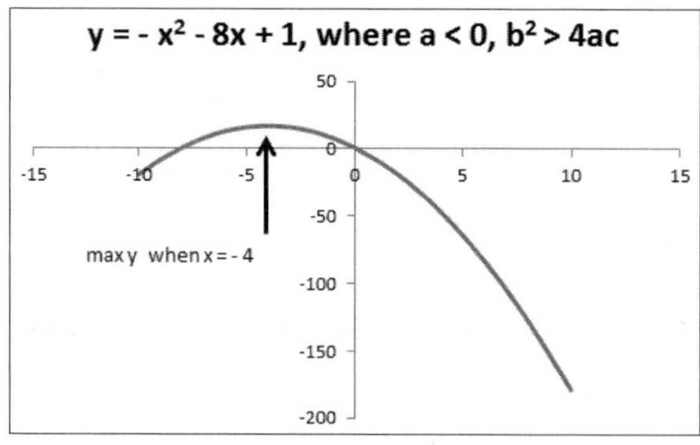

Figure 1.10

Max y = –(–4)^2 – 8*(–4) + 1 = 17.

In this section we will link the concept of minimum and maximum values of a variable y that depends upon a function x to the idea of calculus, and specifically differentiation. Reconsider $y = 2x^2 - 4x + 2$.

Figure 1.11 represents a graphical representation of the relationship between the two variables y and x.

maximum value the maximum value is the largest data value within a data set.

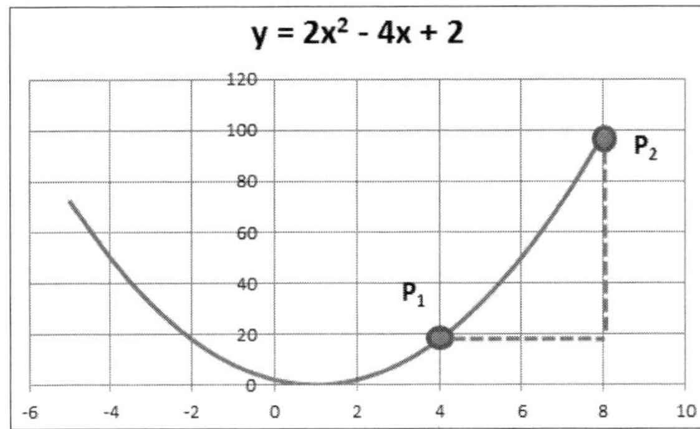

Figure 1.11

At this point let us assume the x coordinate of $P_1 = 4$ and $P_2 = 8$. If we substitute these values of x into the equation for y then we can calculate the value of y at point P_1 and P_2. Substituting each value of x into $y = 2x^2 - 4x + 2$ gives the value of y at each point and therefore the value of (x, y) for each coordinate point for points P_1 and P_2. Therefore, the coordinates for P_1 and P_2 would be (4, 18) and (8, 98) respectively. The gradient between these two would then be $(y_2 - y_1)/(x_2 - x_1) = 20$. If we choose two different points on the curve then we would find that the gradient of the line between the two points would change.

For any quadratic equation of the form $y = ax^2 + bx + c$ it can be shown that the following rules apply: (a) the large gradients would occur for large values of x, (b) the gradient would be zero at the minimum value of y with $x = -b/2a$, (c) the gradient would be positive when $x > -b/2a$, (d) the gradient would be negative when $x < -b/2a$. What we would like to achieve is to calculate the gradient of the curve at a particular point on the curve.

If we move P_2 towards P_1 along the curve then when P_2 coincides with P_1 the line joining the two points would just touch the curve at one place, as illustrated in Figure 1.12.

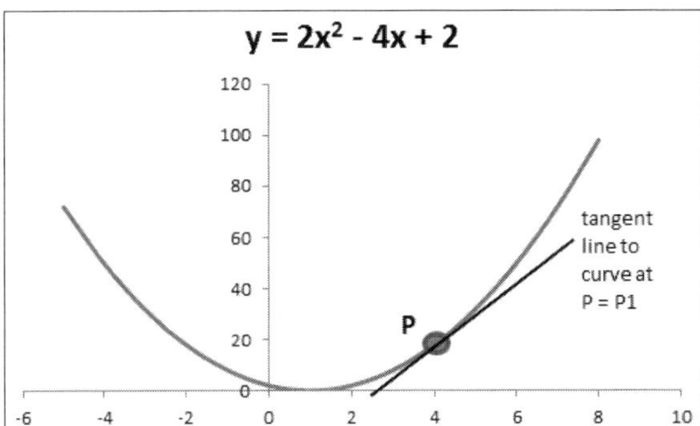

Figure 1.12

Unfortunately, we cannot use the average gradient method since we do not have two distinct values of x.

To calculate the gradient of the curve at a particular point on the curve we use the method of differentiation. Differentiation is a method that can be employed to solve problems where a variable is a function of another variable, for example, if y is a function of x then we can write this as $y = f(x)$ e.g. $y = x^2$, $y = x^3$, $y = x^3 + 3x^2 - 6$. To differentiate this type of relationship we can use the following rule:

$$y = ax^n \tag{1.3}$$

$$\frac{dy}{dx} = anx^{n-1} \tag{1.4}$$

Consider $y = 2x + 4$. From earlier calculations we noted that the gradient of this line is 2. So, let us use differentiation to calculate the same value for the gradient. If we compare $y = ax^n$ with $y = 2x + 4$ then we note that the equation for y has two x terms: $2x$ ($a = 2$, $n = 1$) and 4 ($a = 4$, $n = 0$ (since $x^0 = 1$)). Now use the rules of differentiation to differentiate $y = 2x + 4$:

$$\frac{dy}{dx} = 2(1)x^{1-1} + 4(0)x^{0-1}$$

We can show that this equation simplifies to the following equation:

$$\frac{dy}{dx} = 2$$

Therefore, according to the differentiation of equation $y = 2x + 4$, the gradient of the line is 2 which agrees with the $y = mx + c$ method.

Now reconsider $y = 2x^2 - 4x + 2$. Next use the rules of differentiation to differentiate $y = 2x^2 - 4x + 2$.

$$\frac{dy}{dx} = 2*2x^{2-1} - 4(1)x^{1-1} + 2*0x^{0-1}$$

We can show that this equation simplifies to the following equation:

$$\frac{dy}{dx} = 4x - 4$$

Therefore, according to the differentiation of equation $y = 2x^2 - 4x + 2$, the gradient of the curve is given by equation $dy/dx = 4x - 4$.

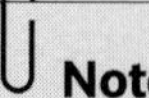

Note

- If $x = 0$, then the gradient of the curve at $x = 0$ is equal to $4(0) - 4 = -4$. Therefore, the tangent of the line would slope downwards (gradient negative) with a unit increase in x producing a 4 unit decrease in y.
- If $x = 1$, then the gradient of the curve at $x = 1$ is $4(1) - 4 = 0$. Therefore, the tangent of the line would be parallel to the x-axis.
- If $x = 3$, then the gradient of the curve at $x = 3$ is equal to $4(3) - 4 = 8$. Therefore, the tangent of the line would slope upwards (gradient positive) with a unit increase in x producing a 8 unit increase in y.

1.3.2 Finding the minimum and maximum value of a function

For a minimum (or maximum) value of y the value of dy/dx would be equal to zero. This implies that at the minimum or maximum value the first derivative is equal to zero:

$$\frac{dy}{dx} = 0 \text{ at a minimum or maximum value}$$

For example, consider $y = 2x^2 - 4x + 2$. The minimum or maximum value of y occurs when $dy/dx = 4x - 4 = 0$. If we solve this equation for x we find $x = 1$ and $y = 2(1)^2 - 4(1) + 2 = 0$. From Figure 1.9 we observe that this point represents a minimum value of y. Therefore, we have a minimum value of $y = 0$ when $x = 0$.

How can you decide if it is a minimum or maximum value?

We will observe that the same first derivative rule applies for a minimum and maximum value, $\frac{dy}{dx} = 0$. So the question that we need to answer is how do we decide whether we have a minimum or maximum value. To answer this question we differentiate the equation $\frac{dy}{dx}$ to give the **second derivative of y on x** (notation for the second derivative is $\frac{d^2y}{dx^2}$).

Second differentiation rule to decide if a minimum or maximum value exists:

1. $\frac{d^2y}{dx^2} > 0$, then we have a minimum value of y.
2. $\frac{d^2y}{dx^2} < 0$, then we have a maximum value of y.

For example, reconsider $y = 2x^2 - 4x + 2$. The minimum or maximum value of y occurs when $4x - 4 = 0$. Solving this equation gives $x = 1$ with Figure 1.9 showing us this is a minimum of $y = 0$.

$$\frac{dy}{dx} = 4x - 4 = 0$$

Now differentiate this equation to give the second derivative of y on x:

$$\frac{d^2y}{dx^2} = 4 > 0$$

Therefore, the equation $y = 2x^2 - 4x + 2$ has a minimum value of y at $x = 1$ when $y = 0$.

For example, consider $y = -x^2 - 8x + 1$.

$$\frac{dy}{dx} = -2x - 8 = 0$$

If $dy/dx = 0$, then solve $-2x - 8 = 0$ to identify the x location of the minimum/maximum. Solving this equation gives $x = -4$ and $y = 17$. Now differentiate this equation to give the second derivative of y on x:

$$\frac{d^2y}{dx^2} = -2 < 0$$

Therefore, the equation $y = -x^2 - 8x + 1$ has a maximum value of y at $x = -4$ and $y = 17$.

1.3.3 Relationship between differentiation and integration

The **concept of integration** is a method that reverses the process of differentiation—in other words, we start with the gradient equation ($\frac{dy}{dx}$) and find the original function, $y = f(x)$. To illustrate the method let us consider the problem $\frac{dy}{dx} = 6x$. The problem we have is that we can state what the original x term was but we do not know what the constant term

X

second derivative of y on x the result of differentiating the first derivative (d^2y/dx^2).

concept of integration is the reverse of differentiation.

was equal too. For example, $y = 3x^2$, $y = 3x^2 + 3$, $y = 3x^2 - 4$. Each of these equations when differentiated would give $\frac{dy}{dx} = 6x$. Thus, if we want to return the first derivative function $\frac{dy}{dx} = 6x$ to its original form $y = f(x)$ then we call this process integration.

$$\int \frac{dy}{dx}\, dx = \int 6x\, dx$$

From the earlier discussion we know that this term is equal to $3x^2 + c$, where c is an unknown constant term (i.e. a number).

$$\int 6x\, dx = 3x^2 + c$$

The general rule to integrate an equation of a term such as $y = f(x)$ is as follows:

$$y = ax^n \tag{1.5}$$

$$\int y\, dx = \frac{ax^{n+1}}{n+1} + c \tag{1.6}$$

In this case we cannot calculate the value of the constant term c therefore we call this an **indefinite integral**. If we know the value of the constant term then we call this a **definite integral**.

Summary

In this chapter we have provided the reader with a brief overview of the numeracy skills required to start a course in quantitative methods. The online refresher course in key numerical skills provides the reader with more detailed notes on the topics mentioned in this chapter. The next chapter will explore visualizing data sets using charts, graphs and calculating measures of average, spread, and shape. For further information please consult the excellent text by Gaulter and Buchanan (2000) or any good introduction to developing numerical skills.

Further reading

Each chapter includes identified further reading resources that can be accessed by students. This list will include traditional text books and online resources in statistics and the application of the Excel spreadsheet.

1. UKCES (UK Commission for Employment and Skills) (2009), available at **http://www.ukces.org.uk/publications/employability-challenge-full-report** (accessed 12 April 2012).
2. G. Davis and B. Pecar (2010) *Business Statistics Using Excel*, Oxford University Press.
3. B. Gaulter and L. Buchanan (2000) *GNVQ Key Skills: Application of Number* (2nd edn), Oxford University Press.

X

indefinite integral the reverse of differentiation.

definite integral evaluation of the indefinite integral at two points to find the difference.

Formula summary

$$y = mx + c \tag{1.1}$$

$$y = ax^2 + bx + c \tag{1.2}$$

$$y = ax^n \tag{1.3}$$

$$\frac{dy}{dx} = anx^{n-1} \tag{1.4}$$

$$y = ax^n \tag{1.5}$$

$$\int y\,dx = \frac{ax^{n+1}}{n+1} + c \tag{1.6}$$

2 Descriptive statistics and basic survey processing

» Overview «

In this chapter we provide the reader with an overview of the key descriptive statistical concepts that will be used in later chapters. This chapter describes:

1. The different data types.
2. How to create tables from raw data using Excel.
3. How to graph this data using Excel.
4. How to provide a summary statistic to measure average, dispersion, and shape using Excel.
5. How to process survey data using Excel.

» Learning outcomes «

On completing this chapter you should be able to:

» Identify the data type for a data set (category, discrete, continuous).

» Tabulate data.

» Identify appropriate graphical representations for each data type.

» Use Excel to tabulate and create graphical representations for each data type.

» Identify and calculate appropriate measures of average, dispersion, and shape to provide appropriate descriptive statistics for the data set.

» Use Excel to calculate and provide appropriate descriptive statistics.

» Recognize a need for formulating different question strategies in a questionnaire.

» Understand that different types of answers require different processing.

» Learn how to pre-process survey data and populate using the Excel spreadsheet.

» Apply pivot table functionality to survey data populated in a spreadsheet.

» Cross-tabulate different questions to get more insight into answers.

» Graph the data and visually identify patterns.

» Prepare data for more complex analysis that might follow.

X

raw data raw facts that are processed to give information.

graph used to refer to any form of graphical display.

statistic a statistic is a quantity that is calculated from a sample of data.

category a set of data is said to be categorical if the values or observations belonging to it can be sorted according to category.

discrete data that is united to integer values.

continuous data where the values or observations belonging to it may take on any value within a finite or infinite interval.

questionnaire set of questions used to collect data.

2.1 Data types

In general, when we deal with data we will find that we have five distinct types of data: discrete, category, ordinal, and continuous/numeric (interval/ratio). A statistic is a quantity that is calculated from a sample of data.

2.1.1 Discrete data

A set of data is said to be discrete if the values/observations belonging to it are distinct and separate, that is, they can be counted (1, 2, 3, . . .). Examples might include the number of kittens in a litter; the number of patients in a doctors surgery; the number of flaws in one metre of cloth; gender (male, female); or blood group (O, A, B, AB).

2.1.2 Category or nominal data

A set of data is said to be a categorical variable if the values or observations belonging to it can be sorted according to category. Each value is chosen from a set of non-overlapping categories. For example, clothes can be sorted according to colour: the characteristic 'colour' can have non-overlapping categories 'black', 'brown', 'red', and 'other'. The choices we make are in specific categories and are not in number form. In other words, we are describing an attribute (or a quality) and we describe this data as qualitative or categorical data. Other examples of categorical data include a person's eye colour, colour of car, the political party they vote for during an election. As we will see, we use pie and bar charts to graphically represent this type of data.

2.1.3 Ordinal data

A set of data is said to be ordinal if the values/observations belonging to it can be ranked (put in order) or have a rating scale attached. You can count and order, but not measure ordinal data. The categories for an ordinal set of data have a natural order: for example, suppose in a race competitor C finished first and is given the number 1 to recognize this achievement. If the competitors finished in the order C, B, A, D, G, we know that C was first, B second, A third, and so on. However, the distinction between neighbouring points on the scale is not necessarily always the same. For instance, the difference in enjoyment expressed by giving a rating of 2 rather than 1 might be much less than the difference in enjoyment expressed by giving a rating of 4 rather than 3. As we will see, we use pie and bar charts to graphically represent this type of data.

2.1.4 Continuous or numeric data

A set of data is said to be a continuous variable if the values/observations belonging to it may take on any value within a finite or infinite interval. You can count, order, and measure continuous data—for example, height, weight, temperature, the amount of sugar in an orange, the time required to run a mile. Continuous data can be subdivided into interval and ratio. An interval scale is a measurement scale in which a certain distance along the

X

types of data are categorized according to several criteria, for example, according to the type of the values used to quantify the observations.

ordinal data that cannot be precisely measured, but that can be ranked or ordered.

interval an interval scale is a scale of measurement where the distance between any two adjacent units of measurement (or 'intervals') is the same but the zero point is arbitrary.

ratio ratio data are continuous data where both differences and ratios are interpretable and have a natural zero.

nominal data data for which there is no useful quantitative measure.

categorical variable is a variable that can be sorted according to category.

qualitative are variables with no natural sense of ordering (see categorical).

bar chart a diagram that represents the frequency of observations in a class by the length of bar.

continuous variable a set of data is said to be continuous if the values belong to a continuous interval of real values.

scale means the same thing no matter where on the scale you are, but where zero on the scale does not represent the absence of the thing being measured. Fahrenheit and Celsius temperature scales are examples. A ratio scale is a measurement scale in which a certain distance along the scale means the same thing no matter where on the scale you are, and where zero on the scale represents the absence of the thing being measured. Thus a 4 on such a scale implies twice as much of the thing being measured as a 2. As we will see, a **histogram** is a way of summarizing data that are measured on an interval/ratio scale.

2.2 Creating tables and graphs

2.2.1 Tables and frequency distributions using Excel

Tables come in a variety of formats, from **simple tables** to **frequency distribution**, which allow data sets to be summarized in a form that allows users to be able to access important information.

Example 2.1

When asked which party would you vote for if there was a general election tomorrow, 1110 students responded as follows: 400 said Conservative, 510 Labour, 78 Democrats, 55 Green, and the rest some other party. We can put this information in a table form indicating the frequency within each category either as a raw score or as a percentage of the total number of responses.

Proposed voting behaviour by 1110 university students				
Party	Frequency		Party	Frequency %
Conservative	400		Conservative	36
Labour	510		Labour	46
Democrat	78	Or	Democrat	7
Green	55		Green	5
Other	67		Other	6
Total	1110		Total	100

Table 2.1 Proposed voting behaviour

Source: University Student Survey, October 2008.

histogram frequency distribution for continuous data.

simple tables a table consisting of an ordered arrangement of rows and columns that allow data and information to be accessible in a visual form.

frequency distribution diagram showing the number of observations in each class.

Example 2.2

For example, consider Figure 2.1 published in the *Daily Telegraph* newspaper that provides a list of exchange rates.

EXCHANGE RATES

£€ RATE 1.2035 CHANGE +0.01c

£$ RATE 1.5201 CHANGE -0.18c

		TOURIST £1=	STERLING £1=	1 EURO=	1 DOLLAR=
AUSTRALIA	*Aus $*	**1.66870**	1.77085	**1.47142**	1.16496
CANADA	*Can $*	**1.50060**	1.59885	**1.32850**	1.05181
DENMARK	*Krone*	**8.43340**	8.97140	**7.45442**	5.90185
EURO	*€*	**1.14240**	1.20350	**-**	0.79172
HONG KONG	*HK $*	**11.1377**	11.8440	**9.84134**	7.79163
INDIA	*Rupee*	N/A	71.4275	**59.3498**	46.9887
ISRAEL	*Shekels*	**5.52380**	N/A	N/A	N/A

Figure 2.1

Source: *Daily Telegraph*: Business Section, p. B4 (Thursday, 8 July 2010)

Figure 2.1 gives information about the exchange rates for a number of countries.

Sometimes categories can be subdivided and tables can be constructed to convey this information together with the frequency of occurrence within the subcategories. For example the following table indicates the frequency of half yearly sales of two cars produced by a large company with the sales split by month.

Example 2.3

Half-yearly sales of XBAR Ltd							
Month	January	February	March	April	May	June	Total
Pink	5200	4100	6000	6900	6050	7000	35,250
Blue	2100	1050	2950	5000	6300	5200	22,600
Total	7300	5150	8950	11,900	12,350	12,200	57,850

Table 2.2 Half yearly sales of XBAR Ltd

When data is collected by survey or by some other form, we initially have a set of unorganized raw data which, when viewed, conveys little information. A first step is to organize the set into a frequency distribution such that 'like' quantities are collected and the frequency of occurrence of the quantities determined.

Example 2.4

Consider the set of data that represents the number of insurance claims processed each day by an insurance agent over a period of 40 days: 3, 5, 9, 6, 4, 7, 8, 6, 2, 5, 10, 1, 6, 3, 6, 5, 4, 7, 8, 4, 5, 9, 4, 2, 7, 6, 1, 3, 5, 6, 2, 6, 4, 8, 3, 1, 7, 9, 7, 2. The frequency distribution can be used to show how many days he took for one claim to be processed, how many days to process two claims, and so on. The simplest way of doing this is by creating a *tally chart*, as illustrated in Table 2.3.

X

chart used to refer to any form of graphical display.

Score	Tally	Frequency, f
1	|||	3
2	||||	4
3	||||	4
4	~~||||~~	5
5	~~||||~~	5
6	~~||||~~ ||	7
7	~~||||~~	5
8	|||	3
9	|||	3
10	|	1
		$\Sigma f = 40$

Table 2.3

Write down the range of values from lowest (1) to the highest (10) then go through the data set recording each score in the table with a tally mark. It's a good idea to cross out figures in the data set as you go through it to prevent double counting (Table 2.3).

In this example there were relatively few cases. However, we may have increased our survey period to one year and the range of claims may have been between 0 and 30. Since our aim is to summarize information we may find it better to group 'likes' into classes to form a grouped frequency distribution. The next example illustrates this point.

Example 2.5

Table 2.4 represents the data set of miles recorded by 120 salesmen in one week.

403	407	407	408	410	412	413	413
423	424	424	425	426	428	430	430
435	435	436	436	436	438	438	438
444	444	445	446	447	447	447	448
452	453	453	453	454	455	455	456
462	462	462	463	464	465	466	468
474	474	475	476	477	478	479	481
490	493	494	495	497	498	498	500
415	430	439	449	457	468	482	502
416	431	440	450	457	469	482	502
418	432	440	450	458	470	483	505
419	432	441	451	459	471	485	508
420	433	442	451	459	471	486	509
421	433	442	451	460	472	488	511
421	434	443	452	460	473	489	515

Table 2.4 Miles recorded by 120 salesmen

This mass of data conveys little in terms of information. Because there are too many value scores, putting the data into an ungrouped frequency distribution does not portray an adequate summary. Grouping the data, however, provides the following grouped frequency table where mileage is organized into a class of values: 400 – 419, 420 – 439, and so forth.

X

range difference between largest and smallest values in a data set.

class range or entry in a frequency distribution.

Mileage	Tally	Frequency, f
400 – 419	~~IIII~~ ~~IIII~~ II	12
420 – 439	~~IIII~~ ~~IIII~~ ~~IIII~~ ~~IIII~~ ~~IIII~~ II	27
440 – 459	~~IIII~~ ~~IIII~~ ~~IIII~~ ~~IIII~~ ~~IIII~~ ~~IIII~~ IIII	34
460 – 479	~~IIII~~ ~~IIII~~ ~~IIII~~ ~~IIII~~ IIII	24
480 – 499	~~IIII~~ ~~IIII~~ ~~IIII~~	15
500 – 519	~~IIII~~ III	8
		$\sum f = 120$

Table 2.5 Grouped frequency distribution data for Example 2.5 data set

The frequency distribution can be constructed using Excel Analysis ToolPak (Data > Data Analysis, see Example 2.8). It is possible that data will be presented in grouped data form where the raw data is already divided into classes. The stated limits for Table 2.5 are the lower and upper limits of each class; for example, for class 2 the lower limit is 419.5 and the upper limit is 439.5.

2.2.2 Creating bar and pie charts using Excel

The next stage of analysis after the data has been tabulated is to graph the data using a variety of methods to provide a suitable graph. In this section we will explore bar charts, pie charts, histograms, frequency polygons, scatter plots, and time series plots. The type of graph you will use to graph the data depends upon the type of variable you are dealing with within your data set, that is, whether category (or nominal), ordinal, or interval (or ratio) data.

Data type	Which graph to use?
Category or nominal	Bar chart, pie chart, cross tab tables (or contingency tables)
Ordinal	Bar chart, pie chart, and scatter plots.
Interval or ratio	Histogram, frequency polygon. Cumulative frequency curve (or ogive) Scatter plots, time series plots.

Table 2.6 Deciding on graph type according to data type

For example, consider Figure 2.2 published in the *Daily Telegraph*, which provides a pie chart and two bar charts to illustrate OCADO's e-tailer market share, gross sales, and pre-tax profit/loss.

Graph and chart are terms that are often used to refer to any form of graphical display. Categorical variable data is represented largely by bar and pie charts. Bar charts are very useful in providing a simple pictorial representation of several sets of data on one graph. Bar charts are used for categorical data where each category is represented by each vertical (or horizontal) bar. In bar charts each category is represented by a bar with the frequency represented by the height of the bar. All bars should have equal width and the distance between each bar is kept constant. It is important that the axes (X and Y) are

X

grouped data raw data already divided into classes.

stated limits the lower and upper limits of a class interval.

bar chart a diagram that represents the frequency of observations in a class by the length of bar.

pie chart diagram that represents the frequency of the observations in a class by the area of a circle.

histogram is a frequency distribution for continuous data.

frequency polygon is a graphical display of a frequency table.

scatter plot graph of a set of points (x, y).

time series a set of data points (x, y) where variable x represents the time point.

cross tab tables are used to summarise categorical data.

contingency tables are used to summarise categorical data.

cumulative frequency curve is a graph that represents the cumulative frequencies of the classes in a frequency distribution.

ogive is a graph of the cumulative frequency against class for continuous data.

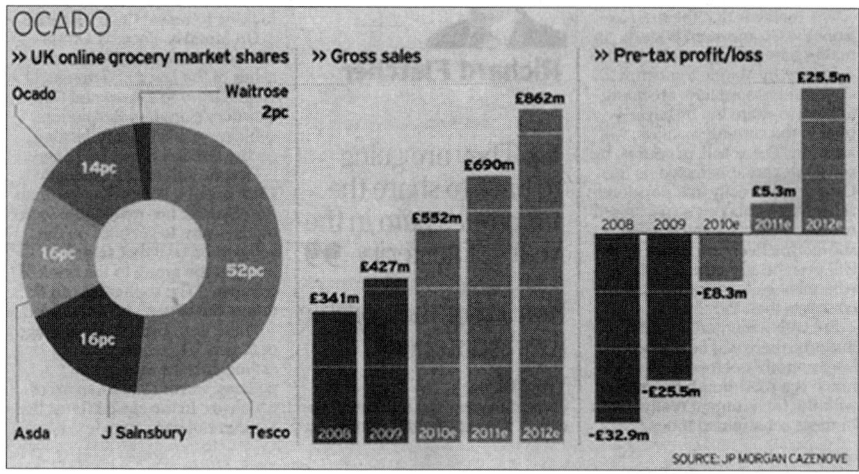

Figure 2.2

Source: *Daily Telegraph*: Business Section, p. B6 (Wednesday, 7 July 2010). Reproduced with permission

labelled and the chart has an appropriate title. What each bar represents should be clearly stated within the chart.

Example 2.6

Consider the categorical data in Example 2.1, which represents the proposed voting behaviour by a sample of university students. Excel can be used to create a bar chart to represent this data set. For each category a vertical bar is drawn with the vertical height representing the number of students in that category (or frequency) with the horizontal distance for each bar representing the category with the distances between each bar kept constant.

Figure 2.3 represents a bar chart for the proposed voting behaviour.

Example 2.6 Bar chart for proposed voting behaviour

Proposed voting behaviour by 1110 university students
(Source: University Student Survey October 2008)

Party	Frequency	or	Party	Frequency %
Conservative	400		Conservative	36
Labour	510		Labour	46
Democrat	78		Democrat	7
Green	55		Green	5
Other	67		Other	6

Proposed Voting Behaviour

600
500
400
300
200
100
0

Conservative Labour Democrat Green Other

Frequency

Figure 2.3

Each bar represents the number of students who would vote for a particular United Kingdom political party. From the bar chart you can easily detect the differences of frequency between the five categories (Conservative, Labour, Democrat, Green, and Other).

Step 1 Input Data Series

The data in Example 2.1 consists of two columns of data. Column 1 represents party membership and column 2 represents the number of students proposing to vote for a particular political party (also called frequency of occurrence). We can use Excel to create a bar chart for this data by placing the data in Excel as follows.

Party: Cells B6:B11 (includes label Party, B6)

Frequency: Cells C6:C11 (includes label Frequency, C6)

Figure 2.4 represents the Excel worksheet.

	A	B	C	D	E	F
1	Example 2.6 Bar chart for proposed voting behaviour					
2						
3						
4		Proposed voting behaviour by 1110 university students				
5		(Source: University Student Survey October 2008)				
6		Party	Frequency	or	Party	Frequency %
7		Conservative	400		Conservative	36
8		Labour	510		Labour	46
9		Democrat	78		Democrat	7
10		Green	55		Green	5
11		Other	67		Other	6

Figure 2.4

Step 2 Highlight B6:C11

Step 3 Now create a chart in Excel by clicking on Insert and then select Column (Figure 2.5).

Figure 2.5

Choose 2D chart and option 1 (Figure 2.6)

Figure 2.6

This will place the bar chart in the location specified. The bar chart will look like the chart in Figure 2.7 but with the title text Frequency changed to Proposed Voting Behaviour, axis labelles Party Frequency and graph legend delete.

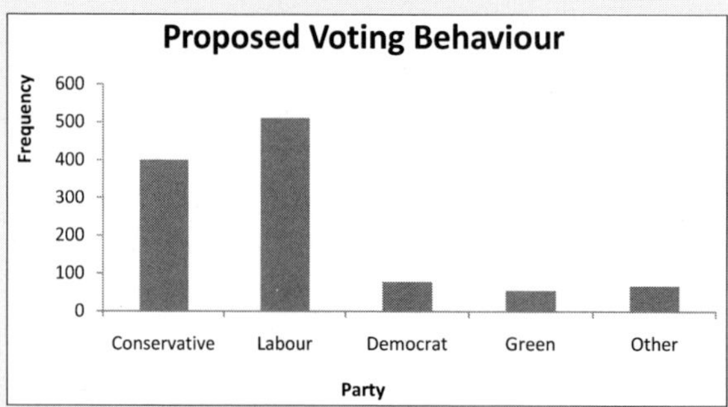

Figure 2.7

Note You can modify this chart quite easily by double-clicking within the chart area. This will enable you to access the Chart Tools option (Figure 2.8):

Figure 2.8

In a pie chart the relative frequencies are represented by a slice of a circle. Each section represents a category, and the area of a section represents the frequency or number of objects within a category. They are particularly useful in showing relative proportions, but their effectiveness tends to diminish for more than eight categories.

Example 2.7

Figure 2.9 represents a Pie chart for proposed voting behaviour created using Excel. We can see that different slices of the circle represent the different choices that people have when it comes to voting. To create this pie chart click on Insert and Select Pie chart (Figure 2.10).

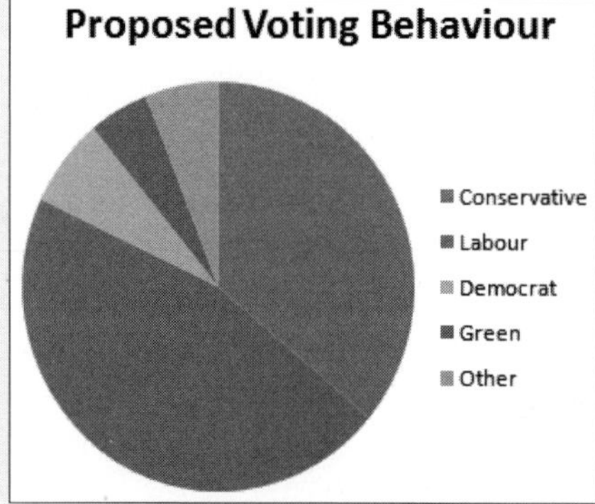

Figure 2.9

Figure 2.10

2.2.3 Creating a histogram using Excel

We have already mentioned the idea of a frequency distribution via the displaying of ordinal level data with tables and bar charts. This concept can now be extended to higher levels of measurement. The method used to graph a **group frequency distribution** is to construct a histogram. A histogram looks like a bar chart but they are different and should not be confused with each other. Histograms are constructed on the following principles: (a) the horizontal axis (x - axis) is a continuous scale, (b) each class is represented by a vertical rectangle, the base of which extends from one true limit to the next, and (c) the area of the rectangle is proportional to the frequency of the class. This is very important since it means that the area of the bar represents the frequency of each category. In the bar chart the frequency is represented by the height of each bar. This implies that if we double the class width for one bar then we would have to half the height of that particular bar. In the special case where all class widths are the same, Excel can be used to create the histogram where the height of the bar can be taken to be representative of the frequency of occurrence for that category. It is important to note that either frequencies or relative frequencies can be used to construct a histogram, but the shape of the histogram will be exactly the same no matter which variable you choose to graph.

Example 2.8

Mileage	Frequency, f
400 – 419	12
420 – 439	27
440 – 459	34
460 – 479	24
480 – 499	15
500 – 519	8
	$\sum f = 120$

Table 2.7

Example 2.5 represents the miles recorded by 120 salesmen in one week as illustrated in Table 2.7.

Figure 2.11 shows what the histogram for miles recorded by 120 salesmen should look like once we have finished.

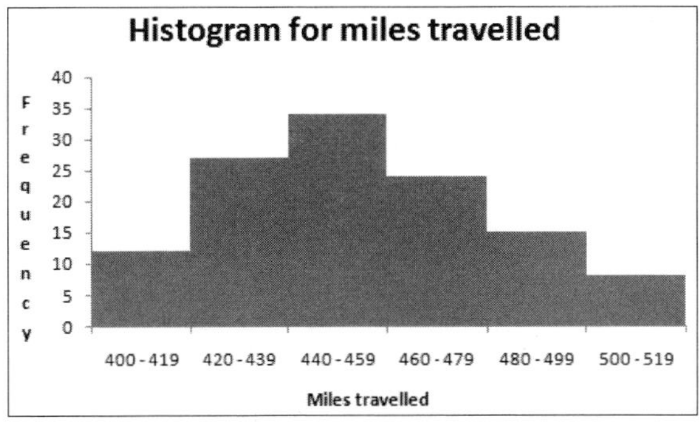

Figure 2.11

group frequency distribution data arranged in intervals to show the frequency with which the possible values of a variable occur.

Step 1 Data Series

Input data into cells A6:H20

See Figure 2.12

	A	B	C	D	E	F	G	H
1	Example 2.5 Miles recorded by 120 salesman in one week							
2								
3	Histogram							
4								
5								
6	403	407	407	408	410	412	413	413
7	423	424	424	425	426	428	430	430
8	435	435	436	436	436	438	438	438
9	444	444	445	446	447	447	447	448
10	452	453	453	453	454	455	455	456
11	462	462	462	463	464	465	466	468
12	474	474	475	476	477	478	479	481
13	490	493	494	495	497	498	498	500
14	415	430	439	449	457	468	482	502
15	416	431	440	450	457	469	482	502
16	418	432	440	450	458	470	483	505
17	419	432	441	451	459	471	485	508
18	420	433	442	451	459	471	486	509
19	421	433	442	451	460	472	488	511
20	421	434	443	452	460	473	489	515

Figure 2.12

Step 2 Excel Spreadsheet Macro Command – Using Analysis ToolPak

Now we can use Excel to create the histogram. Before we use this technique we have to input the lower and upper class boundaries into Excel. Excel calls this the Bin Range. In this example we have decided to create a Bin Range that is based upon equal class widths. Let us choose the following groups with the Bin Range calculated from these group values as illustrated in Table 2.8:

Mileage	LCB – UCB	Class Width	Bin Range
			399.5
400 – 419	399.5 – 419.5	20	419.5
420 – 439	419.5 – 439.5	20	439.5
440 – 459	439.5 – 459.5	20	459.5
480 – 499	479.5 – 499.5	20	499.5
500 – 519	499.5 – 519.5	20	519.5

Table 2.8 Calculation of Bin Range

We can see from Table 2.8 that the class widths are all equal and the corresponding Bin Range is 399.5, 419.5.5, ..., 519.5. We can now use Excel to create the grouped frequency distribution and corresponding histogram for equal classes. If you want, you can leave the Bin Range box blank. The Histogram tool then automatically creates evenly distributed bin intervals using the minimum and maximum values in the input range as beginning and end points. The number of intervals is equal to the square root of the number of input values (rounded down).

Bin Range: Cells B24:B30 (with the label in cell B23)

See Figure 2.13

	A	B	C
22			
23		Bin Range	
24		399.5	
25		419.5	
26		439.5	
27		459.5	
28		479.5	
29		499.5	
30		519.5	

Figure 2.13

Now create the histogram.

Select Data

Select Data Analysis menu (Figure 2.14)

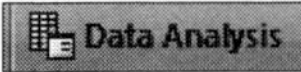

Figure 2.14

Click on Histogram

See Figure 2.15

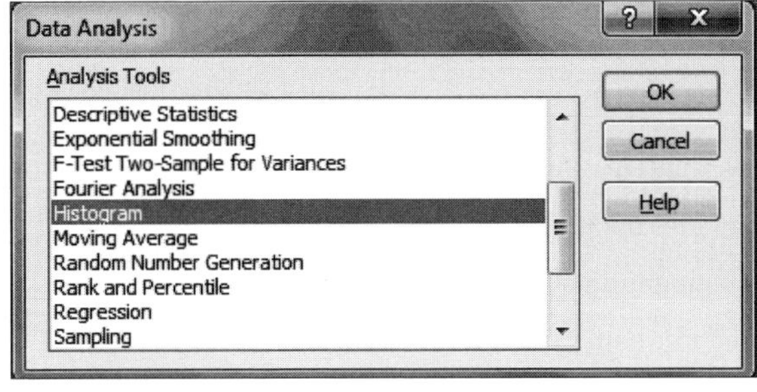

Figure 2.15

Click OK

Input Data Range: Cells A6:H20

Input Bin Range: Cells B24:B30

Choose location of Output range: Cell D23

See Figure 2.16

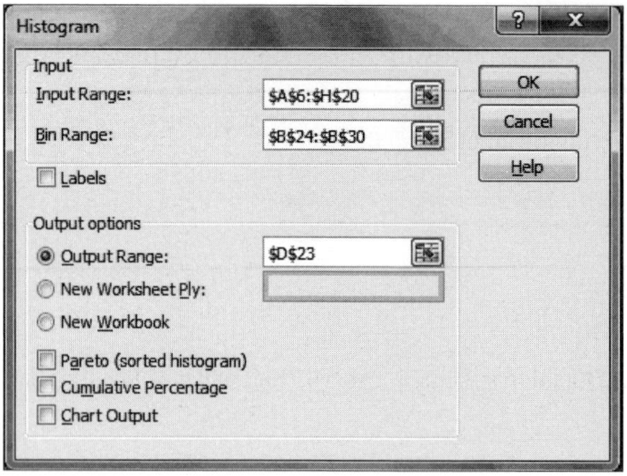

Histogram

Input
Input Range: $A$6:$H$20
Bin Range: $B$24:$B$30
Labels

Output options
Output Range: $D$23
New Worksheet Ply:
New Workbook
Pareto (sorted histogram)
Cumulative Percentage
Chart Output

OK
Cancel
Help

Figure 2.16

Press OK

Excel will now print out the grouped frequency table (Bin Range and frequency of occurrence) as presented in cells D23 – E31.

See Figure 2.17 We can now use Excel to generate the histogram for equal class widths.

	A	B	C	D	E
22					
23		Bin Range		*Bin*	*Frequency*
24		399.5		399.5	0
25		419.5		419.5	12
26		439.5		439.5	27
27		459.5		459.5	34
28		479.5		479.5	24
29		499.5		499.5	15
30		519.5		519.5	8
31				More	0

Figure 2.17

Step 3 Input Data Series using the shaded information in Figure 2.17

Mileage: Cells D34:D40 (includes data label)

Frequency: Cells E34:E40 (includes data label)

See Figure 2.18. This is a grouped frequency distribution table.

	C	D	E
33			
34		Mileage	Frequency
35		400 - 419	12
36		420 - 439	27
37		440 - 459	34
38		460 - 479	24
39		480 - 499	15
40		500 - 519	8

Figure 2.18

Step 4 Highlight D34:E40

Now create a chart in Excel by clicking on Insert and then Insert Bar (Figure 2.19). Choose 2D chart and option 1.

Figure 2.19

This will place the bar chart in the location specified. The bar chart will look like the chart in Figure 2.20.

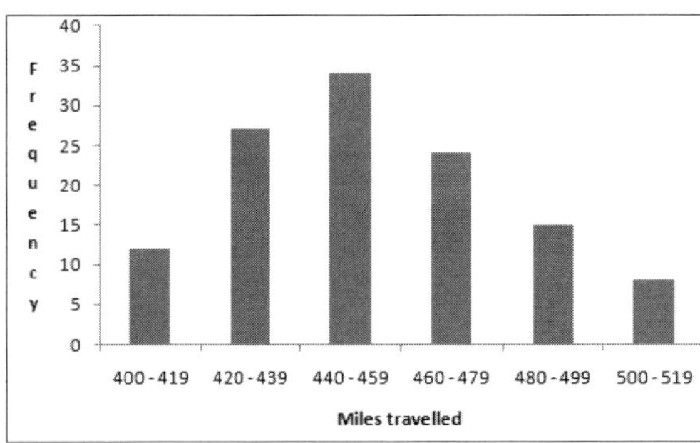

Figure 2.20

Step 5 Transformation of the Bar Chart into a Histogram

Right-click on one of the bars in the chart and choose Format Data Series (Figure 2.21)

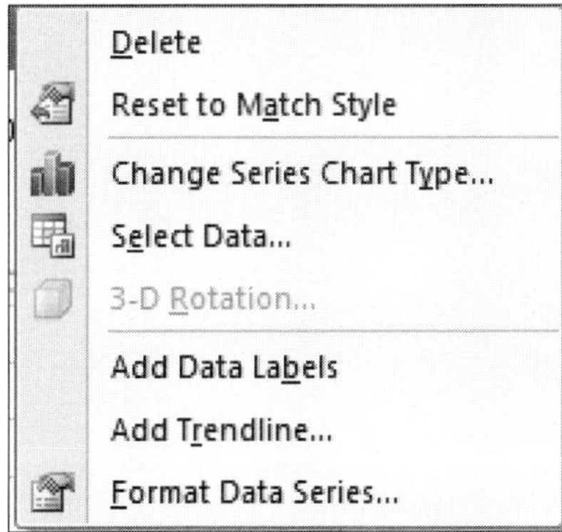

Figure 2.21

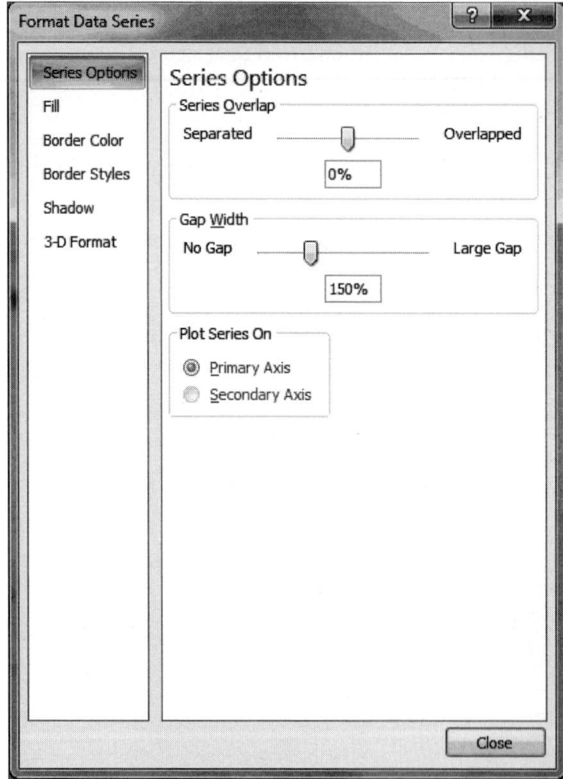

Figure 2.22

Reduce Gap Width to zero (Figure 2.22) and click Close
The histogram will appear on the worksheet (see Figure 2.23).

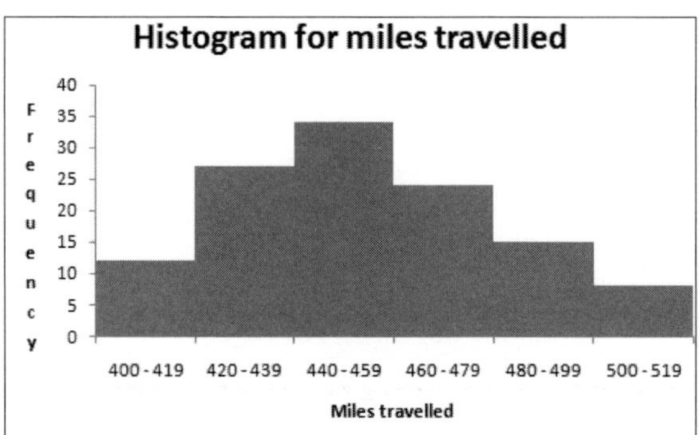

Figure 2.23

Note that we have edited the bar chart to include a main title (Histogram for miles travelled), axes titles and removed legend.

2.2.4 Creating a scatter plot and time series charts using Excel

scatter plot graph of a set of points (x, y).

time series a set of data points (x, y) where variable x represents the time point.

A **scatter plot** is a graph which helps us assess visually the form of relationship between two variables. A special case is when we are interested in plotting a graph of a variable value against time. A **time series** is concerned with data collected over a period of time.

Example 2.9

A manufacturing firm has designed a training programme that is supposed to increase the productivity of employees.

The personal manager decides to examine this claim by analysing the data results from the first group of 20 employees that attended the course.

The results are provided in Table 2.9.

Employee number	Productivity X	Percentage rise in productivity, Y
1	47	4.2
2	71	8.1
3	64	6.8
4	35	4.3
5	43	5.0
6	60	7.5
7	38	4.7
8	59	5.9
9	67	6.9
10	56	5.7
11	67	5.7
12	57	5.4
13	69	7.5
14	38	3.8
15	54	5.9
16	76	6.3
17	53	5.7
18	40	4.0
19	47	5.2
20	23	2.2

Table 2.9 Employee productivity data

Figure 2.24 illustrates the scatter plot. As can be seen from the scatter plot there would seem to be some form of relationship; as productivity increases there is a tendency for the percentage rise in productivity to increase. The data, in fact, would indicate a positive relationship.

The scatter plot can be obtained using Excel.

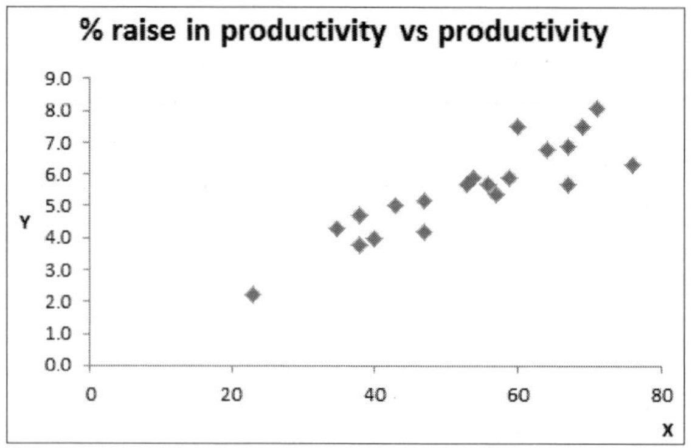

Figure 2.24

Step 1 Input Data Series

X: Cells C5:C24

Y: Cells D5:D24

See Figure 2.25

	A	B	C	D
1	Example 2.9 Scatter plot - % raise in productivity vs productivity			
2				
3		Employee	Productivity	% raise in productivity
4		Number	X	Y
5		1	47	4.2
6		2	71	8.1
7		3	64	6.8
8		4	35	4.3
9		5	43	5.0
10		6	60	7.5
11		7	38	4.7
12		8	59	5.9
13		9	67	6.9
14		10	56	5.7
15		11	67	5.7
16		12	57	5.4
17		13	69	7.5
18		14	38	3.8
19		15	54	5.9
20		16	76	6.3
21		17	53	5.7
22		18	40	4.0
23		19	47	5.2
24		20	23	2.2

Figure 2.25

Step 2 Highlight C4:D24

Step 3 Click the Insert and select Scatter (Figure 2.26).

Figure 2.26

Choose 2D chart and option 1 (see Figure 2.27).

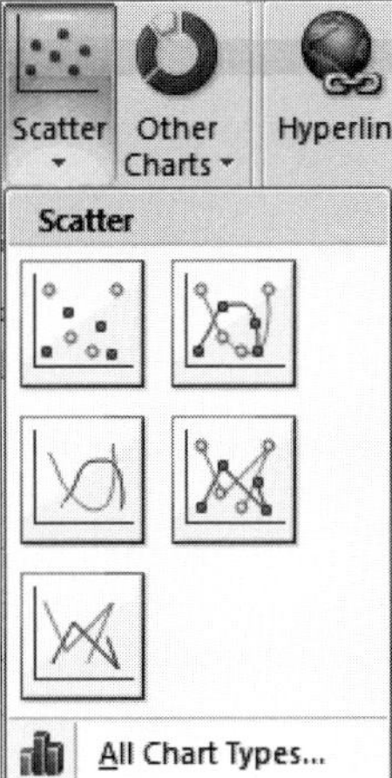

Figure 2.27

This will place the scatter plot in the location specified (see Figure 2.28).

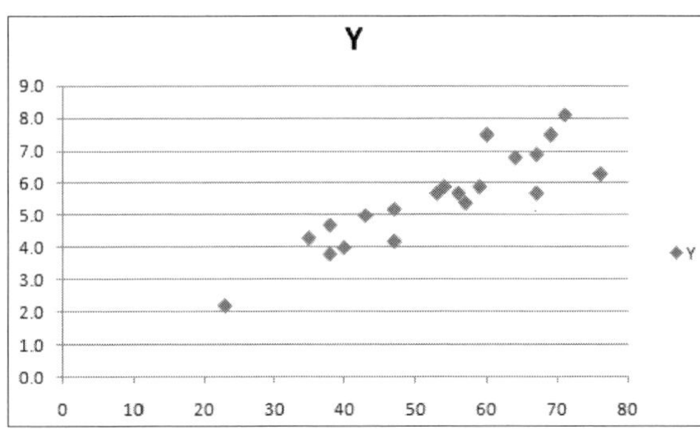

Figure 2.28

Figure 2.29 represents the scatter plot for % raise in productivity vs. productivity (graph re-formatted).

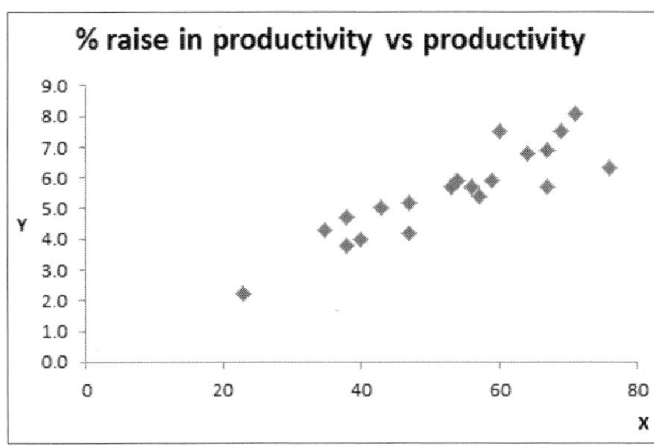

Figure 2.29

Note We can now ask Excel to fit a straight line (linear) to this data by right-clicking on a data point and choose fit trend line.

Student exercises

X2.1 Draw a suitable bar chart for the following data presented in Table 2.10.

Industrial Sources for Consumption and Investment Demand (thousand million)		
Producing industry	Consumption	Investment
Agriculture, mining	1.1	0.1
Metal manufacturers	2.0	2.7
Other manufacturing	6.8	0.3
Construction	0.9	2.7
Gas, electricity & water	1.2	0.2
Services	16.5	0.8
Total	28.5	7.8

Table 2.10

X2.2 Create a pie chart to represent the quarterly sales data shown in Table 2.11.

Northern Region	23%
Southern Region	32%
Central	35%
Out of territory	10%

X2.3 3600 people who work in Bradford were asked about the means of transport which they used for daily commuting. The data collected is shown in Table 2.12.

Type of Transport	Frequency of Response
Private car	1800
Bus	900
Train	300
Other	600

Table 2.12

Construct a pie chart to represent this data.

X2.4 Create a suitable histogram to represent the number of customers visited by a salesman over an 80 week period as presented in Table 2.13.

68	64	75	82	68	60	62	88	76	93	73	79	88	73	60	93
71	59	85	75	61	65	75	87	74	62	95	78	63	72	66	78
82	75	94	77	69	74	68	60	96	78	89	61	75	95	60	79
83	71	79	62	67	97	78	85	76	65	71	75	65	80	73	57
88	78	62	76	53	74	86	67	73	81	72	63	76	75	85	77

Table 2.13

X2.5 Obtain a scatter plot for the data in the table and comment on whether there is a link between road deaths and the number of vehicles on the road (Table 2.14). Would you expect this to be true? Provide reasons for your answer.

Countries	Vehicles per 100 population	Road Deaths per 100,000 population
Great Britain	31	14
Belgium	32	30
Denmark	30	23
France	46	32
Germany	30	26
Irish Republic	19	20
Italy	35	21
Netherlands	40	23
Canada	46	30
USA	57	35

Table 2.14

X2.6 Obtain a scatter plot for this data that represents the passenger miles flown by a UK-based airline (millions of passenger miles) during 2003–2004 (Table 2.15). Comment on the relationship between miles flown and quarter.

Year	Quarter 1	Quarter 2	Quarter 3	Quarter 4
2003	98.9	191.0	287.4	123.2
2004	113.4	228.8	316.2	155.7

Table 2.15

X2.7 The level of faulty goods, expressed in percentages, over the last 12 months is shown to be 1.3, 1.0, 0.9, 0.95, 0.9, 1.05, 1.0, 1.1, 1.15, 1.1, 1.12, and 1.15. Show the data as a time series plot and fit a straight line using Excel built in function. Comment upon the relationship.

2.3 Providing measures of average, dispersion, and shape for raw data

Most people seem to be intuitively familiar with the concept of average. The average is an idea that allows us to visualize or put a measure on what is considered to be the most representative value of the group (measure of location). This value is usually placed somewhere in the middle of the group and as such is the best approximation of all other values. Most of the time average is calculated as the arithmetic mean.

However, there are other possible ways to express an average. The mean (or arithmetic mean), mode, and median are all different measures of central tendency. The concept of central tendency that provides a measure of the middle value of a set of data values only gives a partial description.

A fuller description can be obtained by obtaining a measure of the dispersion (or spread) of the distribution. This kind of measure indicates whether the values in the distribution group closely about an average or whether they are more dispersed. These measures of dispersion are particularly important when we wish to compare distributions.

To illustrate this consider the two hypothetical distributions below which measure the value of sales per week made by two salesmen in their respective sales areas (see Figure 2.30).

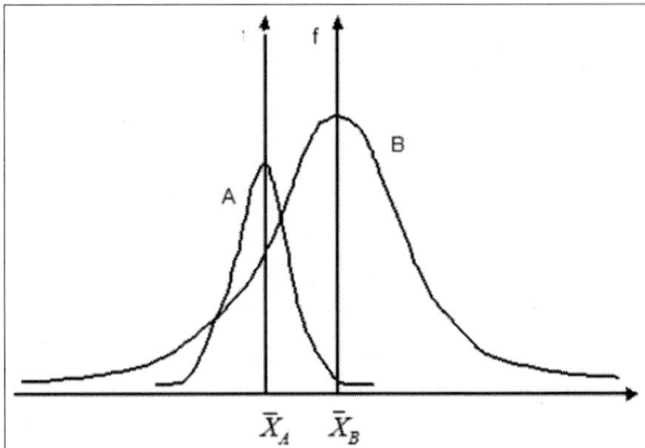

Figure 2.30

Let us say the means of the two distributions, A and B, were 4000 and 5000 respectively. But as you can see their shapes are very different, with B being far more spread out.

What would you infer from the two distributions given about the two salesmen and the areas that they work in? We can see that both distributions, A and B, have different mean values with distribution B being more spread out (or dispersed) than distribution A. Furthermore, distribution B is taller than distribution A.

In this section we shall explore methods that can be used to put a number to this idea of dispersion. The methods we will explain include range, interquartile range, semi-interquartile range, variance, and standard deviation. Beside these, other descriptive statistics are used to provide measures of shape: skewness and kurtosis. Skewness is a measure of the degree of asymmetry of a distribution and kurtosis is a measure of whether the data are peaked or flat relative to a normal distribution. The histogram is an effective graphical technique for showing both the skewness and kurtosis for a data set.

X

measure of location showing the typical value for a set of data values.

arithmetic mean the average of a set of numbers.

mean the average of a set of numbers.

mode the most frequent value in a set of numbers.

median the middle value of a set of numbers.

central tendency measures the location of the middle or the centre of a distribution.

measure of dispersion (or spread) showing how widely data is dispersed about its centre.

interquartile range (IQR) the inter-quartile range is a measure of the spread of or dispersion within a data set.

variance the difference between estimated cost, duration, or effort and the actual result of performance. In addition, it can be the difference between the initial or baseline product scope and the actual product delivered.

standard deviation a measure of the data spread, equal to the square root of variance.

skewness skewness is defined as asymmetry in the distribution of the data values.

kurtosis kurtosis is a measure of the 'peakedness' of the distribution.

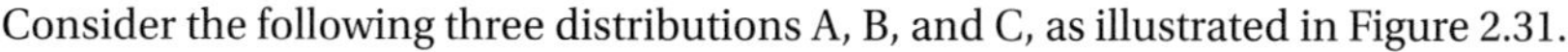

Consider the following three distributions A, B, and C, as illustrated in Figure 2.31.

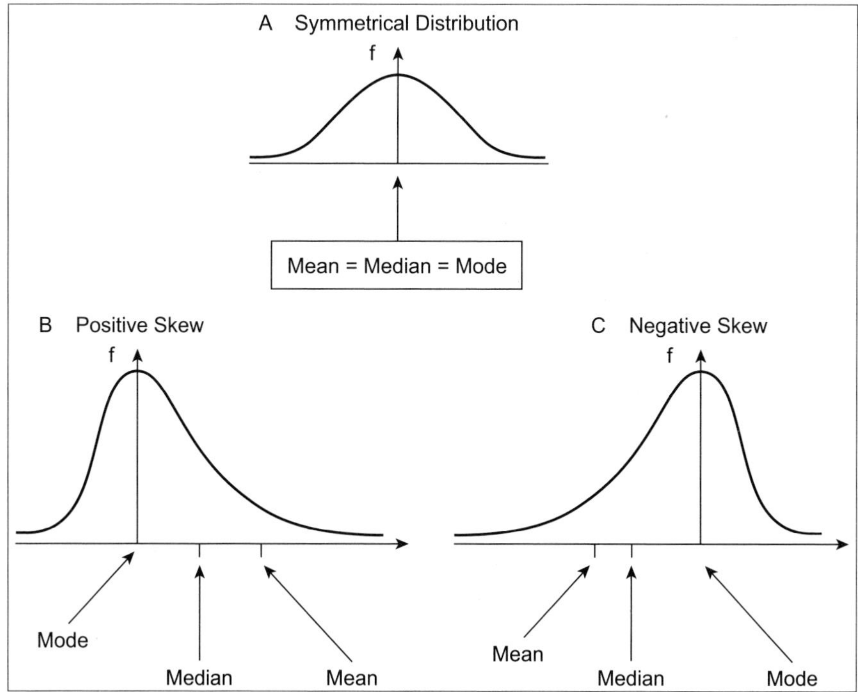

Figure 2.31

Distributions A, B, and C

Distribution A is said to be symmetrical, the mean, median and mode have the same value and thus coincide at the same point of the distribution. Distribution B has a high frequency of relatively low values and a low frequency of relatively high values. Consequently, the mean is 'dragged' toward the right (the high values) of the distribution. It is known as a right or positively skewed distribution. Distribution C has a high frequency of relatively high values and a low frequency of relatively low values. Consequently the mean is 'dragged' toward the left (the low values) of the distribution. It is known as a left or negatively skewed distribution.

The skewness of a frequency distribution can be an important consideration. For example, if your data set is salary, you would prefer a situation that led to a positively skewed distribution of salary to one that is negatively skewed. One measure of skewness is Pearson's coefficient of skewness with Excel using Fisher's skewness coefficient method.

Notes

1. With skewed data, the mean is not a good measure of central tendency because it is sensitive to extreme values. In this case the median is used to provide the measure of central tendency.
2. This value for skewness is zero for symmetric distributions (mean = median).
3. If mean < median, then skewness is negative and the distribution is said to be negatively skewed.
4. If mean > median, then skewness is positive and the distribution is said to be positively skewed.

symmetrical a data set is symmetrical when the data values are distributed in the same way above and below the middle value.

Example 2.10

Reconsider Example 2.5 which records the miles travelled by 120 salesmen during one week (Table 2.4). We can describe the overall performance of these 120 salesmen by calculating: an average score, a measure of spread, and a measure of shape. Figure 2.32 illustrates the Excel solution to Example 2.10 with the data series input into cells A6:H20:

	A	B	C	D	E	F	G	H	I	J	K	L
1	Example 2.10 Miles recorded by 120 salesman in one week											
2												
3												
4												
5												
6	403	407	407	408	410	412	413	413		Mean =	454.2667	=AVERAGE(A6:H20)
7	423	424	424	425	426	428	430	430		Median =	452.0000	=MEDIAN(A6:H20)
8	435	435	436	436	436	438	438	438		Mode =	430.0000	=MODE(A6:H20)
9	444	444	445	446	447	447	447	448				
10	452	453	453	453	454	455	455	456		Range =	112.0000	=MAX(A6:H20)-MIN(A6:H20)
11	462	462	462	463	464	465	466	468		Q1 =	434.7500	=QUARTILE.INC(A6:H20,1)
12	474	474	475	476	477	478	479	481		Q2 =	452.0000	=QUARTILE.INC(A6:H20,2)
13	490	493	494	495	497	498	498	500		Q3 =	473.2500	=QUARTILE.INC(A6:H20,3)
14	415	430	439	449	457	468	482	502		QR =	38.5000	=K13-K11
15	416	431	440	450	457	469	482	502		SIQR =	19.2500	=(K13-K11)/2
16	418	432	440	450	458	470	483	505		varp =	723.3956	=VAR.P(A6:H20)
17	419	432	441	451	459	471	485	508		sdp =	26.8960	=STDEV.P(A6:H20)
18	420	433	442	451	459	471	486	509		Fisher's skew =	0.2587	=SKEW(A6:H20)
19	421	433	442	451	460	472	488	511		Fisher's kurtosis =	-0.6578	=KURT(A6:H20)
20	421	434	443	452	460	473	489	515				
21										n=	120.0000	=COUNT(A6:H20)
22										critical skew =	0.4472	=2*SQRT(6/K21)
23										critical kurt =	0.8944	=2*SQRT(24/K21)

Figure 2.32

Interpretation From the Excel solution we observe the solutions to be:

1. Average: 454.3 (the mean), 452.0 (median), or 430.0 (mode) – note that Excel only provides one value but it is quite possible that more than one modal value may exist in your data set. For this reason we use the mean and median to provide a measure of the middle number.
2. Dispersion: 26.90 (the standard deviation), or 19.25 (semi-interquartile range).
3. Shape: 0.2587 (skewness) and –0.6578 (kurtosis).

The choice of the measure will depend on the type of numbers within the data set.

2.3.1 Measures of average using Excel

The Mean

The explanation of the Excel spreadsheet solution is as follows:

→ Excel method

Mean = Cell K6 Function: = AVERAGE (A6:H20)

From Excel: mean value = 454.3.

❋ **Interpretation** The average mile travelled is taken to be 454.3 miles.

Note In general the mean can be calculated using the formula:

$$\text{Mean }(\bar{X}) = \frac{\text{Sum of Data Values}}{\text{Total Number of Data Values}} = \frac{\sum X}{\sum f} \qquad (2.1)$$

Where $\bar{X}$ (X bar) represents the mean value for the sample data, $\sum X$ represents the sum of all the data values, and $\sum f$ represents the number of data values. If you have a grouped frequency distribution then Equation (2.1) is modified to:

$$\text{Mean} = \frac{\sum fX}{\sum f}.$$

The median

The explanation of the Excel spreadsheet solution is as follows:

➔ Excel method

Median = Cell K7 Function: = MEDIAN (A6:H20)

From Excel: median value = 452.0.

❋ **Interpretation** From the ordered list of numbers we can see that the median mileage travelled is 452.0. We can see from this example that the mean and median are reasonably close (454.3 compared with 452.0). It should be noted that the median is not influenced by the presence of very small or very large data values in the data set (extreme values or outliers). If we have a small number of these extreme values (or *outliers*) we use the median instead of the mean to represent the measure of central tendency.

Note The median is defined as the middle number when the data is arranged in order of size. The position of the median can be calculated as follows:

$$\text{Position of Percentile} = \frac{P}{100}(N + 1) \qquad (2.2)$$

Where P represents the percentile value and N represents the number of numbers in the data set. A percentile is a value on a scale of one hundred that indicates the percent of a distribution that is equal to or below it. To calculate the percentile values (or median or quartiles) you will need to make sure that your data set is stated in order of size and estimate the position of your percentile value (for the median P = 50). The normal textbook method is to use linear interpolation but the method used by Excel is method 1 of J. Freundand B. Perles (1987) 'A New Look at Quartiles of Ungrouped Data', *The American Statistician*, 41.3, 200–3.

X

percentile are values that divide a sample of data into one hundred groups containing (as far as possible) equal numbers of observations.

quartile quartiles are values that divide a sample of data into four groups containing (as far as possible) equal numbers of observations.

The Mode

The explanation of the Excel spreadsheet solution is as follows:

> **→ Excel method**
>
> Mode = Cell K8 Function: = MODE (A6:H20)
>
> Excel 2010 has two new functions that allow for the calculation of the mode: MODE.MULT and MODE.SNGL.

The mode is defined as the number which occurs most frequently (the most 'popular' number). From Excel: modal value = 430.0.

> **Note** At this stage we should remind the reader that the modal value for a data set can have more than one value. Excel will give you only one of these modal values.

The Quartiles

The median represents the middle value of the data set. If a data set is ranked in order of size we can then use the technique described above to calculate the values that would represent individual percentile or quartile values, as follows:

1. First quartile, Q_1, which represents the 25th percentile (P = 25).
2. Second quartile, Q_2, which represents the 50th percentile (P = 50).
3. Third quartile, Q_3, which represents the 75th percentile (P = 75).

Excel can be used to calculate the quartile values as follows:

> **→ Excel method**
>
> First quartile = Cell K11 Function: = QUARTILE.INC (A6:H20, 1)
> Second quartile = Cell K12 Function: = QUARTILE.INC (A6:H20, 2)
> Third quartile = Cell K13 Function: = QUARTILE.INC (A6:H20, 3)
>
> Excel 2010 has two new functions that allow for the calculation of the quartile: QUARTILE.EXC and QUARTILE.INC.

From Excel: 1st quartile Q1 = 434.75, 2nd quartile Q2 = 452.00, and 3rd quartile Q3 = 473.25.

> **Note** The median value also represents the 50th percentile (P = 50) as well as the second quartile (Q_2). These are all alternative expressions for the same statistic.

Interpretation

1. You interpret the 25th percentile of 434.75 to indicate that 25% of students obtained a mark of less than or equal to 434.75.
2. You interpret the 75th percentile of 473.25 to indicate that 75% of students obtained a mark of less than or equal to 473.25.

2.3.2 Measures of dispersion using Excel

In the previous section we explored providing measures of central tendency (or average). The next stage in the analysis is to provide a measure of how wide the distribution is along the variable axis. This can be achieved using a variety of methods, but we will focus on two main concepts: **standard deviation** and **quartile range**.

The range

The range is the simplest measure of dispersion and indicates the 'length' a distribution covers. It is determined by finding the difference between the lowest and highest value in a distribution. The explanation of the Excel spreadsheet solution is as follows:

Excel method

Range = Cell K10 Function: = MAX (A6:H20) - MIN (A6:H20)

Interpretation The range for the travelling salesmen problem is 112, which implies that the achieved distances travelled are scattered over 112 miles between the highest and the lowest mile recorded.

Note For grouped frequency distributions remember to use the upper and lower class boundaries as the largest and smallest data value.

The interquartile range and semi-interquartile range

The interquartile range represents the difference between the third and first quartile and can be used to provide a measure of spread within a data set which includes extreme data values. The interquartile range is little affected by extreme data values in the data set and is considered to be a good measure of spread for skewed distributions. The interquartile range is defined as:

$$\text{Interquartile range} = Q_3 - Q_1 \tag{2.3}$$

The **semi-interquartile range** (SIQR) is defined as:

$$\text{Semi-interquartile range} = \frac{Q_3 - Q_1}{2} \tag{2.4}$$

standard deviation a measure of the data spread, equal to the square root of variance.

quartile range difference in value between the third and first quartiles.

semi-interquartile range half the interquartile range.

The semi-interquartile range is another measure of spread and is computed as one half of the interquartile range which contains half of the data values. With Excel the first quartile value is 434.75 and the third quartile value is 473.25. The explanation of the Excel spreadsheet solution is as follows:

➜ Excel method

QR = Cell K14 Formula: = K13-K11
SIQR = Cell K15 Formula: = (K13-K11)/2

Interpretation Interquartile range is a measure of variation that ignores the extremes and focuses on the middle 50% of the data, i.e. only the data between Q_3 and Q_1.

The interquartile and semi-interquartile ranges are more stable than the range because they focus on the middle half of the data values and, therefore, cannot be influenced by extreme values. The semi-interquartile range is used in conjunction with the median to a highly skewed distribution or to describe an ordinal data set. The inter-quartile range (and semi-interquartile range) are more influenced by sampling fluctuations in normal distributions than is the standard deviation, and therefore are not often used for data that are approximately normally distributed. Furthermore, the actual data values are not used; and so we will now look at a method that provides a measure of spread but uses all the data values within the calculation.

The standard deviation and variance

Standard deviation is the measure of spread most commonly used in statistics when the mean is used to calculate central tendency. The variance and standard deviation provide a measure of how dispersed the data values (X) are about the mean value ($\bar{X}$). Because of its close links with the mean, the standard deviation can be greatly affected if the mean gives a poor measure of central tendency. If we calculated for each data value ($X - \bar{X}$), then some would be positive and some negative. Thus, if we were to sum all these differences, we would find that $\Sigma(X - \bar{X}) = 0$, that is, the positive and negative values would cancel out. To avoid this problem we square each individual difference before undertaking the summation. This provides us with the squared average difference, which is known as the variance (VAR(X)).

Equation (2.5) is used to provide the value of the variance:

$$\text{Variance, VAR(X)} = \frac{\Sigma(X - \bar{X})^2}{\Sigma f} \tag{2.5}$$

To provide us with an average difference we take the square root of the variance to give the standard deviation (SD(X)):

$$\text{Standard deviation, SD(X)} = \sqrt{\frac{\Sigma(X - \bar{X})^2}{\Sigma f}} \tag{2.6}$$

The explanation of the Excel spreadsheet solution is as follows:

→ Excel method

VARP = Cell K16 Function: = VAR.P(A6:H20)
SDP = Cell K17 Function: = STDEV.P(A6:H20)

Excel 2010 has two new functions that allow for the calculation of the population variance: VAR.P and population standard deviation: STDEV.P.

Note You should note that Excel contains two different functions (VAR, VARP) to calculate the value of the variance. The function that you use is dependent upon whether the data set represents the complete population or is a sample from the population being measured.

1. If the data set is the complete population then the population variance (σ^2) is given by the Excel function VAR.P().
2. If the data set is a sample from the population then the sample variance (s^2) is given by the Excel function VAR.S().

This issue is very important when collecting a sample (s) from a population and using the sample to infer population values or undertake hypothesis testing. In most situations the population standard deviation (σ) is unknown and we use the sample standard deviation (s) as an estimate. We can show by algebraic manipulation that Equation (2.5) can be simplified into a form that is easier to solve using pencil/paper/calculator:

$$\text{Variance, VAR}(X) = \frac{\sum X^2}{\sum f} - (\bar{X})^2 \tag{2.7}$$

$$\text{Standard deviation, SD}(X) = \sqrt{\left[\frac{\sum X^2}{\sum f} - (\bar{X})^2\right]} \tag{2.8}$$

These two Excel functions assume that the data set represents the entire population and is not a sample taken from a population. From Excel: population variance = 723.3956 and population standard deviation = 26.8960.

Note Variance describes how much the data values are scattered around the mean value, or, to put it differently, how tightly the data values are grouped around the mean. In a way, the smaller the variance, the more representative the mean value. Unfortunately, the variance does not have the same dimension as the data set or the mean. In other words, if the values are percentages, inches, degrees C, or any other measure, the variance is not expressed in the same values, because it is expressed in squared units. As such, it is very useful as a comparison measure between the two data sets, as we will discover later. To bring the variance into the same units of measure as the data set, the standard deviation needs to be calculated. Although the standard deviation is less susceptible to extreme values than the range, standard deviation is still more sensitive than the semi-interquartile range. If the possibility of outliers presents itself, then the standard deviation should be supplemented by the semi-interquartile range.

❊ **Interpretation** A large proportion of the recorded miles obtained in the salesmen problem, as in the example 2.10, are clustered within 26.90 marks around the mean mileage of 454.3. We will explain later how large this proportion is. Most of the recorded miles are between 427.3707 (454.2667 – 26.8960) and 481.1627 (454.2667 + 26.8960). 78 out of 120 recorded miles are in this interval, which is in our case 65% of all the recorded miles travelled.

2.3.3 Measures of shape using Excel

The final stage in providing descriptive statistics is to provide measures of shape: skewness and kurtosis.

Skewness describes the asymmetry of the distribution relative to the mean. A positive skewness indicates that the distribution has a longer right-hand tail (skewed towards more positive values). A negative skewness indicates that the distribution is skewed to the left (skewed towards less positive values). Excel uses Fisher's skewness coefficient to provide a measure of skewness:

$$\text{Fisher's skewness} = \frac{n}{(n-1)(n-2)} \sum \left(\frac{(X - \bar{X})}{s} \right)^3 \tag{2.9}$$

Where s represents the sample standard deviation (sample variance = $[n/(n-1)]^*$ population variance). This can be calculated using STDEV.S( ).

➜ Excel method

Fisher's skew = Cell K18	Function: = SKEW (A6:H20)
n = Cell K21	Function: = COUNT (A6:H20)
Critical skew = Cell K22	Formula: = 2*SQRT(6/K21)

From Excel: skewness = 0.2587.

❊ **Interpretation** The value of skewness is calculated to be 0.2587.

Note If the skewness value is greater than $\pm 2 \times \sqrt{\frac{6}{N}}$ (where N is the sample size), this would indicate severe skewness. In Example 2.10 we have n = 120 and error measurement is $\pm 2 \times \sqrt{\frac{6}{120}} = \pm 0.4472$. The measured value of skewness 0.2587(cell K18) lies within the region ± 0.4472 (cell K22), and not outside. We conclude that the distribution is not significantly skewed.

Kurtosis describes the peakedness or flatness of a distribution relative to the normal distribution. Positive peakedness indicates a more peaked distribution. A negative kurtosis indicates a flatter distribution. A standard normal distribution has a kurtosis of zero.

Consider the two distributions in Figure 2.33.

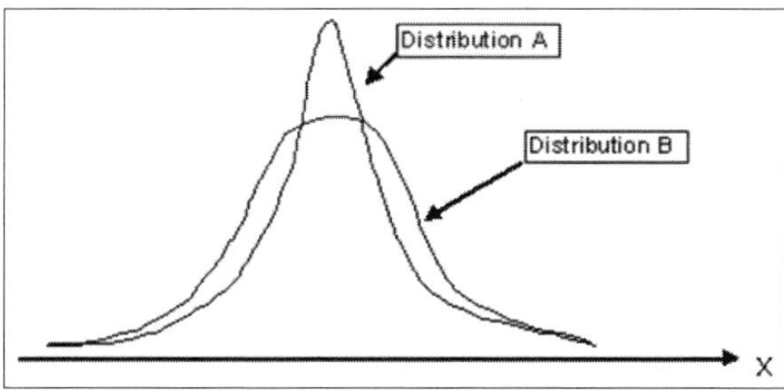

Figure 2.33

We can see from the two distributions that distribution A is more peaked than distribution B but the means and standard deviations are approximately the same.

A measure of whether the curve of a distribution is bell-shaped (Mesokurtic), peaked (Leptokurtic), and flat (Platykurtic) is provided by Fisher's measure of kurtosis given by equation (2.10):

$$\text{Kurtosis} = \frac{n(n+1)}{(n-1)(n-2)(n-3)} \sum \left(\frac{(X - \bar{X})}{s} \right)^4 - \frac{3(n-1)^2}{(n-2)(n-3)} \tag{2.10}$$

This equation is used by Excel to provide an estimate of kurtosis.

➜ Excel method

Fisher's Kurtosis = Cell K19 Function: = KURT (A6:H20)
Critical kurt = Cell K23 Formula: = 2*SQRT(24/K21)

From Excel: kurtosis = −0.6578.

Interpretation The value of kurtosis is calculated to be −0.6578.

Note If the kurtosis value is greater than $\pm 2 \times \sqrt{\frac{24}{N}}$ (where N is the sample size), this would indicate severe kurtosis. In Example 4.10 we have N = 120 and error measurement is $\pm 2 \times \sqrt{\frac{24}{120}}$ = ± 0.8944. The measured value of kurtosis −0.6578 (cell K19) lies within the region ± 0.8944 (cell K23) and not outside. We conclude that the distribution does not have a significant kurtosis problem. Furthermore, the negative value (−0.6578) indicates a flat distribution compared to the normal distribution.

Finally, a **five-number summary** is useful in providing a summary of your data set. It consists of the five most important sample percentiles:

1. The sample minimum (smallest observation).
2. The lower quartile or first quartile.
3. The median (middle value).
4. The upper quartile or third quartile.
5. The sample maximum (largest observation).

five-number summary
a five-number summary is especially useful when we have so many data that it is sufficient to present a summary of the data rather than the whole data set. It consists of 5 values: the most extreme values in the data set (maximum and minimum values), the lower and upper quartiles, and the median.

In order for these statistics to exist the observations must be from a univariate variable that can be measured on an ordinal, interval, or ratio scale. An example to illustrate this method can be found in the next chapter.

Student exercises

X2.8 The average hourly hits to the server over the last six hours were: 320, 295, 334, 456, 300, and 305. Calculate the mean and the median using Excel functions AVERAGE () and MEDIAN (). What can you conclude?

X2.9 Two training classes took a test and the results were marked on the scale of zero to one hundred. The first group got an average score of 75, with the standard deviation of 8. The second group got an average score of 65, with the standard deviation of 4. How do these two groups compare?

X2.10 Cameos Ltd is employed by a leading market research organization based in Berlin. The company is discussing with the firm to expand the catering facilities provided to its employees to include a greater range of products. The initial research by Cameos has identified the following set of weekly spend (€) by individual employees (Table 2.16).

22	16	26	33	33	37	9	23	32	17
20	13	12	18	19	10	21	22	25	22
22	22	34	24	23	21	38	31	41	20

Table 2.16

(a) Use Excel to plot the histogram and visually comment on the shape of the weekly expenditure. Hint: use class width of 10.

(b) Use Excel to calculate appropriate descriptive statistics (average, dispersion, and shape) to provide a numerical summary for the data set.

(c) Use descriptive statistics in conjunction with the histogram to comment on weekly expenditure.

X2.11 Greendelivery.com has recently decided to review the weekly mileage of its delivery vehicles that are used to deliver shopping purchased online to customer homes from a central parcel depot. The sample data collected is part of the first stage in analysing the economic benefit of potentially moving all vehicles to bio fuels from diesel (Table 2.17).

80	165	159	143	140
136	138	118	120	124
159	131	93	145	109
163	136	163	142	80
106	111	123	161	179
144	145	91	112	146
170	105	131	141	122
137	152	109	122	126
114	155	92	143	165

Table 2.17

(a) Use Excel to construct a frequency distribution and plot the histogram with class intervals of 20 and classes 75–94, 95–144, ..., 175–194. Comment on the pattern in mileage travelled by the company vehicles.

(b) Use Excel to determine appropriate descriptive statistics (average, dispersion, and shape).

(c) Use descriptive statistics in conjunction with the histogram to comment on weekly mileage. Explain using your answers to (a) and (b).

2.4 Basic survey processing

Most students will face their first questionnaire processing challenge while working on their final piece of work to get a degree, if not sooner. The practitioners, assuming they are not professional pollsters, will also encounter the same problem of how to process survey data sooner or later, regardless of their area of specialization. If you are dealing with customers, suppliers, quality issues, finance, or any other area, you are about to face the need to process your survey data.

The issue of designing a questionnaire is a separate domain and belongs to a different book such as the excellent Bryman and Bell textbook listed below. Numerous good books on either research methods, or those dedicated to survey design, will provide sufficient guidance on how to design various instruments to gather data. However, most of them do not provide sufficient details on how to process the data, which is precisely what this section will do.

A questionnaire will invariably have different types of questions, such as verbal and numerical, open and closed, and the answers may be binary, interval, ratio. Processing such questions requires that different answers are treated and pre-processed in a different way. However, once this has been accomplished, the data set will always end up looking like one large spreadsheet. To get tables from such a spreadsheet is something that pivot table functionality of Excel does very well: this will be the focus of this section.

2.4.1 A need for questionnaires

The need for questionnaires is to enable a business to make decisions, one needs data as the starting point. Without data, there is no information and without information, the decisions that one makes is arbitrary, subjective and without any rigour. The word 'decision' we use here in its broadest meaning. It does not necessarily mean a discrete; yes/no type of decision, but any situation where analysis before understanding the issue is necessary. A good example is a student thesis.

A thesis will invariably be based around some kind of hypothesis and student's task is to explain the topic and come up with some kind of conclusions that will validate such a hypothesis. Very often these components are not so obvious, so let's give an example. A thesis might be entitled, something like: 'Gender and quantitative methods.' The objective of such a thesis could be to establish if there is a preference for applying certain quantitative methods and if such preferences are gender-dependent. This is effectively a hypothesis. In order to validate it (accept or reject) a lot of research needs to be done. This research can rely on the secondary sources only, or, to suit the purposes of this chapter, we can say that we'll engage in primary methods of data collection.

Questionnaires are one of the most popular and deceptively simple methods of data gathering. It suffices to say that the art of building a questionnaire is not something that can be learned overnight and many questionnaires have failed to collect the data as they were supposed to. Be that as it may, all of us intuitively know that by asking questions we will get some answers and that by aggregating and processing these answers we can gain additional insight into the problem that we have been enquiring about.

To summarize, a questionnaire is an instrument for gathering the primary (field, or original) data and it is used to either supplement the secondary (desk research) data sets, or to provide a genuine new insight into the problem (e.g. a customer survey about the flavour of a new toothpaste).

2.4.2 Types of questions

Without going into the principles and theory of how to construct the questionnaire, one way or the other the questionnaire designer will end up with several different types of questions. The most fundamental division is between open and closed questions. An open question is the one that does not suggest any answers, but allows the respondent to respond in a completely free format. A good example is something like this:

Q: State your favourite colour?

A: ____________________

To reformulate the same question differently, we can turn it into a closed question. Something like this:

Q: State your favourite colour?

A: a) Blue
b) Green
c) Red
d) Brown
e) Yellow
f) Any other colour

As we can see, the closed questions do not necessarily restrict the respondents to only certain colors. This is why we put an option f) giving them a chance to state any colour. However, the way we phrased the question makes it easier for us to process it and it clearly indicates that most of the colours we expect are blue, green, red, brown, and yellow.

What happens if for whatever reason we are not in the position to close the question and we have to go with an open question? How do we process such a question?

First, we must understand that, before processing open questions, they have to be closed. The simplest technique used is the so called content analysis approach. Let us assume that we put forward question as in the above example, that is:

Q: State your favourite colour?

A: ____________________

X

data collection the gathering of facts that can then be used to make decisions.

Let us also assume that we have one hundred respondents in our mini survey. Once we have all the results, we can count the colours people listed. For example, the result could have been something like this:

Blue	20
Green	25
Red	20
Brown	15
Yellow	10
Magenta	5
Pink	3
Orange	1
Black	1
Total =	100

Table 2.18

This example looks very easy for a simple reason that it is very easy to count the colours. What if our question was much more complex? This is why we call the processing technique a 'content analysis'.

Q: Which particular aspect of the last lecture did you find difficult?

A: ____

The way to process this question is to read all the answers and come up with the 'buckets' in which all the answers can be categorized. For example, possible categories might be labelled as follows:

The speed at which it was delivered – 35 answers
Lack of clarity on the second topic – 30 answers
Not enough examples – 20 answers
Not related to real life examples – 5 answers
Difficult language – 3 answers
Poor introduction – 2 answers
Other – 5 answers
TOTAL 100

As we can see, by analysing all the answers, grouping them in similar categories and counting the frequencies, we have effectively come to the same result as if we had the closed question in the first place.

Note We should always attempt to close the questions in a questionnaire before conducting the survey. It is not mandatory to do this, but it helps. Testing and piloting of the questionnaire is often used for such purposes. Questionnaires are usually piloted to test the clarity of the questions and whether the answers are relevant. However, it is also good practice to use this stage to close as many questions as possible.

Processing open questions is the most time consuming activity and the results are most subjective. The simple reason is that two different people could come up with somewhat different labels (or, 'buckets'), which will skew the interpretation of the overall results. As we said, processing the closed questions is much easier; however, they come in numerous 'flavours', depending on types of answers.

2.4.3 Types of answers

Let's state the obvious: answers in fact represent the variables. If we ask a question about the respondent's age, we are essentially defining a variable. In this case, the question that needs answering is: what kinds of variables exist? The first level of separation is to split variables into quantitative and qualitative. Sometimes quantitative variables are called numerical variables and qualitative variables are called categorical variables. The scale used to measure quantitative variables (or numerical variables) can either be an interval, or alternatively a ratio scale. Qualitative variables (or categorical variables), on the other hand, are measured on an ordinal or alternatively on a nominal scale.

Note If a group of business students were asked to name their favourite web browser, the variable would be qualitative. If the time spent on the computer to research a topic were measured, then the variable would be quantitative.

On interval measurement scales, one unit on the scale represents the same magnitude of the characteristic being measured across the whole range of the scale. For example, if student stress was being measured on an interval scale, then a difference between a score of 5 and a score of 6 would represent the same difference in anxiety as would a difference between a score of 9 and a score of 10. Interval scales do not have a true zero point, and therefore it is not possible to make statements about how many times higher one score is than another. For the stress measurement, it would not be valid to say that a person with a score of 6 was twice as anxious as a person with a score of 3.

Ratio scales are like interval scales except they have true zero points. For example, a weight of 100g is twice as much as the weight of 50g. Interval and ratio measurements are also called continuous variables.

Measurements with ordinal scales are ordered in the sense that higher numbers represent higher values. However, the intervals between the numbers are not necessarily equal. For example, on a five-point rating scale measuring student satisfaction, the difference between a rating of 1 ('very poor') and a rating of 2 ('poor') may not represent the same difference as the difference between a rating of 4 ('good') and a rating of 5 ('very good'). The lowest point on the rating scale in this example was arbitrarily chosen to be 1 and this scale does not have a true zero point. The only conclusion you can make is that one is better than the other (or even worse) but you cannot say that one is twice as good as the other.

Nominal measurement consists of assigning items to groups or categories. No quantitative information is conveyed and no ordering of the items is implied. Nominal scales are therefore qualitative rather than quantitative. Football club allegiance, sex or gender, degree type, courses studied are all examples of nominal scales. Frequency distributions are usually used to analyse data measured on a nominal scale. Variables measured on a nominal scale are often referred to as categorical or qualitative variables.

It is very important that you understand the type of data variable that you will be dealing with, since the type of graph or summary statistic calculated will be dependent upon the type of data variable that you are handling. Table 2.19 summarizes the different measurement scales with examples provided of these different scales.

Measurement Scale	Recognizing a measure scale
Nominal data	1. Classification data, e.g. male or female, red or black car. 2. Arbitrary labels, e.g. m or f, r or b, 0 or 1. 3. No ordering, e.g. it makes no sense to state that r > b.
Ordinal data	1. Ordered list, e.g. student satisfaction scale of 1, 2, 3, 4, and 5. 2. Differences between values are not important, e.g. political parties can be given labels: far left, left, mid, right, far right
Interval data	1. Ordered, constant scale, with no natural zero, e.g. temperature, dates. 2. Differences make sense, but ratios do not, e.g. temperature difference.
Ratio data	1. Ordered, constant scale, and a natural zero, e.g. length, height, weight, and age.

Table 2.19

Now we understand different types of variables, let's provide a few examples on how answers in closed question could be constructed. We'll create a very simple list of questions, not a proper questionnaire. The questions used here have only purpose to illustrate how different types of answers are processed.

Sample questions from a questionnaire:

Q1: Respondent's sex?

A1: a) Male
b) Female

Q2: Which political party did you vote for during last election?

A2: a) Conservative
b) Labour
c) Liberal Democrats
d) Other

Q3: How much do you agree with the view that smoking is antisocial?

A3: a) Strongly agree
b) Somewhat agree
c) Not sure
d) Disagree
e) Strongly disagree

Q4: On a scale of 1 to 10, where 1 is the worst and 10 is the best, how would you rank your experience?

A4: _______________

Q5: What is your age?

A5: a) 20 or less
b) 21–35
c) 36–50
d) 51 or more

We'll assume that we used this simple questionnaire and surveyed 20 respondents. How do we process the questionnaires?

2.4.4 Pre-processing of the answers

With Excel it is quite straightforward to pre-process survey answers by entering answers in a spreadsheet and to assign rows to respondents and columns to questions as illustrated in Figure 2.34.

	A	B	C	D	E	F
1		Q1: Sex	Q2: Party	Q3: Smoking	Q4: Experience	Q5: Age
2	R1	a	a	c	2	a
3	R2	a	a	d	3	b
4	R3	b	b	a	2	b
5	R4	a	c	a	1	b
6	R5	b	d	b	6	c
7	R6	a	c	b	2	c

Figure 2.34

Figure 2.34 shows only six respondents. As we can see, we did not enter the full answers to our cells, but just letters representing an answer. The only exception is question 4, because this is a pure numerical variable and we left it in our questionnaire as an open question.

In Section 2.4.5 we will process this spreadsheet and convert into data tables, so it would help us a great deal if we converted all the labels in the cells (letters a, b, c, etc.) into actual answers.

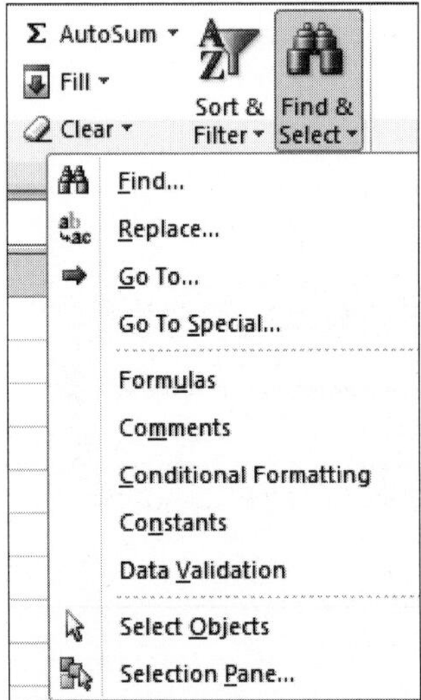

Figure 2.35

In order to do this, go to Home tab, click on Find and Select at the very right of the ribbon and select Replace option (see Figure 2.35).

The next step is to highlight the first column and complete the Find and Replace dialogue box as illustrated in Figure 2.36.

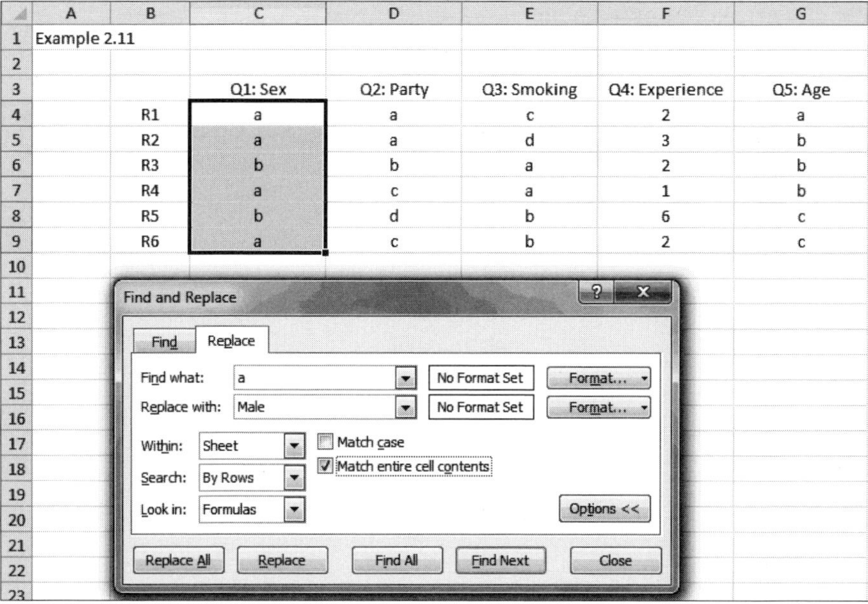

	A	B	C	D	E	F	G
1	Example 2.11						
2							
3			Q1: Sex	Q2: Party	Q3: Smoking	Q4: Experience	Q5: Age
4		R1	a	a	c	2	a
5		R2	a	a	d	3	b
6		R3	b	b	a	2	b
7		R4	a	c	a	1	b
8		R5	b	d	b	6	c
9		R6	a	c	b	2	c

Figure 2.36

Click on the Replace All button.

Excel will automatically report that four replacements have been made and the table will look as shown in Figure 2.37.

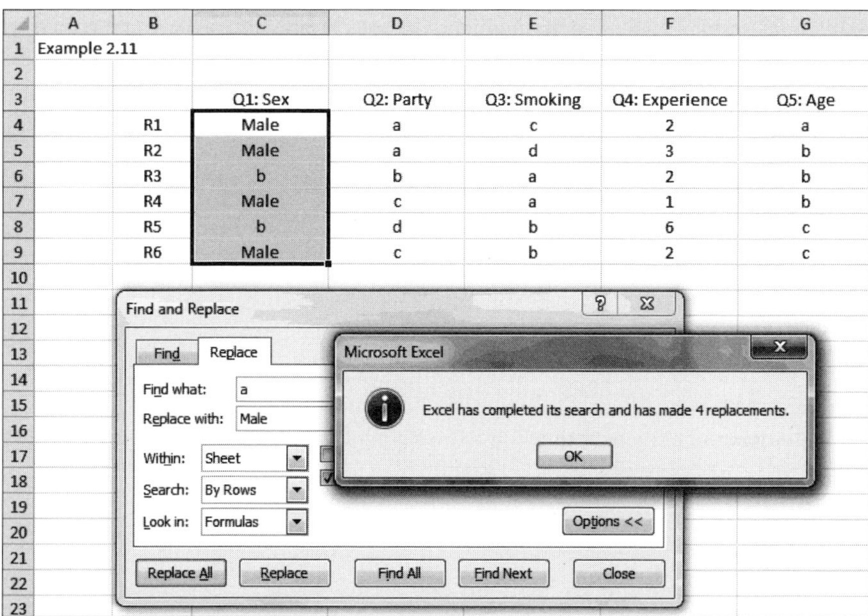

	A	B	C	D	E	F	G
1	Example 2.11						
2							
3			Q1: Sex	Q2: Party	Q3: Smoking	Q4: Experience	Q5: Age
4		R1	Male	a	c	2	a
5		R2	Male	a	d	3	b
6		R3	b	b	a	2	b
7		R4	Male	c	a	1	b
8		R5	b	d	b	6	c
9		R6	Male	c	b	2	c

Figure 2.37

Repeat the process, but replace 'Find what:' from ***a*** to ***b*** and 'Replace with:' to female. If you repeat this procedure for all five questions, you will end up with a spreadsheet as shown in Figure 2.38.

	A	B	C	D	E	F	G
1	Example 2.11						
2							
3			Q1: Sex	Q2: Party	Q3: Smoking	Q4: Experience	Q5: Age
4		R1	Male	Strongly agree	Disagree	2	20 or less
5		R2	Male	Strongly agree	Strongly disagree	3	21 - 35
6		R3	Female	Agree	Strongly agree	2	21 - 35
7		R4	Male	Disagree	Strongly agree	1	21 - 35
8		R5	Female	Strongly disagree	Agree	6	36 - 50
9		R6	Male	Disagree	Agree	2	36 - 50

Figure 2.38

Note The reason why we did not enter full answers in every cell is a strong possibility of an error. A smallest spelling mistake, or inclusion of a space after a word, would automatically indicate to Excel that this is a different answer. By starting with just letters and converting them subsequently into proper answers, we minimize the possibility of this problem. Another way around this problem is to have a data validation for every cell per row (per question); but we will let the reader explore this option.

We are now ready to process our questionnaires and start creating meaningful data tables. In Excel language this is called creating pivot tables.

2.4.5 Pivoting the data

The pivot table is an old concept, although the name pivot came into more frequent use through Microsoft. Pivot tables are the standard ways of tabulating data, but the way it is done is unique to a spreadsheet.

To find it in Excel, just open the Insert tab on the Ribbon and go to pivot table symbol, as shown in Figure 2.39.

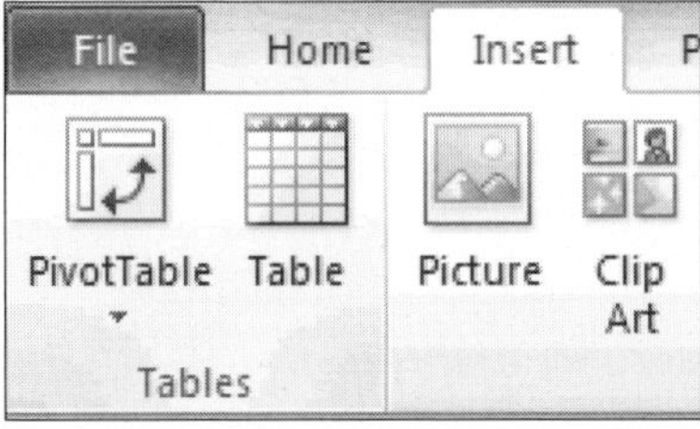

Figure 2.39

For the purpose of demonstrating how to create pivot tables, we'll use our dummy data set as above. The data spreadsheet is given again in Figure 2.40.

	A	B	C	D	E	F	G
1	Example 2.11						
2							
3		Respondent	Q1: Sex	Q2: Party	Q3: Smoking	Q4: Experience	Q5: Age
4		R1	Male	Strongly agree	Disagree	2	20 or less
5		R2	Male	Strongly agree	Strongly disagree	3	21 - 35
6		R3	Female	Agree	Strongly agree	2	21 - 35
7		R4	Male	Disagree	Strongly agree	1	21 - 35
8		R5	Female	Strongly disagree	Agree	6	36 - 50
9		R6	Male	Disagree	Agree	2	36 - 50

Figure 2.40

Note It is very important to note that we have inserted the word 'Respondent' in the cell B3. Why? The most fundamental requirement behind pivoting data is that every column MUST have a title. We put the title 'Respondent' for column B. All other columns already had titles. Without a column heading, Excel will refuse to pivot data.

After we click on the pivot table symbol, a dialogue box will open. Note the range we selected It includes the column headings.

It also includes the location for the pivot table, which will be B12 in the existing spreadsheet as illustrated in Figure 2.41.

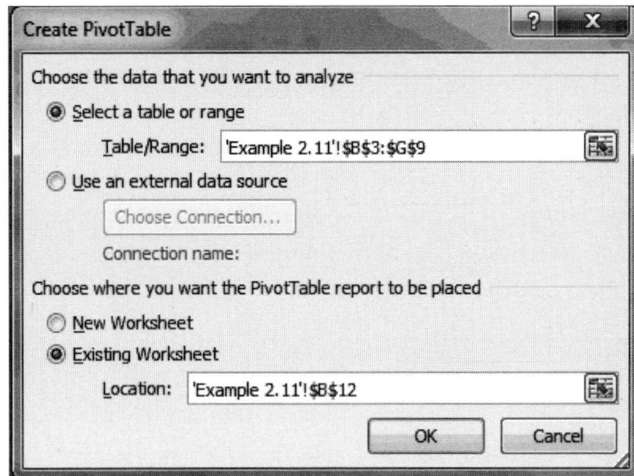

Figure 2.41

As soon as you clicked 'OK', the page will look as illustrated in Figure 2.42.

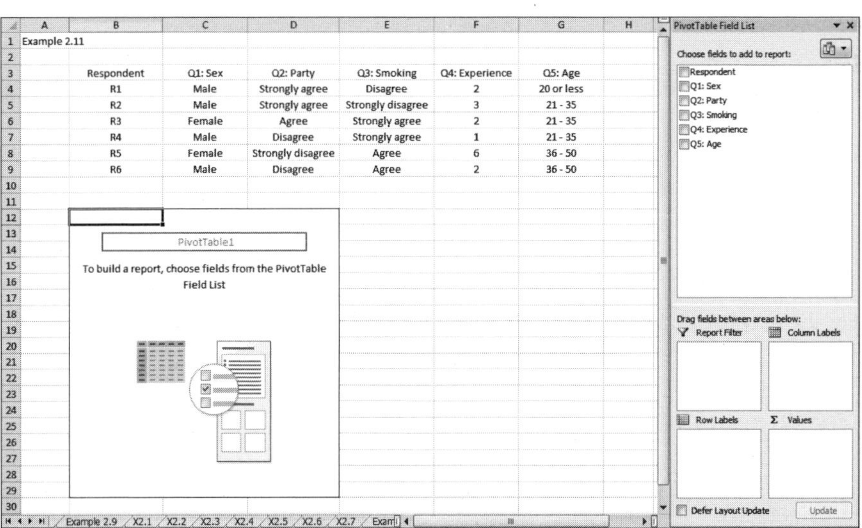

Figure 2.42

Starting from cell B12 we have a pivot table space and as soon as the cursor is on the pivot table space, a Field List pane on the right hand of the screen opens up.

What do we do next?

Let's say that we want to count how many male and female respondents we had in our survey. We go to the Field List pane on the right hand side of the screen and make sure that Q1: Sex is dragged to Row Labels, whilst Respondents are dragged to the Value box (see Figure 2.43):

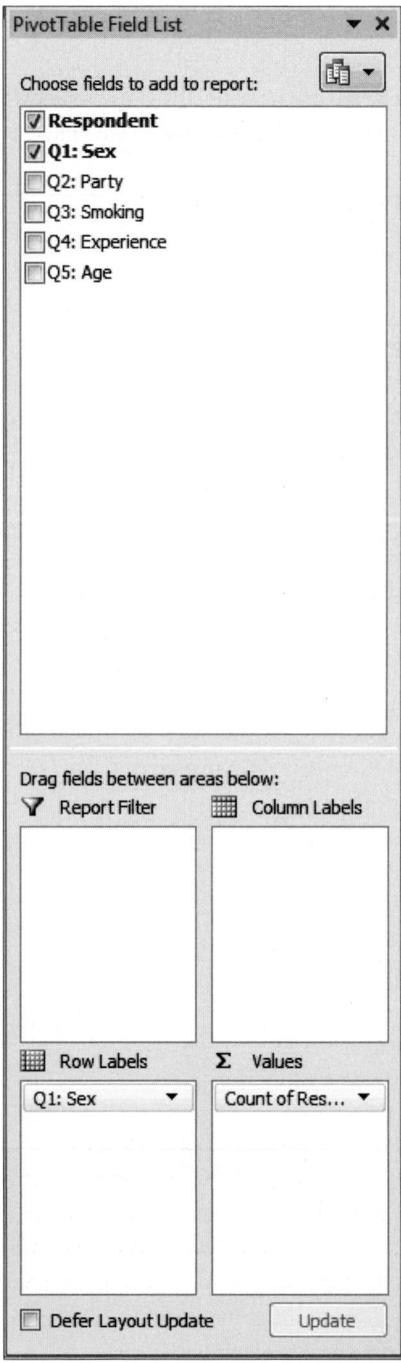

Figure 2.43

The result will be a small table as illustrated in Figure 2.44.

	A	B	C
11			
12		**Row Labels**	**Count of Respondent**
13		Female	2
14		Male	4
15		**Grand Total**	**6**

Figure 2.44

This is our first data tabulation. If we wanted to have data presented as percentages, we should right click on the pivot table, which will give us a dialogue box as illustrated in Figure 2.45.

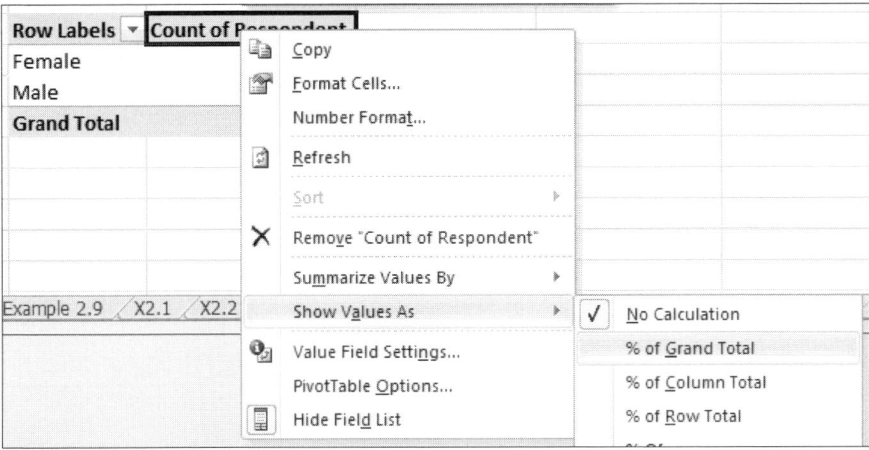

Figure 2.45

If we pick 'Show Values As', a number of options are available. We selected the one called '% of Grand Total.'

The final result is illustrated in Figure 2.46.

	A	B	C
11			
12		**Row Labels**	**Count of Respondent**
13		Female	33.33%
14		Male	66.67%
15		**Grand Total**	**100.00%**

Figure 2.46

In order to create a new pivot table, it is much more economical to copy the pivot table than to start creating a new one. Just highlight the cells from B12:C15, do Copy and Paste to, for example, E12. You will have an identical pivot table.

However, you can now change the questions. Ensure that the cursor is on the pivot table, which will make the right hand pane visible. Drag from the Row Labels box Q1:Sex back to the box above and drag down in its place Q5:Age.

The pivot table will change instantly as illustrated in Figure 2.47.

	D	E	F
11			
12		Row Labels	Count of Q1: Sex
13		20 or less	1
14		21 - 35	3
15		36 - 50	2
16		Grand Total	6

Figure 2.47

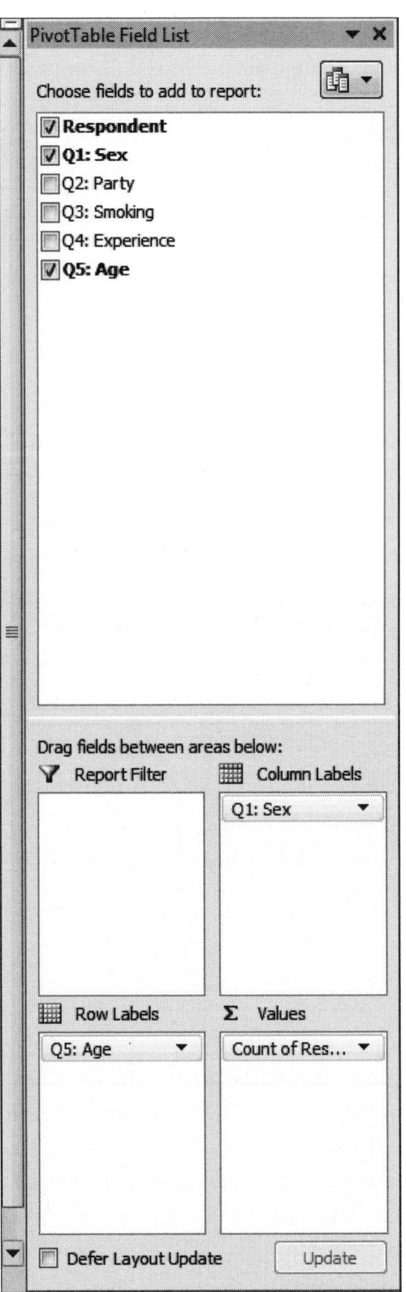

Figure 2.48

Let's see how to provide cross-references. As an example, let's try to see if by cross tabulating age and sex we can get any interesting patterns.

We'll copy/paste one of the existing pivot tables and modify it again.

We'll drag Q5: Age to Row Labels box and Q1: Sex to Column Labels box.

See Figure 2.48

This simple cross tabulation produces the following results illustrated in Figure 2.49.

	D	E	F	G	H
11					
12		**Count of Respondent**	**Column Labels** ▾		
13		**Row Labels** ▾	**Female**	**Male**	**Grand Total**
14		20 or less		1	1
15		21 - 35	1	2	3
16		36 - 50	1	1	2
17		**Grand Total**	**2**	**4**	**6**

Figure 2.49

Even more complicated cross tabulations are possible and we'll let readers experiment with the results.

As we can see, tabulating and cross tabulating data using pivot tables is not very complex. Processing survey data becomes one of the least demanding parts of the overall process, which is the way it should be. It enables researches to quickly tabulate data, experiment with various cross-referencing and focus on the analysis part of the survey. Another advantage of the pivot table functionality in Excel is that it is very easy to chart the data once the tables are created.

2.4.6 Charting the data

To chart the data from a pivot table, you need to click on the pivot table and select Insert tab on the Ribbon, as illustrated in Figure 2.50.

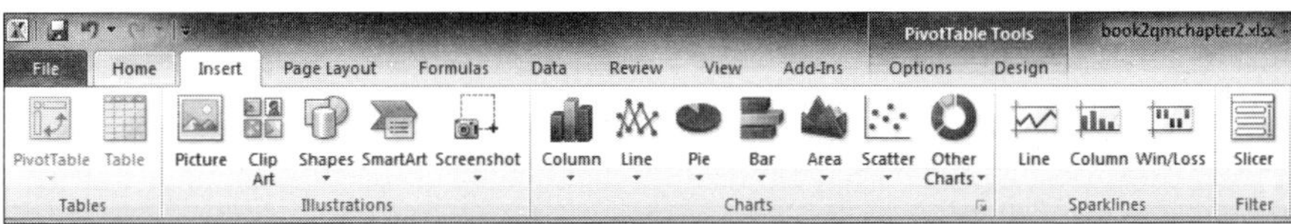

Figure 2.50

From the Charts section select the one that is appropriate for your data set. In our case we selected the Column chart option. The result is illustrated in Figure 2.51.

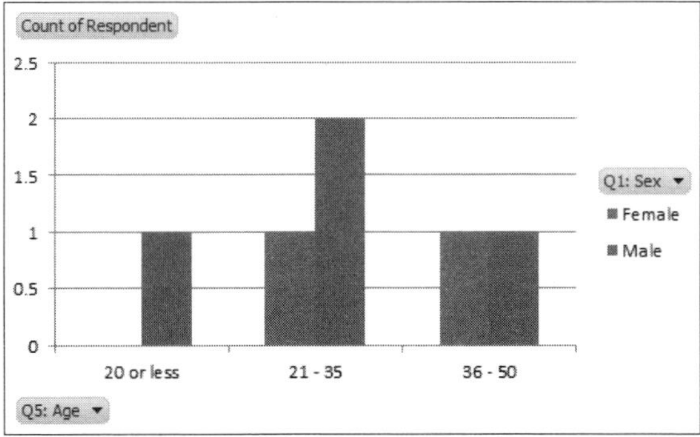

Figure 2.51

Charting pivot tables in Excel is no different from charting any other data table.

2.4.7 Changing the data or data source

In Excel, we can change the data or data source and make some modifications to the answer cells. It would be a waste of time to recreate all the tables that you designed using pivot table function. Fortunately, Excel has an inbuilt function called Refresh that will take care of that. To refresh your pivot tables, because the source data changed, click on the pivot table, which will invoke pivot table Tools, as shown in Figure 2.52, and select Options tab on the Ribbon.

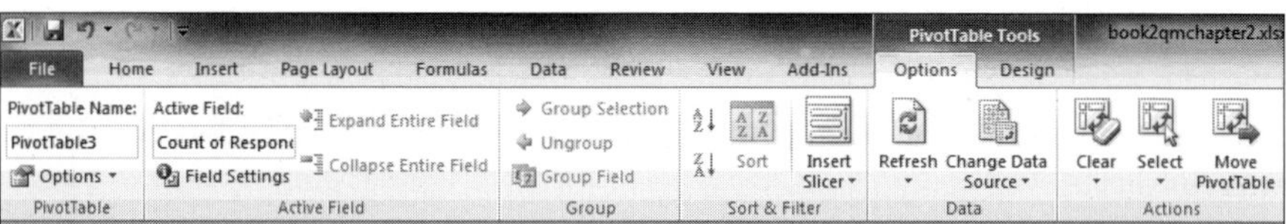

Figure 2.52

Figure 2.53

Figure 2.54

Once you clicked on the Refresh button, all the pivot table results will be refreshed. If, however, you added several new respondents to your source data, the Refresh button will not help you for a simple reason that you have changed the range of source data. Fortunately this is not a problem either. Next to the Refresh button is the button called Change Data Source.

If you click on it, you will get a dialogue box like that illustrated in Figure 2.55.

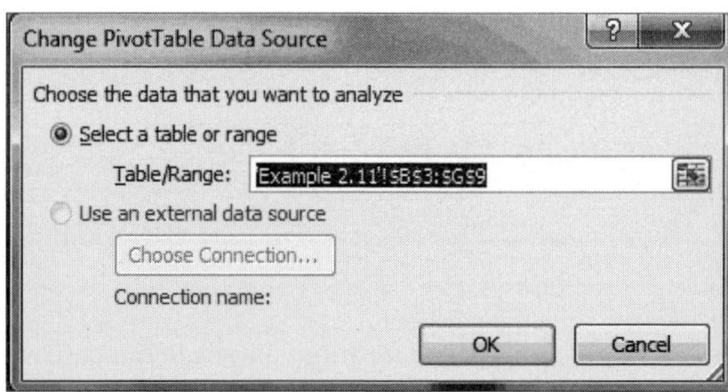

Figure 2.55

If you added two new respondents, i.e. now you have eight respondents that takes you to row 11, then you just change the range in the dialogue box to $G$11. The alternative is to go over the new range with the cursor, which will automatically change the range in the dialogue box.

The final stage in the process is **data presentation** of your findings with suitable use of reporting tools to present your findings.

X

data presentation the method used to present findings in numerical and graphical form.

Student exercises

Please visit the Online Resource Centre which accompanies this textbook for solutions to the student exercises and techniques in practice questions.

X2.12 Why is it important to pilot and test the questionnaire before conducting the full survey?

X2.13 Why is it recommended to use the closed questions in a questionnaire?

X2.14 Why is it mandatory to put the column headings in a table that will be used as a source for pivot tables?

X2.15 How do you change a pivot table after you either changed the data in the original source spread sheet, or if you add new rows to the source spreadsheet?

Techniques in practice

TP1 Skodel Ltd is a small brewery who is undergoing a major expansion after a takeover by a large European brewery chain. Skodel Ltd produces a range of beers and lagers and is renowned for the quality of its beers, winning a number of prizes at trade fairs throughout the European Union. The new parent company are reviewing the quality control mechanisms being operated by Skodel Ltd and are concerned at the quantity of lager in its premium lager brand which should contain a mean of 330 ml and a standard deviation of 15 ml. The bottling plant manager provided the parent company with quantity measurements from 100 bottles for analysis.

334	345	346	317	333	346	297	312	311	334
348	304	328	332	307	334	321	326	319	318
321	342	314	315	348	338	311	300	340	326
357	336	345	344	312	339	354	323	335	346
329	328	327	359	326	363	327	338	322	339
321	351	343	338	338	346	328	330	336	353
321	327	327	338	323	314	342	316	314	329
369	324	326	329	324	336	335	312	311	287
317	321	337	317	340	320	345	332	325	298
345	340	329	343	320	338	322	327	313	348

(a) Use Excel to construct a histogram for this data set and comment on the shape of the distribution.

(b) Calculate a range of appropriate descriptive statistics for this sample.

(c) Based upon your answers to (a) and (b) provide a measure of average, dispersion, and shape. Explain your reasoning for each answer given.

(d) Do the results suggest that there is a great deal of variation in quantity within the bottle measurements? Compare the assumed bottle average and spread with the measured average and spread.

(e) What conclusions can you draw from these results?

TP2 CoCo S.A. is concerned at the time to react to customer complaints and has implemented a new set of procedures for its support centre staff. The customer service director plans to reduce the mean time for responding to customer complaints to 28 days and has collected the following sample data after implementation of the new procedures to assess the time to react to complaints (days):

20	33	33	29	24	30
40	33	20	39	32	37
32	50	36	31	38	29
15	33	27	29	43	33
31	35	19	39	22	21
28	22	26	42	30	17
32	34	39	39	32	38

(a) Construct a histogram for this data set and comment on the shape of the distribution.

(b) Calculate a range of appropriate descriptive statistics. Explain your reasoning for each answer given.

TP3 Skodel Ltd is developing a low calorie lager for the European market with a mean designed calorie count of 43 calories per 100 ml. The new product development team are having problems with the production process and have collected an independent random sample to assess whether the target calorie count is being met.

49.7	45.2	37.7	31.9	34.8	39.8
45.9	40.5	40.6	41.9	51.4	54.0
34.3	47.8	63.1	26.3	41.2	31.7
41.4	45.1	41.1	47.9		

(a) Use Excel to plot a suitable graph and comment upon the shape.

(b) Use Excel to calculate a measure of average, dispersion, and shape. Explain your reasoning for each answer given.

■ Summary

This chapter provides the reader with an introduction to the charting of data and the calculation of summary statistics. The use of Excel has been described and many of these summary statistics will be employed to solve problems in later chapters of this textbook.

The mean is the most commonly calculated average to represent the measure of central tendency, but this measurement uses all the data within the calculation and therefore outliers will affect the value of the mean. This can imply that the value of the mean may not be representative of the underlying data set. If outliers are present in the data set then you can either eliminate these values or use the median to represent the average. The average provides a measure of the central tendency (or middle value) and the next calculation to perform is to provide a measure of the spread of the data within the distribution. The standard deviation is the most common type of measure of dispersion (or spread) but like the mean the standard deviation is influenced by the presence of outliers within the data set. If outliers are present in the data set then you can either eliminate these values or use the semi-interquartile range to represent the degree of dispersion. You can estimate the degree of skewness in the data set by calculating Pearson's coefficient of skewness (or use Fisher's skewness equation) and the degree of 'peakedness' by calculating the kurtosis statistic. The chapter explored the calculation process for raw data.

This chapter introduced some basic terminology from research methods and elementary statistics. We explained different types of variables and how to treat them to match the data set we are handling. The most elementary rules of creating open and closed questions in a questionnaire were explained. After that, simple rules on how to populate the source table with the survey data were given. And finally, the principles of how to create data tables using the pivot table function in Excel were explained. The chapter closed by showing how to cross tabulate the data, create graphs and cope with any changes in data.

Student exercise answers

For all figures listed below, please see the Online Resource Centre.

X2.1 Figure X2.1

X2.2 Figure X2.2

X2.3 Figure X2.3

X2.4 Figure X2.4

X2.5 Figure X2.5

X2.6 Figure X2.6

X2.7 Figure X2.7

X2.8 Figure X2.8

Mean = 335.0 and median = 312.5

X2.9 Figure X2.9

Even though group 1 has a higher average the degree of spread within group 2 is half the size of group 1.

X2.10 Figure X2.10a

(a) Histogram

Using the Excel Bin Range: 4.5, 14.5, 24.5, 34.5, and 44.5.

The histogram shows the weekly spend distribution.

Figure X2.10b

(b) Descriptive statistics

Figure X2.10c

Mean = 23.5333, standard deviation = 8.0818, skewness = 0.3542, skew limit = 0.8944, kurtosis = −0.3538, and kurtosis limit = 1.7889.

X2.11 Figure X2.11a

(a) Histogram
Using the Excel BIN Range: 74.5, 94.5, 114.5, 134.5, 154.5, 174.5, and 194.5. The histogram shows the weekly mileage distribution.

Figure X2.11b

Figure X2.11c

X2.12 Testing of the questionnaire and pilot phase of the survey is important to help us establish whether or not our questions are relevant, to enable us to clarify the questions if they are not understood properly, and to try to close as many open questions as possible.

X2.13 The closed questions are much easier to process and will take less time to analyse them. It is a good practise to close the open questions during the pilot phase, if this make sense, and spend extra time on perfecting the questionnaire strategy, because this saves much more time during the processing phase when we will have to deal with much larger samples.

X2.14 Excel pivot table routine will not function if there is no column heading. The routine relies on the heading columns as they define the variable names that need to be tabulated.

X2.15 If we only changed the content of individual cells in the source spread sheet, the only thing necessary is to refresh the pivot table. This is done by clicking on the Options tab on the Ribbon and selecting the Refresh symbol. If we added new rows, or columns, to the table, then the refresh is not sufficient. We need to modify the range of the source spread sheet. This is done by clicking on the Options tab on the Ribbon and selecting the Change Data Source symbol. Once we clicked on it, we'll redefine the new range and the pivot table will be automatically refreshed including the new range. The same procedure is used if we have to select completely different data source, but we want the pivot table to remain structured as it is.

TP1 Figure tp1a

(a) Histogram - The histogram shows how the quantity of lager is distributed.

Figure tp1b

(b) Descriptive statistics

Figure tp1c
Mean = 329.8100 ≈ median = 329.0000.
Shewness = −0.0942 (which is not significant, critical skewness = ±0.4899)

(c) Therefore, mean = 329.81, standard deviation = 14.9015.

(d) No. Compare bottle average = 330 and standard deviation of 15 with the sample mean = 329.8 and standard deviation = 14.9.

(e) Distribution of the quantity of lager is symmetric with a mean of 330 and standard deviation of 15 likely to be correct, based upon the sample data collected.

TP2 **Figure tp2a**

(a) Histogram - again looks fairly symmetrical.

Figure tp2b

(b) Descriptive statistics

Figure tp2c

The value of skewness suggests that distribution not significantly skewed. Therefore, use the sample mean = 31.2 as the measure of average. The assumed mean of 28 is not that different from the measured average for us to assume that the assumed mean of 28 days might not be correct.

TP3 (a) Histogram - again looks fairly symmetrical.

Figure tp3a

(b) Descriptive statistics

Figure tp3b

The value of skewness suggests that distribution is not significantly skewed (0.39 is not greater than ±1.04). Therefore, use the sample mean = 42.4 as the measure of average. Given that we use the mean we would then use the standard deviation as the measure of dispersion = 8.1.

Further reading

Textbook resources

1. S. C. Albright, C. Zappe, and W. L. Winston (2009) *Data Analysis, Optimization, and Simulation Modelling*, Cengage.
2. A. Bryman and E. Bell (2011) *Business Research Methods* (3rd edn), Oxford University Press.
3. J. Collis and R. Hussey (2009) *Business Research: A Practical Guide for Undergraduate and Postgraduate Students* (3rd edn), Palgrave Macmillan.
4. G. Davis and B. Pecar (2010) *Business Statistics Using Excel*, Oxford University Press.
5. D. Whigham (2007) *Business Data Analysis using Excel*, Oxford University Press.

Web resources

1. StatSoft Electronic Textbook, available at **http://www.statsoft.com/textbook/stathome.html** (accessed 12 May 2012).
2. HyperStat Online Statistics Textbook **http://davidmlane.com/hyperstat/index.html** (accessed 12 May 2012).
3. Eurostat - website is updated daily and provides direct access to the latest and most complete statistical information available on the European Union, the EU Member States, the euro-zone and other countries **http://epp.eurostat.ec.europa.eu** (accessed 12 May 2012).
4. Economagic - contains international economic data sets (**http://www.economagic.com**) (accessed 12th May 2012).
5. The ISI glossary of statistical terms provides definitions in a number of different languages **http://isi.cbs.nl/glossary/index.htm** (accessed 12 May 2012).

■ Formula summary

$$\text{Mean } (\bar{X}) = \frac{\text{Sum of Data Values}}{\text{Total Number of Data Values}} = \frac{\Sigma X}{\Sigma f} \qquad (2.1)$$

$$\text{Position of Percentile} = \frac{P}{100}(N+1) \qquad (2.2)$$

$$\text{Interquartile range} = Q_3 - Q_1 \qquad (2.3)$$

$$\text{Semi-interquartile range} = \frac{Q_3 - Q_1}{2} \qquad (2.4)$$

$$\text{Variance, VAR}(X) = \frac{\Sigma(X - \bar{X})^2}{\Sigma f} \qquad (2.5)$$

$$\text{Standard Deviation, SD}(X) = \sqrt{\frac{\Sigma(X - \bar{X})^2}{\Sigma f}} \qquad (2.6)$$

$$\text{Variance, VAR}(X) = \frac{\Sigma X^2}{\Sigma f} - (\bar{X})^2 \qquad (2.7)$$

$$\text{Standard deviation, SD}(X) = \sqrt{\left[\frac{\Sigma X^2}{\Sigma f} - (\bar{X})^2\right]} \qquad (2.8)$$

$$\text{Fisher's skewness} = \frac{n}{(n-1)(n-2)} \Sigma\left(\frac{(X - \bar{X})}{s}\right)^3 \qquad (2.9)$$

$$\text{Kurtosis} = \frac{n(n+1)}{(n-1)(n-2)(n-3)} \Sigma\left(\frac{(X - \bar{X})}{s}\right)^4 - \frac{3(n-1)^2}{(n-2)(n-3)} \qquad (2.10)$$

Part II

Decision Making in Marketing, Sales, and Business Development

Fundamentals of statistical decision making

3

» Overview «

In this chapter we provide the reader with an overview of the key statistical concepts that will be used in later chapters: introduction to probability and its laws, an overview of the concept of sampling, and an overview of the concept of statistical inference and hypothesis testing.

» Learning outcomes «

On completing this chapter you should be able to:

- » Understand the concept of a probability.
- » Distinguish between subjective, empirical, and a priori probability methods.
- » Identify a sample space.
- » Apply the laws of probability.
- » Understand the concept of dependent and conditional events.
- » Understand the concept of mutually exclusive and independent events.
- » Construct a tree diagram and use this visual aid to solve problems involving probability.
- » Apply Bayes' theorem to modify probabilities with new information.
- » Understand the concept of a population and sample.
- » Distinguish between sampling with and without replacement from a population.
- » Estimate population statistics using sample statistics (mean, standard deviation, and proportion).
- » Understand the concept of the finite correction factor when sampling from a population.
- » Explain the concept of the Central Limit Theorem and its applications.
- » Understand the concept of biased and unbiased estimators.
- » Understand the concept of a sampling distribution for the sample means.
- » Distinguish between the two types of sampling frame (probability and non-probability) and sampling data collection methods and processes.

- » Identify different types of probability distribution.
- » Identify different continuous probability distributions: normal and Student's t distributions.
- » Provide point and interval estimates of the population mean using a sample mean.
- » Understand the concepts of the null and alternative hypotheses, significance levels, and p-values.
- » Perform a hypothesis test using the normal and Student's t distributions.
- » Identify different discrete probability distributions: binomial and Poisson.
- » Solve problems using Microsoft Excel.

3.1 Basic ideas of probability

3.1.1 Basic ideas

There are a number of words and phrases that encapsulate the basic concept of probability: chance, probable, and odds. In all cases we are faced with a degree of uncertainty and concerned with the likelihood of a particular event happening. Statistically these words and phrases are too vague; we need some measure of likelihood of an event occurring. This measure is termed probability and is measured on a scale ranging between 0 and 1.

From Figure 3.1 we observe that the probability values lie between 0 and 1 with 0 representing no possibility of the event occurring and 1 representing the probability is certain to occur. In reality, the value of the probability will lie between 0 and 1.

X

significance level, α the significance level of a statistical hypothesis test is a fixed probability of wrongly rejecting the null hypothesis, H_0, if it is in fact true.

probability provides a number value to the likely occurrence of a particular event.

random experiment is a sampling technique where we select a group of subjects (a sample) for study from a larger group (a population). Each individual is chosen entirely by chance and each member of the population has a known, but possibly non-equal, chance of being included in the sample. By using random sampling, the likelihood of bias is reduced.

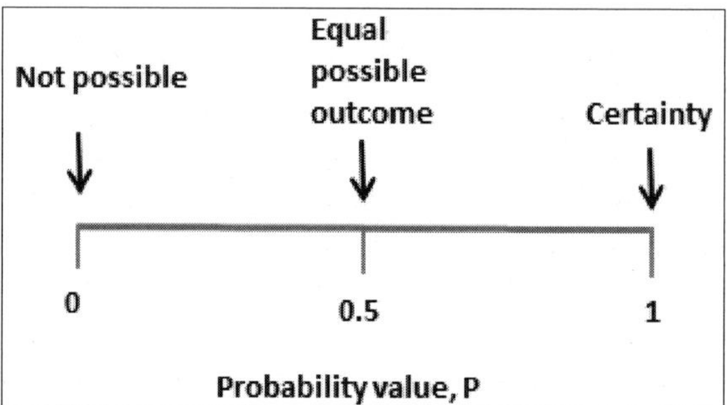

Figure 3.1

In order to determine a probability of an event occurring data has to be obtained. This can be achieved through, for example, experience or observation or empirical methods. The procedure or situation that produces a definite result is termed a random experiment. For example, tossing a coin, rolling a die, recording the income of a factory worker, determining defective items on an assembly line are all examples of experiments. The characteristics of the random experiments are:

- Each experiment is repeatable
- All possible outcomes can be described

- Although individual outcomes appear haphazard, continual repeats of the experiment will produce a regular pattern.

The result of an experiment is called an outcome. It is the single possible result of an experiment: for example, tossing a coin produces 'a head', rolling a die gives a '3'. If we accept the proposition that an experiment can produce a finite number of outcomes then we could in theory define all these outcomes. The set of all possible outcomes is defined as the sample space. For example, the experiment of rolling a die could produce the outcomes 1, 2, 3, 4, 5, and 6, which would thus define the sample space. Another basic notion is the concept of an event and is simply a set of possible outcomes, that is, an event is a subset of the sample space. In the experiment of rolling a die, for example, the event of obtaining an even number would be defined as the subset {2, 4, 6}. Finally, two events are said to be mutually exclusive if they cannot occur together. Thus in rolling a die, the event 'obtaining a two' is mutually exclusive of the event 'obtaining a three'. The event 'obtaining a two' and the event 'obtaining an even number are not mutually exclusive since both can occur together, that is, {2} is a subset of {2, 4, 6}.

Note The value of a probability can be found be using a variety of methods, including:

1. Subjective probability method where the value of a particular probability is estimated from the evidence available or from experience. For example, a market researcher estimates from previous experience that the probability of television commercial being successful is 40% when a particular creative organization is employed to design the commercial. From this data the subjective probability of the commercial being a success is 40% (or 0.4 or 4/10).
2. Empirical probability (also known as relative frequency or experimental probability) method where the value of a probability is based on measurement. For example, a car company finds that a new model car is returned to a particular car dealership 83 times out of 650 cars delivered to the dealership. From this data the empirical probability of the dealership returning this car is 83/650.
3. The a priori probability method assumes that you already know what the probability should be from a theoretical understanding of the experiment being conducted. For example, if we toss a fair coin then we know the probability of a number 1 being face up would be 1/6. This would be true for all the other alternatives: P(1) = P(2) = P(3) = P(4) = P(5) = P(6) = 1/6.

sample space an exhaustive list of all the possible outcomes of an experiment.

mutually exclusive events where only one can happen, but not both.

subjective probability a subjective probability describes an individual's personal judgement about how likely a particular event is to occur.

empirical probability method whereby the value of a probability is based on measurement.

a priori probability method assumes that you already know what the probability should be from a theoretical understanding of the experiment being conducted.

relative frequency relative frequency is another term for proportion; it is the value calculated by dividing the number of times an event occurs by the total number of times an experiment is carried out.

Two or more mutually exclusive events are events that cannot occur at the same time. For example, if we say event A consists of a football team winning and event B consists of the same football team drawing against the same team, then event A and B are mutually exclusive given that the football team cannot win and draw at the same football match.

3.1.2 Relative frequency

Suppose we perform the experiment of throwing a die and note the score obtained. We repeat the experiment a large number of times, say 1000, and note the number of times each score was obtained. For each number we could derive the ratio of occurrence (event A) to the total number of experiments (n = 1000). This ratio is called the relative frequency.

In general, if event A occurs m times out of n attempts, then your **estimate** of the probability that A will occur is

$$P(A) = \frac{m}{n} \tag{3.1}$$

Example 3.1

The result of the die experiment is shown Table 3.1.

Score	1	2	3	4	5	6
Frequency	173	168	167	161	172	159

Table 3.1 Result of die experiment

This notion of relative frequency provides an approach to determine the probability of an event. As the number of experiments increases then the relative frequency stabilizes and approaches the probability of the event. Thus, if we had performed the above experiment 2000 times we might expect 'in the long run' the frequencies of all the scores to approach 0.167, that is, P(2) = 0.167, P(3) = 0.167.

Figure 3.2 illustrates the use of Excel to calculate the relative frequencies for scores 1 to 6.

	A	B	C	D	E	F	G	H
1	Example 3.1							
2								
3		Score	1	2	3	4	5	6
4		Frequency	173	168	167	161	172	159
5		Relative Frequency	0.173	0.168	0.167	0.161	0.172	0.159
6			=C4/$C$8					=H4/$C$8
7								
8		Total frequency =	1000	=SUM(C4:H4)				

Figure 3.2

➜ Excel solution

Frequency = Cells C4:H4	Values
Total frequency = Cell C8	Formula: = SUM(C4:H4)
Relative frequency = Cell C5	Formula: = C4/$C$8
	Copy formula across from C5:H5

There are many situations where probabilities are derived through this empirical approach. If a manufacturer indicates that he is 99% certain (P = 99%) that an electric light bulb will last 200 hours, this figure will have been arrived at from experiments which have tested numerous samples of light bulbs. If we are told that the probability of rain on a June day is 0.42, this will have been determined through studying rainfall records for June over, say, the past 20 years. The relative frequency distribution in Figure 3.2 is also called a **probability distribution**.

estimate an estimate is an indication of the value of an unknown quantity based on observed data.

probability distribution a description of the relative frequency of observations.

Example 3.2

Suppose that a particular production process has been in operation for 200 days with a recorded accident on 150 days. If A = the event that an accident occurs in future, then the probability of an accident occurring in future, P(A) = 150/200 = 0.75. This provides an estimate or probability of 75% that an accident will occur in the future on each separate day.

Example 3.3

Over the last three years a random sample of 1000 students were selected and classified according to their degree classification and gender, as illustrated in Table 3.2.

	1st	2i	2ii	3rd
Male	20	90	200	90
Female	40	150	230	180

Table 3.2 Degree classification by gender

Calculate: (a) probability that a student achieves a 2i and is female, (b) probability that a student achieves a 2i and is male, (c) probability that a student achieves a 2i and is female or male, and (d) the probability that a 2i classification is not achieved.

Figure 3.3 illustrates the Excel solution.

	A	B	C	D	E	F	G	H
1	Example 3.3							
2								
3			1st	2 i	2 ii	3rd	Total	
4		Male	20	90	200	90	400	=SUM(C4:F4)
5		Female	40	150	230	180	600	=SUM(C5:F5)
6		Total	60	240	430	270	1000	
7			=SUM(C4:C5)			=SUM(F4:F5)	=SUM(G4:G5)	
8								
9		P(2i and female) =	0.15	=D5/G6				
10		P(2i and male) =	0.09	=D4/G6				
11		P(2i and being female or ma	0.24	=D6/G6				
12		P(not 2i degree) =	0.76	=(G6-D6)/G6				

Figure 3.3

→ Excel solution

Data: Cells C4:F5	Values
Gender sum: Cell G4	Formula: = SUM(C4:F4)
	Copy formula down G4:G5
Classification sum: Cell C6	Formula: = SUM(C4:c5)
	Copy formula across C6:G6
P(2i and female) = Cell C9	Formula: = D5/G6
P(2i and male) = Cell C10	Formula: = D4/G6
P(2i and being female or male) = Cell C11	Formula: = D6/G6
P(not 2i degree) = Cell C12	Formula: = (G6-D6)/G6

Interpretation The values of the calculated probabilities are as follows:

(a) Probability that a student achieves a 2i and is female = 0.15,

(b) Probability that a student achieves a 2i and is male = 0.09,

(c) Probability that a student achieves a 2i and is female or male = 0.24,

(d) Probability that a 2i classification is not achieved = 0.76.

Note

(a) Probability that a student achieves a 2i and is female

$$P(\text{2i and female}) = \frac{\text{Number of female students with a 2i}}{\text{Total sample size}} = \frac{150}{1000} = 0.15$$

Probability that a student achieves a 2i and is female is 0.15 or 15%.

(b) Probability that a student achieves a 2i and is male

$$P(\text{2i and male}) = \frac{\text{Number of male students with a 2i}}{\text{Total sample size}} = \frac{90}{1000} = 0.09$$

Probability that a student achieves a 2i and is male is 0.09 or 9%.

(c) Probability that a student achieves a 2i and is female or male

$$P(\text{2i student being female or male}) = \frac{\text{Number of male or female students with a 2i}}{\text{Total sample size}}$$

$$= \frac{240}{1000} = 0.24$$

Probability that a student achieves a 2i and is female or male is 0.24 or 24%.

(d) Probability that a 2i degree classification is not achieved

$$P(\text{Not obtaining a 2i}) = \frac{\text{Number of students not obtaining a 2i}}{\text{Total sample size}} = \frac{760}{1000} = 0.76$$

Probability that a 2i degree classification is not achieved is 0.76 or 76%.

A number of important issues emerge from the above examples that concern probability in general:

- The probability of each event lies between 0 and 1.
- The sum of the probabilities of these events will equal 1.
- If we know the probability of an event, then the probability of it not occurring is P(Event not occurring) = 1 – P(Event occurs)

- Since the events in the example are mutually exclusive then the probability of two or more events is the sum of the event probabilities.

3.1.3 Sample space

We already know that the sample space contains all likely outcomes of an experiment and that one or more outcomes constitute an event. Here rather than resort to the notion of relative frequency we will look at probability as

$$P(\text{Event}) = \frac{\text{Number of outcomes in the event}}{\text{Total number of outcomes}} \tag{3.2}$$

A number of examples will be used to illustrate this notion via the construction of the sample space.

Example 3.4

If an experiment consists of rolling a die then the possible outcomes are 1, 2, 3, 4, 5, and 6. The probability of obtaining a 3 can then be calculated using Equation (3.2).

Figure 3.4 illustrates the Excel solution.

	A	B	C	D	E	F	G	H
1	Example 3.4							
2								
3		Outcomes:	1	2	3	4	5	6
4								
5		P(3) =	0.166667	=COUNTIF(C3:H3,3)/COUNT(C3:H3)				

Figure 3.4

→ Excel solution

Outcomes: Cells C3:H3

P(3) = Cell C5 Formula: = COUNTIF(C3:H3,3)/COUNT(C3:H3)

Interpretation The probability of obtaining a 3 = 1/6 or 0.16666....

Note

$$P(\text{obtaining a 3}) = \frac{\text{Number of outcomes producing a 3}}{\text{Total number of outcomes}} = \frac{1}{6} = 0.1666666'$$

Probability of obtaining a 3 is 0.167 or 16 2/3%.

Example 3.5

If an experiment consists of tossing two unbiased coins then the possible outcomes are HH, HT, TH, and TT. We could illustrate the sample space with individual sample points (*) as illustrated in Table 3.3.

		1st Coin	
		H	T
2nd Coin	H	*	*
	T	*	*

Table 3.3 Coin sample space

From this sample space we can calculate individual probabilities. For example, the theoretical probability of achieving at least one head would be calculated as follows:

$$P(\text{at least 1 head}) = \frac{\text{Number of outcomes producing at least 1 head}}{\text{Total number of outcomes}} = \frac{3}{4} = 0.75$$

Therefore, the theoretical probability of achieving at least one head would be 0.75 or 75%.

Example 3.6

An experiment consists of throwing two dice and noting their two scores. The sample space could be illustrated as illustrated in Table 3.4.

		Score on first die (X)					
		1	2	3	4	5	6
Score on second die (Y)	1	*	*	*	*	*	*
	2	*	*	*	*	*	*
	3	*	*	*	*	*	*
	4	*	*	*	*	*	*
	5	*	*	*	*	*	*
	6	*	*	*	*	*	*

Table 3.4 Die sample space

From this sample space calculate the following theoretical probabilities: (a) $P(X = Y)$, (b) $P(X + Y = 5)$, (c) $P(X * Y = 36)$, (d) $P(X < 3 \text{ and } Y > 2)$?

From sample space we can calculate the probability values as follows:

(a) $P(X = Y) = 6/36 = 0.166$, (b) $P(X + Y = 5) = 4/36 = 0.111$, (c) $P(X * Y = 36) = 1/36 = 0.027$, (d) $P(X < 3 \text{ and } Y > 2) = 8/36 = 0.222$.

X
unbiased when the mean of the sampling distribution of a statistic is equal to a population parameter, that statistic is said to be an unbiased estimator of the parameter.

Student exercises

X3.1 Give an appropriate sample space for each of the following experiments:

(a) A card is chosen at random from a pack of cards.

(b) A person is chosen at random from a group containing 5 females and 6 males.

(c) A football team records the results of each of two games as 'win', 'draw' or 'lose'.

X3.2 A group of males and females over the age of 16 of which one is chosen at random. State which pair of events is mutually exclusive

(a) Being a male and aged over 21.

(b) Being a male and being a female.

X3.3 A dart is thrown at a board and is likely to land on any one of eight squares numbered 1 to 8 inclusive. A represents the event the dart lands in square 5 or 8. B represents the event the dart lands in square 2, 3 or 4. C represents the event the dart lands in square 1, 2, 5 or 6. Which two events are mutually exclusive?

X3.4 How would you give an estimate of the probability of a 25-year-old passing the driving test at a first attempt?

X3.5 In an experiment we toss two unbiased coins 100 times and note the frequency of the two possible outcomes (head, tail). We are interested in calculating the probability (or chance) that at least one head will occur from the 100 tosses of the two coins. Calculate (a) the theoretical probability that at least one head occurs, and (b) the value of this probability from your experiment. What would you expect to occur between the theoretical and experimental probability values if the overall number of attempts occurs?

X3.6 The table below provides information about 200 school leavers and their destination after leaving school as illustrated in Table 3.5.

	Leave school at 16 years	Leave school at an higher age
Full time education, E	14	18
Full time job, J	96	44
Other	15	13

Table 3.5 School leaver against destination

Determine the following probabilities that a person selected at random:

(a) Went into full-time education

(b) Went into a full-time job

(c) Either went into full-time education or went into a full-time job

(d) Left school at 16

(e) Left school at 16 and went into full-time education

X3.7 Consider Table in X3.6.

(a) Are the events E and J mutually exclusive

(b) Determine P(E and J)

(c) Using the values of P(E), P(J) and P(E and J) you have already determined in X3.7, evaluate P(E) + P(J). What do you notice when you compare your answer with P(E or J)?

X3.8 A sample of 50 married women was asked how many children they had in their family. The result was as illustrated in Table 3.6.

Number of children	0	1	2	3	4	5+
Number of families	6	14	13	9	5	3

Table 3.6 Distribution of children within families

Estimate the probability that if any married woman is asked the same question, she will answer: (a) none, (b) between 1 and 3 inclusive, (c) more than 3, (d) neither 3 nor 4, and (e) less than 2 or more than 4.

3.2 The probability laws and conditional probability

In this section we will introduce some of the laws of probability, describe the concept of conditional probability, and introduce the concept of independent events.

Example 3.7

An experiment consists of tossing three coins. Let events A, B, C, and D represent the events obtained three heads, obtained three tails, obtained only two heads, and obtained only two tails respectively.

Figure 3.5 illustrates the sample space for this experiment and the four mutually exclusive events using a Venn diagram.

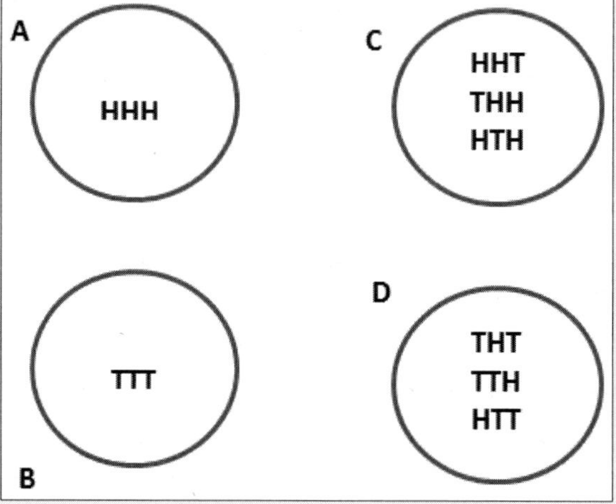

Figure 3.5

From Figure 3.5 we have: P(A) = 0.125, P(B) = 0.125, P(C) = 0.375 and P(D) = 0.375. Since the four mutually exclusive events exhaust the sample space then P(A) + P(B) + P(C) + P(D) = 1.0.

Since A and B are mutually exclusive, then P(A or B) = P(A) + P(B) = 0.25. Similarly, P(A or B or C) = P(A) + P(B) + P(C) = 0.625. Since P(D) = 0.375, then P(D′) = 1 − P(D) = 1 − 0.375 = 0.625.

X

conditional probability the probability that event A occurs, given that event B has occurred, is called a conditional probability.

independent events two events are independent if the occurrence of one of the events has no influence on the occurrence of the other event.

Venn diagram a diagram that represents probabilities as circles that may or may not overlap.

3.2.1 The general addition law

In the above example, we demonstrated the addition law for mutually exclusive events, P(A or B) = P(A) + P(B). When events are not mutually exclusive, that is, two or more events contain common outcomes within a sample space, then this law does not hold.

Note Two events are mutually exclusive when both events cannot occur at the same time.

Example 3.8

To illustrate this case consider a sample space consisting of the positive integers from 1 through 10. Let event A represent all odd integers and event B represent all integers less than or equal to 5. These two events within the sample space are displayed in Figure 3.6.

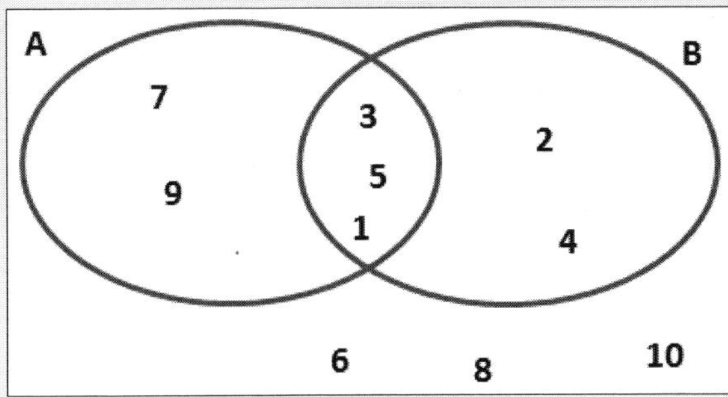

Figure 3.6

While the events A and B overlap (the intersect) common sample points are present and would represent the event {odd integers and integers < 5} or {A and B} or {A n B}. The event {A or B} contains the outcomes of either odd integers or integers < 5. A little thought would indicate that the number containing event A or B is given by the equation n{A or B} = n{A} + n{B} – n{A and B}. Consequently by transforming the events into probabilities the general addition law is as follows:

$$P(A \text{ or } B) = P(A) + P(B) - P(A \text{ and } B) \quad (3.3)$$

Note Thus if two events are mutually exclusive, P(A and B) = 0.

Example 3.9

A card is chosen from an ordinary pack of cards. Write down the probabilities that the card is: (a) black and an ace, (b) black or an ace, and (c) neither black nor an ace. Let event A and B represent the events obtaining an ace card and B a black card respectively. The sample space is represented by Figure 3.7.

addition law the addition rule is a result used to determine the probability that event A or event B occurs or both occur.

general addition law the addition rule is a result used to determine the probability that event A or event B occurs or both occur.

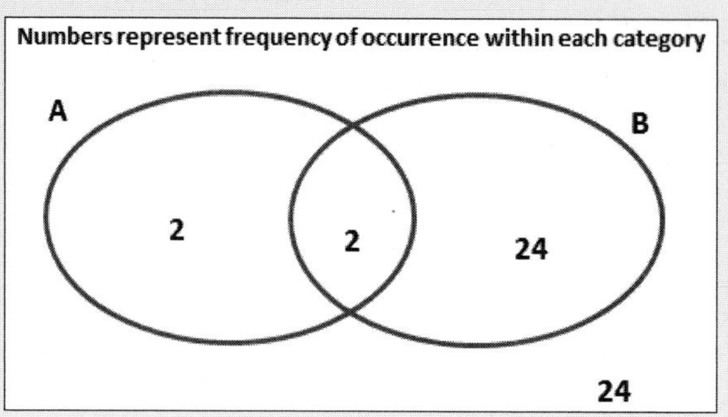

Figure 3.7

(a) $P(\text{B and A}) = \dfrac{\text{Number of outcomes in AnB}}{\text{Total number of outcomes}} = \dfrac{2}{52} = 0.0385$

(b) $P(\text{B or A}) = P(B) + P(A) - P(\text{B and A}) = \dfrac{26}{52} + \dfrac{4}{52} - \dfrac{2}{52} = \dfrac{28}{52} = 0.538462$

(c) $P(\text{neither B nor A}) = 1 - P(\text{B or A}) = 1 - 0.5385 = 0.4615$

3.2.2 Multiplication law and conditional probability

We will now develop the **multiplication law of probability** by considering the concept of conditional probability. Consider the differences between choosing an item at random from a lot with and without replacement. Let us say we have 100 items of which 20 are defective and 80 are not defective and from which two are selected. Let A = event first item defective and B = event second item defective. If an item is replaced after the first selection the number of items defective remains constant and $P(A) = P(B) = 20/100 = 0.2$. If the first item is not replaced then what happens to the value of these probabilities?

The probability of event A is still equal to 0.2. In order to determine P(B) we need to know the composition of the lot at the time of the second selection. By not replacing the first item, the total number of items has been reduced to 99, and if the first item is found to be defective then 19 defective items will remain.

Thus the probability of event B occurring, P(B), will now be conditional on whether event A has occurred. This we denote as $P(B \mid A)$, the **conditional probability** of the event B given that A has occurred. Thus for this example $P(B \mid A) = 19/99 = 0.1919$. In effect, we are computing P(B) with respect to the reduced sample space of A.

X

multiplication law of probability is a result used to determine the probability that two events, A and B, both occur.

conditional probability allows event probability values to be updated when new information is made available.

Example 3.10

The following example will now be used to develop the multiplication law. Of a group of 30 students, 15 are blue-eyed {B}, 5 are left-handed {L}, and 2 are both blue-eyed and left-handed {B and L}.

Figure 3.8 illustrates this situation in a Venn diagram. Picking one student at random then the probabilities would be as follows:

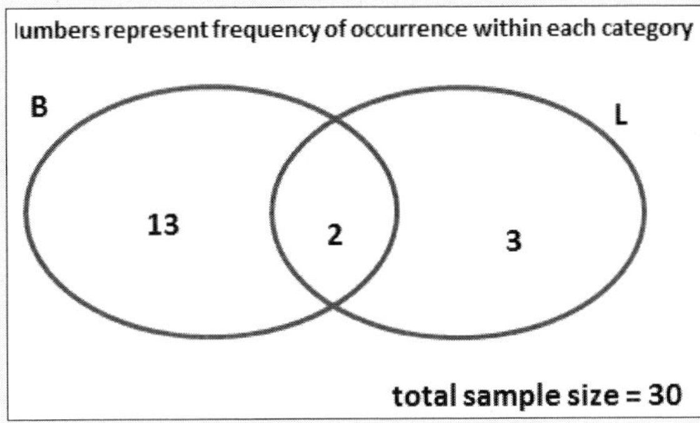

Figure 3.8

P(L) = 5/30

P(B) = 15/30

P(L and B) = P(L ∩ B) = 2/30

If we know that a student is blue-eyed then our sample space will be reduced to 15 students of which 2 are left-handed. Thus, P(L | B) = number in {L and B}/number in {B}. By dividing top and bottom by the total sample space gives:

$$P(A \mid B) = \frac{P(L \cap B)}{P(B)} = \frac{2/30}{15/30} = \frac{2}{15} = 0.133333'$$

In general, if we have two events A and B then the conditional probability of A given that B has occurred is given by Equation (3.4):

$$P(A \mid B) = \frac{P(A \cap B)}{P(B)} \quad (3.4)$$

This general result can be converted to give the multiplication law for joint events as follows:

$$P(A \cap B) = P(A \mid B) * P(B) \quad (3.5)$$

Example 3.11

Consider two events A and B which contain all sample points with P(A ∩ B) = 1/4 and P(A | B) = 1/3. Calculate (a) P(B), (b) P(A), and (c) P(B | A).

(a) P(B)? From Equation (3.4) we have P(B) = P(A ∩ B)/P(A | B) = (1/4)/(1/3) = 3/4. Therefore, the probability of event B occurring is 0.75 or 75%.

(b) P(A)? Because A and B exhaust the sample space, P(A U B) = 1.0. From the addition law, P(A U B) = P(A) + P(B) – P(A ∩ B). Thus, P(A) = P(A ∩ B) + P(A U B) – P(B) = 1.0 + 0.25 – 0.75 = 0.5. Thus, the probability of event A occurring is 0.5 or 50%.

(c) P(B | A)? P(A ∩ B) is the same as P(B ∩ A). Thus, from the multiplication law, P(A ∩ B) = P(B | A) * P(A). Re-arranging this equation gives P(B | A) = P(B ∩ A)/P(A) = 0.25/0.5 = 0.5. Thus, the probability that event B occurs given that even A has already occurred is 0.5 or 50%.

Example 3.12

An office is due to be modernized with new office equipment. To aid the office manager a survey has been undertaken to identify the following information: (a) number of laptops, (b) number of desktops, and (c) whether the computers are old or new. The data collected is provided in Table 3.7 below.

	Laptops, L	Desktops, D	Totals
New, N	40	30	70
Old, O	20	10	30
Totals	60	40	100

Table 3.7 Computer type survey results

If a person picks one computer at random, calculate the following probabilities: (a) the computer is new, (b) the computer is a laptop, and (c) the computer is new given that it is a laptop. Parts (a) and (b) deal with distinct mutually exclusive events within the full sample space. Hence $P(N) = 70/100 = 0.70$ and $P(L) = 60/100 = 0.60$. In part (c) we are dealing with the conditional probability $P(N \mid L)$. By considering the reduced sample space L (60 laptops) then $P(N \mid L) = 40/60 = 0.66'$ or by considering the definition of conditional probability $P(N \mid L) = P(N \cap L)/P(L) = (40/100)/(60/100) = 0.66'$. Both methods will give us the same answer, 66 2/3%, for the probability that it is new given it is a laptop.

Example 3.13

A box contains 6 red and 10 black balls. What is the probability that if three balls are chosen one at a time without replacement that they are all black? Let B_1 = Event first draw black, B_2 = Event second draw black, and B_3 = Event third draw black. In this example we are determining the probability that all three balls chosen are black ($P(B_1$ and B_2 and $B_3)$). On the first draw $P(B_1) = 10/16$. On the second draw the sample space has been reduced to 15 balls and given the condition that the first ball is black then $P(B_2 \mid B_1) = 9/15$. On the third draw the sample space has been reduced to 14 balls and given the condition that the first and second balls are black then $P(B_3 \mid (B_2 n B_1)) = 8/14$. Thus, $P(B_1 \cap B_2 \cap B_3) = P(B_1) * P(B_2 \mid B_1) * P(B_3 \mid (B_2 \cap B_1)) = (10/16) * (9/15) * (8/14) = 0.2143$. Therefore, the probability that all three balls are black when no replacement occurs is 21.43%.

3.2.3 Statistical independence

We have already considered mutually exclusive events i.e. events that cannot occur at the same time. We have also noted that in some situations knowing that one event has occurred yields information that will affect the probability of another event. There will be many situations where the converse is true. For example rolling a die twice, knowing that a six resulted on the first roll cannot influence the outcome of the second roll. Similarly, take the example of picking a ball from a bag. If it were replaced before another was picked nothing changes; the sample space remains the same. Drawing the first ball and replacing it cannot affect the outcome of the next selection (**statistical independence**). In these examples we have the notion of **independent events**. If two (or more) events are independent then the multiplication law for two independent events is as follows:

$$P(A \cap B) = P(A) * P(B) \tag{3.6}$$

From which we can deduce that for independent events $P(A \mid B) = P(A)$ and similarly $P(B \mid A) = P(B)$.

Note The terms independent and mutually exclusive are different and apply to different things. If A and B are events with non-zero probabilities, then we can show:

- P(A and B) = 0, if events A and B are mutually exclusive. Mutually exclusive events cannot occur at the same time and therefore the probability of event A and event B occurring together is zero.
- P(A and B) ≠ 0, if events A and B are independent. Independent events do not influence each other and therefore the probability of A and B is non-zero. In this situation, $P(A \mid B) = P(A)$ and $P(B \mid A) = P(B)$.

Example 3.14

Suppose a fair die is tossed twice. Let A = the first die shows an even number and B = the second die shows a 5 or 6. A and B are intuitively unrelated and therefore are independent events. Thus the probability of A occurring is P(A) = 3/6 = 0.5 and the probability of event B occurring is P(B) = 2/6 = 0.3. Thus, P(A and B) = P(A) * P(B) = 0.5 * 0.3 = 0.16.

Example 3.15

Three marksmen take place in a shooting contest. Their chances of hitting the 'bull' are 1/2, 1/3, 1/4 respectively. If they fire simultaneously, what are the chances that only one bullet will hit the 'bull'? Let A, B, and C represent the events that the first man hits the 'bull', the second man hits the 'bull', and third man hits the 'bull' respectively, with the following probabilities: P(A) = 1/2; P(B) = 1/3; P(C) = 1/4. The probability problem can be written as P(only one bull hit) = $P(A \cap B' \cap C'$ OR $A' \cap B \cap C'$ OR $A' \cap B' \cap C) = P(A \cap B' \cap C') + P(A' \cap B \cap C') + P(A' \cap B' \cap C)$ = 1/2 * 2/3 * 3/4 + 1/2 * 1/3 * 3/4 + 1/2 * 2/3 * 1/4 = 1/4 + 1/8 + 1/12 = 11/24. Thus, the probability that one bull is hit between the three marksmen is 11/24 or 45.83%.

Example 3.16

Two football teams, A and B, are disputing the historical data of who is likely to win. To settle the dispute the following probability data has been collected that measures the probability of each team scoring 0, 1, 2, or 3 goals (see Table 3.8).

X

statistical independence means the occurrence of one event occurring does not affect the outcome of the occurrence of the other event.

independent events are events that do not influence each other.

	Number of goals scored			
	0	1	2	3
Team A	0.3	0.3	0.3	0.1
Team B	0.2	0.4	0.3	0.1

Table 3.8 Result of football experiment

Calculate the probability: (a) team A wins, (b) teams draw, and (c) team B wins.

To solve this problem we need to find the total sample space. From Table 3.9 we observe 16 possible results (events) given the above scores, each of which is mutually exclusive.

		Team A scores			
		0	1	2	3
Team B scores	0	0.06	0.06	0.06	0.02
	1	0.12	0.12	0.12	0.04
	2	0.09	0.09	0.09	0.03
	3	0.03	0.03	0.03	0.01

Table 3.9 Total sample space for football experiment

We will look at these in a joint probability table assuming independence, that is, team A scoring does not influence team B scoring.

Since the events are mutually exclusive then the probabilities are as follows: P(A wins) = 0.06 + 0.06 + 0.02 + 0.12 + 0.04 + 0.03 = 0.33, P(Draw) = 0.06 + 0.12 + 0.09 + 0.01 = 0.28, P(B wins) = 1 – {P(A wins) + P(Draw)} = 1 – {0.33 + 0.28} = 0.39. From these results we can see that team B has the greater chance of winning a game.

Student exercises

X3.9 For each question indicate whether the events are mutually exclusive: (a) thermometers are inspected and rejected if any of the following are found: poor calibration; inability to withstand extreme temperatures without breaking; not within specified size tolerances, and (b) a manager will reject a job applicant for any of the following reasons: lack of relevant experience; slovenly appearance; too old.

X3.10 Consider two events A and B where the associated probabilities are as follows: P(A or B) = 3/4, P(B) = 3/8 and n(A) = 4. Calculate P(A and B) if the total sample size is 8.

X3.11 A survey shows that 80% of all households have a colour television and 30% have a microwave oven. If 20% have both a colour television and a microwave, what percentage has neither?

X3.12 The Gompertz Oil Company drills for oil in old oil fields that the large companies have stated are uneconomic. The decision to drill will depend upon a number of factors, including the geology of the proposed sites. Drilling experience shows that there is a 0.40 probability of a type A structure present at the site if there is a productive well. It is also known that 50% of all wells are drilled in locations with a type A structure and 30% of all wells drilled are productive. Use the information provided to answer the following questions: (a) what is the probability of a well drilled in a type A structure and being productive? (b) what is the probability of having a productive well at the location if the drilling process begins in a location with a type A structure? and (c) is finding a productive well independent of the type A structure?

3.3 Introduction to tree diagrams and Bayes' theorem

3.3.1 Introduction to a tree diagram in solving problems involving probability

The **tree diagram** is a useful visual aid to help map out alternative outcomes of an experiment and associated probabilities.

Example 3.17

A bag contains three red and four white balls. Calculate the following probabilities assuming that one ball is taken at random and then replaced and another ball is taken:

(a) P(Red first and Red second),

(b) P(just one Red),

(c) P(2nd ball White).

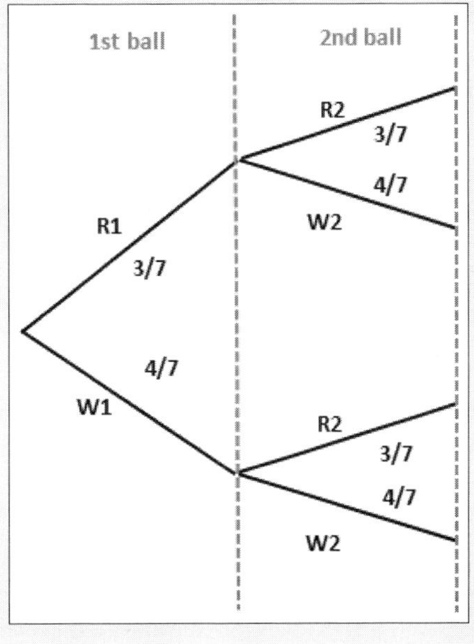

Figure 3.9

Figure 3.9 displays the experiment in a tree diagram. Each branch of the tree indicates the possible result of a draw and associated probabilities.

Multiplying along the branches provides the probability of a final outcome:

(a) $P(R_1 \text{ and } R_2) = P(R_1) * P(R_2) = 3/7 * 3/7 = 9/49$.

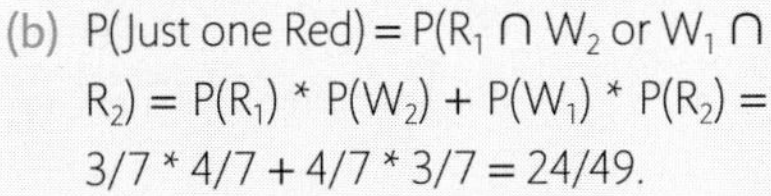

(b) $P(\text{Just one Red}) = P(R_1 \cap W_2 \text{ or } W_1 \cap R_2) = P(R_1) * P(W_2) + P(W_1) * P(R_2) = 3/7 * 4/7 + 4/7 * 3/7 = 24/49$.

(c) $P(\text{2nd Ball White}) = P(R_1 \cap W_2 \text{ or } W_1 \cap W_2) = P(R_1 \cap W_2) + P(W_1 \cap W_2) = 3/7 * 4/7 + 4/7 * 4/7 = 21/49$.

3.3.2 Introduction to Bayes' theorem

In section 3.2.2 we explored the concept of conditional probability and noted that the conditional probability of event A occurring given that an event B has occurred is given by Equation 3.4:

$$P(A \mid B) = \frac{P(A \cap B)}{P(B)}$$

We can think of this as the probability of event A occurring given that we have some new information available, namely, event B has occurred. In this section we can extend the concept of conditional probability to include situations where additional information

Bayes' theorem Bayes' theorem is a result that allows new information to be used to update the conditional probability of an event.

tree diagram is a useful visual aid to help map out alternative outcomes of an experiment and associated probabilities.

is identified, and this new information can be used to update the initial probability value to a new probability value. From this concept we can identify two terms as follows:

1. A **prior probability** is the original probability value before new information is identified.
2. A **posterior probability** is the new probability value based upon the original conditions and the new information identified.

Example 3.18

UK Pro Ltd manufactures footballs for sale by a discount store chain that trades online only. The discount store chain observed a large demand for the footballs in the six months leading up to the last world cup. From past experience the online retailer returned 2% of the footballs to the manufacturer has faulty. Calculate the probability that a football selected at random would be faulty.

From the information provided this probability is 2% and we would write P(faulty football) = 2% or 0.02. This probability is the initial probability and this is called the prior probability. To meet the demand the manufacturer reduced the level of quality testing of the footballs before shipping to the online retailer and found that the probability of a football being rejected given that it is of an acceptable quality is estimated at 8% with the test expected to be correct 95% of the time when the football is faulty.

We observe from the data that the test is a biased test given that the test is less accurate when the football is not faulty. To calculate the probability of a faulty ball we need to modify the prior probability to achieve a new probability that we call the posterior probability.

To calculate the value of this posterior probability we can construct a tree diagram and/or use Bayes' theorem:

$$\text{P(Football defective given failed test)} = \frac{\text{P(Football defective and failed test)}}{\text{P(Failed test)}}$$

To aid understanding we would construct a decision diagram (or tree diagram) as illustrated in Figure 3.10 that provides a visual aid to identify the different alternative options via the branches of the decision tree. From the tree diagram we can observe the four alternative possibilities for this particular scenario using the branches of the tree diagram.

→ Excel solution

P(football faulty) = Cell C4	Value
P(football not faulty) = Cell C5	Formula: = 1-C4
P(football rejected given not faulty) = Cell C7	Value
P(Test when football rejected given faulty) = Cell C8	Formula: = 1-C7
P(Test correct when football faulty) = Cell C10	Value
P(Test not correct when football faulty) = Cell C11	Formula: = 1-C10

Construct the tree diagram – the shaded cells contain formulae linked to the values given in cells C4, C5, C7, C8, C10, and C11.

P(Failing quality test) = Cell C15	Formula: = K15+K22
P(faulty/failed quality test) = Cell C16	Formula: = K22/C15

X

prior probability is the original probability value before new information is identified.

posterior probability is the new probability value based upon the original conditions and the new information identified.

biased a systematic error in a sample.

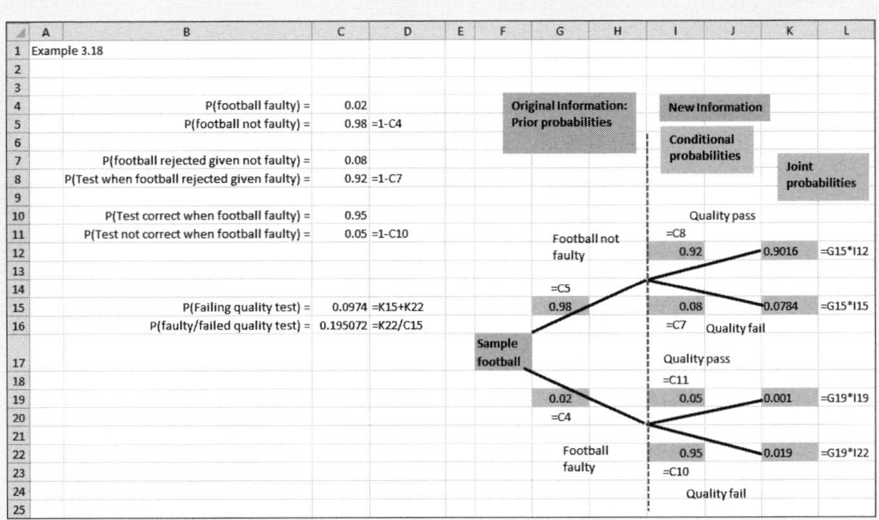

Figure 3.10

❊ **Interpretation** The probability that the football is faulty given that it failed the quality test (called the posterior test) = 0.019/0.0974 = 0.195072 using Equation 3.9.

Note We can now use this tree diagram to calculate the probability that the football is faulty given that it failed the quality test as follows:

1. Probability that the football would fail the test is the sum of the joint probabilities for failing the quality test. From Figure 3.10, this value is simply the sum of the joint probabilities for failing the test (0.0784 and 0.019), which equals 0.0784 + 0.019 = 0.0974.
2. Therefore, the probability that the football is faulty given that it failed the quality test (called the posterior test) = 0.019/0.0974 = 0.195072 using Equation 3.9.

From this analysis, the probability that the football is faulty given that it failed the quality test is 0.195072 or 19.5%. Bayes' theorem is used extensively in the solution to problems involving probabilities and we will use this theorem when exploring the concept of decision making with risk in Chapter 9.

The general form of Bayes' theorem can be used to calculate the conditional probability of event B given that event A has occurred is given by Equation (3.7):

$$P(B_i/A) = \frac{P(A/B_i) \times P(B_i)}{P(A/B_1) \times P(B_1) + P(A/B_2) \times P(B_2) + \ldots\ldots + P(A/B_k) \times P(B_k)} \tag{3.7}$$

Where, B_i is the ith event out of k mutually exclusive and collectively exhaustive events.

Student exercises

X3.13 Each month DINGO Ltd receives a shipment of 100 parts from their supplier which will be checked on delivery for defective parts. Historically the average number defective was three. The new quality assurance procedure involves randomly selecting a sample of three items (without replacement) for inspection. If more than one of the sample is defective the order is returned. What proportion of shipments might be expected to be returned?

X3.14 UK Pro Ltd manufacture footballs for the Far East market with two different standard footballs, standard and professional. As part of the quality assurance process, the manufacturing firm chooses 200 footballs from the manufacturing process and either rejects or accepts the footballs according to specified criteria, with the following results:

Type	Accept	Reject
Standard	89	43
Professional	49	19

Table 3.10 Football quality control results

Calculate: (a) The probability that the football is accepted, (b) the probability that the football is rejected, (c) the probability that the football rejected given selected standard football, and (d) the probability that the football is accepted given selected professional football.

X3.15 A leading book publisher is considering the publication of a new edition of a text book. The publisher has a wealth of information on past sales based upon 20 years in the industry, as illustrated in Table 3.11.

Outcome	Outcome probability
Bestseller	0.3
Average seller	0.4
Breakeven seller	0.2
Loss seller	0.1

Table 3.11

Furthermore, the publisher has the following favourable reviewer data on the probability of each outcome receiving a favourable review, as illustrated in Table 3.12.

Outcome	Outcome probability
Bestseller receiving favourable review	0.84
Average seller receiving favourable review	0.58
Breakeven seller receiving favourable review	0.36
Loss seller receiving favourable review	0.28

Table 3.12

(a) Construct a tree diagram, (b) calculate the conditional probabilities, (c) calculate the proportion resulting in a favourable review, (d) calculate the following probabilities: P(BS/FR), P(AS/FR), P(BE/FR), and P(LS/FR), (e) based upon you answer to part (d) provide a recommendation to the publisher on the possible outcome for this new text book.

3.4 From descriptive statistics to sampling

In Chapter 2 we began by understanding the various types of data, such as discrete, continuous, and category, and then set out to investigate the data through appropriate ordering, tabulation, and illustration, for example Excel sheets, graphs, and tally tables. Subsequently the data was analysed by using a collection of basic descriptive statistical tools and methodologies.

Key to these processes was the availability of quality and representative data, that is, both the data and relative completeness was taken as a given. Further, we did not discriminate between a complete dataset (population) or sub dataset (sample). Put simply, we associated data to dataset.

However, data is not always readily on hand and complete; indeed, data is often a snapshot of what is available or applicable and, at best, is a representation of what is thought to be correct.

In this chapter we set out to consider this ambiguity, its partial representation, and extract as much information and knowledge as possible from the data available. We also devise methods to take these 'snapshots', that is, collect samples that will be used to represent the population data and build a toolkit of quality control methods for the data collected. In this way it is possible to extract the key features of the population without actually having a complete dataset, as well as exploit ways of collecting and concisely expressing this data.

3.4.1 The concepts of population and sampling

So far we have observed that data may come from very diverse sources, ranging from surveys to production quality control measurements. Hence we may have to collect and assess very diverse data, depending on the context in which they were collected in the first place and what is the final intent or expected outcome of the subsequent analysis. For example, exit polls are intended to predict an outcome such as the election results—winner, number of seats won—production quality controls to verify that production quality is under control, customer surveys to capture customer preferences or behaviour and so forth. The data may refer to the entire **population** or, alternatively, be a part of the population.

In the first circumstance, which is often idealistic, all the data of the population are known. Hence, in the case of a census all the inhabitants are actually involved in the survey and a complete dataset is available. Similarly, if we had tested, one by one, all the parts produced in a manufacturing facility the dataset and subsequent findings from the data analysis would concern the entire population of the parts produced. Clearly, the concept of population has many practical implications and repercussions including cost, **data collection**, data exploitation and management, and planning and it is not always feasible or necessary to collect all the population data. For example, measuring the weight and length of *all* the biscuits produced in a biscuit factory is technically feasible but provides little, if any, added value to quality control of the facility and product.

In the second circumstance data concerning part of the population is known as the **sample** and as such would be taken as being representative of the entire population, that is, it is a subset of the complete dataset, as illustrated in Figure 3.11. Each subset of data will

X

population is any entire collection of people, animals, plants or things from which we may collect data.

data collection the gathering of facts that can then be used to make decisions.

sample is a group of units selected from a larger group (the population).

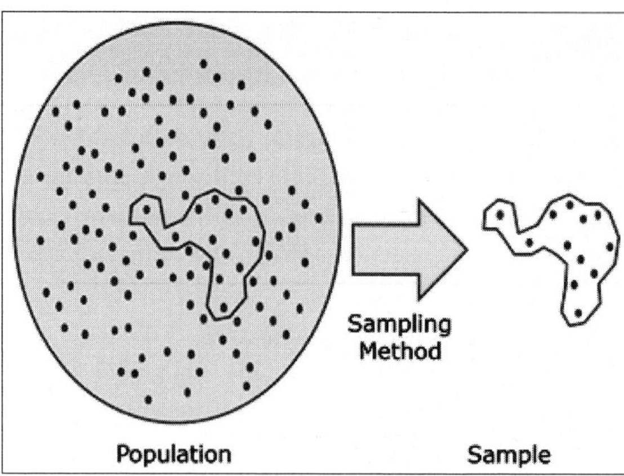

Figure 3.11 Population, sampling method and sample

consist of one or more entities, candidates, data entries, items, observations, and so on. For example, in a survey the people interviewed would be the candidates, whereas in quality control measures the parts assessed would be single entities, and measurements of quantities would be observations; and so forth. The process by which such a subset of data is collected is known as sampling since the data is considered a sample of the entire population.

The population is a generic term and its significance will depend on the context. For example, the population of a town refers to the entire community of inhabitants, the population of a production line refers to whole produce for that particularly line, the population of managers in a corporation refers only to those people (men and women) who have a managerial role. Clearly, all populations are characterized by a collection of entities or candidates and their relative features will reflect the traits of the entire population. Often these features are depicted as classes (categories) and candidates are grouped in classes to reflect these features such as gender. Capturing and understanding (both qualitatively and quantitatively) these features and subsequent extrapolation for the entire population is the whole scope of sampling. Later we will also see that we need to distinguish between finite and infinite populations when sampling.

X

finite population population with a fixed number of items.

infinite population is a population which contains an infinite number of elements; it can be continuous or discrete.

sampling is without replacement sample item not replaced.

simple random sample is a basic sampling technique where we select a group of subjects (a sample) for study from a larger group (a population). Each individual is chosen entirely by chance and each member of the population has an equal chance of being included in the sample. Every possible sample of a given size has the same chance of selection; i.e. each member of the population is equally likely to be chosen at any stage in the sampling process.

3.4.2 Sampling with and without replacement

Suppose a shopping mall has a total of 30 shops and each one has a shop manager. A survey is to be conducted to understand how many have done first aid training. We may want to first conduct a pre-survey based on the random selection of managers. Clearly, we do not want to select a manager more than once, so as soon as a manager has been interviewed that manager is excluded from future random selection. In this case the sampling is without replacement or, more simply, it is known as simple random sampling. If, on the other hand, we do consider replacement as useful (for example, there may be a high turnover of managers or we may want to recheck the responses on different days) then we may want to consider sampling with replacement. Indeed, the number of different simple random samples of size 'n' that can be selected from a (finite) population of size 'N' helps us understand the magnitude of how many combinations is possible: the number of possibilities are given by Equation (3.8).

$$^{N}C_{n} = \frac{N!}{n!(N-n)!} \tag{3.8}$$

Example 3.19

If the population of shopping mall managers is say N = 100 and n is 10 then calculate the number of combinations of samples of size 10 taken from a population of size 100 is given by Equation (3.8).

$$^{100}C_{10} = \frac{100!}{10!(90)!} = 1.71103 \times 10^{13}$$

This is a considerable number of different possible random sample combinations. The Excel function COMBIN () can be used to calculate the number of combinations of n objects from a population of size N, as illustrated in Figure 3.12.

	A	B	C
1	Example 3.19		
2			
3	Population size, N =	100	
4	Sample size, n =	10	
5			
6	Using COMBIN function:		
7	Number of combinations, NCn =	1.73103E+13	=COMBIN(B3,B4)

Figure 3.12

→ Excel solution

Population size, N = Cell B3 Value
Sample size, n = Cell B4 Value
Number of combinations, NCn = Cell B7 Formula: = COMBIN(B3, B4)

Interpretation The number of sample combinations of size 10 taken from a population of size 100 is 1.73103×10^{13}.

The Excel factorial function, FACT (), can be used to solve this type of problem using Equation 3.8 as illustrated in Figure 3.13 for N = 100 and n = 10.

	A	B	C
9	Using Excel FACT function:		
10	N! =	9.3326E+157	=FACT(B3)
11	n! =	3628800	=FACT(B4)
12	(N - n)! =	1.4857E+138	=FACT(B3-B4)
13			
14	Number of combinations, NCn =	1.73103E+13	=B10/(B11*B12)
15	Number of combinations, NCn =	1.73103E+13	=FACT(B3)/(FACT(B4)*FACT(B3-B4))

Figure 3.13

→ Excel solution

N! = Cell B10	Formula: = FACT(B3)
n! = Cell B11	Formula: = FACT(B4)
(N-n)! = Cell B12	Formula: = FACT(B3 - B4)
NCn = Cell B14	Formula: = B10/(B11*B12)
NCn = Cell B15	Formula: = FACT(B3)/(FACT(B4)*FACT(B3-B4))

Interpretation Using Equation (3.8) and Excel FACT (), the number of sample combinations of size 10 taken from a population of size 100 is 1.73103×10^{13}.

Note Excel has limited calculation capabilities and the maximum factorial number it can calculate is 170! = FACT (170) = 7.2574E+306. Try FACT (171) and note the error message #NUM! that Excel inserts in the cell field.

3.4.3 Finite and infinite populations and the effects on sampling

Populations may come in many different (distribution) shapes and sizes but essentially are either considered a finite population (with a fixed and quantifiable size 'N') or infinite population (with an infinite and non-quantifiable size). As will soon be discussed in the following sections, the random selection of items or candidates from a population (finite or infinite) will be associated with the size of the population in general. In finite populations the random selection of items or candidates has the same probability of being selected. In infinite populations the random selection of items or candidates pertains to the population but must also be independent of all others. This independency states that there is no bias since each item or candidate is chosen independently. For example, customers queuing at the ticket office of a train station represent an infinite population because each customer is independent from the others. The key formulae or tools (sampling statistic measures) for the two population circumstances are:

- The sample mean.
- The sample standard deviation.
- The population mean and standard deviation.
- The sample proportion.
- The population proportion.
- **Finite population correction factor**.
- The standard error of proportions.

finite population correction factor it is common practice to use finite population correction factors in estimating variances when sampling from a finite population.

A brief description of these sampling statistic measures in the context of sampling follows.

3.4.4 The sample mean

The sample mean is the average of all the sample elements and observations for the sample size 'n'. It is an estimate of the population mean 'μ', providing the observations are independent random variables $x_1, x_2, \ldots, x_k$, (each one corresponding to a single randomly selected observation). The **sample mean** is calculated using Equation (3.9).

$$\bar{x} = \frac{x_1 + x_2 + x_3 \ldots\ldots x_i}{n} = \frac{\sum_{i=1}^{i=n} x_i}{n} \tag{3.9}$$

Example 3.20

Table 3.13 illustrates five samples taken randomly from an apple processing plant consisting of five observations each (five different apples per sample) with the corresponding weights recorded (in grams). The scope of the sampling is to assess average weight as it is a measure used in the commercial classification of apple size.

Sample ID	Ob. 1	Ob. 2	Ob. 3	Ob. 4	Ob. 5
1	95	111	115	103	98
2	92	110	118	119	105
3	95	97	102	103	108
4	101	100	102	104	104
5	99	92	110	110	109

Table 3.13

Determine the mean of each of the five samples using Excel as illustrated in Figure 3.14.

	A	B	C	D	E	F	G	H
1	Example 3.20							
2								
3	Sample ID	Item 1	Item 2	Item 3	Item 4	Item 5	Sample means	
4	1	95	111	115	103	98	104.4	=AVERAGE(B4:F4)
5	2	92	110	118	119	105	108.8	
6	3	95	97	102	103	108	101.0	
7	4	101	100	102	104	104	102.2	
8	5	99	92	110	110	109	104.0	=AVERAGE(B8:F8)
9								
10						Mean of all samples =	104.1	=AVERAGE(G4:G8)

Figure 3.14

sample mean is an estimator available for estimating the population mean.

→ Excel solution

Sample ID Cells A4:A8	Values
Sample 1 data Cells B4:F4	Values
Sample 2 data Cells B5:F5	Values
Sample 3 data Cells B6:F6	Values
Sample 4 data Cells B7:F7	Values
Sample 5 data Cells B8:F8	Values
Sample means Cells G4	Formula: = AVERAGE(B4:F4)
	Copy formula down from G4:G8
Mean of all samples = Cell G10	Formula: = AVERAGE(G4:G8)

❊ Interpretation From Excel, the sample means are: 104.4, 108.8, 101, 102.2 and 104. The mean for all 25 samples is 104.1 grams so sample 5 provides a better estimate of the mean of all samples than the other sample averages (104.4, 108.8, 101, 102.2).

Note The mean of sample 1 is: $\bar{x} = \frac{95 + 111 + 115 + 103 + 98}{5} = \frac{552}{5} = 104.4.$
If each sample (1 to 5) represented a supplier or production line we would be able to associate the measure of mean as an estimator of quality (in terms of apple weight).

An alternative to the mean calculated in Equation (3.9) is to use frequencies, which is especially useful for very large datasets. The approach consists of organizing and splitting the data into classes where each class is the tally count discussed in Chapter 2. Once this has been done the frequency is multiplied by the class and then summed. Equation (3.10) can then be used to calculate the mean using frequencies:

$$\bar{x} = \frac{\Sigma(\text{frequency} \times \text{class})}{\text{total frequency}} \tag{3.10}$$

3.4.5 The sample standard deviation

The sample standard deviation is defined by Equation (3.11):

$$s = \sqrt{\frac{\Sigma(x_i - \bar{x})^2}{n - 1}} \tag{3.11}$$

Example 3.21

Five samples are taken randomly from a production of small oranges. The samples consist of five observations each with the corresponding weights recorded (in grams), as illustrated in Table 3.14.

Sample ID	Ob. 1	Ob. 2	Ob. 3	Ob. 4	Ob. 5
1	95	92	95	101	99
2	111	110	97	100	92
3	115	97	102	102	110
4	103	100	103	104	110
5	98	92	108	104	109

Table 3.14

Determine the standard deviation of each of the five samples.

	A	B	C	D	E	F	G	H	I	J
1	Example 3.21									
2										
3	Sample ID	Ob. 1	Ob. 2	Ob. 3	Ob. 4	Ob. 5	Sample mean		s	
4	1	95	92	95	101	99	96.4	=AVERAGE(B4:F4)	3.6	=STDEV.S(B4:F4)
5	2	111	110	97	100	92	102		8.3	
6	3	115	97	102	102	110	105.2		7.2	
7	4	103	100	103	104	110	104		3.7	
8	5	98	92	108	104	109	102.2	=AVERAGE(B8:F8)	7.2	=STDEV.S(B8:F8)
9										
10						Mean of all samples =	102.0	=AVERAGE(H4:H8)		

Figure 3.15

→ Excel solution

Sample ID Cells A4:A8	Values
Sample 1 data Cells B4:F4	Values
Sample 2 data Cells B5:F5	Values
Sample 3 data Cells B6:F6	Values
Sample 4 data Cells B7:F7	Values
Sample 5 data Cells B8:F8	Values
Sample means Cells G4	Formula: = AVERAGE(B4:F4)
	Copy formula down from G4:G8
Mean of all samples = Cell G10	Formula: = AVERAGE(G4:G8)
Sample standard deviation, s = Cell I4	Formula: = STDEV.S(B4:F4)
	Copy formula down from I4:I8

❊ **Interpretation** From Figure 3.16, the sample means and sample standard deviations are respectively 96.4, 102, 105.2, 104, 102.2 and 3.6, 8.3, 7.2, 3.7 and 7.2. Furthermore, the overall mean taking into account each sample is 102.0. Again we can use the standard deviation as a quality estimator and sample 1 appears to have the least spread (but also the lowest mean) as shown in Figure 3.15.

3.4.6 The population mean and population standard deviation

The **population mean** (μ) and **population standard deviation** (σ) are defined by Equations (3.12) and (3.13) respectively:

$$\mu = \frac{\sum_{i=1}^{i=N} x_i}{N} \tag{3.12}$$

$$\sigma = \sqrt{\frac{\sum (x_i - \bar{x})^2}{N}} \tag{3.13}$$

Note It will be noted that the differences between sample and population formulae lie essentially in the denominator, later the topic of bias will be tackled to explain these differences.

Example 3.22

A finite population of shoppers were consulted in a medical survey and the amount of fresh fruit purchased measured resulting in the following tabled results:

95	111	115	103	98
92	110	118	**119**	105
95	97	**102**	**103**	108
101	100	102	104	104
99	92	110	110	**109**

Table 3.15

Taking the five smokers indicated in the shaded cells in Table 3.15 compare the sample mean to the population mean and subsequently also the standard deviations. The Excel solution is illustrated in Figure 3.16.

	A	B	C	D	E	F	G
1	Example 3.22						
2							
3		95	111	115	103	98	
4		92	110	118	119	105	
5		95	97	102	103	108	
6		101	100	102	104	104	
7		99	92	110	110	109	
8							
9					Sample mean =	105.600	=AVERAGE(B3,E4,D5,E5,F7)
10					Population mean =	104.080	=AVERAGE(B3:F7)
11					Standard deviation of the sample =	8.989	=STDEV.S(B3,D5,E4,E5,F7)
12					Standard deviation of the population =	7.310	=STDEV.P(B3:F7)

Figure 3.16

population mean (μ) mean value when taking into account the entire population of data values.

population standard deviation (σ) standard deviation value when taking into account the entire population of data values.

→ Excel solution

Data Cells B3:F7	Values
Sample mean = Cell F9	Formula: = AVERAGE(B3,E4,D5,E5,F7)
Population mean = Cell F10	Formula: = AVERAGE(B3:F7)
Sample standard deviation Cell F11	Formula: = STDEV.S(B3,D5,E4,E5,F7)
Population standard deviation Cell F12	Formula: = STDEV.P(B3:F7)

Interpretation From Figure 3.16, we observe that the sample standard deviation (Cell F9 = 8.99) is higher than the population standard deviation (Cell F10 = 7.31). Observe also how the single cells are selected (with commas) for the average and standard deviation of the sample in the Excel worksheet.

Note We have for the sample and population means:

$$\bar{x} = \frac{\sum_{i=1}^{i=n} x_i}{n} = \frac{95 + 119 + 102 + 103 + 109}{5} = 105.6$$

$$\mu = \frac{\sum_{i=1}^{i=N} x_i}{N} = \frac{95 + 111 + 115 + 103 + \ldots 109 + 109}{25} = 104.1$$

The standard deviation of the sample mean (STDEV or STDEV.S function in Excel) is:

$$s = \sqrt{\frac{\Sigma(x_i - \bar{x})^2}{n-1}}$$

$$= \sqrt{\frac{\Sigma(95 - 105.6)^2 + (119 - 106.6)^2 + (102 - 105.6)^2 + (103 - 105.6)^2 + (109 - 105.6)^2}{5-1}}$$

$$s = \sqrt{\frac{(112.36 + 179.56 + 12.96 + 6.76 + 11.56)}{4}} = \sqrt{\frac{323.2}{4}} = 8.99$$

The population standard deviation (STDEV or STDEV.P function in Excel 2010) is:

$$\sigma = \sqrt{\frac{\Sigma(x_i - \bar{x})^2}{N}} = \sqrt{\frac{1335.84}{25}} = 7.31$$

3.4.7 The sample proportion

The **sample proportion** (p) is the ratio of the number elements (m) in the sample to the complete sample size (n), as given by Equation (3.14):

$$p = \frac{m}{n} \tag{3.14}$$

sample proportion is the ratio of the number elements in the sample to the complete sample size.

Example 3.23

If a total of 17 shop managers out of 30 in a shopping mall are trained in first aid procedures what is the sample proportion for this type of training? In Example 3.24, m = 17 and n = 30 hence p is given by Equation (3.14):

$$p = \frac{m}{n} = \frac{17}{30} = 0.567$$

Example 3.24

A class is asked to calculate the sample proportion based on the following field class results. A certain number of bags of M&Ms are taken from several randomly selected vending machines amounting to a total of 420 M&Ms of which 55 are blue in colour. What is the sample proportion for the blue M&Ms? It follows that the sample proportion is:

$$p = \frac{m}{n} = \frac{55}{420} = 0.131$$

3.4.8 The population proportion

The population proportion (π) is the ratio of the sample size (n) to the population size (N), as given by Equation (3.15):

$$\pi = \frac{n}{N} \tag{3.15}$$

3.4.9 The finite population correction factor

As seen in Example 3.22 the exploitation of the sample mean in a finite population provided similar results to the population mean (105.6 vs. 104.1), the same can be said also for the standard deviation of the sample (8.99 vs. 7.31). However, the **sampling distribution** of $\bar{x}$ depends on the population being finite (defined by Equation 3.16) or infinite (defined by Equation 3.17) and leads to two distinct cases for the standard deviation of the mean of these two types of population:

$$\sigma_{\bar{x}} = \sqrt{\frac{N-n}{N-1}}\left(\frac{\sigma}{\sqrt{n}}\right) \tag{3.16}$$

$$\sigma_{\bar{x}} = \left(\frac{\sigma}{\sqrt{n}}\right) \tag{3.17}$$

The difference between these two different standard deviations is known as the finite population correction factor as defined by Equation (3.18):

$$k_n = \sqrt{\frac{N-n}{N-1}} \tag{3.18}$$

X
sampling distribution
the sampling distribution describes probabilities associated with a statistic when a random sample is drawn from a population.

As this factor approaches unity the two standard deviation equations become equivalent, which implies that as the sample size approaches the (finite) population size so our accuracy improves. So when should or can we use these two formulae for the calculation of the standard deviation and consider them equivalent? The key to this decision is the acceptable level of accuracy. To simplify this decision a cut-off value for the correction factor has been established.

The infinite population standard deviation of the mean (Equation 3.17) can be used providing the sample size is equal to or more than 5% of the population, namely:

$$\frac{n}{N} > 0.05$$

Conversely the finite population standard deviation of the mean (Equation 3.16) should be used (together with the correction factor) according to the following condition:

$$\frac{n}{N} \leq 0.05$$

Table 3.16 summarizes for finite and infinite populations:

Finite populations	Infinite populations	Population correction factor
$\sigma_{\bar{x}} = \sqrt{\frac{N-n}{N-1}}\left(\frac{\sigma}{\sqrt{n}}\right)$	$\sigma_{\bar{x}} = \left(\frac{\sigma}{\sqrt{n}}\right)$	$\sqrt{\frac{N-n}{N-1}}$
Use for $\frac{n}{N} \leq 0.05$ i.e. sufficiently large sample sizes	Use for $\frac{n}{N} > 0.05$	When a sample (randomly selected and without replacement) is greater than 5% (or 0.05) of the population from which it is being selected the finite population correction factor should be used.

Table 3.16

Example 3.25

A survey is conducted on the salaries of 3000 public service managers in a regional health authority and a standard deviation of 5000 euros was determined. Following these results a decision was made to conduct and introduce random sampling at regular intervals (every six months) and two sample sizes were to be considered, 30 and 100 samples. (a) Establish if these sample sizes are valid considering both finite and infinite populations. (b) In both cases determine the population correction factor. (c) What is the sample size limit for using the infinite population formula for computing the standard deviation of $\bar{x}$?

(a) Calculate n/N for each sample and compare with 0.05.
The two cases are respectively: $n_1/N = 30/3000 = 0.01 < 0.05$ and $n_2/N = 100/3000 = 0.033 < 0.05$. Both cases satisfy the finite population equation but not the infinite population equation given that $n/N \leq 0.05$.

(b) Calculate the correction factors CF1 and CF2 for each sample using the finite population correction equation:

$$CF1 = \sqrt{\frac{N-n}{N-1}} = \sqrt{\frac{2970}{2999}} = \sqrt{0.99} = 0.995 \cong 1$$

$$CF2 = \sqrt{\frac{N-n}{N-1}} = \sqrt{\frac{2900}{2999}} = \sqrt{0.967} = 0.983$$

(c) Calculate the sample size limit for using the infinite population equation for calculating the standard deviation of the sample means. For an infinite population:

$$n > N \times 0.05 = 3000 \times 0.05 = 150$$

So for sample sizes greater than 150 we would use the infinite population equation. Conversely, if $n \leq 150$ we would use the finite population correction factor equation.

3.4.10 Standard error of proportions

A typical question in sampling is how big does the sample have to be? This could be formulated differently such as 'How accurate do we want the sample to be' or 'What is the error for the sample I am considering' and so forth. The answer is provided by the standard error of proportion formulated as given by Equation (3.19):

$$SE = \sqrt{\frac{p(1-p)}{n}} \tag{3.19}$$

Example 3.26

A company is considering changing the duration of the lunchbreak and 25 workers are randomly consulted. The responses are 68% in favour and the remaining against. What is the error if the sample is taken as being representative of the population (316 workers)? By how much would the error fall if half the population was consulted?

$$SE = \sqrt{\frac{0.68(1-0.68)}{25}} = 0.093$$

This implies that there is a 9.3% error in the estimation for a favourable change hence the percentage could vary from 58.7% to 77.3%. Observe that 32% are against the change so again using SE we would have a variation of 41.3% to 22.7% thus showing that the company should introduce the change based on this sample. If we extend the survey to half the workers we have:

$$SE = \sqrt{\frac{0.68(1-0.68)}{158}} = 0.037$$

This result shows that the margin of error reduces as the sample size grows, in this case roughly by a factor of three.

3.4.11 Central limit theorem

The central limit theorem states that no matter what the shape of the original distribution of the sample dataset the final distribution of the sample means as it approaches the true population will be normal. Mathematically, the central limit theorem states that given a distribution with a mean μ and variance σ^2, the sampling distribution of the mean approaches a normal distribution with a mean (μ) and a variance σ^2/n as n, the sample size, increases. Another interesting feature is that for most distributions a normal distribution will arise surprisingly quickly as n increases, where n is the sample size for each mean and not the total number of samples or items in the dataset. Indeed as sample size grows the sample mean moves towards the population mean, μ. As we will see later, with an ideal normal distribution the sample and population means eventually equate and sit on the centre line of a perfectly symmetrically curve (referred to as the standard normal distribution). Similarly, the standard deviation of the sampling distribution of the mean approaches σ^2/n or $\sigma/\sqrt{n}$ as is commonly reported.

3.4.12 Biased and unbiased estimators

We have seen that estimators are used to establish an approximation of the true value in a population such as the sample mean is used to approximate the population mean. When, for example, the mean value of an estimator equals the true mean value of the population it estimates, then the estimate is considered unbiased. It was also shown that by exploiting the central limit theorem, the mean value of the sample is a very good estimator of the population mean and for this reason the sample mean is considered an unbiased estimator of the population mean providing the sample is not too small.

Formally though, if the mean value of an estimator is either less than or greater than the true value of the quantity it estimates such as the population mean, then the estimator is biased.

In practice, biased sample mean estimators are generally smaller than their unbiased counterparts, which implies that the variance and standard deviation will be too, as shown in Figure 3.17.

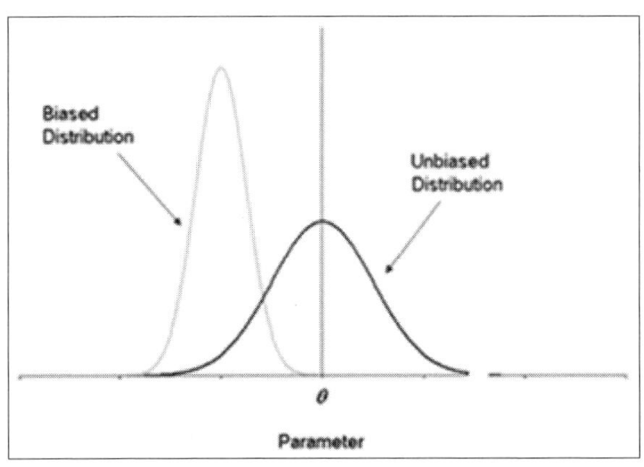

Figure 3.17 Biased versus Unbiased distributions

X

central limit theorem states that whenever a random sample of size n is taken from any distribution with mean μ and variance σ^2, then the sample mean will be approximately normally distributed with mean μ and variance σ^2/n. The larger the value of the sample size n, the better the approximation to the normal.

sampling distribution of the mean distribution of the mean of samples from the population.

standard normal distribution is a normal distribution whose mean is always 0 and a standard deviation is always 1.

Since both the sample variance and standard deviation are based on the sample mean it follows that all three measures will be different with respect to their population counterparts. Moreover, the sample observation x_i will be closer to the sample mean $\bar{x}$ than the population mean μ. To offset this, n – 1 instead of n, is placed in the denominator of the sample variance equation so that for sufficiently large sample sizes the effects of bias between the sample and population variances is negligible. Hence the sample variance is defined by Equation (3.20):

$$s^2 = \frac{\sum_{i=1}^{i=n}(x_i - \bar{x})^2}{n-1} \tag{3.20}$$

Example 3.27

Ten branded chocolate energy bars are selected from a population of 114 different brands of energy bar. The average energy, reported in kCal on each wrapper, is recorded as follows: 275, 205, 198, 289, 302, 189, 225, 256, 289, and 239. Determine the sample mean, sample standard deviation, the population proportion, and the population mean and standard deviation.

Sample mean and standard deviation:

$$\bar{x} = \frac{\sum_{i=1}^{i=n} x_i}{n} = \frac{275 + 205 + 198 + ... + 239}{10} = \frac{2467}{10} = 246.7 \text{ kCal}$$

$$s = \sqrt{\frac{\sum_{i=1}^{i=n}(x_i - \bar{x})^2}{n-1}} = \sqrt{\frac{\Sigma(275 - 246.7)^2 + 205 - 246.7)^2 + ... + (239 - 246.7)^2}{10-1}}$$

$$= \sqrt{1721.57} = 41.5$$

The population proportion is:

$$\pi = \frac{n}{N} = \frac{10}{114} = 0.088 > 0.05$$

The population mean and standard deviation is:

$$\mu = \bar{x} = 246.7$$

$$\sigma = \sqrt{\frac{\Sigma(x_i - \bar{x})^2}{N}} = \sqrt{\frac{15494.1}{10}} = 39.4$$

This is approximately 5% less than the sample estimate.

3.4.13 Standard error of the mean (SEM)

The central limit theorem shows that the sample mean varies around the population mean as though it came from a normal distribution, and this can be observed quickly and with a relatively small sample size. Further, since all the properties of normal distributions for finite populations apply we can also use the standard deviation as a measure of

X
sample variance is a measure of the spread of or dispersion within a set of sample data.

dispersion of the mean, more specifically we use what is called the **standard error of the mean (SEM)**.

The effects of sample size on the accuracy of the sample mean is shown below in Figure 3.18 (not to scale).

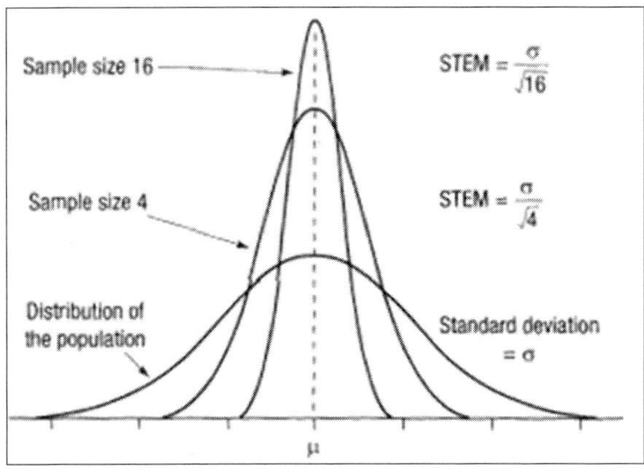

Figure 3.18

The standard deviation of a normal distribution in a finite population states that the behaviour of the sample mean is equal to the standard deviation of the individual observations divided by the square root of the sample size, namely SEM, as illustrated in Equation (3.21):

$$\mathrm{SEM} = \frac{s}{\sqrt{n}} \tag{3.21}$$

Due to the fact we refer to normal distribution properties we may also use the same guidelines as found for standard deviation, that is:

- For 68% of the occurrences, the sample mean and population mean will be within 1 SEM of each other;
- For 95% of the occurrences, the sample mean and population mean will be within 2 SEMs of each other;
- For 99% of the occurrences, the sample mean and population mean will be within 2.57 SEMs of each other;
- For 99.7% of the occurrences, the sample mean and population mean will be within 3 SEMs of each other and so forth.

Example 3.28

The standard deviation for radiation measurements on a sample of the local population following a nuclear incident at a nuclear power plant is 25.75. Determine and study the effects on the sample size for three different cases n = 10, n = 50, n = 1000. What conclusions can you make for these results? Substituting the value of n into Equation (3.21) gives: (a) n = 10, SEM = 8.143, (b) n = 50, SEM = 3.642, and (c) n = 1000, SEM = 0.814.

X

standard error of the mean (SEM) standard deviation of the sampling error of the mean.

Note As the sample size grows so the standard error of the mean reduces, or, as the sample size grows the estimate of the sample mean becomes more reliable, accurate, and approaches the population mean. Moreover, the mean of the sample can lie anywhere within the bounds of the normal curve for sampling conducted, although it will more likely be closer to the centre rather than the tails of the curve. In order to establish the sample size it would be necessary to understand more about the measurement of the radiation and what it entails hence the answer is only mathematical. Clearly, since such a measure is precautionary in nature and regards human health the scope is to accurately measure the likelihood that the value measured is safe or otherwise. Hence larger and targeted samples such as children, low weight, and frail people (see multi-stage sampling) are taken, or, more convincingly, the measurements are extended to the whole population.

3.4.14 Types of sampling frames: probability and non-probability

There are essentially two types or categories of sampling frame, probability and non-probability:

1. The concept of probability sampling assumes some form of random selection of the data and it is assumed that such data, even though random, represents the population. Hence there are equal opportunities or probabilities for the selection of data. A good example of probability sampling is picking a name out of a hat or choosing the shortest or longest straw. As such the selection is representative of the population because we know that the odds (or probability) of representing the population. In probability sampling the actual random selecting method varies according to the selection procedure behind it and the procedure identifies the process used such as simple random selection, stratified random sampling, and so forth.
2. The non-probability sampling approach on the other hand does not involve random selection and is also known as non-representative sampling because not always do we know if the sample represents well the population. Broadly speaking we may categorize the non-probabilistic approach under accidental or purposive, the latter being the most common since it involves a specific data collection plan. Hence for obvious reasons researchers prefer the probabilistic approach since it is considered more rigorous and accurate and we are able to determine the confidence intervals for the statistics.

sampling frame a list of every member of the population.

probability sampling the concept of probability sampling assumes some form of random selection of the data and it is assumed that such data, even though random, represents the population.

non-probability sampling involves a sample of units where the selected units in the sample have an unknown probability of being selected.

3.4.15 Sampling data collection methods and process

The purpose of a sample (e.g. obtained through a survey or quality control check) in which data is collected is to obtain information and possibly knowledge about the population. The purpose of data collection is to obtain information to monitor a situation, make fact based decisions on issues important for those who promote the survey and/or to report on important information and knowledge about the population useful for third parties or others. The purpose of the sampling will depend on the scope, for example, in scientific fields data is collected because the data offers empirical answers to theoretical research questions or validates theoretical reasoning. Key to sampling is the following interpretation given for data, information and knowledge, as illustrated in Table 3.17.

	Description	Usefulness and competitive advantage
Data	Are the numerical and non-numerical responses or measurements. For example, physical measurements, binary (Yes or No), nominal and categorical data, etc.	Indispensable for descriptive analysis; limited CA; usefulness depends on reliability and degree of obsolescence of the data.
Information	Information is the interpretation of the data such as a tally diagram, scatter plot, histogram, quality control chart etc. Information is therefore a pre-packaged and summarized report of data. To a certain extent also descriptive statistics perform this task.	Indispensable for summarizing data and communication purposes; medium CA if exploited properly, facilitates decision making; relies on data.
Knowledge	Is the exploitation of data and information in a cognitive manner and decision making circumstance? For example, in the case of quality control if the plotted data is between the UCL and LCL the process is said to 'under control'. Knowledge is often difficult to state in writing and is usually tacit in nature. A good example of tacit knowledge is the tying of shoelaces, which even with a mathematical explanation of the knot model is virtually impossible to convey. To a certain extent reporting (a form of information) captures knowledge.	Difficult to capture and state; requires experience and interpretation; very strong CA and difficult to replicate by the competition; knowledge is not necessarily a true indicator or response or quality since it can be biased; data and information take second place in knowledge based decision processes.

Table 3.17 Data, information and knowledge

There are essentially two types of data: primary and secondary:

1. The collection of **primary data** is considered to be less biased, the most relevant, the most up to date and directly collected or collectable at the source. It is often managed and in the custody of professional bodies such as quality control staff, professional bodies such as National Statistics Institutes. For this reason it is often referred to as source or first-hand data and comes unpackaged or is available in its 'raw' form and not 'rolled up' or summarized. It may therefore often have additional data, such as metadata, for example a customer's address.
2. The collection of **secondary data** is pre-processed data, second-hand and often summarized or rolled-up into an information-type of format such as graphs, summary charts, and tables. Often the methods, tools, and procedures used in rolling up are unknown or vague. Typical sources are magazines, journals, presentations, and media.

It is often assumed in data collection and sampling that the data has already been 'cleaned', accepted as valid and all errors have been removed (i.e. validated) before actually progressing to the analysis. Sometimes sampling includes these tasks and involve adhering to rules before the sample data is accepted, such as in quota or stratified sampling. Hence if a survey is being conducted on a certain part of the population, such as car owners, there may be a question such as 'Do you own more than two cars in your

X

primary data is data collected by the user.

secondary data is data collected by someone other than the user.

family or do you own a specific brand of car?,' ambient temperature sampling has been set at ten samples per minute. Consequently, the data collection process can be summarized in Figure 3.19.

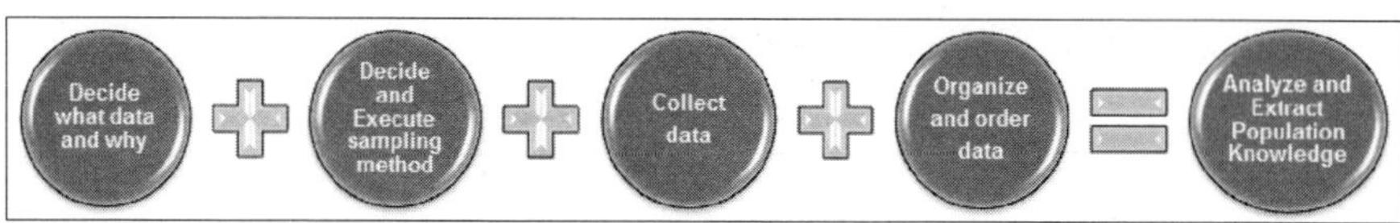

Figure 3.19 Sampling and data collection process

sampling error sampling error refers to the error that results from taking one sample rather than taking a census of the entire population.

continuous probability distribution if a random variable is a continuous variable, its probability distribution is called a continuous probability distribution.

normal (or Gaussian) distribution is a continuous probability distribution that has a bell-shaped probability density function.

student's t-distribution is a family of continuous probability distributions that arises when estimating the mean of a normally distributed population in situations where the sample size is small and population standard deviation is unknown.

chi-square distribution with k degrees of freedom is the distribution of a sum of the squares of k independent standard normal random variables. It is useful because, under reasonable assumptions, easily calculated quantities can be proven to have distributions that approximate to the chi-square distribution if the null hypothesis is true.

F distribution a continuous statistical distribution which arises in the testing of whether two observed samples have the same variance.

In statistics, **sampling error** is the amount of inaccuracy in estimating some value that is caused by only a portion of a population (i.e. a sample) rather than the whole population. The sampling distribution describes probabilities associated with a statistic when a random sample is drawn from a population.

3.5 Continuous probability distributions

In this section we will introduce the concept of the normal and standard normal distribution, which we will use in later chapters to solve specific problems. There are many **continuous probability distributions**, such as: uniform distribution, **normal distribution**, the **student's t-distribution**, the **chi-square distribution**, exponential distribution, and **F distribution**.

3.5.1 The normal distribution and Excel

When a variable is continuous, and its value is affected by a large number of chance factors, none of which predominates, then it will frequently appear as a normal distribution. This distribution does occur frequently and is probably the most widely used statistical distribution. Some of the real-life variables having a normal distribution can be found, for example, in manufacturing (weights of tin cans), or can be associated with the human population (people's heights). The normal distribution curve (also called the bell curve or Gaussian curve) is illustrated in Figure 3.20 and is defined by the Gaussian function (Equation 3.22):

$$f(X) = \frac{1}{\sigma\sqrt{2\pi}} e^{\left(-\frac{(X-\mu)^2}{2\sigma^2}\right)} \tag{3.22}$$

Where:

f(X) is the probability density function, PDF.

μ is the population mean.

σ is the population standard deviation.

$\pi \approx 3.14$

$e \approx 2.71$

This equation can be represented by Figure 3.20 and illustrates the symmetrical characteristics of the normal distribution.

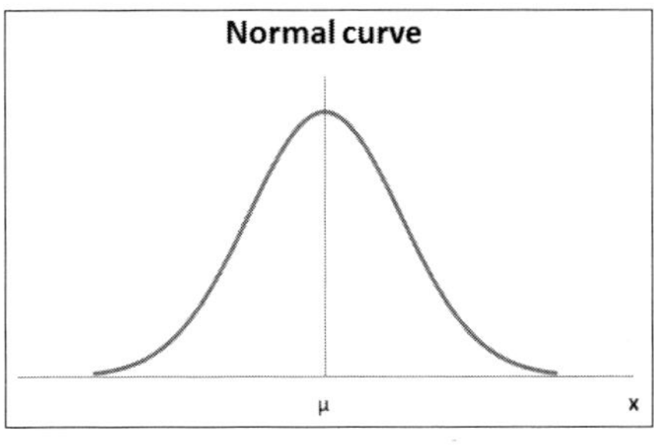

Figure 3.20

For the normal distribution the mean, median, and mode all have the same numerical value.

Note The normal distribution and function relates to sampling and populations and in particular:

1. The horizontal axis represents the value of the variable and all relative estimators of the features of the population. Hence the centre is the location of the mean and the width is measured by the variance or more commonly the standard deviation. The more variance the wider the curve.
2. The vertical axis of the normal distribution curve represents the frequency of the samples but in the analysis of samples and quality control cases it refers to the probability density function or probability or relative frequencies.

Other key features of the normal distribution are:

- Since the mean, mode and median coincide these are represented by the population mean μ and its relative location on the X-axis. For this reason population mean μ is recognized as the location parameter of the curve.
- The standard deviation of the population σ is known as the scale parameter of the curve.
- Skewness is zero since the distribution is perfectly symmetric.
- Kurtosis is equal to zero
- Range is infinity ..... in both directions of the X-axis
- Coefficient of variation is represented by σ/μ.

To calculate the probability of a particular value of X occurring we would calculate the appropriate area represented in Figure 3.20 and use Excel (or tables) to find the corresponding value of the probability.

coefficient of variation measures the spread of a set of data as a proportion of its mean. It is often expressed as a percentage.

Example 3.29

A manufacturing firm quality assures components manufactured and historically the length of a tube is found to be normally distributed with the population mean of 100 cm and a standard deviation of 5 cm. Calculate the probability that a random sample of one tube will have a length of at least 110 cm? From the information provided we define X has the tube length in cm and population mean μ = 100 and standard deviation = 5. This can be represented using the notation $X \sim N(100, 5^2)$. The problem we have to solve is to calculate the probability that one tube will have a length of at least 110 cm.

The Excel solution is illustrated in Figure 3.21.

	A	B	C	D
1	Example 3.29 and 3.30			
2				
3		Normal distribution		
4				
5		Mean μ =	100	
6		Standard deviation σ =	5	
7				
8		X =	110	
9				
10		P(X <= 110) =	0.97725	=NORM.DIST(C8,C5,C6,TRUE)
11				
12		P(X => 110) =	0.02275	=1-C10

Figure 3.21

From Excel, the NORM.DIST () function can be used to calculate $P(X \geq 110) = 0.02275$.

→ Excel solution

Mean = Cell C5	Value
Standard deviation Cell C6	Value
X = Cell C8	Value
P(X <= 110) = Cell C10	Function: = NORM.DIST(C8,C5,C6,TRUE)
P(X => 110) = Cell C12	Formula: = 1-C10

Excel 2010 has a new function that allows for the calculation of the normal cumulative distribution: NORM.DIST.

✻ Interpretation We observe that the probability that an individual tube length is at least 110 cm is 0.02275 or 2.3% ($P(X \geq 110) = 0.02275$).

Note To solve these types of probability distribution problems it is helpful to sketch a normal distribution curve and note on this sketch the problem we wish to solve.

Example 3.29 can be written as $P(X \geq 110)$ and is represented by the shaded area illustrated in Figure 3.22.

The Excel function NORM.DIST will calculate the region to the left of X = 110. Remember we want to know $P(X \geq 110)$ which is the region to the right of X = 110.

This problem can be solved by using the Excel function NORM.DIST (X, μ, σ^2, TRUE).

This function calculates the area illustrated in Figure 3.23.

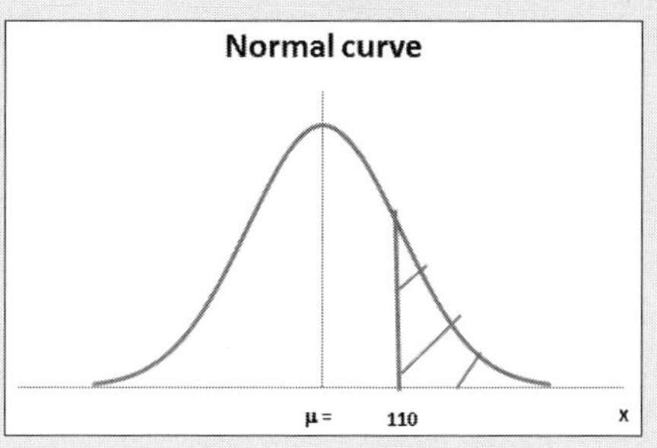

Figure 3.22

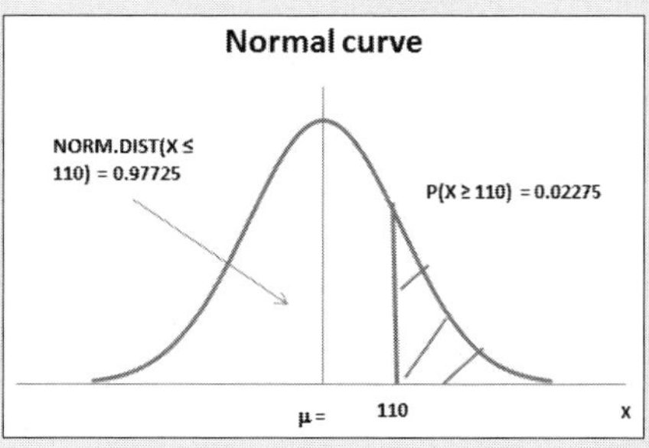

Figure 3.23

3.5.2 The standard normal distribution and Excel

If we have two different populations, both following normal distribution, it could be difficult to compare them as the units might be different, the means and variances might be different. If this is the case, we would like to be able to standardize these distributions so that we can compare them. This is possible by creating the **standard normal distribution**. The standard normal distribution is a normal distribution whose mean is always 0 and a standard deviation is always 1. Normal distributions can be transformed to standard normal distribution by Equation (3.23):

$$Z = \frac{(X - \mu)}{\sigma} \tag{3.23}$$

Where, X, μ, and σ are the variable score value (or observation values), population mean, and population standard deviation respectively taken from the original normal distribution. Any distribution can be converted to a standardized distribution using Equation (3.23) and the shape of the standardized version will be the same as the original distribution. If the original was symmetric then the Z transformed version would still be symmetric, and if the original was skewed then the Z transformed version would still be skewed. The advantage of this method is that the Z values are not dependent on the original data units and this allows tables of Z values to be produced with corresponding areas under the curve. This allows for probabilities to be calculated if the Z value is known, and vice versa, which allows a range of problems to be solved.

standard normal distribution is a normal distribution with zero mean and unit standard deviation.

Note From calculation we can show that the proportion of values between ±1, ±2, and ±3 population standard deviations from the population mean of zero is 68%, 95%, and 99.7% respectively. To state this differently, the mean value ±1 standard deviation will include 68% of all the values in the distribution.

Example 3.30

Using the data from Example 3.29, if a variable X varies as a normal distribution with a mean of 100 and a standard deviation of 5, then the value of Z when X = 110 would be equal to Z = (100 – 100)/5 = +2.

The value of P(Z ≥ 2) can be calculated using Excel's NORM.S.DIST() function. The Excel solution is illustrated in Figure 3.24.

	A	B	C	D
1	Example 3.29 and 3.30			
2				
3		Normal distribution		
4				
5		Mean μ =	100	
6		Standard deviation σ =	5	
7				
8		X =	110	
9				
10		P(X <= 110) =	0.97725	=NORM.DIST(C8,C5,C6,TRUE)
11				
12		P(X => 110) =	0.02275	=1-C10
13				
14		Z =	2	=(C8-C5)/C6
15		Z =	2	=STANDARDIZE(C8,C5,C6)
16		P(Z <= +2) =	0.97725	=NORM.S.DIST(C14,TRUE)
17		P(Z => +2) =	0.02275	=1-C16

Figure 3.24

→ Excel solution

Mean = Cell C5	Value
Standard deviation Cell C6	Value
X = Cell C8	Value
P(X <= 110) = Cell C10	Function: = NORM.DIST(C8,C5,C6,TRUE)
P(X => 110) = Cell C12	Formula: = 1-C10
Z = Cell C14	Formula: = (C8-C5)/C6
Z = Cell C15	Formula/Function: = STANDARDIZE(C8,C5,C6)
P(Z <= +2) = Cell C16	Function: = NORM.S.DIST(C14, TRUE))
P(Z => +2) = Cell C17	Formula: = 1-C15

Excel 2010 has a new function that allows for the calculation of the normal cumulative distribution: NORM.DIST.

This solution can be represented graphically by Figure 3.25.

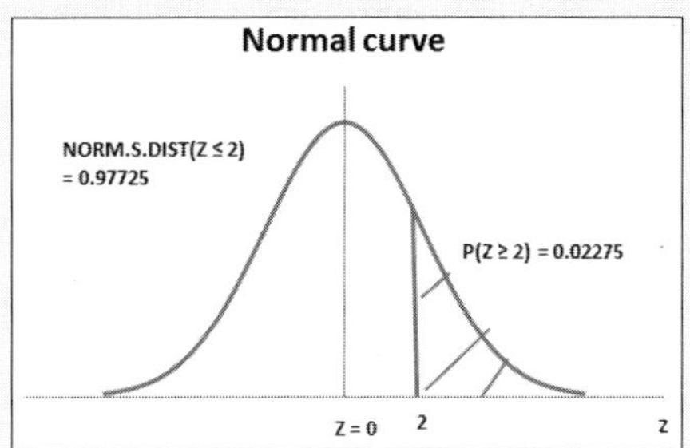

Figure 3.25

From Excel, the NORM.S.DIST () function can be used to calculate P(Z ≥ +2) = 0.02275.

Interpretation We observe that the probability that an individual tube length is at least 110 cm is 0.02275 or 2.3% (P(X ≥ 110) = 0.02275), just as in the example where we used the raw data rather than the standardized values.

Notes

1. The Excel function NORM.DIST () calculates the value of the normal distribution for the specified mean and standard deviation.
2. The Excel function NORM.S.DIST () calculate the value of the normal distribution for the specified Z score value.
3. The value of the Z score can be calculated using the Excel function STANDARDIZE ().

We can use standard normal distribution tables to look up the value of the probability for particular values of z as illustrated in Figure 3.26 for z = +2. For PZ ≥ +2) = 0.02275.

	A	B	C	D	E	F	G	H	I	J	K
1	**Critical values of the standardised normal distribution Z ~ N(0,1)**										
2											
3	**Right Hand Tail Test**					**e.g. 2 tail 5% Z_{cri} = - + 1.96**					
4	**Using Excel function NORMSDIST()**					**e.g. 1 tail 5% Z_{cri} = - 1.645 or + 1.645**					
5											
6	**Z**	**0.00**	**0.01**	**0.02**	**0.03**	**0.04**	**0.05**	**0.06**	**0.07**	**0.08**	**0.09**
7	**0.0**	0.50000	0.49601	0.49202	0.48803	0.48405	0.48006	0.47608	0.47210	0.46812	0.46414
8	**0.1**	0.46017	0.45620	0.45224	0.44828	0.44433	0.44038	0.43644	0.43251	0.42858	0.42465
26	**1.9**	0.02872	0.02807	0.02743	0.02680	0.02619	0.02559	0.02500	0.02442	0.02385	0.02330
27	**2.0**	0.02275	0.02222	0.02169	0.02118	0.02068	0.02018	0.01970	0.01923	0.01876	0.01831
28	**2.1**	0.01786	0.01743	0.01700	0.01659	0.01618	0.01578	0.01539	0.01500	0.01463	0.01426

Figure 3.26

3.5.3 Sampling from a normal population

If we select a random variable X from a population that is normally distributed with population mean μ and standard deviation σ, then we can state this relationship using the notation $X \sim N(\mu, \sigma^2)$.

Figure 3.27 illustrates the relationship between the variable and the distribution.

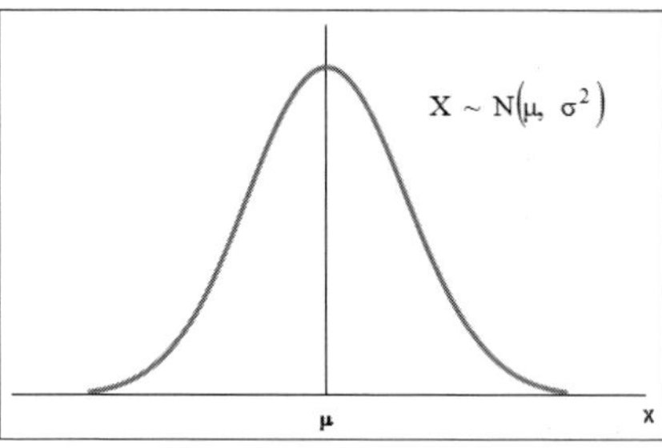

Figure 3.27

If we choose a **sample from a normal population** then we can show that the sample means are also normally distributed with a mean of μ and a standard deviation of the sampling mean given by Equation (3.17), where n is the sample size on which the sampling distribution was based. Figure 3.28 illustrates the relationship between the sampling mean and the normal distribution:

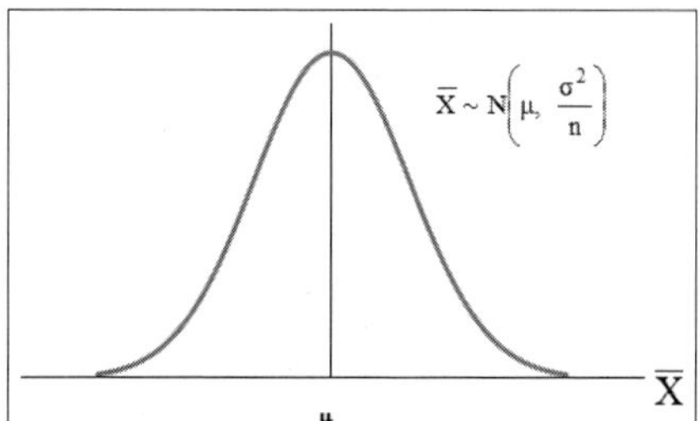

Figure 3.28

Example 3.31

Consider the problem of selecting 1000 random samples from a population that is assumed to be normally distributed with mean £45,000 and standard deviation of £10,000. The population values are based on 40 data points and the sampling distribution is illustrated in Figure 3.29 where we observe that the distribution is approximately normal.

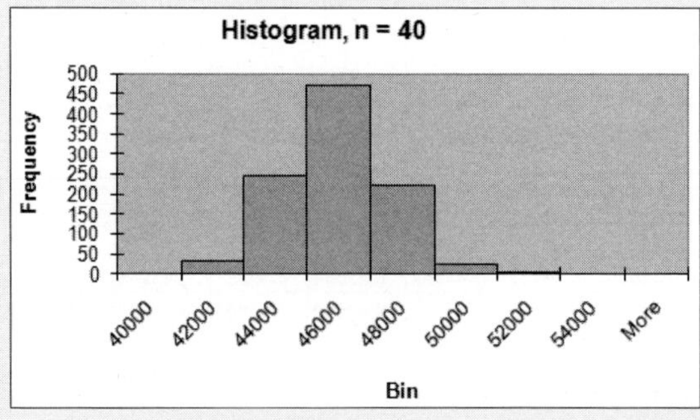

Figure 3.29

sample from a normal population collection of a sample from a normal population.

We can repeat this experiment for samples of size 2, 5, 10, and 40,000 and we would observe that the sample mean histograms show a normal shape but we observe that the sample means are less spread out about the mean as the sample sizes increase.

Note From these observations we conclude that if we sample from a population that is normally distributed with mean μ and standard deviation σ ($X \sim N(\mu, \sigma^2)$), then the sampling mean is normally distributed with mean μ and standard deviation of the sample means of $\sigma_{\bar{x}} = \sigma/\sqrt{n}$.

This relationship is represented by Equation (3.24) as follows:

$$\bar{X} \sim N\left(\mu, \frac{\sigma^2}{n}\right) \quad (3.24)$$

The standardized sample mean Z value is given by Equation (3.25) as follows:

$$Z = \frac{\bar{X} - \mu}{\sigma/\sqrt{n}} \quad (3.25)$$

3.5.4 Checking for normality using Excel

The issue of checking whether the population is normally distributed is an important concept and can be achieved by either constructing a five-number summary (or box-and-whisker plot) or by constructing a normal probability plot. A normal probability plot consists of constructing a graph of data values against a corresponding Z value where Z is based upon the ordered value.

Example 3.32

The manager at BIG JIMS restaurant is concerned at the time it takes to process credit card payments at the counter by counter staff.

The manager has collected the following processing time data (time in minutes) and requested that the data be checked to see if it is normally distributed (see Table 3.18).

Processing credit cards (n = 19)				
0.64	0.71	0.85	0.89	0.92
0.96	1.07	0.76	1.09	1.13
1.23	0.76	1.18	0.79	1.26
1.29	1.34	1.38	1.5	

Table 3.18

Figure 3.30 illustrates the Excel solution to Example 3.32.

sample mean an estimator available for estimating the population mean.

five-number summary a five-number summary is especially useful when we have so many data that it is sufficient to present a summary of the data rather than the whole data set. It consists of 5 values: the most extreme values in the data set (maximum and minimum values), the lower and upper quartiles, and the median.

box and whisker plot is a way of summarizing a set of data measured on an interval scale.

normal probability plot graphical technique to assess whether the data is normally distributed.

	A	B	C	D	E	F	G	H	I	J
1	Example 3.32 - Normal Probability Plot									
2										
3		n =	19		Ordered Value	Area		Z value		Ordered data value
4					1	0.05	=1/(C3+1)	-1.6449	=NORM.S.INV(F4)	0.64
5					2	0.10	=F4+$F$4	-1.2816		0.71
6					3	0.15		-1.0364		0.76
7					4	0.20		-0.8416		0.76
8					5	0.25		-0.6745		0.79
9					6	0.30		-0.5244		0.85
10					7	0.35		-0.3853		0.89
11					8	0.40		-0.2533		0.92
12					9	0.45		-0.1257		0.96
13					10	0.50		0.0000		1.07
14					11	0.55		0.1257		1.09
15					12	0.60		0.2533		1.13
16					13	0.65		0.3853		1.18
17					14	0.70		0.5244		1.23
18					15	0.75		0.6745		1.26
19					16	0.80		0.8416		1.29
20					17	0.85		1.0364		1.34
21					18	0.90		1.2816		1.38
22					19	0.95	=F21+$F$4	1.6449	=NORM.S.INV(F22)	1.5

Figure 3.30

Data values (from Table 3.18) are ordered in order of size and placed in cells J4:J22.

→ Excel solution

n = Cell C3	Value
Ordered value Cells E4:E22	Values
Area Cell F4	Formula: = 1/(C3+1)
Cell F5	Formula: = F4+$F$4
	Copy formula from F5:F22
Z value Cell H4	Formula: = NORM.S.INV(F4)
	Copy function from H4:H22
Ordered data value Cell J4:J22	Values

Excel 2010 has a new function that allows for the calculation of the inverse of the normal cumulative distribution: =NORM.S.INV.

The method to create the normal probability plot is as follows:

- Order the data values (1, 2, 3, ..., n) with 1 referring to the smallest data value and n representing the largest data value.
- For the first data value (smallest) calculate the cumulative area using the formula: = 1/(n + 1).
- Calculate the value of Z for this cumulative area using the Excel Function: =NORM.S.INV (Z value).

- Repeat for the other values where the cumulative area is given by the formula: = old area + 1/(n + 1).
- Input data values with smallest to largest value.
- Plot data value y against Z value for each data point.

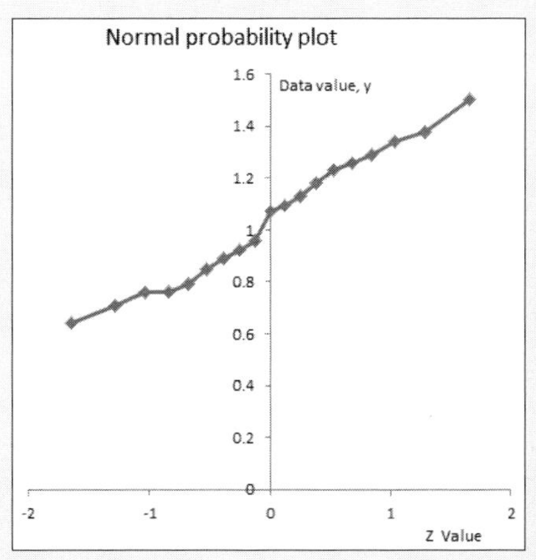

Figure 3.31

Figure 3.31 illustrates the normal probability curve plot for Example 3.32. We observe from the graph that the relationship between the data values and Z is approximately a straight line.

For data that is normally distributed we would expect the relationship to be linear. In this situation we would accept the statement that the data values are approximately normally distributed.

> **Interpretation** Given that the normal probability plot shows more or less a straight line, we conclude that the data is approximately normally distributed.

Note The decision on the symmetry of a distribution is as follows together with the shape of the normal probability plot:

(a) Figure 3.32 illustrates a normal distribution where Largest value – Q_3 = Q_1 – Smallest value.

In Example 3.32 we have: Largest value – Q_3 = 0.18 approximately equal to Q_1 – Smallest value = 0.26.

(b) Figure 3.33 illustrates a left-skewed distribution where Q_1 – Smallest value greatly exceeds Largest value – Q_3.

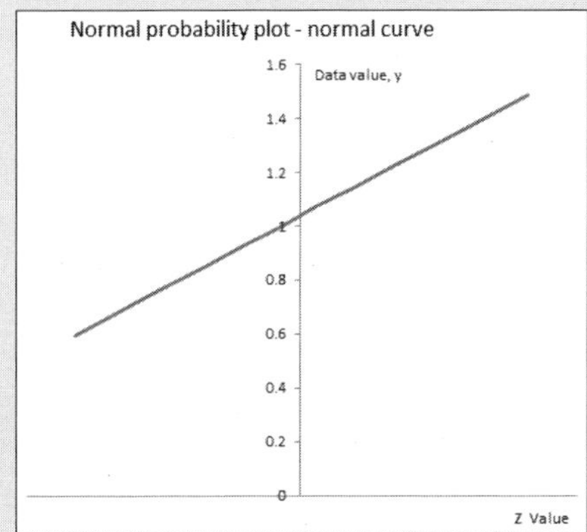

Figure 3.32

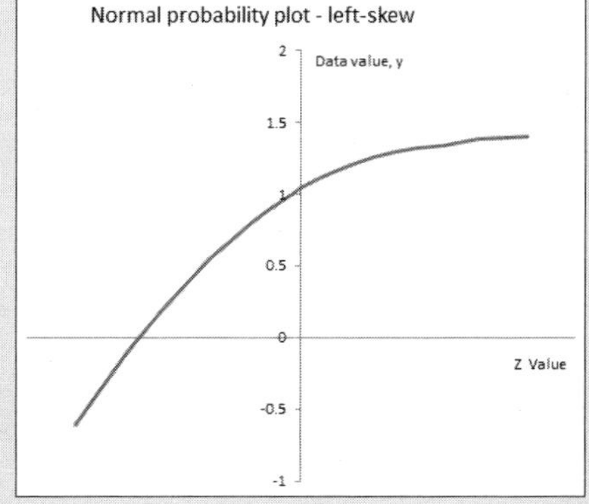

Figure 3.33

(c) Figure 3.34 illustrates a right-skewed distribution where Largest value – Q_3 greatly exceeds Q_1 – Smallest value.

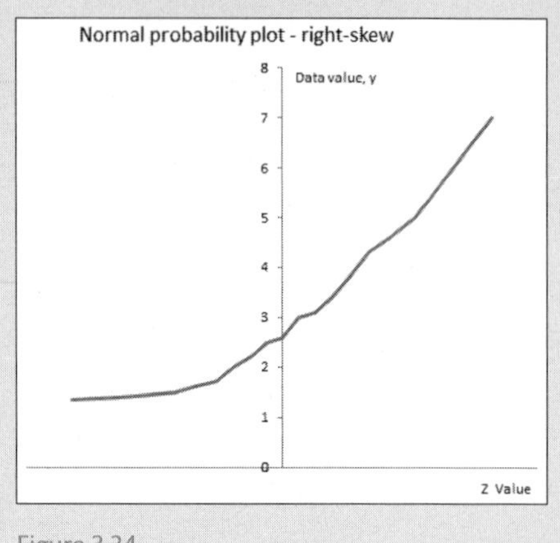

Figure 3.34

3.5.5 Other continuous probability distributions

A number of other probability distributions fall in the continuous distribution category: Student's t distribution, chi-squared distribution, and F distribution.

1. The Student's t distribution is distribution that is used to estimate a mean value when the population variable is normally distributed but the sample chosen to measure the population value is small and the population standard deviation is unknown. It is the basis of the popular student's t-tests for the statistical significance of the difference between two sample means, and for confidence intervals for the difference between two population means. Excel functions include T.DIST () and T.INV ().
2. The chi-squared distribution (χ^2 distribution) is a popular distribution that is used to solve **statistical inference** problems involving contingency tables and assessing the significance of a model to sample data (goodness-of-fit). Excel functions include CHISQ.DIST () and CHISQ.INV ().
3. The F distribution is a distribution that can be used to test whether the ratios of two variances from normally distributed statistics are statistically different. The shape of the distribution depends upon the **degrees of freedom**. Excel functions include F.DIST () and F.INV ().

X

statistical inference
process of collecting data from a random sample of a population and using it to estimate features of the whole population.

degrees of freedom
refers to the number of independent observations in a sample minus the number of population parameters that must be estimated from sample data.

Note The normal Student's, t, and chi-squared distributions are special cases of the F distribution, as follows:

- Normal distribution = F(n_1 = 1, n_2 = infinite) distribution
- T distribution = F(n_1 = 1, n_2) distribution
- Chi-squared distribution = F(n_1, n_2 = infinite) distribution

Two other continuous probability distributions that are less frequently used are the uniform distribution and exponential distribution. The uniform distribution is used in the generation of random numbers for different probability distributions and the exponential probability distribution is important in the area of queuing theory.

3.5.6 Point and confidence interval estimates using Excel

In the previous section we described the sampling distribution of the mean (or proportion) and stated that the distribution can be considered to be normal with particular population parameters (μ, σ^2). For many populations, it is likely that we do not know the value of the population mean (or proportion). Fortunately, we can use the sample mean (or proportion) to provide an estimate of the population value. The objective of estimation is to determine the approximate value of a population parameter on the basis of a sample statistic (also called **statistical inference**). The method described in this section is dependent upon the sampling distribution being normally distributed (or approximately) and we can provide two estimates of the population value: **point estimate** and **interval estimate**.

Figure 3.35 illustrates the relationship between population mean point, and interval estimates.

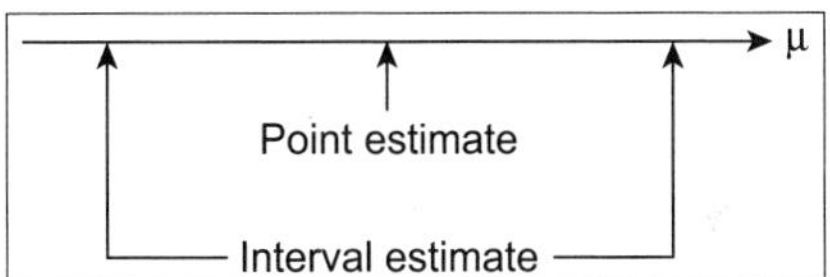

Figure 3.35

A point estimator draws inferences about a population by estimating the value of an unknown parameter using a single point or data value. The sample mean is the best estimator of the population mean. It is unbiased, consistent, and the most efficient estimator as long as the sample was either (a) drawn from a normal population or (b) if the population was not normal but the sample was sufficiently large then the sampling distribution can be approximated by the normal distribution.

Point estimates

Thus a point estimate of the population mean ($\hat{\mu}$) is given by Equation (3.26):

$$\hat{\mu} = \bar{X} \tag{3.26}$$

We would expect the point estimator to get closer and closer to the true population value as the sample size increases. The degree of error is not reflected by the point estimator but we can employ the concept of the interval estimator to put a probability to the value of the population parameter lying between two values, with the middle value being represented by the point estimator. If we assume that the sample data represents the entire population of data points then we can use Equation (3.13) to provide the value of the population standard deviation (given by the Excel function STDEV.P ()).

Unfortunately, when we take a sample from the population we cannot use Equation (2.8) but will have to modify the equation by replacing $\sum f$ with $n - 1$ in the denominator as given by Equation (3.11) to give the sample standard deviation s which represents the unbiased estimator of the population standard deviation (given by the Excel function STDEV.S ()). This value of the sample standard deviation (s) is called an unbiased estimator of the population standard deviation ($\hat{\sigma}$):

$$\hat{\sigma} = s \tag{3.27}$$

X

statistical inference concerns the problem of inferring properties of an unknown distribution from data generated by that distribution.

point estimate a point estimate (or estimator) is any quantity calculated from the sample data that is used to provide information about the population.

interval estimate is a range of values within which, we believe, the true population parameter lies with high probability.

$$\hat{\sigma}_{\bar{X}} = \frac{\hat{\sigma}}{\sqrt{n}} = \frac{s}{\sqrt{n}} \qquad (3.28)$$

The sampling distribution of the mean is a distribution of sample means where Equations (3.26) defines the relationship between the population mean and overall sample mean value and the standard error of the mean given by Equation (3.28).

Confidence interval

A population parameter can be estimated from a sample if we take just one sample from a population. Our knowledge of sampling error would indicate that the standard error provides an evaluation of the likely error associated with a particular estimate. If we assume that the sampling distribution of the sample means are normally distributed then we can provide a measure of this error in terms of a probability value that the value of the population mean will lie within a specified interval. This interval is called an interval estimate (or confidence interval) where the interval is centred at the point estimate for the population mean. Assuming that the sampling distribution of the mean follows a normal distribution then we can allocate probability values to these interval estimates. From Equation (3.25) we can re-structure the equation to Equation (3.29):

$$\mu = \bar{X} - Z \times \frac{\sigma}{\sqrt{n}} \qquad (3.29)$$

From our knowledge of the normal distribution we know that 95% of the distribution lies within ±1.96 standard deviations of the mean. Thus for the distribution of sample means, 95% of these sample means will lay in the interval defined by Equation (3.29): $\mu = \bar{X} \pm 1.96 \times \sigma/\sqrt{n}$.

Therefore, this equation tells us that an interval estimate (or confidence interval) is centred at $\bar{X}$ with a lower value of $\mu_1 = \bar{X} - 1.96 \times \sigma/\sqrt{n}$ and upper value of $\mu_2 = \bar{X} + 1.96 \times \sigma/\sqrt{n}$ as illustrated in Figure 3.36.

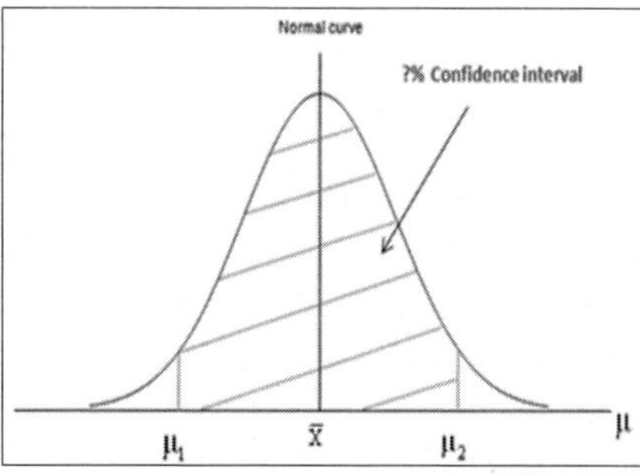

Figure 3.36

A) Confidence interval estimate of the population mean, μ (σ known)

If a random sample of size n is taken from a normal population $N(\mu, \sigma^2)$ then the sampling distribution of the sample means will be normal, $\bar{X} \sim N(\mu, \sigma^2/n)$, and the confidence interval of the population mean is given by Equation (3.30):

$$\bar{X} - Z \times \frac{\sigma}{\sqrt{n}} \le \mu \le \bar{X} + Z \times \frac{\sigma}{\sqrt{n}} \qquad (3.30)$$

Example 3.33

Eight samples measuring the length of cloth are sampled from a population where the length is normally distributed with population standard deviation 0.2. Calculate a point estimate and 95% confidence interval (or confidence level) for the population mean based on a sample of 8 observations: 4.9, 4.7, 5.1, 5.4, 4.7, 5.2, 4.8, and 5.1.

Figure 3.37 illustrates the Excel solution

	A	B	C	D	E	F	G
1	Confidence interval for μ - population standard deviation known						
2	Example 3.33						
3							
4		Sample Data			Population standard deviation σ =	0.2	Known
5		X			2 tails, 95% confidence interval =	0.05	Chosen 5%
6		4.9			CDF =	0.975	=1-F5/2
7		4.7			Z_{cri} =	1.95996398	=NORM.S.INV(F6)
8		5.1					
9		5.4			n =	8	=COUNT(B6:B13)
10		4.7			Sample mean x =	4.9875	=AVERAGE(B6:B13)
11		5.2			Estimate of population mean =	4.9875	=F10
12		4.8			Standard error of the mean =	0.07071068	=F4/F9^0.5
13		5.1			μ_1 =	4.8489096	=F10-CONFIDENCE.NORM(F5,F4,F9)
14					μ_2 =	5.1260904	=F10+CONFIDENCE.NORM(F5,F4,F9)

Figure 3.37

→ Excel solution

X: Cell B6:B13	Values
Population standard deviation σ = Cell F4	Value
2 tails, 95% confidence interval = Cell F5	Value
CDF = Cell F6	Formula: = 1-F5/2
Z_{cri} = Cell F7	Function: = NORM.S.INV(F6)
n = Cell F9	Function: = COUNT(B6:B13)
Sample mean x = Cell F10	Function: = AVERAGE(B6:B13)
Estimate of population mean = Cell F11	Formula: = F10
Standard error of the mean = Cell F12	Formula: = F4/F9^0.5
μ_1 = Cell F13	Formula/Function: = F10-CONFIDENCE.NORM(F5,F4,F9)
μ_2 = Cell F14	Formula/Function: = F10+CONFIDENCE.NORM(F5,F4,F9)

The value of the lower and upper confidence interval is given by Equation (3.30). From Excel: population standard deviation σ = 0.2 (known), sample mean $\bar{X}$ = 4.9875, sample size = 8, and value of Z for 95% confidence = ±1.96. Substituting values into Equations (3.28) and (3.30) gives:

$$\text{Standard error } \sigma_{\bar{X}} = \frac{\sigma}{\sqrt{n}} = \frac{0.2}{\sqrt{8}} = 0.0707$$

$$\mu_1 = \bar{X} - Z \times \frac{\sigma}{\sqrt{n}} = 4.9875 - 1.96 \times 0.0707 = 4.8489$$

confidence level the confidence level is the probability value (1 – α) associated with a confidence interval.

$$\mu_2 = \bar{X} + Z \times \frac{\sigma}{\sqrt{n}} = 4.9875 + 1.96 \times 0.0707 = 5.1261$$

Figure 3.38 illustrates the 95% confidence interval for the population mean.

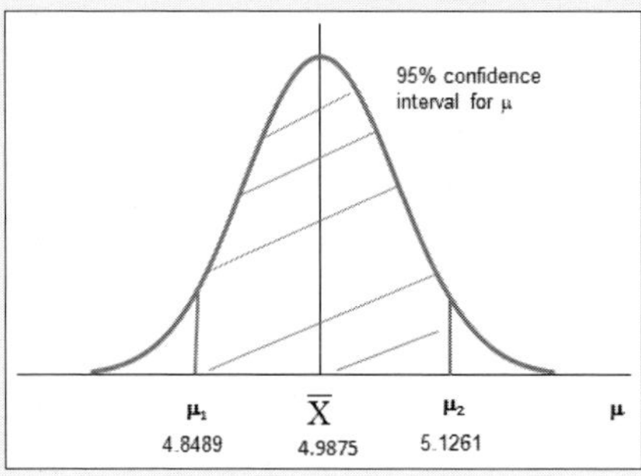

Figure 3.38

Thus, the 95% confidence interval for μ is = 4.9875 ± 1.96 * 0.0707 = 4.9875 ± 0.1386 = 4.8489 to 5.1261.

Interpretation The point estimate of the population mean is 4.9875 with a 95% confidence interval for the population mean of 4.8489 to 5.1261, i.e. there is 95% certainty that the true value is in this interval.

This calculation can be repeated if dealing with a proportion rather than a mean.

B) Confidence interval estimate of the population mean, μ (σ unknown, $n < 30$)

In the previous example we calculated the point and interval estimates when the population was normally distributed but the population standard deviation was known. In most cases the population standard deviation would be an unknown value and we would have to use the sample value to estimate the population value with associated errors. The population mean estimate is still given by the value of the sample mean but what about the confidence interval? In the previous example the sample mean and size where used to provide this interval but in the new case we have an extra unknown, that as to be estimated from the sample data, to find this confidence interval.

Note This is often the case in many student research projects. They handle small sizes and the population standard deviation is unknown.

This problem was solved by W. S. Gossett, who determined the distribution of the mean when divided by an estimate of the standard error. The resultant distribution is called the Student's t distribution as defined by Equation (3.31):

$$t_{df} = \frac{\bar{X} - \mu}{s/\sqrt{n}} \tag{3.31}$$

Where, $\bar{x}$ is the sample mean, μ is the population mean, s is the sample standard deviation, and n the sample size. Given that we are comparing one sample mean against an assumed population mean value we call this a one sample t test. This distribution is similar to the normal probability distribution when the estimate of the variance is based on many degrees of freedom ($df = n - 1$) but the left and right tails have more values in compared to the normal distribution.

Note The t distribution is very similar to the normal distribution when the estimate of variance is based on many degrees of freedom but has relatively more scores in its tails when there are fewer degrees of freedom. The t distribution is symmetric, like the normal distribution, but flatter.

Figure 3.39 shows the t distribution with 5 degrees of freedom and the standard normal distribution. The t distribution is flatter than the normal distribution.

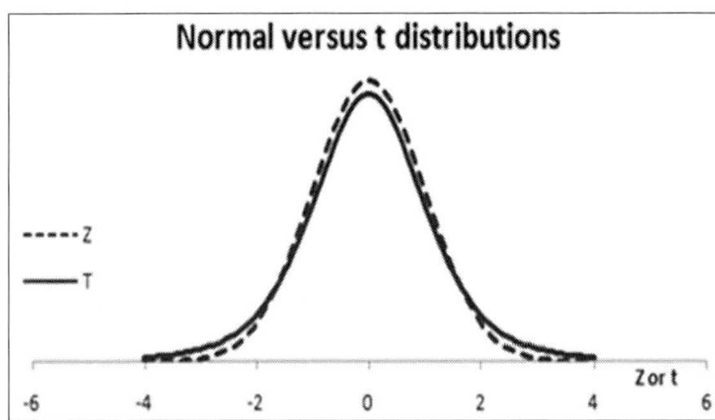

Figure 3.39

Since the t distribution is flatter, the percentage of the distribution within 1.96 standard deviations of the mean is less than the 95% for the normal distribution.

However, if the number of degrees of freedom (df) is large ($df = n - 1 \geq 30$) then there is very little difference between the two probability distributions. The sampling error for the t distribution is given by the unbiased sample standard deviation (s) and sample size (n), as follows defined by Equation (3.32):

$$\sigma_{\bar{X}} = \frac{\hat{\sigma}}{\sqrt{n}} = \frac{s}{\sqrt{n}} \tag{3.32}$$

With the degrees of freedom and confidence interval given by Equations (3.33) and (3.34) respectively:

$$df = n - 1 \tag{3.33}$$

$$\bar{X} - t_{df} \times \frac{s}{\sqrt{n}} \leq \mu \leq \bar{X} + t_{df} \times \frac{s}{\sqrt{n}} \tag{3.34}$$

one sample t test a one sample t test is a hypothesis test for answering questions about the mean where the data are a random sample of independent observations from an underlying normal distribution $N(\mu, \sigma^2)$, where σ^2 is unknown.

Example 3.34

For the following sample of 8 observations from a normal population find the sample mean and standard deviation and hence determine the standard error, the population standard deviation and a 95% confidence interval for the mean: 10.3, 12.4, 11.6, 11.8, 12.6, 10.9, 11.2, and 10.3.

Figure 3.40 illustrates the Excel solution.

	A	B	C	D	E	F
1	Confidence interval for μ - population standard deviation unknown, n small					
2	Example 3.34					
3						
4		Sample Data		2 tails, 95% confidence interval =	0.05	
5		X		df = n - 1 =	7	=E8-1
6		10.3		t_{cri} =	2.3646243	=T.INV.2T(E4,E5)
7		12.4				
8		11.6		n =	8	=COUNT(B6:B13)
9		11.8		Sample mean =	11.388	=AVERAGE(B6:B13)
10		12.6		Sample variance =	0.7641071	=VAR.S(B6:B13)
11		10.9		Sample standard deviation =	0.8741322	=STDEV.S(B6:B13)
12		11.2		Estimate of population mean =	11.388	=E9
13		10.3		Standard error of the mean =	0.3090524	=E11/E8^0.5
14				Confidence Interval for μ_1 =	10.656707	=E9-E6*E13
15				Confidence Interval for μ_2 =	12.118293	=E9+E6*E13

Figure 3.40

→ Excel solution

X: Cells B6:B13	Values
2 tails, 95% confidence interval = Cell E4	Value
d = n − 1 = Cell E5	Formula: = E8-1
t_{cri} = Cell E6	Function: = T.INV.2T(E4,E5)
n = Cell E8	Function: = COUNT(B6:B13)
Sample mean = Cell E9	Function: = AVERAGE(B6:B13)
Sample Variance Cell E10	Function: = VAR.S(B6:B13)
Sample standard deviation = Cell E11	Function: = STDEV.S(B6:B13)
Estimate of population mean = Cell E12	Formula: = E9
Standard error of the mean = Cell E13	Formula: = E11/E8^0.5
μ_1 = Cell E14	Formula: = E9-E6*E13
μ_2 = Cell E15	Formula: = E9+E6*E13

Excel 2010 has three new functions that allow for the calculation of the t-value of the Student's t-distribution: T.INV, sample variance: VAR.S, and sample standard deviation: STDEV.S.

The value of the lower and upper confidence interval is given by Equation (3.34). From Excel: sample mean, $\bar{X}$ = 11.3875, sample size = 8, sample variance = 0.7641071, sample standard deviation = 0.8741322, and value of t_8 for 95% confidence = ±2.3646243. Figure 3.41 illustrates the 95% confidence interval for the population mean.

Thus, the 95% confidence interval for μ is = 11.3875 ± 2.3646243 * 0.3090524 = 10.6567 → 12.1183.

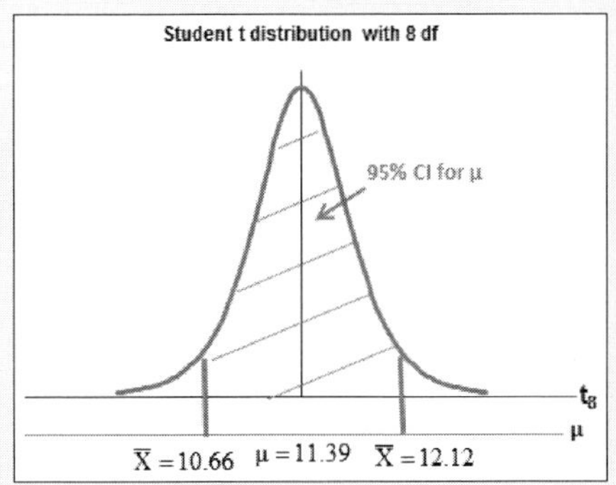

Figure 3.41

Note Equation (3.34) can be used to calculate the lower and upper value of the population mean (μ) as follows:

$$\text{Standard error } \sigma_{\bar{X}} = \frac{s}{\sqrt{n}} = \frac{0.8741322}{\sqrt{8}} = 0.3090524$$

$$\mu_1 = \bar{X} - t_8 \times \frac{s}{\sqrt{n}} = 11.3875 - 2.3646243 \times 0.3090524 = 10.656707$$

$$\mu_2 = \bar{X} - t_8 \times \frac{s}{\sqrt{n}} = 11.3875 + 2.3646243 \times 0.3090524 = 12.118293$$

Interpretation We are 95% confident that, on the basis of the sample, the true population mean is between 10.6567 and 12.1183.

C) Confidence interval estimate of the population mean, μ (σ unknown, $n \geq 30$)

If the population standard deviation is unknown but sample size is large then we can use the normal distribution as an approximation with $\sigma = s$. Similar approaches are available for estimating population proportions based upon the sample proportion.

3.5.7 Simple hypothesis testing using Excel

A hypothesis is a statement of the perceived value of a variable or perceived relationship between two or more variables that can be measured. For example, the average salary of accountants is €31,000 can be classed as a hypothesis statement which can be measured and assessed. It contains one variable that can be classed as salary. In another example, Teesside and Leeds University undergraduate business degree students have similar entry qualifications that can be written as a hypothesis statement. When dealing with a hypothesis test we have to formulate our initial research hypothesis into two statements which can then be evaluated: **null hypothesis** and **alternative hypothesis**.

X

null hypothesis the original hypothesis that is being tested.

alternative hypothesis a hypothesis that is true when we reject the null hypothesis.

Hypothesis statements H_0 and H_1

The null hypothesis (H_0) is known as the hypothesis of no difference and is formulated in anticipation of being rejected as false. The alternative hypothesis (H_1) is a positive proposition which states that a significant difference exists. In our first example, the average salary of accountants is €31,000 and can be stated as: H_0: μ = €31,000 and the alternative hypothesis H_1: $\mu \neq$ €31,000. In our second example, we state that there is no difference between the mean Teesside and Leeds entry scores which can be stated as H_0: Teesside mean = Leeds mean and the alternative hypothesis H_1: Teesside mean ≠ Leeds mean.

Note The rejection of the null hypothesis in favour of the alternative hypothesis cannot be taken as conclusive proof that the alternative hypothesis is true, but rather as a piece of evidence that increases the belief in the truth of the alternative hypothesis.

Example 3.35

The historical output by employees is a mean rate of 100 units per hour with a standard deviation of 20 units per hour. A new employee is tested on 36 separate random occasions and found to have an output of 90 units per hour. Does this indicate that the new employee's output is significantly different from the population mean output? Figure 3.42 illustrates the Excel solution to solve the problem outlined in Example 3.35. As we can see, we have used several built in Excel functions, which we will explain shortly, to help us make a decision. What is our decision? In this example we would reject H_0 in favour of H_1 and conclude that there is a significant difference between new employee's output and the firms existing employee output. In fact, this test gives us power to state that we are 95% certain of our decision. How did we do this? The hypothesis test procedure requires only a few strict steps and these are as follows:

1. State hypothesis.
2. Select the test.
3. Set the level of significance.
4. Extract relevant statistic.
5. Make a decision.

	A	B	C	D	E	F
1	**Hypothesis Testing Example - One Sample Z Test of the Population Mean**					
2						
3			State Hypothesis			
4				H_0 : population mean μ = 100	(1)	
5				H_1 : population mean μ not equal to 100		
6				Two tail test		
7			Select Test	One Sample Z Test for Mean	(2)	
8				Population distribution unknown but large n		
9				Population standard deviation known σ		
10			Set level of significance	Significance Level =	0.05	(3)
11						
12			Extract relevant statistic	Population		
13				Mean μ =	100	
14				Standard Deviation σ =	20	
15				Sample		
16				n =	36	
17				Xavg =	90	
18				Standard Error =	3.33333333	=E14/E16^0.5
19				(4) Z_{cal} =	-3	=STANDARDIZE(E17,E13,E18)
20						
21				P-value and Critical Z		
22				Two tail p-value =	0.0026998	=2*(1-NORM.S.DIST(ABS(E19),TRUE))
23				Lower Z_{cri} =	-1.95996	=NORM.S.INV(E10/2)
24				Upper Z_{cri} =	1.95996	=NORM.S.INV(1-E10/2)
25						
26			Decision:	Since Z_{cal} < Lower Z_{cri}, Accept H_1	(5)	
27						

Figure 3.42

hypothesis test procedure a series of steps to determine whether to accept or reject a null hypothesis, based on sample data.

Tests of hypothesis are usually classified into two methods: parametric and non-parametric. Parametric methods make assumptions about the underlying distribution from which sample populations are selected. Nonparametric methods make no assumptions about the sample population distribution. Parametric statistical tests assume that your data is approximately normally distributed (follows a classic bell-shaped curve) and that the data is at the interval/ratio level of measurement. Nonparametric methods do not make any assumptions about the sample population distribution and are often based upon data that has been ranked, rather than actual measurement data. In many cases it is possible to replace a parametric test with a corresponding nonparametric test. Another division is between one and two (or sometimes multiple) sample tests.

A one-sample test involves testing a sample parameter (e.g. mean value) against a perceived population value (e.g. accountant salary €31,000) to ascertain whether there is not a significant difference between a sample statistic and a population parameter (e.g. H_0: μ = €31,000 and H_1: $\mu \neq$ €31,000).

For a two-sample test we test a sample against another sample to ascertain whether or not there is a significant difference between two samples and, consequently, whether or not the two samples represent different populations. In both cases we use tests that utilize the normal probability distribution and will test for differences between the means (or proportions) as follows: one-sample z test for the population mean, one-sample t test for the population mean, two-sample z test for the population mean, two-sample z test for the population proportion, two-sample t test for population mean (independent samples), two-sample t test for population mean (dependent samples), F test for two population variances (variance ratio test).

Another crucial concept related to hypothesis testing is the level of significance. The level of significance represents the amount of risk that an analyst will accept when making a decision. Whenever research is undertaken we will always have the possibility that the data values are subject to chance. The use of the significance level is to seek to put beyond reasonable doubt the notion that the findings are due to chance. The level of significance is usually denoted by the Greek letter alpha (α) and represents the amount of error associated with rejecting the null hypothesis when it is true. The value of α is normally 5% (0.05) or 1% (0.01), but the value of α depends upon how sure you want to be that your decisions are an accurate reflection of the true population relationship.

Interpretation If an analyst states that the results are significant at the 5% level then what they are saying is that there is a 5% probability that the sample data values collected have occurred by chance. An alternative expression is to use the concept of a confidence interval and apply different language. In this case we can say that we are 95% confident that the results have not occurred by chance.

Note Most of the examples in this chapter use 0.05 for the level of significance. In practice you will notice that sometimes certain hypotheses can be accepted at that level of significance but would have to be rejected if we used 0.01 as the level of significance. What do we do in such situations? The answer is not simple and depends upon how important it is to accept or reject the hypothesis.

X

parametric any statistic computed by procedures that assume the data were drawn from a particular distribution.

non-parametric tests are often used in place of their parametric counterparts when certain assumptions about the underlying population are questionable.

one-sample test is a statistical hypothesis test which uses one sample from the population.

two-sample test is a statistical hypothesis test which uses two samples from the population.

alpha, α Alpha refers to the probability that the true population parameter lies outside the confidence interval. In a time series context, i.e. exponential smoothing, alpha is the smoothing constant.

Earlier we stated that the alternative hypotheses were of the form H_1: $\mu \neq$ €31000 or H_1: $\mu_T \neq \mu_L$. The ≠ sign tells us that we are not sure what the direction of the difference will be (< or >) but that a difference exists. In this case we have a two-tailed test. It is possible that we are assessing that the average accountant salary is greater than €31,000 (implying H_1: $\mu >$ €31,000) or is smaller than €31,000 (implying H_1: $\mu <$ €31,000). In both cases the direction is known and these are known as one-tail test. The region of rejection is located in the tail(s) of the distribution. The exact location is affected by the way H_1 is expressed.

If H_1 simply states that there is a difference, e.g. H_1: $\mu \neq 100$ then the region of rejection is located in both tails of the sampling distribution with areas equal to $\alpha/2$, e.g. if α is set at 0.05 then the area in both tails will be 0.025 (see Figure 3.43). This is known as a two-tail test.

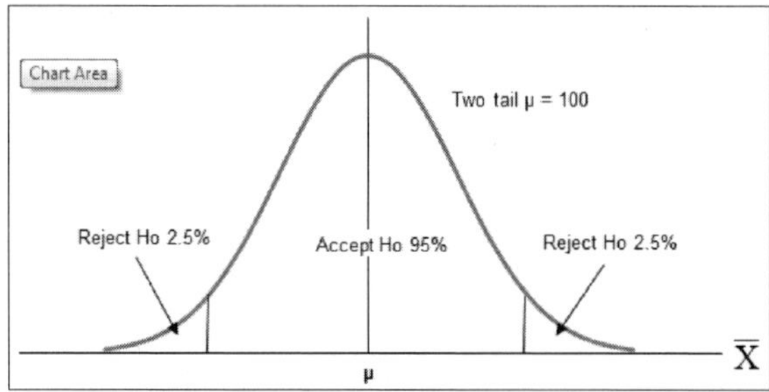

Figure 3.43

If H_1 states that there is a direction of difference e.g. $\mu < 100$ or $\mu > 100$, then the region of rejection is located in one tail of the sampling distribution, the tail being defined by the direction of the difference. Hence, if we are considering a less than direction ($\mu < 100$) then the left-hand tail would be used (see Figure 3.44). This is known as a lower one-tail test.

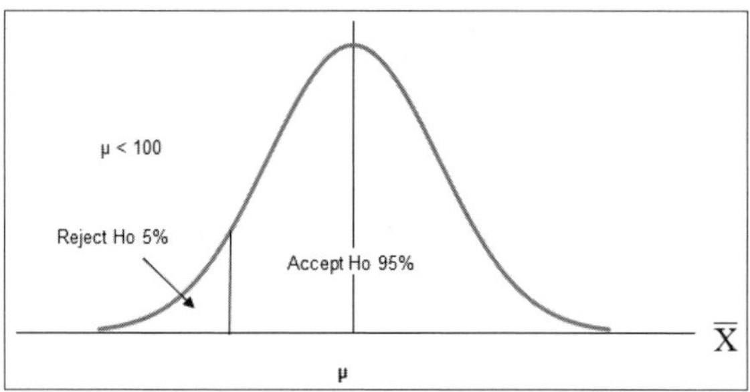

Figure 3.44

Hence, if we are considering a greater than direction ($\mu > 100$) then the right-hand tail would be used (see Figure 3.45). This is known as an upper one-tail test.

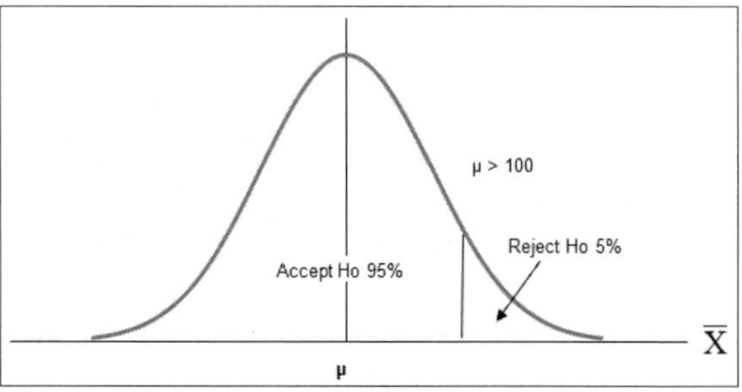

Figure 3.45

X

two-tail test a two-tailed test is a statistical hypothesis test in which the values for which we can reject the null hypothesis, H_0, are located in both tails of the probability distribution.

one-tail test is a statistical hypothesis test in which the values for which we can reject the null hypothesis, H_0 are located entirely in one tail of the probability distribution.

Note The hypothesis test set up (H_0 and H_1) will automatically tell you whether you have a one- or two-tailed test.

The actual location of this critical region will be determined by whether the variable being measured varies as a normal or Student's t distribution. When making a decision, in hypothesis testing we can distinguish between two types of possible errors as illustrated in table 3.19: type I and type II. A type I error is committed when we reject a null hypothesis when it is true whilst a type II error occurs when we accept a null hypothesis when it is not true.

		Truth	
		H_0 true	H_1 true
Decision	Reject H_0	Type I error	Correct
	Do not reject H_0	Correct	Type II error

Table 3.19 Types of error

A type I error is called a false positive and a type II error is called a false negative:

1. A false positive occurs when a test is performed and shows an effect, when in fact there is no effect. For example, the lecturer claims that the proportion passing his module examination is 46%, when in fact this is false. The test shows a positive result (what you were looking for is there), but the test result is false.
2. A false negative occurs when a test is performed and shows no effect, when in fact there is an effect. For example, the lecturer fails to use the proportion passing the examination, when it is true. The test result shows a negative result (what you are looking for is not there), but the test is false.

For example, in an assessment of the spending habits of shoppers in a supermarket at two time points, the null hypothesis might be that the spending habits in the supermarket at time 1 is no better, on average, than at time point 2.

A type I error would occur if we concluded that the spending habits at time point 1 and 2 produced different effects when in fact there was no difference between them (reject H_0 when H_0 true). A type II error occurs when the null hypothesis H_0, is not rejected when it is in fact false. A type II error would occur if it was concluded that the shopping habits produced the same effect when an affect exists (fail to reject H_0 when H_0 false).

A type I error is often considered to be more serious, and therefore more important to avoid, than a type II error. The hypothesis test procedure is adjusted so that there is a guaranteed 'low' probability of rejecting the null hypothesis wrongly. This probability of a type I error can be precisely computed as P(type I error) = significance level = α (Greek letter alpha) with the significance level set at 5% (or 1%) for business related hypothesis tests. The probability of a type II error is generally unknown, but is symbolized by the Greek letter beta (β) and is written as P(type II error) = β.

There are two fundamental ways to do the calculations needed to conduct hypothesis testing. We can either use the p-values or use the critical test statistics, which is a classical

X

type I error occurs when the null hypothesis is rejected when it is in fact true; that is, H_0 is wrongly rejected.

type II error occurs when the null hypothesis H_0, is not rejected when it is in fact false.

beta, β Beta refers to the probability that a false population parameter lies inside the confidence interval.

probability value (p-value) of a statistical hypothesis test is the probability of getting a value of the test statistic as extreme as or more extreme than that observed by chance alone, if the null hypothesis H_0 is true.

critical test statistic the critical value for a hypothesis test is a limit at which the value of the sample test statistic is judged to be such that the null hypothesis may be rejected.

approach. Unlike the classical approach using the critical test statistic, the p-value is easier to use in Excel to decide on accepting or rejecting H_0. The p-value represents the probability of the calculated random sample test statistic being this extreme if the null hypothesis is true. This p-value can then be compared to the chosen significance level (α) to make a decision between accepting or rejecting the null hypothesis H_0.

Interpretation If $p < \alpha$, then we would reject the null hypothesis H_0 and accept the alternative hypothesis H_1.

Microsoft Excel can be used to calculate a p-value depending upon whether the variable being measured varies as a normal or Student's t distribution.

Note The Excel screenshots will identify each of these stages in the solution process.

The p-value will automatically be generated by Excel when using the Data Analysis solution method. Classical alternative to using the p-value is to calculate the test statistic and compare the value with a critical test statistic estimate from an appropriate table or via Excel. The value of the critical test statistic will depend upon the following factors: (i) significance level for Z test problems, and (ii) the significance level and number of degrees of freedom for t test problems. This critical test statistic can then be compared to the calculated test statistic to make a decision between accepting or rejecting the null hypothesis H_0.

Interpretation If test statistic > critical test statistic then we would reject the null hypothesis H_0 and accept the alternative hypothesis H_1.

Microsoft Excel can be used to calculate the critical test statistic values depending upon whether the variable being measured varies as a normal or student's t distribution. These values will automatically be generated by Excel when using the Data Analysis solution method. To illustrate the solution process we will look at a one sample Z test for the population mean. This test assumes that the sample data is randomly collected from a population that is normally distributed. In this particular case we know the value of the population standard deviation.

Example 3.36

Employees of a firm produce units at a rate of 100 units per hour with a standard deviation of 20 units. A new employee is tested on 36 separate random occasions and found to have an output of 90 units per hour. Does this indicate that the new employee's output is significantly different from the average output? Figure 3.46 illustrates the Excel solution.

	A	B	C	D	E	F
1	**Hypothesis Testing Example - One Sample Z Test of the Population Mean**					
2						
3			State Hypothesis			
4				H_0 : population mean μ = 100	(1)	
5				H_1 : population mean μ not equal to 100		
6				Two tail test		
7			Select Test	One Sample Z Test for Mean	(2)	
8				Population distribution unknown but large n		
9				Population standard deviation known σ		
10			Set level of significance	Significance Level =	0.05	(3)
11						
12			Extract relevant statistic	Population		
13				Mean μ =	100	
14				Standard Deviation σ =	20	
15				Sample		
16				n =	36	
17				Xavg =	90	
18				Standard Error =	3.33333333	=E14/E16^0.5
19				(4) Z_{cal} =	-3	=STANDARDIZE(E17,E13,E18)
20						
21				P-value and Critical Z		
22				Two tail p-value =	0.0026998	=2*(1-NORM.S.DIST(ABS(E19),TRUE))
23				Lower Z_{cri} =	-1.95996	=NORM.S.INV(E10/2)
24				Upper Z_{cri} =	1.95996	=NORM.S.INV(1-E10/2)
25						
26			Decision:	Since Z_{cal} < Lower Z_{cri}, Accept H_1	(5)	

Figure 3.46

→ Excel solution

Significance level Cell E10	Value = 0.05
Population mean Cell E13	Value = 100
Population standard deviation Cell E14	Value = 20
Sample size n Cell E16	Value = 36
Sample mean Xavg Cell E17	Value = 90
Sample standard error Cell E18	Formula: = E14/E16^0.5
Z_{cal} Cell E19	Formula: = STANDARDIZE(E17,E13,E18)
Two tail p-value Cell E22	Formula: '= 2*(1-NORM.S.DIST(ABS(E19),TRUE))
Lower Zcri = Cell E23	Function: = NORM.S.INV(E10/2)
Upper Zcri = Cell E24	Function: = NORM.S.INV(1-E10/2)

Excel solution using the p-value and Z_{cri} value.

To use the p-value statistic method to make a decision:

1. State hypothesis

   Null hypothesis H_0: $\mu = 100$ (population mean is equal to 100 units per hour)

   Alternative Hypothesis H_1: $\mu \neq 100$ (population mean is not 100 units per hour)

   The $\neq$ sign implies a two tail test.

2. Select test

   We now need to choose an appropriate statistical test for testing H_0. From the information provided we note:

   - Number of samples – one sample.
   - The statistic we are testing – testing for a difference between a sample mean ($\bar{x} = 90$) and population mean ($\mu = 100$). Population standard deviation is known ($\sigma = 20$).

- Size of the sample - large (n = 36).
- Nature of population from which sample drawn - population distribution is not known but sample size is large. For large n, the central limit theorem states that the sample mean is distributed approximately as a normal distribution.

One sample Z test of the mean is therefore selected.

3. Set the level of significance (α) = 0.05 (see Cell E10)
4. Extract relevant statistic

   When dealing with a normal sampling distribution we calculate the Z statistic using Equation (3.25):

$$Z_{cal} = \frac{(\bar{x} - \mu)}{\sigma/\sqrt{n}}$$

   From Excel, population mean = 100 (see Cell E13), population standard deviation = 20 (see Cell E14), sample size n = 36 (see Cell E16), sample mean $\bar{x}$ = 90 (see Cell E17), standard error of the mean $\sigma_{\bar{x}}$ = 3.33333′ (see Cell E18):

$$Z_{cal} = \frac{\bar{X} - \mu}{\sigma/\sqrt{n}} = \frac{90 - 100}{20/\sqrt{36}} = -3 \text{ (see Cell E19)}$$

   In order to identify region of rejection, in this case, we need to find the p-value. The p-value can be found from Excel by using the NORM.S.DIST () function. In the example H_1: $\mu \neq 100$ units/hour. From Excel, the two-tail p-value = 0.0026998 (see Cell E22).

Note For two tail tests the p-value is given by the Excel formula:

=2*(1-NORM.S.DIST(ABS(z value or cell reference), TRUE))

For one tail tests the p-value is given by the Excel formula:

=NORM.S.DIST(z value or cell reference, true) for lower tail p value, where Z as a negative value =1-NORM.S.DIST(z value or cell reference, true) for upper tail p value, where Z as a positive value

5. Make a decision

   Does the test statistic lie within the region of rejection? Compare the chosen significance level (α) of 5% (or 0.05) with the calculated two-tail p-value of 0.0026998. We can observe that the p value < α and we conclude that given two-tail p-value (0.0026998) < α (0.05), we reject H_0 and accept H_1.

Interpretation Conclude that there is a significant difference, at the 0.05 level, between new employee's output and the firms existing employee output. In other words, the sample mean value (90 units per hour) is not close enough to the population mean value (100 units per hour) to allow us to assume that the sample comes from that population.

Note Figure 3.47 illustrates the relationship between the p-value and test statistic.

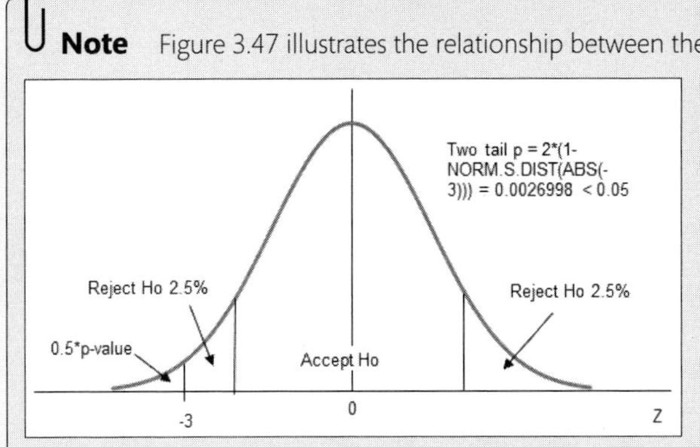

Figure 3.47

Excel solution using the critical test statistic, Z_{cri}

The solution procedure is exactly the same as for the p-value except that we use the critical test statistic value to make a decision:

1. State hypothesis
2. Select test
3. Set the level of significance ($\alpha = 0.05$)
4. Extract relevant statistic

The calculated test statistic $Z_{cal} = -3.0$ (see Cell E19). We need to compare it with the critical test statistic, Z_{cri}. In the example H_1: $\mu \neq 100$ units/hour. The critical Z values can be found from Excel by using the NORM.S.INV() function, two tail $Z_{cri} = \pm 1.96$ (see Cells E23 and E24).

Note We can calculate the critical two-tail value of z as follows:

=NORM.S.INV(significance level/2) for lower critical Z value
=NORM.S.INV(1-significance level/2) for upper critical Z value

The corresponding one tail critical z values are given as follows:

=NORM.S.INV(significance level) for lower tail
=NORM.S.INV(1-significance level) for upper tail

6. Make decision

   Does the test statistic lie within the region of rejection? Compare the calculated and critical Z values to determine which hypothesis statement (H_0 or H_1) to accept. In Figure 3.48 we observe that Z_{cal} lies in the lower rejection zone ($-3 < -1.96$). Given Z_{cal} (-3) < lower two tail Z_{cri} (-1.96), we will reject H_0 and accept H_1.

❊ **Interpretation** Conclude that there is a significant difference, at the 0.05 level, between new employee's output and the firms existing employee output. In other words, the sample mean value (90 units per hour) is not close enough to the population mean value (100 units per hour) to allow us to assume that the sample comes from that population.

Note Figure 3.48 illustrates the relationship between the critical Z value and test statistic.

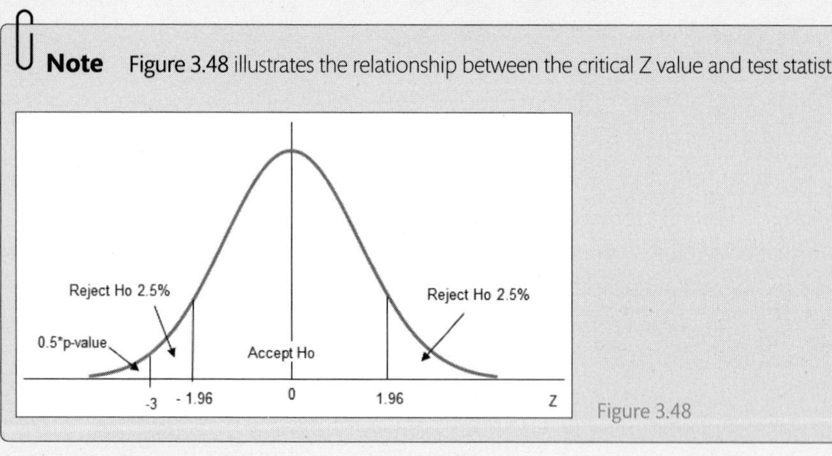

Figure 3.48

A range tests are available for one, two and greater than two samples using both parametric and non-parametric tests.

Note As emphasized, the use of the p-value or comparison of z-calculated vs. z-critical value is a matter of preference. Both methods yield identical results. In conventional statistics textbooks z-critical values are given in a special table usually found in the textbook appendices. In this textbook we rely on Excel to calculate these values and no tables were used.

Note For the Student's t test

a) We can calculate the one and two-tail p-values using the Excel functions: =T.DIST, T.DIST.RT, or T.DIST.2T.
b) The critical two-tail ⊕ values are calculated using the Excel function T.INV.2T.
c) The corresponding one-tail ⊕ values are given by the Excel function T.INV.

Student exercises

X3.16 Use NORM.DIST to calculate the following probabilities, X ~ N(100, 25): (a) P(X ≤ 95), (b) P(95 ≤ X ≤ 105), (c) P(105 ≤ X ≤ 115), (d) P(93 ≤ X ≤ 99)?

X3.17 Use NORM.S.DIST to calculate the following probabilities, X ~ N(100, 25): (a) P(X ≤ 95), (b) P(95 ≤ X ≤ 105), (c) P(105 ≤ X ≤ 115), (d) P(93 ≤ X ≤ 99)? In each case convert X to Z. Compare your answers with your answers to X3.16.

X3.18 The lifetimes of certain types of car battery are normally distributed with a mean of 1248 days and standard deviation of 185 days. If the supplier guarantees them for 1080 days, what proportion of batteries will be replaced under guarantee?

X3.19 What is the critical z values for a significance level of 2%: (i) two tail, (ii) lower one tail, and (iii) upper one tail?

X3.20 A local Indian restaurant advertises home delivery times of 30 minutes. To monitor the effectiveness of this promise the restaurant manager monitors the time that the order was received and the time of delivery. Based upon historical data the average time for delivery is 30 minutes with a standard deviation of 5 minutes. After a series of complaints from customers regarding this promise the manager decided to analyse the last 50 data orders, which resulted in an average time of 32 minutes. Conduct an appropriate test at a significance level of 5%. Should the manager be concerned?

X3.21 Calculate the critical t values for a significance level of 2% and 12 degrees of freedom: (i) two-tail, (ii) lower one-tail, and (iii) upper one-tail?

X3.22 A new low-fat fudge bar is advertised as having 120 calories. The manufacturing company conducts regular checks by selecting independent random samples and testing the sample average against the advertised average. Historically the population varies as a normal distribution and the most recent sample consists of the numbers: 99, 132, 125, 92, 108, 127, 105, 112, 102, 112, 129, 112, 111, 102, and 122. Is the population value significantly different from 120 calories (significance level 5%)?

3.6 Discrete probability distributions

In this section we shall explore probability distributions when dealing with discrete random variables. Two specific discrete probability distributions are the binomial probability distribution and the Poisson probability distribution.

3.6.1 The binomial probability distribution and Excel

One of the most elementary discrete random variables—binomial—is associated with questions that only allow success or failure type answers, or a classification such as male or female, or recording a component as defective or not defective. If the outcomes are also independent, for example, the possibility of a defective component does not influence the possibility of finding another defective component then the variable is considered to be a binomial variable. Consider the example of a supermarket that runs a two week television campaign in an attempt to increase the volume of trade. During the campaign all

X

discrete probability distribution if a random variable is a discrete variable, its probability distribution is called a discrete probability distribution.

binomial probability distribution is the discrete probability distribution of the number of successes in a sequence of n independent yes/no experiments, each of which yields success with probability p.

Poisson probability distribution is a discrete probability distribution that expresses the probability of a given number of events occurring in a fixed interval or time and/or space if these events occur with a known average rate and independently of the time since the last event.

customers are asked if they came to the supermarket because of the television advertising. Each customer response can be classified as either yes or no. At the end of the campaign the proportion of customers that responded yes is determined. For this study the experiment is the process of asking customers if they came to the supermarket because of the television advertising. The random variable, X, is defined as the number of customers that responded yes. Clearly, the random variable can assume only the values 0, 1, 2, 3, ..., n, where n is the total number of customers. Consequently the random variable is discrete. Consider the characteristics that define this experiment:

- The experiment consists of n identical trials.
- Each trial results in one of two outcomes which for convenience we can define as either a success or a failure.
- The outcomes from trial to trial are independent.
- The probability of success (p) is the same for each trial.
- The probability of failure (q), where $q = 1 - p$.
- The random variable equals the number of successes in the n trials and can take the value from 0 to n.

These characteristics define the binomial experiment and are applicable for situations of sampling from finite populations with replacement or for infinite populations with or without replacement.

Example 3.37

A marksman shoots 3 rounds at a target. His probability of getting a 'bull' is 0.3. Develop the probability distribution for getting: 0, 1, 2, 3, 'bulls'. This experiment can be modelled by a binomial distribution since:

- Three identical trials ($n = 3$)
- Each trial can result in either a 'bull' (success) or not a 'bull' (failure)
- The outcome of each trial is independent
- The probability of a success ($P(\text{a bull}) = p = 0.3$) is the same for each trial
- The random variable is discrete

We can show that Equation (3.35) will calculate the probability of 'r' successes given 'n' attempts of the experiment:

$$P(X = r) = \binom{n}{r} p^r q^{n-r} \tag{3.35}$$

The term $\binom{n}{r}$ calculates the binomial coefficients as given by Equation (3.36):

$$\binom{n}{r} = \frac{n!}{r!(n-r)!} \tag{3.36}$$

Where n! (n factorial) is defined by Equation (3.37):

$$n! = n^*(n-1)^*(n-2)^*(n-3) \text{ .... } 3^*2^*1 \tag{3.37}$$

Note

1. $\binom{n}{r}$ is equivalent to the equation to calculate the number of combinations of obtaining 'r' successes from 'n' attempts of the experiment. This term can be re-written using alternative notation ^nC_r.
2. It is important to note that 3! = 3*2*1 = 6, 2! = 2*1 = 2, 1! = 1, 0! = 1.

It can be shown that the mean and variance for a binomial distribution is given by Equations (3.38) and (3.39) as follows:

$$\text{Mean of binomial distribution, } E(X) = np \tag{3.38}$$

$$\text{Variance of binomial distribution, } VAR(X) = npq \tag{3.39}$$

Reconsidering Example 3.37: n = 3, p = 0.3, and q = 1 − p = 0.7. Substituting these values into Equations (3.35) gives: P(no bulls) = P(X = 0) = $^3C_0(0.3)^0(0.7)^3$. Inspecting this formula we note that the problem consists of three terms that are multiplied together to provide the probability of no bulls being hit. The terms are: (a) $^3C_0$, (b) $(0.3)^0$, and (c) $(0.7)^3$. Parts (b) and (c) are straight forward to calculate, and part (a) can be calculated from Equation (3.36) as follows:

$$^3C_0 = \frac{3!}{0!(3-0)!} = \frac{3!}{0!\,3!} = \frac{3 \times 2 \times 1}{1 \times 3 \times 2 \times 1} = 1$$

Therefore, substituting this value into the problem solution gives:

$$P(\text{no bulls}) = P(X = 0) = {}^3C_0(0.3)^0(0.7)^3 = 1 \times 1 \times (0.7)^3 = 0.343$$

Figure 3.49 illustrates the Excel solution for Example 3.37:

	A	B	C	D	E	F
1	Binomial distribution					
2	Example 3.37					
3			Number of trials n =	3		
4			Probability of hitting the bull p =	0.3		
5			Probability of missing the bull q =	0.7	=1-D4	
6						
7			Let X represent the number of bulls hit (r) out of 3 attempts (n)			
8						
9			Probability Distribution	r	P(X = r)	
10				0	0.343	=BINOM.DIST(D10,$D$3,$D$4,FALSE)
11				1	0.441	
12				2	0.189	
13				3	0.027	=BINOM.DIST(D13,$D$3,$D$4,FALSE)
14				Total =	1	=SUM(E10:E13)
15						
16			Number of combinations	r	nCr	
17				0	1	=COMBIN($D$3,D17)
18				1	3	
19				2	3	
20				3	1	=COMBIN($D$3,D20)
21						
22			Factorials	r	r!	
23				0	1	=FACT(D23)
24				1	1	
25				2	2	
26				3	6	=FACT(D26)

Figure 3.49

number of combinations number of ways of selecting r items from n, when the order of selection does not matter.

- Binomial probability of 'r' successes from 'n' attempts using BINOM.DIST ().
- Binomial coefficients using COMBIN ().
- Factorial values using FACT ().

➜ Excel solution

Number of trials Cell D3	Value
Probability of hitting bull, p Cell D4	Value
Probability of missing bull, q Cell D5	Formula: = 1-D4
Probability distribution	
r Cells D10:D13	Values
P(X = r) Cells E10:E13	Function: = BINOM.DIST(D10,$D$3,$D$4,FALSE)
	Copy formula from E10:E13
Total Cell E14	Formula: = SUM(E10:E13)
Number of combinations	
r Cells D17:D20	Values
^nC_r Cells E17:E20	Function: = COMBIN($D$3,D17)
	Copy formula from E17:E20
Factorials	
r Cells D23:D26	Values
r! Cells E23:E26	Function: = FACT(D23)
	Copy function from E23:E26

Excel 2010 has one new function that allows for the calculation of the individual term binomial distribution probability: BINOM.DIST. The Excel 2010 function BINOM.INV will return the smallest value for which the cumulative binomial distribution is less than or equal to a criterion value.

Note Total probability for the experiment: $\sum P(X = r) = 1$.

From these calculations we can now note the probability distribution for this experiment (see Table 3.20).

X	P(X)
0	0.343
1	0.441
2	0.189
3	0.027
Total =	1.000

Table 3.20

This probability distribution is illustrated graphically in Figure 3.50.

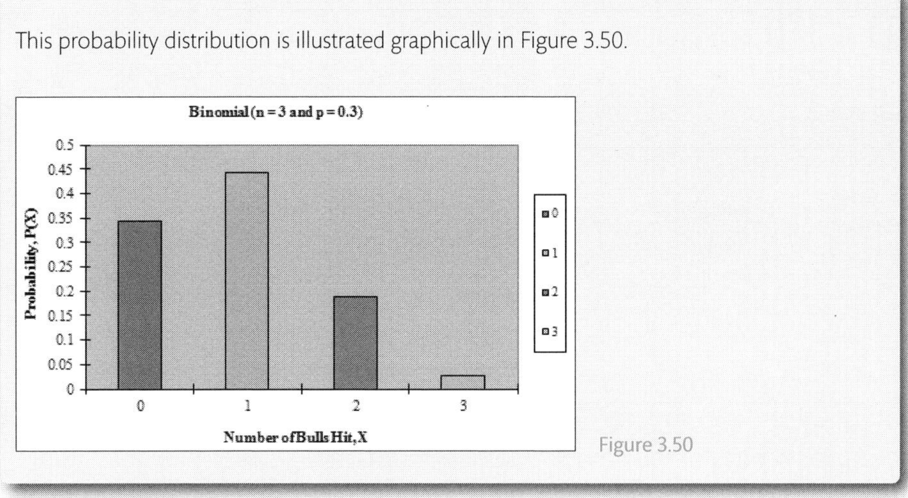

Figure 3.50

3.6.2 The Poisson probability distribution and Excel

Like the binomial, the Poisson probability distribution is used to describe a discrete random variable. With the binomial distribution we have a sample of definite size and we know the number of successes and failures. There are situations, however, when to ask how many failures would not make sense and/or the sample size is indeterminate. For example if we watch a football match we can report the number of goals scored but we cannot say how many were not scored. In such cases we are dealing with isolated cases in a continuum of space and time, where the number of experiments (n), probability of success (p) and failure (q) cannot be defined. What we can do is divide the interval (time, distance, area, volume) into very small sections and calculate the mean number of occurrences in the interval. This gives rise to the Poisson probability distribution defined by Equation (3.40):

$$P(X = r) = \frac{\lambda^r e^{-\lambda}}{r!} \tag{3.40}$$

Where:

- $P(X = r)$ is the probability of event r occurring.
- The symbol r represents the number of occurrences of an event and can take the value $0 \to \infty$ (infinity).
- r! is the factorial of r calculated using the Excel function: FACT ().
- λ is a positive real number that represents the expected number of occurrences for a given interval. For example, if we found that we had an average of 4 stitching errors in a 1 metre length of cloth, then for 2 metres of cloth we would expect the average number of errors to be $\lambda = 4*2 = 8$.
- The symbol e represents the base of the natural logarithm (e = 2.71828...).

Unlike other distributions, the Poisson probability distribution mean and variance are identical, or very close in practice.

Example 3.38

The following data, derived from the past 100 years, concerns the number of times a river floods in a wet season. Check if the distribution may be modelled using the Poisson probability distribution and determine the expected frequencies for a 100-year period (see Table 3.21).

Number of floods (X)	Number of years with 'X' floods (f)
0	24
1	35
2	24
3	12
4	4
5	1
Total =	100

Table 3.21

Excel solution is provided in Figures 3.51 and 3.52 below.

	A	B	C	D	E	F	G	H	I
1	POISSON PROBABILITY DISTRIBUTION EXAMPLE								
2		Example 3.38							
3		(a) Calculate frequency distribution mean and variance							
4									
5		Number of Floods	Number of Years with X Floods						
6		X	f	Xf		X^2		fX^2	
7		0	24	0	=B7*C7	0	=B7^2	0	=C7*F7
8		1	35	35		1		35	
9		2	24	48		4		96	
10		3	12	36		9		108	
11		4	4	16		16		64	
12		5	1	5	=B12*C12	25	=B12^2	25	=C12*F12
13		Totals =	100	140				328	
14			=SUM(C7:C12)	=SUM(D7:D12)				=SUM(H7:H12)	
15									
16		mean =	1.4	=D13/C13					
17		variance =	1.32	=H13/C13-C16^2					

Figure 3.51

	J	K	L	M	N
2	Example 3.38				
3	(b) Calculate the Poisson probabilities and fit probability model to data set				
4					
5				Expected Frequencies	
6	r	P(X = r)		EF	
7	0	0.2466	=POISSON.DIST(J7,$C$16,FALSE)	24.66	=$C$13*K7
8	1	0.3452		34.52	
9	2	0.2417		24.17	
10	3	0.1128		11.28	
11	4	0.0395		3.95	
12	5	0.0111	=POISSON.DIST(J12,$C$16,FALSE)	1.11	=$C$13*K12
13					
14	Total =	0.9968		99.68	
15		=SUM(K7:K12)		=SUM(M7:M12)	

Figure 3.52

The first stage is to estimate the average number of floods per year, λ, based upon the sample data. Figure 3.51 illustrates the Excel solution.

→ Excel solution

(a) Calculate frequency distribution mean and variance

Number of floods X Cells B7:B12	Values
Number of years with X floods, f Cells C7:C12	Values
xf Cells D7	Formula: = B7*C7
	Copy formula from D7:D12
$\sum X$ = Cell C13	Function: = SUM(C7:C12)
$\sum Xf$ = Cell D13	Function: = SUM(D7:D12)
X^2 Cells F7	Formula: = B7^2
	Copy formula from F7:F12
fX^2 Cells H7	Formula: = C7*F7
	Copy formula from H7:H12
Mean = Cell C16	Formula: = D13/C13
Variance = Cell C17	Formula: = H13/C13-C16^2

The average number of floods per year, λ, and variance is calculated from this frequency distribution:

$$\text{Mean } \lambda = \frac{\Sigma fX}{\Sigma f} = \frac{140}{100} = 1.4 \text{ floods per year and}$$

$$\text{Variance VAR}(X) = \frac{\Sigma fX^2}{\Sigma f} - (\text{mean})^2 = 1.32.$$

Interpretation The average number of floods, i.e. the mean, is 1.4 floods per year with a variance of 1.32. They seem to be in close agreement (only 5.7% difference), which is one of the characteristics of the Poisson distribution. The mean and variance of the Poisson distribution have the same numerical value and given the closeness of the two values in this numerical example we would conclude that the Poisson distribution should be a good model for the sample data.

Thus, we can now determine the probability distribution using Equation (3.40) as illustrated in Figure 3.52 above.

➜ Excel solution

(b) Calculate the Poisson probabilities and fit the probability model to the data set

r Cells J7:J12	Values
P(X = r) Cells K7	Function: = POISSON.DIST(J7,$C$16,FALSE)
	Copy formula K7:K12
Total = Cell K14	Function: = SUM(K7:K12)
Expected frequencies Cells M7	Formula: = $C$13*K7
	Copy formula from M7:M12
Total = Cell M14	Function: = SUM(M7:M12)

Excel 2010 has one new function that allows for the calculation of the Poisson distribution probability: POISSON.DIST.

❋ Interpretation

(a) The probability distribution is given in Table 3.22 as follows:

r	P(X = r)
0	0.2466
1	0.3452
2	0.2417
3	0.1128
4	0.0395
5	0.0111

Table 3.22

(b) To check how well the Poisson probability distribution fits the data set we note that the observed frequencies are given in the original table and that the expected frequencies can be calculated from the Poisson probability fit using the equation EF = (Σf) × P(X = r). The solution is now presented in Table 3.23 as follows:

r	P(X = r)	Observed frequency	Expected frequency
0	0.2466	24	24.66
1	0.3452	35	34.52
2	0.2417	24	24.17
3	0.1128	12	11.28
4	0.0395	4	3.95
5	0.0111	1	1.11
	Totals =	100	99.68

Table 3.23

We note that the expected frequencies are approximately equal to the observed frequency values. Table 3.24 illustrates the calculation of the Poisson probability values for $\lambda = 1.4$ by applying Equation (3.40) as follows:

r	Poisson Value	Excel
0	$P(X=0)=\frac{1.4^0e^{-1.4}}{0!}=0.2466$	=POISSON.DIST(J7,$C$16,FALSE)
1	$P(X=1)=\frac{1.4^1e^{-1.4}}{1!}=0.3452$	=POISSON.DIST(J8,$C$16,FALSE)
2	$P(X=2)=\frac{1.4^2e^{-1.4}}{2!}=0.2417$	=POISSON.DIST(J9,$C$16,FALSE)
3	$P(X=3)=\frac{1.4^3e^{-1.4}}{3!}=0.1128$	=POISSON.DIST(J10,$C$16,FALSE)
4	$P(X=4)=\frac{1.4^4e^{-1.4}}{4!}=0.0395$	=POISSON.DIST(J11,$C$16,FALSE)
5	$P(X=5)=\frac{1.4^5e^{-1.4}}{5!}=0.0111$	=POISSON.DIST(J12,$C$16,FALSE)

Table 3.24

Figure 3.53 illustrates a Poisson probability plot for the number of floods example.

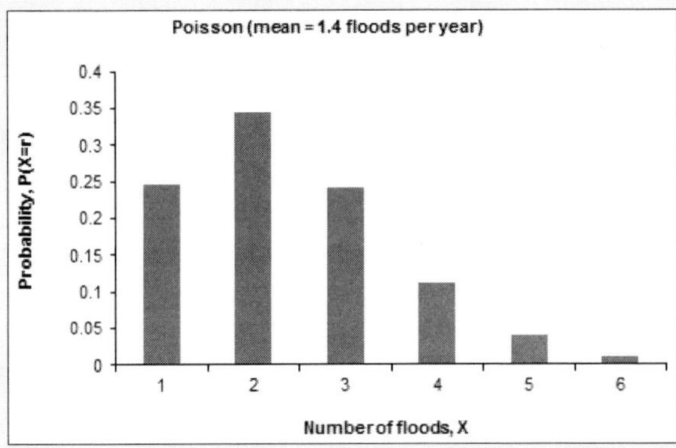

Figure 3.53

The skewed nature of the distribution can be clearly seen (left skewed).

If we determine the mean and the variance either using the frequency distribution or the probability distribution we would find:

$$\lambda = VAR(X) \tag{3.41}$$

To recap, for Poisson distribution to be applicable:

- Mean = Variance
- Events discrete and randomly distributed in time and space
- Mean number of events in a given interval is constant
- Events are independent
- Two or more events cannot occur simultaneously.

Note Once it has been identified that the mean and variance have the same numerical value, ensure that the other conditions above are satisfied, indicating that the sample data most likely follow the Poisson probability distribution.

3.6.3 Other discrete probability distributions

Other types of discrete probability distributions include the hypergeometric discrete probability distribution which measures, like the binomial distribution, the number of successes from n observations of the experiment. Unlike the binomial which involves replacement and therefore the probability of success (p) is constant the hypergeometric distribution involves sampling without replacement. In this case the probability of success (p) is dependent upon the outcome of the previous run of the experiment.

Student exercises

Please visit the Online Resource Centre which accompanies this textbook for figures solutions in Excel to the student exercises and Techniques in Practice.

X3.23 Evaluate the following: (a) ${}^{3}C_{1}$, (b) ${}^{10}C_{3}$, (c) ${}^{2}C_{0}$?

X3.24 Historically 70% of all the attendees of a sales conference are men and only 30% women. If you pick a random sample of six people at the conference, find the probabilities that:

(a) All women are selected.

(b) Three men are selected.

(c) Less than three women are selected.

X3.25 A small tourist resort has a weekend traffic problem and is considering whether to provide emergency services to help mitigate the congestion that results from an accident or breakdown. Past records show that the probability of a breakdown or an accident on any given day of a four day weekend is 0.25. The cost to the community caused by congestion resulting from an accident or breakdown is as follows:

- a weekend with 1 accident day costs £20,000
- a weekend with 2 accident days costs £30,000
- a weekend with 3 accident days costs £60,000
- a weekend with 4 accident days costs £125,000

As part of its contingency planning, the resort needs to know:

(a) The probability that a weekend will have no accidents.

(b) The probability that a weekend will have at least two accidents.

(c) The expected cost that the community will have to bear for an average weekend period.

(d) Whether or not to accept a tender from a private firm for emergency services of £20,000 for each weekend during the season.

X3.26 A garage has three cars available for daily hire. Calculate the following probabilities if the variable is a Poisson variable with a mean of 2: (a) Find the probability that on a given day that exactly none, one, two, and three cars will be hired and determine the mean number of cars hired per day. (b) The charge of hire of a car is £25 per day and the total outgoings per car, irrespective of whether or not it is hired, are £5 per day. Determine the expected daily profit from hiring these three cars.

Techniques in practice

TP1 Skodel Ltd is a small brewery that is undergoing a major expansion after a takeover by a large European brewery chain. Skodel Ltd produces a range of beers and lagers and is renowned for the quality of its beers; winning a number of prizes at trade fairs throughout the European Union. The new parent company are reviewing the quality control mechanisms being operated by Skodel Ltd and are concerned at the quantity of lager in its premium lager brand which should contain a mean of 330 ml and a standard deviation of 15 ml. The bottling plant manager provided the parent company with quantity measurements from 100 bottles for analysis.

334	345	346	317	333	346	297	312	311	334
348	304	328	332	307	334	321	326	319	318
321	342	314	315	348	338	311	300	340	326
357	336	345	344	312	339	354	323	335	346
329	328	327	359	326	363	327	338	322	339
321	351	343	338	338	346	328	330	336	353
321	327	327	338	323	314	342	316	314	329
369	324	326	329	324	336	335	312	311	287
317	321	337	317	340	320	345	332	325	298
345	340	329	343	320	338	322	327	313	348

(a) Construct a histogram for this data set and comment on the shape of the distribution.

(b) Calculate a range of appropriate descriptive statistics for this sample.

(c) Based upon your answers to (a) and (b) provide a measure of average, dispersion, and shape. Explain your reasoning for each answer given.

(d) Do the results suggest that there is a great deal of variation in quantity within the bottle measurements? Compare the assumed bottle average and spread with the measured average and spread.

(e) Do we have any evidence that the distribution could be modelled using a normal distribution?

(f) What conclusions can you draw from these results?

TP2 Bakers Ltd is concerned about the time taken to react to customer complaints and has implemented a new set of procedures for its support centre staff. The customer service director plans to reduce the mean time for responding to customer complaints to 28 days and has collected the following sample data after implementation of the new procedures to assess the time to react to complaints (days):

20	33	33	29	24	30
40	33	20	39	32	37
32	50	36	31	38	29
15	33	27	29	43	33
31	35	19	39	22	21
28	22	26	42	30	17
32	34	39	39	32	38

(a) Construct a histogram for this data set and comment on the shape of the distribution.

(b) Calculate a range of appropriate descriptive statistics. Explain your reasoning for each answer given.

(c) Do we have any evidence to suggest that this distribution can be modelled using a normal distribution?

(d) Calculate point estimates for the population mean and standard deviation.

(e) Calculate the probability that the mean time to react is not greater than 28 days. Explain any assumptions you have made in calculating this answer.

TP3 Skodel Ltd is developing a low-calorie lager for the European market with a mean designed calorie count of 43 calories per 100 ml. The new product development team are having problems with the production process and have collected an independent random sample to assess whether the target calorie count is being met.

49.7	45.2	37.7	31.9	34.8	39.8
45.9	40.5	40.6	41.9	51.4	54.0
34.3	47.8	63.1	26.3	41.2	31.7
41.4	45.1	41.1	47.9		

(a) Calculate point estimates for the population mean and standard deviation based upon the sample data. Explain your reasoning for each answer given.

(b) State the value of calorie count if the production manager would like this value to be $43 \pm 5\%$.

(c) Do we have any evidence to suggest that the mean calorie count can be assumed to be normally distributed?

(d) Estimate the probability that the mean calorie count lies between $43 \pm 5\%$. Explain any assumptions you have made in calculating this answer.

■ Summary

In this chapter we have explored the concept of probability, the key laws that allow calculations to be performed, and explanation of the key definitions such as mutually exclusive and independent events. Furthermore, we have explored the concept of sampling from a population and provided the reader with an introduction to using date samples to infer a population value and check statistically whether a population mean is likely to be correct given a sample of data values.

Student exercise answers

For all figures listed below, please see the Online Resource Centre.

X3.1 (a) Set of 52 playing cards, (b) gender of males and females, (c) sample space consists of 9 sample points (*) is as follows:

		1st Game		
		Win	Draw	Lose
2nd Game	Win	*	*	*
	Draw	*	*	*
	Lose	*	*	*

X3.2 (a) Not mutually exclusive, (b) mutually exclusive.

X3.3 Only events A and B are mutually exclusive.

X3.4 Use official records to correlate the number of 25 year olds passing a driving test at the first attempt with the total number sitting the test. This would be undertaken for a particular time frame and the probability would represent the probability for this time frame only. This is likely to change if you were to repeat the calculation for a different time frame (different sample).

X3.5 (a) theoretical value of probability of at least one head for two unbiased coins = 0.75, (b) estimated probability of at least one head from the experiment. If the two coins are unbiased then we should find that as the number of trials increases that the experiment probability value approaches the theoretical value.

X3.6 (a) 4/25, (b) 7/10, (c) 43/50, (d) 5/8, (e) 7/100.

X3.7 (a) Events E and J mutually exclusive (since they cannot occur at the same time), (b) P(E and J) = 0, (c) P(E) + P(J) = 43/50, we notice that P(E or J) = P(E) + P(J) if E and J are mutually exclusive.

X3.8 (a) 3/25, (b) 18/25, (c) 4/25, (d) 18/25, and (e) 23/50.

X3.9 (a) not mutually exclusive - since all can occur at the same time, (b) not mutually exclusive - since all can occur at the same time.

X3.10 P(A and B) = 1/8.

X3.11 10% have neither.

X3.12 (a) P(A n P) = 0.12, (b) P(P/A) = 0.24, and (c) P(A n P) $\neq$ P(A) * P(P).

X3.13 P(X > 1) = 0.0059 or 0.6%.

X3.14 (a) 0.69, (b) 0.31, (c) 0.36, (d) 0.72.

X3.15 (a) tree diagram and (b) Conditional probabilities:

Figure X3.15a

Figure X3.15b

(c) Proportion resulting in favourable response

Figure X3.15c

(d) **Figure X3.15d**

(e) From (d) the option that is most likely to occur is best seller.

X3.16 (a) 0.1587, (b) 0.6826, (c) 0.1574, and (d) 0.3379.

X3.17 (a) 0.1587, (b) 0.6826, (c) 0.1574, and (d) 0.3379.

X3.18 P(replaced) = 0.1814.

X3.19 (i) ±2.326, (ii) −2.054, (iii) +2.054.

X3.20 Accept H_1, a significant difference exists at 5% (Zcal = 2.83, 2 tail p-value = 0.0047, Zcri = ±1.96).

X3.21 (i) ±2.681, (ii) −2.303, (iii) +2.303.

X3.22 Accept H_1, a significant difference exists at 5% (tcal = −2.37, 2 tail p-value = 0.038, tcri = ±2.145).

X3.23 (a) 3, (b) 120, (c) 1.

X3.24 (a) 0.004, (b) 0.028, (c) 0.5443.

X3.25 (a) 0.3164, (b) 0.2617, (c) £18,066.41, and (d) reject bid based upon expected cost.

X3.26 (a) P(X = 0) = 0.1353, P(X = 1) = 0.2707, P(X = 2) = 0.2707, P(X = 3) = 0.1804, mean = 1.3533, (b) expected daily profit = £27.07.

TP1 (a) **Figure tp3P1a**

Figure tp3P1b

Figure tp3P1c From Figure tp1c the distribution is relatively symmetric.

(b) **Figure tp3P1d**

From the histogram it looks like the distribution is fairly symmetric (skewness = −0.0942 with critical value = ±0.4899 – distribution not significantly skewed, (confirms part a) since −0.0942 is not greater than −0.4899. Mean = 329.8100 ≈ median = 329.0000 (confirms part (a)), and standard deviation = 14.9015.

(c) Use mean = 329.8, standard deviation = 14.9 as the measures of average and dispersion, where the value of skewness = −0.0942.

(d) Assumed mean = 330, standard deviation = 15. Comparing the values there is very little difference between the assumed and sample values.

(e) Distribution is fairly symmetric with mean ≈ median and therefore it may be possible to model the distribution with a normal distribution.

TP2 (a) **Figure tp3.2a**

Figure tp3.2b

Figure tp3.2c From Figure tp3.2c the distribution is relatively symmetric.

(b) **Figure tp3p2d**

From the histogram it looks like the distribution is fairly symmetric (skewness = −0.1225 with critical value = ±0.7559 – distribution not significantly skewed (confirms part a) since −0.1225 is not greater than −0.7559. Mean = 31.2381 ≈ median = 32.0000 (confirms part (a)), and standard deviation = 7.6216.

(c) Distribution is fairly symmetric with mean ≈ median and therefore it may be possible to model the distribution with a normal distribution.

(d) Point estimate of the population mean = 31.2381 and population standard deviation = 7.6216.

(e) $P(X \le 28) = 0.00295$ (or 0.3%).

TP3 Figure tp3p3

(a) Point estimates of population mean = 42.4 and standard deviation = 8.26.

(b) Values range from 40.85 to 45.15.

(c) The value of skewness = 0.39 with a critical value of ±1.04. Since 0.39 is not greater than 1.04 we can state the level of skewness is not significant and the distribution is approximately symmetric. Therefore, we will assume a normal distribution to calculate part d.

(d) $P(X\ 43 \pm 5\%) = P(40.85 \le X \le 45.15) = 0.7535$ (or 75.4%).

Further reading

Textbook resources

1. S. C. Albright, W. L. Winston, C. Zappe (199) *Data Analysis and Decision Making with Microsoft Excel*, Dusbury Press.
2. D. Anderson, D. Sweeney, D. and T. Williams (2011) *Essentials of Statistics for Business and Economics* (6th edn), Cengage.
3. G. Burton, G. Carrol, and S. Wall (1999) *Quantitative Methods for Business and Economics*, Longman.
4. G. Davis and B. Pecar (2010) *Business Statistics Using Excel*, Oxford University Press.
5. D. Levine, D. Stephan, T. C. Krehbie, and M. Berenson (2011) *Statistics for Managers using MS Excel* (6th edn), Pearson.
6. J. K. Lindsey (2004) *Introduction to Applied Statistics: A Modelling Approach* (2nd edn), Oxford University Press.
7. D. Whigham (2007) *Business Data Analysis Using Excel*, Oxford University Press.

Web resources

1. Dr Arsham's statistics site **http://home.ubalt.edu/ntsbarsh/Business-stat/opre504.htm** (accessed 12 May 2012).
2. Economagic - contains international economic data sets (**http://www.economagic.com**) (accessed 12 May 2012).
3. Eurostat - website is updated daily and provides direct access to the latest and most complete statistical information available on the European Union, the EU Member States, the euro-zone and other countries **http://epp.eurostat.ec.europa.eu** (accessed 12 May 2012).
4. HyperStat Online Statistics Textbook **http://davidmlane.com/hyperstat/index.html** (accessed 12 May 2012).
5. The ISI glossary of statistical terms provides definitions in a number of different languages **http://isi.cbs.nl/glossary/index.htm**.
6. StatSoft Electronic Textbook **http://www.statsoft.com/textbook/stathome.html** (accessed 12 May 2012).

Formula summary

$$P(A) = \frac{m}{n} \tag{3.1}$$

$$P(\text{Event}) = \frac{\text{Number of outcomes in the event}}{\text{Total number of outcomes}} \tag{3.2}$$

$$P(A \text{ or } B) = P(A) + P(B) - P(A \text{ and } B) \tag{3.3}$$

$$P(A \mid B) = \frac{P(A \cap B)}{P(B)} \tag{3.4}$$

$$P(A \cap B) = P(A \mid B) * P(B) \tag{3.5}$$

$$P(A \cap B) = P(A) * P(B) \tag{3.6}$$

$$P(B_i/A) = \frac{P(A/B_i) \times P(B_i)}{P(A/B_1) \times P(B_1) + P(A/B_2) \times P(B_2) + \ldots\ldots + P(A/B_k) \times P(B_k)} \tag{3.7}$$

$$^{N}C_{n} = \frac{N!}{n!(N-n)!} \tag{3.8}$$

$$\bar{x} = \frac{x_1 + x_2 + x_3 \ldots\ldots x_i}{n} = \frac{\sum_{i=1}^{i=n} x_i}{n} \tag{3.9}$$

$$\bar{x} = \frac{\Sigma(\text{frequency} \times \text{class})}{\text{number} \cdot \text{of} \cdot \text{data}} \tag{3.10}$$

$$s = \sqrt{\frac{\Sigma(x_i - \bar{x})^2}{n-1}} \tag{3.11}$$

$$\mu = \frac{\sum_{i=1}^{i=N} x_i}{N} \tag{3.12}$$

$$\sigma = \sqrt{\frac{\Sigma(x_i - \bar{x})^2}{N}} \tag{3.13}$$

$$p = \frac{m}{n} \tag{3.14}$$

$$\pi = \frac{n}{N} \tag{3.15}$$

$$\sigma_{\bar{x}} = \sqrt{\frac{N-n}{N-1}}\left(\frac{\sigma}{\sqrt{n}}\right) \tag{3.16}$$

$$\sigma_{\bar{x}} = \left(\frac{\sigma}{\sqrt{n}}\right) \tag{3.17}$$

$$k_n = \sqrt{\frac{N-n}{N-1}} \tag{3.18}$$

$$SE = \sqrt{\frac{p(1-p)}{n}} \tag{3.19}$$

$$s^2 = \frac{\sum_{i=1}^{i=n}(x_i - \bar{x})^2}{n-1} \quad (3.20)$$

$$SEM = \frac{s}{\sqrt{n}} \quad (3.21)$$

$$f(X) = \frac{1}{\sigma\sqrt{2\pi}} e^{\left(-\frac{(X-\mu)^2}{2\sigma^2}\right)} \quad (3.22)$$

$$Z = \frac{(X - \mu)}{\sigma} \quad (3.23)$$

$$\bar{X} \sim N\left(\mu, \frac{\sigma^2}{n}\right) \quad (3.24)$$

$$Z = \frac{\bar{X} - \mu}{\sigma/\sqrt{n}} \quad (3.25)$$

$$\hat{\mu} = \bar{X} \quad (3.26)$$

$$\hat{\sigma} = s \quad (3.27)$$

$$\hat{\sigma}_{\bar{X}} = \frac{\hat{\sigma}}{\sqrt{n}} = \frac{s}{\sqrt{n}} \quad (3.28)$$

$$\mu = \bar{X} - Z \times \frac{\sigma}{\sqrt{n}} \quad (3.29)$$

$$\bar{X} - Z \times \frac{\sigma}{\sqrt{n}} \leq \mu \leq \bar{X} + Z \times \frac{\sigma}{\sqrt{n}} \quad (3.30)$$

$$t_{df} = \frac{\bar{X} - \mu}{s/\sqrt{n}} \quad (3.31)$$

$$\sigma_{\bar{X}} = \frac{\hat{\sigma}}{\sqrt{n}} = \frac{s}{\sqrt{n}} \quad (3.32)$$

$$df = n - 1 \quad (3.33)$$

$$\bar{X} - t_{df} \times \frac{s}{\sqrt{n}} \leq \mu \leq \bar{X} + t_{df} \times \frac{s}{\sqrt{n}} \quad (3.34)$$

$$P(X = r) = \binom{n}{r} p^r q^{n-r} \quad (3.35)$$

$$\binom{n}{r} = \frac{n!}{r!(n-r)!} \quad (3.36)$$

$$n! = n^*(n-1)^*(n-2)^*(n-3) \ldots\ldots\ldots\ldots 3^*2^*1 \quad (3.37)$$

Mean of binomial distribution, $E(X) = np$ (3.38)

Variance of binomial distribution, $VAR(X) = npq$ (3.39)

$$P(X = r) = \frac{\lambda^r e^{-\lambda}}{r!} \quad (3.40)$$

$$\lambda = VAR(X) \quad (3.41)$$

4 Prediction and forecasting

» Overview «

In this chapter we will introduce situations that require some data modelling, trending, and forecasting. The methods used fall in the regression analysis and time series analysis category.

» Learning outcomes «

On completing this chapter you should be able to:

- » Understand that it is possible to model the relationship between two variables using a mathematical equation.
- » Graph the data and visually identify patterns.
- » Fit a linear and non-linear model to a data series.
- » Assess the reliability of this model fit to the data.
- » Recognize the main problems associated with this technique and identify possible solutions.
- » Understand the forecasting pre-requisites.
- » Fit an appropriate model using appropriate time series methods such as classical, moving averages, smoothing, and stochastic methods.
- » Calculate a measure of error for the model fit to the data set.
- » Use the identified model to provide a forecast.
- » Solve problems using the Microsoft Excel functions.

X

regression a generic name for a method that describes and predicts movements of one variable with another related variable.

equation algebraic formula that shows the relationship between variables, saying that the value of one expression equals the value of the second expression.

pattern a recurring and predictable sequence of values that look identical or similar.

moving averages a series of averages calculated for a rolling, or a moving, number of periods. Every subsequent interval excludes the first observation from the previous interval and includes the next observation following the previous period.

error a difference between the actual and predicted value (in the context of time series).

function in this context a subprogram or a mini routine that converts a formula or an algorithm into a single value, or an array of values.

4.1 Introduction to regression and time series models

Prediction and forecasting are the two terms often used interchangeably, though we would like to suggest that there is a difference between these two concepts. Prediction is more closely related to causality. In other words, if we know how one of the decision making elements is behaving, we can predict the other. The most intuitive example would be the revenues and profit. If we know how profit and revenues were linked historically, and if we are given an assumption that the revenue is going to be 'X', then we can predict that the value of the profit will be 'Y'. This is most of the time modelled through regression analysis methods.

Forecasting, on the other hand, does not require the knowledge of more than one variable. If we know how the profits behaved historically, by extrapolating past behaviour, we can forecast what the future values will be. A different family of methods, called time series analysis methods, is used to make forecasts. If we use regression method for these purposes, but use the time as the independent variable, then regression produces forecasts, just like any time series analysis method. We'll explain this as we move through this chapter.

Note Predictions are estimates of one variable, based on some other related variable (or several other variables). Regression analysis is a typical prediction method. Forecasts are projections of one single variable based on the extrapolations of the historical values of this variable. Time series analysis methods are typical forecasting methods.

Prediction, and the related regression method, imply that the method can be used in the time domain (predict the future values) or in the structural domain (predict one variable from the other). Before we move into the time domain, let's explore a simple structural case.

Companies typically use numerous spreadsheets to track various aspects of their business. Two variables that will with absolute certainty appear in every company's spreadsheet are revenues and profits. Sometimes alternative expressions are used, such as the sales, income, and turnover for the revenues and margin and net income for profits. Regardless of the semantics, the first one describes the 'top line' and the second one the 'bottom line'. There is no doubt that revenues and profits are related. The fact is that profit depends on revenues, or to put it differently: it is a function of the revenues. If this is the case, then we can state that: Profit $= f$(Revenue). To make this relationship more universal, we can assign the letter y to profit and the letter x to revenues. In this case the above relationship, expressed in the most abstract terms, is: $y = f(x)$.

Why do we prefer abstract terms? For a simple reason that we might like to create some universal principles and stop reinventing the wheel every time we have a similar problem. We could find ourselves in a situation where we are trying to analyze the relationship between costs and the level of inventory. By using most abstract approach, we can easily apply the principles from the revenue/profit case to cost/inventory case. If we state that $y = f(x)$, we can ask ourselves a logical question, which is: but what kind of function? The answer is that we do not know, but we can look at the data and, hopefully, the relationship will determine the function that will become a model. Let's say, hypothetically, that an increase in one variable by, say 2, results with the increase in the other by 4, and then an increase of 3 results with 9. If this was the case and we had enough data points to validate it, we could say that the relationship between these two variables is described by some kind of exponential function. In reality, the relationships are less obvious, but still not too difficult to spot.

model an abstraction of reality i.e. a simplified method of representing reality.

Example 4.1

Let us assume that in our hypothetical company the profit and the revenue over the last ten months were related, as in Table 4.1.

Revenue	Profit
320	20
200	10
190	10
350	45
1200	130
330	30
700	80
450	60
700	100
1000	110

Table 4.1

If we chart this performance, the graph in Figure 4.1 reveals that the relationship between the profit and revenue, in this case, is probably linear. Why? Because the dots that represent the intersection of every Profit and Revenue point seem to be forming almost a straight line. In fact, we drew a straight line through these data points, just to confirm it.

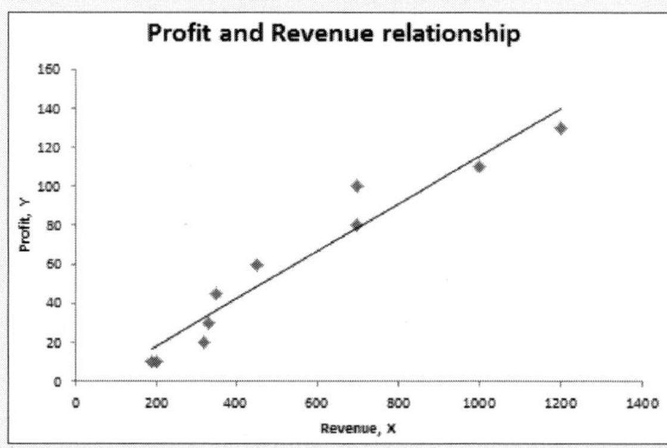

Figure 4.1

Profit and revenue relationship for the hypothetical company

In other words, changes in revenue are followed, in a linear fashion, by the changes in profit. Interestingly enough, the data set shown in Table 4.1 could represent, say, ten different branches of the same company, or, it can represent ten different time periods in which revenue and profit measurement were recorded. This implies that regression analysis can be applied in both the time domain and in the structural domain. Let's ignore the revenue and concentrate on profit only, as illustrated in Figure 4.2.

Example 4.2

We'll use a profit per month time series that consists of only 30 observations as in Table 4.2. If we use the letter *y* for the profit, in this case, we can write y as a function of time: y = f(t).

Period	Profit	Period	Profit
1	20	16	130
2	10	17	120
3	10	18	130
4	45	19	130
5	130	20	140
6	30	21	120
7	80	22	150
8	60	23	140
9	100	24	130
10	110	25	150
11	90	26	140
12	90	27	160
13	100	28	180
14	120	29	170
15	100	30	180

Table 4.2

Figure 4.2 illustrates a time series graph based upon Example 4.2

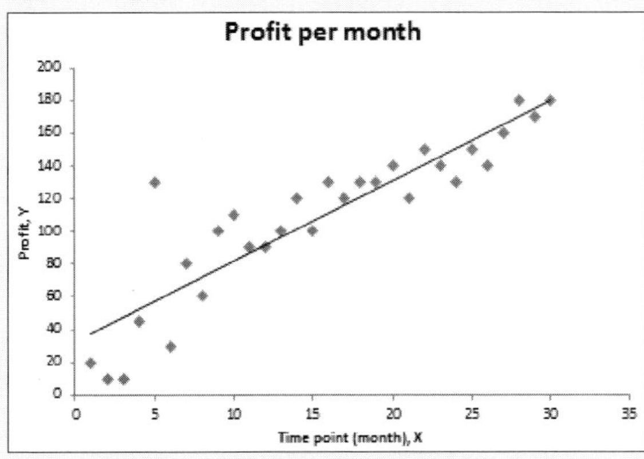

Figure 4.2

The point to remember is that the model that we have built is equally applicable to time domain problems as well as to structural problems. These kinds of models fall into the regression analysis and time series category. What is common for all of them is that they are designed to approximate the potential relationships via regression analysis models. In the simplest case we will show how to fit a straight line (or trend line) to the data set of the form Y = a + bX, where 'a' and 'b' in the equation are called the regression coefficients.

4.2 Modelling linear relationships between data variables

The type of relationship between two variables, y and x (or y and t, if one of the variables is the time), can be represented by a straight line (linear model) or by a non-straight line (non-linear model). In sections 4.2.1–4.2.5 we will explore linear relationships with section 4.3.1 introducing the reader to non-linear relationships.

4.2.1 Least squares regression using Excel

If we said that in our case there is no doubt that the relationship between profits and revenues can be described by a straight line, then the function must be linear. What is the equation for the straight line? It is:

$$y = bx \tag{4.1}$$

The above equation describes a straight line that can be put through the dots representing the relationship between profits and revenues (see Figure 4.1). *Y* is the profit, *x* are the revenues and *b* is some number (a parameter) that we need to use to multiply the revenues in order to get the profit value. We know that a straight line, if it does not start from the origin (zero point where the two axes on the graph intersect), needs a parameter *a*, which defines by how many units the line is shifted from the zero point. Let's change the notation and call these two parameters b_0 for the intercept, and b_1 for the slope. As you can imagine, the slope parameter will determine how steep this line will be and whether it will have an upward or downward direction. So the equation should be written as:

$$y = b_0 + b_1 x \tag{4.2}$$

The question is, how do we calculate the values of the parameters b_0 and b_1 that define this specific line? The parameters (or coefficients) of any equation can be calculated in a variety of ways, some of which are more accurate than others. Statisticians prefer the least squares method.

Note The logic of the least squares method for estimating unknown parameters is very simple. It states that: whatever the value of the parameter, if this guarantees that the sum of all squared values of the deviations of the trend from the actual data is a minimum, then this is the best possible parameter value for that data set. According to the least squares methods, the formulae for calculating b_0 and b_1 are given below:

$$b_0 = \frac{\Sigma y}{n} - b\frac{\Sigma x}{n} \tag{4.3}$$

$$b_1 = \frac{\Sigma xy - \frac{(\Sigma x \Sigma y)}{n}}{\Sigma x^2 - \frac{(\Sigma x)^2}{n}} \tag{4.4}$$

X

parameter a single value (quantity) used to multiple a variable in an equation.

intercept a point at which the function crosses vertical y-axis (at this point the value of x = 0).

slope also called a gradient, describes the steepness of the line.

deviation a difference between the actual values in the series and the trend that approximates the time series. Could also mean the errors.

The least squares method formulae look unfriendly, but they are not difficult to reproduce in Excel. Fortunately, we do not even have to do this. Excel has built in functions that will calculate b_0 and b_1 and they are called =INTERCEPT() and =SLOPE(). All we need to do is click on the function symbol on the Formulas resource tab and from the Statistical functions category select Intercept. This triggers the wizard, as explained in earlier chapters. The same procedure is used for calculating the slope.

Example 4.3

Consider Example 4.1 data set.

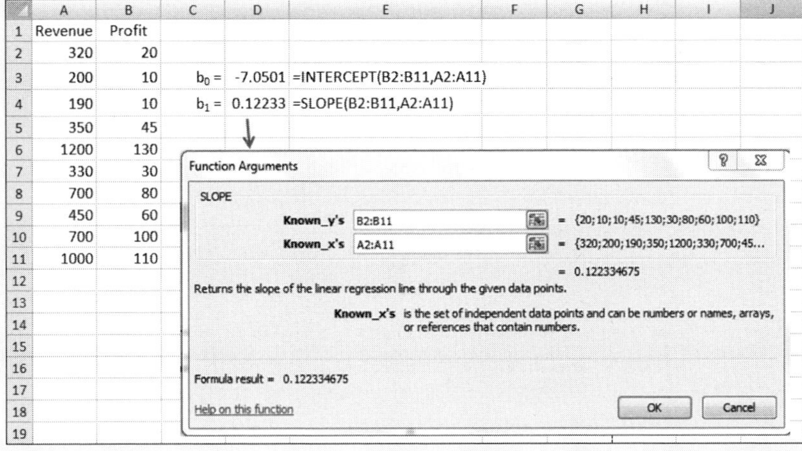

Figure 4.3

Calculating the intercept and the slope for linear trend (regression)

To access this menu in Excel 2007 select Insert > Formulas > Insert Function and choose Slope function.

For the given data set in our example, the value of $b_0 = -7.050$ and the value of $b_1 = 0.122$, which means that the equation that describes this particular relationship using Equation 4.2 is: $Y = -7.050 + 0.122X$. Let us just for the moment look at the above formula and interpret its meaning. The reason for this is quite important. It might not be too obvious to us, but we have in fact created our first business model. The above equation, first and foremost, says that for every unit in revenue, our profit will grow by a factor of 0.122. In other words, whatever the value of revenue, we simply need to multiply it by 0.122 to see the corresponding profit. This number 0.122, if multiplied by 100, becomes a percentage. In other words, our profit rate is 12.2%. It also says that if we do not make any revenue (the value of revenue is zero), then the profit will be a negative value of −7.050 (a loss). We obtained this in a simple way by substituting 0 for X. In addition, it tells us that if we want to break even (the value of profit is zero) we must have the revenue of at least 57.786. We obtained this by simply assigning 0 to y, such that:

$$0 = -7.05 + 0.122X$$

$$7.05 = 0.122X$$

$$X = 7.05 / 0.122$$

$$X = 57.786$$

X

factor a coefficient or the value that indicates the rate of change of variable (a multiplier).

So, we have our first model, and we can say that if we knew what the revenues are we could predict the profit.

We could have asked ourselves if there was a way to quantify the strength of the relationship between our two variables by using some measure or a statistic. The answer is, yes, we could have used a coefficient correlation. In Excel the function for this is =CORREL(array1, array2). In our example the formula was =CORREL(A2:A11,B2:B11), giving us a value of 0.9379. As we can see, the two variables are highly correlated variables, which also justifies our initial impression that the variables are related in a linear fashion.

Interpretation The value of the coefficient of correlation can vary from −1 to +1, where −1 implies completely negative correlation (growth in one variable is accompanied by the decline of the other) and +1 implies perfect positive correlation (growth in one variable is accompanied by exactly the same move by the other variable). If we have the value of the coefficient correlation equal to zero, then there is absolutely no correlation between the two variables. In our case the value of 0.9379 indicates very high positive correlation between profits and revenues.

We will observe that linear relationships between data variables (Y, X) is not the only one possible, and that non-linear relationships are possible too. These non-linear relationships can take a variety of forms which will be described below.

Note Linear relationship between two variables is just one possible type of relationships. Sometimes the data set will indicate that there is some other type of relationship that could be described by, for example, a parabolic curve, some sort of S-type curve or any polynomial equation. Remember that all these equations are only models and they describe the underlying trend of the relationship and, if needed, can be extrapolated into the future to predict future values. The way they are calculated is just a bit more complex than for the linear models.

4.2.2 How good is our linear model

If we look at Figure 4.1, we'll see that the straight line that represents our model does not go through most of the dots that represent actual data. This is often the case. This is why we all know that models are not perfect. They are only approximations of the reality. However, some of them are better than the others. How do we measure how good is the model? We'll start by analysing the graph. To explain variations around the regression line, we can use a simple graph, as in Figure 4.4.

We assigned y to the actual value of the series. The predicted value $\hat{y}$ (or, the value fitted by the model) is the value from the regression line that approximates the actual value y, and $\bar{y}$ is the mean value of the actual series. This indicates that the explained variation is the difference between the predicted value and the mean. The unexplained

X

coefficient of correlation a value that indicates the strengths of relationship between two variables.

curve a curved line that visualizes a non-linear function.

variation a difference between the regression line values and the actual time series values that the regression line approximates.

mean the average of a set of numbers.

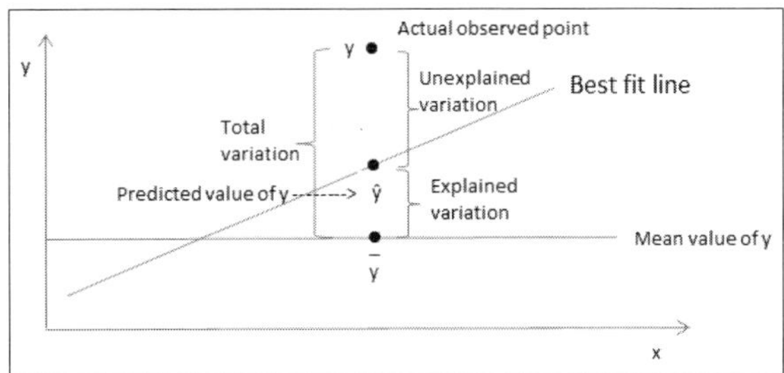

Figure 4.4
Variations around the actual value in regression analysis

variation is the difference between the actual value and the predicted value. The total variation is the difference between the actual value and its mean. Let us look at a series consisting of just four values, as in Figure 4.5.

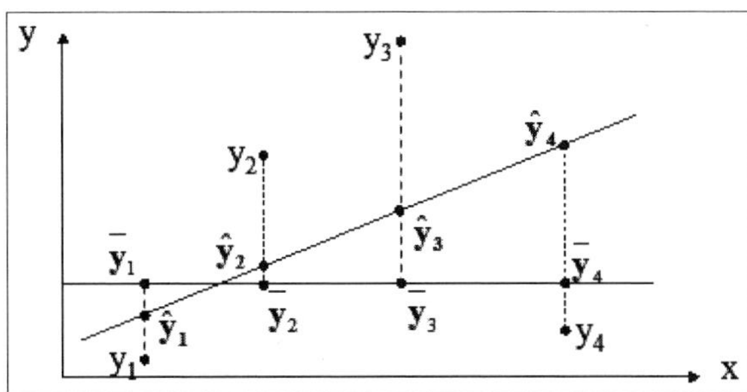

Figure 4.5
Variations from the regression line

To eliminate negative values, variations are actually expressed as squared values. This means that for each and every one of these points the variations are calculated as in Table 4.3. As Table 4.3 indicates, by summing up all the variations for individual points, we get the variation for the whole variable.

Type of variation	One point	The whole variable
Total variation	$(y - \bar{y})^2$	$\Sigma(y - \bar{y})^2$
Explained variation	$(\hat{y} - \bar{y})^2$	$\Sigma(\hat{y} - \bar{y})^2$
Unexplained variation	$(y - \hat{y})^2$	$\Sigma(y - \hat{y})^2$

Table 4.3 Variations in one point and the whole variable (time series)

If we take the ratio between the explained variation and the total variation we get a formula to calculate the **coefficient of determination** R:

$$R = \frac{\Sigma(\hat{y} - \bar{y})^2}{\Sigma(y - \bar{y})^2} \tag{4.5}$$

Essentially this tells us that R indicates the percentage of the total variation in *y* accounted for by the variable *x*, or as in this case, by the value of ŷ.

Note In time series analysis *x* is always a time unit, so R tells us the degree to which variations in a time series values *y* are dependent on time.

X
coefficient of determination the ration of the explained and the total variance. It provides a measure of how well the model describes the data set.

We should also remember that the coefficient of determination R can be used to calculate the coefficient of correlation r. As a matter of fact, we know that $r^2 = R$. This means that the coefficient of correlation is simply a square root of R:

$$r = \sqrt{R} \tag{4.6}$$

Note By definition, the value of R will always be between zero and one. The closer R is to 0, the less impact *x* has on *y*, and the closer R to 1, the more is *y* dependent on *x*.

If, for example, we calculate the regression between profit and revenue and get R = 0.96, then r is simply a square root of that, that is, 0.98. This indicates a very high correlation between the two variables. It also tells us that 96% (R can be interpreted as percentages) of the total variation in profit can be explained by variations in revenue and that only 4% is not explained by this relationship.

Let us return to our equation that describes the relationship between profits and the revenues. If a relationship between two variables can be modelled in this form, then this is called a simple regression. The word 'regression' means that we can we can return, or revert, one variable from the other. However, simple regression implies that it is applicable only to the specific range of values included in this data set. In other words, the revenue in the above data set has the smallest value of 190 and the largest of 1200. The line of regression implies that the profit changes with the revenues in accordance with the equation we calculated only providing the values of revenue stay in this range.

Note A regression model does not necessarily hold if we try to use the revenue values that are outside the range for which the model was calculated. Exercise caution if using regression analysis outside the initial variable range.

Another important point is that the **residuals** (differences between the actual and regression calculated values) must be **random**. If there is any kind of pattern present in these residuals, then the regression equation is false and does not constitute a true representation of the relationship. The whole issue of deviations from the regression line is quite complex and we refer to it here only briefly.

Note Just as simple regression applies to linear relationships, other types of regression equations apply to other non-linear types of relationships. It is also important to understand that more than one variable can be used to create a model. In case of multiple regression, we have one dependent variable and a series of independent (or predictors) variables.

In summary, the following assumptions need to be obeyed in order to make the results of simple regression analysis valid:

- Relationship between the dependent and independent variables must be linear;
- The errors have to be independent of each other (no **serial correlation**);

residual the same as errors, i.e. the differences between the actual and predicted values. Also used for unexplained variations after fitting a regression model.

random a property that implies impossibility to predict precisely the future value. The general shape of a random time series is that without a trend and any regularity. This is the shape and the property that a series of errors should have after fitting a forecasting model to a time series and subtracting the corresponding values.

serial correlation same as autocorrelation, i.e. a relationship between a variable and itself over different time intervals. The use 'serial correlation' is mainly used in regression analysis to describe a relationship of errors over different time intervals.

- Errors have to follow normal distribution;
- The regression errors must have a constant variance (**homoscedasticity**);
- Dependent variables should not be related (colinearity) – in case of multiple regression.

4.2.3 Linear regression in Excel

To illustrate how to apply simple regression and how to interpret the results, we will use the two variables from Table 4.1 (the data set is given in Figure 4.6), each with ten observations and run Regression analysis in Excel. The way to do this is to go to the Data tab, select Data Analysis on the Analysis resource block (far right on your Excel ribbon), and then select Regression option from the dialogue box. We need to fill in the wizard box, as in Figure 4.7. The data set is in cells A2:A11 (Revenue variable, or X) and in cells B2:B11 (Profit variable, or Y). The labels for these two variables are in cells A1 and in B1. We have, therefore, ticked the box marked 'Labels' in the wizard. In this particular case, we have chosen to see all possible Output options in the dialogue box. However, we will only describe the most important one(s).

	A	B
1	Revenue	Profit
2	320	20
3	200	10
4	190	10
5	350	45
6	1200	130
7	330	30
8	700	80
9	450	60
10	700	100
11	1000	110

Figure 4.6

Data set for the simple regression

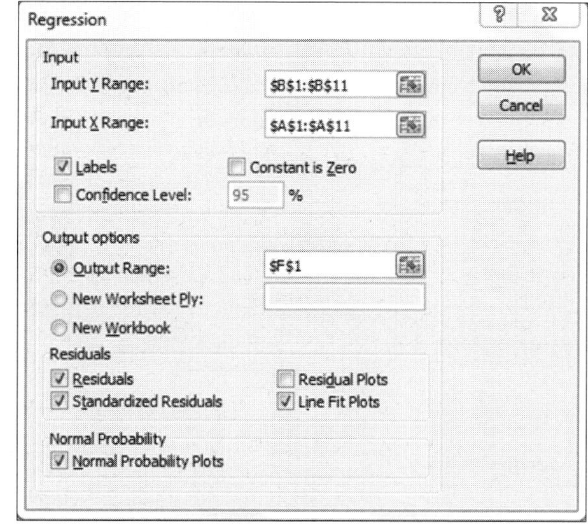

Figure 4.7

Excel Regression analysis wizard box (Data > Data Analysis > Regression)

Once we have clicked the OK button, Excel will produce a Summary Output for the regression analysis. The report begins from the cell F1, as specified in the wizard under the Output Range (see Figure 4.8). The first table that constitutes this Summary Output (printout) is given in Figure 4.9.

	F	G
1	SUMMARY OUTPUT	
2		
3	*Regression Statistics*	
4	Multiple R	0.968442727
5	R Square	0.937881316
6	Adjusted R Square	0.93011648
7	Standard Error	11.5305419
8	Observations	10

Figure 4.8

Summary Regression statistics output

Multiple R in cell G4 is the coefficient of correlation. Exactly the same number can be

homoscedasticity also called homogeneity or uniformity of variance. Implies that the variance is finite, i.e. the variance around the regression line is constant for all values of the predictor.

obtained if we used functions: =CORREL(A2:A11,B2:B11) or =PEARSON(A2:A11,B2:B11). R Square in G5 is the coefficient of determination. The formula =RSQ(A2:A11,B2:B11) would have also given us the same number. As we said, the coefficient of correlation is the square root of the coefficient of determination, so Multiple R is a square root of R Square. This means that for the cell G4 we could have used a formula =SQRT(G5) to get the same value.

Adjusted R Square (cell G6) is a refined version of the coefficient of determination achieved by eliminating the R^2 bias. It does so by adjusting the R Square for the sample size and the number of dependent variables. The following formula does this:

$$\text{Adjusted R Square} = 1 - \left[(1 - R^2)\frac{n-1}{n-2}\right] \tag{4.7}$$

Or:

$$\text{Adjusted R Square} = 1 - \left[\left(\frac{SSE}{SST}\right)\left(\frac{n-1}{n-2}\right)\right] \tag{4.8}$$

Where, n is the number of observations and SSE and SST are the residual sum of squares and the total sum of squares, as explained below. This is very useful for comparing models with a different number of variables. In a simple case like ours, Adjusted R Square and R Square will be almost identical. The standard error of the estimate from cell G7 is the same value as the one calculated by using the function: =STEYX(B2:B11,A2:A11). It represents the value of standard deviation for this estimate.

The second table that Excel produces is as per Figure 4.9.

	F	G	H	I	J	K
10	ANOVA					
11		*df*	*SS*	*MS*	*F*	*Significance F*
12	Regression	1	16058.87283	16058.87283	120.78573	4.177E-06
13	Residual	8	1063.627171	132.9533964		
14	Total	9	17122.5			

Figure 4.9
ANOVA table

Note The term degrees of freedom (df) refers to the number of restrictions, or, a penalty we 'pay' for selecting a certain number of parameters. Unfortunately, the same concept can be calculated in several different ways, dependent upon the application. If we use df in the context of regression line, then the number of degrees of freedom (or v_1) is equal to m, where m = number of independent variables. If we use df in the context of residuals (degrees of freedom are represented as v_2), then $v_2 = n - m - 1$, where n = number of observations and m as above.

standard error standard deviation of the actual values around the regression line. Calculated by dividing the error sum of squares (unexplained variations) by the degrees of freedom.

standard deviation a measure of the data spread, equal to the square root of variance.

degrees of freedom refers to the number of independent observations in a sample minus the number of population parameters that must be estimated from sample data.

The number of degrees of freedom for regression (cell G12) corresponds to v_1 described earlier, whilst v_2 (cell G13) is the number of degrees of freedom for residuals ($v_2 = n - m - 1 = 10 - 1 - 1 = 8$). 'SS' (cell H11) refers to sum of squares and these correspond to the proportion of explained (cell H12) and unexplained variance (H13), described below. The naming conventions used by Excel differs somewhat from those used in this book and those used by statisticians. The relationship between the labels found in Excel and the phrases we used earlier in this chapter is as follows:

- Regression sum of squares (SSR) = explained variation (cell H12)
- Residual (error) sum of squares (SSE) = unexplained variation (cell H13)
- Total sum of squares (SST) = SSR + SSE (cell H15)
- Mean square for regression (MSR) = SSR/v_1 (cell I12)
- **Mean square for error (MSE)** = SSE/v_2 (cell I13)

We have to remember that:

$$R^2 = \frac{SSR}{SST} = \frac{SST - SSE}{SST} = \frac{1 - SSE}{SST} \tag{4.9}$$

In other words, we could have also calculated the R Square value if we used the formula = H12/H13 or = 1 – (H13/H14):

$$R^2 = \frac{SSR}{SST} = \frac{16058.87}{17122.5} = 0.937881$$

or

$$R^2 = 1 - \frac{SSE}{SST} = 1 - \frac{1063.627}{17122.5} = 0.937881$$

Cell I13 contains MSE. Just as a pointer, if you take the square root of this value (=SQRT(I13)), you will get 11.53054 which is the value of the Standard Error displayed in cell G7.

Cells D33 (I12) and D34 (I13) are used to calculate the F-statistic. The formula is:

$$F = \frac{MSR}{MSE} \tag{4.10}$$

In order to accept that there is a significant relationship between the dependent and independent variable(s), the value of F-calculated needs to be higher than F-critical. The value of F-statistic (cell J12) of 120.7857 is used to find the **p-value** for the regression. This is shown as 4.17671E-06 (cell K12), which is Excel's way of saying that the level of **significance** is 0.00000417671. The number is close to zero, which implies that the variations in the independent variable significantly explain the variations in the dependent variable.

And finally, the excerpt from the Excel regression summary, shown in Figure 4.10, gives the values of the regression coefficients, namely the intercept and the slope, and the associated measures.

	F	G	H	I	J	K	L	M	N
15									
16		*Coefficients*	*Standard Error*	*t Stat*	*P-value*	*Lower 95%*	*Upper 95%*	*Lower 95.0%*	*Upper 95.0%*
17	Intercept	-7.050063371	7.068439829	-0.99740021	0.3477785	-23.349915	9.2497881	-23.349915	9.2497881
18	Revenue, x	0.122334675	0.011131194	10.99025607	4.177E-06	0.0966661	0.1480033	0.0966661	0.1480033

Figure 4.10

The second table in ANOVA output

The intercept, or coefficient *a*, is exactly the same as that calculated previously (see Figure 4.10), as is coefficient *b*, or the slope. The standard error for the slope (called Revenue (X) as per Excel printout in Figure 4.10) is exactly the same number that we would have got had we applied the formula for SE_b (see the Note box below). Cells I17 and I18 contain the t-Stat for testing the significance of coefficients *a* and *b*.

X

mean square for error (MSE) the mean value of all the squared differences between the actual and forecasted values in the time series.

p-value the p-value is the probability of getting a value of the test statistic as extreme as or more extreme than that observed by chance alone, if the null hypothesis is true.

significance a percentage that indicates if some event is random or a result of some pattern. Most frequently used levels of significance are 1%, 5% and 10%. They are the thresholds indicating the probability beyond which an event or relationship is random (due to chance).

Note Several important points should also be remembered. First, in the equation $y = b_0 + b_1x$, b_0 and b_1 represent just a sample of the total population (our data set covers only ten months!). The total population parameters are represented by α and β, such that: $Y = \alpha + \beta X$. In other words b_0 and b_1 are just estimates of α and β. Particularly problematic is the estimation of b_1 (because b_0 is just the intercept level), so we'll focus on b_1 here. How do we know how well b_1 represents β? In fact we do not, unless we test it. Here is just a brief, one paragraph reminder of how to use the t-statistic to test this.

We set the null hypothesis that β is equal to zero (H_0: $\beta = 0$) and the alternative hypothesis that it is not equal to zero (H_1: $\beta \neq 0$). We hope to prove that that $\beta \neq 0$ at the 0.05 level of significance, which is 95% level of certainty (any other level of significance can be used). We calculate the t-statistic (the Excel function can be used) and if it is greater than the critical value of t, then we can reject H_0 and accept H_1, i.e. we are 95% confident that our parameter 'b' is representative of the true relationship.

The standard error of estimate for the parameter 'b' (cell H17) is calculated as:

$$SE_b = \sqrt{\frac{\frac{\Sigma(y-\hat{y})^2}{(n-2)}}{\Sigma(x-\bar{x})^2}} \tag{4.11}$$

The nominator is SSE divided by n – 2 and the denominator is sometimes called SSX (sum of squares for X). Once we have SE_b, we can calculate the t-value to be compared with the t-critical value from the table. This is calculated as:

$$t_{calc} = \frac{b-\beta}{SE_b} \tag{4.12}$$

In our case $b_1 = 0.122334675$ (cell G18), $\beta = 0$ (which is the H_0 hypothesis) and $SE_b = 0.011131194$ (cell H18). The result is $t_{calc} = 10.99025607$ (cell I18). If we were using the tables, this would be compared against the t_{crit} value and if it is higher than t_{crit}, then we can conclude that parameter 'b' represents the population well. However, in Excel we rely on P-value (cell J18).

The P-value (cell J18) helps us assess the meaning of this t-Stat. The lower the p-value, the more relevant the values of the intercept and the slope. In the language of hypothesis testing, we can reject null hypothesis that these parameters are zero. In Figure 4.10, the t Stat values (cells I17 and I18) are calculated by simply dividing the value of the coefficient by its standard error, i.e. I17 = G17/H17 = –7.050063371/7.068439829. The same applies to cell I18. These t-values are relevant at the level of significance given in column J, entitled P-value. In other words, the value of the coefficient *b* given in cell G18 = 0.122334675 is acceptable because the P-value (cell G18) is 0.00000417671 (or to use Excel notation, 4.17671E-06), which is the level of significance. Generally speaking, if this P-value exceeds 0.05, for example, we cannot reject the null hypothesis and assume that this parameter is significant.

You can also see that the P-value (cell J18) for the slope (called Revenue (X) in the Excel Summary) is exactly the same as the F-significance for the regression (cell K12, Figure 4.9). This is always the case with regression equations containing only one explanatory variable

t-value a calculated value that will be compared with the critical t-value from Student t-distribution to decide if a hypothesis will be accepted or rejected.

(due to the fact that this is the only independent variable). Columns K and L give us the permissible region (confidence interval) for the values of ***a*** and ***b*** at the given level of significance, in this case a 95% interval is applied because alpha is assumed to be 0.05.

The final table of the Excel Summary Report is shown in Figure 4.11. Column G (G25:G34) contains the predicted values calculated as a result of the regression formula. Column H, or Residuals, are the actual values of Profit (given in B2:B11), minus the Predicted Profit values (G25:G34). And finally, Standard Residuals are the Residuals divided by their standard error, which tells us how far in unites of standard deviation is every residual from their mean value (very similar to Z score in standard normal distribution). The columns K and L in Figure 4.11 are just the percentiles for every value of Profit. In other words, more than 95% of the variable has the value of 130, between 85% and 95% of the profits are 110 or less, between 75% and 85% of the profits are 100, and so on.

	F	G	H	I	J	K	L
22	RESIDUAL OUTPUT					PROBABILITY OUTPUT	
23							
24	*Observation*	*Predicted Profit, y*	*Residuals*	*Standard Residuals*		*Percentile*	*Profit, y*
25	1	32.09703273	-12.09703273	-1.112769975		5	10
26	2	17.41687169	-7.416871692	-0.682255914		15	10
27	3	16.19352494	-6.193524938	-0.569723894		25	20
28	4	35.76707299	9.232927011	0.849309429		35	30
29	5	139.751547	-9.751547007	-0.897015736		45	45
30	6	33.32037948	-3.320379483	-0.305431809		55	60
31	7	78.58420935	1.415790651	0.130234361		65	80
32	8	48.00054052	11.99945948	1.103794502		75	100
33	9	78.58420935	21.41579065	1.969974733		85	110
34	10	115.2846119	-5.284611944	-0.486115697		95	130

Figure 4.11
Residual output

4.2.4 Fitting regression trend line to scatter plot using Excel

Excel can be used to automatically fit a regression line to the data set described in Figure 4.1, as illustrated in Figures 4.12 to 4.14.

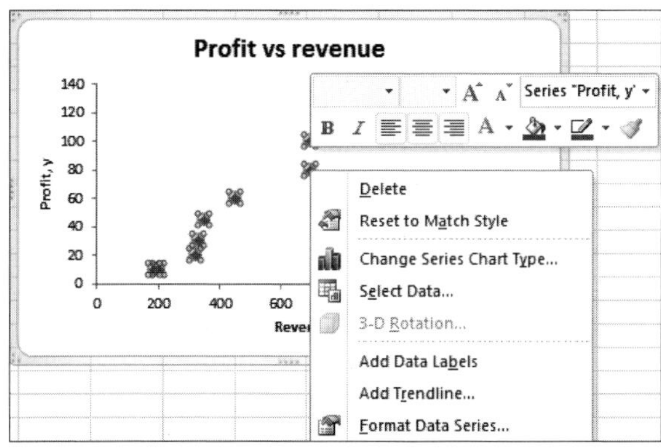

Figure 4.12
Using Excel to Fit trend line

An alternative approach to calculating the regression line, although the results printout is not as comprehensive, is to right click on one of the data points in the graph and select Add Trendline option from the box.

permissible region
a region inside the confidence interval that implies that certain values are not a result of random variations.

confidence interval
a confidence interval specifies a range of values within which the unknown population parameter may lie, e.g. mean.

From the selection of curves that is presented after the Trendline option was selected, chose the second one, that is, the linear option.

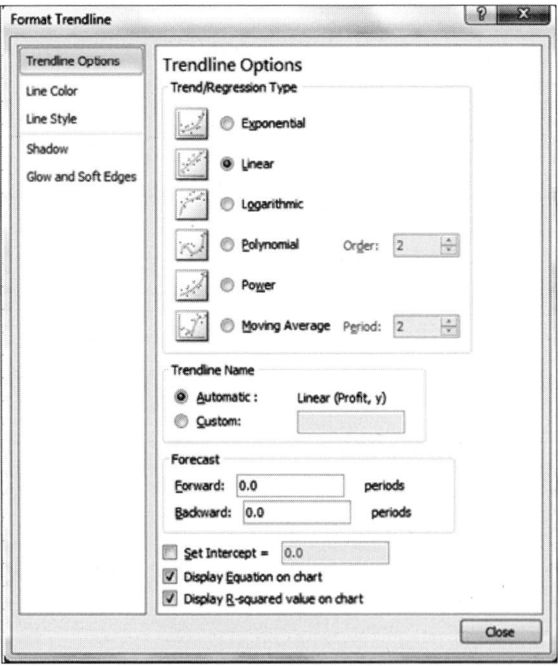

Figure 4.13
Select the type of curve to fit the data

Excel will automatically insert the regression line in the graph. In order to see the actual equation that defines this linear regression, after you have selected the type of regression, select 'Display equation on chart'.

Note

You can use this menu to display the equation and R^2 values on the chart.

Click Close.

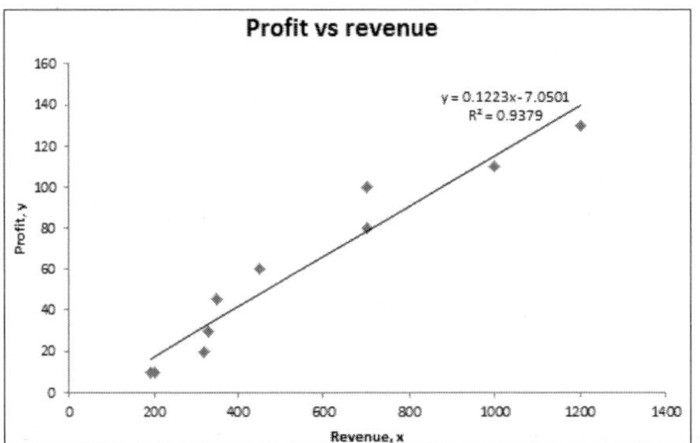

Figure 4.14
Trend line fit

We now get not just the regression line, but the equation, which is identical to the one we calculated using Excel functions SLOPE and INTERCEPT.

In order to demonstrate the above points, we'll show here yet another method of calculating linear regression using the TREND () function.

	A	B	C	D	E	F
1	Revenue, x	Profit, y	Estimated, y^		Error, e = Y^ - y	
2	320	20	32.09703273	=TREND($B$2:$B$11,$A$2:$A$11,A2)	12.09703273	=C2-B2
3	200	10	17.41687169		7.416871692	
4	190	10	16.19352494		6.193524938	
5	350	45	35.76707299		-9.232927011	
6	1200	130	139.751547		9.751547007	
7	330	30	33.32037948		3.320379483	
8	700	80	78.58420935		-1.415790651	
9	450	60	48.00054052		-11.99945948	
10	700	100	78.58420935		-21.41579065	
11	1000	110	115.2846119	=TREND($B$2:$B$11,$A$2:$A$11,A11)	5.284611944	=C11-B11

Figure 4.15

Linear regression calculation using Excel =TREND() function

➜ Excel solution

Estimated y ($\hat{y}$) = Cells C2:C11 Formula = TREND($B$2:$B$11,$A$2:$A$11,A2)
Copy down C2:C11

Error = Cells E2:E11 Formula = C2-B2
Copy down E2:E11

The syntax for the above Excel function is =TREND (known_y's, known_x's, New_x's, Const). We have ignored the constant element here, as it is not relevant. Known_x's is the set of all known Revenue values, and as it does not change from cell to cell, we had to put the whole range as absolute references ($B$2:$B$11). Known_y's is the set of all known Profit values, and again as it does not change from cell to cell, we had to put the whole range as absolute references ($A$2:$A$11). The value of New_x' changes from cell to cell and it is therefore left as a relative reference in this formula.

Note We showed four ways to establish a regression model between two variables. They are:

1. Using the =SLOPE() and =INTERCEPT() Excel functions
2. Using regression from the Data Analysis Tool Pak
3. Fitting a trend to a chart
4. Using the =TREND() function

Every approach has some advantages and disadvantages, and the richness of the output varies accordingly.

4.2.5 Prediction interval for an estimate of Y

Very closely related to the concept of forecasting error is the notion of confidence. The errors measure the accuracy of our forecasts, whilst the confidence interval provides the measure of reliability. In other words, we are trying to assign a probability percentage, which will define how confident we are that our forecasts will be within a certain interval.

Let us look back to our regression models to see how to deal with confidence intervals in this context. The regression equation ($\hat{y} = b_0 + b_1x$) provides a relationship that can then be used to provide an estimate of y based upon an x value. For example, we may want to know what the value of one variable would be if the other variable was set at some particular value. The prediction interval for y at a particular value of $x_p = x$ is given by Equation (4.13):

$$\hat{y} - e < y < \hat{y} + e \tag{4.13}$$

Where the error term is calculated using Equation (4.14)

$$e = t_{cri} SEE \sqrt{1 + \frac{1}{n} + \frac{n(\hat{x} - \bar{x})^2}{n(\sum x^2) - (\sum x)^2}} \tag{4.14}$$

Where SEE is the standard error of estimate, $\hat{x}$ is the predicted value of x, and $\bar{x}$ is the mean value.

Excel Spreadsheet Solution - calculation of the prediction interval

Let's examine an Excel solution to calculate the prediction interval for $\hat{x}$ = 300. Figure 4.16 illustrates the Excel solution to calculate the predictor interval.

	A	B	C	D	E	F	G
1	Revenue, X	Profit, y	X^2				
2	320	20	102400		Regression coefficients		
3	200	10	40000		b0 =	-7.05006337	=INTERCEPT(B2:B11,A2:A11)
4	190	10	36100		b1 =	0.122334675	=SLOPE(B2:B11,A2:A11)
5	350	45	122500		Prediction interval		
6	1200	130	1440000		n =	10	=COUNT(A2:A11)
7	330	30	108900		level =	0.05	
8	700	80	490000		df =	8	=F6-2
9	450	60	202500		tcri =	2.306004135	=TINV(F7,F8)
10	700	100	490000		x =	300	
11	1000	110	1000000		xbar =	544	=AVERAGE(A2:A11)
12					y^ =	29.65033922	=F3+F4*F10
13					Σx =	5440	=SUM(A2:A11)
14					Σx^2 =	4032400	=SUM(C2:C11)
15					SEE =	11.5305419	=STEYX(B2:B11,A2:A11)
16					E =	28.58193791	=F9*F15*SQRT(1+(1/F6)+(F6*(F10-F11)^2)/(F6*F14-F13^2))
17					Lower PI =	1.068401315	=F12-F16
18					Upper PI =	58.23227713	=F12+F16

Figure 4.16

→ Excel function method

b_0 = Cell F3	Formula = INTERCEPT (B2:B11,C2:C11)
b_1 = Cell F4	Formula = SLOPE (B2:B11,C2:C11)
n = Cell F6	Formula = COUNT (A2:A11)
level = Cell F7	Value
df = Cell F8	Formula = F6-2
t_{cri} = Cell F9	Formula = TINV (F7,F8)
x = Cell F10	Value
Xbar = Cell F11	Formula = AVERAGE (A2:A11)
Y^ = Cell F12	Formula = F3 + F10*F4
Σx = Cell F13	Formula = SUM (A2:A11)
Σx^2 = Cell F14	Formula = SUM (C2:C11)
SEE = Cell F15	Formula = STEYX (B2:B11,A2:A11)
E = Cell F16	Formula = F9*F15*SQRT(1+(1/F6)+(F6*(F10-F11)^2)/ (F6*F14-F13^2))
Lower PI = Cell F17	Formula = F12-F16
Upper PI = Cell F18	Formula = F12+F16

From Excel: $x_p = 30$, $n = 10$, significance level = 5%, $t_{cri} = 2.306004$, SEE = 11.53054, $\bar{x} = 544$, $\sum x = 5440$, and $\sum x^2 = 4{,}032{,}400$.

$$e = 2.306004 * 11.53054 * \sqrt{1 + \frac{1}{10} + \frac{10 * (300 - 544)^2}{10 * (4{,}032{,}400) - (5440)^2}} = 28.58194$$

Equation (4.13) then gives the 95% prediction interval for $x_p = 300$ to be between 1.068401 and 58.23228.

Interpretation If the revenue level was at 300 units then we predict the value of the profit of 29.65034 with a 95% confidence between 1.068401 to 58.23228. This shows that the actual value can vary greatly from the predicted value of 29.65034.

Student exercises

X4.1 If y = Profit and x = Revenue, what does the following regression equation tell you: $y = -4.4 + 0.085x$?

X4.2 Given the equation in X4.1, at what point would you expect to break even?

X4.3 If you reach a revenue of 370, what is the expected profit?

X4.4 If, after you conducted regression analysis, the ANOVA table from Excel printout shows the following values. How would you interpret them?

ANOVA					
	df	*SS*	*MS*	*F*	*Significance F*
Regression	1	608.6012	608.6012	44.302659	0.000159807
Residual	8	109.8988	13.73735		
Total	9	718.5			

4.3 Non-linear relationships and regression analysis

In the previous two sections we have explored methods of measuring and fitting relationships between one variable and another variable. These one-predictor models have assumed that the relationship between y and x is linear and this simple situation in known as simple linear regression modelling. In most cases the situation is more complicated, and we will now briefly consider:

- Identifying and fitting non-linear relationships;
- Non-linear regression analysis.

4.3.1 Identifying and fitting non-linear relationships (or trends) using Excel

In reality, the relationships between the variables are more often non-linear than linear. In fact, as opposed to only one linear form, which is $y = b_0 + b_1x$, there are numerous non-linear forms. One of the more often used models is the parabolic model:

$$y = b_0 + b_1x + b_2x^2 \tag{4.15}$$

Another frequently deployed model is the exponential model:

$$y = b_0e^{b1x} \tag{4.16}$$

There are numerous other non-linear models to choose from.

Example 4. 4

Suppose that the following demand versus discount information has been collected (Table 4.4).

The first step is to graph demand versus discount to see what the possible relationship may be between the two variables y and x.

Discount	Demand	Discount	Demand
1	5000	7	71005
2	11001	8	89008
3	19001	9	109000
4	29003	10	131010
5	41003	11	155006
6	55003	12	181008

Table 4.4

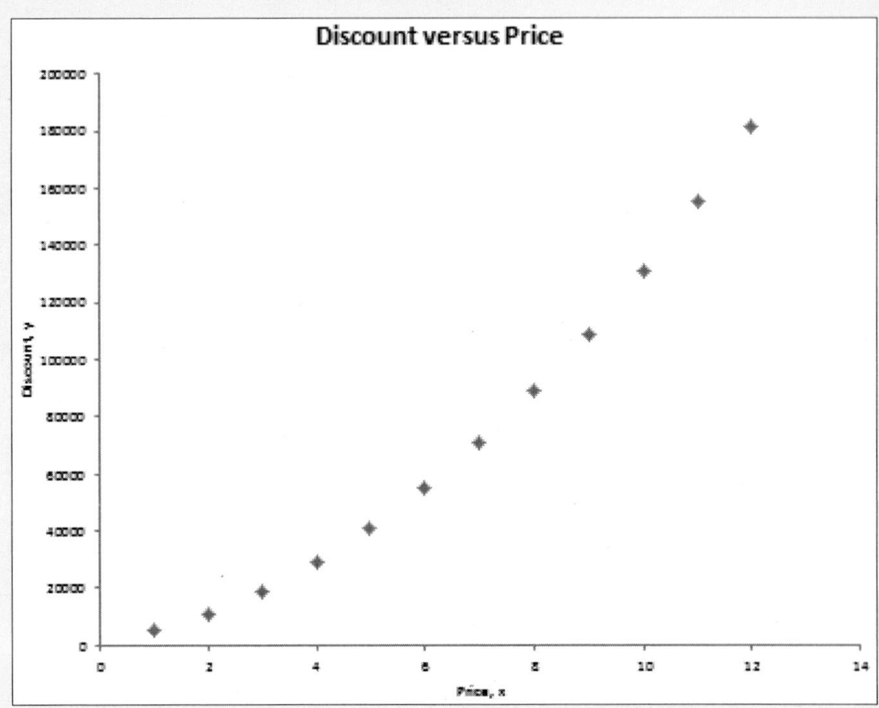

Figure 4.17

Scatter plot of demand versus discount

We observe from the scatter plot that the relationship between y and x could be a line or a possibility exists that a non-linear (or curve) relationship may exist between the two variables.

Some of the most commonly used theoretical curves and their respective equations are shown below.

a. Line

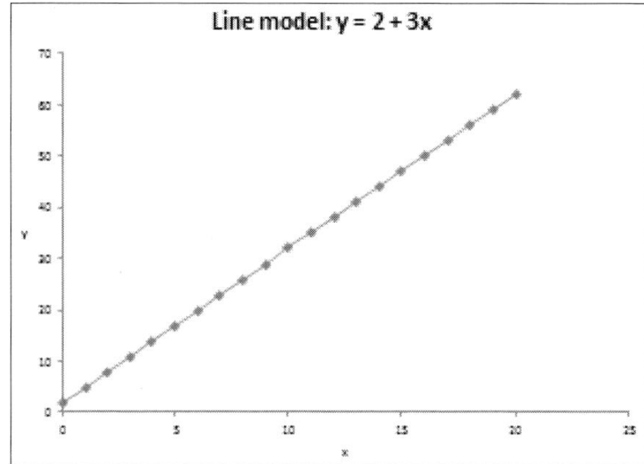

Figure 4.18

$y = b_0 + b_1x$

b. Parabola curve

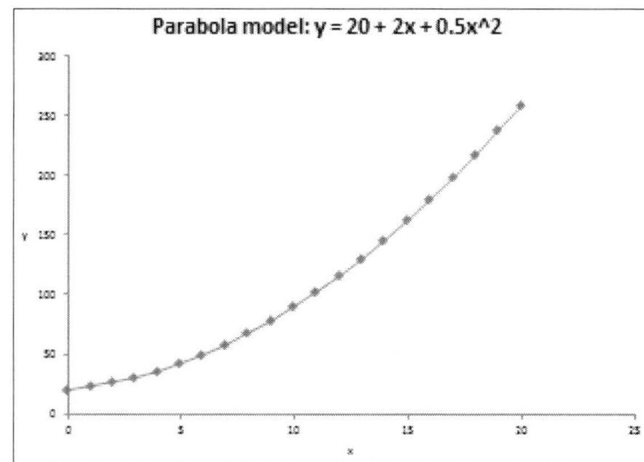

Figure 4.19

$y = b_0 + b_1x + b_2x^2$

c. Hyperbola curve

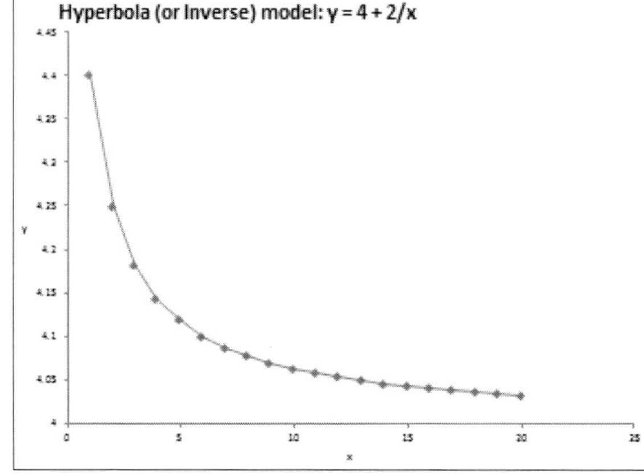

Figure 4.20

$y = b_0 + b_1/x$

d. Exponential curve

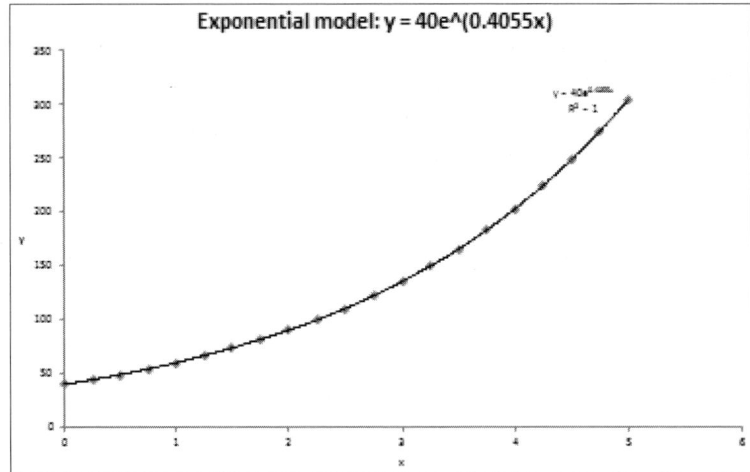

Figure 4.21
$y = b_0e^{b1x}$

We already excluded the linear model and by looking at the remaining three curves above and the example data set scatter plot in Figure 4.17, we observe that the parabola, may be the most appropriate relationship of the form $y = b_0 + b_1x + b_2x^2$. The regression coefficients can be calculated using formulae, but we will use the Excel built in 'Add Trendline' method to calculate these coefficients.

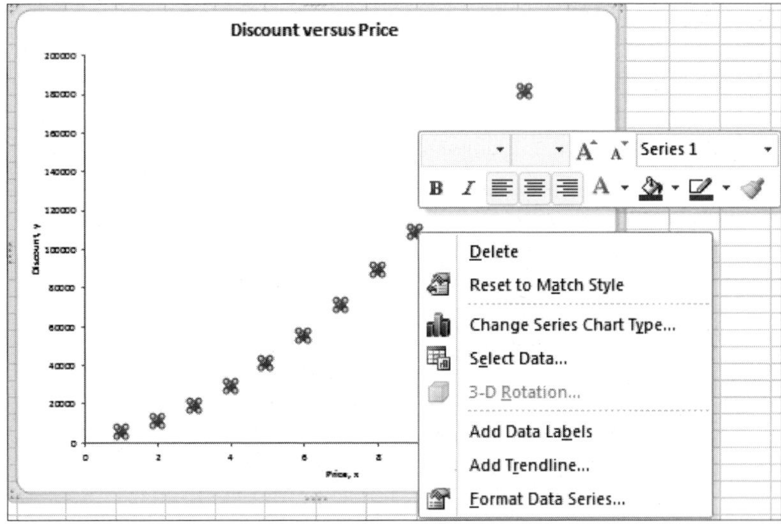

Figure 4.22
Fitting trend line to scatter plot

Right click on a data point in the scatter plot

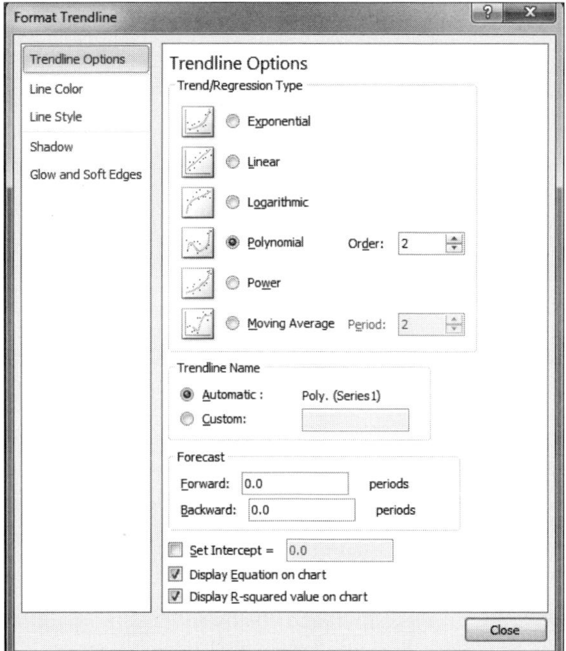

Figure 4.23

Fitting trend line to scatter plot

Choose the 'Add trendline' option and select Polynomial of Order 2 since we wish to fit the model $y = b_0 + b_1x + b_2x^2$ to the data set.

Select display equation on chart and display R-squared on chart.

Click Close

The trendline dialogue box gives you 6 options. When selecting a polynomial you need to set the order of the polynomial (2 is quadratic, 3 is cubic). At the bottom of the Format Trendline box choose Display Equation and Display R squared. Note also that you can choose to give the equation a name, choose to have the equation extrapolated forward or backward, and set a fixed intercept value.

Note Forecasting: You can extend the model (trendline) forward or backward beyond the data set: Right click on the trendline and go to format trendline. This brings up the original dialog box that allows you to adjust the forecast value forward or backwards.

Setting the decimal places in a model: Once a trendline has been added to a graph you may need to add decimal places to the equation, especially if Excel starts using scientific notation (significant digits are often lost when excel does this). Highlight the equation that you want to edit, right click and choose Format Trendline label. Choose Number and then you will be able to set the decimal places. As a rule it seems safe to go one more decimal place than needed to get rid of the scientific notation. Note also that when you highlight and right click the equation you can change the font size.

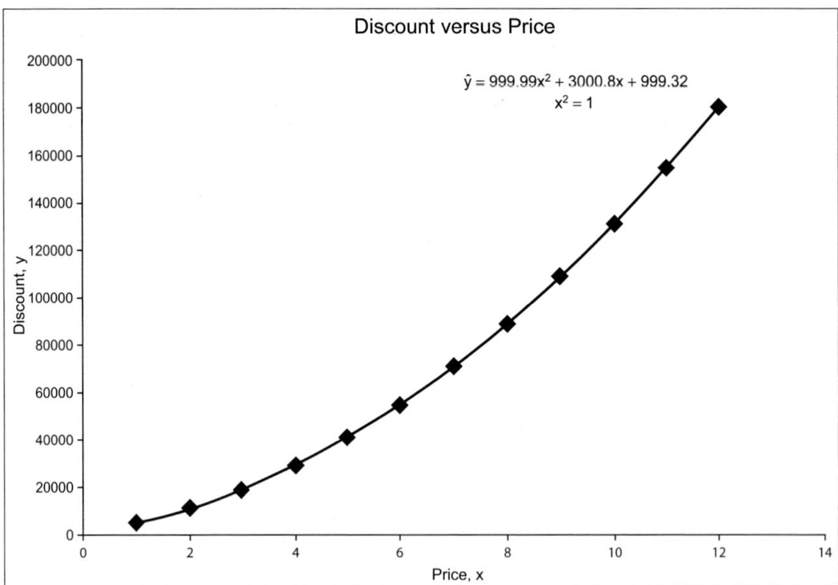

Figure 4.24

Figure 4.24 illustrates the scatter plot with the equation and coefficient of determination included.

We observe that Excel fits the curve (solid line) to the data points and calculates the regression coefficients to give the polynomial of order 2 regression equation: $\hat{y} = 999.99x^2 + 3000.8x + 999.32$, with coefficient of determination = 1 or 100%.

Note When you want to add a trendline to a chart in Microsoft Office Excel 2007, you can choose any one of six different trend or regression types: linear trendlines, logarithmic trendlines, polynomial trendlines, power trendlines, exponential trendlines, or moving average trendlines. The type of data that you have determines the type of trendline that you should use. A trendline is most accurate when its R-squared value is at or near 1. When you fit a trendline to your data, Excel automatically calculates its R-squared value. If you want to, you can display this value on your chart.

1. Linear trendlines: A linear trendline is a best-fit straight line that is used with simple linear data sets. Your data is linear if the pattern in its data points resembles a straight line. A linear trendline usually shows that something is increasing or decreasing at a steady rate. Equation: $y = b_0 + b_1x$, where b_0 and b_1 are regression coefficients.
2. Logarithmic trendlines: A logarithmic trendline is a best-fit curved line that is used when the rate of change in the data increases or decreases quickly and then levels out. A logarithmic trendline can use both negative and positive values. Equation: $y = b_0 + b_1x$, where b_0 and b_1 are regression coefficients.
3. Polynomial trendlines: A polynomial trendline is a curved line that is used when data fluctuates. It is useful, for example, for analyzing gains and losses over a large data set. The order

of the polynomial can be determined by the number of fluctuations in the data or by how many crests and troughs appear in the curve. Equation: $y = b_0 + b_1x + b_2x^2 + ... + b_nx^n$, where $b_0, b_1, \ldots, b_n$ are regression coefficients.

4. Power trendlines: A power trendline is a curved line that is used with data sets that compare measurements that increase at a specific rate—for example, the acceleration of a race car at 1-second intervals. You cannot create a power trendline if your data contains zero or negative values. Equation: $y = b_0x^{b1}$, where b_0 and b_1 are the regression coefficients. This option is only available for positive values.
5. Exponential trendlines: An exponential trendline is a curved line that is used when data values rise or fall at constantly increasing rates. You cannot create an exponential trendline if your data contains zero or negative values. Equation: $y = b_0e^{b1x}$, where b_0 and b_1 are regression coefficients. This option is only available for positive values.
6. Moving average trendlines: A moving average trendline smoothes out fluctuations in data to show a pattern or trend more clearly. A moving average uses a specific number of data points (set by the Period option), averages them, and uses the average value as a point in the line.

Student exercises

X4.5 Assume that inventory is growing in the following way:

134	267	456	390	777	978	1510	1800	2560	4250

Chart the variable and use Add Trendline function to fit three trends: power, exponential and power with three parameters (parabola). Which one fits the data best and why?

4.4 Trending data (single variable) and introduction to time series analysis

Simple regression created a model that described relationship between two variables. In our simple case the profit was *y* and the revenues were *x*. What would happen if we did not have the values for revenues, only profit, but measured over the same ten periods? This means that the time will become an independent variable and we could still use the same principle to model our data, but this time as a single variable dependent on time.

This is one of the most common approaches to modelling and it is called time series analysis. There is no difference between a simple regression model between two business variable and a time series model between one variable and the time. There are many situations where trying to establish dependencies between two or more variables will be too complex and too time consuming. In this case if we are trying to trend and predict the future values of this one single variable, we are much better off using the time series analysis approach. This is the domain of forecasting, as opposed to prediction. We have already indicated that time series models are those to be used for forecasting.

Note The main assumption of time series analysis is simple: it doesn't matter what influenced the movements of the variable that we are trending and extrapolating. Whatever it was, it is all embedded in the dynamics of the historical movements of this variable. If we can work out some regularity of the historical movements, we can assume that they will continue in the same fashion, which will enable us to extrapolate the future values.

Time series analysis goes beyond using simple regression models and substituting one variable for the time. The simple regression principles are used, but only to calculate the underlying trend. Time series analysis attempts to identify other components beyond trend that could be used to make the predictions more accurate and more reliable. We'll first show again how to calculate the trend in Excel and what kinds of trends are available to us.

4.4.1 Fitting trend line using Excel

Example 4.5

Consider a time series consisting of the closing daily values of Microsoft stocks between 2 December 2010 and 13 January 2011. In total, there are 30 observations.

Period, X	Revenue, y	Period, X	Revenue, y
1	26.89	16	28.3
2	27.02	17	28.07
3	26.84	18	28.01
4	26.87	19	27.97
5	27.23	20	27.85
6	27.08	21	27.91
7	27.34	22	27.98
8	27.25	23	28.09
9	27.62	24	28
10	27.85	25	28.82
11	27.99	26	28.6
12	27.9	27	28.22
13	27.81	28	28.11
14	28.07	29	28.55
15	28.19	30	28.19

Table 4.5 Microsoft closing daily stock values between 2 December 2010 and 13 January 2011

The data set is plotted in Figure 4.25 and this scatter plot helps to visualize the possible trend fit between y and x, where y are Microsoft daily closing stock values and x are the days in the given interval. The scatter plot includes a trend line fit to the data set.

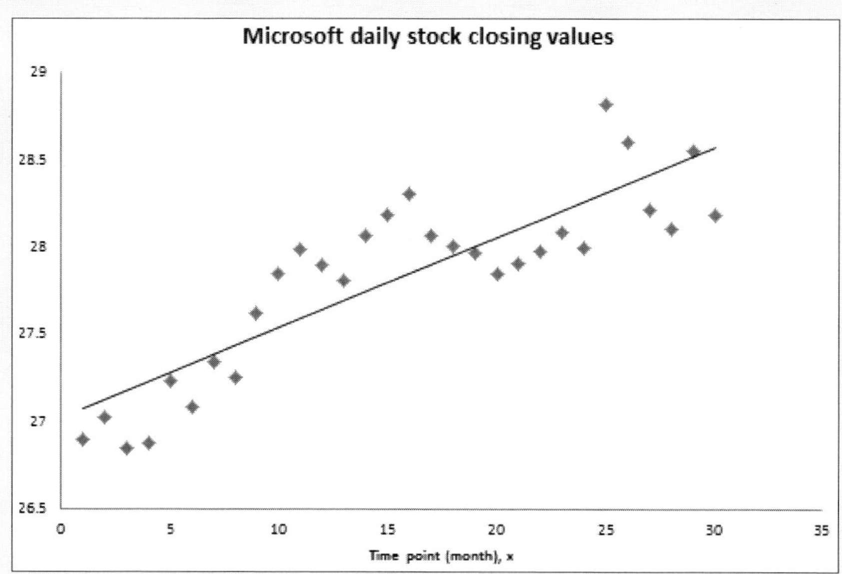

Figure 4.25

We'll show here two methods for trending the variable. One uses the TREND () function and the other one calculate the coefficients b_0 and b_1 (see Figs 4.3 and 4.15 for similar examples for regressing two variables).

	A	B	C	D	E	F
1	Period, X	Revenue, y	Trend, y^		Trend, y^	
2	1	26.89	27.06860215	=$C$33+$C$34*A2	27.06860215	=TREND($B$2:$B$31,$A$2:$A$31,A2)
3	2	27.02	27.12046867		27.12046867	
4	3	26.84	27.17233519		27.17233519	
26	25	28.82	28.31339859		28.31339859	
27	26	28.6	28.36526511		28.36526511	
28	27	28.22	28.41713163		28.41713163	
29	28	28.11	28.46899815		28.46899815	
30	29	28.55	28.52086466		28.52086466	
31	30	28.19	28.57273118	=$C$33+$C$34*A31	28.57273118	=TREND($B$2:$B$31,$A$2:$A$31,A31)
32						
33		b_0 =	27.01673563	=INTERCEPT(B2:B31,A2:A31)		
34		b_1 =	0.051866518	=SLOPE(B2:B31,A2:A31)		

Figure 4.26

Linear regression calculation using Excel =TREND () function (only the first three and last five observations shown).

→ Excel solution

Period, x Cells A2:A31

Revenue, y Cells B2:B31

b_0 = Cell C33 Formula = INTERCEPT(B2:B31,A2:A31)

b_1 = Cell C34 Formula = SLOPE(B2:B31,A2:A31)

Trendy, ($\hat{y}$) = Cells C2 Formula = $G$2+$G$3*A2

Copy down C2:C31

Trendy, ($\hat{y}$) = Cells E2:E31 Formula = TREND($B$2:$B$31,$A$2:$A$31,A2)

Copy down E2:E31

Note The syntax for the above Excel function is = TREND (known_y's, known_x's, New_x's, Const). Known_x's is the set of all known revenue values, and as it does not change from cell to cell, we had to put the whole range as absolute references ($B$2:$B$31). Known_y's is the set of all known time periods values, and again as it does not change from cell to cell, we had to put the whole range as absolute references ($A$2:$A$31). The value of New_x' changes from cell to cell and it is therefore left as a relative reference in this formula.

The equation y = 0.051x + 27.016 is a trending model fitted to our data set. A generic Excel linear trend equation that we used before is: $Y = b_0 + b_1x$. In most of the textbooks this equation is written as y = ax + b or y = a + bx. Whatever the case, the letter that stands alone (without x) is called an intercept and the other letter associated with x is called the slope. To avoid further confusion, let's standardize to a formula: $y = b_0 + b_1x$. Clearly b_0 is an intercept and b_1 is a slope. In our case, the value of the intercept is 27.016 and the value of the slope is 0.051. To calculate our past and future trend values we just need these two parameters. The values of x are represented by the sequential numbers that represent time periods. The forecast are produced in the same way as illustrated in Figure 4.27.

	A	B	C	D
36	x		Forecast	
37	31		28.625	=$C$33+$C$34*A37
38	32		28.676	
39	33		28.728	
40	34		28.78	
41	35		28.832	=$C$33+$C$34*A41

Figure 4.27

Figure 4.27 illustrates the calculation of the future values.

Note The future values of *x* should always be a sequential continuation of the period numbers used in the past. In our case, the last observation is for period 30, which means that the future values of *x* are 31, 32, . . . , 35.

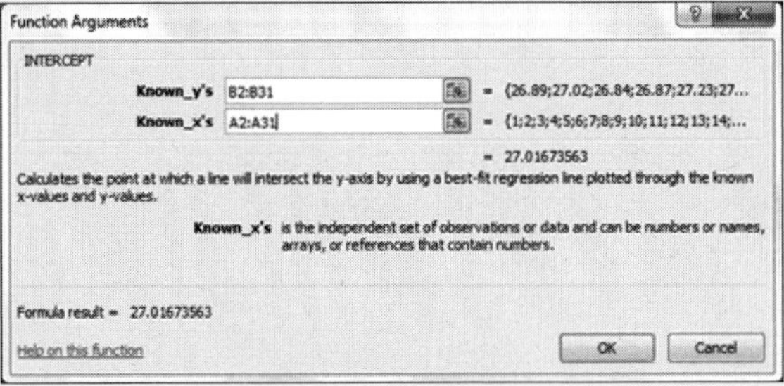

Figure 4.28
Details for the Intercept function

Insert > Formulas > Statistical > Intercept.

The slope function is invoked in exactly the same way and placed in cell H2. Both functions need to know the ranges for the values of *y* and *x* as follows: Y: B2:B31, and X: A2:A31.

Let's repeat that *y* represents the values of the time series and the *x* represents the values of time period numbers. In Figure 4.26 the cells C33 and C34 could have been calculated as follows:

→ Excel Method 1

Intercept Value = Cell C33	Formula = INTERCEPT(B2:B31,A2:A31)
Slope Value = Cell C34	Formula = SLOPE(B2:B31,A2:A31)
Linear trend formula Cell C2	Formula = $C$33+$C$34*A2
	Copy formula from C2:C31

Another approach is to use already 'pre-packaged' Excel functions dedicated to trend estimation.

In cell C2, where we want the first value of trend to be calculated, we invoke the TREND function as illustrated in Figure 4.29.

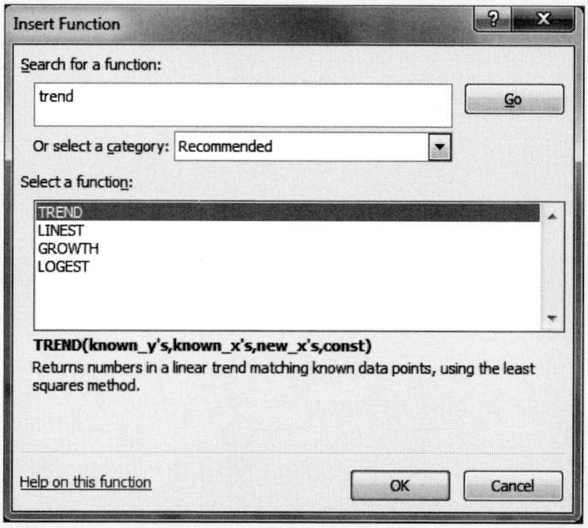

Figure 4.29

This will trigger another dialogue box that should be completed. The values of *y*, as we have seen, are the values of the time series (B2:B31) and the values of *x* are the values of time periods (A2:A31). New *x* is a specific period for which we are trying to calculate the trend value, which in our case is the period 1 (cell A2).

Note Pay attention to the values of *y* and *x*. They are entered as $B$2:$B$31 and $A$2:$A$31, respectively. They have to be referenced as fixed cells with the $ sign because if we copy down the formula, which we will, the range changes.

We can now copy the TREND function down from C2 to all the way to C36, which will cover the historical and the future trend values.

Note As before, the values of *x* have to be the sequential numbers that continue from the last historical period number.

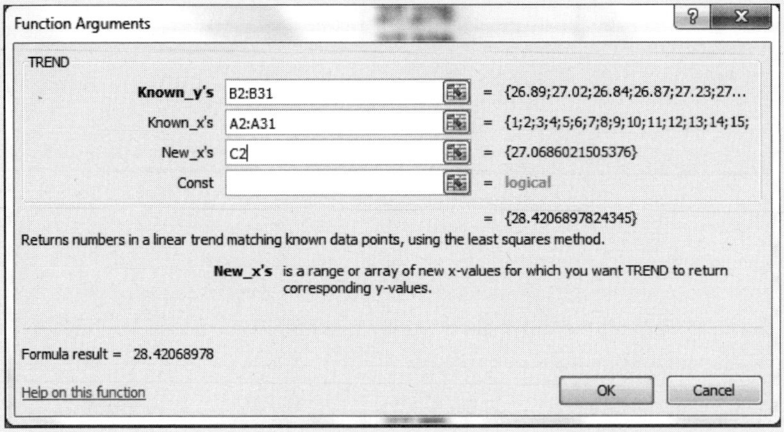

Function Arguments

TREND

Known_y's B2:B31 = {26.89;27.02;26.84;26.87;27.23;27...

Known_x's A2:A31 = {1;2;3;4;5;6;7;8;9;10;11;12;13;14;15;

New_x's C2 = {27.0686021505376}

Const = logical

= {28.4206897824345}

Returns numbers in a linear trend matching known data points, using the least squares method.

New_x's is a range or array of new x-values for which you want TREND to return corresponding y-values.

Formula result = 28.42068978

Help on this function

OK Cancel

Figure 4.30

Using trend function

The future trend values are calculated just as in previous examples, i.e. by copying the TREND function all the way to the last future observation.

→ Excel Method 2

Linear trend formula Cell C2 Formula = TREND($B$2:$B$31,$A$2:$A$31,A2)
Copy formula down E2:E31

Note The principles of calculating linear trend, as described here, can be applied to other types of curves. Besides the TREND function, Excel offers the GROWTH function. GROWTH is Excel function that describes exponential trends. It is invoked and used exactly in the same way as the TREND function used for linear time series.

Just in case you were wondering what happened with the actual daily closing values of Microsoft stocks vs. our forecast, the table and the associated chart are as follows shown in Figure 4.31 and 4.32.

	F	G	H
35			
36	x	Forecast	Actual
37	31	28.6246	28.3
38	32	28.67646	28.66
39	33	28.72833	28.47
40	34	28.7802	28.35
41	35	28.83206	28.02

Figure 4.31

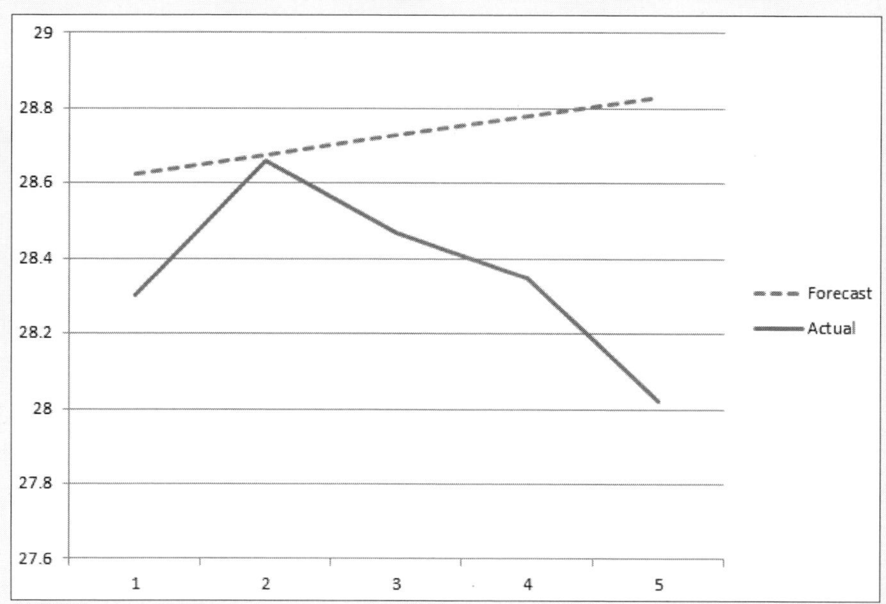

Figure 4.32

We will learn soon that extrapolating trend is a good method for long-term forecasts, but not so good for the purposes of short-term forecasting, as demonstrated above. Out of five future values, we only forecasted one with perfect accuracy.

4.4.2 Difference between regression and time series analysis

As it was the case with simple regression models, there is obviously a degree of error between observed values of y and those estimated by the trend line ($\hat{y}$). This *error*, or difference, is known as the residual and is given by the formula:

$$\text{Residual} = y - \hat{y} \tag{4.17}$$

In simple regression analysis, we treated all these errors just as residuals deviating from the regression line (or in this case a trend line). However, in time series analysis, the residuals can be subdivided into three further components:

- **Cyclical variations** (C),
- **Seasonal variations** (S),
- **Irregular variations** (I).

This means that in order to model the data, we can say that our best approximation (model) could be written something like:

$$Y = T + C + S + I \tag{4.18}$$

X

Cyclical variations variations around the trend line that take place over a larger number of years.

Seasonal variations variations around the trend line that take place within one year.

Irregular variations any variations around the trend line that are neither cyclical nor seasonal. Also used as another expression for errors or residuals.

Where T is a symbol for the trend and the remaining three components are as described above. The components do not have to be necessarily in additive relationship. If they are and this is the simplest of all models, then this is called an additive model.

Note In addition to an *additive* model, a *multiplicative* model can also be used. Sometimes the most appropriate model is a *mixed* one. Here are two example of these models:

Multiplicative model: $Y = T \times C \times S \times I$

Mixed model: $Y = (T \times C \times S) + I$

The character of the data in time series will determine which model is the most appropriate.

Underlying trend is almost self-explanatory. It suffice to say that it describes the underlying direction the variable is moving to, as well as the shape (linear vs. non-linear). The *cyclical* component consists of the long-term variations that happen over a period of several years. If the time series is not long enough, sometimes we might not even be able to observe this component, because the cycle is either longer than out time series, or it is just not obvious. On the other hand, the *seasonal* component applies to seasonal effects happening within one year. Therefore, if the time series consists of annual data, there is no need to worry about the seasonal component. At the same time, if we have monthly data and our time series is several years long, then it will (potentially) consist of the seasonal as well as of the cyclical component. And finally, the *irregular* component is everything else that does not fit into any of the previous three components, or, a proper residual.

Note A method of isolating different components in a time series, or decomposing the time series, is called the classical time series decomposition method. This is one of the oldest approaches to forecasting.

The whole area of classical time series analysis is concerned with the theory and practice of how to decompose a time series into these components, estimate them and then recompose to produce forecasts.

4.4.3 A trend component

Let's say that, for practical purposes, we are only interested in estimating the trend and that all the remaining components can be grouped into something that we will call the *residuals* (R), just as was the case with simple regression models. In other words, time series Y in this simplified model now consists of only two components:

$$Y = T + R \tag{4.19}$$

If a trend represents an underlying pattern that the time series follows, than the residuals are something that should randomly oscillate around the trend, which is the assumption we already used in regression analysis. In other words, if we can estimate the underlying trend of a time series, we will not worry about these random residuals fluctuating around the trend line. We can then extrapolate this trend. The trend becomes our forecast of the time series. Admittedly, this forecast will not be 100% accurate as some residual value will be oscillating around the trend, but for all practical purposes, this might be exactly what we want. We are interested in just isolating the trend and extrapolating it into the future, which produces the forecast value for our time series.

Note Fitting a trend to a time series and extrapolating it into the future is the most elementary form of forecasting.

4.4.4 Using a trend chart function to forecast time series

Earlier when we described how to right click on the time series chart to invoke the Trendline dialogue box, we have not described how to extrapolate the trend line using the built-in option. Let's look at it.

Under the forecast section in the dialogue box we have opted for automatic trend line that will move five periods in the future.

We also opted to display on the chart the trend equation as well as the R-squared value. How will this look like and what is the meaning of all of this? Figure 4.33 illustrates the Add Trendline dialogue box.

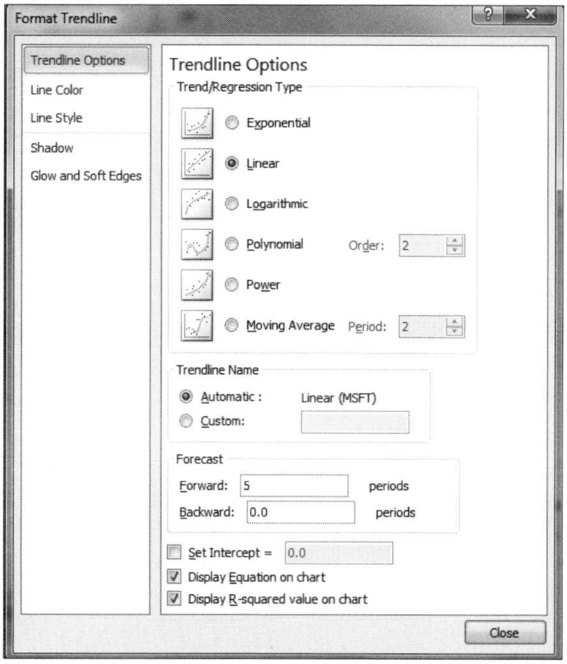

Figure 4.33

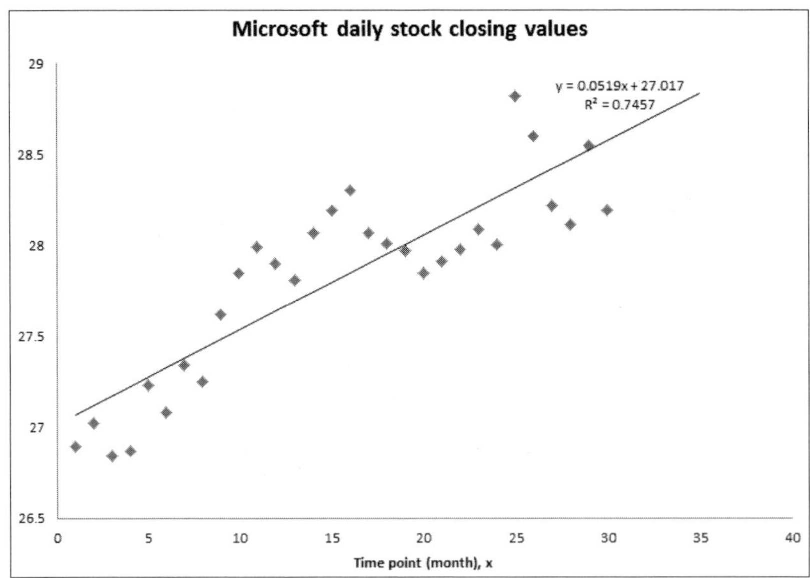

Figure 4.34

The final chart with the trend line, equation of the trend and R-squared value.

First, we can see that the trend has now being extended five periods in the future, as expected. This is effectively our forecast.

We can see that the actual time series is not a smooth straight line, but it oscillates around the linear trend. By extrapolating our straight line, or linear trend in the future, we are stating that the actual values might be a bit a drift, but we believe that they will be inside some confidence factor, as we will describe later on. Excel does not just gives us a pictorial of this trend line, but the actual equation of this line. By ticking an option in a dialogue box, we can see that this trend line is moving in accordance with the equation: y = 0.0519x + 27.017. We'll explain this in a minute. The R-squared (or R^2) value is 0.74. Let's refresh what we know about this statistic. When fitting a line to a data set we measure how closely the trend line fits the actual data. Every deviation is squared and all these values are summed to create the Total Sum of Squares (SST). The theory suggests that the SST consists of the Regression Sum of Squares (SSR) and the Residual Sum of Squares (SSE). R-squared is a coefficient that measures how closely is the actual time series approximated (or fitted) by a trend line. The formula is:

$$R^2 = 1 - \frac{SSE}{SST} \tag{4.20}$$

R-squared is actually the coefficient of determination. As we know, the square root of this value would give us the coefficient of correlation. Clearly this coefficient is checking how closely the trend line and the actual time series are related. In effect it tells us how much of the time series variations are 'left out' after we fitted the trend line.

Note The closer R^2 is to the value of 1, the better the fit of the trend to time series. In our case R-squared is 0.74, which is OK. This confirms that our trend is approximating, or fitting, the data reasonably well. Some 26% (1 – 0.74 = 0.26) of data variations are not captured by the trend line. This is acceptable.

4.4.5 Moving averages as a trend function

Moving averages, as the word implies, are a series of averages that track the movements of a time series often much better than a single average value. This is especially true if a time series shows non-stationary (upward or downward) movements.

Example 4.6

We created a short time series and calculated moving averages of order 3 and 5 in Figure 4.35.

	A	B	C	D	E	F
1	Period	Series	3MA	3MA Formulae	5MA	5MA Formulae
2	1	150			252	=SUM($B$2:$B$6)/5
3	2	250	200.00	=SUM(B2:B4)/3	252	=SUM($B$2:$B$6)/5
4	3	200	270.00	=SUM(B3:B5)/3	252	=SUM($B$2:$B$6)/5
5	4	360	286.67	=SUM(B4:B6)/3	252	=SUM($B$2:$B$6)/5
6	5	300			252	=SUM($B$2:$B$6)/5

Figure 4.35

→ Excel manual method

Moving average formula Cell C3 Formula = SUM(B2:B4)/3
Cell C4 Formula = SUM(B3:B5)/3, etc.
Copy down

Moving averages are dynamical averages that change in accordance with the number of periods for which they are calculated. A general formula for moving averages is:

$$M_t = \frac{x_t + x_{t-1} + \ldots + x_{t-N+1}}{N} = \frac{\sum_{i=t}^{t-N+1} x_i}{N} \tag{4.21}$$

In this formula t is the time period and N is the number of observations taken into calculation. In column C in Fig. 4.32 we are using three observations as a basis for calculating moving averages. The advantage of using an odd number for N and taking an odd number of elements into a formula, is that we can centre the moving average value in the middle of the interval, as per Figure 4.32. This implies that most of the time we'll use the odd number of interval, as it is easier to centre the values. In our case, the moving average of order 3 would be centred at period two (position $= \frac{1}{2}(3 + 1) = 2^{nd}$ number) is calculated as:

$$M_2 = \frac{x_3 + x_2 + x_1}{3} = \frac{150 + 250 + 200}{3} = 200$$

If we had a moving average of order 5 then the first moving average value would be centered at t = 3 (position $= \frac{1}{2}(5 + 1) = 3^{rd}$ number).

Note Equation 4.21 can also be rewritten as: $M_t = M_{t-1} + \frac{x_t - x_{t-N}}{N}$. In other words, if we do not know the value of the first observation in the moving average interval, we can still estimate the current moving average from the previous value of the moving average, plus the other value from the interval. Although this might appear to be a useless fact here, you will see why we mentioned it when we discuss exponential smoothing.

Let us now use a little longer time series and see how to use moving averages for forecasting purposes. If a series is horizontal (stationary) and we just want to predict a single future value of this series, we already said that using a simple average value of the series is almost as good as any other method. Let's see what happens with the non-stationary series, i.e. the one with an upward or downword trend.

Example 4.7

Consider the data series as in Example 4.5, i.e. Microsoft stock daily closing values.

Figure 4.36 represents a scatter plot of series against time point and we observe that the data shows an upward trend.

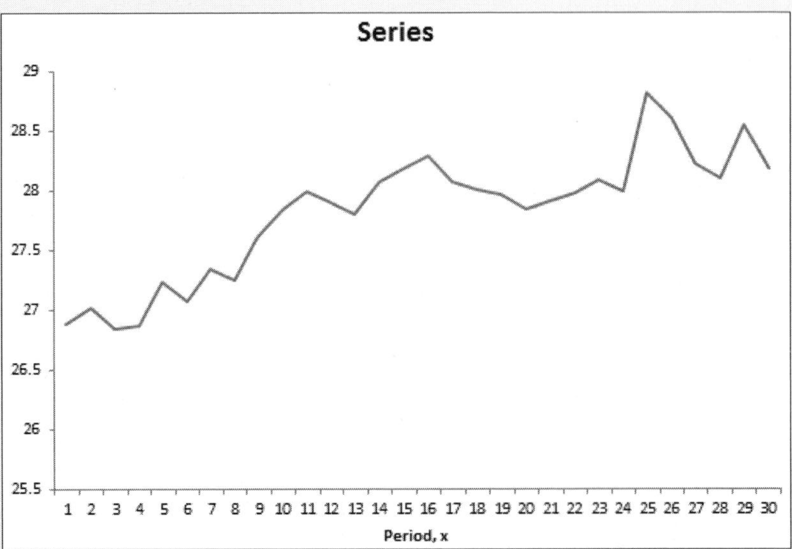

Figure 4.36

If the data values were fluctuating about a horizontal line then we could have just extended this horizontal line (which actually represents the average) in the future. This type of time series is called a stationary time series. In case of a stationary time series, the mean is its best predictor. This method does not produce very accurate forecasts, but the results will be precise enough.

Note In case of a stationary, namely horizontally moving time series, the mean value line becomes effectively a trend that can be fitted to the time series and used for extrapolations.

However, the mean value line is completely unusable if we have a dynamic time series showing strong non-stationarity and exhibiting either a growth, or decline. Figure 4.36 suggests that the mean value is not necessarily the best trend line, so, rather than using a linear trend line, we will use moving averages as an effective trend. One of the Trendline functions that Excel offers is called Moving Averages. If we right click on the time series this, as we know, invokes a dialogue box with several options included.

If we click on the option called 'Add Trendline...', this invokes the next dialogue box, and we select the moving averages option. This option gives us a chance to put the number of observations we can include in the moving average and in our case we inserted 3 as the number of periods to be include, as illustrated in Figure 4.37.

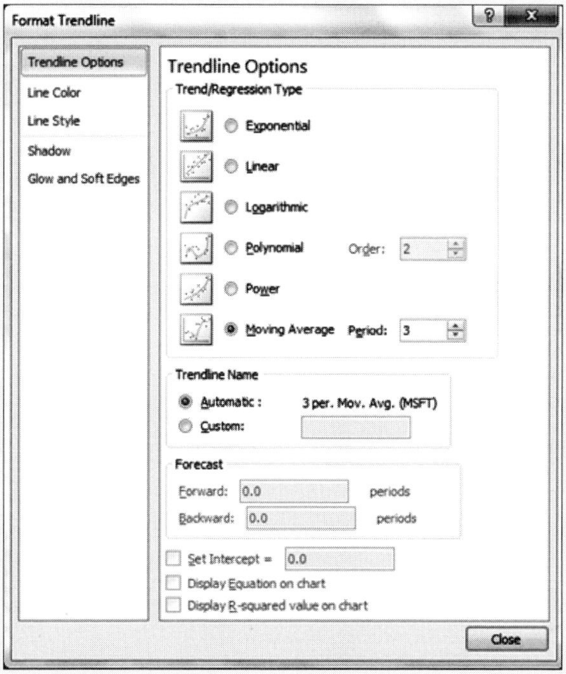

Figure 4.37

Excel will automatically start charting the moving average from the last observation in the period specified (in this case three). This is somewhat different to what we did earlier when we placed the moving average in the centre of the interval for which it is calculated. A simple reason for this is that here we are trying to predict the series, and this is going to help us to achieve this.

Note Click on Trending Name: Automatic to update trendline name in menu e.g. should say 3 per. Mov. Avg (Series).

Figure 4.38 illustrates the point for three-period moving averages.

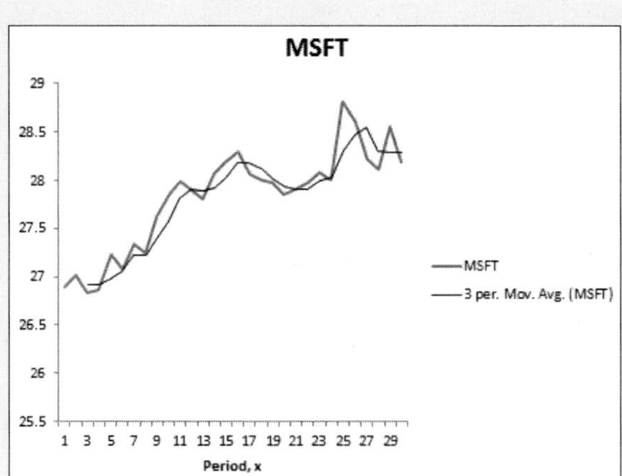

Figure 4.38

So, how is the moving average approach used to produce forecasts? All we need to do is to shift the moving average plot, as produced by Excel, by one observation. In other words, the moving average value for the first three observations (assuming we are using moving averages for three periods) becomes the forecast for the fourth observation. The fifth observation is predicted by using the second three period moving average (observations two to four), and so on. Unfortunately, this is not possible using the Excel method described here. Excel just produces a graph, without any numbers, so shifting the data is not possible.

In this case it is much more practical to calculate moving averages manually. Figure 4.39 shows how they were calculated in this particular case.

	A	B	C	D
1	Period	MSFT	3MA	
2	1	26.89		
3	2	27.02		
4	3	26.84		
5	4	26.87	26.92	=AVERAGE(B2:B4)
6	5	27.23	26.91	=AVERAGE(B3:B5)
30	29	28.55	28.31	=AVERAGE(B27:B29)
31	30	28.19	28.29	=AVERAGE(B28:B30)
32	31		28.28	=AVERAGE(B29:B31)

Figure 4.39

→ Excel Formula Method

Moving averages Cell C5	Formula = AVERAGE(B2:B4)
	Copy down C4:C32
Forecast Cell C32	Formula = AVERAGE(B29:B31)

As stated earlier, we need to remember that the more we extend the number of periods used for calculating the moving average, the smoother this newly created curve will be. If we take into account all the observations in the series, needless to say, we will have only one moving average value and it will be identical to the mean value of the overall time series.

Note Moving averages as a technique are acceptable for trending and forecasting, providing we are interested in forecasting only one future period.

Let's go back to an attempt to create this data automatically. An option is to use the Excel ToolPak macro by selecting Data > Data Analysis > Moving Average.

Figure 4.40 illustrates the Moving Average menu for this problem with series data in Cells B2:B31, moving average is of order 3, output range is C2, and choose chart output.

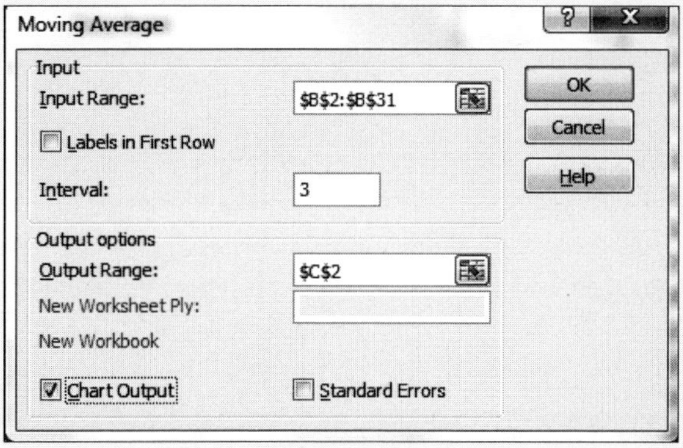

Figure 4.40

Figure 4.41 illustrates the Excel solution.

	A	B	C
1	Period	MSFT	
2	1	26.89	#N/A
3	2	27.02	#N/A
4	3	26.84	26.91667
5	4	26.87	26.91
6	5	27.23	26.98
7	6	27.08	27.06
8	7	27.34	27.21667
9	8	27.25	27.22333
10	9	27.62	27.40333
11	10	27.85	27.57333
12	11	27.99	27.82
13	12	27.9	27.91333
14	13	27.81	27.9

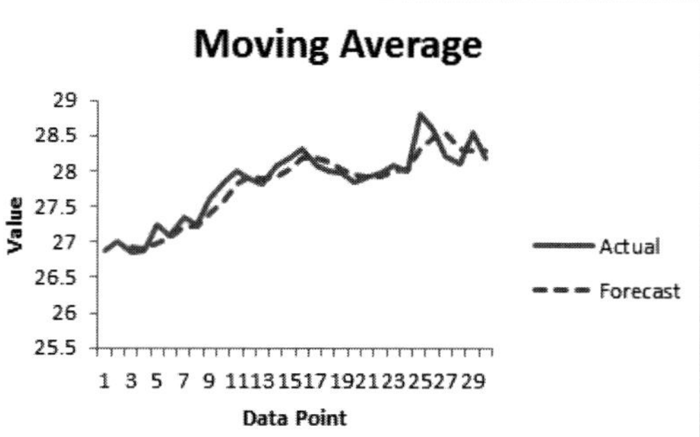

Figure 4.41

The screenshot includes 13 time points illustrated but remember that we have 30 time points in total.

In this case it is easy to insert just one blank cell in C2. This will shift the moving averages time series by one observation and the last moving average value for B29:B31 becomes a forecast for period B32, that is, the future 31st observation. The graph in Figure 4.42 shows the final result.

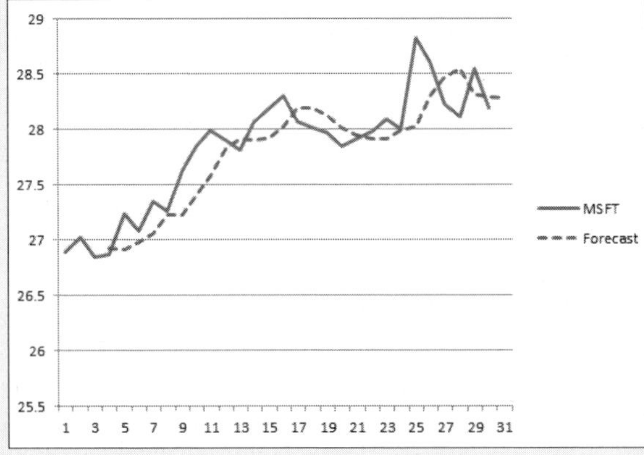

Figure 4.42

Just for the record, the forecast produced using moving averages for period 31 has the value of 28.28. Using the trend extrapolation, we predicted 28.62. The actual value was 28.3. As we can see, the moving averages method produced much more accurate value. Unfortunately, the major limitation of this method is that you can only predict one value in the future. Trend, although less accurate in the short run, was capable of extending the values well into the future.

Student exercises

X4.6 Take Microsoft data from Table 4.5 fit 3-period moving averages using Data Analysis Tool Pak. Select Standard Errors on the dialogue box. The values will be produced in the column next to the moving average column. What do you think these standard errors mean?

4.5 Classical time series decomposition

If we are not satisfied by just extrapolating the trend, or calculating moving averages as the trend values, we already indicated the various components that a time series consists of can isolated and used for a bit more sophisticated forecasts. These components, once identified, can be put together in two different fundamental models, and they are:

$$Y = T + C + S + I \tag{4.22}$$

$$Y = T \times C \times S \times I \tag{4.23}$$

As we can see, the components could be either in an additive relationship or a multiplicative relationship. Hence, these models are called: the additive model and the multiplicative model.

Note Unfortunately, many real-life time series do not fall into those two categories. It is not unusual to find time series that comply broadly with a multiplicative model, but should not be multiplied with some sort of irregular component. A more realistic model, in this case, is a mixed multiplicative model with the irregular component just added to other components:

$$Y = (T \times C \times S) + I \tag{4.24}$$

In addition to the pseudo additive model above, a pseudo multiplicative model is also sometimes found to fit some real-life data most closely:

$$Y = T \times (C + S + I) \tag{4.25}$$

For the sake of simplicity we will refer to the models that do not fall into an additive or multiplicative model category as mixed models.

How do we estimate all these components and what are the rules for selecting the appropriate model? The method that is based on this approach is called the classical time series decomposition method. The main objective of this approach to forecasting is to identify the components present in the time series, separate them, i.e. decompose the series, and finally recompose them using one of the models. We will start with the multiplicative model and show how, by using use some basic mathematical operations, the components can be isolated. For the sake of simplicity, in our first example we shall ignore the seasonal component. The time series, in this case, consists of only the T, C and I components and has a form: $Y = T \times C \times I$. We already know how to calculate the **Trend component**, so let's focus on the rest.

4.5.1 Cyclical time series only

If we divide the time series with the calculated trend values of this time series, we obtain some interesting results. A simple formula describes this operation:

$$\frac{Y}{T} = \frac{T \times C \times I}{T} = C \times I \tag{4.26}$$

Example 4.8

In order to illustrate better what we are doing, we'll take a real life series as an example. We'll take the time series that describes the UK Gross Fixed Capital Formation; Business Investment in GBP mill from 1983 to 2005. The data set is given in Table 4.6.

X

trend component one of the components that a time series is built of. It represents a long range direction any underlying shape of the time series.

Period	Series	Period	Series	Period	Series
1	41856	11	60912	21	109218
2	46689	12	63839	22	111765
3	50476	13	68840	23	115116
4	49581	14	76053		
5	54993	15	83481		
6	64247	16	100225		
7	72052	17	104205		
8	71666	18	108933		
9	65802	19	110390		
10	63277	20	111678		

Table 4.6

Figure 4.43 shows the original time series for which we are trying to identify constituent components and the underlying trend.

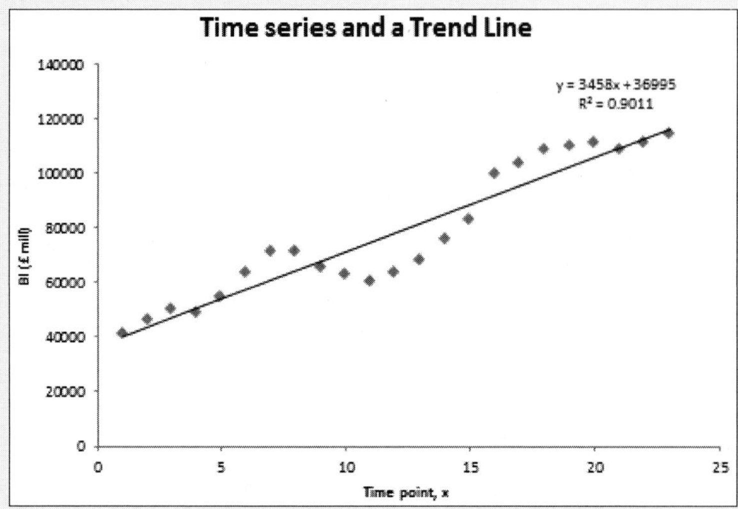

Figure 4.43

According to Equation (4.26) we need to divide every observation in the time series by the corresponding trend values. What is left over is a cyclical component containing irregular variations. Figure 4.44 illustrates the Excel solution.

These two components in column D, still combined into one set of values, can be visualized as jumping up and down around the trend (see Figure 4.45).

Figure 4.46 illustrates how C and I component were segregated and how to calculate the typical C.

	A	B	C	D
1	Period, x	Series, y	T	C*I
2	1	41856	40453.14	1.03
3	2	46689	43911.13	1.06
4	3	50476	47369.12	1.07
5	4	49581	50827.11	0.98
6	5	54993	54285.11	1.01
7	6	64247	57743.10	1.11
8	7	72052	61201.09	1.18
9	8	71666	64659.08	1.11
10	9	65802	68117.07	0.97
11	10	63277	71575.06	0.88
12	11	60912	75033.05	0.81
13	12	63839	78491.04	0.81
14	13	68840	81949.03	0.84
15	14	76053	85407.03	0.89
16	15	83481	88865.02	0.94
17	16	100225	92323.01	1.09
18	17	104205	95781.00	1.09
19	18	108933	99238.99	1.10
20	19	110390	102696.98	1.07
21	20	111678	106154.97	1.05
22	21	109218	109612.96	1.00
23	22	111765	113070.95	0.99
24	23	115116	116528.95	0.99

Figure 4.44

Calculation of C × I (the combined cyclical and irregular components)

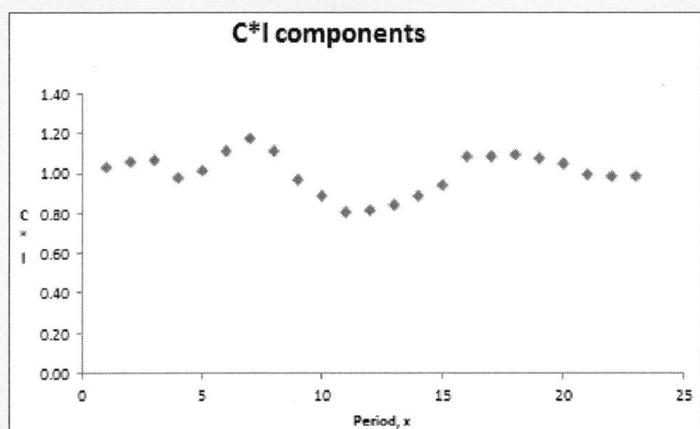

Figure 4.45

Combined cyclical and irregular component

	A	B	C	D	E	F	G
1	Period, x	Series, y	T	C*I	MA CI = C	I	Typ C
2	1	41856	40453.14	1.03			
3	2	46689	43911.13	1.06	1.05	1.01	0.94
4	3	50476	47369.12	1.07	1.03	1.03	0.94
5	4	49581	50827.11	0.98	1.02	0.96	0.95
6	5	54993	54285.11	1.01	1.03	0.98	1.00
7	6	64247	57743.10	1.11	1.10	1.01	1.07
8	7	72052	61201.09	1.18	1.13	1.04	1.11
9	8	71666	64659.08	1.11	1.08	1.02	1.09
10	9	65802	68117.07	0.97	0.99	0.98	1.03
11	10	63277	71575.06	0.88	0.89	1.00	0.96
12	11	60912	75033.05	0.81	0.84	0.97	0.92
13	12	63839	78491.04	0.81	0.82	0.99	0.91
14	13	68840	81949.03	0.84	0.85	0.99	0.94
15	14	76053	85407.03	0.89	0.89	1.00	0.95
16	15	83481	88865.02	0.94	0.97	0.97	1.00
17	16	100225	92323.01	1.09	1.04	1.05	1.07
18	17	104205	95781.00	1.09	1.09	1.00	1.11
19	18	108933	99238.99	1.10	1.09	1.01	1.09
20	19	110390	102696.98	1.07	1.07	1.00	1.03
21	20	111678	106154.97	1.05	1.04	1.01	0.96
22	21	109218	109612.96	1.00	1.01	0.98	0.92
23	22	111765	113070.95	0.99	0.99	1.00	0.91
24	23	115116	116528.95	0.99			0.94

Figure 4.46

→ Excel solution

Period (year) Cells A2:A24	Values
Data/Time series Cell B2:B24	Values
Trend Cells C2:C24	Formula = TREND($B$2:$B$24,$A$2:$A$24,A2)
	Copy formula C2:C24
C × I component Cell D2:D24	Formula = B2/C2
	Copy formula D2:D24
Just C component Cells E3:E23	Formula = SUM(D2:D4)/3
	Copy formula E3:E23
Just I component Cells F3:F23	Formula = D3/E3
	Copy formula F3:F23
Typical C comp. Cells G3	Formula = (E3+E13)/2
	Copy formula G3:G13
Cells G14	Formula = (E4+E14)/2
	Copy formula G14:G23

In column C of Figure 4.46, we used the Excel function TREND to calculate the trend. These two columns B and C are charted in Figure 4.43. Column D divides every observation by its corresponding trend value, as per Equation (4.21), which gave us the values to produce the chart as in Figure 4.45.

Column E eliminates the irregular component by calculating moving averages of column D. In previous chapters we stated that moving averages, as a technique, smooth the curve to which they are applied. This means that by taking the moving averages of the above combined values (i.e. cyclical and irregular component together) we can eliminate the irregular variations and isolate the pure cyclical component. Therefore:

$$\text{Moving Averages of } C \times I = C \tag{4.27}$$

Figure 4.47 shows what this newly isolated cyclical component (column E) looks like. We can see that our series consists of two cycles. The cycles are not identical, which is to be expected,

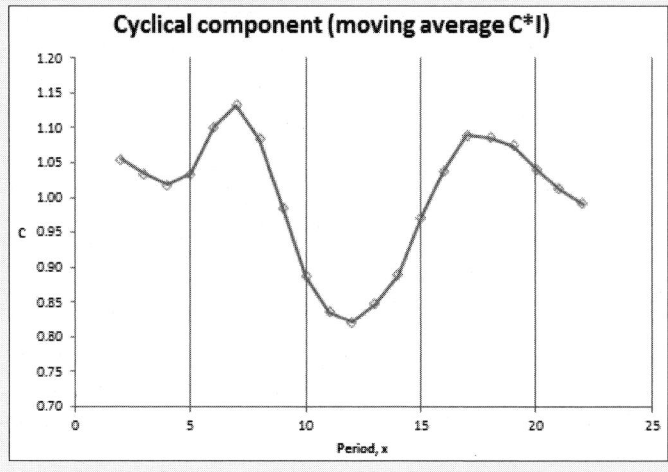

Figure 4.47
Pure cyclical component isolated in the series

so for forecasting purposes they need to be made more regular. One way to do this is to find average values for every corresponding value in the cycle.

If we look at the two peaks, they are ten periods apart (Cell G8 to G18), where the first one belongs to period seven, whilst the second one to period seventeen. From this we can build an average value by adding up these two values and dividing it by two. We copy the cells from G3 to G13. When we reached the cell G14, there are no future values from column F to take into account. Check the spreadsheet on the web and you will see that at this point we take the first historical cycle value that is available. In this case, G14 = (E4 + E14)/2 and copy this formula from G14 to G23. Figure 4.48 gives us the final value of what we would call typical cyclical values.

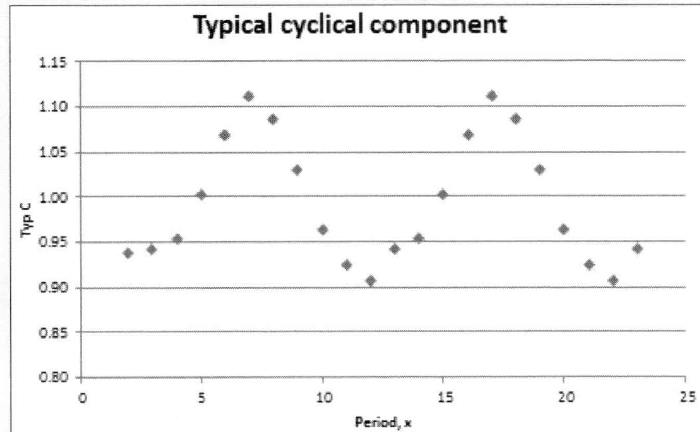

Figure 4.48 Typical cyclical component

> **Note** If we had three cycles, for example, to calculate the typical value for every specific cycle we would add up the three corresponding values from every cycle and divide them by three.

Column F now contains pure Irregular component that we obtained by dividing the values from column D by E. This an intuitive operation. As column D contains both the component C and I mixed up, if we divide it by just C (column E), what remains is a pure component I. In other words:

$$\frac{C \times I}{C} = I \tag{4.28}$$

The values of just component I are given in Figure 4.49.

The irregulars (residuals) appear to be random, so our procedure looks promising (a more rigorous approach to confirm this is needed, as in regression analysis, but we'll conveniently skip this step). How do we produce the forecasts now? This process constrasts stongly with the decomposition. We need to 'recompose' the components. As in our case we only have the T (trend) and C (cyclical component), and this was a multiplicative model, we just need to multiply them.

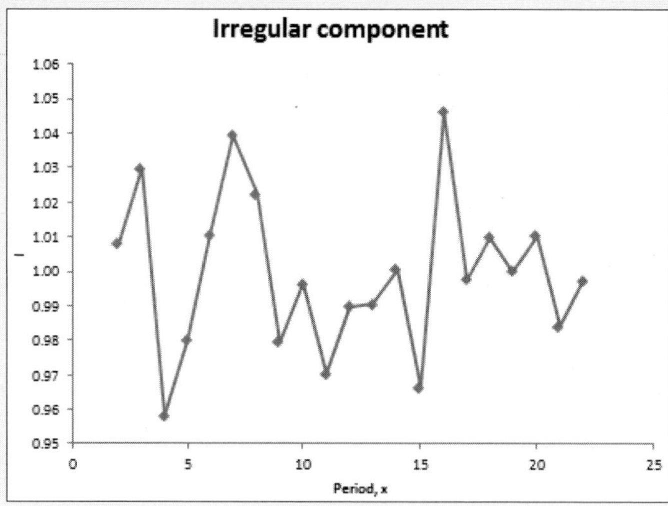

Figure 4.49
Decomposition of the time series

Figure 4.50 shows just a few first and the last periods.

	A	B	C	D	E	F	G	H
1	Period, x	Series, y	T	C*I	MA CI = C	I	Typ C	Re-composition
2	1	41856	40453.14	1.03				
3	2	46689	43911.13	1.06	1.05	1.01	0.94	41193.71674
20	19	110390	102696.98	1.07	1.07	1.00	1.03	105830.3819
21	20	111678	106154.97	1.05	1.04	1.01	0.96	102354.8916
22	21	109218	109612.96	1.00	1.01	0.98	0.92	101320.2031
23	22	111765	113070.95	0.99	0.99	1.00	0.91	102477.8383
24	23	115116	116528.95	0.99			0.94	109695.9388
25	24		119986.94				0.95	114468.2806
26	25		123444.93				1.00	123787.2835
27	26		126902.92				1.07	135700.0345
28	27		130360.91				1.11	144907.5907
29	28		133818.90				1.09	145243.1071
30	29		137276.89				1.03	141465.3651
31	30		140734.88				0.96	135696.929

Figure 4.50
Re-composition of the time series and forecasts

→ Excel solution

Forecast Period Cells A25:A31 — Values

Extrapolate trend Cell C25 — Copy formula from C24:C31.

Recomposed values Cells H3 — Formula = C3*G3
Copy H3:H23

Extrapolated typical C Cells G24 — Formula = (E4 + E14)/2
Copy G24:G31

Future forecasts Cells H24 — Formula = C24*G24
Copy H24:H31

Figure 4.51 shows the shape of the recomposed series as well as the forecasts.

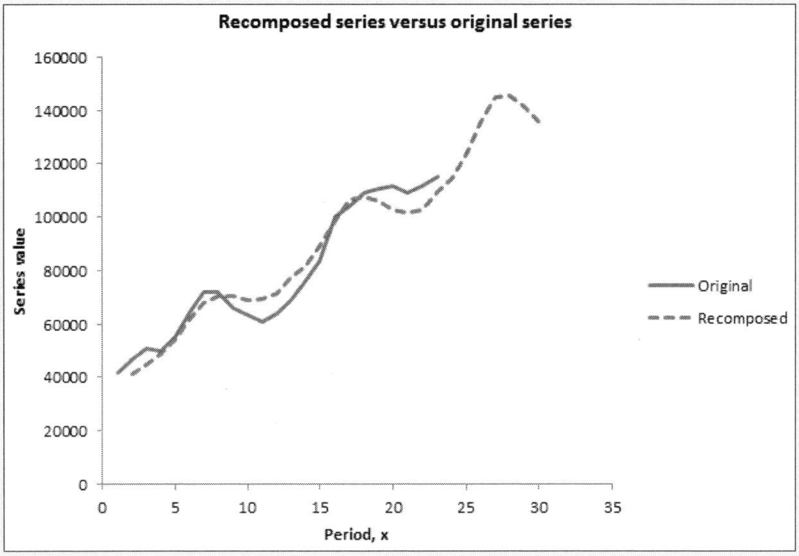

Figure 4.51

As we can see we managed to mimic the past movements reasonably well and fit the data using this method. We also produced a forecast that looks credible.

4.5.2 Seasonal time series only

We will now explore how to treat time series with a seasonal component. If we have monthly data and the seasonal component needs to be isolated, it is done in a similar way as with the cyclical component, although there are several different ways to perform calculations. Let us use a time series without a cyclical component. As in the previous example, the seasonal component is extracted as follows:

$$\frac{Y}{T} = \frac{T \times S \times I}{T} = S \times I \tag{4.29}$$

By dividing the original series with the trend values we get, in this case, the seasonal and irregular variations (components) combined together.

Example 4.9

Figure 4.52 shows a spreadsheet of one such example. The time series depicts US Total New Privately Owned Housing Units Started in thousands between 2002 and 2005. Column E in Figure 4.48 contains the series with trend component eliminated. However, in this example we are going to call this column an Index column, as it is actually telling us how much, in terms of index numbers, every month is above or below the trend line.

	A	B	C	D	E	F	G	H
1	TIME	PERIOD	SERIES	Trend	Index	Deseasonal	Residual	Recomp
2	Jan 2002.	1	110.4	137.3	80.38			
3	Feb	2	120.4	138.2	87.11			
4	Mar	3	138.2	139.1	99.36			
5	Apr	4	148.8	140.0	106.32			
6	May	5	165.5	140.8	117.52			
7	Jun	6	160.3	141.7	113.12			
8	Jul	7	155.9	142.6	109.35			
9	Aug	8	147.0	143.4	102.48			
10	Sep	9	155.6	144.3	107.82			
11	Oct	10	146.8	145.2	101.11			
12	Nov	11	133	146.1	91.06			
13	Dec	12	123.1	146.9	83.78			
14	Jan 2003.	13	117.8	147.8	79.70			
15	Feb	14	109.7	148.7	73.78			
16	Mar	15	147.2	149.6	98.43			
17	Apr	16	151.2	150.4	100.51			
18	May	17	165.0	151.3	109.06			
19	Jun	18	174.5	152.2	114.67			
20	Jul	19	175.8	153.0	114.87			
21	Aug	20	163.8	153.9	106.42			
22	Sep	21	171.3	154.8	110.67			
23	Oct	22	173.5	155.7	111.46			
24	Nov	23	153.7	156.5	98.19			
25	Dec	24	144.2	157.4	91.61			
26	Jan 2004.	25	124.5	158.3	78.66			
27	Feb	26	126.4	159.2	79.42			
28	Mar	27	173.8	160.0	108.61			
29	Apr	28	179.5	160.9	111.56			
30	May	29	187.6	161.8	115.97			
31	Jun	30	172.3	162.6	105.94			
32	Jul	31	182	163.5	111.31			
33	Aug	32	185.9	164.4	113.09			
34	Sep	33	164	165.3	99.24			
35	Oct	34	181.3	166.1	109.13			
36	Nov	35	138.1	167.0	82.69			
37	Dec	36	140.2	167.9	83.52			
38	Jan 2005.	37	142.9	168.7	84.68			
39	Feb	38	149.1	169.6	87.90			
40	Mar	39	156.2	170.5	91.62			
41	Apr	40	184.6	171.4	107.72			
42	May	41	197.9	172.2	114.90			
43	Jun	42	192.8	173.1	111.38			
44	Jul	43	187.6	174.0	107.83			
45	Aug	44	192	174.9	109.81			
46	Sep	45	187.9	175.7	106.93			
47	Oct	46	180.4	176.6	102.15			
48	Nov	47	160.7	177.5	90.55			
49	Dec	48	136.0	178.3	76.26			

Figure 4.52

Extracting seasonal component

→ Excel solution

Year/months Cells A2:A49	Values
Period Cell B2:B49	Values
Data/Time series Cell C2:C49	Values
Trend Cells D2	Formula = TREND($C$2:$C$49,$B$2:$B$49,B2)
	Copy down D2:D49
Index Cells E2	Formula = (C2/D2)*100
	Copy down E2:E49

The irregular component needs to be eliminated from the indices in column E. There is a very elegant and easy way of doing this. If we take the same months in every year of our time series (see Figure 4.53), and find the average value of them, we can get rid of irregulars. It is important to stress that we should not use the mean as an average value but, rather, the median. The mean is very sensitive to extremes, which might affect our average for the month.

To calculate the medians we used Excel MEDIAN function. Unfortunately, the median values do not eliminate irregulars completely. If there is no influence of a seasonal component then, in theory, the value of each month should be equal to 100 (and we can call it a monthly index).

Of course, the total value of all the indices for the year should then be equal to 1,200. If we add our monthly indices the value could be somewhat above or below 1,200 (in our case, in Figure 4.53 it was 1,203). Dividing 1,200 with our annual value, we get a correction factor of 0.998 (cell F78) with which we have to multiply our seasonal indices, that is, median values (see column G in Figure 4.53).

	A	B	C	D	E	F	G
63			YEAR				
64	Month	2002	2003	2004	2005	Average	Seasonal Indices
65	Jan	80.38	79.70	78.66	84.68	80.04	79.85
66	Feb	87.11	73.78	79.42	87.90	83.27	83.07
67	Mar	99.36	98.43	108.61	91.62	98.89	98.66
68	Apr	106.32	100.51	111.56	107.72	107.02	106.77
69	May	117.52	109.06	115.97	114.90	115.44	115.17
70	Jun	113.12	114.67	105.94	111.38	112.25	111.99
71	Jul	109.35	114.87	111.31	107.83	110.33	110.07
72	Aug	102.48	106.42	113.09	109.81	108.11	107.86
73	Sep	107.82	110.67	99.24	106.93	107.37	107.12
74	Oct	101.11	111.46	109.13	102.15	105.64	105.40
75	Nov	91.06	98.19	82.69	90.55	90.80	90.59
76	Dec	83.78	91.61	83.52	76.26	83.65	83.45
77	SUM					1202.81	1200.00
78	C. F.					1.00	

Figure 4.53

Calculating typical seasonal indices

➔ Excel solution

Months Cells A65:A76	Values
Monthly indices 2002–05 Cells B65:E76	Values
Average monthly indices Cells F65	Formula = MEDIAN(B65:E65)
	Copy down F65:F76
Sum of monthly indices Cell F77	Formula = SUM(F65:F76)
Correction factor Cell F78	Formula = 1200/F77
Seasonal indices Cells G65	Formula = F65*$F$78
	Copy down G65:G76
Check Index sum Cell G77	Formula = SUM(G65:G76)

These typical seasonal indices from column G are charted in Figure 4.54.

Before we proceed, let us just step back to explain columns F and G in Figure 4.53. Column F shows how the time series would look if there were no seasonal influences at all (we just divided each actual value with the corresponding typical seasonal index value). These deseasonalized values, still containing some irregular component, are shown in Figure 4.54.

We eliminated the irregular component by dividing the deseasonalized values of the series with the trend. What we are left with is a measure of other influences or an index of irregular fluctuations (column G in Figure 4.55). Each value is telling us how much a particular month is affected by other influences, and not only seasonal fluctuations. Figure 4.56 shows the chart of this component and Figure 4.57 the remaining component—the residuals.

X

seasonal indices are the values that indicate by how much a time series deviates from the trend in every seasonal period. As the deviation is typically multiplied by 100, the value are called 'indices'.

typical seasonal index a single value for every seasonal period that represents all corresponding seasonal periods.

deseasonalized values of the variable from which any seasonal influences have been removed.

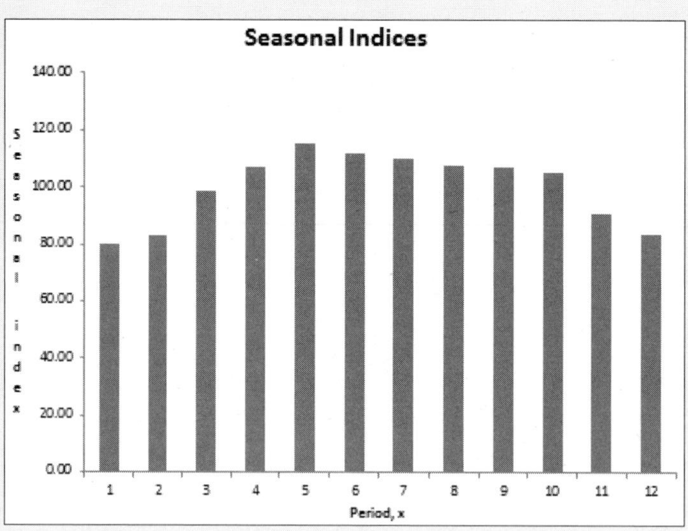

Figure 4.54

Typical seasonal indices

	A	B	C	D	E	F	G	H
1	TIME	PERIOD	SERIES	Trend	Index	Deseasonal	Residual	Recomp
2	Jan 2002.	1	110.4	137.3	80.38	138.25	100.66	109.67
3	Feb	2	120.4	138.2	87.11	144.93	104.86	114.82
4	Mar	3	138.2	139.1	99.36	140.07	100.71	137.23
5	Apr	4	148.8	140.0	106.32	139.36	99.57	149.44
6	May	5	165.5	140.8	117.52	143.71	102.04	162.19
7	Jun	6	160.3	141.7	113.12	143.14	101.01	158.69
8	Jul	7	155.9	142.6	109.35	141.64	99.34	156.93
9	Aug	8	147.0	143.4	102.48	136.29	95.01	154.73
10	Sep	9	155.6	144.3	107.82	145.26	100.65	154.60
11	Oct	10	146.8	145.2	101.11	139.28	95.93	153.03
12	Nov	11	133	146.1	91.06	146.81	100.51	132.32
13	Dec	12	123.1	146.9	83.78	147.51	100.39	122.62
14	Jan 2003.	13	117.8	147.8	79.70	147.52	99.80	118.03
15	Feb	14	109.7	148.7	73.78	132.05	88.82	123.51
16	Mar	15	147.2	149.6	98.43	149.19	99.76	147.55
17	Apr	16	151.2	150.4	100.51	141.61	94.14	160.61
18	May	17	165.0	151.3	109.06	143.27	94.69	174.24
19	Jun	18	174.5	152.2	114.67	155.82	102.40	170.41
20	Jul	19	175.8	153.0	114.87	159.72	104.36	168.45
21	Aug	20	163.8	153.9	106.42	151.86	98.66	166.02
22	Sep	21	171.3	154.8	110.67	159.91	103.31	165.81
23	Oct	22	173.5	155.7	111.46	164.62	105.75	164.06
24	Nov	23	153.7	156.5	98.19	169.66	108.39	141.80
25	Dec	24	144.2	157.4	91.61	172.80	109.78	131.36
26	Jan 2004.	25	124.5	158.3	78.66	155.91	98.50	126.39
27	Feb	26	126.4	159.2	79.42	152.16	95.61	132.21
28	Mar	27	173.8	160.0	108.61	176.16	110.08	157.88
29	Apr	28	179.5	160.9	111.56	168.12	104.49	171.79
30	May	29	187.6	161.8	115.97	162.90	100.70	186.30
31	Jun	30	172.3	162.6	105.94	153.86	94.60	182.14
32	Jul	31	182	163.5	111.31	165.35	101.13	179.97
33	Aug	32	185.9	164.4	113.09	172.35	104.85	177.31
34	Sep	33	164	165.3	99.24	153.10	92.64	177.02
35	Oct	34	181.3	166.1	109.13	172.02	103.54	175.09
36	Nov	35	138.1	167.0	82.69	152.44	91.28	151.29
37	Dec	36	140.2	167.9	83.52	168.00	100.08	140.09
38	Jan 2005.	37	142.9	168.7	84.68	178.95	106.05	134.75
39	Feb	38	149.1	169.6	87.90	179.48	105.82	140.90
40	Mar	39	156.2	170.5	91.62	158.32	92.86	168.21
41	Apr	40	184.6	171.4	107.72	172.89	100.89	182.96
42	May	41	197.9	172.2	114.90	171.84	99.77	198.36
43	Jun	42	192.8	173.1	111.38	172.16	99.45	193.86
44	Jul	43	187.6	174.0	107.83	170.44	97.97	191.50
45	Aug	44	192	174.9	109.81	178.01	101.80	188.60
46	Sep	45	187.9	175.7	106.93	175.41	99.82	188.24
47	Oct	46	180.4	176.6	102.15	171.16	96.92	186.13
48	Nov	47	160.7	177.5	90.55	177.39	99.96	160.77
49	Dec	48	136.0	178.3	76.26	162.97	91.38	148.83

Figure 4.55

Extracting seasonal component

→ Excel solution

Deseasonalized series	Cells F2	Formula = (C2/G65)*100
		Copy down F2:F13
	Cell F14	Formula = (C14/G65)*100
		Copy down F14:F25
		Repeat for F26:F37 and F38:F49
Residuals	Cells G2	Formula = (F2/D2)*100
		Copy down G2:G49
Recomposition	Cells H2	Formula = (D2*G65)/100
		Copy down H2:H13
	Cell F14	Formula = (D14/G65)*100
		Copy down H14:H25
		Repeat for H26:H37 and H38:H49

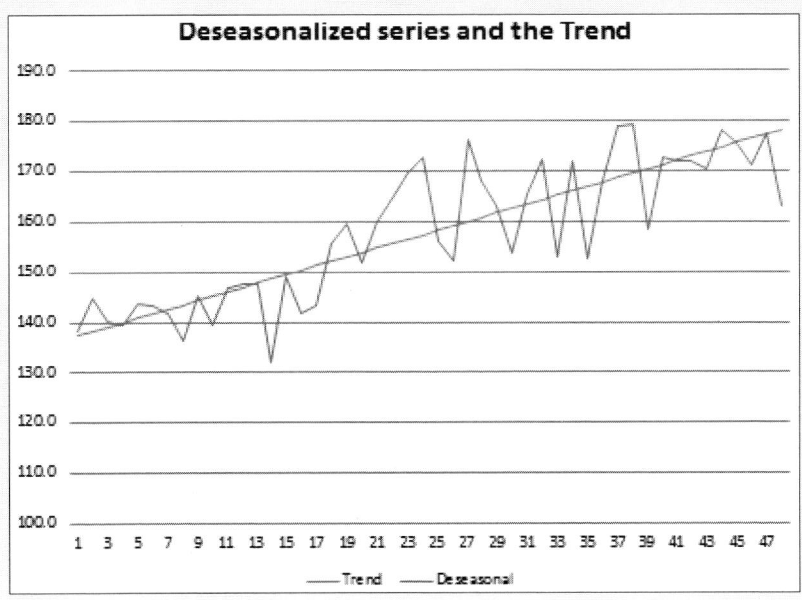

Figure 4.56
Deseasonalized values and the trend

As in the example with the cyclical component, it is easy to recompose the time series and make forecasts. All we need to do is to multiply the trend values with the typical monthly indices.

Figure 4.58 shows how the forecasts were produced for both historical and future periods (the first 12 historical, the last 2 historical and the future 12 observations are only shown). Pay attention to cells H14 and down in this column when copying and pasting the formulae. In cell H13, the formula is =D13*G76/100, that is, the trend value (D13) multiplied by the corresponding index value (G76). The next cell, H14, contains formula =D14*G65/100, because we are back to January and the corresponding typical index is in cell G65.

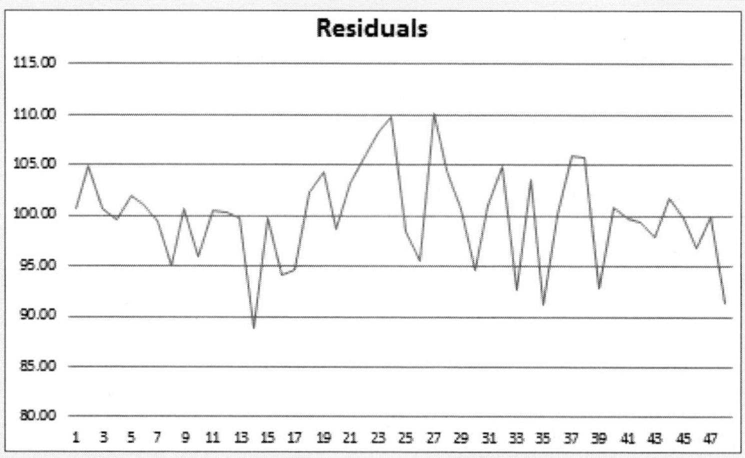

Figure 4.57

Residual component (as an index of irregular influences)

	A	B	C	D	E	F	G	H
1	TIME	PERIOD	SERIES	Trend	Index	Deseasonal	Residual	Recomp
2	Jan 2002.	1	110.4	137.3	80.38	138.25	100.66	109.67
3	Feb	2	120.4	138.2	87.11	144.93	104.86	114.82
4	Mar	3	138.2	139.1	99.36	140.07	100.71	137.23
5	Apr	4	148.8	140.0	106.32	139.36	99.57	149.44
6	May	5	165.5	140.8	117.52	143.71	102.04	162.19
7	Jun	6	160.3	141.7	113.12	143.14	101.01	158.69
8	Jul	7	155.9	142.6	109.35	141.64	99.34	156.93
9	Aug	8	147.0	143.4	102.48	136.29	95.01	154.73
10	Sep	9	155.6	144.3	107.82	145.26	100.65	154.60
11	Oct	10	146.8	145.2	101.11	139.28	95.93	153.03
12	Nov	11	133	146.1	91.06	146.81	100.51	132.32
13	Dec	12	123.1	146.9	83.78	147.51	100.39	122.62
48	Nov	47	160.7	177.5	90.55	177.39	99.96	160.77
49	Dec	48	136.0	178.3	76.26	162.97	91.38	148.83
50	Jan 2006.	49		179.21	79.85			143
51	Feb	50		180.09	83.07			150
52	Mar	51		180.96	98.66			179
53	Apr	52		181.83	106.77			194
54	May	53		182.70	115.17			210
55	Jun	54		183.58	111.99			206
56	Jul	55		184.45	110.07			203
57	Aug	56		185.32	107.86			200
58	Sep	57		186.19	107.12			199
59	Oct	58		187.06	105.40			197
60	Nov	59		187.94	90.59			170
61	Dec	60		188.81	83.45			158

Figure 4.58

Re-composition of the components (back-forecasts) and the future forecasts

→ Excel solution

Future trend Cells D50 Formula = TREND($C$2:$C$49,$B$2:$B$49,B50)
Copy formula D50:D61

Future Indices Cells E50 Formula = G65
Copy formula E50:E61

Future forecasts Cells H50 Formula = (D50*G65)/100
Copy formula H50:H61

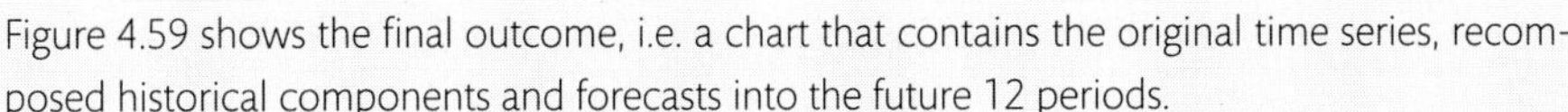

Figure 4.59 shows the final outcome, i.e. a chart that contains the original time series, recomposed historical components and forecasts into the future 12 periods.

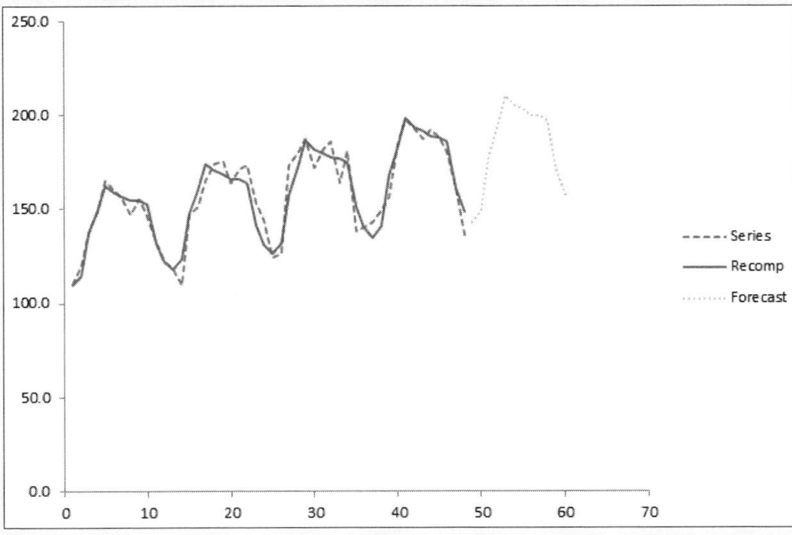

Figure 4.59

Classical decomposition is a very intuitive and simple method. Unfortunately, there is more than one way of achieving the same objective. This might automatically imply that the method is not particularly accurate. Fortunately, that is not true. It is a fairly accurate method, but the problem with it is that it is very arbitrary, as the results can vary depending on who is doing the forecasting. Classical decomposition method is applied in numerous forecasting packages, although hardly ever in its original form as explained in this chapter. Methods, such as Census II, X-11 or X-12-ARIMA are typical examples of the modified decomposition method.

Student exercises

X4.7 Which one of the two time series model is appropriate for modelling monthly ice cream consumption data: Y = (T × C) + I or Y = T + S + I?

4.6 Smoothing methods

Unlike the classical decomposition method, or just straightforward trend extrapolation, which are fundamentally long-term forecasting methods, there is another family of forecasting methods predominantly concerned with short-term forecasts. They fall generally into a class of the so-called smoothing methods. Sometimes we are not interested in long term trends. All we want is the next observation forecast. A good example is forecasting the next month's financial performance, or the sales volume for the next year, or the level

X

classical decomposition method approach to forecasting that decomposes a time series into constituent components (trend, cyclical, seasonal, and random component), makes estimates of every component and then re-composes the time series and extrapolates the values into the future.

ARIMA Auto Regressive Integrated Moving Average. A type of the stochastic model that describes the time series by using both the auto regressive and the moving average component.

of inventory required for the next week. Whatever the need, a long-term trend method is not equipped to give us the best answer. However, a group of methods, fundamentally built around the concept of moving average, is designed to address these needs. These methods 'morphed' into a category called exponential smoothing, another powerful group of methods, and we'll provide overview of the most fundamental forms for all these methods.

4.6.1 Exponential smoothing concept

In order to introduce the exponential smoothing method, we need to assume that one of the ways to think about observations in a time series is to say that the previous value in the series, plus some error element, is the best predictor of the current value (in particular if we are dealing with a stationary time series) as given by Equation (4.30):

$$\hat{y}_t = y_{t-1} + e_t \tag{4.30}$$

We can extend this logic and we can say that every forecasted value in the series can be built that way, that is, it depends on the previous forecasted value, plus some error term. The error term is defined as a difference between the actual value and the forecasted value, i.e. $e_t = y_t - F_t$. This means we can rewrite the above formula as:

$$F_t = F_{t-1} + (y_{t-1} - F_{t-1}) \tag{4.31}$$

Let us now assume that the error element, i.e. $(y_t - F_t)$ is zero. In this case the current forecast is the same as the previous forecast. However, if it is not zero, then under certain circumstances we might be interested in taking just a fraction of this error:

$$F_t = F_{t-1} + \alpha(y_{t-1} - F_{t-1}) \tag{4.32}$$

Note Why a fraction of an error? If every current forecast/observation depends on the previous one and this one depends on the one before, then all the previous errors are in fact embedded in every current observation/forecast. By taking a fraction of error, we are in fact discounting the influence that every previous observation and its associated error has on current observations/forecasts.

We use letter α to describe the fraction and the word 'fraction' implies that α takes values between zero and one. If $\alpha = 0$, then current forecast is the same as the forecast for the previous period. If $\alpha = 1$, then current forecast is also the same as the previous actual value. In order to take just a fraction of that deviation, α has to be greater than zero and smaller than one, i.e. $0 < \alpha < 1$. The forecasts calculated in such a way are in fact smoothing the actual observations. If we plot both the original observations and these newly calculated 'back-forecasts' of the series, we'll see that the back-forecast curve is eliminating some of the dynamics that the original observations exhibit. It is a smoother time series. We'll change the notation and start referring to F_t as S'_t, or the smoothed values. The previous formula is in this case:

$$S'_t = S'_{t-1} + \alpha(y_{t-1} - S'_{t-1}) \tag{4.33}$$

The above formula can be rewritten differently, which is often used, as:

$$S'_t = \alpha y_{t-1} + (1-\alpha)S'_{t-1} \tag{4.34}$$

Note We could have derived to formula (4.34) in a different way. You will recall from the section on moving averages that we've said that: $M_t = M_{t-1} + \frac{y_t - y_{t-N}}{N}$, which can be rewritten as $M_t = \frac{1}{n}y_t + (1-\frac{1}{n})M_{t-1}$. If we say that $\alpha = \frac{1}{n}$ and that M_t is another expression for S_t, then we can see how we got Equation (4.34).

Equations (4.33) and (4.34) are identical and it is a matter of preference which one to use. They both provide identical smoothed approximations of the original time series. This approach to forecasting is called single exponential smoothing method, and we will explain shortly why the word 'exponential' is used.

Note We implied that the smaller the α (i.e. the closer α to zero), the smoother is the series of newly calculated values. Conversely, the larger the α (i.e. the closer α to one), the more impact the deviations have and potentially the more dynamic the fitted series is. When $\alpha = 1$, the smoothed values are identical to the original values, that is, no smoothing is taking place.

The smoothing constant α and the number of elements in the interval for calculating moving averages are in fact related. The formula that defines this relationship is:

$$\alpha = \frac{2}{M+1} \tag{4.35}$$

In the formula above, M is a number of observations used to calculate the moving average. The formula indicates that the moving average for three observations that we used earlier is equivalent to $\alpha = 0.5$. Equally, $\alpha = 0.2$ is equivalent to $M = 9$. So, the smaller the value of the smoothing constant, the more horizontal the series will be, just like in the case when larger number of moving averages is used.

Note If we substituted in the formula for exponential smoothing all the previous values from the series we would see that effectively we are multiplying the newer observations with higher values of α and the older data in the series with the smaller values of α. By doing this we are in effect assigning a higher importance to the more recent observations. As we move further in the past, the value of α falls exponentially. This is the reason why we call it exponential smoothing. In essence, every value in the series is affected by all those that precede it, but the relative weight (importance) of these preceding values declines exponentially the further we go in the past.

X

smoothing constant alpha a constant used in exponential smoothing to predict the future values by 'smoothing' or 'discounting' the influence that all the past values in the series have on this future value. The influence decreases exponentially the further in the past we go.

4.6.2 Forecasting with exponential smoothing

The formula for exponential smoothing can easily be applied in Excel. As an example, we can use the same short time series we used to demonstrate how to use moving averages, illustrated in Figure 4.60.

Example 4.10

	A	B	C	D
1	Period	Yt	Si'	
2	1	150	150	=B2
3	2	250	150	=$B$7*B2+(1-$B$7)*C2
4	3	200	180	
5	4	360	186	
6	5	300	238.2	=$B$7*B5+(1-$B$7)*C5
7	α =	0.3		

Figure 4.60
Applying simple exponential smoothing to data given in Example 4.60.

→ Excel Formula Method

Constant α Cell B7 Value = 0.3

Exponential smoothing

Cell C3 Formula = $B$7*B2+(1-$B$7)*C2

Copy down C3:C6

As was the case with moving averages, in order to forecast one value in the future, we need to shift the exponential smoothing calculations by one period ahead. The last exponentially smoothed value will in effect become a forecast for the following period.

Note Simple Exponential Smoothing, just like the Moving averages method is an acceptable forecasting technique, providing we are interested in forecasting only one future period.

As an alternative to this formula method, Excel gives us an option to use exponential smoothing method from the Data Analysis add-in pack.

Example 4.11

To illustrate, consider the data that represent FTSE100 index values from 18 April 2011 until 25 May 2011, as in Table 4.7.

Period	FTSE100	Period	FTSE100
1	5870.1	13	6018.9
2	5896.9	14	5976
3	6022.3	15	5945
4	6018.3	16	5925.9
5	6069.4	17	5923.7
6	6068.2	18	5861
7	6069.9	19	5923.5
8	6082.9	20	5956
9	5984.1	21	5948.5
10	5920	22	5835.9
11	5976.8	23	5858.4
12	5942.7	24	5870.1

Table 4.7

To activate the Data Analysis option click on Data > Data Analysis > Exponential Smoothing as illustrated in Figure 4.61.

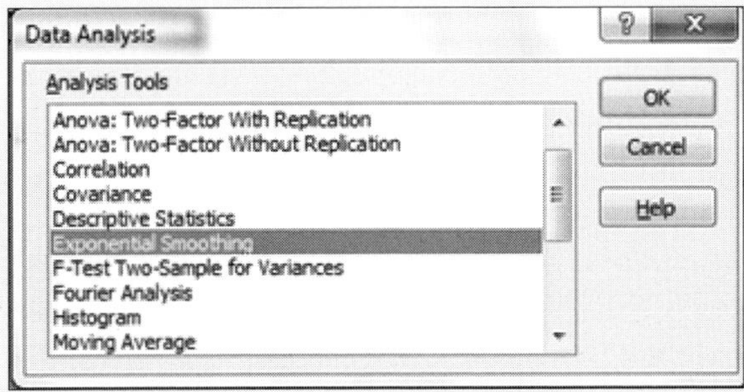

Figure 4.61

Activating the Data Analysis Add-in pack

Selecting the Data Analysis option will trigger another dialogue box in which some of the parameters need to be defined. Figure 4.62 shows an example of selecting a data range B2:B25.

Exponential Smoothing
Input
Input Range: $B$2:$B$25
Damping factor: 0.7
Labels
Output options
Output Range: $C$2
New Worksheet Ply:
New Workbook
Chart Output
Standard Errors
OK
Cancel
Help

Figure 4.62

Selecting data set for exponential smoothing from Data Analysis add-in

> **Note** WARNING: Excel uses the expression 'Damping factor', rather than smoothing constant, or α. Damping factor is defined as $(1-\alpha)$. In other words, if you want α to be 0.3, you must specify in Excel the value of damping factor as 0.7.

If in the dialogue box we select the options to display the chart as well as the standard errors:

Input range: B2:B25

Damping factor: 0.7 (equivalent to $\alpha = 0.3$)

Output range: C2

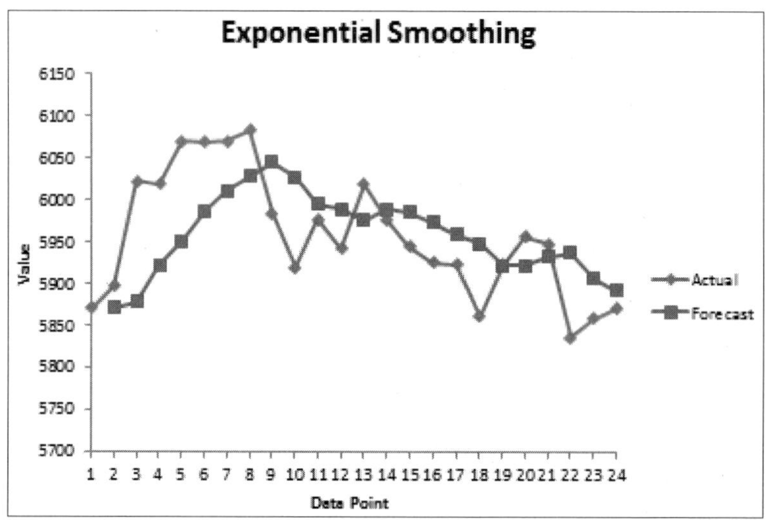

Figure 4.63

Data analysis chart output for Exponential smoothing option

	A	B	C	D	E	F
1	Period	FTSE100			Col C formula	Col D formula
2	1	5870.1	#N/A	#N/A	#N/A	#N/A
3	2	5896.9	5870.1	#N/A	=B2	#N/A
4	3	6022.3	5878.14	#N/A	=0.3*B3+0.7*C3	#N/A
5	4	6018.3	5921.388	#N/A		#N/A
6	5	6069.4	5950.4616	101.4762392		=SQRT(SUMXMY2(B3:B5,C3:C5)/3)
7	6	6068.2	5986.14312	121.5461289		
8	7	6069.9	6010.760184	100.4516638		
9	8	6082.9	6028.502129	90.14283552		
10	9	5984.1	6044.82149	66.30730926		
11	10	5920	6026.605043	58.14850412		
12	11	5976.8	5994.62353	77.4830368		
13	12	5942.7	5989.276471	71.5760966		
14	13	6018.9	5975.30353	67.95018054		
15	14	5976	5988.382471	38.24350971		
16	15	5945	5984.66773	37.52041872		
17	16	5925.9	5972.767411	34.77310537		
18	17	5923.7	5958.707188	36.1635569		
19	18	5861	5948.205031	40.80680554		
20	19	5923.5	5922.043522	60.62665761		
21	20	5956	5922.480465	54.25969032		
22	21	5948.5	5932.536326	53.94564551		
23	22	5835.9	5937.325428	21.45164664		
24	23	5858.4	5906.8978	62.35787988		
25	24	5870.1	5892.34846	65.55911558	=0.3*B24+0.7*C24	=SQRT(SUMXMY2(B22:B24,C22:C24)/3)
26			5885.673922	66.16682948		

Figure 4.64

Exponential smoothing Data analysis add-in sheet output

Part of the Excel output is also the spreadsheet, and Figure 4.64 displays the formulae contained in this spreadsheet (only the first 15 cells are shown here).

First, Excel always ignores the first observation and produces exponential smoothing from the second observation. It also cuts short with the exponential smoothing values, as the last exponentially smoothed value corresponds with the last observation in the series. You can easily extend the last cell one period in the future to get a short term forecast.

The second thing that becomes obvious is that you cannot change the values of α and see automatically what effect this has on your forecasts. This means that you would be better off producing your own set of formulae, as shown in Figure 4.65.

	A	B	C	D	E	F
1	Period	Series	Exp Smoothing			
2	1	5870.1			constant =	0.3
3	2	5896.9	5870.10	=B2		
4	3	6022.3	5878.14	=$F$2*B3+(1-$F$2)*C3		
5	4	6018.3	5921.39			
6	5	6069.4	5950.46			
7	6	6068.2	5986.14			
8	7	6069.9	6010.76			
9	8	6082.9	6028.50			
10	9	5984.1	6044.82			
11	10	5920	6026.61			
12	11	5976.8	5994.62			
13	12	5942.7	5989.28			
14	13	6018.9	5975.30			
15	14	5976	5988.38			
16	15	5945	5984.67			
17	16	5925.9	5972.77			
18	17	5923.7	5958.71			
19	18	5861	5948.21			
20	19	5923.5	5922.04			
21	20	5956	5922.48			
22	21	5948.5	5932.54			
23	22	5835.9	5937.33			
24	23	5858.4	5906.90			
25	24	5870.1	5892.35	=$F$2*B24+(1-$F$2)*C24		

Figure 4.65
Manual calculations for exponential smoothing

The advantage of this formulae approach is that, providing we have a chart open that includes the data from the column B and exponentially smoothed values from the column C, we can see immediately the effects of changing the value of α (cell F2) on our overall forecast.

Figure 4.66 shows the impact two different values of α have on forecasts. As expected, smaller α makes forecasts smoother and larger α makes them more dynamic.

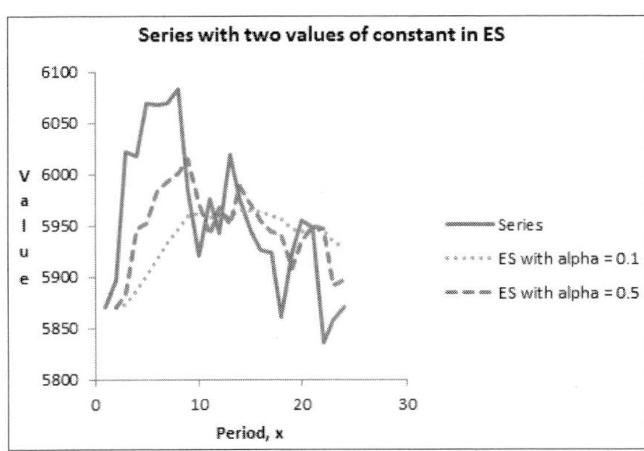

Figure 4.66

The formulae in column D in Figure 4.65 are Excel equivalent of equation (4.36). This essentially means that the current smoothed value is the forecast for the next period, or: $S_t = \hat{Y}_{t+1}$. In this case we can rewrite the formula as:

$$\hat{Y}_{t+1} = \alpha y_t + (1 - \alpha)\hat{Y}_t \qquad (4.36)$$

Another way to express the same formula is:

$$\hat{Y}_{t+1} = \hat{Y}_t + \alpha e_t \qquad (4.37)$$

Or, indeed, yet another way to say the same is:

$$\hat{Y}_{t+1} = y_t - (1 - \alpha)e_t \qquad (4.38)$$

This last formula takes us back to Equation (4.36), confirming that the forecasts in this method are exponentially weighted moving averages. Remember, the word weighted is equivalent of saying discounted, where $(1 - \alpha)$ is the discount factor (or, a damping factor as it is termed in Excel).

Note It is important to remember that formulae (4.33), (4.34), (4.36), (4.37) and (4.38) all say the same thing and we are free to use whichever we think is easiest to implement.

If we go back to Excel's printout (Figure 4.64) we will see that it does provide one interesting and useful piece of information, that is, we automatically get the value of the standard error. The formula that Excel uses to calculate this starts in cell D6 as: =SQRT(SUMXMY2(B3:B5,C3:C5)/3) and the value in the last cell, that is, cell D25 is: =SQRT(SUMXMY2(B22:B24,C22:C24)/3). As we can see, Excel uses the principle of moving averages to calculate a 'moving standard error'.

Just out of interest, and for the record, we forecasted the next value of FTSE100 to be 5885.674. The actual value on 26 May 2011 was 5881. Using this value of alpha, we were only 4 points above the actual value. With little bit of experimenting with the smoothing constant, we could have even improved this forecast.

4.6.3 Forecasting seasonal series with exponential smoothing

Earlier in this chapter we fitted a time series using linear trend. The formula for the straight line used as a trend was: $Y = b_0 + b_1x$. You will also recall that we said that various time series components (trend, cyclical, seasonal, and irregular) can be added together to form a time series decomposition model. As we said, this additive relationship is only a one of several possible. In fact, sometime the components form not an additive, but a multiplicative model. Which one is the correct one is beyond the scope of this book, but it suffices to say that it will primarily depend on the type of time series used. In order to introduce one of the possible approaches to handling the seasonal time series, we need to accept that we can use either an additive or a multiplicative model. They are defined as follows:

$$F_{t+m} = a_t + S_{t-s+m} \qquad (4.39)$$

$$F_{t+m} = a_t S_{t-s+m} \qquad (4.40)$$

Note As a general guidance, multiplicative models are better suited for time series that show more dramatic growth or decline, whilst additive models are more suited for less dynamic time series.

Just as with the linear trend, the coefficient a_t is an intercept of the series, but in this case a dynamic one. We'll explain this. S_{t-s+m} have a function of a slope, but it is called a seasonal component. The meaning of the symbols s and m in the subscript $t + m$ and $t - s + m$ is: s = number of periods in a seasonal cycle, and m = number of forecasting periods (forecasting horizon). The main feature of this approach is that we can use exponential smoothing to estimate dynamical values of not just the seasonal component, but of the intercept too. For an additive model, these two factors are calculated as follows:

$$a_t = \alpha(y_t - S_{t-s}) + (1-\alpha)a_{t-1} \tag{4.41}$$

$$S_t = \delta(y_t - a_t) + (1-\delta)S_{t-s} \tag{4.42}$$

For a multiplicative model, these two factors are calculated as follows:

$$a_t = \alpha\left(\frac{y_t}{S_{t-s}}\right) + (1-\alpha)a_{t-1} \tag{4.43}$$

$$S_t = \delta\left(\frac{y_t}{a_t}\right) + (1-\delta)S_{t-s} \tag{4.44}$$

As we can see, unlike the simple exponential smoothing which required only one smoothing constant, here we are using two smoothing constants, alpha (α) and delta (δ). In both cases we need to initialize the values of a_t and S_t. This is achieved, for additive models, by calculating a_s, from Equation (4.45):

$$a_s = \sum_{t=1}^{s} \frac{y_t}{s} \tag{4.45}$$

Where, $t = 1, 2, \ldots, s$ and $a_t = a_s$. In other words, the first s number of a_s are calculated as an average of all the corresponding actual observations. The initial values of S_t are calculated as:

$$S_t = y_t - a_t \tag{4.46}$$

For the multiplicative model a_s is calculated in the same way as in Equation (4.45) and S_t is calculated as:

$$S_t = \frac{y_t}{a_t} \tag{4.47}$$

The forecasts are produced as follows. To produce back forecasts (i.e. $m = 0$) for a current period, for example at $t = 15$, and assuming that $s = 4$, we would use the following equation:

$$F_{15+0} = a_{15} + S_{15-4+0} = a_{15} + S_{11}.$$

If the series has only 20 observations, for example, and we want to produce the forecast for the 23rd period, the forecast is calculated as:

$$F_{20+3} = a_{20} + S_{20-4+3} = a_{20} + S_{19}.$$

For a multiplicative model we use the same principle, except that the components are not added but multiplied. Figure 4.63 gives an example of an additive model.

Example 4.12

Let's now look at the data set describing the US Total New privately owned housing units per quarter (in 000) from 2000 to 2005.

Year	Quarter	Data	Year	Quarter	Data
2000	Q1	357.1	2003	Q1	374.7
2000	Q2	448.7	2003	Q2	490.7
2000	Q3	405.3	2003	Q3	510.9
2000	Q4	357.5	2003	Q4	471.4
2001	Q1	347.8	2004	Q1	424.7
2001	Q2	460.5	2004	Q2	539.4
2001	Q3	429.2	2004	Q3	531.9
2001	Q4	365.4	2004	Q4	459.6
2002	Q1	369	2005	Q1	448.2
2002	Q2	474.6	2005	Q2	575.3
2002	Q3	458.5	2005	Q3	567.5
2002	Q4	402.9	2005	Q4	477.1

Table 4.8 US Total New privately owned housing units started per quarter (in 000) from 2000 to 2005

	A	B	C	D	E	F	G	H
1	Period	Quarter	Series	at	St	Seasonal Forecast	alpha =	0.5
2	1	1	357.1	386.92	-29.82		delta =	0.5
3	2	2	448.7	498.20	-49.50		MSE =	728.238
4	3	3	405.3	483.88	-78.58			
5	4	4	357.5	422.32	-64.82			
6	5	1	347.8	399.97	-40.99	370.15		
7	6	2	460.5	454.98	-21.99	405.48		
8	7	3	429.2	481.38	-65.38	402.80		
9	8	4	365.4	455.80	-77.61	390.98		
10	9	1	369	432.90	-52.44	391.90		
11	10	2	474.6	464.74	-6.07	442.75		
12	11	3	458.5	494.31	-50.60	428.93		
13	12	4	402.9	487.41	-81.06	409.80		
14	13	1	374.7	457.28	-67.51	404.83		
15	14	2	490.7	477.02	3.80	470.95		
16	15	3	510.9	519.26	-29.48	468.66		
17	16	4	471.4	535.86	-72.76	454.80		
18	17	1	424.7	514.04	-78.42	446.52		
19	18	2	539.4	524.82	9.19	528.62		
20	19	3	531.9	543.10	-20.34	513.62		
21	20	4	459.6	537.73	-75.44	464.97		
22	21	1	448.2	532.18	-81.20	453.75		
23	22	2	575.3	549.14	17.68	558.34		
24	23	3	567.5	568.49	-10.66	548.15		
25	24	4	477.1	560.52	-79.43	485.07		
26	25	1				530.70		
27	26	2				511.02		
28	27	3				481.93		
29	28	4				495.70		

Figure 4.67
Calculating seasonal forecasts using the simple seasonal additive exponential smoothing model

→ Excel Formula Method – Seasonal additive exponential smoothing method

Alpha α Cell H1	Value = 0.5
Delta δ Cell H2	Value = 0.5
MSE Cell H3	Formula = SUMXMY2(C6:C21,F6:F21)/COUNT(C6:C21)
a_t Cell D2	Formula = (C2+C6+C10+C14+C18+C22)/6
	Copy down D2:D5
Cell D6	Formula = \$H\$1*(C6-E2)+(1-\$H\$1)*D5
	Copy down D6:D25
S_t Cells E2	Formula = C2-D2
	Copy down E2:E5
Cells E6	Formula = \$H\$2*(C6-D6)+(1-\$H\$2)*E2
	Copy down E6:E25
Forecast F_t Cell F6	Formula = D6+E2
	Copy down F6:F25
Cell F26	Formula
	Copy down F26:F29

Cells H1 and H2 contain the values of constants alpha and delta, whilst cell H3 contains MSE (mean square error). We assigned the initial values to both alpha and delta as 0.5 each.

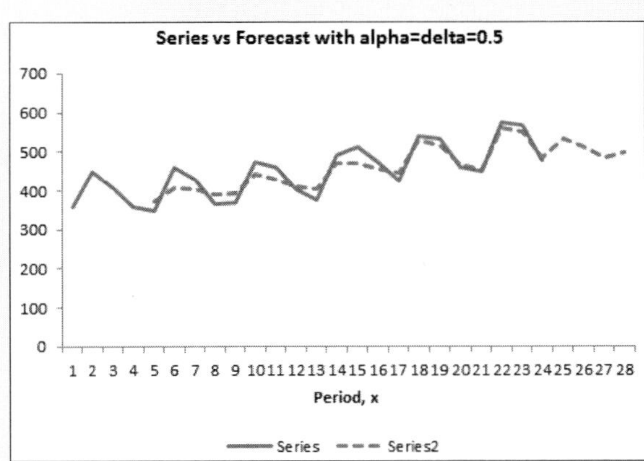

Figure 4.68
Initial forecast chart

By inputting manually the value of 0.5 in cells H1 and H2 as the values of constants alpha and delta, we automatically get in cell H3 the value of 2.036.

Cell H3 contains MSE (Mean Square Error) and Excel formula we used for MSE is: MSE=SUMXMY2(C6:C21,F6:F21)/COUNT(C6:C21). This formula will be fully explained in the next section and we'll use it here just as a method for estimating the values of alpha and delta. We used Excel's solver function to find the optimum values of alpha and delta. Let us explain how this is done. We put manually any value to cells H1 and H2, in our example 0.5 in each cell. After that we put together all the formulae and calculate forecasts. Once this is done, we click on cell H3 where the formula for MSE resides. Now select Solver from Data > Solver and enter values as illustrated in Figure 4.69.

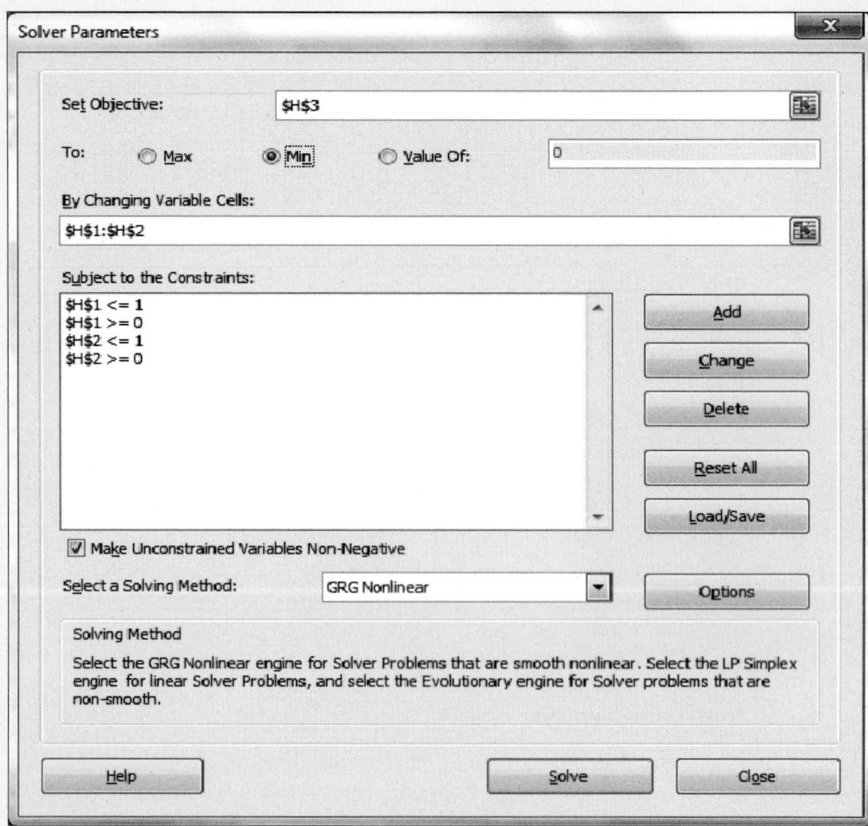

Figure 4.69
Solver parameters dialogue box.

In the solver dialogue box we specify that we want cell H3 to take the minimum value, by changing cell H1 and H2, under the condition that both cells H1 and H2 should never exceed zero or 1.

> **Note** If the Solver Add-In does not show in the Tools menu and go to Tools > Add-Ins and switch on the Solver Add In.

This changes all the calculated cells automatically and produces the forecast as per Figure 4.66. As we can see, the Solver has changed the values of alpha and delta, which in turn had an effect on all our formulae and forecast.

	A	B	C	D	E	F	G	H
1	Period	Quarter	Series	at	St	onal Fore	alpha =	1
2	1	1	357.1	386.92	-29.82		delta =	0.57013
3	2	2	448.7	498.20	-49.50		MSE =	1.8E-27
4	3	3	405.3	483.88	-78.58			
5	4	4	357.5	422.32	-64.82			
6	5	1	347.8	377.62	-29.82	347.80		
7	6	2	460.5	510.00	-49.50	460.50		
8	7	3	429.2	507.78	-78.58	429.20		
9	8	4	365.4	430.22	-64.82	365.40		
10	9	1	369	398.82	-29.82	369.00		
11	10	2	474.6	524.10	-49.50	474.60		
12	11	3	458.5	537.08	-78.58	458.50		
13	12	4	402.9	467.72	-64.82	402.90		
14	13	1	374.7	404.52	-29.82	374.70		
15	14	2	490.7	540.20	-49.50	490.70		
16	15	3	510.9	589.48	-78.58	510.90		
17	16	4	471.4	536.22	-64.82	471.40		
18	17	1	424.7	454.52	-29.82	424.70		
19	18	2	539.4	588.90	-49.50	539.40		
20	19	3	531.9	610.48	-78.58	531.90		
21	20	4	459.6	524.42	-64.82	459.60		
22	21	1	448.2	478.02	-29.82	448.20		
23	22	2	575.3	624.80	-49.50	575.30		
24	23	3	567.5	646.08	-78.58	567.50		
25	24	4	477.1	541.92	-64.82	477.10		
26	25	1				512.10		
27	26	2				492.42		
28	27	3				463.33		
29	28	4				477.10		

Figure 4.70
Revised forecast

Figure 4.71 illustrates the forecast using the seasonal exponential smoothing method. We observe from Figure 4.71 that the forecast values are a perfect fit to the actual data values. As we can see this method, although fairly simple, produces impressive results.

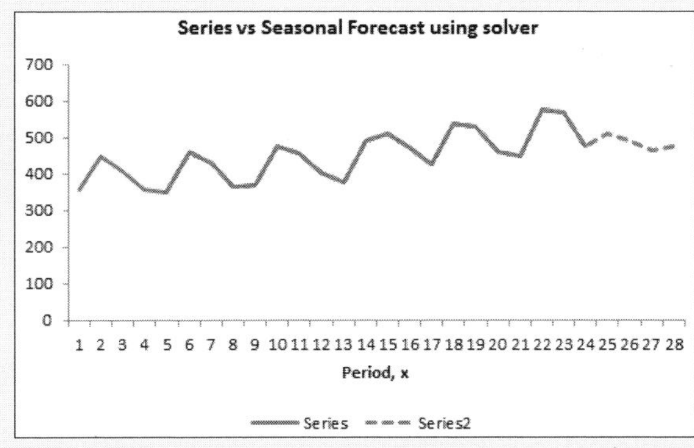

Figure 4.71

Student exercises

X4.8 What is the corresponding value of moving averages if the value of alpha = 0.1? Conversely, what is the value of alpha if the value of moving averages is equivalent to 12?

X4.9 Use the time series as below:

10	12	13	11	14	13	12	15	16	15

Show in a spread sheet by constructing the columns that the following formulae all yield the same results:

$$S'_t = S'_{t-1} + \alpha(y_{t-1} - S'_{t-1}) \tag{4.33}$$

$$S'_t = \alpha y_{t-1} + (1 - \alpha)S'_{t-1} \tag{4.34}$$

$$\hat{Y}_{t+1} = \alpha y_t + (1 - \alpha)\hat{Y}_t \tag{4.36}$$

$$\hat{Y}_{t+1} = \hat{Y}_t + \alpha e_t \tag{4.37}$$

$$\hat{Y}_{t+1} = y_t - (1 - \alpha)e_t \tag{4.38}$$

X4.10 If you had to model a very dynamic, non-stationary and seasonal time series, would you rather use a multiplicative or an additive seasonal model? Why?

4.7 Forecast error analysis

One of the primary reasons for using forecasting as a tool is to try to reduce uncertainty. The better the forecasts, the lower the uncertainty that surrounds the variable we forecast. We can never eliminate uncertainty, but good forecasts can reduce it to an acceptable level. What would we consider to be a good forecast? An intuitive answer is that it has be the one that shows the smallest error when compared with actual event. The problem with this statement is that we cannot measure the error until the event has happened, by which time it is too late to say that our forecast was, or was not, good. Ideally, we would like to measure the error before the future unfolds. How do we do this? As we have demonstrated in this chapter, when forecasting, we always used the model to back-fit the existing time series. This is sometimes called back-casting, or more appropriately, ex post forecasting. Once we produced ex-post forecasts, it is easy to measure deviations from the actual data. These deviations are forecasting errors and they will tell us how good our method or model is.

Interpretation The main assumption we make here is that whichever model shows the smallest errors in the past, it will probably make the smallest errors when extrapolated in the future. In other words, the model with smallest historical errors will reduce the uncertainty that the future brings. This is the key assumption.

4.7.1 Error measurement

Calculating errors is one of the easiest tasks. We already defined an error as a difference between what actually happened and what we thought would happen. In the context of forecasting time series and models, error is the difference between the actual data and the data produced by a model, or ex-post forecasts. This can be expressed as a formula:

$$e_t = A_t - F_t, \text{ or } e_t = y_t - F_t \tag{4.48}$$

Where e_t is an error for a period *t*, A_t is the actual value in a period *t* and F_t is forecasted value for the same period *t*. Figure 4.72 shows an example of how to calculate forecasting errors.

	A	B	C	D	E
1	Period	Actual	Forecast	Error	
2	1	100	130	-30	=B2-C2
3	2	250	150	100	
4	3	150	210	-60	
5	4	220	250	-30	
6	5	320	320	0	=B6-C6
7	Sum =	1040	1060	-20	
8		=SUM(B2:B6)		=SUM(D2:D6)	

Figure 4.72
An example of calculating the forecasting errors.

In the above example, using some simple method, we produced back-forecasts that clearly deviate from the actual historical values. Figure 4.73 shows the results in a graphical way.

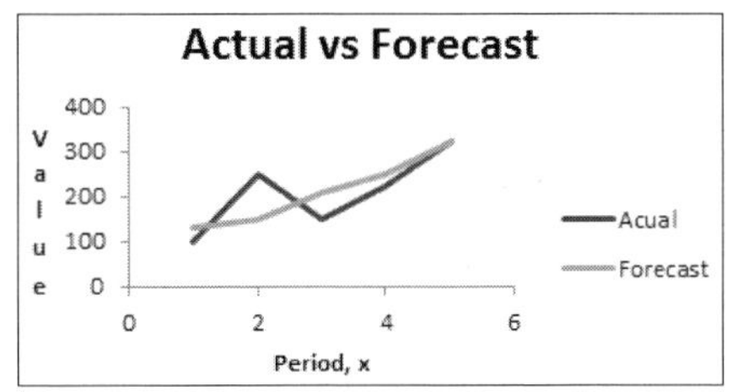

Figure 4.73
A chart showing actual and forecasted values

For period 1 (t = 1) our method exceeded actual values, which is presented as -30, because errors are calculated as actual minus forecasted. For period t = 2, our method underscored by 100. For period 6 (t = 6), for example, our method was perfect and it had not generated any errors. What can we conclude from this? If these were the first 5 weeks of our new business venture, and if we add all these numbers together, than our cumulative forecast for these five weeks would have been 1060. In reality the business generated 1040. This implies that the method we used made a cumulative error of –20, or given the above formula, it overestimates the reality by 20 units. If we divide this cumulative value by the number of weeks to which it applies, 5, we get the average value of our error:

$$\bar{e} = \frac{\Sigma(A_t - F_t)}{n} = \frac{-20}{5} = -4$$

Interpretation The average error that our method generates per period is –4 and because errors are defined as differences between the actual and forecast values, this means that in average the actual values are by 4 units *higher* than our forecast. Given earlier assumptions that the method will probably continue to perform in the future as in the past (assuming there are no dramatic or step changes), our method will probably generate similar errors in the future.

Assuming that we decided to experiment with some other method and assuming that the average error that this other method generated was 2, which method would you rather use to forecast your business venture? The answer, hopefully, is very straightforward. The second method is somewhat pessimistic (the actual values are by 2 units per period *below* the forecasted values), but in absolute terms 2 is less than 4. Therefore we would recommend the second method as a much better model for forecasting this particular business venture. In the above example, we have not only decided which forecasting method reduces uncertainty more, but we have also learned how to use two different ways of measuring this uncertainty. Using errors as measures of uncertainty, we learned how to calculate an average, or mean error, and we implied that an absolute average error also makes sense to be estimated. In practice, other error measurements are used too.

4.7.2 Types of errors

In fact, many different error measurements formulae are used to assess how good the forecasts are. The four more commonly used error measurements are the mean error (ME), the mean absolute error (sometimes called the mean absolute deviation and abbreviated as MAD), the means square error (MSE) and the mean percentage error (MPE). These errors are calculated as follows:

$$ME = \frac{\Sigma(A_t - F_t)}{n} \tag{4.49}$$

$$MAD = \frac{\Sigma|A_t - F_t|}{n} \tag{4.50}$$

$$MSE = \frac{\Sigma(A_t - F_t)^2}{n} \tag{4.51}$$

$$MPE = \frac{\Sigma\left(\frac{A_t - F_t}{A_t}\right)}{n} = \frac{\Sigma\left(\frac{e_t}{A_t}\right)}{n} \tag{4.52}$$

Sometimes MPE causes problems in Excel (due to negative values), in which case it is better to estimate the mean absolute percentage error (MAPE):

$$MAPE = \frac{\Sigma\left(\frac{|A_t - F_t|}{A_t}\right)}{n} = \frac{\Sigma\left(\frac{|e_t|}{A_t}\right)}{n} \tag{4.53}$$

In Excel it is very easy to calculate these errors. Using our previous example, these errors are calculated as shown in Figure 4.74.

	A	B	C	D	E	F	G	H	I
1	Period	Actual	Forecast	Error	MAD	MSE	MPE	MPE %	MAPE
2	1	100	130	-30	30	10000	-0.3	-30	0.3
3	2	250	150	100	100	3600	0.4	40	0.4
4	3	150	210	-60	60	900	-0.4	-40	0.4
5	4	220	250	-30	30	0	-0.1364	-13.636	0.13636
6	5	320	320	0	0	400	0	0	0
7	Sum =	1040	1060	-20	220	14900	-0.4364	-43.636	1.23636
8	Average =	208	212	-4	44	2980	-0.0873	-8.7273	0.24727

Figure 4.74
Calculating various errors

➔ Excel Formula Method

ME Cell D2	Formula = B2-C2
	Copy down D2:D6
MAD Cell E2	Formula = ABS(D2)
	Copy down E2:E6
MSE Cell F2	Formula = D2^2
	Copy down F2:F6
MPE Cell G2	Formula = D2/B2
	Copy down G2:G6
MPE % Cell H2	Formula = D2/B2*100
	Copy down H2:H6
MAPE Cells I2	Formula = E2/B2
	Copy down I2:I6
SUM Actual Cell B7	Formula = SUM(B2:B6)
Average Actual Cell B8	Formula = AVERAGE(B2:B6)
SUM Forecast Cell C7	Formula = SUM(C2:C6)
Average Forecast Cell C8	Formula = AVERAGE(C2:C6)
SUM ME Cell D7	Formula = SUM(D2:D6)
Average ME Cell D8	Formula = AVERAGE(D2:D6)
SUM MAD Cell E7	Formula = SUM(E2:E6)
Average MAD Cell E8	Formula = AVERAGE(E2:E6)
SUM MSE Cell F7	Formula = SUM(F2:F6)
Average MSE Cell F8	Formula = AVERAGE(F2:F6)
SUM MPE Cell G7	Formula = SUM(G2:G6)
Average MPE Cell G8	Formula = AVERAGE(G2:G6)
SUM MPE % Cell H7	Formula = SUM(H2:H6)
Average MPE % Cell H8	Formula = AVERAGE(H2:H6)
SUM MAPE Cell I7	Formula = SUM(I2:I6)
Average MAPE Cell I8	Formula = AVERAGE(I2:I6)

The column H in Figure 4.70 is identical to the column G. The only difference is that we used Excel percentage formatting to present the numbers as percentages, rather than decimal values.

Rather than calculating individual errors (as in columns D to I) and adding all the individual error values (as in row 7) or calculating the average (as in row 8), we could have calculated all these errors with a single formula line for each type of error.

Using some of the built-in Excel functions, these errors can be calculated as:

➔ Excel Formula Method – Alternative

ME Cell D8	Formula = (SUM(B2:B6)-SUM(C2:C6))/COUNT(B2:B6)
MAD Cell E8	Formula {= SUM(ABS(D2:D6))/COUNT(D2:D6)}
MSE Cell F8	Formula = SUMXMY2(B2:B6,C2:C6)/COUNT(B2:B6)
MPE Cell G8	Formula {= SUM(((B2:B6)-(C2:C6))/(B2:B6))/COUNT(B2:B6)}
MAPE Cell I8	Formula {=SUM(ABS((B2:B6)-(C2:C6))/(B2:B6))/COUNT(B2:B6)}

Note Observe that MAD, MPE and MAPE formulae have curly brackets on both sides of the formulae. Do not enter these brackets manually. Excel enters the brackets automatically if after you typed the formula you do not just press the Enter button, but CTRL+SHIFT+ENTER button (i.e. all three at the same time). This means that the range is treated as an array.

	A	B	C	D
1	Period	Actual	Forecast	Error
2	1	100	130	-30
3	2	250	150	100
4	3	150	210	-60
5	4	220	250	-30
6	5	320	320	0
7	Sum =	1040	1060	-20
8	verage =	208	212	-4
9				
10		ME =	-4	
11		MAD =	44	
12		MSE =	3080	
13		MPE =	-0.087272727	
14		MAPE =	0.247272727	

Figure 4.75

For the sake of clarity, Figures 4.75 and 4.76 reproduces the spreadsheet, as it should look like if the single cell formulae for the error calculations were used. Again, note that the curly brackets for MAD, MPE and MAPE are not visible by observing formulae in cells D10, D12 and D13. However, they are visible in the formula bar.

C11 fx {=SUM(ABS(D2:D6))/COUNT(D2:D6)}

	A	B	C	D
1	Period	Actual	Forecast	Error
2	1	100	130	=B2-C2
3	2	250	150	=B3-C3
4	3	150	210	=B4-C4
5	4	220	250	=B5-C5
6	5	320	320	=B6-C6
7	Sum =	=SUM(B2:B6)	=SUM(C2:C6)	=SUM(D2:D6)
8	Average =	=AVERAGE(B2:B6)	=AVERAGE(C2:C6)	=AVERAGE(D2:D6)
9				
10		ME =	=(SUM(B2:B6)-SUM(C2:C6))/COUNT(B2:B6)	
11		MAD =	=SUM(ABS(D2:D6))/COUNT(D2:D6)	
12		MSE =	=SUMXMY2(B2:B6,C2:C6)/COUNT(B2:B6)	
13		MPE =	=SUM(((B2:B6)-(C2:C6))/(B2:B6))/COUNT(B2:B6)	
14		MAPE =	=SUM(ABS((B2:B6)-(C2:C6))/(B2:B6))/COUNT(B2:B6)	

Figure 4.76

Single cell formulae for calculating the ME, MAD, MSE, MPE and MAPE

The ability to calculate all these aggregate errors with a single formula is a useful feature that can be used to explore and compare forecasts.

4.7.3 Interpreting errors

How do we interpret the above five different error measurements? We have already said that ME indicates that the actual data are on average four units per period above the forecasted values. This is a good indication, but the problem is that positive and negative deviations eliminate each other, so we might end up with a forecast that jumps up and down around the actual values, never providing exact forecasts, yet the ME could be zero. To eliminate the above problem with ME, we can calculate MAD. MAD indicates that if we eliminate overestimates and underestimates of our forecasts, a typical bias that our method shows (regardless whether it is positive or negative) is 44 units per period. This is typical error, regardless of the direction in which our forecasts went when estimating the actual values.

The meaning of the MSE is more difficult to interpret, for a simple reason that we have taken the square values of our errors. What is a square value of something? The rational is as follows: if there are some big deviations of our forecast from the actual values, then in order to magnify these deviations even further, we need to square them. Let's take an example of two hypothetical errors for a period. Let one error reading shows two and the other ten. The second error is five times larger than the first one. However, when we square these two numbers, number 100 (10×10) is 25 times larger than number 4 (2×2). This is what we mean by magnifying large errors. So, the higher the MSE, the more extreme deviations from the actual values are contained in our forecast. This is particularly useful when comparing two forecasts. If MSE obtained from the first forecast is larger than the MSE from the second, than the first forecast contains more extreme deviations than the second one.

The interpretation of the MPE is very intuitive. It tells us that on average an error constitutes x% of the actual value, or as in our case, MPE = –8.73%. This means that on average our forecasting errors overshot the actual values by 8.73% (remember that negative error means forecasts overshooting the actual values and positive error means undershooting). However, this implies that just like with the ME we could have a series of overshoots and undershoots (as in our example), yet gaining an average value of almost zero. The mean absolute percentage error (MAPE) addresses this problem. It shows us the value of 0.2473. In other words, if we disregard positive and negative variations of our forecasts from the actual values, we are on average making an absolute error of 24.73%.

4.7.4 Error inspection

When we introduced time series in this chapter, we mentioned that forecasting errors should be treated as the residual element, in other words, something that is moving completely randomly when observed visually. The same applies to regression analysis. Regardless of the forecasting method, errors should always be calculated and inspected. Should these errors follow any kind of pattern, the forecasting method must be treated as suspect. In fact, forecasting errors are often required to adhere to some formal assumptions, such as: independence, normality and homoscedasticity. The meaning of some of these terms is not just that we do not want to see any pattern among the errors (residuals), but also that they should be independent of each other, normally distributed and have a constant variance (homoscedasticity). Some rigorous tests exist to help us determine if the residuals violate any of these assumptions, but they are beyond the scope of this book.

Note Homoscedasticity is a complicated word that explains relatively simple concept. Imagine a series that has a constant mean (stationary time series), but it variance is changing, i.e. it is growing, contracting, or oscillating. This kind of time series is not considered to be homoscedastic, but heteroscedasticity. In case with residuals, we always aim to make them homoscedastic, as otherwise it means that our model is not good and some of the 'pattern' is still left in residuals.

One of the most elementary steps to take after we produced our forecasts is to visually check the residuals/errors. Figure 4.77 shows an example of plotting forecasting errors. It appears that the residuals are flowing in a random fashion and do not show any pattern, which is exactly what we wanted.

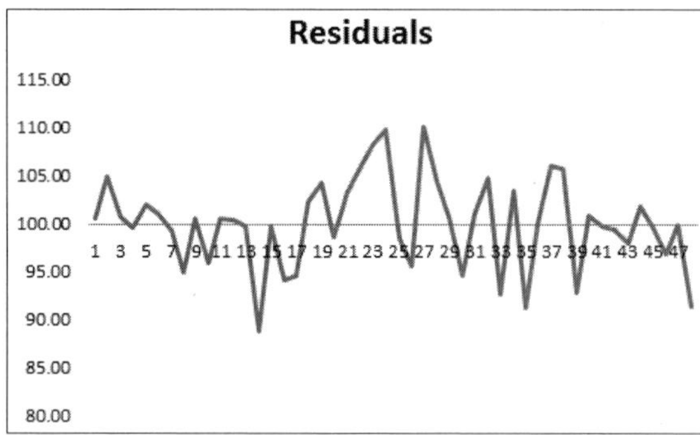

Figure 4.77
Error/residual plot

In addition to visually checking that forecasting errors are behaving randomly, we also need to ensure that they are not dependent of one another. In other words, errors must not be correlated. There are other properties that errors need to comply with, but this is beyond the scope of the chapter on basic forecasting.

Note One of the methods of verifying whether residuals are correlated is the autocorrelation plot. Autocorrelations are the coefficients that we calculate and they form an autocorrelation function. They can be used for various purposes, but here we are referring to the series of autocorrelations of residuals. Essentially, we lag the residuals by one time period, then by another and another, etc., and then measure correlations between all these lagged series of residuals. This is called a residual autocorrelation function.

X
autocorrelation
Correlation between the time series with itself, but where the observations are shifted by a certain number of periods. The series of these autocorrelation coefficients for every time shift produces the autocorrelation function.

Student exercises

Please visit the Online Resource Centre which accompanies this textbook for figures solutions in Excel to the student exercises and Techniques in Practice.

X4.11 If your average error, calculated as ME, is zero, does this mean that you have a perfect forecast?

X4.12 By using two different forecasting methods on a same data set you get two respective MSE values of 323.5 and 655.8. What would you conclude about these two forecasting methods?

X4.13 If the residuals, after you produced forecasts, do not show random behaviour, what would you conclude?

X4.14 One of the most frequently used methods to examine if the residuals are correlated is:

a) Residual scattergram.

b) Autocorrelation function.

c) Residual bar function.

X4.15 Homoscedasticity and heteroscedasticity are interchangeable terms used depending if we are using endogenous or exogenous variables. True/False?

Techniques in practice

TP1 Figure TP4p1 is a table containing Microsoft weekly adjusted closing values of shares from 06/06/2011 to 09/01/2012. Your task is to produce a forecast for the shares closing value for the next six weeks:

Make sure that you:

- Chart the series
- Use the forecasting method that you think is best suited for this task
- Use an error measurement method to validate your forecasts
- Examine the residuals and discuss how appropriate is your method
- Decide if this is best way to produce forecasts for this objective

TP2 Figure TP4p2 is a table containing Emerson daily adjusted closing values of shares from 8 August 2011 to 31 January 2012. Your task is to produce the forecast the shares closing value for the following day, that is, 1 February /2012.

Make sure that you:

- Chart the series
- Use several alternative forecasting methods
- Use several different error measurement methods
- Examine the residuals and ensure that all the methods are appropriate
- Decide what is the forecast for 1 February 2012
- Why do you believe that this is the right forecast

Summary

In this chapter we have introduced a concept that relationships between two variables can be modelled using a mathematical equation. As the most fundamental models are the linear models, we used the concept of regression analysis to model two variable via the so called linear regression model. This was followed by a simple introduction to the non-linear modelling and non-linear regression analysis.

If one of the variables is the time variable, then linear regression is effectively using for trending the data. Trending the variable also means that we can extrapolate it and forecast the future values of this variable. Rather than just extrapolating the simple trend, we also introduced the concept of classical decomposition method. This method enables a better breakdown of a time series into constituent components. Once these components were identified and extrapolated, they can be recomposed to produce more accurate forecasts.

An alternative method to classical decomposition is the smoothing method. A particular model we demonstrated is the exponential smoothing method, which is especially suited for short-term forecasts.

We concluded the chapter with the analysis of forecasting errors. Irrespective of which method we use, the forecasts are bound to deviate from what will actually happen in the future. To measure how good our method is potentially, we analysed the past errors. Different types of errors were introduced and explained how to be interpreted to ensure the best possible future forecasts.

Student exercise answers

For all figures listed below, please see the Online Resource Centre.

X4.1 From the equation $y = -4.4 + 0.085x$ we can see that the profit is growing in a linear fashion as the revenues grow. In fact, the profit will grow at the rate of 0.085 (or 8.5%) and for the given data set (not for all cases!) if we have zero revenue ($x = 0$), we will make a loss of 4.4 on average.

X4.2 The breakeven point is when the profit is equal to zero. We need to substitute zero for y in the equation $y = -4.4 + 0.085x$:

$$y = -4.4 + 0.085x$$

$$0 = -4.4 + 0.085x$$

$$4.4 = 0.085x$$

$$x = +4.4/0.085$$

$$x = +51.7647$$

We will break even at the value of revenue of $x = -51.7647$.

X4.3 If we reach the revenue of 370, we expect the profit to be 27.05:

$$y = -4.4 + 0.085x$$

$$y = -4.4 + 0.085(370)$$

$$y = 27.05$$

X4.4 The number of degrees of freedom for the regression is 1, whilst the number of degrees of freedom for the residuals is 8. The regression sum of squares (SSR), or the proportion of the explained variance, is 608.6012. The residual or error sum of squares (SSE), or the proportion of the unexplained variance, is 109.8988. The total variance, or the sum of squares (SST) is 718.5.

	ANOVA				
	df	*SS*	*MS*	*F*	*Significance F*
Regression	1	608.6012	608.6012	44.302659	0.000159807
Residual	8	109.8988	13.73735		
Total	9	718.5			

The mean square error for regression (MSR) is 608.6012 (which is SSR/df for regression). The mean square error for residuals (MSE) is 13.73735 (which is SSE/df for residuals). The F statistic is 44.302659 and it was obtained as MSR/MSE. As the level of significance is very small, 0.000159807, which is virtually zero, this means that the variations in the profit are significantly explained by the variations in revenue.

X4.5 The best fit for the given time series of inventory is the parabolic curve. It shows the coefficient of determination R^2 of 0.9868. Power curve shows R^2 of 0.9217 and the exponential curve shows R^2 of 0.9772.

X4.6 The formula for standard errors is shown as =SQRT(SUMXMY2(B4:B6,C4:C6)/3). This is the square root of the squares of differences between two arrays, divided by three. This error type is also called RMSE (Root Mean Square Error). The first of the two arrays represents the actual time series and second one the fitted values using the moving average method of forecasting. The squared differences between these two time series are effectively squared errors. However, only three of them are summed at the time and divided by three. This means that the RMSE metric that is used is a dynamic one, just like the moving average forecasts. In other words, it is not a one single indicator for the whole time series, but a moving error measurement for only three observations at the time.

X4.7 As the consumption of ice cream in this example has been captured as monthly data, this means that there will be a strong seasonal component and we need to take it into modelling. The second model, Y = T + S + I includes the seasonal component, whilst the first one does not. It is, therefore, the model Y = T + S + I that is appropriate for this time series.

X4.8 The formula for converting moving averages into the smoothing constant alpha is: alpha = 2/(M + 1), where M is the number of moving averages. If M = 12, then alpha = 0.15. Equally to do the inverse conversion: M = (2-alpha)/alpha, which for alpha = 0.1 gives us M = 19.

X4.9 See Figure X4.9.

X4.10 Multiplicative models are better suited for the time series that are moving upwards or downwards. A non-stationary time series is moving upwards or downwards, unlike the stationary one that follows some general horizontal trend. A multiplicative seasonal model is for this reason much better suited for any non-stationary time series, including the seasonal ones.

X4.11 The problem with an average error is that all the positives deviations are cancelled by all the negative deviations once they are all summed up. This could give us a zero value as the mean error (deviation), but this does not mean that our forecast had no deviations from the actual time series. By observing just the ME, we cannot conclude that our forecast is 'perfect'.

X4.12 Mean square error (MSE) is very sensitive to larger deviations, for a simple reason that the deviations are squared before the average is taken. A greater deviation, when squared, will exaggerate how far is the fitted model line from the actual time series. For this reason MSE is said to be biased towards smaller deviations. If one method shows much higher MSE value than the other, then it was either one or several larger outliers that caused this dramatic increase in the MSE value. It doesn't necessarily mean that the method with the smaller MSE will be a better predictive model, it just means that it was historically more conservative and that it had fewer larger deviations than the method that produced a higher MSE. This is the reason why we often use more than one type of error measurement to evaluate the forecasting method.

X4.13 If the residuals still show some regularity or a pattern in their behaviour, then this means that our model is not the best fit for the time series. This means that the model have 'left' some of the regularities in the residuals and is not the best representation of the time series that is being modelled. In this case, we should start all over again, or modify the model parameters.

X4.14 The autocorrelation function is used to determine if the residuals still contain any pattern. The autocorrelation coefficients that constitute the autocorrelation function are all expected to be insignificant and close to zero.

X4.15 False. Homoscedasticity and heteroscedasticity are two opposite terms, one describing the uniformity of variance and the other describing the changing variance.

TP1 The time series is charted as below:

Figure TP4.1a

The time series appears to be non-stationary, with just a slight upward trend. On the face of it, it appears that there is some seasonality in the time series, so we decided to use a seasonal forecasting method. The one we picked was an additive seasonal exponential smoothing method. After the values of alpha and delta smoothing constants were optimized using Excel Solver add-in, the final values of forecasts were calculated as: 29.03, 28.76, 28.27, 29.06, 29.59, and 29.87. These values are result of minimizing the MSE measurement and by assigning the optimal value of alpha and delta by the Solver. These optimal values are 0.873623 for alpha and 0.365335 for delta. Our ex post forecasts overlap with the actual observations in almost perfect manner and the future forecasts are charted as follows:

Figure TP4p1b

However, after we had charted the errors, the graph for errors indicated that there is still some trend left in them:

Figure TP4.1c

This implied that we picked the wrong method. The conclusion is that the selected method is not appropriate for this time series. The question that remains is which method is appropriate for this time series? Here is what we think. Because the time series are the weekly closing values of stock movements, we do not think that any of the methods described in this book is capable of capturing virtually random movements of stocks. They would all fall short of acceptable results, especially because we wanted to forecast six weeks ahead. If our objective was just one week ahead, then perhaps some of the methods from this book could have been used.

Is there a possible alternative? Surprisingly, we could have used the linear trend extrapolation, although the forecasts would be equally inaccurate. However, from the statistical perspective, the linear regression method, or trend extrapolation, would give us statistically more acceptable results. As we can see and as far as we know, no method is robust enough to capture almost random movements of the stock exchange.

TP2 The time series is charted as below:

Figure TP4.2a

The time series appears to be non-stationary, with just an upward trend. As our task is to produce just one single forecast for the following day, we decided to go for a simple exponential smoothing method. However, we will use three different values of the smoothing constant alpha and then by measuring the errors, we'll decide which forecast is the final forecast for this time series. The three values of alpha that we will use are 0.1, 0.5 and 0.9. The alpha value of 0.9 gave us the most credible ex-post forecasts:

Figure TP4.2b

We calculate five different types of error metrics for every ex-post forecast. They are ME, MAD, MSE, MPE and MAPE. They are as follows:

	F1	F2	F3
ME =	0.671666	0.158318	**0.086921**
MAD =	1.597153	0.981207	**0.900193**
MSE =	3.709493	1.545881	**1.351138**
MPE =	0.013052	0.002859	**0.001521**
MAPE =	0.033729	0.021074	**0.019343**

For all five error indicators, the forecasts with the value of alpha of 0.9 had the lowest value. We used this method to forecasts the next day value of stock and our forecast is 51.88. We graphed the errors for the given method, and the chart was as below.

Figure TP4p2c

Our conclusion is as the series of errors appears to be random and without any trend or pattern embedded in it and on the basis of this visual inspection, we conclude that the choice of this forecasting method was acceptable.

Further reading

1. G. C. S. Wang (2003) *Regression Analysis, Modelling & Forecasting*, Graceway.
2. J. E. Hanke and D. W. Wichern (2009) *Business Forecasting* (9th edn), Prentice Hall.
3. S. Makridakis, S. C. Wheelwright, and R. J. Hyndman (1998) *Forecasting; Methods and Applications* (3rd edn), John Wiley.

Web resources

1. http://en.wikipedia.org/wiki/Forecasting
2. http://forecasters.org/

Formula summary

$$y = bx \tag{4.1}$$

$$y = b_0 + b_1x \tag{4.2}$$

$$b_0 = \frac{\Sigma y}{n} - b\frac{\Sigma x}{n} \tag{4.3}$$

$$b_1 = \frac{\Sigma xy - \frac{(\Sigma x \Sigma y)}{n}}{\Sigma x^2 - \frac{(\Sigma x)^2}{n}} \tag{4.4}$$

$$R = \frac{\Sigma(\hat{y} - \bar{y})^2}{\Sigma(y - \bar{y})^2} \tag{4.5}$$

$$r = \sqrt{R} \tag{4.6}$$

$$\text{Adjusted R Square} = 1 - \left[(1 - R^2)\frac{n-1}{n-2}\right] \tag{4.7}$$

$$\text{Adjusted R Square} = 1 - \left[\left(\frac{SSE}{SST}\right)\left(\frac{n-1}{n-2}\right)\right] \tag{4.8}$$

$$R^2 = \frac{SSR}{SST} = \frac{SST - SSE}{SST} = 1 - \frac{SSE}{SST} \tag{4.9}$$

$$F = \frac{MSR}{MSE} \tag{4.10}$$

$$SE_b = \sqrt{\frac{\frac{\Sigma(y - \hat{y})^2}{(n-2)}}{\Sigma(x - \bar{x})^2}} \tag{4.11}$$

$$t_{calc} = \frac{b - \beta}{SE_b} \tag{4.12}$$

$$\hat{y} - e < y < \hat{y} + e \tag{4.13}$$

$$e = t_{cri}SEE\sqrt{1 + \frac{1}{n} + \frac{n(\hat{x} - \bar{x})^2}{n(\Sigma x^2) - (\Sigma x)^2}} \tag{4.14}$$

$$y = b_0 + b_1x + b_2x^2 \tag{4.15}$$

$$y = b_0e^{b1x} \tag{4.16}$$

$$\text{Residual} = y - \hat{y} \tag{4.17}$$

$$Y = T + C + S + I \tag{4.18}$$

$$Y = T + R \tag{4.19}$$

$$R^2 = 1 - \frac{SSE}{SST} \tag{4.20}$$

$$M_t = \frac{x_t + x_{t-1} + \ldots + x_{t-N+1}}{N} = \frac{\sum_{i=t}^{t-N+1} x_i}{N} \tag{4.21}$$

$$Y = T + C + S + I \tag{4.22}$$

$$Y = T \times C \times S \times I \tag{4.23}$$

$$Y = (T \times C \times S) + I \tag{4.24}$$

$$Y = T \times (C + S + I) \tag{4.25}$$

$$\frac{Y}{T} = \frac{T \times C \times I}{T} = C \times I \tag{4.26}$$

$$\text{Moving Averages of } C \times I = C \tag{4.27}$$

$$\frac{C \times I}{C} = I \tag{4.28}$$

$$\frac{Y}{T} = \frac{T \times S \times I}{T} = S \times I \tag{4.29}$$

$$\hat{y}_t = y_{t-1} + e_t \tag{4.30}$$

$$F_t = F_{t-1} + (y_{t-1} - F_{t-1}) \tag{4.31}$$

$$F_t = F_{t-1} + \alpha(y_{t-1} - F_{t-1}) \tag{4.32}$$

$$S'_t = S'_{t-1} + \alpha(y_{t-1} - S'_{t-1}) \tag{4.33}$$

$$S'_t = \alpha y_{t-1} + (1 - \alpha)S'_{t-1} \tag{4.34}$$

$$\alpha = \frac{2}{M + 1} \tag{4.35}$$

$$\hat{Y}_{t+1} = \alpha y_t + (1 - \alpha)\hat{Y}_t \tag{4.36}$$

$$\hat{Y}_{t+1} = \hat{Y}_t + \alpha e_t \tag{4.37}$$

$$\hat{Y}_{t+1} = y_t - (1 - \alpha)e_t \tag{4.38}$$

$$F_{t+m} = a_t + S_{t-s+m} \tag{4.39}$$

$$F_{t+m} = a_t S_{t-s+m} \tag{4.40}$$

$$a_t = \alpha(y_t - S_{t-s}) + (1 - \alpha)a_{t-1} \tag{4.41}$$

$$S_t = \delta(y_t - a_t) + (1 - \delta)S_{t-s} \tag{4.42}$$

$$a_t = \alpha\left(\frac{y_t}{S_{t-s}}\right) + (1-\alpha)a_{t-1} \tag{4.43}$$

$$S_t = \delta\left(\frac{y_t}{a_t}\right) + (1-\delta)S_{t-s} \tag{4.44}$$

$$a_s = \sum_{t=1}^{s} \frac{y_t}{s} \tag{4.45}$$

$$S_t = y_t - a_t \tag{4.46}$$

$$S_t = \frac{y_t}{a_t} \tag{4.47}$$

$$e_t = A_t - F_t, \text{ or } e_t = y_t - F_t \tag{4.48}$$

$$ME = \frac{\Sigma(A_t - F_t)}{n} \tag{4.49}$$

$$MAD = \frac{\Sigma|A_t - F_t|}{n} \tag{4.50}$$

$$MSE = \frac{\Sigma(A_t - F_t)^2}{n} \tag{4.51}$$

$$MPE = \frac{\Sigma\left(\frac{A_t - F_t}{A_t}\right)}{n} = \frac{\Sigma\left(\frac{e_t}{A_t}\right)}{n} \tag{4.52}$$

$$MAPE = \frac{\Sigma\left(\frac{|A_t - F_t|}{A_t}\right)}{n} = \frac{\Sigma\left(\frac{|e_t|}{A_t}\right)}{n} \tag{4.53}$$

Part III

Decision Making in Manufacturing and Quality

5 Optimization

» Overview «

In this chapter we will provide the reader with an introduction to the concept of resource allocation and optimization within business. Linear programming is one of the most powerful decision making techniques for optimization in business. Its job is to recommend allocations of resources that will be the most efficient required for that decision.

As with so many techniques, linear programming was developed during the Second World War for military applications as the prime driver in solving complex planning problems during wartime operations. When the war ended linear programming was introduced into industrial applications, initially to aid production planning. Initially, linear programming, and the many derivatives within the mathematical programming family, were under the control of specialists (e.g. operational research scientists) who understood the algorithms, programmes, and how to enter the information and interpret the output. Mainframe computers were, by today's standards, slow, huge, and expensive.

With the advent of faster, much smaller, and cheaper computers, linear programming can be run very effectively on desktop or laptop machines and so is not always in the domain of specialists, although for truly large models specialist software and people with expertise in construction and interpretation of linear programming is still required.

Even though linear programming may not be constructed within business departments, the output should be understood and interpreted by all managers whether they be in accountancy, finance, banking, production, marketing, human resources, logistics, supply or sales, to name but a few, because linear programming can help form many of the decision strategies within those departments.

Quite large linear programming models can now be run within Excel, so anyone with a computer and Microsoft Office has access to software that can perform quite powerful linear programming calculations. The terminology learnt from that is exactly the same as that used by more powerful specialist software, so the manager will understand the types of problems that linear programming can be used for and be able to converse with the specialist if required.

X

linear programming a mathematical model with a linear objective function, a set of linear constraints, and non-negative variables.

» Learning outcomes «

On completing this chapter you should be able to:

- » Understand the concept of linear programming.
- » Know how to express linear programming problems.
- » Understand the meaning of the objective function and constraints.
- » Know how to formulate and solve both maximizing and minimizing problems.
- » Know how to solve problems using the graphical method.
- » Know how to identify the optimum value, binding and slack constraints, and the application of sensitivity analysis.
- » Understand the idea of shadow pricing and the effect of profit or cost changes on solutions.
- » Understand the meaning of the limits of sensitivity.
- » Solve problems using the Microsoft Excel spreadsheet.
- » Formulate and solve transportation models.

objective function a mathematical expression that describes the problem's objective.

constraints restrictions or limitations imposed on a problem.

maximizing the greatest value in the domain of a variable is its maximum.

minimizing the smallest value in the domain of a variable is its minimum.

sensitivity analysis the study of how changes in the coefficients of a linear programming problem affect the optimal solution.

sensitivity the size of a response value to changes of one of the input values.

allocating resources apportioning shared resources e.g. men, machines, time, finance among the users of those resources, usually in a measured economic fashion to reduce cost for example.

objectives what we are trying to achieve or optimize towards, e.g. maximizing profit.

optimizing the specific decision-variable value(s) that provide the 'best' output for the model.

5.1 Introduction to linear programming

The essence of management in business is to make decisions about allocating resources (men, machines, materials, money, etc) in order to satisfy certain objectives—perhaps to make as much profit as we can or perhaps at as small a cost as we are able. We use the word optimizing to cover both directions: if we want to make the most of something, then we are maximizing; if we want to make the least of something, then we are minimizing. Optimizing means to maximize or minimize, whichever suits the particular occasion.

Usually, the resources available are not enough to cover all that we require, because they are scarce. For example, we may be manufacturing 500 42-inch televisions and 300 36-inch televisions. If a particular circuit board is used once in each television and we have over 800 of them we have no problem. But what do we do if we only have 450 circuit boards? We try to allocate the circuit board to the television that is going to make us the most profit. Very often many items (including labour) that make up the televisions will be scarce, usually in different ways. The problem for the manager is to allocate the items (resources) to make the most profit from what we have available.

The essence of linear programming is a technique that helps the manager to decide on the allocation of scarce resources to finished products that are themselves subject to constraints, in order to optimize an objective (profit, cost, machine hours, machine spare hours, manpower hours, etc.)

The term linear means that all the relationships involved must be linear in fashion, without economies of scale; if we double the input then we double the output. The word programming just means that the solution (in a computer) is found by an iterative repeatable programme method.

Although linear programming is very powerful, and in reality is always done on a computer, using specialist software, its main features can be demonstrated by hand. From this we can learn the terms used in linear programming and can understand the output obtained from computer software in real-life 'huge' problems.

5.1.1 Example uses of linear programming

The application of linear programming solutions is huge, covering all kinds of sectors. Today solutions are more readily available because computers are becoming much faster and smaller so we can solve realistic problems much quicker. When I began linear programming in the 1970s they were run overnight (usually all night) on large mainframe computers. Now the same size problems could almost run in Excel on a laptop computer in a few minutes!! Linear programming can help decision making in many different areas just a few are mentioned here.

i Manufacturing: Product mix problem (allocating parts to finished products to maximize profit).

ii Distribution: Transportation problem (ensuring supplies are distributed from warehouses to customers in the most cost effective manner).

iii Blending: ensuring that mixes of materials such as oils, vitamins, and animal feeds reach the minimum requirements of the finished blend in the most cost effective manner.

iv Investment Appraisal: financial applications (given a certain amount of money to allocate to a portfolio of investments we can balance maybe risk factors to guarantee, as far as possible, a minimum return on investment with minimum combined risk).

5.1.2 Limitations of linear programming

i The variables must be continuous, not discrete.

ii Only one objective can be solved at any one time i.e. cannot optimize on two or more things at once. For example, we cannot maximize profit and minimize cost at the same time—they are two different things.

iii The relationships of the variables for the objectives and constraints must be linear.

If it essential that one or more of these limitations should be broken then there are members of the **mathematical programming (MP)** family that can be used. For example, **integer programming** is a form of mathematical programming for use when discrete values are absolutely necessary. **Non-linear programming** can overcome times when powers in the relationships are essential. **Goal programming** can be used if there is more than one objective to be achieved (e.g. minimize cost, satisfy shareholders). There are many others. However, they may take significantly longer to solve, can be much larger, and usually require very specialist knowledge to perform and decipher.

These forms are all specialist derivatives of mathematical programming but usually linear programming is sufficient for us to have solutions that can be accurate enough for the occasion (with maybe rounding or approximation of the results). They can be used to give an initial solution to aid decision making.

X

mathematical programming (MP) a family of techniques to optimize objectives when the resources are constrained.

integer programming a linear programme with the additional requirement that one or more of the variables must be integer.

non-linear programming an optimization problem that contains at least one non-linear term in the objective function, or a constraint.

goal programming a linear programming approach to multicriteria decision problems whereby the objective function is designed to minimize the deviations from goals.

5.1.3 Linear relationships

In Chapter 1 you had a refresher in basic mathematics. Linear programming needs an appreciation of linear relationships.

To recap:

In the manufacturing process we will incur a cost before we make any items. This is known as the fixed cost; it includes such things as the cost of setting up the machinery. Furthermore, if the cost of material for each item is £20, then we have what we call a variable cost of £20 per item produced. What is the relationship between the number produced at the end of the day and the overall cost?

(1) We can show the relationship as a function (relationship, formulae)

Overall cost (£) = fixed cost + total variable cost

Overall cost (£) = 200 + 20*N

Where N is the number of items produced

(2) We can show the relationship as a table

No of Items	Overall cost formula	Overall cost (£)
0	200 + 20 * 0	200
1	200 + 20 * 1	220
2	200 + 20 * 2	240
5	200 + 20 * 5	300
10	200 + 20 * 10	400

Table 5.1

Or, this relationship observed in table 5.1 can be visualized in Figure 5.1.

(3) We can show the relationship as a graph

Figure 5.1 illustrates the relationship between overall cost and number of items produced for the equation: overall cost = 200 + 20 * N.

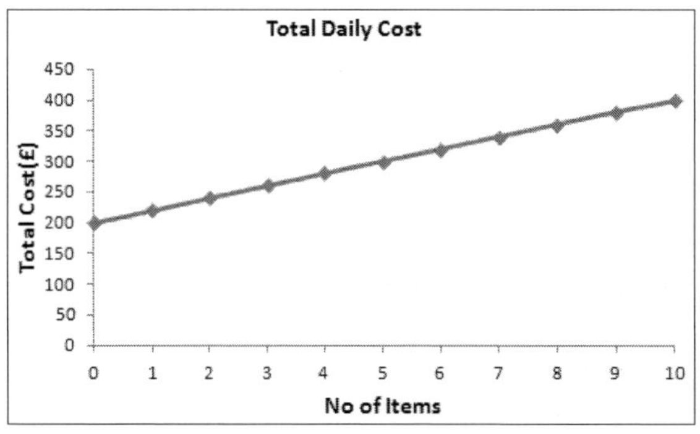

Figure 5.1
Linear graph

Compared with the general line equation: y = mx + c.

We observe, fixed cost = Intercept (c) of line, and variable cost = Slope (m) of line.

So a linear equation is just one which graphs as a straight line.

What determines a straight line is that there are no powers or multiplying of variables: $y = 3 + 2x$, $y = 3$, $y = x_1 + x_2 + 3x_3$ (in several variables), but not $y = 3/x$, $y = 2x^2$, and $y = 4 + xz$. The last three examples which when plotted would make a curve or a parabola. Generally for a straight line in two variables, $y = mx + c$, where x is the independent variable, y is the dependant variable, m is the slope and c is the y-intercept.

The dependent variable is normally drawn vertically and the independent variable horizontally.

$$\text{Slope, } m = \frac{\text{Difference in y values}}{\text{Difference in x values}} = \frac{y_2 - y_1}{x_2 - x_1}$$

The general form of a linear equation for multiple variables is

$$y = m_1X_1 + m_2X_2 + m_3X_3 + \ldots\ldots\ldots\ldots + c$$

where: m_1, m_2, m_3, ... are constant coefficients and X_1, X_2, X_3 .... are different variables. As we will shortly see these are the type of equations used for linear programming but the equations are best formed to have all of the variables on the left hand side of the equation. That is: $ay + bx = \text{constant}$ rather than $y = mx + \text{constant}$.

For example, $2Y + 3X = 12$ would be used rather than $Y = -3X/2 + 6$.

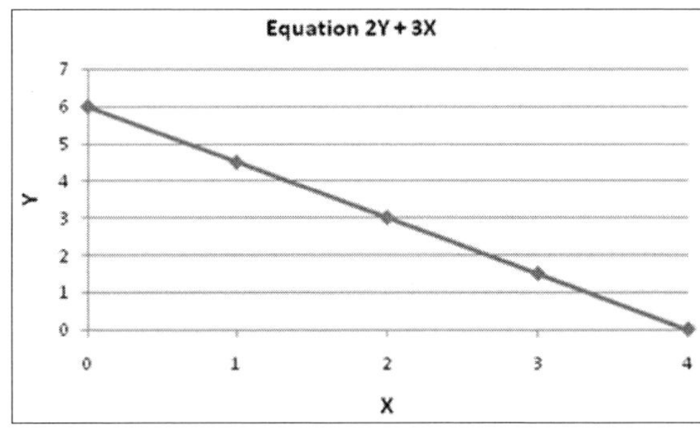

Figure 5.2
Graph of $2y + 3x = 12$

Therefore, $2Y + 3X = 12$ would be plotted as illustrated in Figure 5.2.

Student exercises

X5.1 Which of the following equations are linear? If in your view an equation is not linear then briefly state why this is the case.

(i) $Y = 2X - 3$ (ii) $10 = 2X$

(iii) $Y = 3X^2$ (iv) $2Y - X = 4 + 3Y - 2X$

(v) $T/4 = 3S$ (vi) $4/T = 3S$

(vii) $0 = L - 2M$ (viii) $3A - 5B = 15$

(ix) $P = 2 + 3^Q$ (x) $Y = 0$

5.2 Linear programming with two variables

In practice linear programming solves problems of many variables (sometimes thousands) and equations; however, if we use two variables we can demonstrate all of the main features of linear programming in order to introduce the terminology. We will give both a maximization example and a minimization example.

5.2.1 Example of maximization problem

Example 5.1

Consider the following:

The Great Outdoors Ltd manufactures speciality clothing for hiking, skiing, and mountain climbing. They have decided to start production of two new parkas designed for use in extreme cold weather: to be called the Snowdon and the Nevis.

The following information has been assembled:

- Each Snowdon requires one hour of cutting time & 45 minutes of sewing time. A Nevis requires 30 minutes of cutting time and 15 minutes for sewing.
- Their mid-Wales manufacturing plant has 180 hours of cutting time & 120 hours of sewing time per day available for producing these two parkas.
- Labour & materials costs per parka amount to: Snowdon £80, Nevis £75.
- The parkas are to be sold by mail order at the price of: Snowdon £250, Nevis £150.
- Because management believe that the Snowdon is a unique coat that will enhance the image of the firm, they have decided that at least 20% of total parka production must consist of this model.
- Great Outdoors believe that it can sell all the parkas it chooses to produce.

How many of each parka should Great Outdoors make per day to maximize contribution (i.e. selling price – variable cost)?

5.2.2 Formulation of linear programme

Because LPs are normally large and can be very complicated there is a formal way of formulating the problem. When we discuss computer input you will find that the programme software input is in the order of this formulation.

a. What is it that has to be decided? That is, how many Snowdon or Nevis do we make per day?

What variables can we change in order to meet the objective?

These are called decision variables. We have to decide on the value of these to solve the problem. It helps to use symbols (i.e. letters) instead of words. So, let S = daily output of Snowdon parkas and N = daily output of Nevis parkas.

contribution the value of each variables contribution within the linear programming objective function and constraints.

formulation formulating the linear programming equations based upon the information provided.

decision variables a controllable set of inputs for a linear programming model.

b. What is the objective that we are trying to achieve? In this case we are trying to maximize the contribution (note: this is not profit because the fixed costs such as heating, lighting, warehouse costs etc. are not included).

The contribution per Snowdon is: £250 – £80 = £170.

The contribution per Nevis is: £150 – £75 = £75.

So if we make S Snowdon's then the contribution is £170S; for example, if we make 10 then the contribution is 170*10 = £1700. Similarly, the contribution of Nevis per day is £75N.

So the total contribution is 170S + 75N and we must choose S and N to maximize this number.

Formally, the objective is:

Maximize contribution 170S + 75N

c. However, we cannot choose to make as many of S and N as we like, since if we do there is no problem. We have constraints that prevent us from choosing whatever S and N we would like. Sometimes the constraints are physical and easy to see, sometimes they are softer, for example marketing constraints, but the effect is still the same in that they force the production of S and N—they do not allow us to choose whatever numbers we wish.

Production of the parkas requires the use of resources—in this case cutting and sewing time—which we are told are scarce. In this example we have a sewing constraint, that is, each Snowdon requires 45 minutes of sewing time and each Nevis requires 15 minutes but the manufacturing plant has 120 hours of sewing time per day available for producing these two parkas.

How do we 'formulate' this in terms of our decision variables?

Total daily sewing time for Snowdon is 0.75S; e.g., if S is 10 then we use 7.5 hours sewing.

Total daily sewing time for Nevis is 0.25N; e.g., if N is 20 then we use 0.25 * 20 = 5 hours sewing.

So the total sewing time is 0.75S + 0.25N.

There are only 120 hours per day available for sewing (maybe labour or machinery hours—it doesn't matter the reason, but sewing hours are constrained). So the number of sewing hours used must be less than number of hours available. Therefore, whatever we choose for S and N we must ensure that 0.75S + 0.25N are less than 120. Or, more mathematically:

$$0.75S + 0.25N \leq 120$$

The constraint for cutting is developed similarly.

Therefore, each Snowdon requires one hour of cutting time and each Nevis requires 30 minutes but the manufacturing plant has 180 hours of cutting time per day available for producing these two parkas. Total daily cutting time for Snowdon is 1S; e.g. if S is 10 then we use ten hours cutting. Total daily cutting time for Nevis is 0.5N; e.g., if N is 20 then we use ten hours for cutting (0.5*20). So the total cutting time is 1S + 0.5N.

There are only 180 hours per day available for cutting. So the number of cutting hours used must be less than the number of hours available. Therefore, 1S + 0.5N is less than 180. Or, more mathematically:

$$1S + 0.5N \leq 180$$

Is that all of the constraints?

Well, no: there is another statement that prevents us choosing S and N as we wish. That is the management constraint:

'Because management believe that the Snowdon is a unique coat that will enhance the image of the firm, they have decided that at least 20% of total parka production must consist of this model.'

Whatever reason management has, this is a genuine constraint upon production and therefore is just as important as the others.

It may not be as neat as the others but it is still linear: daily output $= S + N$, therefore 20% is $0.2(S+N)$. So S must be at least $0.2(S+N)$ or $S \geq 0.2(S+N)$. Linear Programming requires all of the variables on the left so this equation should be arranged to read

$$S - 0.2(S+N) \geq 0$$

$$0.8S - 0.2N \geq 0$$

$$8S - 2N \geq 0$$

$$4S - 1N \geq 0$$

Lastly, it may look as though all the constraints have been covered. However, the solution depends upon all values being zero or more; that is, you cannot make a negative number of Snowdon parkas! This may appear obvious but if it was being solved by a computer then you must tell it. This is taken care of by adding **non-negativity constraints**:

$$S \geq 0$$

$$N \geq 0$$

Note If a lower limit has been put on to the variables previously then non-negativty constraints could be omitted. If you are not sure then add them anyway.

Final Formulation:

Decision Variables

Let S = daily output of Snowdon parkas

Let N = daily output of Nevis parkas

Objective Function

Maximize contribution: $170S + 75N$

Subject to Constraints

Sewing	$0.75S + 0.25N \leq 120$
Cutting	$1S + 0.5N \leq 180$
Management	$4S - 1N \geq 0$
Non-negativity	$S \geq 0$
	$N \geq 0$

non-negativity constraints a set of constraints that requires all variables to be non-negative.

5.2.3 Solution of two variable maximization linear programme

With only two variables we can represent the solutions on a graph. With more than two variables, that is, in real-life problems, we have to solve by an algorithm (usually the **Simplex method**) hidden within special computer software. MS Office Excel has an 'add on' feature called **Solver** which will deal with quite large linear programme problems.

Example 5.2

Using Great Outdoors Ltd. as an example the linear programming formulation is as follows:

Decision variables

Let S = daily output of Snowdon parkas

Let N = daily output of Nevis parkas

Objective function

Maximize contribution: 170S + 75N

Subject to constraints

Sewing	$0.75S + 0.25N \leq 120$
Cutting	$1S + 0.5N \leq 180$
Management	$4S - 1N \geq 0$
Non-negativity	$S \geq 0$
	$N \geq 0$

The first step in the graphical solution method is to graph the constraints.

Say we graph the Snowdon on the vertical axis and the Nevis on the horizontal, as illustrated in Figure 5.3.

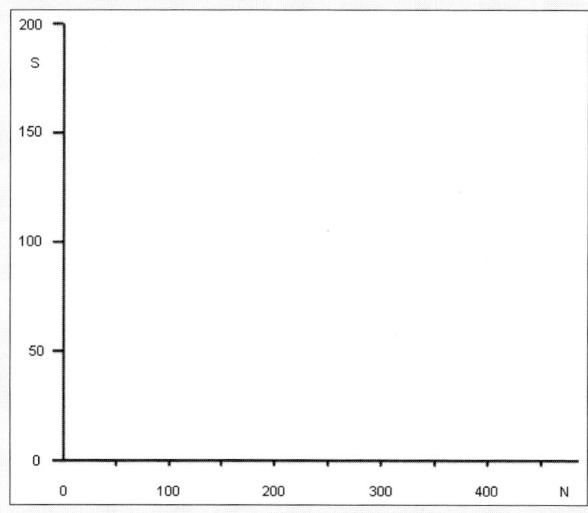

Figure 5.3

Snowdon/Nevis production mix

Simplex method an algebraic procedure for solving linear programming problems. The simplex method uses elementary row operations to iterate from one basic feasible solution (extreme point) to another until the optimal solution is reached.

Solver a software package for solving certain types of mathematical models, such as linear programming models.

Note: because the variables are on the left hand side of the equation we do not think in terms of dependant and independent variables, the axis that they are drawn on only depends on the look of the graph.

Now we see a plane of possible bivariate solutions of make at the end of the day.

For example, three possible combinations of Nevis and Snowdon are shown in Figure 5.4.

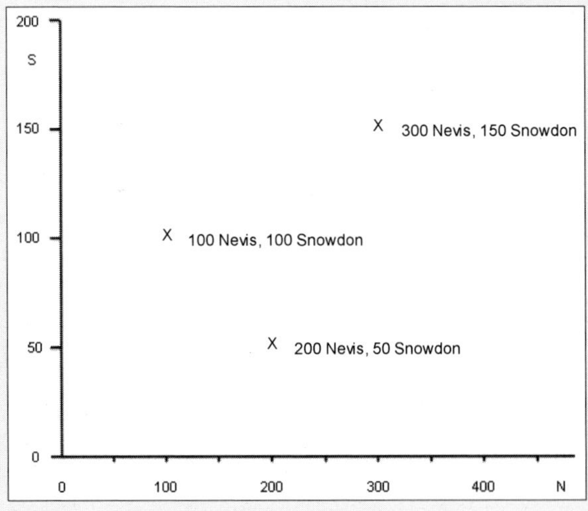

Figure 5.4
Example production combinations

How do we know how best to scale the axes?

Let us start by checking the maximum values required for each of the variables, in each of the constraints.

Consider the cutting time constraint, $S + 0.5N \leq 180$.

If S is 0 (i.e. we only cut Nevis) then maximum we could make would be $0.5N = 160$, $N = 360$.

If N is 0 (i.e. we only cut Snowdon) then maximum we could make would be $S = 180$.

And now, the sewing time constraint, $0.75S + 0.25N \leq 120$.

If S is 0 (i.e. we only sew Nevis) then maximum we could make would be $0.25N = 120$, $N = 480$.

If N is 0 (i.e. we only sew Snowdon) then maximum we could make would be $0.75S = 120$, $S = 160$.

The management constraint has no maximums.

Thus, our daily maximum values for each constraint must be within N: 0 – 480 and S: 0 – 180. Thus the scales indicated in Figure 5.3 would cover all possible combinations that we could make.

Now let us graph the constraints.

Consider the cutting time constraint: $S + 0.5N \leq 180$. This is really two equations: all S and N such that $S + 0.5N = 180$, and all S and N such that $S + 0.5N < 180$.

First if we just take the equality. Remember in order to show all points on the graph that satisfy a linear equation we can just find two points and draw the line between them (we can only draw one straight line between two points!). The easiest points to calculate are on the axes:

- If $S = 0$ then $0 + 0.5N = 180$, and we find $N = 360$,
- If $N = 0$ then $S + 0.5 * 0 = 180$, and we find $S = 180$.

This line is shown in Figure 5.5. So every combination of S, N on this line will add up to 180 hours

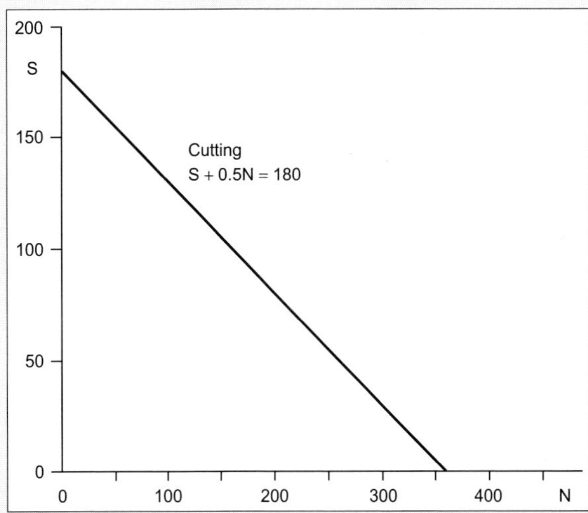

Figure 5.5
Cutting time constraint

What about the less than?

What happens with inequalities is that the line separates the space into two areas. One area will be less than the right-hand side of the equation and the other area will be greater than the right-hand side. To see which is which, just try any point.

For example, in Figure 5.6, the point S = 50 N = 100 will give a cutting time of 50 + 0.5(100) = 100 hours this is less than 180 so this combination could be cut.

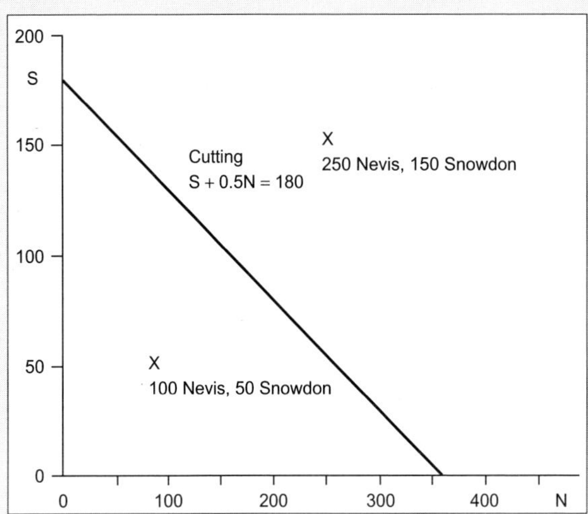

Figure 5.6
Can we cut it?

However, in Figure 5.6, the point S = 150 and N = 250 will give a time of 150 + 0.5(150) = 225 hours: this is greater than 180 so the combination cannot be cut.

Thus in this case we can make everything on the line or to the left of it as illustrated in Figure 5.7.

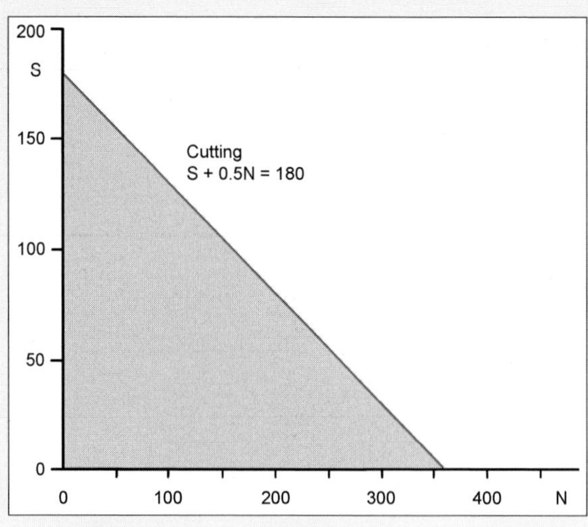

Figure 5.7

Region that satisfies the cutting constraint

The region allowed by the sewing constraint $0.75S + 0.25N \leq 120$ is as illustrated in Figure 5.8.

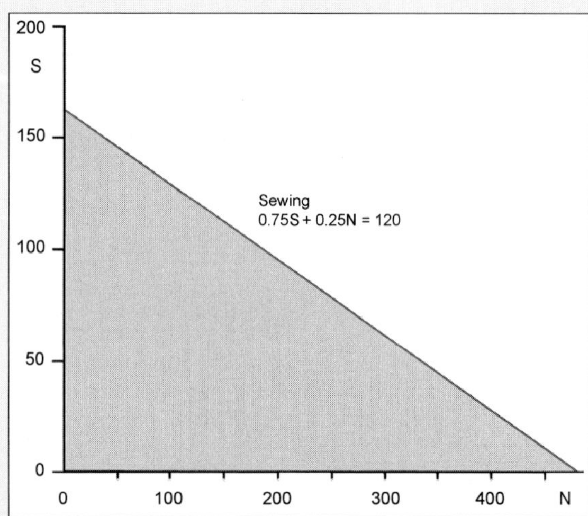

Figure 5.8

Region that satisfies the sewing constraint

How can we draw the management constraint $4S - N \geq 0$?

If $S = 0$ then $N = 0$.

This gives one point but for another point we can choose any N (or S); e.g. if $N = 160$ then $4S - 160 = 0$ so $S = 40$.

This line can be plotted as Figure 5.9.

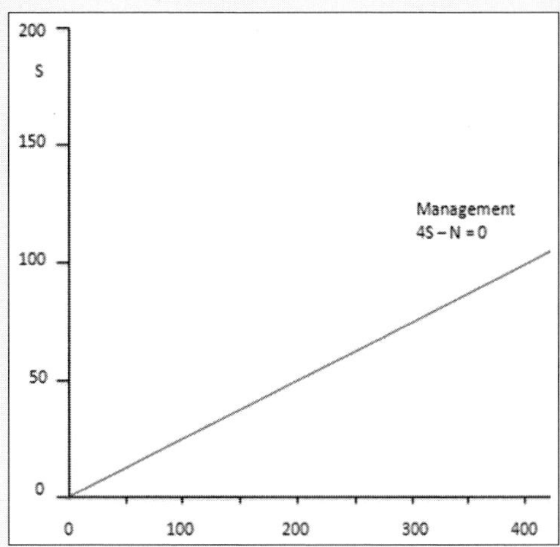

Figure 5.9

Management constraint

Finding the side of the line that satisfies the > constraint can be done by trying one point; e.g. S = 100 N = 100.

This is 4(100) – 100 = 300 which is > 0.

Because that point satisfies the inequality then all that side of the line satisfies the inequality. So the area prescribed by the management constraint is as in Figure 5.10.

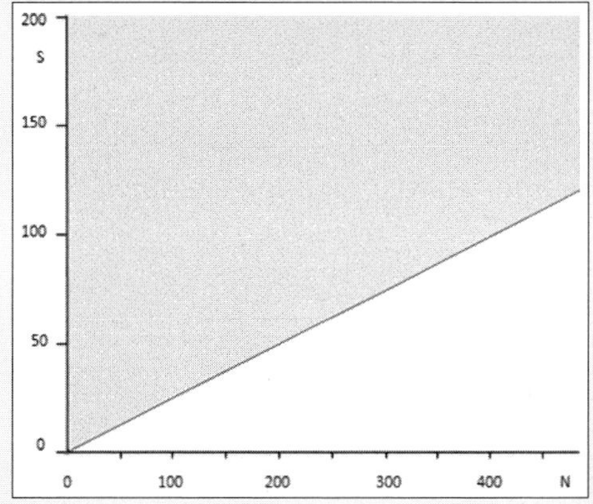

Figure 5.10

Region that satisfies the management constraint

If we superimpose all of these regions together and shade the area that is in the common to all of them we have the graph in Figure 5.11.

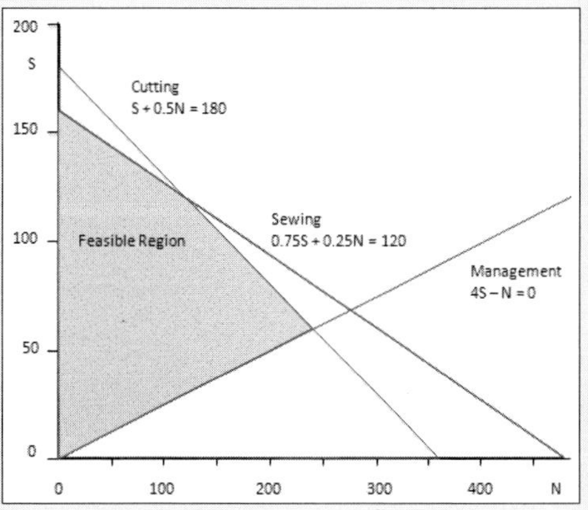

Figure 5.11

Feasible region of Snowdon and Nevis

feasible region the set of all feasible solutions.

The area in common to all of the regions is called the feasible region. This is the region where each point satisfies the constraints. Any mix of Snowdon and Nevis within that area can be made; anything outside that area must break at least one of the constraints and so cannot be made.

Now all we have to do is to find the point in this region that gives us the maximum contribution (satisfies the objective)! This can seem quite daunting but a feature of the shape helps us to simplify this. Notice that the shape of the feasible region is a polygon, where all of the points (vertices) are outwards. In many dimensions (we only have two at the moment) this is called a convex polyhedron. Remember the objective function is to maximize contribution 170S + 75N. On its own we cannot plot this. But we can plot a line where the contribution equals, say, £12,750. (I have chosen this because 170 * 75 = 12,750 so when we are finding the points, as follows, we do not have a lot of calculation!), that is, 170S + 75N = 12,750, because this follows the general form of a straight line.

So if I choose points:

When N = 0,

170S + 75(0) = 12,750,

S = 75

When S = 0,

170(0) + 75N = 12,750,

N = 170

Plot this line and we have Figure 5.12.

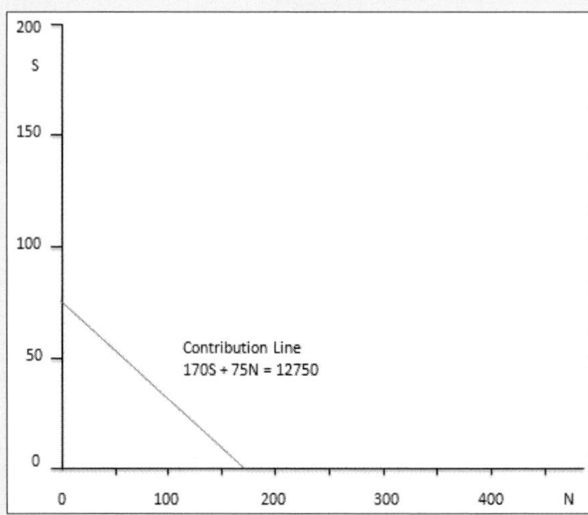

Figure 5.12
Contribution = £12,750 line

This means that all the combinations on our example objective line will earn £12,750. What happens if we vary the value of the objective function?

Figure 5.13 shows lines with various objective values.

X

convex polyhedron geometrically, the linear constraints define a convex polyhedron, which is called the feasible region.

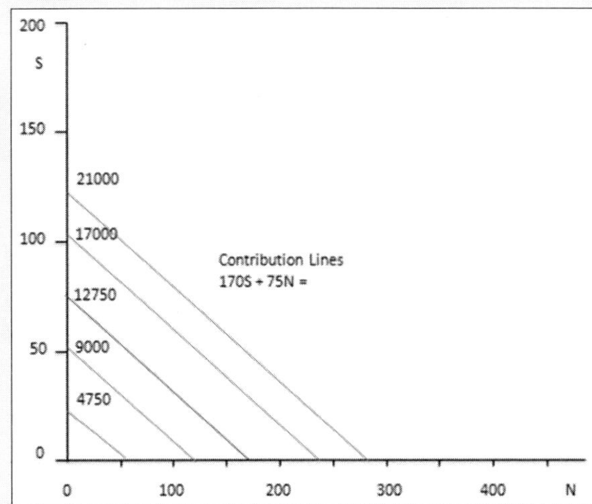

Figure 5.13
Varying contribution lines

The important thing to notice is that as the value of the objective increases the line moves outwards from the origin and as the value decreases, than the line moves towards the origin, but the slope of the line remains the same i.e. it is only the intercept that is changing.

From the graph in Figure 5.14 you can see that the objective line crosses the feasible region and all points where they overlap gives a Snowdon, Nevis combination at that particular contribution. For example, the black dashed lines give a contribution of £12,750.

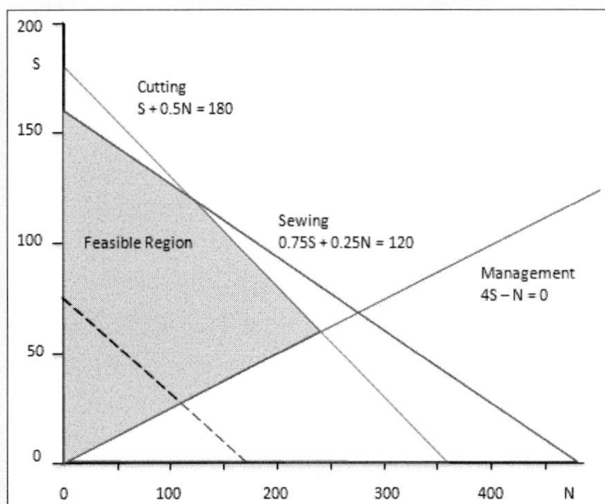

Figure 5.14
Feasible points giving a contribution of £12,750

But there are feasible points to the right of this line so those covered by the next line on Figure 5.15 may all give 18,000 and so on.

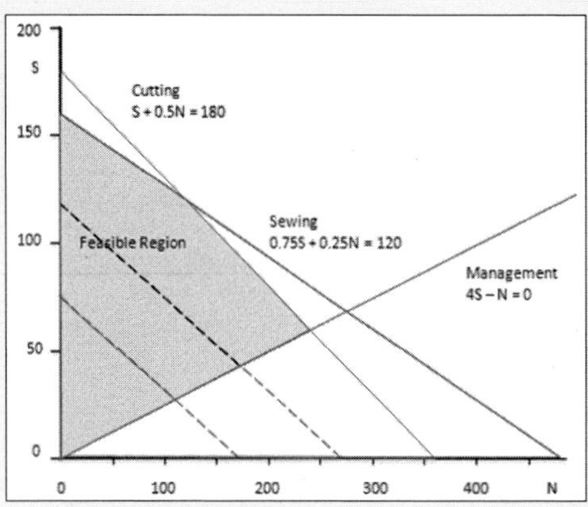

Figure 5.15
Feasible points giving an £18,000 contribution

If we draw the objective line overlapping the very last point of the feasible region, then this is the combination that gives the maximum contribution as illustrated in Figure 5.16.

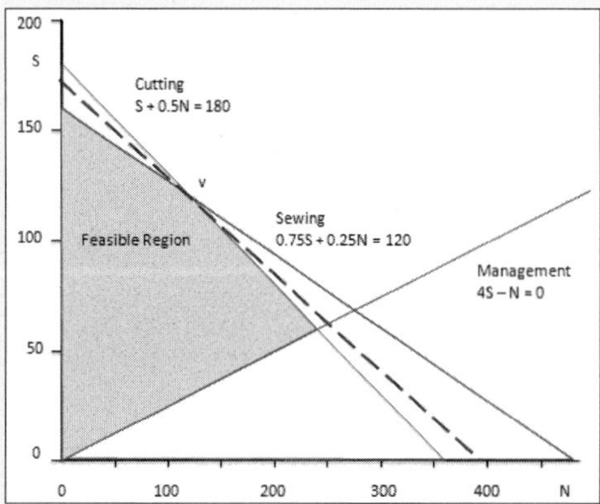

Figure 5.16
Point giving maximum contribution

This point is always available because the corners always point outwards! If the contribution increased any more, the line would move outwards and it will no longer cross the feasible region, so nothing can be made.

If the objective line is exactly parallel to a constraint line then we will have all of the Snowdon, Nevis combinations on this line giving the maximum contribution, but this will mean that the two corners (at each end of the line) will be the same! This demonstrates a very important feature of LPs – the solution of a linear programme is always at a vertex (corner), never in the middle, of the feasible region! So we have established that the best point to make is point 'v' on Figure 5.16. How do we find the coordinates of this? Graphs are notoriously bad to read accurate values so we resort to algebra, noticing that the point lies at the intersection of two lines. The lines are:

Cutting $S + 0.5N = 180$ .... (i)

Sewing $0.75S + 0.25N = 120$ .... (ii)

This means that the cutting time and the sewing constraints are fully utilized.

By using simultaneous equations, in this case:

Multiply (ii) by 2 $1.5S + 0.5N = 240$ .... (iii)

X
vertex the point or corner of a feasible region. Where two or more constraints intersect on the feasible region.

Now, because we have the same term in both equations (0.5N), subtract (iii) from (i) and we obtain:

$$0.5S = 60$$
$$S = 120$$

Put into (i) gives:

$$120 + 0.5N = 180$$
$$0.5N = 60$$
$$N = 120$$

So the optimal solution is to make 120 Snowdon and 120 Nevis parkas. This will give a contribution of $170S + 75N = 170(120) + 75(120) = 20{,}400 + 9000 = £29{,}400$.

If we make this combination then we use:

Cutting:

$S + 0.5N = 120 + 0.5(120) = 120 + 60 = 180$ hours.

Sewing:

$0.75S + 0.25N = 0.75(120) + 0.25(120) = 90 + 30 = 120$ hours.

Management:

$4S - N = 4(120) - 120 = 360$, it is difficult to visualize the meaning of this but $120 > 0.2(120 + 120) = 48$ so S is certainly greater than 20% of the total.

The cutting time and sewing time are fully used up and so are said to be a 'tight', 'scarce' or 'binding' constraints. Management is not on the limit and so is a 'slack' constraint.

Student exercises

X5.2 Computer problem

Electron Ltd is a small company manufacturing industrial computers, related control hardware and systems. The PC division of Electron produces two types of industrial computer: the Standard and the Super. During manufacture, components of the computers are processed in various departments, without constraint. They are finally put together, into finished products, in two main areas of the plant—assembly, and finishing/packaging. The time taken by each product in each department is summarized in the following Table 5.2.

Plant	Standard (hours)	Super (hours)	Total time available (hours per week)
Assembly	2	3	300
Finishing/Packaging	3	2	300

Table 5.2

A Super computer requires 30 minutes specialized testing on one of two test machines, each working for 20 hours per week. Standard and Super computers have control circuit boards in common: the Standard requires four but the Super only requires two. Electron only has capacity to make 320 of these boards per week. An automatic soldering process needs to be kept in regular use, implying that a minimum of 20 Supers must be made per week.

The Standard computer is made under licence from Industrial Computer Supplies, implying that Electron is not allowed to manufacture more than 65 Standards in any week. However, they can produce as many Supers as they are able. An agreement with the union specifies that at least 50 units, Standards, Supers or a combination of both, must be manufactured each week. Electron does not manufacture finished computers for stock, but sells everything that it builds. The accountants attribute a contribution of £210 to each Standard and £135 to each Super computer.

Formulate the problem as a linear program.

X5.3 Solve this linear programming problem by graphical means.

$$\text{Maximize } 2X + Y$$

Subject to:

$$\begin{aligned} 2X + 2Y &\leq 32 \\ X \quad\;\; &\leq 10 \\ 4X + 6Y &\geq 48 \\ X \quad\;\; &\geq 0 \\ Y &\geq 0 \end{aligned}$$

X5.4 Solve this linear programming problem by graphical means.

$$\text{Maximize } 3X + 2Y$$

Subject to:

$$\begin{aligned} 2X - 2Y &\leq 80 \\ -2X + 3Y &\leq 90 \\ X + Y &\leq 55 \\ X \quad\;\; &\geq 0 \\ Y &\geq 0 \end{aligned}$$

X5.5 Referring to the computer problem formulated in X5.2. Solve it graphically.

5.3 A two variable minimization problem

As an example of a minimization problem in two variables we will use a different application of linear programming – an investment example.

5.3.1 Example of minimization problem

Example 5.3

ABC Investments manages funds for a number of companies and wealthy clients. For a new client ABC has been authorized to invest up to £1.2 million in two investments: an equity fund and bonds. Each unit of the equity fund costs £50 and provides an expected annual return of 10%. Each bond costs £100 and provides an annual return of 4%. The client wishes to minimize risk subject to the requirement that the annual income from the investment be at least £60,000. According to ABC's risk measurement system each unit invested in the equity fund has a risk index of 8 and each bond has a risk index of 3: the higher risk index associated with the equity fund simply indicates that it is the riskier investment. The client has also specified that at least £300,000 be invested in bonds.

5.3.2 Formulation of linear programme

a. What is it that has to be decided? That is how many bonds or equities do ABC buy, ie what variables can we change in order to meet the objective?
These are called decision variables. We have to decide on the value of these to solve the problem. So let B = number of bonds purchased, and let E = number of equities purchased.

b. What is the objective that we are trying to achieve? In this case we are trying to minimize the risk for the client.

   Risk per equity is 8, risk per bond is 3.

   So if we buy E equities then risk is 8E, B bonds risk is 3B.

   So the total risk is $3B + 8E$ and we must choose B and E to minimize this number.

   Formally the objective is: minimize risk $8E + 3B$.

c. However, we have constraints which prevent us from choosing whatever E and B we would like.

   Total invested must be less than or equal to £1,200,000.

   An equity unity costs £50 and a bond costs £100.

   So E equities costs £50E and B bonds cost £100B.

   Total cost is $50E + 100B$.

   This cannot exceed the total invested,

   Therefore, $50E + 100B \leq 1{,}200{,}000$

   Next, annual income must exceed £60,000.

   Income from equity is 10% with a cost of £50 and from a bond is 4% with a cost of £100.

   So the return from equity is £5 and from a bond is £4.

   Therefore, $5E + 4B \geq 60{,}000$

Lastly, at least £300,000 must be invested in bonds.

This is a lot simpler in that bonds cost £100.

Therefore, $100B \geq 300{,}000$

Remember that we must include non-negativity constraints. Notice though that B already has a lower limit ($100B \geq 3000$) so we only need to have a lower limit on E (although if $B \geq 0$ is included it does not matter but is just a redundant constraint).

So non-negativity constraints: $E \geq 0$

Final Formulation:

Decision Variables

So Let B = Number of bonds purchased

Let E = Number of equities purchased.

Objective Function

Minimize Risk $8E + 3B$

Subject to Constraints

Investment	$50E + 100B \leq 1{,}200{,}000$
Return	$5E + 4B \geq 60{,}000$
Bonds	$100B \geq 300{,}000$
Non-negativity	$E \geq 0$

5.3.3 Solution of two variable minimization linear programmes

Again we will solve it graphically with the axes of E and B.

How do we know what scales to put onto the graph?

Let us start putting the possible combinations that can be made; that is, we plot the constraints. To do this we check the maximum values required for each of the variables.

Consider the investment constraint, $50E + 100B \leq 1{,}200{,}000$.

- If E is 0 (i.e. we only bought bonds) then maximum we could buy would be $100B = 1{,}200{,}000$, $B = 12{,}000$.
- If B is 0 (i.e. we only buy equities) then maximum we could buy would be $50E = 1{,}200{,}000$, $E = 24{,}000$.

The minimum returns constraint is a greater than constraint, therefore there is no upper limit:

$$5E + 4B \geq 60{,}000$$

To draw the minimum line if E is 0 (i.e. only buy bonds) then minimum $B = 15{,}000$.

If B is 0 (i.e. we only buy equities) then minimum we could buy would be $E = 12{,}000$.

The minimum bonds constraint, $100B \geq 300{,}000$, means that $B = 3000$ is minimum

Thus E must be at least 0 – 24,000, B must be 0 - 15,000.

So the scales in Figure 5.17 would be sufficient.

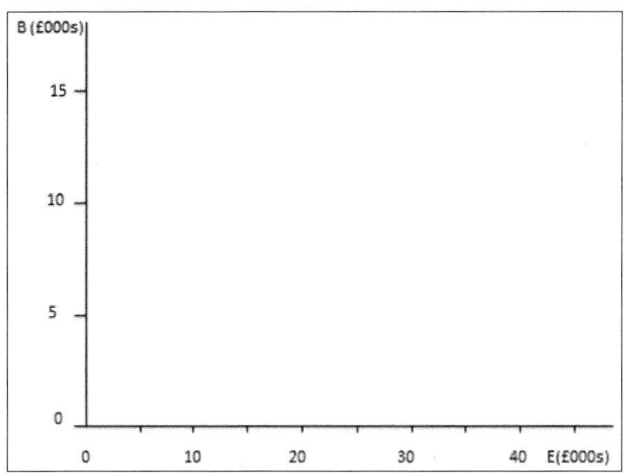

Figure 5.17
Scales for ABC investments

Now let us graph the constraints and the areas of inequality.

Consider the investment constraint $50E + 100B \leq 1{,}200{,}000$.

This is really two equations:

- All E and B such that $50E + 100B = 1{,}200{,}000$
- All E and B such that $50E + 100B < 1{,}200{,}000$

First if we just take the equality.

If $E = 0$ then $0 + 100B = 1{,}200{,}000$, and $B = 12{,}000$

If $B = 0$ then $50E = 1{,}200{,}000$, and $E = 24{,}000$

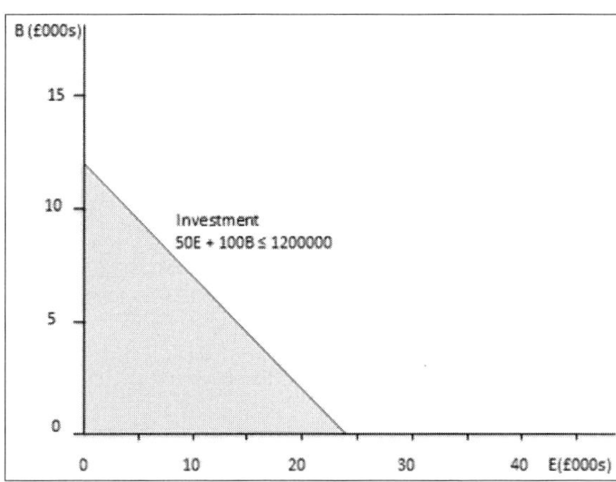

Figure 5.18
Region that satisfies the investment constraint

This line and region is shown in Figure 5.18. So every combination of E, B on this line will add up to £1,200,000 and in the shaded area will be less than £1,200,000.

The region allowed by the Returns constraint

$$5E + 4B \geq 60{,}000$$

is as in Figure 5.19.

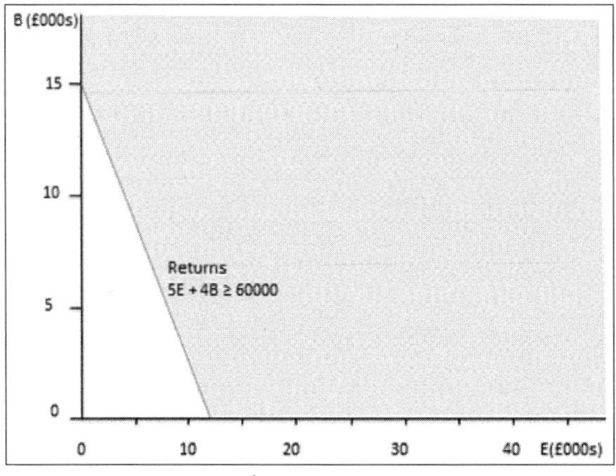

Figure 5.19

Region that satisfies the returns constraint

The region allowed by the minimum bond constraint.

$$100B \geq 300{,}000$$

is as in Figure 5.20.

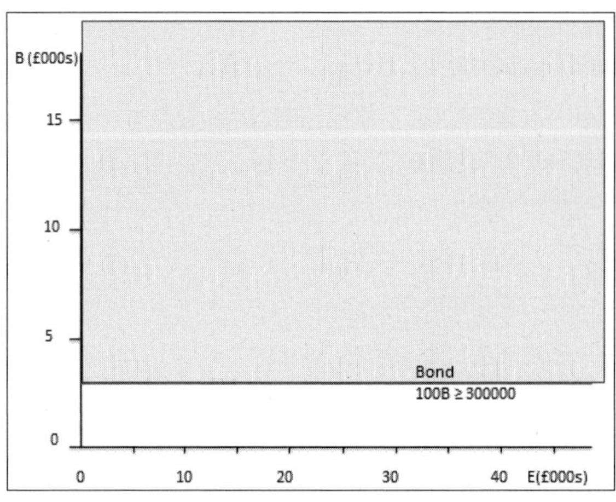

Figure 5.20

Region that satisfies the bond constraint

If we superimpose all of these regions together and shade the area that is in the common to all of them we have the graph in Figure 5.21.

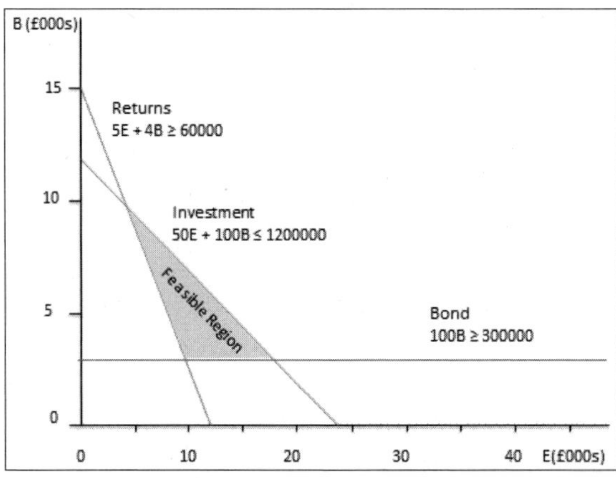

Figure 5.21

Feasible region of equities and bonds

The objective is to minimize risk 8E + 3B.

From our previous discussion there are two ways to find the minimum point:

(i) Evaluate every vertex because we know that the solution is always at a vertex. Hence find the coordinates of each corner and calculate the risk. The objective is the minimum value.

(ii) Draw an example objective line and move it until the first point of the Feasible Region nearest to the origin, then find the coordinates of that point.

Using Method (ii), if I draw the line 8E + 3B = 48,000

When E = 0, B = 16,000

When B = 0, E = 6000.

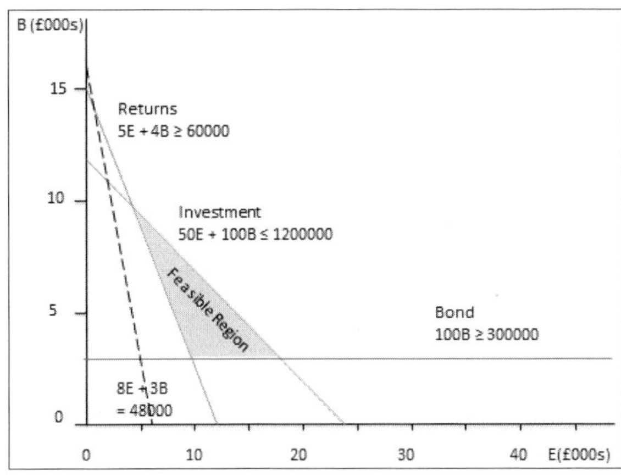

Figure 5.22
Feasible region with example objective line

Figure 5.22 illustrates this line (dotted) superimposed on to the graph.

If we draw the objective line overlapping the very first point of the feasible region, then this is the combination that gives the minimum contribution as illustrated in Figure 5.23.

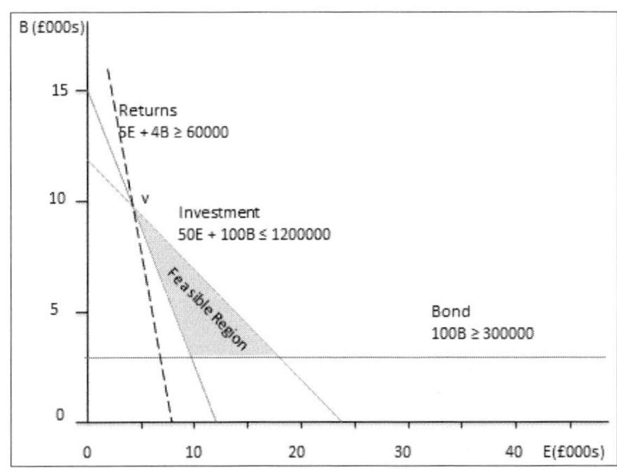

Figure 5.23
Point giving minimum risk

If the risk decreased then the line moves inwards and it will no longer cross the feasible region.

So we have established that the best combination to buy is shown at point 'v' on Figure 5.23. To find the coordinates of this point notice that it is where the maximum Investment and minimum Returns constraints cross. The lines are:

Investment $50E + 100B = 1{,}200{,}000$ .... (i)

Returns $5E + 4B = 60{,}000$ .... (ii)

To solve, multiply (ii) by 10: $50E + 40B = 600{,}000$ .... (iii)

Now, because we have the same term in both equations (50E), subtract (iii) from (i) and we obtain:

$$60B = 600{,}000$$

$$B = 10{,}000$$

Put into (ii):

$$5E + 4(10{,}000) = 60{,}000$$

$$5E = 20{,}000$$

$$E = 4000$$

So the optimal solution is to buy 10,000 bonds and 4000 equities. This will have a risk factor of only $8(4000) + 3(10{,}000) = 62{,}000$. If we buy this combination then we use:

Investment $50(4000) + 100(10{,}000) = 200{,}000 + 1{,}000{,}000 = 1{,}200{,}000$

Return $5(4000) + 4(10{,}000) = 20{,}000 + 40{,}000 = 60{,}000$

Bonds $100(10{,}000) = 1{,}000{,}000 \geq 300{,}000$

The investment is at a maximum and returns are at a minimum so are binding. The bonds are way above the minimum required so this is a slack constraint.

Student exercises

X5.6 Solve this linear programming problem by graphical means:

Minimize $3X + 4Y$

Subject to:

$X + 3Y \geq 6$

$X + Y \geq 4$

$X \geq 0$

$Y \geq 0$

X5.7 Solve this linear programming problem by graphical means:

Minimize $5X + 4Y$

Subject to:

$X + Y \geq 8$

$X + 3Y \geq 12$

$3X + Y \geq 12$

$X \geq 0$

$Y \geq 0$

5.4 Sensitivity of linear programmes

Whenever we suggest a solution to a problem we should see how the solution would change if we vary the input parameters of the problem slightly. It's to be hoped that the solution will not change very much, in which case it is said to be robust. Sensitivity should be studied in all decision making techniques, but here we just study the measurement of sensitivity of linear programming problems. In particular we are assuming that we may vary constraint levels or the coefficients of the objective function (in the Great Outdoor Ltd. problem the contributions of Snowdon or Nevis). During sensitivity we do not attempt to change too many numbers at once, if we did then we wouldn't understand the effect of each change. So we just change one thing with everything else remaining the same.

Example 5.4

Reconsider the Great Outdoor Ltd. problem.

Final Formulation

Decision Variables

Let S = daily output of Snowdon parkas

Let N = daily output of Nevis parkas

Objective Function

Maximize contribution 170S + 75N

Subject to Constraints

Sewing	$0.75S + 0.25N \leq 120$
Cutting	$1S + 0.5N \leq 180$
Management	$4S - 1N \geq 0$
Non-negativity	$S \geq 0$
	$N \geq 0$

The solution (at point v) was to make 120 each of Snowdon and Nevis giving a contribution of £29,400.

5.4.1 Constraint levels

What is the effect of changing the constraint level, ie the right-hand side of the equations?

As we have seen with the objective function, as the right-hand side of the equation increases then the constraint line moves outwards from the origin, and if it decreases then the line moves inwards. So if we have more cutting time available then the line will move outwards, because it is a binding constraint the feasible region will increase to the new line.

(i) Thus, the point where the lines cross moves, and we will have a new optimum solution (v′ instead of v), as illustrated in Figure 5.24.

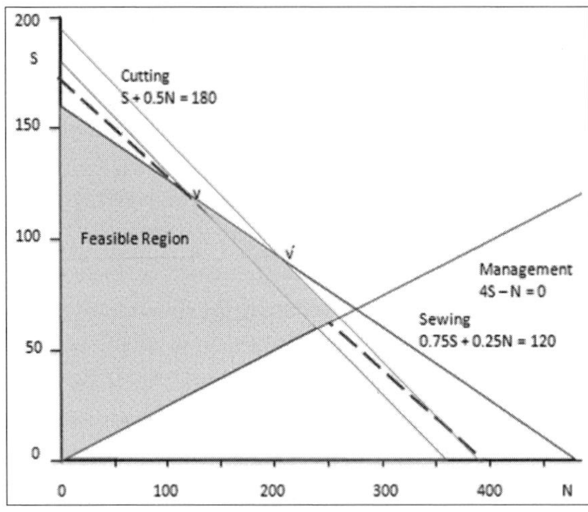

Figure 5.24
Moving cutting constraint

In practice we would like to increase the line as far as we are able to increase cutting time, but as an indication of the effect, just increase the line by 1.

The same two lines are binding:

Cutting time	$S + 0.5N = 181$	.............(i)
Sewing	$0.75S + 0.25N = 120$	.............(ii)
Multiply (ii) by 2:		
	$1.5S + 0.5N = 240$	...........(iii)
(iii)–(i) gives	$0.5S = 59$	
So	$S = 118$	
Put into (i)		

$$118 + 0.5N = 181$$
$$0.5N = 181 - 118 = 63$$
$$N = 126$$

So the effect of having one more hour of cutting means that we make six more Nevis and two less Snowdon. More importantly, what is the change in the contribution value? Remember the objective function is 170S + 75N so at our new solution point this represents:

$$= 170(118) + 75(126) = 20{,}060 + 9450 = £29{,}510$$

Previously we made a £29,400 contribution, so by having one more hour of cutting time we have gained £110 extra contribution. This is called the 'shadow price' of the cutting constraint. **Shadow price** is the change in the objective function value that would arise if the constraint level is adjusted by 1 without changing the optimal constraints. Obviously we cannot increase the cutting constraint by one hour forever gaining £110 each time we do it. As illustrated in the graph in Figure 5.25, the cutting time can move outwards as the constraint level increases, pulling the feasible region with it as it goes.

But after point 'a' the feasible region is constrained by the sewing line and the management constraint and any increase in the cutting hours will add £0 to the contribution; i.e., there will be slack time in the cutting constraint.

> **shadow price** is the change in the objective function value that would arise if the constraint level is adjusted by 1 without changing the optimal constraints.

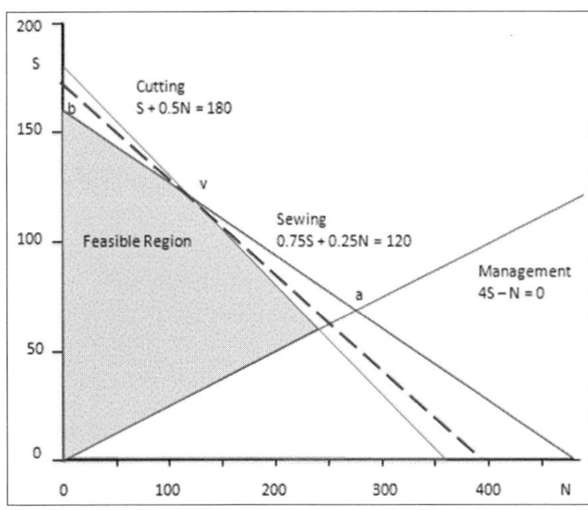

Figure 5.25
Showing limits of cutting time

How can we find the value of this upper limit of the cutting constraint?

Notice that it is where the sewing and management constraint cross so we can solve these equations simultaneously to find the coordinates of this point.

Sewing $0.75S + 0.25N = 120$ .... (i)

Management $4S - \quad 1N = 0$ .... (ii)

Multiply (i) by 4 gives:

$3S + \quad 1N = 480$ .... (iii)

Add (iii) and (i) (to eliminate N!)

$$7S = 480$$

$$S = 480/7 = 68.57$$

Put into (ii) to find N

$$4(480/7) - N = 0$$

$$N = 4*480/7 = 274.29$$

It doesn't matter that they are fractions because in practice we would round them down and say, at this point, we would make 68 Snowdon and 274 Nevis (remember that a linear programming solution has to be continuous).

What would be the cutting time to make this combination?

$68 + 0.5 * 274 = 68 + 137 = 205$ hours

Cutting time could be increased to approximately 205 hours before it ceased to be scarce.

Of course, the shadow price also acts in the other direction, that is, if the cutting time is decreased by one hour then the contribution will reduce by £110.

What is the lower limit of the cutting time shadow price?

According to the graph in Figure 5.25, if the cutting line moves towards the origin then the point where sewing and cutting crosses moves up the sewing line until the point 'b' where the sewing line meets the S axis. If the cutting line moves lower then, even though the cutting line is still binding it, it crosses a different line and so will have a different shadow price. Remember the definition of shadow price is only true 'without changing the optimal constraints.'

To find the lower limit of the cutting constraint we solve the equations:

Sewing $0.75S + 0.25N = 120$ .... (i)

Snowdon Axis $N = 0$ .... (ii)

So (ii) into (i) give: $0.75S + 0 = 120$, $S = 160$

What is the cutting hours when the line passes through $S = 160$, $N = 0$?

Cutting Time $S + 0.5N = 160 + 0 = 160$

Thus we can decrease cutting time to 160 hours from 180 hours and we reduce by £110 per hour.

> **Interpretation** Shadow price for Cutting = £110 Original value = 180 Lower Limit = 160, Upper limit = 205.

If the cutting time level goes outside these limits then there may be different constraints which are optimal or we may have a different shadow price. The linear programme would have to be recalculated.

Important decision making can be made from knowing the shadow price and its limits. For example, if someone offered to sell us 50 extra cutting hours for £80, how many, if any, should we take?

We know that for every extra cutting hour we gain £110 extra contribution, so if we pay £80 then we are still gaining £30 per hour. We would certainly buy the extra hours. However, we also know that after an extra 25 then the cutting time is no longer scarce and so the shadow price becomes £0, so we would lose £80 per hour.

We would be happy to buy an extra 25 hours at £80, but no more!

To find the shadow price and limits for sewing time we proceed as follows:

We add one hour to sewing but leave the cutting time unchanged.

Cutting time $S + 0.5N = 180$ .... (i)

Sewing $0.75S + 0.25N = 121$ .... (ii)

Multiply (ii) by 2

$1.5S + 0.5N = 242$ .... (iii)

Subtract (iii)—(i)

$$0.5S = 62$$
$$S = 124$$

Substitute into (i)

$$124 + 0.5N = 180$$
$$0.5N = 56$$
$$N = 112$$

Thus if we gain one extra sewing time hour then we can make four more Snowdon and eight less Nevis.

The effect on contribution is: $170(124) + 75(112) = 21{,}080 + 8400 = £29{,}480$.

Previously we made a £29,400 contribution, so by having one more hour of sewing time we have gained £80 extra in contribution.

This is very valuable because imagine we had £500 to spend on capacity. Where would we put it? Cutting has a shadow price of £110 and sewing has a shadow price of £80, for each extra hour. Obviously we would spend on cutting because we have a much bigger return.

How can we find the value of the upper limit of the sewing constraint?

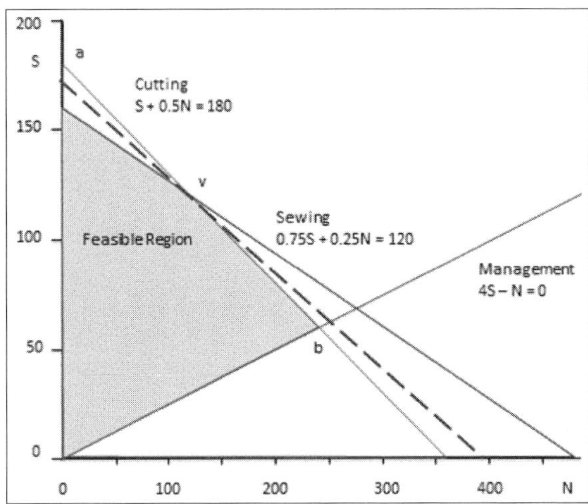

Figure 5.26
Showing limits of sewing time

According to the graph in Figure 5.26 if the sewing line moves outwards then the point where sewing and cutting crosses moves up the cutting line until point 'a' where the cutting line meets the S axis.

To find the upper limit of the sewing constraint we solve the equations;

Cutting $S + 0.5N = 180$ .... (i)

Snowdon Axis $N = 0$ .... (ii)

Thus from (ii) into (i) $S + 0 = 180$, $S = 180$

What is the sewing hours when the line passes through $S = 180$, $N = 0$?

Sewing time $0.75S + 0.25N = 0.75(180) + 0 = 135$

Thus we can increase sewing time to 135 hours from 120 hours and we increase by £80 per hour. Of course, the shadow price also acts in the other direction ie if sewing time is decreased by one hour then the contribution will reduce by £80.

What is the lower limit of the sewing time shadow price?

How can we find the value of the lower limit of the sewing constraint?

Notice that it is at point 'b' where the cutting and management constraint cross so we can solve these equations simultaneously to find the coordinates of this point. If the sewing line moves lower then, even though the sewing line is still binding it crosses a different line (management) and so will have a different shadow price. Remember the definition of shadow price is only true 'without changing the optimal constraints.'

Cutting	$1S + 0.5N = 180$	(i)
Management	$4S - 1N = 0$	(ii)

Multiply (i) by 2 gives

$$2S + 1N = 240 \text{ .... (iii)}$$

Add (iii) and (ii) (to eliminate N!)

$$6S = 360,\ S = 360/6 = 60$$

Put into (ii) to find N

$$4(60) - N = 0,\ N = 240$$

What would be the sewing time to make this combination?

$$0.75(60) + 0.25(240) = 45 + 60 = 105 \text{ hours}$$

So sewing time could be decreased to 70 hours before it ceased to be scarce.

> ✻ **Interpretation** Shadow price for Sewing = £80 Original value = 120 Lower Limit = 105, Upper limit = 135

What is the shadow price for management constraint?

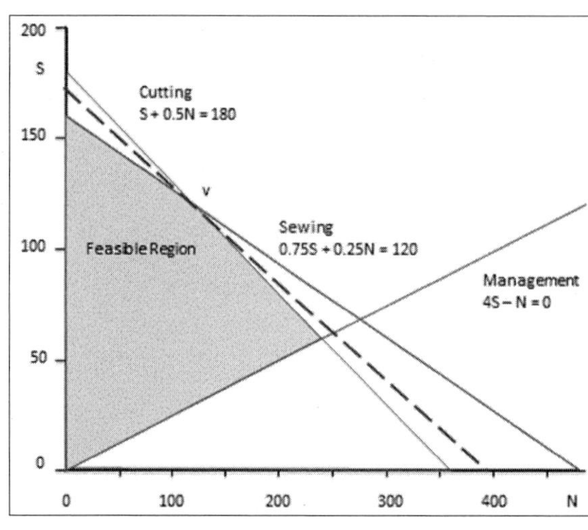

Figure 5.27
Showing management constraint

From Figure 5.27, we observe that if we move the constraint by 1 then it will not interfere with the solution. Therefore the contribution remains the same.

Therefore the shadow price of any slack constraint is £0.

Note: they do have a shadow price, but it is £0.

What about the limits over which this shadow price is applicable?

First, let's interpret the meaning of 1 on the right hand side of the management constraint. Remember the original constraint is that Snowdon has to be greater than 20% of the total production:

$$S \geq 0.2(S + N)$$

$$S \geq 0.2S + 0.2N$$

$$0.8S - 0.2N \geq 0$$

$$4S - \quad N \geq 0$$

So every increase on the right-hand side is an increase in Snowdon manufacture above 20% of total. Looking at the graph in Figure 5.27 we can move the line to the right and it does not affect the solution—in fact it is moving away from the solution. So there is no limit that way. However, if the line moves towards the solution then when it goes through the solution point it will affect the optima. In terms of management constraint this is when 4(120) – 120 = 360. Thus when the equation becomes 4S – N = 360 then the £0 shadow price will end.

To put back into the original form this is saying that $0.8S - 0.2N \geq 360/5$, $S \geq 0.2S + 0.2N + 360/5$ so total Snowdon is greater than 20% of the total + 72.

Interpretation Shadow price for management £0, Original value = 0, Lower Limit = 0, Upper limit = 360.

5.4.2 Coefficients of objective

Another number that would be interesting to have information about is how susceptible the solution is to changes in the contribution figures. For example, if the contribution of Snowdon had to drop to £100 instead of £170 (a combination of either selling price decreased or costs increased or both), then would the optimal build of (120, 120) still be the best? Or, what we would like to know is, for what contribution ranges is the solution of (120, 120) still the best one?

As before, sensitivity analysis is best carried out if all factors remain the same apart from one, which is the parameter we are testing the sensitivity upon. The objective function coefficients (contributions in this case) are presently 170 for Snowdon and 75 for Nevis.

If Nevis stayed at 75 over what range could the coefficient for Snowdon range while the solution is still Snowdon 120 and Nevis 120? Then we would reverse the analysis.

Let us see on the graph in Figure 5.28 the effect of changing the coefficient of Snowdon, but keeping Nevis at 75.

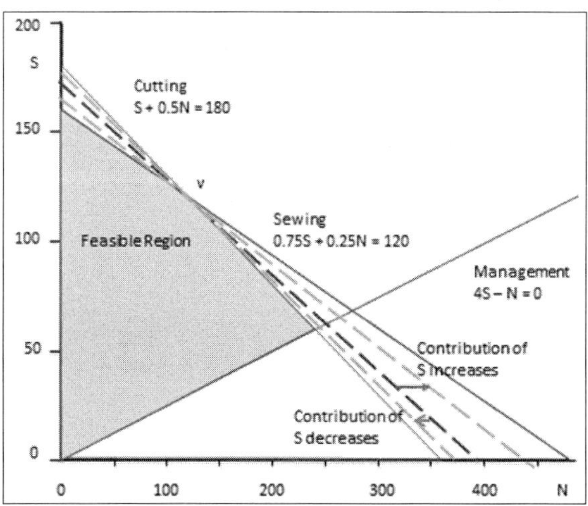

Figure 5.28

Effect of altering the Snowdon contribution while keeping Nevis fixed

coefficients of objective the variable multiplier in the objective function.

We can see that changing these numbers has an effect on the gradient of the line.

Remember that the form of a straight line is $y = mx + c$, m is the gradient. If m is bigger the line becomes steeper. If m is smaller the line becomes more shallow (m is negative the line points downwards).

The objective line for this example is $170S + 75N = \text{constant}$.

To put it into the general form of the straight line, divide throughout by 170 and we obtain:

$$S + (75/170)N = \text{constant, or } S = -(75/170)N + \text{constant.}$$

$$\text{Or, } S = -(\text{contribution of N}/\text{contribution of S})N + \text{constant.}$$

Thus, the gradient of the line is –(contribution of N/contribution of S).

So, the line becomes steeper if N's contribution increases or if S's contribution decreases, keeping the other contribution fixed. The line becomes shallower if N's contribution decreases or S's contribution increases, keeping the other contribution fixed.

What happens if the objective line becomes shallower?

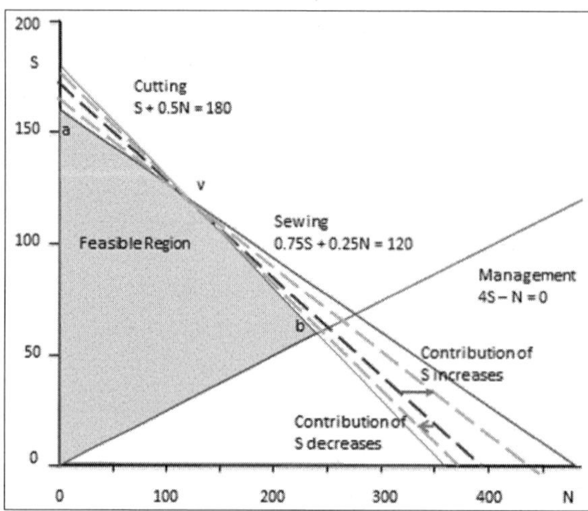

Figure 5.29
Neighbouring solution points

According to the graph in Figure 5.29, if the gradient of the objective line falls below the gradient of the sewing line (green) then the solution jumps to point 'a' on the graph.

i.e., the sewing line is $0.75S + 0.25N = 120$

So $S = -(0.25/0.75)N + 120$

So the gradient of sewing line $= -0.25/0.75 = -1/3$

What happens if the objective line becomes steeper? Looking at the graph in Figure 5.29, if the gradient of the objective line goes above the gradient of the cutting line (blue) then the solution jumps to point 'b' on the graph.

The cutting line is $S + 0.5N = 180$

So $S = -(0.5/1)N + 180$

So gradient of the cutting line $= -0.5/1 = -\frac{1}{2}$

So, provided the gradient of the objective, –(N's coefficient / S's coefficient), stays between the above gradients then the solution will stay at point (120,120). That is:

$-1/2 \leq -$N's coefficient / S's coefficient $\leq -1/3$.

If we divide by -1 then we change the signs so

$1/2 \geq$ N's coefficient / S's coefficient $\geq 1/3$

If we keep S's coefficient constant at 170 then we can vary N's coefficient, but it must keep the above relationship.

$1/2 \geq$ N's coefficient / $170 \geq 1/3$

Multiply by 170, $170/2 \geq$ N's coefficient $\geq 170/3$

$85 \geq$ N's coefficient ≥ 56.67

Interpretation Thus if S's contribution stays at £170 then N's contribution, original value £75, can vary between £56.67 and £85 and the solution will stay at 120, 120

If we keep N's coefficient constant at 75 then we can vary coefficient of S but it must keep the above relationship.

$1/2 \geq 75/$coefficient of S $\geq 1/3$

So $1/2 \geq$ (75/S's coefficient), or S's coefficient $\geq 75 * 2 = 150$.

Or (75 / S's coefficient) $\geq 1/3$, S's coefficient $\leq 75 * 3 = 225$.

Interpretation Thus if N's contribution stays at £75 then S's contribution, whose original value is £170, can vary between £150 and £225 and the solution will stay at S = 120, N = 120

Obviously sensitivity is quite difficult to do if we follow the graphical method; fortunately, as we will see in the next section computer software can generate this output for us.

Student exercises

X5.8 Referring to the computer problem X5.2 and X5.5

(a) Establish the shadow prices for the assembly, specialized testing and circuit board constraints.

(b) Electron have found a supplier of the common control circuit board who, although not yet ready to supply them on a regular basis, has offered a one off immediate delivery of up to 50 units at a price of £15 each, above the present cost of manufacture. Electron cannot stock these boards and so must use them within the week. Should Electron accept these or even some of them? How would the production plan be affected?

(c) Assuming that Electron does not purchase additional circuit boards, they are considering reducing the price of Supers by £35 in an attempt to fight off increasing foreign competition. This will reduce the unit contribution from £135 to £100. How would this affect your production plan when maximizing contribution? Advise on the range of variation in the contribution for Supers, for which the production plan will remain optimal.

(d) Electron would like to assemble a new control computer, the 'Elite'. The Elite uses 4 hours in Assembly and 2 hours in Finishing and Packaging. It requires only 1 of the common circuit boards, but no special testing facilities. The number of Elite computers manufactured would be included in the union's minimum manufacture agreement. Under present conditions what is the minimum contribution that the Elite should generate in order to make it a feasible proposition? Explain.

5.5 Use of Excel Solver for two variable problems

The graphical method of solution is excellent for finding solutions to problems with two variables. However, real-life decision problems have a lot of variables; for example, Snowdon and Nevis will just be two of many products made by Great Outdoor Ltd, all of which will compete for the same resources and so should be included in the constraint and objective equations. Similarly they will have lots of constraints. Great Outdoor Ltd will have many process, machine, labour or marketing constraints on production. These problems can only be effectively solved using computer software. The software will contain an algorithm, usually the Simplex Method, which solves large numbers of equations very quickly. However, we still have to formulate the problem and interpret the solutions.

We are going to demonstrate computer software using Excel 'Solver'. Later, in the Inventory chapter, you will also use Solver to solve other difficult sets of equations. Access to Solver is obtained through the Data Menu, under the Analysis group.

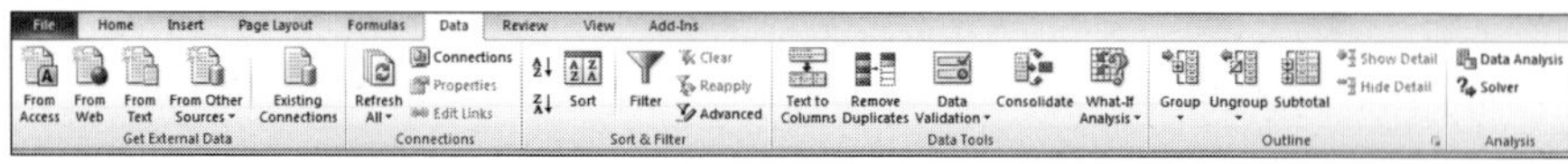

Figure 5.30
Menu ribbon with Solver under data menu

If it does not appear on your Excel then it hasn't been loaded initially. To rectify this choose File>Options>Add Ins.

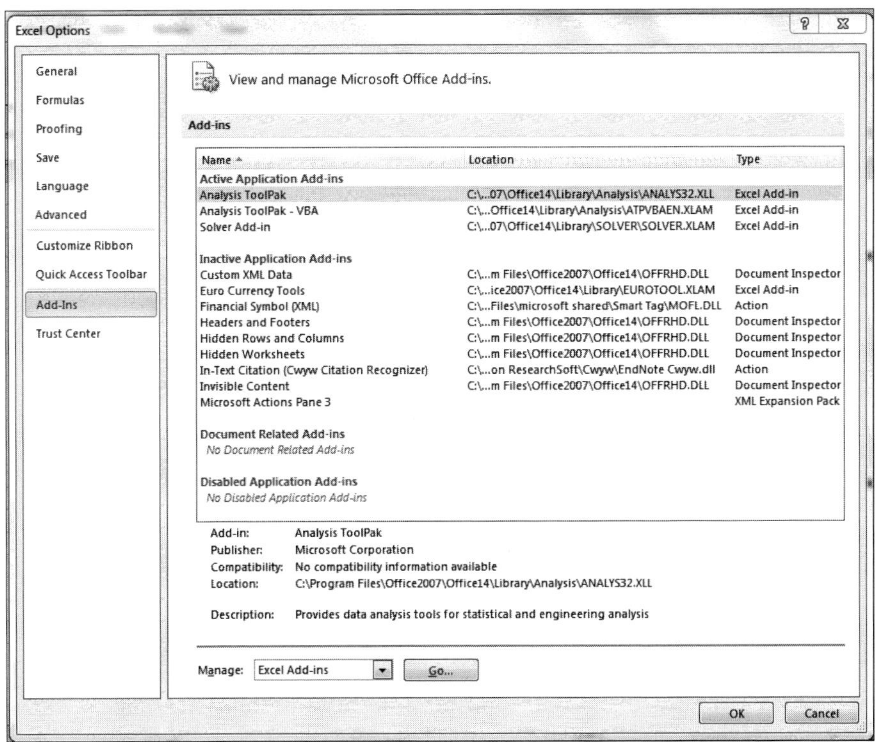

Figure 5.31

Excel options page

Choose 'Go' at Manage Excel Add Ins.

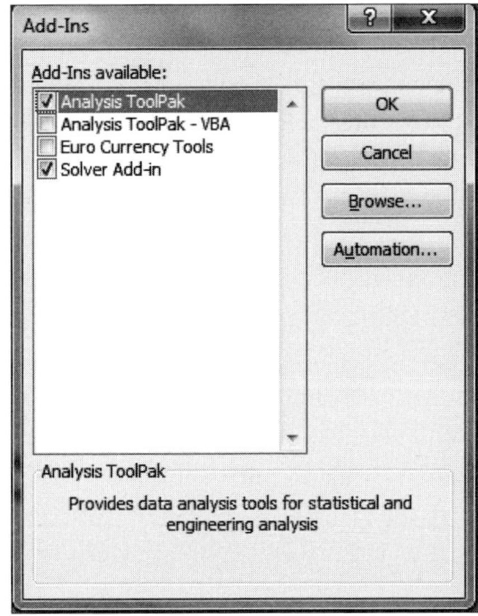

Figure 5.32

Excel add ins

In Figure 5.32 ensure that 'Solver Add-In' is selected, and then select 'OK'.

Then Choose File> Data to find Solver as before.

Example 5.5

First I will introduce the Solver in helping us with the Great Outdoor Problem and then introduce a special type of linear programme use—the transportation problem, for another example of multi-variable problems (more than two). Before we access Solver let us set up an Excel spreadsheet ready to solve the problem; that is, we will lay out the formulation of the problem as in Figure 5.33.

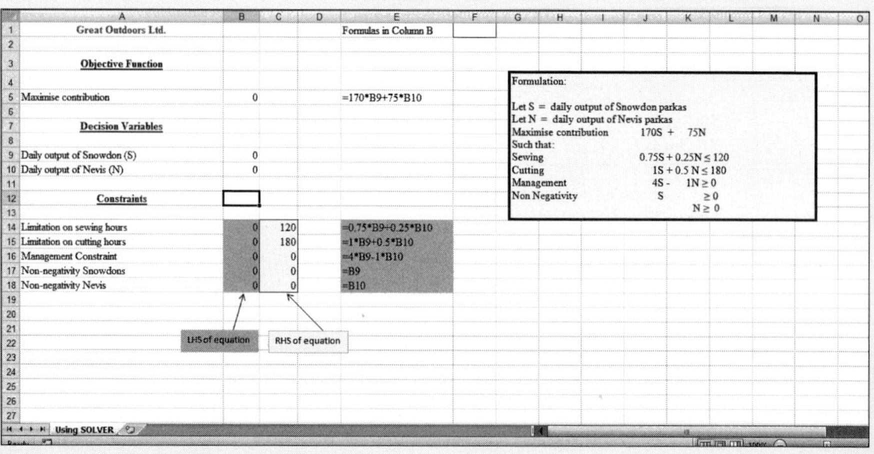

Figure 5.33

Setup of Great Outdoors in Excel

→ Excel solution

Target Cell

Objective Value Cell B5 — Formula = 170*B9 + 75*B10

Changing

Output of Snowdon (S) Cell B9

Output of Nevis (N) Cell B10

Constraints

Sewing Cell B14	Formula = 0.75*B9 + 0.25*B10
Limit Cell C14	Value
Cutting Cell B15	Formula = 1*B9 + 0.5*B10
Limit Cell C15	Value
Management Cell B16	Formula = 4*B9 – 1*B10
Limit Cell C16	Value
Non Neg (S) Cell B17	Formula = B9
Cell C17	Value
Non Neg (N) Cell B18	Formula = B10
Cell C18	Value

Column A has the titles and names within the problem formulation. Column B has the values. Running your cursor down column B you will find that the Decision values will be in B9 and B10. All other cells in Column B are formulae connecting the cell via B9 and

B10. Thus B9 is S and B10 is N. If we look at the cell B5 this calculates the Objective Function (Contribution) from B9 and B10, that is, 170*B9 + 75*B10. So whatever values are placed in B9, B10 will be automatically calculated in the other cells. For example if we put 50 in B9 (S) and 100 in B10 (N) then the spreadsheet calculates as in Figure 5.34.

	A	B	C	D	E
1	Great Outdoors Ltd.				Formulas in Column B
2					
3	**Objective Function**				
4					
5	Maximise contribution	16000			=170*B9+75*B10
6					
7	**Decision Variables**				
8					
9	Daily output of Snowdon (S)	50			
10	Daily output of Nevis (N)	100			
11					
12	**Constraints**				
13					
14	Limitation on sewing hours	62.5	120		=0.75*B9+0.25*B10
15	Limitation on cutting hours	100	180		=1*B9+0.5*B10
16	Management Constraint	100	0		=4*B9-1*B10
17	Non-negativity Snowdons	50	0		=B9
18	Non-negativity Nevis	100	0		=B10
19–23		LHS of equation	RHS of equation		

Formulation:

Let S = daily output of Snowdon parkas
Let N = daily output of Nevis parkas
Maximise contribution 170S + 75N
Such that:
Sewing 0.75S + 0.25N ≤ 120
Cutting 1S + 0.5 N ≤ 180
Management 4S - 1N ≥ 0
Non Negativity S ≥ 0
N ≥ 0

Figure 5.34
Outdoor Excel with example values

The contribution would calculate as 16,000 and the constraint values would also be calculated.

In Column C we put the limits of the Constraint equations. Column E is just an explanation of the formulae in B. Return the values to B9 = 0, B10 = 0 and select Solver.

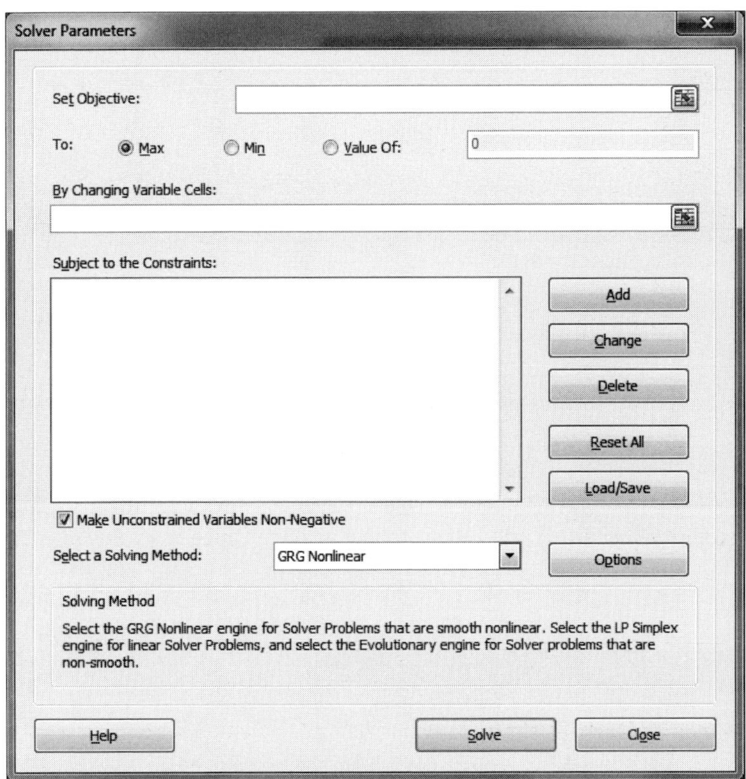

Figure 5.35
Solver input window

Solver allows us select cells in Excel and change the value of the objective cell (maximize). By changing variable cells (decision variables), subject to constraints. So it is repeating the expressions in the formulation.

To complete the Solver screen for linear programmes. The objective cell is (refer to Figure 5.34 or the Excel sheet) B5, which we are maximizing, by changing cells B9:B10.

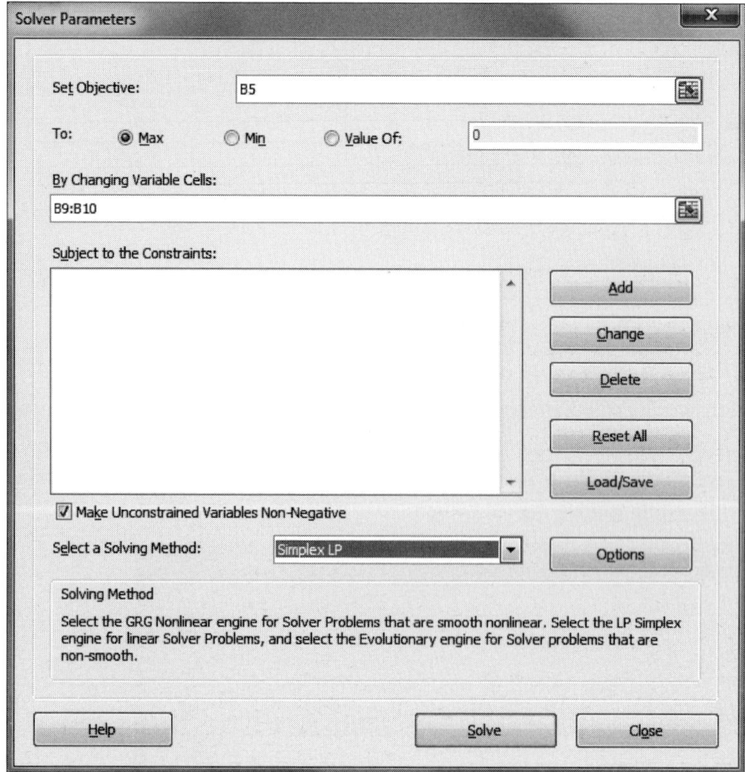

Figure 5.36

Start of Solver data input

So the Solver input screen now looks like Figure 5.36. Change 'Select a Solving Method' to Simplex LP.

Here as well you could select to make unconstrained variables non-negative. This will automatically include non-negativity values, which is useful on very large models.

To enter constraint values select Add and the following screen appears as illustrated in Figure 5.37.

Add Constraint

Cell Reference: <= Constraint:

OK Add Cancel

Figure 5.37

Solver constraints input

This is where we can tell Solver where the constraint inequalities are. Notice on the spreadsheet that for the sewing constraint the value in B14 must be ≤ C14. B14 changes according to the values in B9 and B10. Thus this section of Solver ensures that B14 never exceeds 120 (C14). So under 'Cell reference' enter (or click to select) B14. Under 'Constraint' select C14.

Notice that the drop-down menu in the middle ranges through the variety of relationships that can be chosen (<=, =, >=, int, bin, or dif). If 'Add' is selected then the other constraints can be entered in the same way as illustrated in Figure 5.38.

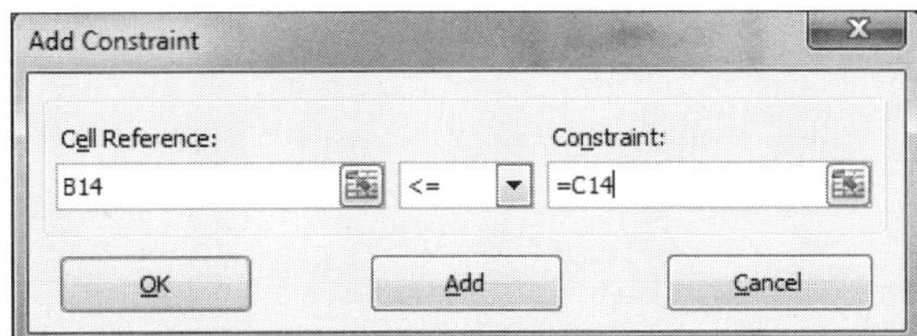

Figure 5.38
Entering constraints

After the last constraint select 'OK' instead of 'Add' and the screen in Figure 5.39 is returned.

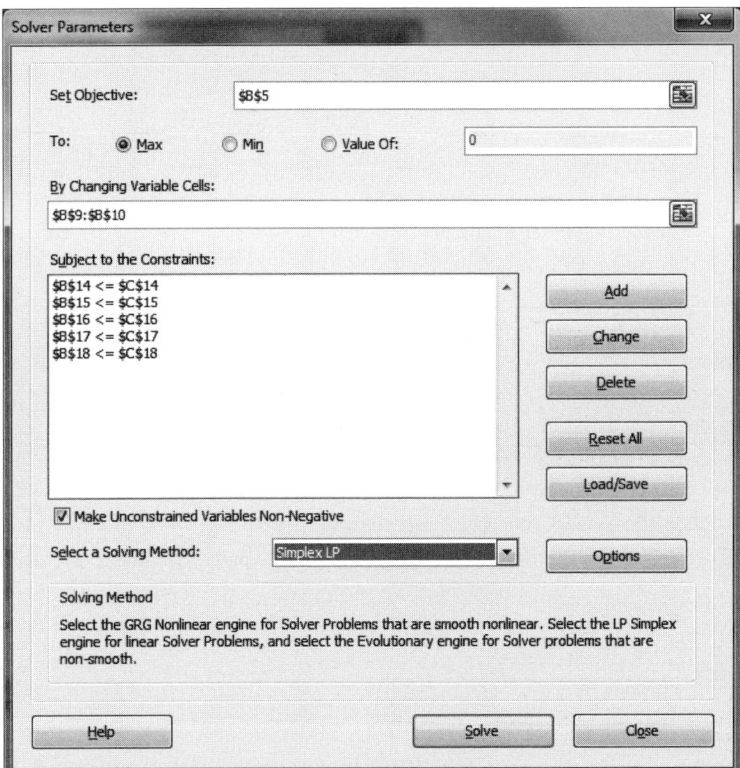

Figure 5.39
Final constraint input

If mistakes are made in the constraints then they can be changed or deleted by selecting the appropriate choice.

The Options Selection just allows the computer tolerances to be changed, so do not change any of this.

Select 'Solve'.

Figure 5.40 tells us that a solution has been found.

Solver Results

Solver found a solution. All Constraints and optimality conditions are satisfied.

Reports

Answer
Sensitivity
Limits

◉ Keep Solver Solution

○ Restore Original Values

☐ Return to Solver Parameters Dialog

☐ Outline Reports

OK | Cancel | Save Scenario...

Solver found a solution. All Constraints and optimality conditions are satisfied.

When the GRG engine is used, Solver has found at least a local optimal solution. When Simplex LP is used, this means Solver has found a global optimal solution.

Figure 5.40

Solver results

Select all of the reports and 'OK' and the Excel Spreadsheet as in Figure 5.41 is returned:

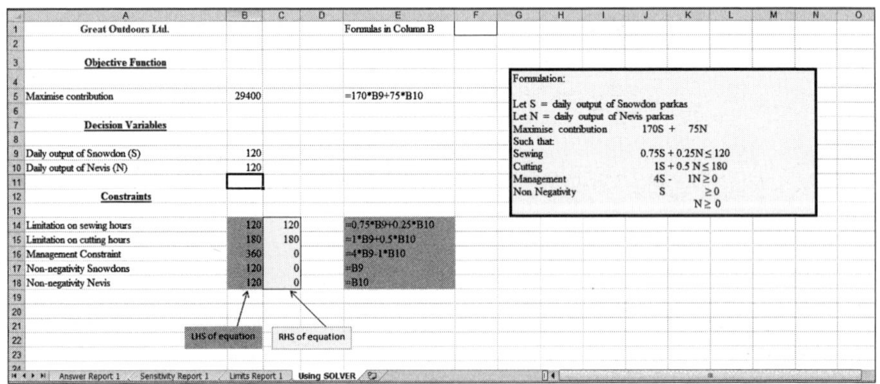

	A	B	C	D	E
1	Great Outdoors Ltd.				Formulas in Column B
2					
3	Objective Function				
4					
5	Maximise contribution	29400			=170*B9+75*B10
6					
7	Decision Variables				
8					
9	Daily output of Snowdon (S)	120			
10	Daily output of Nevis (N)	120			
11					
12	Constraints				
13					
14	Limitation on sewing hours	120	120		=0.75*B9+0.25*B10
15	Limitation on cutting hours	180	180		=1*B9+0.5*B10
16	Management Constraint	360	0		=4*B9-1*B10
17	Non-negativity Snowdons	120	0		=B9
18	Non-negativity Nevis	120	0		=B10

Figure 5.41

Solution spreadsheet

Note that the solution confirms our Graphical Method. It is to make 120 Snowdon, 120 Nevis and the contribution is £29,400. It also provides the constraint levels. There are also separate sheets produced for the three reports chosen. Select **Answer Report** 1:

Objective Cell (Max)

Cell	Name	Original Value	Final Value
\$B\$5	Maximise contribution	0	29400

Variable Cells

Cell	Name	Original Value	Final Value	Integer
\$B\$9	Daily output of Snowdon (S)	0	120	Contin
\$B\$10	Daily output of Nevis (N)	0	120	Contin

Constraints

Cell	Name	Cell Value	Formula	Status	Slack
\$B\$14	Limitation on sewing hours	120	\$B\$14<=\$C\$14	Binding	0
\$B\$15	Limitation on cutting hours	180	\$B\$15<=\$C\$15	Binding	0
\$B\$16	Management Constraint	360	\$B\$16>=\$C\$16	Not Binding	360
\$B\$17	Non-negativity Snowdons	120	\$B\$17>=\$C\$17	Not Binding	120
\$B\$18	Non-negativity Nevis	120	\$B\$18>=\$C\$18	Not Binding	120

Answer Report 1 | Sensitivity Report 1 | Limits Report 1 | Using SOLVER

Figure 5.42

Answer report

Answer Report a report obtainable from using Solver indicating the solution variables and their values.

This provides the information as on the spreadsheet but also tells us that sewing and cutting constraints are binding. We also have the slack amounts of the other constraints. If we select Sensitivity Report 1 we obtain:

Variable Cells

Cell	Name	Final Value	Reduced Cost	Objective Coefficient	Allowable Increase	Allowable Decrease
$B$9	Daily output of Snowdon (S)	120	0	170	55	20
$B$10	Daily output of Nevis (N)	120	0	75	10	18.33333333

Constraints

Cell	Name	Final Value	Shadow Price	Constraint R.H. Side	Allowable Increase	Allowable Decrease
$B$14	Limitation on sewing hours	120	80	120	15	15
$B$15	Limitation on cutting hours	180	110	180	25.71428571	20
$B$16	Management Constraint	360	0	0	360	1E+30
$B$17	Non-negativity Snowdons	120	0	0	120	1E+30
$B$18	Non-negativity Nevis	120	0	0	120	1E+30

Answer Report 1 | Sensitivity Report 1 | Limits Report 1 | Using SOLVER

Figure 5.43

Sensitivity report

Here we have the Objective Function sensitivity values followed by the shadow price values and limits. Again it confirms the graphical solution that we found earlier.

Cell	Objective Name	Value
$B$5	Maximise contribution	29400

Cell	Variable Name	Value	Lower Limit	Objective Result	Upper Limit	Objective Result
$B$9	Daily output of Snowdon (S)	120	30	14100	120	29400
$B$10	Daily output of Nevis (N)	120	0	20400	120	29400

Answer Report 1 | Sensitivity Report 1 | Limits Report 1 | Using SOLVER

Figure 5.44

Limits report

Sensitivity Report a report obtainable from using Solver indicating the ranges over which solution variables may hold true. For example the sensitivity values of a linear programme.

The **limits report** is a more specialized report that is not really of any use here. It gives the limits of each decision variable if the value of the other decision variable stays unchanged and the constraints are not broken. For example, if we keep Nevis at 120 then Snowdon can vary between 30 and 120 without breaking constraints. Then apply the same to Snowdon constant.

 **Student exercises**

X5.9 Referring to the computer problem X5.2, X5.5, X5.8, set up the formulation (X5.2) in Excel and solve using Solver.

5.6 Multivariable problems

Multivariable problems are formulated in the same way as two variable problems but obviously Solver will have to be used for the solution method. The formulation takes care of the extra variables. To demonstrate multiple variable problems we will use one particular application of linear programmes called network flow models. This one is the transportation model.

Example 5.6

RockHardy Brewers produce a special commemorative beer. Currently the beer is brewed at just two of its plants, located at Northside, and Southside, and is sold at just four warehouse outlets located at Upperton, Middleton, Lowerton, and Netherton. The beer is transported in barrels and the cost of transport per barrel from each supplier to each warehouse is shown in Table 5.3. This table also gives information about how much the plant can produce (supplier) and how much the warehouses require (demand).

	Outlet				
Plant	Upperton	Middleton	Lowerton	Netherton	Supply
Northside	£30	£90	£90	£30	500
Southside	£15	£30	£75	£105	300
Demand	140	320	200	140	800

Table 5.3 Transport costs per barrel

Table 5.3 shows it costs £30 to transport a barrel from Southside to Middleton. Southside can produce 300 barrels and Lowerton requires 200 barrels. Notice that supply and demand is equal at 800 barrels, so in this example we have a balanced supply. If we didn't then we would have to add dummy variables on supply or demand to take up the excess and remake it into a balanced situation. So how can RockHardy transport from plants to outlets as cheaply as possible?

X

limits report a report obtainable from using Solver. Range over which decision variables can change without breaking constraints while keeping one fixed.

5.6.1 Formulation of transportation problems

Decision variables

How much is transported from each Supplier to each Outlet?

In shorthand we use the symbol X_{ij} to mean how much is transported from plant i to outlet j, per week.

Plants: let Northside be 1 and Southside be 2.

Outlets: let Upperton be 1, Middleton be 2, Lowerton be 3 and Netherton be 4.

So Amount transported from Southside to Lowerton per week is X_{23}.

For example, the cost of transporting 10 barrels from Northside to Middleton is £90 * 10 = £900.

So cost of transporting X_{12} barrels from Northside to Middleton is £90X_{12}.

The objective function is to minimize total cost:

Minimize $30X_{11} + 90X_{12} + 90X_{13} + 30X_{14} + 15X_{21} + 30X_{22} + 75X23 + 105X_{24}$.

Constraints are how many barrels can be supplied at each plant or how many are required at each outlet per week.

For example supply from Northside must be less than or equal to 500,

So $X_{11} + X_{12} + X_{13} + X_{14} \leq 500$

Supply from Southside must be less than or equal to 300,

So $X_{21} + X_{22} + X_{23} + X_{24} \leq 300$

Similarly a demand constraint could be at Lowerton which requires 200 per week,

So $X_{13} + X_{23} = 200$

Therefore, the complete equation formulation is as follows:

Complete formulation:

Decision Variables

Let X_{11} = Number of barrels transported from Northside to Upperton per week

Let X_{12} = Number of barrels transported from Northside to Middleton per week

Let X_{13} = Number of barrels transported from Northside to Lowerton per week

Let X_{14} = Number of barrels transported from Northside to Netherton per week

Let X_{21} = Number of barrels transported from Southside to Upperton per week

Let X_{22} = Number of barrels transported from Southside to Middleton per week

Let X_{23} = Number of barrels transported from Southside to Lowerton per week

Let X_{24} = Number of barrels transported from Southside to Netherton per week

Objective Function

Minimize Cost $30X_{11} + 90X_{12} + 90X_{13} + 30X_{14} + 15X_{21} + 30X_{22} + 75X23 + 105X_{24}$

Subject to Constraints

Supply at Northside	$X_{11} + X_{12} + X_{13} + X_{14} \leq 500$
Supply at Southside	$X_{21} + X_{22} + X_{23} + X_{24} \leq 300$
Demand at Upperton	$X_{11} + X_{21} = 140$
Demand at Middleton	$X_{12} + X_{22} = 320$
Demand at Lowerton	$X_{13} + X_{23} = 200$
Demand at Netherton	$X_{14} + X_{24} = 140$

Non-negativity $X_{ij} \geq 0$ for all i, j

5.6.2 Use of Excel Solver to solve transportation problems

Before we access Solver let us set up an Excel spreadsheet ready to solve the problem; that is, we will lay out the formulation of the problem.

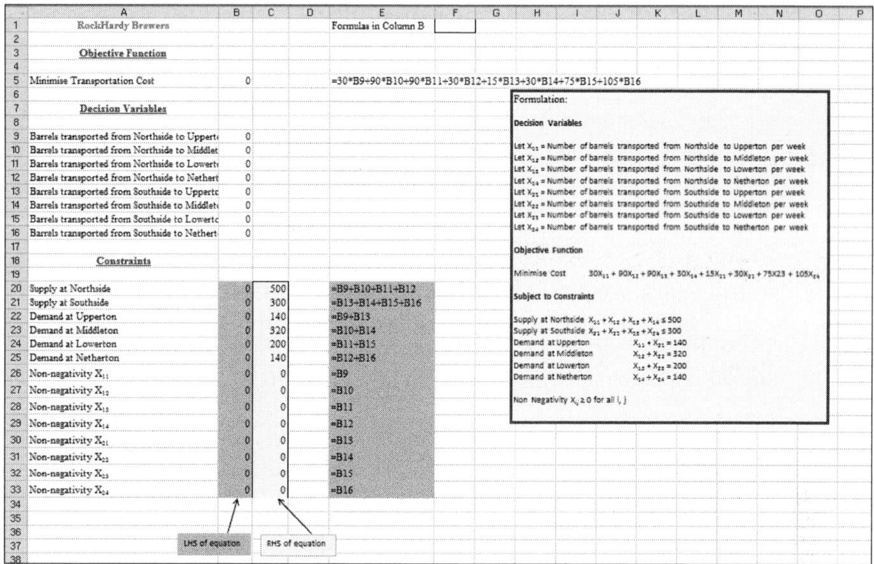

	A	B	C	D	E
1	RockHardy Brewers				Formulas in Column B
2					
3	**Objective Function**				
4					
5	Minimise Transportation Cost	0			=30*B9+90*B10+90*B11+30*B12+15*B13+30*B14+75*B15+105*B16
6					
7	**Decision Variables**				
8					
9	Barrels transported from Northside to Upperto	0			
10	Barrels transported from Northside to Middlet	0			
11	Barrels transported from Northside to Lowerto	0			
12	Barrels transported from Northside to Nethert	0			
13	Barrels transported from Southside to Upperto	0			
14	Barrels transported from Southside to Middlet	0			
15	Barrels transported from Southside to Lowerto	0			
16	Barrels transported from Southside to Nethert	0			
17					
18	**Constraints**				
19					
20	Supply at Northside	0	500		=B9+B10+B11+B12
21	Supply at Southside	0	300		=B13+B14+B15+B16
22	Demand at Upperton	0	140		=B9+B13
23	Demand at Middleton	0	320		=B10+B14
24	Demand at Lowerton	0	200		=B11+B15
25	Demand at Netherton	0	140		=B12+B16
26	Non-negativity X_{11}	0	0		=B9
27	Non-negativity X_{12}	0	0		=B10
28	Non-negativity X_{13}	0	0		=B11
29	Non-negativity X_{14}	0	0		=B12
30	Non-negativity X_{21}	0	0		=B13
31	Non-negativity X_{22}	0	0		=B14
32	Non-negativity X_{23}	0	0		=B15
33	Non-negativity X_{24}	0	0		=B16

Figure 5.45

Setup of RockHardy Brewers

→ Excel solution

Target Cell

Objective Value Cell B5 Formula = 30*B9+90*B10+90*B11+30*B12
+15*B13+30*B14+75*B15+105*B16

Changing

Northside–Upperton Cell B9

Northside–Middleton Cell B10

Northside–Lowerton Cell B11

Northside–Netherton Cell B12

Southside–Upperton Cell B13

Southside–Middleton Cell B14

Southside–Lowerton Cell B15
Southside–Netherton Cell B16
Constraints
Supply

Northside Cell B20	Formula = B9+B10+B11+B12
Limit Cell C20	
Southside Cell B21	Formula = B13+B14+B15+B16
Limit Cell C21	
Demand	
Upperton Cell B22	Formula = B9+B13
Limit Cell C22	
Middleton Cell B23	Formula = B10+B14
Limit Cell C23	
Lowerton Cell B24	Formula = B11+B15
Limit Cell C24	
Netherton Cell B25	Formula = B12+B16
Limit Cell C25	
Non Negativities Cell B26:B33	Formula = B9:B16
Limits Cell C26:C33	

Select Solver

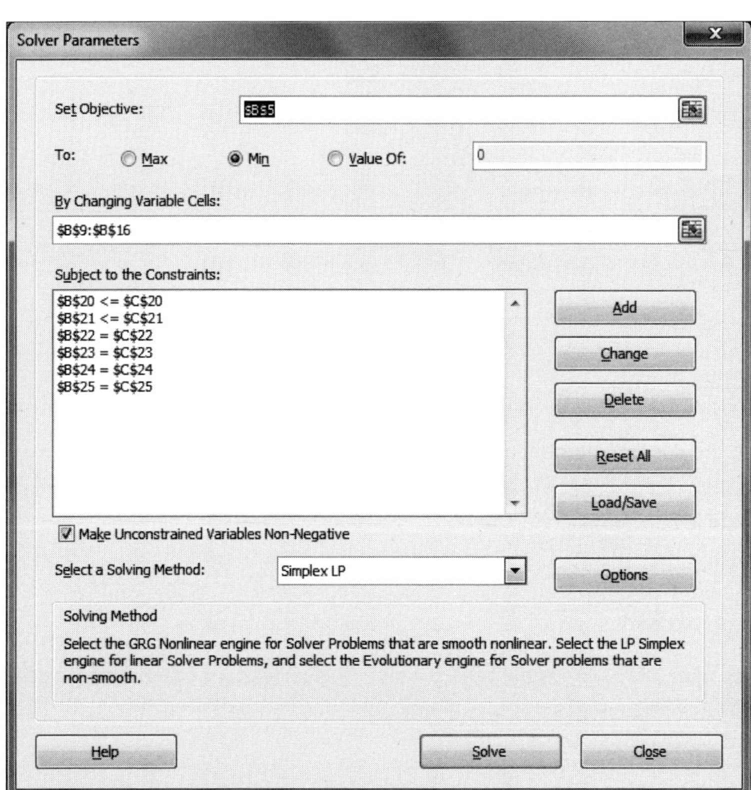

Figure 5.46
Solver input for RockHardy Brewers

See two variable Solver (5.5) for instructions but note here:

(i) the problem has been set to minimize

(ii) The demand constraints are '='

(iii) I have let Solver insert the non-negativity constraints by ticking the box

(iv) I have chosen Simplex LP for the Solving Method

Select 'Solve'

Solver found a solution as follows on the spread sheet (NB we are not interested in the reports in this case because they do not help us)

	A	B	C
1	**RockHardy Brewers**		
2			
3	**Objective Function**		
4			
5	Minimise Transportation Cost	37200	
6			
7	**Decision Variables**		
8			
9	Barrels transported from Northside to Upperton	140	
10	Barrels transported from Northside to Middleton	20	
11	Barrels transported from Northside to Lowerton	200	
12	Barrels transported from Northside to Netherton	140	
13	Barrels transported from Southside to Upperton	0	
14	Barrels transported from Southside to Middleton	300	
15	Barrels transported from Southside to Lowerton	0	
16	Barrels transported from Southside to Netherton	0	
17			
18	**Constraints**		
19			
20	Supply at Northside	500	500
21	Supply at Southside	300	300
22	Demand at Upperton	140	140
23	Demand at Middleton	320	320
24	Demand at Lowerton	200	200
25	Demand at Netherton	140	140
26	Non-negativity X_{11}	140	0
27	Non-negativity X_{12}	20	0
28	Non-negativity X_{13}	200	0
29	Non-negativity X_{14}	140	0
30	Non-negativity X_{21}	0	0
31	Non-negativity X_{22}	300	0
32	Non-negativity X_{23}	0	0
33	Non-negativity X_{24}	0	0

Figure 5.47

RockHardy Brewers transport solution

So we can see the supply and demand requirements are met and the cheapest cost of doing so is £37,200. The number of barrels transported from each plant to each outlet can be read in Figure 5.47.

Student exercises

Please visit the Online Resource Centre which accompanies this textbook for solutions to the student exercises and techniques in practice questions.

X5.10 Jessel Holdings manufacture blodgets at their plants in Swansea, Glasgow, and Cambridge. The table below shows the maximum monthly supply (in units) that can be produced at each plant.

Plant	Swansea	Glasgow	Cambridge
Monthly supply	135	56	93

All Jessel's blodgets are stored at depots in Brighton, Leeds, Coventry, and Margate. Currently their monthly requirements for blodgets (in units) are as shown in the table below.

Depot	Brighton	Leeds	Coventry	Margate
Maximum demand	72	91	39	82

Jessel's accountant has just come up with some new figures for the unit cost (in £s) of transporting blodgets from each plant to each depot.

Plant	Depot			
	Brighton	Leeds	Coventry	Margate
Swansea	132	94	97	103
Glasgow	85	91	88	100
Cambridge	106	89	100	98

(i) Formulate and solve a linear programming problem to determine how blodgets should be transported from plant to depot at minimum monthly cost. You will require to use Solver to obtain the solution.

(ii) Suppose that the monthly demand from Margate increases by 10 units. Reformulate your model as appropriate and obtain the revised solution. Compare this with the solution to (i).

Techniques in practice

TP 5.1 The Blending problem

RMC is a small firm that produces a variety of chemical products. In a particular production process three raw materials are blended to produce two products, a fuel additive and a solvent base. Each kg of fuel additive is a mixture of 0.4 kg of material 1 and 0.6 kg of material 3. A kg of solvent base is a mixture of 0.5 kg of material 1, 0.2 kg of material 2 and 0.3 kg of material 3. After deducting relevant costs the contribution (sales price – variable cost) is £40 for every kg of fuel additive produced and £30 for every kg of solvent base produced.

RMC's production is constrained by a limited availability of the three raw materials. For the current production period RMC has the following quantities available:

Raw material	Amount available (kgs)
Material 1	20
Material 2	5
Material 3	21

RMC is interested in maximizing contribution and wishes to know the optimal output of fuel additive and solvent base to achieve the maximum contribution.

TP5.2 Klunk Klick

A manufacturer produces two products, Klunk and Klick. Klunk has a selling price of £21 per unit and Klick of £26 per unit. The manufacturer wishes to establish the weekly production plan that will maximize contribution. Market research data confirms that there will be no problem in selling whatever outputs of the two products are determined.

Klunk and Klick both need time in the machining department. Each unit of Klunk requires four hours of machining time, while a unit of Klick requires two hours. Also, making a unit of Klunk will require four hours of labour, while Klick needs six hours per unit. Both Klunk and Klick use 1 kg of metal for each unit produced.

Metal costs the firm £2 per kg, machine time is costed at £1 per hour, while labour is paid at the rate of £3 per hour. Because of resource limitations only 100 hours of machine time, 180 hours of labour time and 40 kg of metal are available per week. Also, a trade agreement limits sales of Klunk to a maximum of 20 per week and another agreement, with a trading partner, commits the manufacturer to produce at least five units of Klick per week.

Required:

(a) Formulate the above as a linear programming problem.

(b) Solve the problem using the graphical method and determine the production plan to maximize weekly contribution.

(c) Which resources are scarce? Considering each situation separately, what is the shadow price for:

- labour time
- machine time
- metal

(d) With a holiday period looming, the unions have offered the availability of up to 50 extra labour hours per week, at the same rate of £3 per hour. How should the firm respond to this offer?

(e) The manufacturer is considering production of a new product called Klank. Each unit of Klank will use up four machine hours, four labour hours and 2 kgs of metal. Determine the minimum contribution per unit at which production of Klank becomes worthwhile.

TP 5.3 Tingaki Group

The Tingaki Group distil and supply ouzo to four outlets, located in Kardamena, Kefalos, Marmari, and Mastahari. All outlets pay a price of €100 per case. Tingaki has three plants, located in Platoni, Antimahia,and Pyli. The cost of producing ouzo varies slightly from plant to plant due to differing labour and water costs.

The production cost per case, and monthly capacity, at each of the three plants is given in table TP5.3a.

Plant	Cost per case (€)	Monthly capacity
Platoni	58	4000
Antimahia	54	2500
Pyli	56	7500

Table TP5.3a Unit cost and capacity by plant

Transport costs per case (in €s) and outlet demands per month are as shown in table TP5.3b.

	Outlet			
Plant	Kardamena	Kefalos	Marmari	Mastahari
Platoni	24	21	18	26
Antimahia	12	16	14	20
Pyli	16	24	20	15
Monthly Demand	5000	4000	2000	3000

Table TP5.3b Transport costs (€s) and monthly outlet demand

For example, every case transported from Platoni to Kardamena costs €24.

Required:

(a) How many cases should Tingaki transport from each plant to each outlet so as to maximize monthly contribution?

(b) Operational problems at Tingaki now prevent more than 1000 cases per month being transported from Antimahia to Kardamena. Also, it has been determined that at least 1000 cases per month must be transported from Pyli to Kefalos. How will this affect the shipping schedule (and resulting monthly contribution) that you determined in part (a)?

(c) Tingaki has now learned that Marmari's monthly demand has risen from 2,000 to 3,000 cases. What impact will this have upon the shipping schedule (and resulting monthly contribution) that you established in part (a)? Note: in producing a solution to part (c) you should remove the restrictions imposed in part (b).

■ Summary

In this chapter we discussed the technique of linear programming, which allows us to solve problems where there is an objective (e.g. profit) that has to be optimized, but the variables (resources) that will contribute to this objective are constrained—for example, there is not enough manpower or machine hours to make everything that we would like to do. How can we best allocate these resources to the decision variables to make the objective optimal? For example, make the most profit given the constraints that we have. The technique is just one of a family of resource allocation techniques but as it stands it has applications in areas such as manufacturing, blending, logistics and supply, warehousing, finance and investment portfolio, to name just a few.

Linear programming in practice is carried out using a computer and specialized languages, but the technique can be demonstrated for two variables using a graph. For more than two variables Excel solver is very powerful computer software for medium size problems.

In Chapter 2 variable problems of minimization and maximization were demonstrated manually, as well as using computer software, Excel Solver, to find the same solutions. Formulation of the problem is the same for two or multivariable problems, so a section is first given about formulating problems into a form suitable for linear programming.

For multivariable solutions an introduction to a special type of problem, transportation, is demonstrated using Solver. For example, these problems are concerned with supply, from manufacturers, to customers, in as cheap a way as possible. These problems are demonstrated in balanced and unbalanced form.

Sensitivity analysis is important to all decision making techniques—that is, how robust is the solution to changes in input parameters. Linear programming is a very helpful technique to demonstrate this. Variation of resource levels and objective function coefficient values was demonstrated.

Student exercise answers

For all figures listed below, please see the Online Resource Centre.

X5.1 (i) Linear.
(ii) Linear.
(iii) Not linear.
(iii) Linear.
(iv) Linear.
(v) Not linear.
(vi) Linear.
(vii) Linear.
(viii) Not linear.
(ix) Linear.

X5.2 Let:

St = the weekly output of Standard computers

Su = the weekly output of Super computers

Then the formulated problem is:

Maximize 210St + 135Su

Subject to:

2St	+	3Su	≤	300	assembly time
3St	+	2Su	≤	300	finishing/packaging time
		0.5Su	≤	40	specialized testing
4St	+	2Su	≤	320	circuit boards
		Su	≥	20	automatic soldering
St			≤	65	licensing limitation
St	+	Su	≥	50	union agreement
St			≥	0	non-negativity condition

X5.3 Solution X = 10, Y = 8, Objective = 28.

X5.4 Solution X = 40, Y = 0, Objective = 120.

X5.5 Solution Standards = 45, Supers = 70, Objective = £18,900.

X5.6 Solution X = 3, Y = 1, Objective = 13.

X5.7 Solution X = 2, Y = 6, Objective = 34.

X5.8 (a) The shadow prices for assembly is £45, specialized testing £0, circuit boards £15.

(b) Electron should accept 40 of them. The production plan would be to make 60 Standards and 60 Supers.

(c) If the selling price of Electrons dropped by £35, the production plan would make 65 Standards and 30 Supers. The range of variation in contribution of Supers to keep to the present production plan would be £105 to £315.

(d) The minimum contribution of an Elite should be £105.

X5.9 Figure X5.9c

X5.10 (i) Solution:

Minimize Cost	26,854
Decision Variables	
Blodgets Swansea - Brighton	0
Blodgets Swansea - Leeds	91
Blodgets Swansea - Coventry	39
Blodgets Swansea - Margate	5
Blodgets Glasgow - Brighton	56
Blodgets Glasgow - Leeds	0
Blodgets Glasgow - Coventry	0
Blodgets Glasgow - Margate	0
Blodgets Cambridge - Brighton	16
Blodgets Cambridge - Leeds	0
Blodgets Cambridge - Coventry	0
Blodgets Cambridge - Margate	77

(ii) Solution of revised model:

Minimize Cost	26,774
Decision Variables	
Blodgets Swansea - Brighton	0
Blodgets Swansea - Leeds	4
Blodgets Swansea - Coventry	39
Blodgets Swansea - Margate	92
Blodgets Glasgow - Brighton	56
Blodgets Glasgow - Leeds	0
Blodgets Glasgow - Coventry	0
Blodgets Glasgow - Margate	0
Blodgets Cambridge - Brighton	6
Blodgets Cambridge - Leeds	87
Blodgets Cambridge - Coventry	0
Blodgets Cambridge - Margate	0
Blodgets Dummy - Brighton	10
Blodgets Dummy - Leeds	0
Blodgets Dummy - Coventry	0
Blodgets Dummy - Margate	0

TP1 RMC produce 25 kgs of fuel additive and 20 kgs of the solvent base. The maximized contribution will be £1600.

TP2 (a) The formulated problem is:

$$\begin{aligned}
&\text{Maximize } 3Klu + 4Kli\\
&\text{Subject to:}\\
&4Klu + 2Kli \le 100\\
&4Klu + 6Kli \le 180\\
&Klu + Kli \le 40\\
&Klu \le 20\\
&Kli \ge 5\\
&Klu \ge 0
\end{aligned}$$

(b) The production plan is to make 15 Klunks and 20 Klicks per week. The weekly contribution to profit is £125.

(c) The shadow price for labour time is £0.625, machine time is £0.125 and metal is £0.

(d) Accept all 50 hours.

(e) The minimum unit contribution for a Klank is £3.

TP3 (a) The solution is as below:

Maximize contribution	380,000
Decision variables	
Platoni to Kardamena	0
Platoni to Kefalos	2000
Platoni to Marmari	2000
Platoni to Mastahari	0
Antimahia to Kardamena	500
Antimahia to Kefalos	2000
Antimahia to Marmari	0
Antimahia to Mastahari	0
Pyli to Kardamena	4500
Pyli to Kefalos	0
Pyli to Marmari	0
Pyli to Mastahari	3000

(b) The solution because of Operational problems of Tingaki as below:

Maximize contribution	372,500
Decision variables	
Platoni to Kardamena	500
Platoni to Kefalos	1500
Platoni to Marmari	2000
Platoni to Mastahari	0
Antimahia to Kardamena	1000
Antimahia to Kefalos	1500
Antimahia to Marmari	0
Antimahia to Mastahari	0
Pyli to Kardamena	3500
Pyli to Kefalos	1000
Pyli to Marmari	0
Pyli to Mastahari	3000

(c) The solution due to rise in Marmari's schedule:

Maximize contribution	384,500
Decision variables	
Platoni to Kardamena	0
Platoni to Kefalos	500
Platoni to Marmari	3500
Platoni to Mastahari	0
Antimahia to Kardamena	500
Antimahia to Kefalos	2000
Antimahia to Marmari	0
Antimahia to Mastahari	0
Pyli to Kardamena	4500
Pyli to Kefalos	0
Pyli to Marmari	0
Pyli to Mastahari	3000
Dummy to Kardamena	0
Dummy to Kefalos	1500
Dummy to Marmari	0
Dummy to Mastahari	0

■ Further reading

Textbook resources

1. D. R., Anderson, D. J. Sweeney, T. A. Williams, and K. Martin (2008) *An Introduction to Management Science: Quantitative Approaches to Decision Making* (12th edn), Thomson Learning.
2. F. Hillier, M. Hillier, K. Schemedders, and M. Stephens (2008) *Introduction to Management: Science: A Modeling and Case Studies Approach with Spreadsheets* (3rd edn), McGraw Hill.
3. C. Morris (2008) *Quantitative Approaches in Business Studies* (7th edn), Prentice Hall.
4. L. Oakshott (2012) *Essential Quantitative Methods for Business, Management and Finance* (5th edn) Palgrave.
5. S. G. Powel and K. R. Baker (2010) *Management Science: The Art of Modeling with Spreadsheets* (3rd edn) John Wiley & Sons.
6. B. Render, R. Stair, and M. Hanna (2012) *Quantitative Analysis for Management* (11th edn), Pearson Education.

6 Inventory and stock control

» Overview «

Nearly all organizations need to hold a variety of items in the form of inventories (stocks). Raw materials, energy inputs, finished, and semi-finished components are all examples of essential inputs that must be available if the final production process is to be carried out efficiently.

In an ideal world sufficient inventories would be readily on hand to allow scheduled production tasks to be carried out. However, in practice, inventory must be ordered in advance of production runs and must be held as stock until the various items are required. This means that, from the cost perspective, at the simplest level there are four major components in the total inventory associated costs:

1. The ordering cost which will depend upon the number of orders placed, through administration, delivery and other charges.
2. The actual unit cost of the items and the number of items ordered.
3. The cost to the firm of holding inventory. This will include warehousing and handling charges but also an opportunity cost element reflecting the lost interest that could have been earned on the value of inventories held. Clearly there is a time dimension to this last aspect since the higher is the value of the inventory, and the longer it is held, the greater is the amount of interest or other revenue forgone.
4. There may be considerable costs associated with running out of inventory, and these are not always easy to estimate. They will, however, depend largely on the costs of not being able to meet an order, which will obviously include the loss of revenue as well as any penalties that may be incurred.

Of course, costs are only one dimension of the overall issue of determining best practice inventory management. Inventory is only a means to an end—production—and production is only the means of achieving the ultimate objective of satisfying demand for the end product.

If demand were stable and easily forecast, then it is relatively easy to determine the ideal inventory management strategy, but in the absence of such certainty firms must rely upon demand forecasts, which, of course may be less than completely accurate.

X

ordering cost the cost of ordering a delivery of inventory from the supplier.

» Learning outcomes «

After studying this chapter and after completing the exercises you should be able to:

- » Understand the key principles of inventory control.
- » Understand the reasons for holding inventory.
- » Understand the four main costs associated with inventory: ordering, acquiring, holding, and stockout costs.
- » Define commonly used inventory control terms: lead time, stockout time, economic order quantity.
- » Know what is meant by Pareto analysis.
- » Solve problems using Microsoft Excel.

6.1 Inventory usage

The basic model of inventory usage presumes that the current level of inventory (S) is given by the quantity ordered (Q) minus the per period usage rate (u) times the number of time periods (t).

In other words, we presume a linear relationship of the form:

$$S = Q - u^*t$$

Clearly, when $t = 0$, then $S = Q$; that is, the current stock level is equal to the quantity ordered.

However, with the passage of time, u units of inventory are used per period, and so eventually the current stock level will become zero (i.e. $S = 0$ and is called a stockout).

This will happen when:

$0 = Q - u^*t$, implying $Q = u^*t$, and that $t = Q/u$ is when the stockout will happen.

$$\text{Stockout time} = Q/u \qquad (6.1)$$

Example 6.1

With an initial order of $Q = 100$, a per period usage rate of $u = 20$, then: $t = 100/20 = 5$ periods until stockout. Over the entire length of a production run this process can be viewed as shown in Figure 6.1.

X

stockout a situtation in which there is no stock left and output still to be produced.

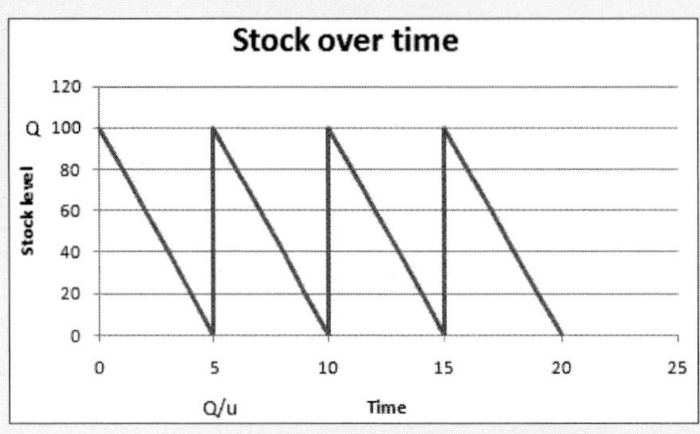

Figure 6.1

Now suppose that the firm in question requires a total of d units of inventory over the entire length of a production run. It follows that with Q units being ordered in each order period the total number of orders for the run (n) will be given by:

$$n \text{ (number of orders)} = d/Q \qquad (6.2)$$

Example 6.2

With a demand of d = 1000, an initial order of Q = 100 then: d/Q = 10 orders per run. It is important to note another implication of the model. Since the ordered quantity varies between Q and zero over the order period, it follows that the average inventory level over this period is given by Q/2. That is:

$$\text{Average inventory level} = Q/2 \qquad (6.3)$$

This is a significant result that will be used later in this chapter.

At this last stage of the current discussion, note two crucial assumptions upon which the model is based:

(a) There is full knowledge of the demand behaviour of the product for which the inventory is used.

(b) Once an order is placed, it is assumed that it is met by the supplier instantaneously and in full.

If (a) applies, then inventory levels may fluctuate around planned levels, and the extent of this fluctuation may depend upon the accuracy of the demand forecast. If (b) applies, the basic model is easily adjusted to accommodate lags in the time before an order is received (known as the lead time), and the possibility of the order being delivered in periodic batches rather than in full.

For example, suppose that the time between ordering and receiving the inventory is given by m. This means that the order must be placed m periods before a stockout occurs. Now, since we know that this will happen when t = Q/u, an inventory order must be placed when:

$$t = Q/u - m$$

Example 6.3

With an initial stock level of Q = 100, a usage rate of u = 20 and a lead time of m = 2, Then:

$$Q/u = 5, \text{ and } t = Q/u - m = (5 - 2) = 3.$$

Inventory must be ordered three time periods from now: this is known as the re-order time. Also, if we know the re-order time we can calculate what is known as the re-order stock level. This is simply given by m*u, since a lead time of m periods will require a total of m*u units of inventory to meet demand from what is left in stock. So:

$$\text{Re-order stock level} = m*u.$$

And in our current example we have m*u = 2*20 = 40. Inventory should be re-ordered either after three time periods and/or when the current stock level has fallen to 40.

As a concluding point, we should consider a situation in which there is not only a lead time for delivery, but also the order quantity being filled by the supplier in stages rather than in its entirety. Suppose that the supplier meets the order quantity at a rate of r per period and with a lead time of m periods before these deliveries commence. It follows that the supplier will take Q/r days to complete the order, which, including the lead time of m periods before deliveries commence, means that the order must be placed Q/r + m days before a stockout will occur (Q/u as before).

This means that the re-order time becomes:

$$\text{Re-order time} = Q/u - (Q/r + m) \tag{6.4}$$

and the re-order stock level becomes:

$$\begin{aligned}\text{Re-order stock level} &= Q - u*(\text{Re-order time}) = Q - u*(Q/u - Q/r - m)\\ &= u*(Q/r + m)\end{aligned} \tag{6.5}$$

Example 6.4

With an initial order of Q = 100, a usage rate of u = 20, a lead time of m = 2 and a replenishment rate of r = 50, we have:

$$\text{Re-order time} = 100/20 - (100/50 + 2) = 5 - (2 + 2) = 5 - 4 = 1 \text{ and:}$$

$$\text{Re-order stock level} = 20*(100/50 + 2) = 20*4 = 80$$

The order must be placed one period from now, when the current stock level has fallen to 80.

X

re-order time the time at which an order for more inventory must be placed. This will depend upon the usage rate, the lead time, the replenishment rate, and the initial amount of stock that was received.

re-order stock level the level of current inventory that triggers an order for more stock.

lead time the length of time between placing an inventory order and receipt of the delivery from the supplier. A lead time of zero implies immediate delivery, although this may either be in full or in batches.

replenishment rate the rate at which inventory that has been ordered is delivered by the supplier. This may be in full or in lots or batches over a period of time.

Example 6.5

These formulae are easily transferred to Excel and are shown in Figure 6.2.

	A	B	C
1	Example 6.5		
2	Usage per time period = u	20	
3	Replenishment per time period = r	50	
4	Order size = Q	100	
5	Lead time = m	2	
6	Stockout time = Q/u	5	=B4/B2
7	Time to supply order = Q/r + m	4	=B4/B3+B5
8	Re-order time = Q/u - (Q/r + m)	1	=B6-B7
9	Re - order stock level = Q - u(Re-order time)	80	=B4-B2*B8

Figure 6.2

→ Excel solution

B2:B5 are given values

Stockout time Cell B6 Formula: = B4/B1
Time to supply order Cell B7 Formula: = B4/B3+B5
Re-order time Cell B8 Formula: = B6-B7
Re-order stock level Cell B9 Formula: = B4-B2*B8

Interpretation The order must be placed one period from now, when the current stock level has fallen to 80.

Note The worksheet is designed as follows:

First, all the givens of the model (known as parameters) are entered at the top of the sheet.

Then, formulae that use these givens (or previously written formulae) are built up in a step-by-step manner. This continues until the model is complete.

In this way, a bottom-up hierarchical structure is created that is simple to follow and amenable to tracing the formulae links that have been created. This can be crucial when things go wrong, but Excel's audit facility can help here.

To see how this works locate the cursor in the B8 cell then select Formulas from the main menu and then Trace Precedents. Arrows will appear showing which cells affect the selected cell (in this case B2, B4 and B8). To remove the arrows simply click Remove Arrows.

We should also note that the validity of the model depends upon the values of m and r. For example, if m is greater than Q/u then the order will not be available by stockout time. Similarly, if r is less than u then replacement is unable to match usage and so there will insufficient inventory to prevent a stockout. Finally, if m + Q/r is greater than Q/u then once again the stockout cannot be prevented.

As a final point note that the model can be made to collapse to the basic model (Example 2.1) if we set the lead time (m) equal to zero and the replenishment rate (r) equal to a very large number such as a billion. As making these alterations to the model shown in Figure 6.2 will confirm, re-order should happen once again when t = 5 and the stock level has fallen to zero.

Student exercises

X6.1 Given an initial stock level of 1000 units and a daily usage rate of 20 units, calculate the length of time before a stockout.

X6.2 Given an initial stock level of 3000 units, a daily usage rate of 50 units and a current stock level of 1000 units, calculate the length of time that the production process has been operating.

X6.3 Given that the current stock level is 4000 units, that 6000 units were initially ordered and that the process has been operating for 10 days, calculate the daily rate of usage.

X6.4 Given that a stockout occurred after 25 days when the daily usage rate was 50 units, calculate the initial order quantity.

X6.5 A producer orders inventory from a supplier who can start delivery in 5 days time at a rate of 50 units per day. Daily usage of the item is 20 units and the producer has decided to order 800 units. Calculate the re-order time and the re-order stock level.

X6.6 A producer had to re-order stock after 20 days. Given that the initial order level was 1000 units, that the daily usage and replenishments rates were 20 and 40 units respectively, calculate the lead time implied.

X6.7 A firm's re-order stock level is known to be 100 units. The initial order level was 1000 units, the daily replenishment rate was 50 units and the lead time was 5 days. Calculate the implied daily usage rate.

X6.8 An order quantity of 2000 units is used up at a rate of 50 units per day. The item is replenished at a daily rate of 40 units with a lead time of 7 days. Calculate the re-order stock level.

6.2 An inventory control model

Having established the factors influencing the inventory costs and the usage of that inventory it is now time to combine these ideas in order to develop rules for determining the optimal quantity of inventory that should be ordered. This is known as the Economic Order Quantity (EOQ), and is defined as the optimal level of inventory to be ordered at regular intervals over the length of the production run. Clearly the EOQ will be the optimal (i.e. least cost) value of Q.

To determine this we can proceed as follows:

Suppose that c_o is defined as the unit cost of ordering a batch of Q units of inventory. This unit cost is assumed to be the same regardless of the size of the order. The total ordering cost (TOC) associated with the production run is therefore:

$$TOC = c_o*(\text{number of orders})$$

However, we have seen that the number of orders is given by d/Q, So:

$$TOC = c_o*d/Q$$

EOQ the optimal level of an inventory item that should be ordered periodically so that all relevant costs are minimized.

As regards **holding costs**, these are usually taken to be a percentage rate (representing the internal cost of capital) of the purchase cost of the inventory item. So, denoting the percentage rate by c_h and the cost of the item by c_i, the unit holding cost will be given by:

$$\text{Unit holding cost} = c_h{*}c_i$$

Being a unit cost, this must be applied to the average stock level over each order period, which we saw earlier to be given by Q/2. The total holding costs (THC) are therefore given by:

$$THC = c_h{*}c_i{*}Q/2$$

Finally, we must include the total purchasing cost (TPC) of the actual inventory and this is given by:

$TPC = c_i{*}d$ – whereas before d is the total inventory demand

Taking these three costs together we then have the overall total cost (TC) being given by:

$$TC = c_o{*}d/Q + c_h{*}c_i{*}Q/2 + c_i{*}d$$

The EOQ can now be seen to be that value of Q that minimizes TC in the above expression and can be found by differentiating TC with respect to Q, setting this derivative equal to zero and then solving for Q. That is:

$d(TC)/d(Q) = -c_o{*}d/Q^2 + c_h{*}c_i/2 = 0$ whereby:

$Q^2 = (2{*}c_o{*}d)/c_h{*}c_i$ and:

$$Q = EOQ = [2{*}c_o{*}d/c_h{*}c_i]^{0.5} \tag{6.6}$$

Example 6.6

With the total inventory demand = 6000, $c_o = 20$, $c_h = 0.15$ and $c_i = 1.6$, then:

$$EOQ = [2{*}20{*}6000/0.15{*}1.6]^{0.5} = (240{,}000/0.24)^{0.5} = 1000 \text{ units}$$

Interpretation The firm should place six orders of 1000 units over the length of the production run.

Example 6.7

Of course this formula is easily transferred to Excel as indicated in Figure 6.3.

	A	B	C
1	Example 6.7 The EOQ		
2	Unit ordering cost:c_o	20	
3	Unit holding cost:c_h	0.15	
4	Unit cost of stock:c_i	1.6	
5	Demand :d	6000	
6	Economic Order Quantity EOQ	1000	=((2*B2*B5)/(B3*B4))^0.5
7	Total holding cost	120	=B3*B4*B6/2
8	Total ordering cost	120	=B2*B5/B6
9	Total purchase cost	9600	=B4*B5
10	Total cost	9840	=B7+B8+B9

Figure 6.3

holding costs the cost of holding a given level of inventory of a period of the production run. It is assumed to depend upon the average stock level, the purchase cost of the item, and a percentage of this cost representing the opportunity cost of the funds tied up.

➜ Excel solution

B2:B5 are given values

Economic Order Quantity Cell B6 Formula: = ((2*B2*B5)/(B3*B4))^0.5
Total holding cost Cell B7 Formula: = B3*B4*B6/2
Total ordering cost Cell B8 Formula: = B2*B5/B6
Total purchase cost Cell B9 Formula: = B4*B5
Total cost Cell B10 Formula: = B7+B8+B9

Interpretation From this it is clear the total cost of ordering, acquiring, and holding the required inventory is minimized when the EOQ equals £9840 and when six orders for 1000 units are placed.

But it should be clear that, even with this simple model, solving for the EOQ is not entirely straightforward, and as the complexity of the models increases then so too do the algebraic difficulties. For this reason many practical problems need to make use of the Excel Solver facility. This should now be explained.

Student exercises

X6.9 A production run of 250,000 units requires use of an inventory item that is available immediately and in full. The cost of the item is £80, the ordering costs are £4 and the holding cost is 10% of the value of the item. Determine the EOQ.

X6.10 Using the given values from Exercise 6.9 calculate the change in the EOQ that would result from a 10% increase in the ordering cost of the inventory item

X6.11 With the original values given in Exercise 6.9, if it had been the purchase cost of the item that had increased by 10%, what is the new EOQ value?

6.3 Using the Excel Solver

The Excel Solver is an invaluable assistant in the process of solving difficult equations, so to understand how it should be used we can approach the process of equation solving from first principles. An equation is simply a symbolic statement of the equality between two mathematical expressions—the left-hand side (LHS) and the right-hand side (RHS). Thus: LHS = RHS, is an equation that has been written in its explicit form i.e. with the equals sign in the middle. However equations can also be written in what is known as their implicit form as: LHS – RHS = 0.

In either form the information that is being conveyed is the same, but as we will see with regards to using the Excel Solver the implicit form will often be more useful. In most practical cases both the LHS and the RHS will comprise a number of terms. The known

Excel Solver is an Excel add in that can solve for the values of one or more unknowns in a spreadsheet model.

terms will either be numbers or symbols representing the givens of the equation. The unknown terms will be the variables of the equation and it is usually these for which we require to find solution values. Taking a simple example, suppose we have the equation: $2x = 6$ or $2x - 6 = 0$. The solution is easily obtained from simple algebra by writing: $x = 6/2 = 3$, since then $2(3) = 6$ and $2(3) - 6 = 0$.

But can we have found this simple solution in any other (non-analytical) way? One way would be to try various values for x until we found one that made $2x - 6$ equal to zero. That is:

Let $x = 0$ then $2x - 6 = 0 - 6 = -6$

Let $x = 1$ then $2x - 6 = 2 - 6 = -4$

Let $x = 2$ then $2x - 6 = 4 - 6 = -2$

Let $x = 3$ then $2x - 6 = 6 - 6 = 0$

When we have reached the last line above then we have found the solution by a process known as trial and (observation of) error.

Given this idea we can transfer the procedure to an Excel worksheet as shown in Figure 6.4.

	A	B	C
1	Value of x	0	Trial value for x
2	LHS	0	= 2*B1
3	RHS	6	RHS given as 6
4	LHS - RHS	-6	=B2-B3

Figure 6.4

→ Excel solution

The only difference between this and the previous process is that we have written an Excel formula in B2 to calculate the value of the LHS (2x) in formula term of the value that we have tried in B1 (so the entry in B2 is = 2*B1. Then, with B3 containing the fixed RHS data we calculate the difference between the two sides in B4 from: =B2-B3. If the model has been constructed properly the B4 cell will return a value of –6 as shown.

Clearly the equation has not yet been solved, so we should increase the trial value of x in B1 from 0 to 1, from 1 to 2 and then from 2 to 3 (when we find the solution). It should be apparent that we are just doing the same thing as we did earlier by hand, but now we are letting Excel do the calculations. If we take note of this Excel process then it comprises the following:

1. First, we are changing the value in the B1 cell. This represents letting the value of x vary.
2. Next, we observe the value in the B4 cell and note the effect of the change that has been made.
3. Finally, we compare the observed effect with our knowledge of the effect that we are seeking (a value of zero in B4).

On the basis of this comparison we either try another value for x if the value in B4 is not zero; stop if the B4 value is equal to zero. In Excel parlance the cell that we observe in order to note the effect of the change in the value of x is known as the **target cell**. The effect that we are looking for is known as the **target cell value** (zero in this case). Finally, the cell that we are changing in order to achieve our target is known as the **changing cell**. Notice that in all Solver models the changing cell(s) will always be numerical values (not

X

target cell a cell in a worksheet that is to be minimized, maximized or made equal to a defined value by the Solver on the basis of one or more defined changing cells in the same or another linked worksheet. It must always contain a formula that is linked to the changing cells.

target cell value is the value that the target cell is required to adopt. This can be a maximum, minimum or specified value.

changing cell in a Solver model, one or more cells that feed into a target cell whose value is to be determined by the Solver. Changing cells will always be numerical values and will never contain formulae.

formulae) while the target cell must always contain a formula (that links the changing cell to the target cell). This means that the Solver must be supplied with at least three pieces of essential information. These are:

1. The changing cell (or cells): B1 in this case.
2. The target cell: B4 in this case.
3. The target cell (required) value: zero.

Once apprised of these three essentials, Excel can do the solving for us. To do this, make sure that B1 in Figure 6.4 contains a value other than three (so that the equation is not yet solved). Now access the Solver from the Data option of the main menu.[1] The dialogue box shown in Figure 6.5 will appear.

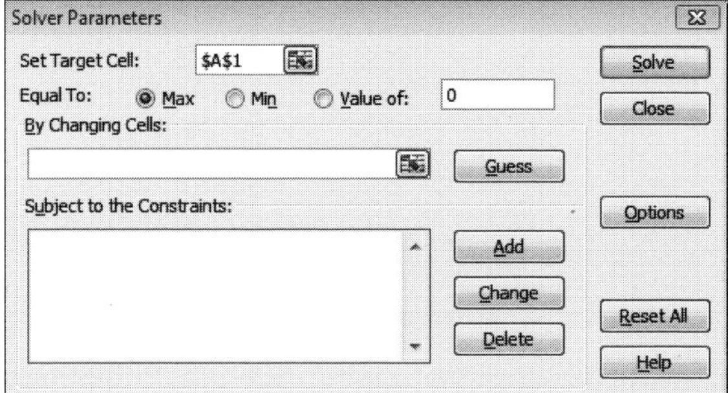

Figure 6.5

As was explained above, we now feed the three essentials into the dialogue box, so that it looks like Figure 6.6.

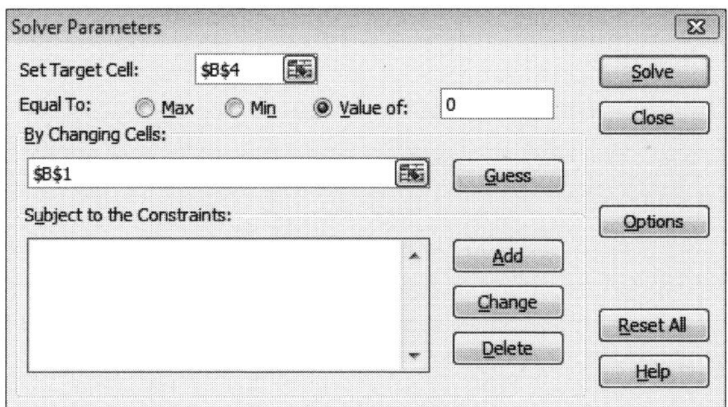

Figure 6.6

Now click on solve and the solution screen will resemble Figure 6.7.

	A	B	C	D	E	F
1	Value of x	3	Trial value for x			
2	LHS	6	= 2*B1			
3	RHS	6	RHS given as 6			
4	LHS - RHS	0	=B2-B3			

Solver Results

Solver found a solution. All constraints and optimality conditions are satisfied.

Reports: Answer, Sensitivity, Limits

Keep Solver Solution

Restore Original Values

OK | Cancel | Save Scenario... | Help

Figure 6.7

[1] The excel Solver is and Add-in that may not always be automatically installed. To add it in select the Office icon and then Excel options. Now choose Add-ins and select the Solver Add-in, then Go. The Solver will be added as the last option under the Data menu.

Interpretation As is clear, the simple solution of x = 3 has been found as the value for the changing cell.

Importantly however, the same simple procedure can be employed for equations of much greater complexity than the one used in the example.

Note We now see the reason for using the implicit equation form. This is because Excel's default value for the target cell value is zero. So if the RHS were to change (from 6 to 8 say) there is no need to adjust the solver target cell value setting—simply change the value in the B3 cell.

Student exercises

X6.12 Use the worksheet developed in Figure 6.7 to solve the following equation: $x^3 + x^2 + x = 14$.

X6.13 Use the Excel Solver to solve the following equation: $2^x + x^2 = 17$.

So far, the Solver has only been used to solve a simple equation. But as the second lines of Figures 6.5 and 6.6 show maximum and minimum options (i.e. optimization) are also available. If either of these is selected then the Solver will attempt to find the value of the changing cell that optimizes the value of the target cell. So, in the context of inventory control the changing cell would be the EOQ, and the target cell would be the minimum value of Total Cost.

To see how the Solver approaches this problem Figure 6.3 is reproduced as Figure 6.8—with one important alteration—there is no longer a formula in the B5 cell. Rather, a trial value of 200 for the EOQ has been entered.

	A	B	C
1	Unit ordering cost:c_o	20	
2	Unit holding cost:c_h	0.15	
3	Unit cost of stock:c_i	1.6	
4	Demand :d	6000	
5	Economic Order Quantity EOQ	200	<-- Trial value for EOQ
6	Total holding cost	24	=B2*B3*B5/2
7	Total ordering cost	600	=B1*B4/B5
8	Total purchase cost	9600	=B3*B4
9	Total cost	10224	=B6+B7+B8

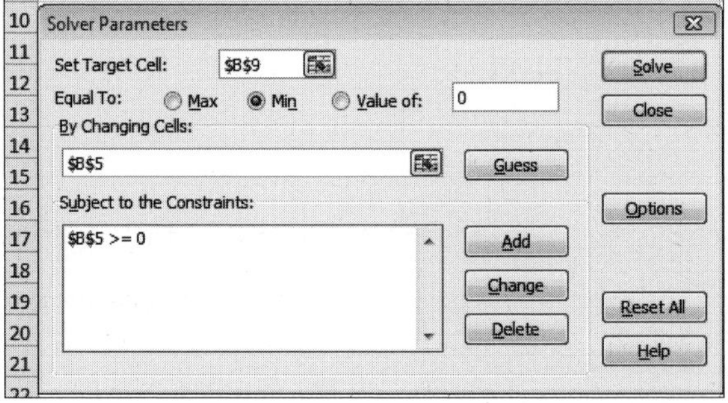

Solver Parameters
Set Target Cell: $B$9
Equal To: Max Min Value of: 0
By Changing Cells: $B$5
Subject to the Constraints: $B$5 >= 0
Solve Close Guess Options Add Change Delete Reset All Help

Figure 6.8

→ Excel solution

Cells B1:B4 contain given values and B4 contains our trial value for the EOQ.
C9 is the target cell.

Unit ordering cost:co Cell B1
Unit holding cost:ch Cell B2
Unit cost of stock:ci Cell B3
Demand :d Cell B4
Economic Order Quantity EOQ Cell B5 <-- Trial value for EOQ
Total holding cost Cell B6 Formula: = B2*B3*B5/2
Total ordering cost Cell B7 Formula: = B1*B4/B5
Total purchase cost Cell B8 Formula: = B3*B4
Total cost Cell B9 Formula: = B6+B7+B8

Interpretation With the Solver settings shown in Figure 6.8, click on Solve and the solution that was found by formula in Example 6.6 (EOQ = 1000) will be reproduced. This is shown in Figure 6.9.

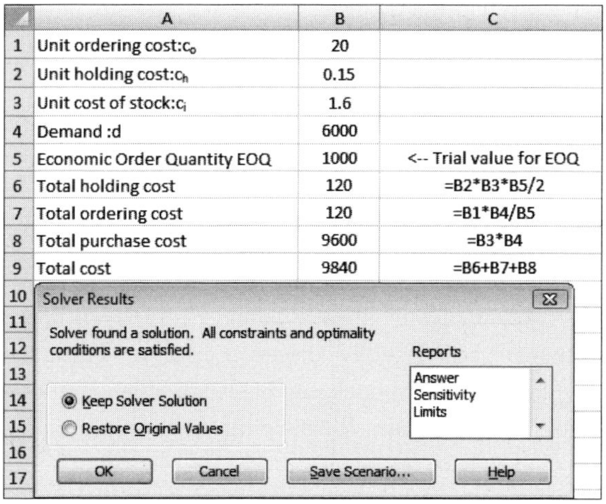

	A	B	C
1	Unit ordering cost:c_o	20	
2	Unit holding cost:c_h	0.15	
3	Unit cost of stock:c_i	1.6	
4	Demand :d	6000	
5	Economic Order Quantity EOQ	1000	<-- Trial value for EOQ
6	Total holding cost	120	=B2*B3*B5/2
7	Total ordering cost	120	=B1*B4/B5
8	Total purchase cost	9600	=B3*B4
9	Total cost	9840	=B6+B7+B8

Solver Results

Solver found a solution. All constraints and optimality conditions are satisfied.

Reports: Answer, Sensitivity, Limits

◉ Keep Solver Solution
○ Restore Original Values

OK | Cancel | Save Scenario... | Help

Figure 6.9

Student exercises

X6.14 Repeat Exercise 6.9 using the worksheet developed in Figure 6.8.

X6.15 Repeat Exercise 6.10 using the worksheet developed in Figure 6.8.

X6.16 Repeat Exercise 6.11 using the worksheet developed in Figure 6.8.

There are a few further points to be made about the Solver. As the Solver dialogue box shown in Figure 6.7 indicates, there is the option to introduce constraints to the model. These can tell the Solver to restrict the value of any of the cells that have been used to be

constraints limitations upon the values that can be adopted by a target cell and/or changing cells that reflect the logical requirements of the model.

confined within certain limits. For example, in the EOQ discussion the inventory item may take the form of complete units, meaning that EOQ values that are not whole numbers (discrete) are not possible. In other cases the inventory may be effectively continuous (powders, fluids, etc.) and so the solution that the Solver finds can be non-integer (continuous). For our current EOQ example we would expect at the very least that the optimal value would be greater than zero—and perhaps integer—depending upon the nature of the item.

An illustration of how to use the constraint dialogue box is shown in Figure 6.10. Here, we simply clicked on the middle tab of the Add Constraint option and selected integer. At the same time we also required that the value of the changing cell (B5) had to be positive.

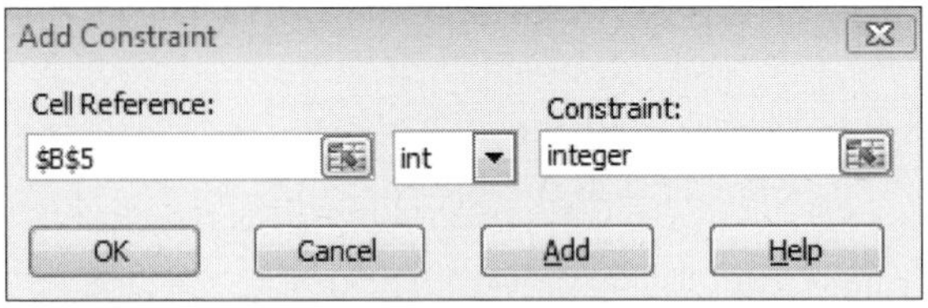

Add Constraint
Cell Reference: $B$5 | int | Constraint: integer
OK | Cancel | Add | Help

Figure 6.10

The full dialogue box is shown in Figure 6.11.

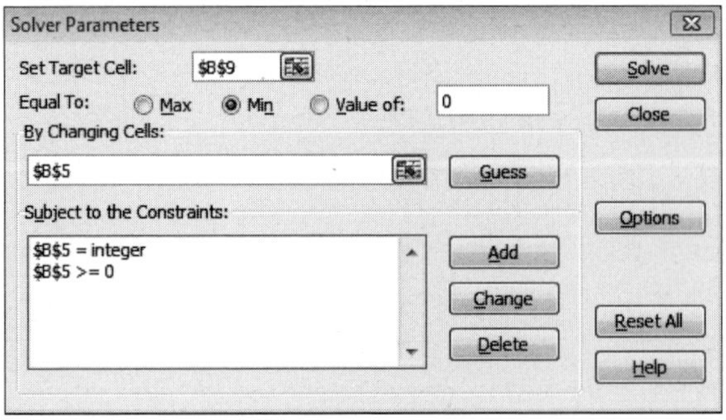

Solver Parameters
Set Target Cell: $B$9
Equal To: Max | Min | Value of: 0
By Changing Cells: $B$5
Subject to the Constraints:
$B$5 = integer
$B$5 >= 0
Solve | Close | Guess | Options | Add | Change | Delete | Reset All | Help

Figure 6.11

Another point to note about the Solver is that although there can only ever be one target cell defined, there can be several changing cells. If each of these feed into the value of the target cell in different ways then highly complex models can be constructed, and then solved for the optimal values of the variables represented by the changing cells.

Lastly, a source of difficulty with the Solver must be mentioned.

Since the routine always requires a trial value for the changing cell, this raises the question of what values should or should not be used as the trial. There is no easy answer to this difficulty.

For example, the equation: $(x-2)*(x-6)=0$ has two obvious solutions: $x=2$ and $x=6$ $(2-2)*(x-6)=0*(x-6)=0$ and $(x-2)*(6-6)=(x-2)*0=0$. Using the Solver, either solution is easily found, but finding both in the absence of this prior knowledge is not straightforward. This is because if the trial value chosen is less than 2, the Solver will find the $x=2$ solution, while if the trial value is greater than 6 then the $x=6$ solution will be found. For trial values between 2 and 6 then the Solver will usually (but not always) find that solution value closest to the trial value.

Finally, sometimes there may be a need to constrain the changing cell value to be non-negative, since, especially when there are multiple solution values, the model must be prevented from finding mathematically valid but logically meaningless negative values.

Student exercises

X6.17 By making regular changes to the trial value for x in B1, use the model from Figure 6.7 to confirm that $x = 2$ and $x = 6$ are both valid solutions to the equation: $(x - 2)*(x - 6) = 0$.

X6.18 Suppose that the total cost (TC) of producing an item of inventory is given in terms of the quantity produced (x) by: $TC = 0.02x^3 - 0.8x^2 + 12x + 100$. Prepare a Solver model that will determine the value of output at which average total cost (i.e. total cost per unit produced) is minimized.

6.4 The EOQ with non-instantaneous replenishment

Earlier in this chapter it was noted that the simplest version of the EOQ formula was based on the assumption that **inventory replacement** was instantaneous (without lead time) and delivered in full. Fortunately, the introduction of a positive lead time of m periods does not alter the EOQ formula. All that happens is that the order must be placed m periods in advance of the expected stockout, and that the re-order stock level will no longer be zero. The actual value of the EOQ will not be affected.

This is not true, however, if replenishment is periodic rather than in full. When replenishment is periodic the usage will take place concurrently and the EOQ will have to be adjusted to take account of this. For example, suppose that replenishment takes place at a rate of r per time period, while usage is at a rate of u over the same period.

The main implication of this process is that the average stock level is no longer given by Q/2. This is because it will take Q/r periods to resupply the required level of stock over a period of time at which the level of inventory is being replaced at a rate of $(r - u)$.

Consequently the maximum stock is given by:

$$(Q/r)*(r - u) = Q*(1 - u/r)$$

And the average stock level by:

$$Q*(1 - u/r)/2$$

Now, since it is this average stock level that influences holding costs, we would expect that the derived formula for the EOQ must be adjusted to reflect this fact. This can be seen as follows where the new expression for the average stock level has replaced Q/2 in the expression for Total Cost, that is, what was previously Q/2 is now $Q/2*(1 - u/r)$. So:

$$TC = c_o*d/Q + c_h*c_i*\ Q/2*(1 - u/r) + c_i*d$$

Differentiating with respect to Q, setting this derivative equal to zero and solving for Q gives the formula for the EOQ as:

$$EOQ = [2*c_o*d/(c_h*c_i*(1 - u/r))]^{0.5} \qquad (6.7)$$

inventory replacement is the rate at which the required amount of new inventory can be bearded to existing stock.

Example 6.8

With demand for the item d = 6000, respective ordering, holding and purchase cost of $c_o = 20$, $c_h = 0.15$ and $c_i = 1.6$, then we saw earlier (Example 6.6) that the EOQ was calculated to be 1000 units. Now suppose that inventory is used at a rate of 20 per period (i.e. u = 20) and that replenishment takes place at a rate of 80 per period (i.e. r = 80). This makes (1 – u/r) = (1 – 0.25) = 0.75 and the EOQ becomes: $EOQ = [2*20*6000/0.15*1.6*0.75]^{0.5} = 1154.70$ or 1155 if the item is discrete.

Interpretation As might be expected the effect has been to increase the EOQ form its previous value of 1000 by about 15.5%.

Once again this version of the EOQ can be made to collapse to the original form if r is very large in relation to u. For instance, if r is infinitely large (implying that replenishment is made in full), then u/r is effectively zero and (1 – u/r) becomes 1. This has the effect of making the EOQ once again equal to 1000 units.

Example 6.9

Of course, it is now an easy matter to transfer these calculations to Excel. This is shown in Figure 6.12.

	A	B	C
1	Example 6.9 The EOQ version 2		
2	Unit ordering cost:c_o	20	
3	Unit holding cost:c_h	0.15	
4	Unit cost of stock:c_i	1.6	
5	Demand :d	6000	
6	Usage per time period: u	20	
7	Replenishment rate: r	80	
8	Average inventory level	433.01	=(1-B6/B7)*B9/2
9	Economic Order Quantity EO(	1154.7	=((2*B2*B5)/(B3*B4*(1-B6/B7)))^0.5
10	Total holding cost	103.92	=B3*B4*B8
11	Total ordering cost	103.92	=B2*B5/B9
12	Total purchase cost	9600	=B4*B5
13	Total cost	9807.8	=B10+B11+B12

Figure 6.12

→ Excel solution

Cells B2:B7 are the given values.

Unit ordering cost:co Cell B2
Unit holding cost:ch Cell B3
Unit cost of stock:ci Cell B4
Demand :d Cell B5
Usage per time period: u Cell B6
Replenishment rate: r Cell B7
Average inventory level Cell B8 Formula: = (1-B6/B7)*B9/2
Economic Order Quantity EOQ Cell B9 Formula: = ((2*B2*B5)/(B3*B4*(1-B6/B7)))^0.5
Total holding cost Cell B10 Formula: = B3*B4*B8
Total ordering cost Cell B11 Formula: = B2*B5/B9
Total purchase cost Cell B12 Formula: = B4*B5
Total cost Cell B13 Formula: = B10+B11+B12

Interpretation As we saw earlier from the manual calculation the EOQ produced by the model is the same (1154.7).

Note Observe the entry in B8. Here we have calculated the average inventory in the way explained above (i.e. from Q*(1 – u/r)/2). Then the EOQ is calculated from our most recent expression, and finally the Total Holding Cost is defined in terms of the Average Inventory level contained in B8.

Furthermore, this model can now be used to confirm that as r becomes very large (10^{12} say); the model collapses to produce the same results as those obtained earlier (Figure 6.3), with an EOQ value of 1000.

Of course, the Solver could have been used to obtain the same result.

This is shown in Figure 6.13 where a trial value of 900 has been used for the EOQ to start with.

Simply click on Solve with the settings shown and the last result for the EOQ (1155) will be obtained as illustrated in Figure 6.13.

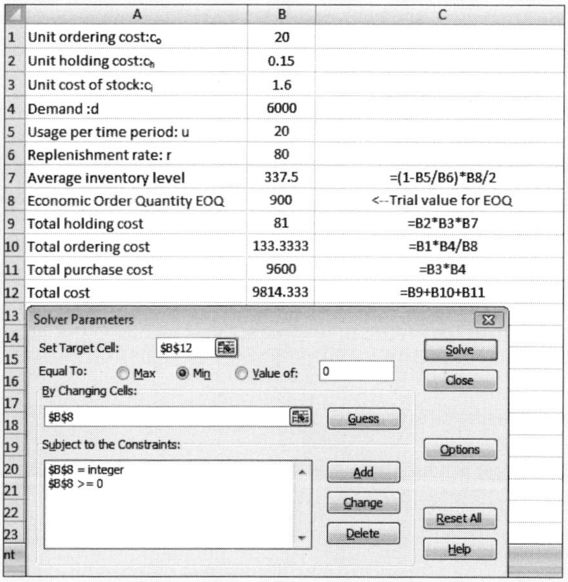

	A	B	C
1	Unit ordering cost:c_o	20	
2	Unit holding cost:c_h	0.15	
3	Unit cost of stock:c_i	1.6	
4	Demand :d	6000	
5	Usage per time period: u	20	
6	Replenishment rate: r	80	
7	Average inventory level	337.5	=(1-B5/B6)*B8/2
8	Economic Order Quantity EOQ	900	<--Trial value for EOQ
9	Total holding cost	81	=B2*B3*B7
10	Total ordering cost	133.3333	=B1*B4/B8
11	Total purchase cost	9600	=B3*B4
12	Total cost	9814.333	=B9+B10+B11

Solver Parameters
Set Target Cell: $B$12
Equal To: Max Min Value of: 0
By Changing Cells: $B$8
Subject to the Constraints:
$B$8 = integer
$B$8 >= 0
Solve Close Guess Options Add Change Delete Reset All Help

Figure 6.13

Lastly, it is an easy matter to get Excel to chart the relationship between the EOQ and the u/r ratio.

This is done in Figure 6.14 and confirms our earlier contention that as u/r increases, so too does the EOQ (from its lowest value of 1000 when replenishment is made in full and u/r is indistinguishable from zero).

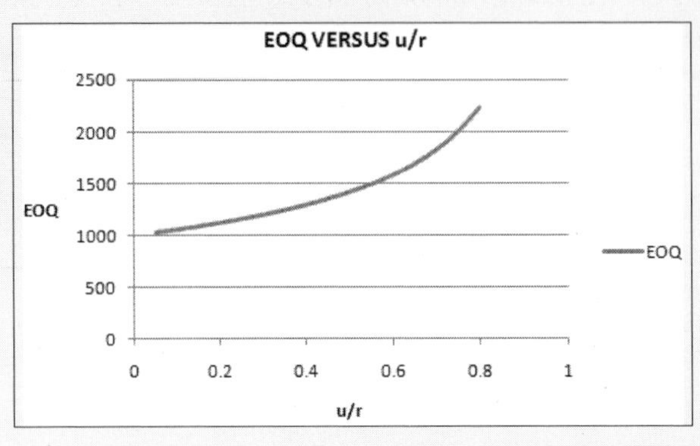

Figure 6.14

Student exercise

X6.19 A producer orders inventory items from a supplier who can start delivery in four days time at a rate of 50 units per day. A production run of the end product will require 250,000 units of the item, and will use up inventory at a rate of 20 units per day. Ordering, purchase and holding costs are, respectively, £4, £80 and 10%. Calculate the EOQ.

6.5 The effect of quantity discounts

So far we have assumed that the cost of the item (c_i) was fixed regardless of the size of the order. Sometimes however suppliers find it profitable to offer a discount for order sizes that are above certain threshold amounts. As an illustration, suppose that the supplier offers the following discounts on the purchase cost of the item:

0% for all order sizes less than 100 units.

1% for all order sizes of 100 units or more but less than 150.

1.5% for all order sizes of 150 units or more but less than 200.

2% for all order sizes of 200 units or more.

Since we know that the purchase cost is given by c_i this means that, with the discount offered being given by k, then the true cost of each item is given by:

$$c_i - kc_i = c_i{*}(1 - k)$$

For example, with the purchase cost of the item being £100, then the true cost for various order sizes (Q) would be as shown below:

Q = 99: £100 per item

Q = 101–149: £99 per item

Q = 150–199: £98.5 per item

Q = 200 plus : £98 per item

Now suppose that the company has to fulfil an order that requires 300 units, with relevant costs given by: $C_0 = £18$, $c_h = 0.15$ and $c_i = £20$. The EOQ without any discount is easily seen to be 60 units.

But how would this EOQ be affected by the discount possibility?

The ideas involved can be seen in Figure 6.15.

	A	B	C	D	E
1	Unit ordering cost:co	18	18	18	18
2	Unit holding cost:ch	0.15	0.15	0.15	0.15
3	Unit cost of stock:ci	20	20	20	20
4	Demand :d	300	300	300	300
5	Discount: k	0	0.01	0.015	0.02
6	Threshold	0	100	150	200
7	Economic Order Quantity EOC	60	60	60	60
8	Total holding cost	90	89.1	88.65	88.2
9	Total ordering cost	90	90	90	90
10	Total cost of stock items	6000	5940	5910	5880
11	Total cost	6180	6119.1	6088.7	6058.2
12					EOQ=60

Figure 6.15

→ Excel solution

Here we have taken a basic EOQ model such as the one developed in Figure 6.3 and added two rows to contain the given discount and threshold values for which these discounts apply. With these given data the EOQ is calculated to be EOQ = [2*18*300/0.15*20]0.5 = 60 units.

So B1:B7 are given values. Column B was then copied into columns C to E. In line with the parameters given, we then changed the values for the discount and the threshold for this to apply, in the C to E columns. With the previously calculated EOQ value of 60 replicated in each column, it would appear that the total cost unambiguously declines from left to right. However, it is clear that the EOQ values in columns C to E are all less than the threshold values for the discount. So the discount will not actually prevail.

Consequently, we applied the Solver to each of columns C to E - each time requiring that the target cell was the one containing total cost (row 11), and the changing cell was the one containing the EOQ (row 7).

Importantly, we also added the constraint that the changing cell was greater than or equal to the threshold value at which the discount would apply. In other words, C7 ≥ C6, D7 ≥ D6, etc. When this process was carried out the results shown in Figure 6.16 are obtained.

	A	B	C	D	E
1	Unit ordering cost:co	18	18	18	18
2	Unit holding cost:ch	0.15	0.15	0.15	0.15
3	Unit cost of stock:ci	20	20	20	20
4	Demand :d	300	300	300	300
5	Discount: k	0	0.01	0.015	0.02
6	Threshold	0	100	150	200
7	Economic Order Quantity EOC	60	60	60	60
8	Total holding cost	90	89.1	88.65	88.2
9	Total ordering cost	90	90	90	90
10	Total cost of stock items	6000	5940	5910	5880
11	Total cost	6180	6119.1	6088.7	6058.2
12					EOQ=60

Solver Parameters

Set Target Cell: $C$11

Equal To: Max ◉ Min Value of: 0

By Changing Cells: $C$7

Subject to the Constraints:

$C$7 = integer
$C$7 >= $C$6
$C$7 >= 0

Solve | Close | Guess | Options | Add | Change | Reset All | Delete | Help

Figure 6.16

✻ **Interpretation** From this it is clear that discounts of 1% and 1.5% both produce a lower total cost than when the discount is either 0% or 2%, and that of the former two options an EOQ of 100 units that qualifies for the 1% discount is unambiguously superior.

Note Observe the results shown in row 12 These were obtained from a conditional formula (written in B12 and then copied into (C12:E12). The formula was =IF(B11=MIN($B$11:$E$11),"EOQ="&B7,"").

For each of columns B to E this compares the actual total costs with the minimum total cost value of the values in B11:E11 and returns the EOQ value from any of columns B to E if that should be the minimum. A blank is returned otherwise.

Student exercise

X6.20 A firm requires 6000 units of an inventory item for which the ordering, purchase and holding costs are £30, £25 and 10% respectively. The supplier offers discounts of 1%, 1.5%, and 1.75% respectively for order sizes between 400 and 799, 800, and 1499, and 1500 units or more. Calculate the EOQ for each of the discount possibilities and then indicate the optimal EOQ.

6.6 Probabilistic demand

In the discussion to date it has always been assumed that the demand for the inventory item is a known given. However, as previously suggested it is more likely that the demand for the item has an element of randomness that could lead to a stockout and failure to meet the order. To appreciate the implications of this probabilistic demand, suppose that from experience it is known that the behaviour of demand is well desribed by a Poisson distribution with mean = d. This means that the probability of a stockout is given by the probability that the calculated EOQ is exceeded in a Poisson distribution with mean = d; that is, P(d > d).

Now consider Figure 6.17 where we have calculated this probability in B4 from the function:

=1-POISSON(B7,B6,1)

	A	B	C
1	Unit ordering cost:co	30	
2	Unit holding cost:ch	0.1	
3	Unit cost of stock:ci	25	
4	Demand :d	6000	
5	Prob(d > d)	0.1004	=1-POISSON(B7,B6,1)
6	Economic Order Quantity EOQ (formula)	379.47	=((2*B1*B4)/(B2*B3))^0.5
7	Economic Order Quantity EOQ (trial)	404	404
8	Total holding cost	505	=B2*B3*B7/2
9	Total ordering cost	445.54	=B1*B4/B7
10	Total cost of stock items	150000	=B3*B4
11	Total cost	150951	=B8+B9+B10

Figure 6.17

probabilistic demand
a situation in which the estimated demand for the end product, and therefore the inventory item, is subject to random variation rather than being known for certain.

→ Excel solution

B1:B4 are given values.

Prob(d > d) Cell B5	Formula: = 1-POISSON(B7,B6,1)
Economic Order Quantity EOQ (formula) Cell B6	Formula: = ((2*B1*B4)/(B2*B3))^0.5
Economic Order Quantity EOQ (trial) Cell B7	Trial value
Total holding cost Cell B8	Formula: = B2*B3*B7/2
Total ordering cost Cell B9	Formula: = B1*B4/B7
Total cost of stock items Cell B10	Formula: = B3*B4
Total cost Cell B11	Formula: = B8+B9+B10

Since the calculated value of the EOQ in B6 is based upon the average demand, this is taken as the mean of the distribution. The Poisson formula in B5 calculates the probability that with this mean the trial value for the EOQ in B7 will be exceeded.

Interpretation As is clear from Figure 6.17 with a trial value of 404 for the EOQ and a Poisson mean value of 379.4 (the calculated EOQ) there is a 10% probability that demand exceeds 379.4 and that there will be a stockout.

Note =POISSON (B7,B6,1) calculates the probability that that with a mean value for the distribution given in B6 (i.e. the calculated value of the EOQ), the value of demand contained in B7 will lie between zero and d. Consequently: =1-POISSON (B7,B6,1) will calculate the probability that demand exceeds the calculated EOQ value.

Now suppose that the firm is only willing to take a risk of stockout of no more than 5%. We can use the model to set up a Solver routine that will find the new value of the EOQ that will cause the risk of stockout to be less than or equal to 0.05.

The solver settings are shown in Figure 6.18, as well as the results of running the Solver

	A	B	C
1	Unit ordering cost:co	30	
2	Unit holding cost:ch	0.1	
3	Unit cost of stock:ci	25	
4	Demand :d	6000	
5	Prob(d > d)	0.0465	=1-POISSON(B7,B6,1)
6	Economic Order Quantity EOQ (formul	379.47	=((2*B1*B4)/(B2*B3))^0.5
7	Economic Order Quantity EOQ (trial)	412	Trial value
8	Total holding cost	515	=B2*B3*B7/2
9	Total ordering cost	436.89	=B1*B4/B7
10	Total cost of stock items	150000	=B3*B4
11	Total cost	150952	=B8+B9+B10

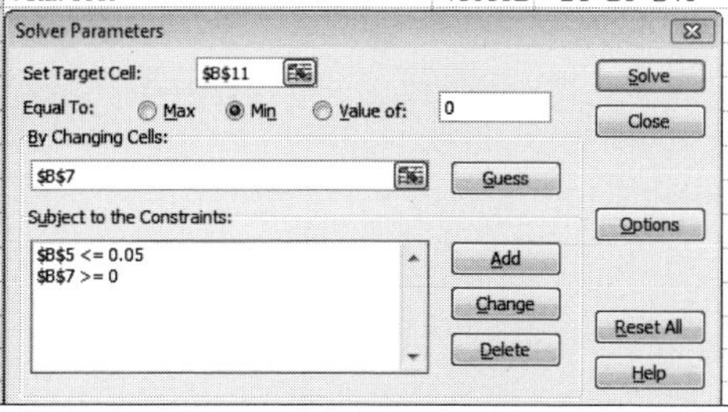

Solver Parameters
Set Target Cell: $B$11
Equal To: Max Min Value of: 0
By Changing Cells:
$B$7
Subject to the Constraints:
$B$5 <= 0.05
$B$7 >= 0
Solve Close Guess Options Add Change Delete Reset All Help

Figure 6.18

Interpretation From this we see that the EOQ must increase from 379 to 404 units if there is to be a risk of no more than 10% of there being a stockout. The extra amount added to the EOQ can be thought of as a safety stock, and clearly can become quite large if demand conditions are particularly volatile.

Of course, whether this risk is worth bearing depends upon the financial consequences of a stockout, and this would require a much more detailed study of both the costs borne and revenues lost if this were to happen.

Student exercise

X6.21 If the demand for an item of inventory is known to be distributed as a Poisson variable with mean equal to 120 units. Calculate the probability that there will be a stockout if the firm uses an EOQ of 125 units. What EOQ value ensures that the risk of a stockout is no more than 5%?

6.7 Pareto analysis

Pareto analysis is a method of drawing attention to situations in which a proportionately small number of events can be associated with a relatively large number of other events. For example, it may be noticed that in 80% of all cases where an order has not been received, it can be attributed to only 20% of suppliers. Or, when there is a production stoppage, on 82% of occasions it can be associated with only 18% of inventory items that are out of stock. This is the so-called 80:20 rule and provides a useful method of identifying bottlenecks in systems that are dependent upon many contributing items. To appreciate the value of this method consider a production process that requires eight essential inventory components (comp 1 : comp 8).

Also suppose that from experience of a large number of production runs it is found that production stoppages can be attributed to stockouts of each of the components as shown in Figure 6.19.

	A	B	C	D
1	Component	Number of stockouts	Abs %	Cum %
2	comp1	60	0.3	0.3
3	comp2	50	0.25	0.55
4	comp3	40	0.2	0.75
5	comp4	15	0.075	0.825
6	comp5	12	0.06	0.885
7	comp6	10	0.05	0.935
8	comp7	8	0.04	0.975
9	comp8	5	0.025	1

Figure 6.19

safety stock the amount of inventory held in excess of the EOQ to prevent random variations in the level of demand, causing a stockout.

Pareto analysis a statistical method of identifying the extent to which the majority of stoppages in production can be attributed to stockouts in relatively few items.

→ Excel solution

The values in B2:B9 are the given values.

In C2: =B2/SUM(B$2:B2) copied into C3:C9

This calculates the absolute percentage frequencies.

In D2: =SUM(C$2:C2) copied into D3:D9

This calculates the running (cumulative) totals of the absolute percentage frequencies.

Given these data, Pareto analysis simply involves constructing absolute and cumulative percentage frequencies for each of the components involved.

The results are shown in Figure 6.20.

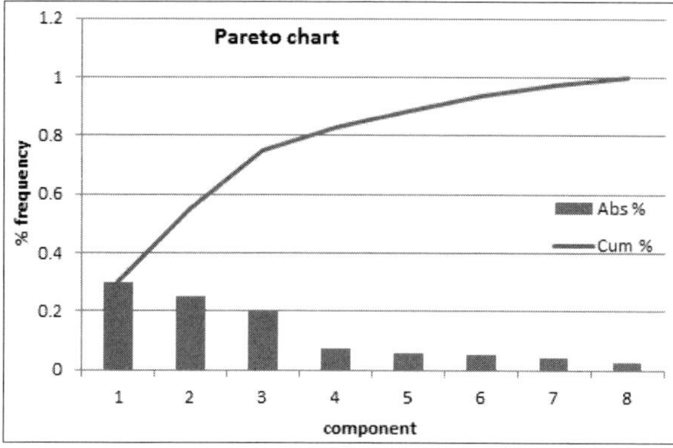

Figure 6.20

→ Excel solution

The chart was constructed using C2:D9 as the data range and then inserting a column chart. Then, by clicking on the Cum% series it was turned into a line graph.

Interpretation The vertical bars represent the percentage of occasions on which each component was responsible for a stoppage. The line curve shows the cumulative percentage frequencies of stoppages from all components.

6.8 Models to determine the EOQ and the selling price

The analysis to date has only focused on the cost dimension of inventory control. However, since firms typically attempt to maximize profits we should consider how the introduction of revenue considerations interact with costs in order to determine profit.

By way of illustration, consider a company that simply imports inventory items and then sells them on to domestic clients.

Up until now it has been assumed that apart from random variations, the demand for the item is given, and beyond the firm's control. However, it is clearly likely that the price that the firm charges will influence the demand for its items. Consequently, suppose that the demand (d) for a particular item is subject to the following dependency upon the price charged (p): $d = a - b*p$. This has two effects:

1. First, it means that revenue (R) can be calculated as: $R = p*d = p*(a - b*p) = a*p - b*p^2$
2. Second, it means that the expression for ordering costs (c_o*d/Q) can now be expressed as : $c_o*(a - bp)/Q$

Now (and using the same notation as before), taking costs and revenue together gives the following expression for profit (π): $\pi = p*(a - b*p) - c_0*(a - b*p)/Q - c_h*c_i*Q/2 - c_i d$. This is equivalent to the formula that was derived earlier for the basic EOQ when d is replaced by (a – b*p). Expressed in this way it is apparent that the firm now has to make two choices – the price to charge (p) and the EOQ (Q). And, since p and Q do not interact independently, resolution for the optimal values of each is not entirely straightforward.

Consequently, an Excel Solver routine for the given parameters for costs and demand should be used as shown in Figure 6.21.

	A	B	C
1	Unit ordering cost:c_o	10.00	
2	Unit holding cost:c_h	0.15	
3	Unit cost of stock:c_i	40.00	
4	Demand constant: a	250.00	
5	Demand constant: b	2.00	
6	Price: P	82.80	<--Trial value
7	Economic Order Quantity EOQ	16.77	<--Trial value
8	Demand: D	84.40	=B4-B5*B6
9	Revenue: R	6988.48	=B6*B8
10	Total holding cost	50.32	=B2*B3*B7/2
11	Total ordering cost	50.32	=B1*B8/B7
12	Total cost of stock items	3376.15	=B3*B8
13	Total cost	3476.79	=B10+B11+B12
14	Profit	3511.68	=B9-B13

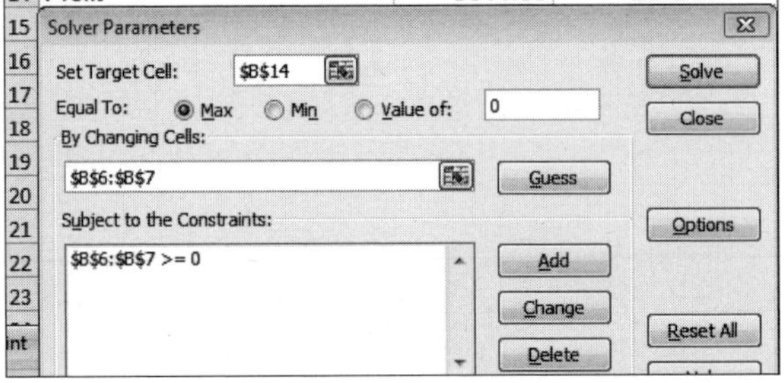

Solver Parameters

Set Target Cell: $B$14

Equal To: Max Min Value of: 0

By Changing Cells:

$B$6:$B$7

Subject to the Constraints:

$B$6:$B$7 >= 0

Solve Close Guess Options Add Change Reset All Delete

Figure 6.21

→ Excel solution

B1:B5 are given values, while B6 and B7 contain trial values for the price and the EOQ

Demand: D Cell B8	Formula: = B4-B5*B6
Revenue: R Cell B9	Formula: = B6*B8
Total holding cost Cell B10	Formula: = B2*B3*B7/2
Total ordering cost Cell B11	Formula: = B1*B8/B7
Total cost of stock items Cell B12	Formula: = B3*B8
Total cost Cell B13	Formula: = B10+B11+B12
Profit Cell B14	Formula: = B9-B13

The target cell is B14 (profit) and this is to be maximized by changing the values in B6:B7 (price and the EOQ respectively, subject to the constraint that the latter two values are greater than or equal to zero.

Interpretation From this it can be seen that the optimal strategy is to charge a price of £82.8 and use an EOQ of 16.77 units.

Student exercise

Please visit the Online Resource Centre which accompanies this textbook for solutions to the student exercises and techniques in practice questions.

X6.22 Use the model developed in the last illustration (Figure 6.21) to calculate the effect upon price and the EOQ of an increase in the ordering cost from £10 to £20.

Techniques in practice

The forgoing discussion has outlined the basic principles involved in inventory and stock control, and shown how Excel can be an invaluable assistant. In practice, inventory control is a highly complex process, especially when large numbers of different items are involved in the production process. Usually, this will require dedicated software either in the form of ready made Excel templates, or more sophisticated software packages.

Another practical issue concerns the accounting and management procedures that current auditing and reporting regulations require. Once again, dedicated software packages are available to assist in this, yet are nontheless based on the fundamental principles that have been explained.

Practical issues also arise from the need to make accurate demand forecasts. Once again, highly sophisticated statistical techniques and associated software packages can be invaluable in predicting future demand patterns and trends.

Having said this, we conclude this section with three illustrations of techniques in practice that can be managed within the Excel environment.

TP 6.1 Hummer plc is a company producing simple transistor radios. The production process involves assembling two prefabricated components (Twitters and Bangers) into a plastic casing. The expected demand for the radios over the production period is for 100,000 units, and the production process can assemble 1000 units per day. For Twitters, the ordering, purchase and holding costs are £20, £0.45, and £15 respectively, and replenishment occurs at a rate of 150 Twitters per day. For Bangers, the ordering, purchase and holding costs are £18, £0.55 and £15 respectively, and replenishment occurs at a rate of 160 Bangers per day. For cases, the ordering, purchase and holding costs are £5, £0.25, and £15 respectively and replenishment occurs at a rate of 120 cases per day. Calculate the EOQ values for Twitters, Bangers, and cases.

TP 6.2 Hummer now finds itself in a position where the demand for radios depends upon the price (p) charged as: Demand = 200,000 – 15,000p. Calculate the price that Hummer should charge and the new EOQ values for each of the inventory items.

TP 6.3 Hummer has a total suitable inventory storage capacity of 4,000,000 cm^3. The volumes of Twitters, Bangers and cases are 90, 180 and 270 cm^3 respectively. Compared with the results found in TP 6.2, how do these storage restrictions affect the EOQ values for each item of inventory?

Summary

This chapter has explained the principles involved in developing best practice rules for inventory management. Simple formulae were derived for the optimal re-order stock level and the economic order quantity (EOQ). These were then adapted to deal with non zero delivery lead times and non-instantaneous replenishment.

Use of the Excel Solver was also explained and then used to assist solving more mathematically challenging inventory models.

The advantages and limitations of Pareto analysis were explained in an inventory control environment, and the analysis extended in a probabilistic manner to take account of uncertainty in the derived demand for inventories.

Student exercise answers

For all figures listed below, please see the Online Resource Centre.

X6.1 We have Q = 1000 and u = 20, and require t such that S = 0. Therefore: 0 = 1000 – 2t and: t = 1000/20 = 50 days.

X6.2 We have Q = 3000, u = 50 and S = 1000, and require to find the value of t that would produce this scenario. Therefore: 1000 = 3000 – 50t, 50t = 2000 and t = 2000/50 = 40 days.

X6.3 We have S = 4000, Q = 6000 and t = 10, and require to find the value of u that this implies. Therefore: 4000 = 6000 – 10u and u = (6000 – 4000)/10 = 200 units per day.

X6.4 We have t = 25 when S = 0 and u = 50. Therefore: 0 = Q – 50(25) and Q = 1250 units.

X6.5 In terms of our established notation we have: u = 20, Q = 800, m = 5 and r = 50. So: Re-order time = Q/u – (Q/r + m) = 800/20 – (800/50 + 5) = 40 – 21 = 19 days. Re-order stock level = Q – u*(Re-order time) = 800 – 20*19 = 420 (i.e re-order when there are 420 units left in stock.

X6.6 We have Q =1000, u = 20, r = 40 and re-order time = 20. The lead time (m) is unknown. Therefore: 20 = 1000/20 – (1000/40 + m) and 20 = 50 – (25 + m) and m = 50 – 25 – 20 = 5 days.

X6.7 We have the re-order stock level = 100, Q = 1000, r = 50 and m = 5, and require to find the value of u that this implied. Therefore: 100 = u(1000/50 + 5) and 100 = 25u so: u = 4 units per day.

X6.8 We have Q = 2000, u = 50, r = 40 and m = 7. Therefore: Re-order stock level = 50(2000/40 + 7) = 50(50 +7) = 2850 units. Since this value exceeds the order quantity (2000) it is impossible to achieve. Alternatively, re-order time is: Re-order time = 2000/50 – (2000/40 + 7) = 40 – 57 = –17 days. Clearly a negative re-order time makes no logical sense, and is therefore an invalid calculation.

X6.9 We can see that: c_o = £4, d = 250,000, c_i = £80 and c_h = 0.1. The EOQ is therefore given by: EOQ = $[2*250,000*4/0.1*80]^{0.5}$ = 500 units. The solution could also have been obtained from the model developed in Figure 6.3 simply by inputting the four given values to the appropriate cells of the worksheet (B1:B4).

X6.10 We now have c0 = £4 + 0.10(£4) = £4.40 and the rest of the givens being the same as before. Therefore: EOQ = $[2*250,000*4.4/0.1*80]^{0.5}$ = 524.4 units. Once again, this solution could have been obtained from Figure 6.3 simply by changing the value in the B2 cell to 4.4.

X6.11 We now have ci = £80 + 0.10(£80) = £88 and the rest of the givens being the same as before. Therefore: EOQ = $[2*250,000*4/0.1*88]^{0.5}$ = 476.73 units. Again, the Figure 6.3 model will produce this result if the value in B4 is made equal to 8.8.

X6.12 Two simple changes to the model developed in Figure 6.7 are all that is needed to solve this (non-trivial) equation. First, edit the formula in B2 to express the equation in terms of the B1 cell. That is: =B1^3+B1^2+B1. Second, change the RHS value in B3 to 14. With the Solver settings as shown in Figure 6.7, click on Solve to obtain the solution of x = 2.

X6.13 Use the worksheet that was developed in Figure 6.7 with the following changes: In B2: =2^B1+B1^2. In B3: 17 (i.e. the value 17). A solution value of x = 3 will be returned.

X6.14 After inputting the given values to the B1:B4 cells (4, 0.1, 80 and 250,000) of the worksheet in Figure 6.8, the solution will be obtained from the Solver settings shown in Figure 6.8, and confirms the earlier answer of 500 units for the EOQ.

X6.15 After inputting the given values to the B1:B4 cells (4.4, 0.1, 80 and 250,000) of the worksheet in Figure 6.8, the solution will be obtained from the Solver settings shown in Figure 6.8, and confirms the earlier answer of 524.4 units for the EOQ.

X6.16 After inputting the given values to the B1:B4 cell (4, 0.1, 88 and 250,000) of the worksheet in Figure 6.8, the solution will be obtained from the Solver settings shown in Figure 6.8, and confirms the earlier answer of 467.73 units for the EOQ.

X6.17 Simply change the formula in B2 of the worksheet shown in Figure 6.7 to: =(B1-2)*(B1-6) and the value in B3 to zero. Now use a trial value in B1 of zero, and the Solver will find the solution $x = 2$. Next, Increase the trial value to 3 and the solution: $x = 2$ will still prevail. However if the trial value is set at 4 the Solver finds the $x = 6$ solution.

X6.18 Total cost per unit produced is given by: $TC/x = 0.02x^2 - 0.8x + 12 + 100/x$. Consequently, use the B1 cell (say) to contain a trial value for x (positive non-zero is best). Then use the B2 cell to contain the expression for TC/x in terms of the B1 cell. That is, in B2 enter: =0.02*B1^2-0.8*B1+12+100/B1. This is also the target cell, and it should be minimized subject to the constraint that x (cell B1) must be greater than or equal to zero. When the Solver is run with these settings a solution value of x = 24.25 units will be obtained.

X6.19 Using the most recent version of the EOQ formula we have: $d = 250{,}000$, $u = 20$, $r = 50$, $c_o = £4$, $c_i = £80$ and $c_h = 0.1$. Meaning: $EOQ = [2*c_o*d/c_h*c_i*(1 - u/r)]^{0.5} = [(2*4*250{,}000)/(0.1*80*(1 - 20/50))]^{0.5} = 646$ units. Alternatively, the same answer could have been obtained from the models shown in Figure 6.12 (using formula) and Figure 6.13 (using the Solver), simply by entering the given values to the appropriate cells.

X6.20

→ Excel solution

The easiest solution is to use the model created in Figure 6.15 after entering the new given values. This initial situation is shown in Figure X6.1 where the Solver has been applied to column B to minimize a target cell of B11 using a changing cell of B7, subject to the constraints that B7 is integer, zero or more, and greater than or equal to the threshold value in B6.

An EOQ of 379 units is obtained when there is no discount applicable.

Figure X6.20a

We now run the Solver with the equivalent settings on each of columns C to E and get the results shown in Figure X6.20b.

Figure X6.20b

❊ Interpretation Clearly the EOQ is now 800 units (qualifying for the 1.5% discount). Increasing the EOQ to 1500 in order to qualify for the 1.75% discount is not justified since the benefit of the discount is outweighed by the burden of the holding costs that must be borne in order to qualify for the discount.

X6.21 (a) Use any cell of an Excel worksheet to contain: =1-Poisson(125,120,1) to obtain a result of 0.3038.

(b) Set up a worksheet as shown in Figure X6.3.

Figure X6.21

> **→ Excel solution**
>
> The entries in B1:B2 are the given values, and B3 is a trial value for the changing cell, which is also the target cell to be minimized, subject to the constraint that B4 (the Poisson probability) is below the required risk level contained in B2.
>
> Poisson Probability Cell B4 Formula: = 1 – POISSON(B3,B1,1)
>
> An EOQ = 138 units satisfies the defined minimum risk requirement.

X6.22 Simply change the value in the B1 cell from 10 to 20 and rerun the Solver with the same settings. Excel will find that the price should be reduced to £82.92 and the EOQ increased to 26.69 (or 27 if the item is discrete).

TP6.1 Solution

We can use the worksheet developed in Figure 6.12 as a template which can be extended to address this problem. The method is shown in Figure TP6.1.

Figure TP6.1

> **→ Excel solution**
>
> The entries in B3:D8 are the givens of the problem.
>
> | | |
> |---|---|
> | Average inventory level Cell B9 | Formula: = (1-B7/B8)*B10/2 |
> | Economic Order Quantity EOQ Cell B10 | Formula = ((2*B3*B6)/(B4*B5*(1-B7/B8)))^0.5 |
> | Total holding cost Cell B11 | Formula: = B4*B5*B9 |
> | Total ordering cost Cell B12 | Formula: = B3*B6/B10 |
> | Total purchase cost Cell B13 | Formula: = B5*B6 |
> | Total cost Cell B14 | Formula: = B11+B12+B13 |
>
> Then B9:B13 was copied across into columns C and D, and produces the EOQ values for each item shown in B10, C10 and D10.

TP6.2 Solution

The model developed in TP 6.1 can easily be used as a template to address this new variant of the problem.

> **→ Excel solution**
>
> | | |
> |---|---|
> | Demand :d Cell B6 | = B$16-B$17*E$10 copied into C6:D6 |
> | Economic Order Quantity Cells B10:D10 | trial values for the EOQ – not formulae. |
> | Price Cell E10 | trial value for price. |
> | Demand parameter b Cell B16 | given value |
> | Demand parameter a Cell B17 | given value |
> | Profit Cell B18 | = E$10*B6-B14-C14-D14 |
>
> Target cell: B17 (profit) to be maximized
>
> Changing cells: B10:E10
>
> Constraints: B10:E10>=0

Interpretation The firm should charge £7.29 for the radios and the EOQ values have been reduced in comparison with the values obtained in TP 6.1.

TP6.3 Solution

The model developed in TP 6.2 can be used as a convenient template when modified as shown in Figure TP 6.3.

Figure TP 6.3

→ Excel solution

Unit volume Cells B19:D19	given values.
Total volume Cell B20	= B10*B19 copied into C20:D20 and summed to give the grand total in E20.
Additional constraint	E20 < = B21(the given warehouse space)

When the Solver is invoked the results shown in Figure TP 6.3 are obtained.

Interpretation There has been a very small increase in the price to be charged, but the EOQ values have all fallen significantly as a result of the storage restriction.

Further reading

1. S. Axsater (2010) *Inventory Control* (2nd edn), Springer.
2. S. Bragg (2011) *Inventory Best Practices*, Wiley
3. W. Hui-Ming (2011) *Inventory Systems: Modelling and Research Methods*, Novan Science.

Formula summary

Stockout time = Q/u (6.1)

n (number of orders) = d/Q (6.2)

Average inventory level = Q/2 (6.3)

Re-order time = Q/u – (Q/r + m) (6.4)

Re-order stock level = u(Q/r + m) (6.5)

EOQ (version 1) = $[2*c_o*d/c_h*c_i]^{0.5}$ (6.6)

EOQ (version 2) = $[2^*c_o{}^*d/c_h{}^*c_i{}^*(1 - u/r)]^{0.5}$ (6.7)

For Excel:

If a random variable - x - is Poisson distributed with a mean value of m, then:

The probability that x lies between 0 and k inclusive is returned by:
= POISSON(k,m,1)

From this:

The probability that x exceeds k is given by:
= 1 – POISSON(k,m,1)

For an exact value of a single Poisson occurrence then we change the last argument of the Excel function from 1 (cumulative) to 0 (discrete)

So:

= POISSON(k,m,0)

Returns the probability that a Poisson random variable X is exactly equal to k when the mean of the Poisson distribution is equal to m.

7 Statistical quality control

X

quality control actions or methods that are used to ensure the quality of a product or service.

decision making make decisions based upon the data and information available.

acceptance sampling acceptance sampling is used by industries worldwide for assuring the quality of incoming and outgoing goods.

accuracy it is the difference between the average, or mean, of a number of readings and the true, or target, value.

precision is a measure of how close an estimator is expected to be to the true value of a parameter.

outlier in statistics, an outlier is an observation that is numerically distant from the rest of the data.

z-score in statistics, a standard score indicates how many standard deviations an observation is above or below the mean value.

Cherbyshev's theorem is an empirical rule that enables us to consider the proportion of packets of data within a specific number of standard deviations. Henceforth it is an extension of the z-Score approach where instead of examining a single data value we assess a group of data with respect to the whole data set.

» Overview «

The aim of this chapter is to introduce the basic concepts of statistical quality control and exploit further the basic descriptive statistical tools discussed in Chapter 3 but in the context of data analysis as a process.

Therefore the emphasis in this chapter is the real world of datasets with a special focus on datasets in the context of surveys, quality control of processes, products, and services. The chapter is split into three parts. In the opening part we explain the background to data quality and quality control versus quality assurance. We look at the process of data analysis with a wider scope, which includes the need to acquire and use 'clean' data. In particular, we will see the importance of data quality and cleaning within the process of data analysis. We then return to some of the basic descriptive statistical tools introduced in Chapter 2 and show how combinations of such tools can be exploited not only to summarize datasets but also grasp their key features. In the second and core part of this chapter we examine the basic quality control tools, including indicators and charting methods, that help us monitor quality in processes, whether these be manufacturing or business processes. The objective is to provide the reader with a collection of methods that provide better insight into process quality and use a fact-based approach in decision making. In the third and concluding part of this chapter, acceptance sampling and general decision making are discussed.

» Learning objectives «

After studying this chapter and after completing the exercises you should be able to:

- » Understand the concepts of quality control and assurance in datasets.
- » Discriminate between accuracy and precision and why not always do they co-exist.
- » Understand the cleaning of datasets prior to analysis; that is, the elimination of outliers.
- » Understand the data analysis process, from collecting data to reporting findings.
- » Understand the two key data cleaning methods: z-score and Cherbyshev's theorem.

- Understand the management of outliers and the effects they might have on the results of an analysis.
- Understand the summarization of datasets through the combination of basic descriptive statistical tools.
- Understand the box and whisker plot.
- Understand the basics of statistical process control.
- Assess quality control and conformance via different types of control chart and point estimators.
- Assess quality control and conformance via acceptance sampling.
- Understand the application of statistical quality control procedures and relative tools in decision making.
- Explain why management decisions are often a compromise.
- Introduce acceptance sampling in quality control and as a process.
- Understand the binomial probability function and operation curve in acceptance sampling.

7.1 Quality control versus quality assurance

When dealing with data the issues of quality control and quality assurance will surface sooner or later. Both can be viewed in terms of sampling. In sampling the quality of the data refers to the completeness of the data. For example, a quality check applied to an interview file may state that the file must hold all the basic information of the interviewee such as name, surname, address, and country in order for it to be qualitatively acceptable. Such checks are obviously part of a quality control procedure and carried out before any formal processing or analysis is conducted. In this case incompleteness is a measure of quality or rather lack of quality. On the other hand, and from a quality assurance stand point, the same data is evaluated on its correctness. For example, if an interviewee is born in Paris but the assigned country code is that of the UK something is obviously wrong. So we may have data that is acceptable from a quality control perspective but which is unacceptable from a quality assurance perspective. The goal is therefore is to have datasets that are both complete and correct. We may also add that the dataset is to be coherent and consistent with the scope of the analysis.

Online surveys provide an added advantage over manual versions because it is possible to embed in the survey software rules that ensure that the data is complete. For example, you can't submit a survey until it is complete, indeed many online web applications have this functionality. In terms of quality assurance even online surveys can fall foul of correctness: for instance, if a 'free text' box is provided in a survey for comments but what the actual respondent writes is difficult to check. Indeed many surveys now provide a printed or onscreen version at the end of the survey so that they can be read and checked before

X

box and whisker plot is a way of summarizing a set of data measured on an interval scale.

statistical process control statistical process control involves using statistical methods to monitor processes.

point estimators in statistics, point estimation involves the use of sample data to calculate a single value which is to serve as a 'best guess' of an unknown population parameter.

binomial probability function the binomial distribution is a type of discrete probability distribution. It shows the probability of achieving 'd' successes in a sample of 'n' taken from an 'infinite' population where the probability of a success is 'p'.

submission. Manual or face-to-face surveys provide the interviewer and interviewee the opportunity to provide extra detail, and in-focus groups' tape and video recordings of the group are also assessed to make sure that data is as correct and truthful as possible. These latter surveys also afford the opportunity to capture the subtle comments from the interviewee.

The following six quality indicators have been identified and used, where possible, for quality checks and quality assurance for datasets.

1. Accuracy versus precision

   In general, both datasets and data values need to be accurate and therefore 'accurately' reflect the population we are sampling. Accuracy is often semantically confused with precision, but in datasets they have two very different meanings, as depicted in Figure 7.1.

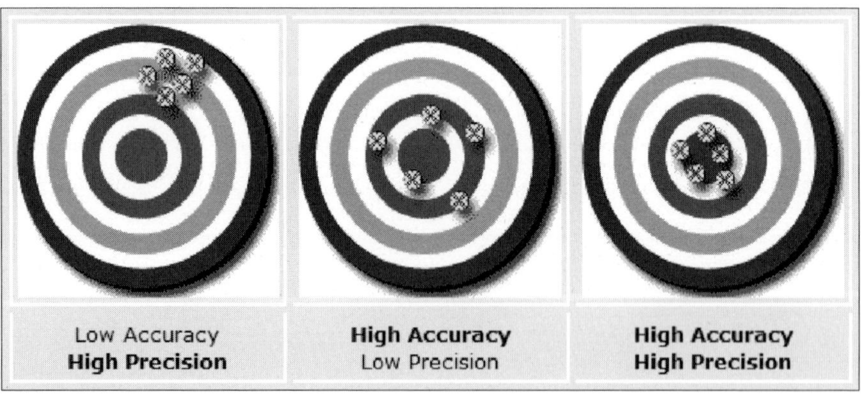

Figure 7.1
Accuracy versus precision

   We may have a dataset that has high precision but low accuracy, or high accuracy and low precision. In quality assessments of manufacturing processes the ideal is to have high accuracy and high precision, and indeed in such circumstances we often refer to high quality production. On the other hand, in surveys much will depend on the scope of the survey. If a survey is preliminary or investigative—we wish to home in on the population needs or preferences—then we may well have low accuracy and low precision; yet the dataset is valid for analysis. If the survey is hunting for or confirming population classes of customers then high accuracy and high precision are recommended, as in systematic and cluster sampling. As a rule of thumb ask yourself if data homogeneity, accuracy, and precision are needed (or expected) to match the scope of the sampling. Note also that survey questions are often representative of clusters or categories, which implies that each question may have different accuracy and precision needs in the responses. Once again, the intent or expected outcome of the question will drive the accuracy and precision choices.

2. Completeness

   The data needs to be as complete, factual, and comprehensive as possible. It is possible to conduct several test assessments, that is, use different parts of the dataset, to verify the findings. Indeed, a typical mistake in sampling is that when sample sizes are established samples are often reduced to the essential because of the cost and organizational issues involved. However, this not only inhibits the thorough testing of the datasets but also forces the use of techniques such as interpolation and extrapolation. As discussed in Chapter 4 concerning time series analysis and regression extrapolation in particular, this often leads to additional and unnecessary uncertainty in the findings.

3. Consistency
   Consistency implies that the form and meaning of the data must be coherent with the different sources and scope of the analysis. For example, if assessing populations were height (in cm) and weight (in kgs) then correlation and consistency become important and will obviously alter the findings if they are mixed, misaligned. So, if we associate a weight of 60kg and/or a height of 180cm with a baby, then consistency is obviously an issue, even though the data is fundamentally complete.
4. Redundancy
   Although replicated data is certainly possible in a survey or sample and may perfectly be acceptable since it genuinely reflects the population, the reader should be wary of accidentally replicated, redundant, or instrument error prone data.
5. Relevancy
   When ordering or pre/processing the data, and/or possibly doing some preliminary analysis, ensure that the data is relevant for the scope of the analysis. For example, in surveys where quota sampling is necessary eliminate the data that is in excess or use it as a test case for the analysis and reporting steps. In multi-stage sampling, ensure that data is not accidentally mixed or from previous stages of sampling unless absolutely coherent with the analysis.
6. Interpretability
   The meaning and significance of the data can only be understood if they fit the scope of the analysis; if they do not, interpretation may be difficult or impossible. For example, samples that are too small, inappropriately mixed, or when outliers are present, the data may be rendered worthless and confusing. In the case of outliers, such data should be removed from the dataset or, if cluster sampling, you should make sure that the data being analysed reflects the cluster(s) under examination. Later in this chapter we will see how data can be cleaned and outliers removed or exploited better.

7.2 Data cleaning, the z-score, Cherbyshev's theorem, and outliers

7.2.1 Data cleaning

The cleaning of data and the relative tools used fit within a process of data validation and overall preliminary assessment before actually conducting the analysis and reporting the findings. The process is depicted in Figure 7.2 and consists of six steps:

1. The first step is to collect the data which usually involves or implies also some form of pre-processing or organization of the data, such as preparing datasets or sub-datasets or importing data from files, exporting to Excel from an online survey and so forth.

2. With the data loaded into a database, table, or Excel worksheet the next step is to order the data. This step may also involve some processing such as sorting the data, adding metadata (titles, subtitles, descriptions, notes, etc.).
3. A preliminary assessment is carried out using descriptive statistical tools. As will be seen, there are several ways of spotting 'bad' data values in the dataset before analysis—such as spotting and eliminating outliers. In step 3 this usually doesn't involve data removal; rather, the scope is the location of 'bad' data through a graph or frequency count, for example.
4. The same descriptive statistical tools are also usually employed in assessing the data and developing rules for classification, mining and cleaning. Step 4 is used in particular to pinpoint patterns in the data and clean-out 'bad' data or irrelevant values in preparation for the analysis.
5. The analysis is conducted and key findings established. This usually involves preparing the data in an informative format such as graphs and summarized tables. Step 5 also involves trends analysis, regression, packaging the results in preparation for decisions and summarizing.
6. In the final step the findings are reported and the results concluded. This also involves exploiting graphical tools that provide a synthetized grouping of the results in the form of maps, explanation of processes, flow charts, preparing executive summaries, and so forth.

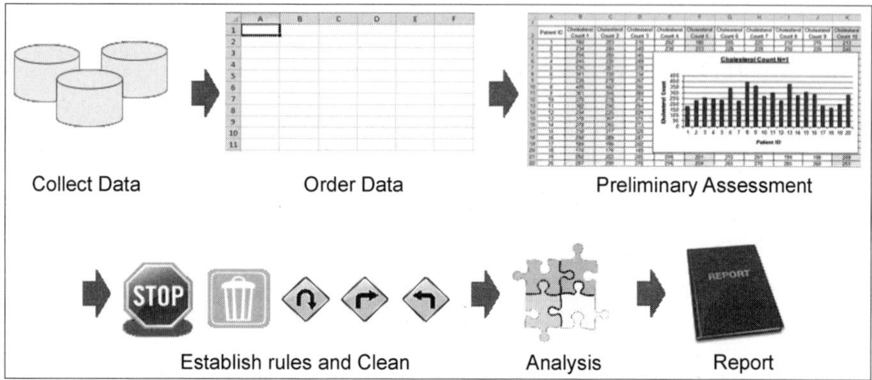

Figure 7.2
Data cleaning and data analysis process

A key part of the process depicted in Figure 7.2 is obviously the preparation and cleaning of data. In this context we will now examine two useful tools, the z-score and apply Cherbyshev's method or theorem and then look at other tools to spot outliers.

Table 7.1 provides further information on data cleaning and analysis.

7.2.2 Z-score

Cherbyshev's theorem is an empirical rule that enables us to identify outliers.

All the tools discussed so far envisaged the need to analyse and classify clusters of data or the entire dataset where all the data were considered to be suitable for the analysis. However, it may also be useful or needed to consider the importance of a single data value with respect to the whole dataset. For example, one may need to know if a particular

Step	Scope	Description	Examples	Excel functions, features, and options
1	Collect data	In surveys, questionnaires are usually compiled or notes taken in focus groups or measurements recorded in production.	Figure 7.3	In Excel 2010 no specific function is foreseen but data should be imported in the classic row and column format. To this end two import functions are useful: FILE OPEN and DATA, which lead to the Get External data section. Here the 'From Text' function can be exploited, as illustrated in Figure 7.4: Figure 7.4
2	Order data	Once the data has been complied and entered into a database (e.g. Access) or put directly into an Excel worksheet, the data can be pre-treated: this may involve sorting, adding metadata (e.g. column titles), formatting (e.g. number format), etc.	Patient ID / Cholesterol Count 1: 1 / 180; 2 / 234; 3 / 256. Table 7.2	There are several useful functions, the most common being Sort and Filter as shown below in the 'Data' toolbar menu, as illustrated in Figure 7.5. Figure 7.5
3	Preliminary assessment	There are many tools available for this, but two common ones are plotting and z-score.	Figure 7.6	The sparkline function also allows the use of WIN/LOSS and Bar graphs. Figure 7.6 illustrates a sparkline graph for each row of data. The z-score compares each single data value against the mean and standard deviation of the dataset.
4	Establish rules and clean	If the z-score is used it is common practice to set a range of acceptable values	$-3 \leq z \leq +3$	Delete those data values that are deemed extreme or not coherent with the scope of the analysis.
5	Analysis	Descriptive statistics are usually exploited first, followed by inferential statistics if applicable. The chart options are also very helpful.	Figure 7.7	Formulae tool bar options are illustrated in Figure 7.8. Figure 7.8
6	Reporting	The final step of the process involves reporting and providing the executive summary and the findings, conclusions, and recommendations.	Figure 7.9	The reporting may also involve the use of PowerPoint or the more sophisticated graphing functions of Excel, such as multi-coloured column graphs.

Table 7.1 Data cleaning and data analysis

data value, observation or measurement is useful or detrimental for the analysis. A simple and effective tool that allows this is the so called z-score, sometimes known as the standardized value. In essence the z-score represents the number of standard deviations from the mean of the population or sample for the data value under observation. Consequently, it is applied by taking each data value and compares this with both a measure of spread and a measure of centrality to the entire dataset. By doing so we can establish just how far the particular data value is from the mean as well as relate this distance in terms of the standard deviation for the dataset. The z-score is especially useful in deciding if a particular data value is reasonable, prone to error, or irrelevant for the dataset and therefore a potential candidate for being classified as an outlier.

In this sense an outlier is defined as a single data value that does not pertain to the dataset or scope of the analysis and therefore should be removed before it can condition the outcome of the analysis. Hence the z-score is a data cleaning tool. The z-score is determined using Equation (7.1):

$$Z_i = \frac{x_i - \bar{x}}{s} \tag{7.1}$$

The cut-off value for the z-score will depend on the application but, in general, values outside the range of $-2 \leq z \leq +2$ are considered as potential outliers. Sometimes the cleaning process is multistage in the sense that a wider range for the z-score is applied e.g. $-3 \leq z \leq +3$ before homing-in and deciding what to do with a doubtful data value. The following indications are provided for generic reference:

$-1 \leq z \leq +1$	captures 68% of the dataset
$-2 \leq z \leq +2$	captures 95% of the dataset
$-3 \leq z \leq +3$	captures 99.7% of the dataset

Example 7.1

Suppose the mean for a given data set is 41 and the standard deviation, s, is 10. Using the z-score determine if a particular data of value equal to 11 is a potential outlier and should be eliminated from the analysis.

We have:

$$Z = \frac{x_i - \bar{x}}{s} = \frac{11 - 41}{10} = \frac{-30}{10} = -3$$

Interpretation So for x = 11 we see that the z-score is –3 and therefore this particular data value is 3 standard deviations from the mean. Since the value is negative the particular data value is 3s to the left of the mean. Hence it is highly likely that this data value is an outlier or an extreme value of the data set and should be eliminated.

Example 7.2

For a given dataset the following information is known: mean = 26, z-score 1.5 and for a selected data value we have $x_i = 22$. Determine the standard deviation and comment if this selected data value is a possible outlier.

Rearranging the z-score formula we have: $z_i = \frac{x_i - \bar{x}}{s}$

After rearranging we obtain: $s = \frac{x_i - \bar{x}}{z_i}$

Hence we have: $s = \frac{x_i - x}{z_i} = \frac{22 - 26}{3/2} = \frac{2(22 - 26)}{3} = -2.66'$

Interpretation Since the selected data is minus 4 units from the mean (22 – 26), which is greater than one standard deviation and the z-score is 1.5, then we may conclude that the data value is relatively far from the mean but not that far so as to be classified as an outlier.

Example 7.3

For a given dataset the following data is known: $z = 1.5$, $s = 0.55$ and $x_i = 4$. What is the mean for the dataset? Also is the data value provided to the left or right of the mean? Rearranging Equation 7.1 to make $\bar{x}$ the subject: $\bar{x} = x_i - (z \times s)$. Substituting actual values into this equation gives: $\bar{x} = x_i - (z \times s) = 4 - (1.55 \times 0.55) = 3.1475$.

Interpretation Since this mean value is lower than the data value provided (i.e. 4) it is to the right of the mean.

Example 7.4

The dataset illustrated in Table 7.3 has been collected, but before proceeding to the analysis it has to be checked for outliers. Using the z-score tool, evaluate each data value and conclude which ones should be removed and which ones should be kept for the analysis.

35	39	36	22	29	30	31
42	22	28	24	27	29	33
33	39	40	25	26	28	30
20	45	22	25	31	32	27

Table 7.3 Dataset

In this dataset the number of data values is limited so we can proceed using several different options. For example, we can plot the data, we can calculate the standard deviation and mean values and then pre-spot the values that are near the mean (thus showing these are 'good' values), or, as suggested, use the z-score for each data value.

In file Example 7.4 the data has been sorted (see column A) from the smallest to largest value, as illustrated in Figure 7.10. The same can be done for other parts and the rest of the dataset (see Figure 7.12).

	A	B	C	D	E	F	G
1	20	45	22	25	31	32	27
2	33	39	40	25	26	28	30
3	35	39	36	22	29	30	31
4	42	22	28	24	27	29	33

Figure 7.10

The ordering technique is a useful way of concentrating on the extreme values first and then work inwards, i.e. towards those values that will be closer to the mean (see Figure 7.11).

	A	B	C	D	E	F	G
1	20	45	22	25	31	32	27
2	33	39	40	25	26	28	30
3	35	39	36	22	29	30	31
4	42	22	28	24	27	29	33
5							
6	Mean	30.4					
7	Std. Dev. (sample)	6.5					
8	Std. Dev. (pop)	6.4					

Figure 7.11

Even better is to copy the listed values into a column format and then sort them as shown in Figure 7.12.

P	Q	R	S
Listed	Sorted		
20	20		
22	22		
22	22		
22	22		
24	24		
25	25		
25	25		
26	26		
27	27		
27	27		
28	28		
28	28		
29	29		
29	29		
30	30		
30	30		
31	31		
31	31		
32	32		
33	33		
33	33		
35	35		
36	36		
39	39		
39	39		
40	40		
42	42		
45	45		
Mean	30.4		
Std. Dev. (sample)	6.5		
Std. Dev. (pop)	6.4		

Figure 7.12

Next we calculate the mean and standard deviation (sample and population) as illustrated in Figure 7.11 and 7.5 to provide a complete picture of the dataset.

The final stage is to calculate the z-score as illustrated in Figure 7.12.

❊ **Interpretation** Both the sample and population standard deviations have been computed since this is not specified in the question, although in such circumstances and as a rule of thumb, take the value with the lowest std. deviation value since this provides the highest z-score for each data value assessed. The completed analysis should look like this:

J	K
Data Value	zScore
20	-1.62716
22	-1.31295
22	-1.31295
22	-1.31295
24	-0.99874
25	-0.84163
25	-0.84163
26	-0.68453
27	-0.52742
27	-0.52742
28	-0.37032
28	-0.37032
29	-0.21321
29	-0.21321
30	-0.05611
30	-0.05611
31	0.100996
31	0.100996
32	0.258101
33	0.415206
33	0.415206
35	0.729417
36	0.886522
39	1.357837
39	1.357837
40	1.514943
42	1.829153
45	2.300468

Figure 7.13

As we can see, the only data value that is over $z = 2$ is the last one, which is 45. The next candidate would be 42 ($z = 1.829$), the 20 ($z = 1.627$). So the first data value that should be removed is 45 after which the analysis should be conducted and the results assessed. Since only one data value seems to be an outlier (which represents approximately 3% of the dataset) and its numerical value is not dramatically high, it is unlikely that it will impact the overall analysis. Nevertheless, it is worth removing, especially if a trend line (e.g. linear function fit) is foreseen in the analysis.

Example 7.5

Reconsider Example 7.4 but this time build two different scatter plots and then, with data value 45 included and excluded from the plots, fit a linear function to both plots.

Comment on the results:

The first scatter plot with a linear function fitted and data value 45 included is as illustrated in Figure 7.14.

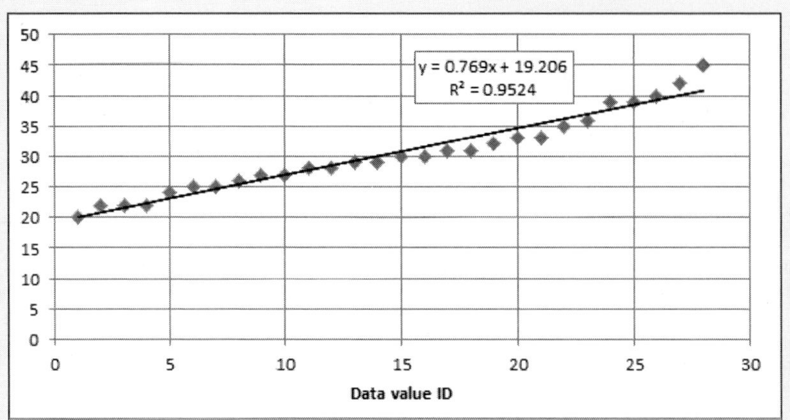

Figure 7.14

The second scatter plot with data value 45 excluded is as illustrated in Figure 7.15.

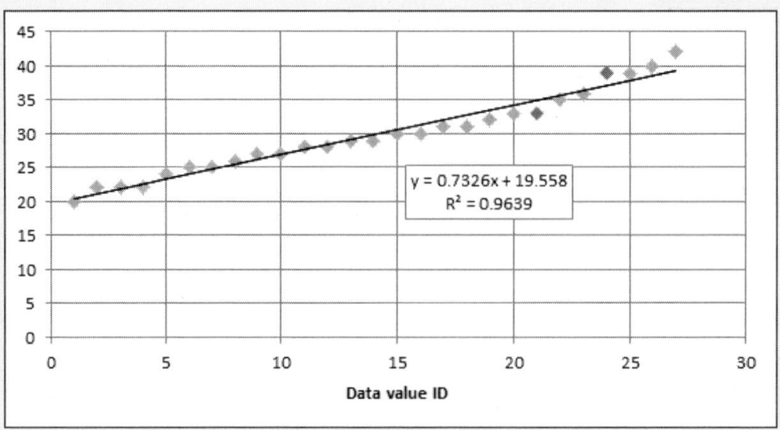

Figure 7.15

Comparing the two equations and correlation coefficient we have:

Example	Linear equation	Correlation coefficient, r^2
With data value 45 included	$y = 0.769x + 19.206$	0.9524
With data value 45 excluded	$y = 0.7326x + 19.558$	0.9639

Table 7.4

Interpretation We may conclude that by removing the outlier (data value 45) the estimation of the linear function is better since the correlation coefficient has improved and is closer to unity (where unity or $r^2 = 1$ represents a perfect linear fit). Interestingly there are two other potential candidates (see red diamonds in the second scatter plot) but these only become truly apparent in the second scatter plot i.e. once data value 45 is excluded (see Figure 7.15).

7.2.3 Cherbyshev's theorem

Cherbyshev's theorem is an empirical rule that enables us to consider the proportion of *packets* of data within a specific number of standard deviations. Henceforth it is an extension of the z-score approach where instead of examining a single data value we assess a group of data with respect to the whole data set.

It is known that for any normal distribution that:

- Approximately 68% of the data will be within 1 standard deviation from the mean.
- Approximately 95% of the data will be within 2 standard deviations from the mean.
- Approximately 99.7% of the data will be within 3 standard deviations from the mean.

These three cases are shown in Figure 7.16.

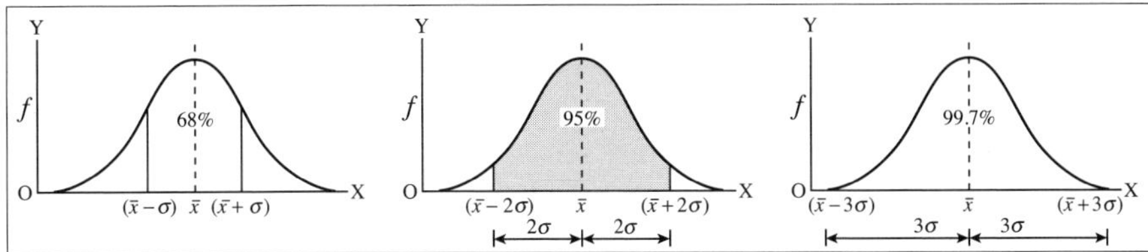

Figure 7.16
Normal distribution and standard deviations

The theorem may be stated as follows:

> At least $(1 - 1/z^2) \times 100\%$ of the data values pertaining to a given data set must be within 'x' standard deviations of the mean where z is any value greater than unity.

Henceforth about 68% of results will fall between +1 and –1 standard deviations from the mean, and about 95% will fall between +2 and –2 standard deviations. Chebyshev's theorem allows you to extend this idea to any distribution, even if that distribution isn't normal. Chebyshev's theorem is applicable for standard deviations over 1.

Example 7.6

Consider the following four arbitrary z-score values namely 2, 3, 4, and 5 using Chebyshev's theorem establish the relative coverage with these values. When z-score = 2

$$(1 - 1/z^2) \times 100\% = \left(1 - \frac{1}{2^2}\right) \times 100\% = (1 - 0.25) \times 100\% = 75\%$$

Interpretation In other words at least 75% of the data values must be within z = 2 from the mean.

Similarly:

- When z-score = 3, at least 89% of the data values must be within z = 3 from the mean.
- When z-score = 4, at least 93.75% of the data values must be within z = 4 from the mean.
- When z-score = 5, at least 96% of the data values must be within z = 5 from the mean.

Example 7.7

In a survey conducted among a group of customers concerning after-sales support the mean customer satisfaction index was 7.5 out of 10; that is, 75 out of 100 customers were satisfied with the after-sales services and the standard deviation for the same survey was 0.7. A recent sales promotion has caused a spurt of customer calls and in particular one customer provided a satisfaction index value of 5, should this customer be classified as a special case?

$$Z_i = \frac{x_i - \bar{x}}{s} = \frac{5 - 7.5}{0.7} = \frac{-2.5}{0.7} = -3.57$$

Interpretation Since the z-score is greater than 3 this is certainly a special case.

Example 7.8

Following on from the previous case what is the (lower) limit satisfaction index value for special cases?

After rearranging Equation 7.1 for the z-score to make x_i the subject of the equation gives:

$$x_i = Z_i \cdot s + \bar{x}$$

The upper limit is given when $s = +0.7$:

$$x_i = Z_i \cdot s + \bar{x} = 3 \times (0.7) + 7.5 = 2.1 + 7.5 = 9.6$$

The lower limit is given when $s = -0.7$:

$$x_i = Z_i \cdot s + \bar{x} = 3 \times (-0.7) + 7.5 = -2.1 + 7.5 = 5.4$$

Interpretation All customers that provide a customer satisfaction index value lower than 5.4 should be classified as special cases.

Example 7.9

Following the implementation of the satisfaction index discussed in Examples 7.7 and 7.8, if a customer returns a value of $x_i = 9.7$, is this customer a special case?

Mathematically yes, but since we are speaking of the satisfaction index this customer is really very satisfied about the service/product. Maybe the customer should be contacted to understand why he/she is so satisfied.

7.2.4 Managing outliers: a closer look

In the examples seen so far, outliers have been detected by calculating the z-score and then applying a rule (i.e. range) in which data values have been accepted or rejected as good or bad data values respectively. We have also seen that a scatter plot may be useful in sifting out outliers and conducting a regression analysis may also help. Indeed there are several tools available that help spot outliers but before doing so the following check list is suggested.

- What is the scope of the final analysis?
- Do rules, filters or procedures already exist that should have spotted the outlier before?
- Will a specific tool be used in the final analysis to establish key findings e.g. running average, regression analysis?
- What are the effects of leaving the outlier in the dataset?
- If there is more than one outlier what is the proportion of outliers to the actual dataset?
- On what grounds have the rules for data value inclusion and exclusion been established?
- Could an outlier be the key finding or used instead as a test data value for the analysis
- Can the outlier be a 'catalyst' or seed for future analysis?

If the scope of the analysis is comparison (comparing two different datasets) then it may be that outliers are more beneficial for the outcome of the analysis. For example, in quality control the outlier becomes the warning signal that indicates that something is wrong in the production process. If there is more than one outlier and these tend to cluster in succession there may be a trend starting, as we see in the graphs shown in Example 7.5. In fact when trends are key to the findings it is these outliers that become the justification for understanding why such swings occur in electorate preferences and customer complaint analysis, for example. In Example 7.4 data value 45 was judged as being an outlier but in reality the dataset came from a survey where the data values represented the age of the interviewee and one rule for this particular survey was 'only respondents in the age range of 25 to 45 yrs are to be considered'. From this it is clear that 45 is not an outlier: the true outliers would lie on the lower part of the dataset, that is, with data values of 20, 22, and 24, since these are outside the age range foreseen for the survey. Statistical tools like mean, mode, median, standard deviation, and regression are tools that in some ways help to organize and assess the dataset. Some of these tools are more prone to error than others, or rather are conditioned more than others. Here is simple table that compares some of these tools:

Tool A	Competing tool B	Possible discrepancies
Variance	Standard deviation	Variance suffers from very large or small data values so standard deviation is better.
Range	Deviation about the mean	Ranges are susceptible to large or small data values especially if the majority of data hangs about a certain value.
Mean	Mode or median	Mean values tend to provide fractions (rather than whole numbers) and also tell little, if nothing, about the spread of the dataset. Hence mode and median are preferred or better used in tandem with the mean value.
Linear Regression plots	Alternative regression plots such as moving average	Linear regression plots do not dampen large swings in data values. Sometimes it is more beneficial to apply a moving (running) average that suppress some of the swing.
Scatter plot	Histogram	Scatter plots usually take the whole dataset and not always is it possible to see the type of distribution. Histograms on the other hand provide a better view, especially for larger datasets with pre-established classes.
Histogram	Box and whisker (B & W) plot	Histograms are ideal for the representation of classes but cannot simultaneously illustrate outliers and summarized descriptive statistics as for B & W plots.

Table 7.5 Spotting and managing outliers. Examples of tool comparisons

The question 'what are the effects of leaving the outlier in the dataset?' is not a trick question; rather, it is one that addresses the usefulness of including a data value just for the simple purpose of seeing its effects on the analysis, such as a regression plot. Indeed, in the analysis of residuals (the difference between some given datum, e.g. mean and the data value) the idea is to see how far the data value is from a datum. The next figure is taken from Example 7.4 and shows, for each data value, the difference with respect to the mean of the dataset.

Figure 7.17 shows which data values are outside a certain range, e.g. −10 and +10, and obviously leaving out outliers is usually not recommended for residual plots.

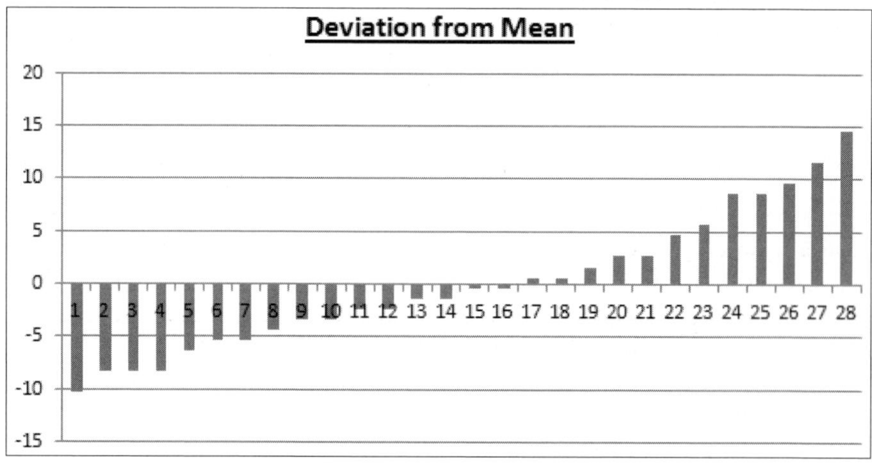

Figure 7.17

Example of deviation from mean

In Examples 7.4 and 7.5, leaving out one or two data values does not seriously affect the validity of the analysis or plots. This is because the remaining part of the dataset compensates for their inclusion or exclusion. So, as a general 'rule of thumb,' it is better to first include and then exclude a suspected outlier to see the effects on the analysis. As the proportion of potential outliers increases so do the effects, so it is generally recommended to set a limit for such values, for example 5%, depending on the size of the sample or population.

The definition of an outlier is somewhat vague and is usually referred to the mass of data values or observations in the dataset being assessed. One definition is 'an outlier is any value that is unusually small or large with respect to the rest of the dataset.' So outliers tend to be extreme values or appear awkward in some way. In general a data value should remain in the dataset only if all circumstances of doubt (e.g. measurement or human error) have been excluded in the collection and recording of the data value. In exploiting tools such as the z-score caution should be applied to establish the range for which a data value is considered acceptable. For this reason the following z-score ranges are suggested in Table 7.6.

Accept data value	Evaluate data value before removing	Exclude data value
$-2 \le z \le +2$	$-2 < z > +2$	$-3 < z > +3$

Table 7.6 Inclusion or exclusion of data values

Extreme data values are not always detrimental to the findings, so they should be first considered as a friend rather than foe. In the words of an unknown statistician 'Whenever I come across an outlier I ask myself should I remove it or patent it?' As a further 'rule of thumb,' use outliers to prove results and strengthen findings as well as criticize or emphasis the validity of the rigour of the analysis undertaken. It also highlights the reasoning applied in assessing the dataset. On a closing note, outliers may well turn out to make sense in future investigations and analyses. Actually an outlier may be the catalyst for the next round of surveys or the inclusion of one or more specific questions in a new survey. Moreover, when a data value is removed the z-scores should be recalculated because often other suspect data values arise (see Example 7.11).

Example 7.10

The following data set 10, 20, 12, 17 and 16 is provided, is there an outlier here? Let us compare the z-scores for this data set; hence we obtain the values illustrated in Figure 7.18.

	A	B	C	D	E
1	Example 7.10				
2					
3		Data ID	Data value	zScore	
4		1	10	-1.40	=($C4-$C$10)/$C$11
5		2	20	1.40	
6		3	12	-0.84	
7		4	17	0.56	
8		5	16	0.28	=($C8-$C$10)/$C$11
9					
10		Mean	15.00	=AVERAGE(C4:C8)	
11		Std. Deviation	3.58	=STDEV.P(C4:C8)	

Figure 7.18

→ Excel solution

Data ID Cells B4:B8	Values
Data value Cells C4:C8	Values
Mean = Cell C10	Formula: = AVERAGE(C4:C8)
Std deviation = Cell C11	Formula: = STDEV.P(C4:C8)
z-score Cell D4	Formula: = ($C4-$C$10)/$C$11
	Copy formula from D4:D11

✻ Interpretation The z-scores confirm that there are no outliers in the data set even though the values of 10 and 20 probably (initially) looked suspicious. Moreover the value of the z-score helps us to see just how far we are from classifying the data values as outliers. In all cases the worst z-score is 1.4 which is far from the limit of 3 set for an outlier.

Example 7.11

At the end of each academic year a university campus director wishes to compare professor teaching performance by assessing end-of-course survey data. To do this the director decides to use statistics to spot potential weak and strong professor teaching skills and this is done using the z-scores, mean and standard deviation computations.

The data set obtained from the surveys, where the performance scale is 0–5 (where 5 is ideal) is as illustrated in Table 7.7.

Professor ID	Rating	Professor ID	Rating
A	4.00	K	4.67
B	4.12	L	2.14
C	3.82	M	4.09
D	4.00	N	4.17
E	4.56	O	4.88
F	4.32	P	4.26
G	4.33	Q	2.32
H	4.5	R	4.5
I	4.64	S	4.17
J	4.2	T	2.17

Table 7.7

After the z-score analysis the results are summarized, as illustrated in Figure 7.19.

	A	B	C	D	E
1	Example 7.11				
2					
3					
4		Professor ID	Rating	zScore	
5		A	4	0.00885	=(C5-$C$26)/$C$27
6		B	4.12	0.16059	
7		C	3.82	-0.21876	
8		D	4	0.00885	
9		E	4.56	0.71697	
10		F	4.32	0.41349	
11		G	4.33	0.42614	
12		H	4.5	0.64110	
13		I	4.64	0.81814	
14		J	4.2	0.26175	
15		K	4.67	0.85607	
16		L	2.14	-2.34313	
17		M	4.09	0.12266	
18		N	4.17	0.22382	
19		O	4.88	1.12162	
20		P	4.26	0.33762	
21		Q	2.32	-2.11552	
22		R	4.5	0.64110	
23		S	4.17	0.22382	
24		T	2.17	-2.30519	=(C24-$C$26)/$C$27
25					
26		Mean	3.99300	=AVERAGE(C5:C24)	
27		Std. Deviation	0.79082	=STDEV.P(C5:C24)	

Figure 7.19

→ Excel solution

Professor ID Cells B5:B24	Values
Rating Cells C5:C24	Values
Mean Cell C26	Formula: = AVERAGE(C5:C24)
Std.Deviation Cell C27	Formula: = STDEV.P(C5:C24)
rScore Cell D5	Formula: = (C5-$C$26)/$C$27
	Copy formula down from D5:D24

Interpretation As was probably noticed even before the results of the analysis were computed, three professors are well below the average, namely L, Q, and T. However, none (at least statistically) of the professors can be classified as outliers although 'L' and 'T' look the best candidates for being poor performers.

In Figure 7.20 we have removed cells I16 and I24.

	H	I	J	K	L
1					
2		Professors L and T excluded			
3					
4		Professor ID	Rating	zScore	
5		A	4	-0.37419	=(J5-$J$26)/$J$27
6		B	4.12	-0.14651	
7		C	3.82	-0.71570	
8		D	4	-0.37419	
9		E	4.56	0.68830	
10		F	4.32	0.23295	
11		G	4.33	0.25192	
12		H	4.5	0.57446	
13		I	4.64	0.84008	
14		J	4.2	0.00527	
15		K	4.67	0.89700	=(J15-$J$26)/$J$27
16		L			
17		M	4.09	-0.20343	=(J17-$J$26)/$J$27
18		N	4.17	-0.05165	
19		O	4.88	1.29543	
20		P	4.26	0.11911	
21		Q	2.32	-3.56165	
22		R	4.5	0.57446	
23		S	4.17	-0.05165	=(J23-$J$26)/$J$27
24		T			
25					
26		Mean	4.19722	=AVERAGE(J5:J14,J15:J24)	
27		Std. Deviation	0.52707	=STDEV.P(J5:J14,J15:J24)	

Figure 7.20

This means that cells J16 and J24 are no longer calculated and the z-score for Q now becomes −3.56165.

If we decide to eliminate the two worst values (not the professors!), i.e. L and T, we have the following new scenario illustrated in Figure 7.20.

Now we see that Q is an outlier and should also be removed.

Student exercises

X7.1 Return to Example 7.4 and set a z-score limit for data acceptance of +/– 1.5; then plot the cleaned data.

X7.2 Repeat Example 7.5 but compare the linear function with a second order polynomial plot based on the correlation coefficient. Which of the two plots provides a better result and why?

X7.3 What is the 'deviation of the mean'? Plot the 'deviation of mean' column graph (i.e. deviation for each data value with respect to the mean) for the uncleaned data in Example 7.4.

X7.4 In a normal distributed population 68% are to be considered acceptable for a given trial. What is the limit value for such a case if the mean is 50 and the standard deviation is 10?

X7.5 What would be the answer if the limit in exercise X 7.4 was now raised to 97%?

7.3 Two, three, four, and five data summaries

In Chapter 2, basic concepts and measures such as mean, standard deviation, min–max, range, quartiles, median, and variance were introduced not only to summarize the meaning of the data being analysed but also to highlight the key features of the dataset. Indeed, population estimation and relative estimators provide much more detail if they are used collectively. To this end to aid the analysis four potential groupings of descriptive statistical tools can be introduced, namely:

1. **Two data summary.**
2. **Three data summary.**
3. **Four data summary.**
4. **Five data summary.**

7.3.1 Two data summary: mean and standard deviation

The mean is the most common indicator of central tendency while the standard deviation is a popular and normalized measure of dispersion. Together these form an outline of the dataset orientation towards an average value and by how much the data differs from this average value. As is observed in the control charts for quality control by plotting the running data (e.g. samples) of a process it is possible to visualize the current situation of the process and understand if process quality is within the quality bounds for the process. In addition we may also observe the trend of the data and if the process has always remained within the bounds or not. The drawback for the two data summary is that we do not have a measure of skewness and more than one peak maybe present in the dataset.

7.3.2 Three data summary: mean, median, and mode

The mean ($\bar{x}$), median (Me) and mode (Mo) are all measures of central tendency since all three provide an understanding of where the majority of the data hang out and tend to centralize. However, when used together they can also provide an indication of the skewness of the distribution and therefore indicate just how normal or skewed the dataset actually is. The key is to understand the relationship between mean, median, and mode and three circumstances or cases arise. The method is called the three data summary as illustrated in Figures 7.21–7.23.

Case 1 When the distribution curve is skewed to the left (right tail) resulting from the mode (Mo) being less than the median (Me) which is less than the mean $\bar{x}$, as shown in Figure 7.21.

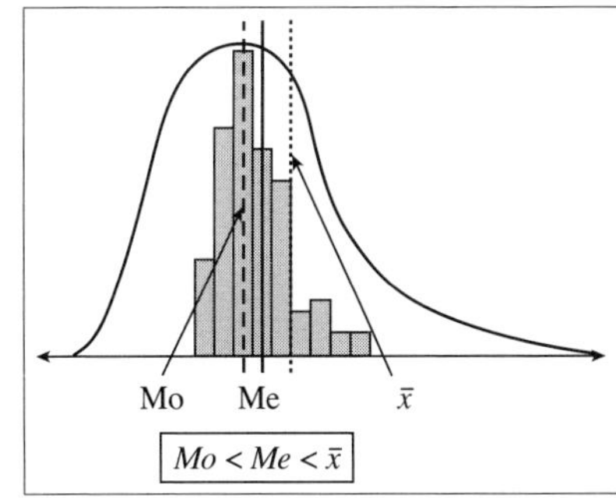

Figure 7.21

X

quartile quartiles are values that divide a sample of data into four groups containing (as far as possible) equal numbers of observations.

two data summary the mean is the most common indicator of central tendency while the standard deviation is a popular and normalized measure of dispersion.

three data summary the mean, median, and mode are all measures of central tendency since all three provide an understanding of where the majority of the data hang out and tend to centralize.

four data summary the four data summary exploits a measure of dispersion together with quartiles that can also represent skewness.

five data summary consists of using also the minimum and maximum values together with the quartiles to summarize data.

Case 2 The dataset reflects a perfect normal distribution when Mean = Median = Mode are coincident as shown in Figure 7.22.

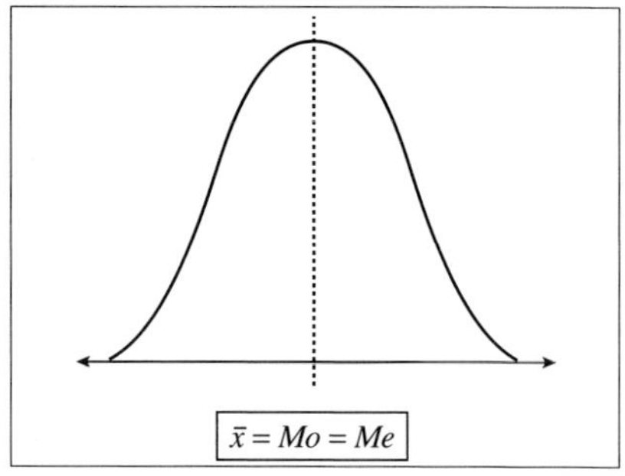

Figure 7.22

Case 3 When the distribution curve is skewed to the right (left tail) resulting from the mean $\bar{x}$ being less than the median (Me) which is less than the mode (Mo), as shown in Figure 7.23.

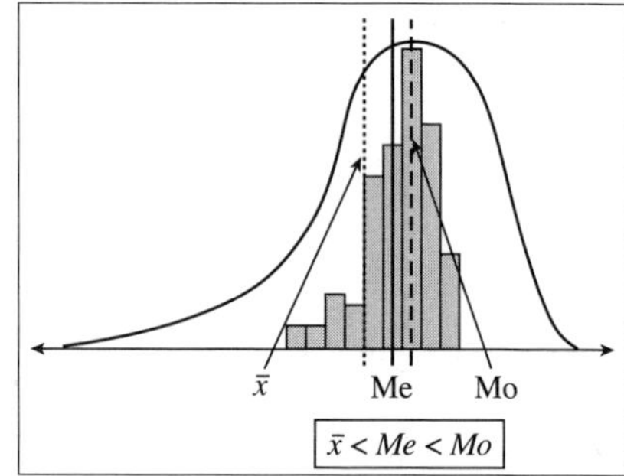

Figure 7.23

The drawback for the three data summary is that not always are all three measures so clear cut, especially if the dataset small in size.

7.3.3 Four data summary

The four data summary exploits a measure of dispersion together with quartiles that can also represent skewness and this is based on the following reasoning. In Chapter 2 it was mentioned that the measure of variance has one disadvantage that is, for high data values the variance can be very large which often makes it difficult to use when comparing datasets which have very different magnitudes of data value such as annual sales, house prices versus monthly gas bills. To alleviate such situations the standard deviation was exploited. In both cases the concept was to obtain a measure of dispersion by assessing the difference between a single data value and the mean, that is, $(x_i - \bar{x})$. This was squared to remove eventual negative differences, that is, $(x_i - \bar{x})^2$. Another way of looking at the dispersion and difference is to consider the average absolute deviation that is:

$$\frac{1}{n}\sum_{i=1}^{n}|x_i - \bar{x}| \tag{7.2}$$

In other words, the difference is not squared to remove negative values rather the absolute value is taken instead. However, by itself this measure has limited use so quartiles are introduced to provide an idea of dispersion and/or skewness. Quartiles in fact indicate the distribution of the data by assigning a location for such data with respect to a certain percentage of the data (see also percentile, Chapter 2 and Figure 7.24). The three quartile measures are summarized below and depicted in Figure 7.24.

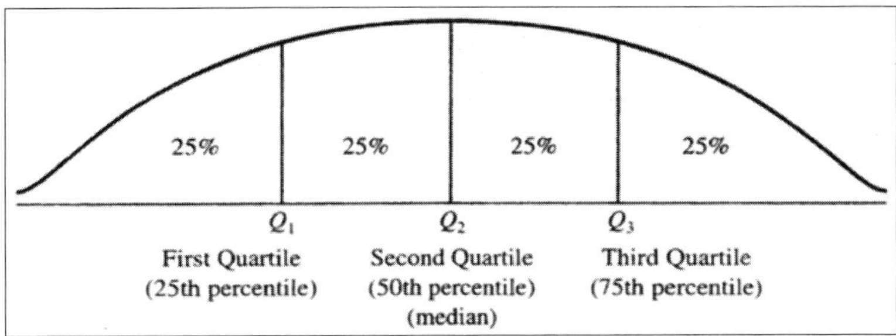

Figure 7.24
Quartiles

1. Q_1 = first quartile or 25th percentile.
2. Q_2 = second quartile or 50th percentile which is the equivalent to the median.
3. Q_3 = third quartile or 75th percentile.

The first and third quartiles are used to indicate the dispersion while the second quartile operates as an indication of the centrality of the data, as we have seen for the mean or median. But the first and third quartiles when compared to the second quartile can also be applied to indicate the skewness of the distribution of the dataset. For example, if the first and third quartiles are equally distanced from the second quartile then the data distribution will be normally distributed; if not normally distributed, then the data will be skewed to the left or right. It follows that by determining differences in the quartiles we can obtain further insight into the dataset, its dispersion and distribution. In fact, in Chapter 2 the difference between first and third quartiles, known as the interquartile range (IQR), was said to be the middle 50% of the data or IQR = $Q_3 - Q_1$ and this provides an idea of dispersion within the central part of the dataset. If, however, we compare the differences between $Q_2 - Q_1$ and $Q_3 - Q_2$ then we may make an assumption of the skewness as well:

Skewed to the left (Positive skewness, longer tail to the right)	Normal distribution (No skewness)	Skewed to the right (Negative skewness, longer tail to the left)
$Q_2 - Q_1 < Q_3 - Q_2$	$Q_2 - Q_1 = Q_3 - Q_2$	$Q_3 - Q_2 < Q_2 - Q_1$

Table 7.8 Data distribution and quartiles

Example 7.12

Consider the following dataset: 1780, 1830, 1960, 2010, 2050, 2090, 2100, 2110, 2150, 2170, 2200, 2200. Determine the first, second, and third quartiles and then compare them so as to determine if the dataset is skewed or not. Table 7.8 illustrates the data set sorted in order of size and split into 25% or four equal parts:

1780, 1830, 1960	2010, 2050, 2090	2100, 2110, 2150	2170, 2200, 2200
25%	25%	25%	25%

Table 7.9

From Table 7.9 we observe:

$$\text{The first quartile is } Q_1 = \frac{2010 - 1960}{2} + 1960 = 1985$$

$$\text{The second quartile is } Q_2 = \frac{2100 - 2090}{2} + 2090 = 2095$$

$$\text{The third quartile is } Q_3 = \frac{2170 - 2150}{2} + 2150 = 2160$$

Since $Q_2 - Q_1 = 2095 - 1985 = 110$ and $Q_3 - Q_2 = 2160 - 2095 = 65$ it follows that the data is certainly skewed: that is, we can exclude the case where $Q_2 - Q_1 = Q_3 - Q_2$.

In fact we have $Q_3 - Q_2 < Q_2 - Q_1$; hence the data is skewed to the right, as is shown in the plotted data in Figure 7.25.

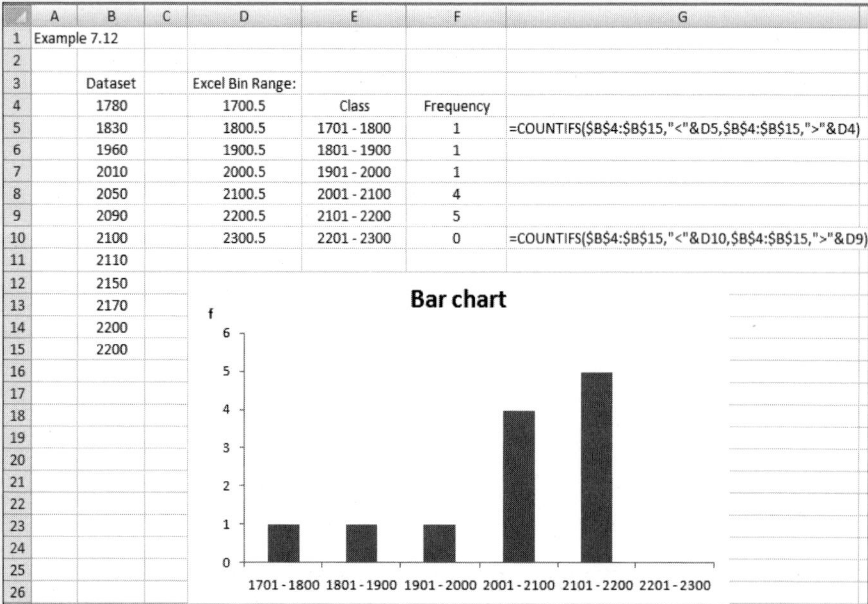

	A	B	C	D	E	F	G
1	Example 7.12						
2							
3		Dataset		Excel Bin Range:			
4		1780		1700.5	Class	Frequency	
5		1830		1800.5	1701 - 1800	1	=COUNTIFS($B$4:$B$15,"<"&D5,$B$4:$B$15,">"&D4)
6		1960		1900.5	1801 - 1900	1	
7		2010		2000.5	1901 - 2000	1	
8		2050		2100.5	2001 - 2100	4	
9		2090		2200.5	2101 - 2200	5	
10		2100		2300.5	2201 - 2300	0	=COUNTIFS($B$4:$B$15,"<"&D10,$B$4:$B$15,">"&D9)
11		2110					
12		2150					
13		2170					
14		2200					
15		2200					

Figure 7.25

→ Excel solution

Dataset Cells B4:B15	Values
Excel Bin Range Cells D4:D10	Values
Class Cells E5:E10	Values
Frequency Cell F5	
	Formula: = COUNTIFS($B$4:$B$15,"<"&D5,$B$4:$B$15, ">"&D4)
	Copy formula down F5:F10

Interpretation Note that the Mean < Median < Mode and are respectively, 2054.2, 2095 and 2200. This confirms that the data is skewed to the right.

Note To create Figure 7.25 use Excel Bin Range: 1700.5, 1800.5, 1900.5, 2000.5, 2100.5, 2200.5, and 2300.5. See Chapter 2 for creating a histogram using Excel.

7.3.4 Five data summary

So far we have seen examples of data summaries that contemplated measures of centricity, dispersion and skewness. Another method, known as the five data summary, consists of using also the minimum and maximum values together with the quartiles. The aim is to use all five in a special graphical tool known as the box and whisker plot as well as to provide a simple way of summarizing data and spotting outliers in the dataset. The five data summary is based on:

- Minimum value
- First quartile (Q_1)
- Median (Q_2)
- Third quartile (Q_3)
- Maximum value

Example 7.13

During the annual health checks at a factory 12 volunteers were called for a medical. Their weight was recorded in kg as follows: 67, 99, 101, 78, 90, 69, 110, 78, 80, 90, 86, and 94. Use the five data summary to summarize the key features of this dataset.

First we place the dataset in ascending order from left to right; then we calculate the quartiles:

67, 69, 78	78, 80, 86	90, 90, 94	99, 101, 110
25%	25%	25%	25%

Table 7.10

Figure 7.26 illustrates the Excel solution to calculate the five number summaries and bar chart for this data set.

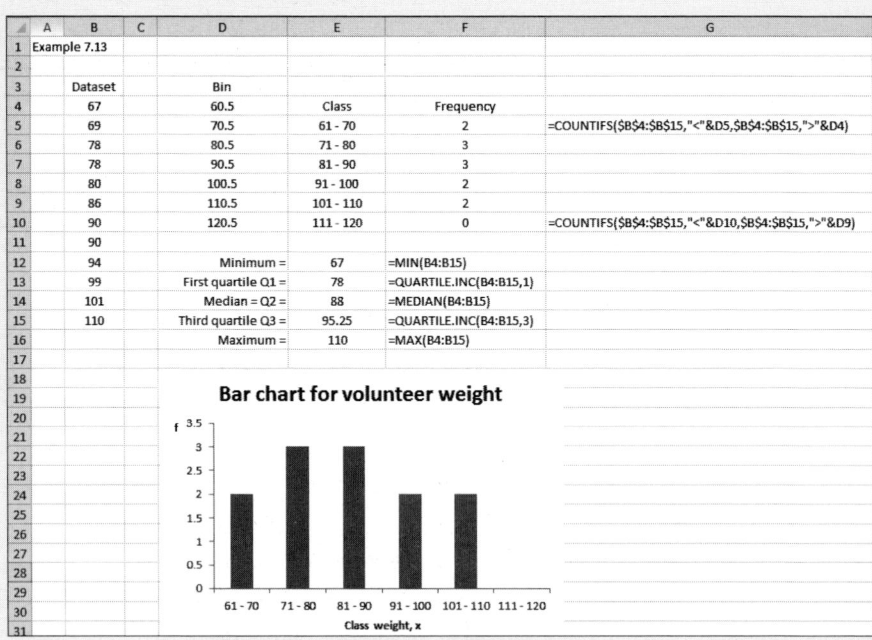

	A	B	C	D	E	F	G
1	Example 7.13						
2							
3		Dataset		Bin			
4		67		60.5	Class	Frequency	
5		69		70.5	61 - 70	2	=COUNTIFS($B$4:$B$15,"<"&D5,$B$4:$B$15,">"&D4)
6		78		80.5	71 - 80	3	
7		78		90.5	81 - 90	3	
8		80		100.5	91 - 100	2	
9		86		110.5	101 - 110	2	
10		90		120.5	111 - 120	0	=COUNTIFS($B$4:$B$15,"<"&D10,$B$4:$B$15,">"&D9)
11		90					
12		94		Minimum =	67	=MIN(B4:B15)	
13		99		First quartile Q1 =	78	=QUARTILE.INC(B4:B15,1)	
14		101		Median = Q2 =	88	=MEDIAN(B4:B15)	
15		110		Third quartile Q3 =	95.25	=QUARTILE.INC(B4:B15,3)	
16				Maximum =	110	=MAX(B4:B15)	

Figure 7.26

→ Excel solution

Dataset Cells B4:B15	Values
Excel Bin Range Cells D4:D10	Values
Class Cells E5:E10	Values
Frequency Cell F5	Formula: = COUNTIFS($B$4:$B$15,"<"&D5,$B$4:$B$15," >"&D4)
	Copy formula down F5:F10
Minimum Cell E12	Formula: = MIN(B4:B15)
First quartile Cell E13	Formula: = QUARTILE.INC(B4:B15,1)
Median Cell E14	Formula: = MEDIAN(B4:B15)
Third quartile Cell E15	Formula: = QUARTILE.INC(B4:B15,3)
Maximum Cell E16	Formula: = MAX(B4:B15)

The minimum and maximum values are 67 and 110 respectively. So the summary is:

- Minimum value = 67
- First quartile (Q_1) = 78
- Median (Q_2) = 88
- Third quartile (Q_3) = 95.25
- Maximum value = 110

Example 7.14

During the same annual health checks discussed in Example 7.13, the same 12 volunteers at a factory were checked for high blood pressure. The following results were recorded (Table 7.10):

	V1	V2	V3	V4	V5	V6	V7	V8	V9	V10	V11	V12
Minimum - mmHg	75	90	85	100	65	70	80	90	95	80	70	60
Maximum - mmHg	115	145	120	160	110	135	120	125	135	115	100	95

Table 7.11

Use the five data summary to summarize the key features of this dataset.

Figure 7.27 illustrates the Excel solution.

Volunteer	Minimum - mmHg	Maximum - mmHg
1	75	115
2	90	145
3	85	120
4	100	160
5	65	110
6	70	135
7	80	120
8	90	125
9	95	135
10	80	115
11	70	100
12	60	95

Five data Summary

	Minimum - mmHg	Maximum - mmHg
Minimum	60	95
First Quart	70	111
Median - Q	80	120
Third Quar	90	135
Maximum	100	160

Figure 7.27

→ Excel solution

Volunteer Cells A4:A15 Values
Minimum mmHg Cells B4:B15 Values
Maximum mmHg Cells C4:C15 Values
Minimum mmHg:
Minimum Cell F6 Formula: = MIN(B4:B15)
First quartile Cell F7 Formula: = QUARTILE.INC(B4:B15,1)
Median Cell F8 Formula: = MEDIAN(B4:B15)
Third quartile Cell F9 Formula: = QUARTILE.INC(B4:B15,3)
Maximum Cell F10 Formula: = MAX(B4:B15)
Maximum mmHg:
Minimum Cell G6 Formula: = MIN(C4:C15)
First quartile Cell G7 Formula: = QUARTILE.INC(C4:C15,1)
Median Cell G8 Formula: = MEDIAN(C4:C15)
Third quartile Cell G9 Formula: = QUARTILE.INC(C4:C15,3)
Maximum Cell G10 Formula: = MAX(C4:C15)

7.3.5 Box and whisker plots

Box and whisker (B-W) plots are based on the five data summary method but with the addition of the IQR measure. box and whisker plots are intended to graphically represent the key features of a dataset and, if needed, spot outliers. In this sense a box and whisker plot can be viewed as a data cleaning tool and a quick way of grasping normality, skewness and distribution in general in datasets (see Figure 7.28).

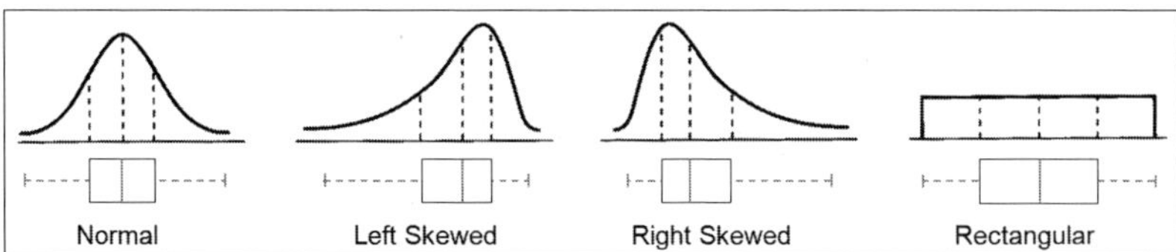

Figure 7.28
Different types of distribution and relative box and whisker plots

Here an outlier is defined as any data value that does not reflect the true normality of the dataset and would be classified as extreme and outside the normal bounds of the dataset. Such values are 'one-offs', such as erratic measurements in process control. In surveys, an outlier would be an answer that does not pertain to the question being posed and/or is not useful for the scope of the survey and/or the value provided is not contemplated in the survey. The process for developing the box and whisker plot is as follows:

1. First, the data is put into ascending order; then the number line for the dataset is prepared, bearing in mind the extreme values of the dataset.
2. Next draw a box above the number line bearing in mind that; a. the box width is measured by the IQR value, b. the left hand side of the box represents the first quartile value and c. the right hand side of the box represents the third quartile value and position. The box can be of any scale as it reflects the number scale below it.
3. Next, the length of the whiskers (that are represented by dotted lines) are established. The dotted lines are connected to the lower and upper limits of the plot and are located at +1.5IQR and at −1.5IQR. These limits are those used to determine outliers in the dataset.
4. Finally if an outlier exists within the dataset this is located on the plot, usually with an asterisk (*) or other evident graphical symbol.

The complete box and whisker plot is shown below in Figure 7.29.

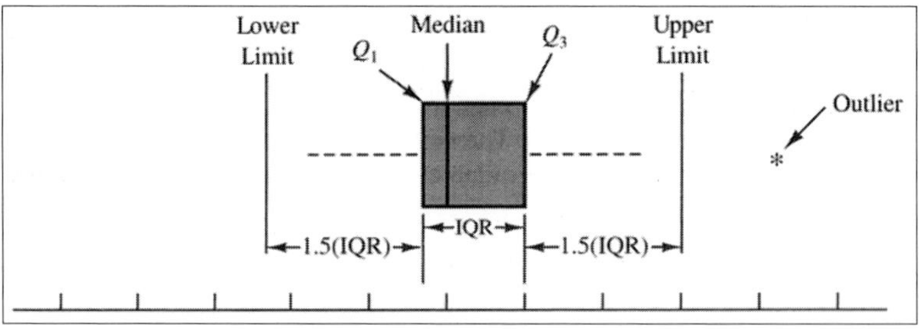

Figure 7.29
Box and whisker plot (number line is not numbered here)

An example will show how the box and whisker plot is constructed and interpreted.

process control is the manipulation of the conditions of a process to bring about a desired change in the output characteristics of the process.

Example 7.15

A company has annual sales of 100.4 milion euros obtained over 12 months, as illustrated in Table 7.12.

Month	Revenues in thousands of euros	Month	Revenues in thousands of euros
January	8100	July	6720
February	2555	August	7770
March	10,600	September	8900
April	11,700	October	12,670
May	7850	November	9810
June	4500	December	9240

Table 7.12

Determine the five data summary and provide the box and whisker plot. In ascending order we have: 2555, 4500, 6720, 7770, 7850, 8100, 8900, 9240, 9810, 10,600, 11,700, and 12,670. Table 7.12 illustrates these numbers split into 25% or four equal parts.

2555, 4500, 6720	7770, 7850, 8100	8900, 9240, 9810	10600, 11700, 12670
25%	25%	25%	25%

Table 7.13

Table 7.13 indicates $Q_1 = 7245$, $Q_2 = 8500$, $Q_3 = 10205$. Note that for Q1, Q2, and Q3 the median values are determined between two adjacent values, respectively 6720–7770, 8100–8900 and 9810–10,600. The minimum and maximum values are 2555 and 12,670 respectively. So the summary is:

- Minimum value = 2555
- First quartile (Q_1) = 7245
- Median (Q_2) = 8500
- Third quartile (Q_3) = 10205
- Maximum value = 12670

The interquartile range is 2960; hence the limits for the whiskers are:

- Lower limit = $Q_1 - 1.5$ IQR = 7245 − 4440 = 2805
- Upper limit = $Q_3 + 1.5$ IQR = 10205 + 4440 = 14645

It follows that the month of February was indeed an outlier since value 2555 < 2805. The box and whisker plot is illustrated in Figure 7.30.

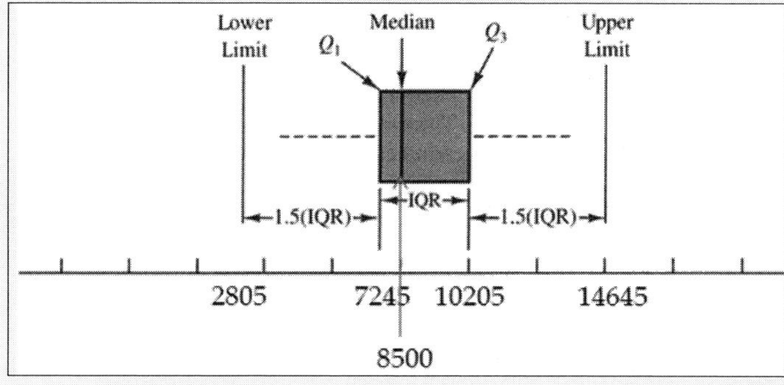

Figure 7.30

Example 7.16

The same problem tackled in Example 7.15 will now be tackled using Excel. Excel 2003 and 2007 provide only ONE version of quartile function defined as QUARTILE, which includes the median value for all the dataset. Excel 2010 provides two additional versions, namely: QUARTILE.EXC, which excludes the median value for all the dataset or array, QUARTILE.INC, which includes the median value for all the dataset or array.

Note The dataset or array, as it is called in Excel, is arbitrary since it is selected by the user. Hence the version of Excel may provide several possible computations for Q1 and Q3. Q2 will always be the median for the all the dataset irrespective of the version of Excel you use.

Case 1

Condition: Array is all the dataset:

Q1	QUARTILE = 7507.5	QUARTILE.INC = 7507.5	QUARTILE.EXC = 6982.5
Q3	QUARTILE = 10007.5	QUARTILE.INC = 10007.5	QUARTILE.EXC = 10402.5

Table 7.14

Case 2

Condition: Array is only the relative 50% of the dataset, hence for Q1 we use the lower half and for Q3 we use the upper half. Note that the calculated median is excluded (since it pertains to the whole of the dataset).

Q1	QUARTILE.EXC = 4013.8
Q3	QUARTILE.EXC = 11942.5

Table 7.15

Case 3

Array refers only to the two values near the true locations of Q1 and Q3 and as such reflects the work done in the previous example and where the median of the data set is excluded.

Q1	MEDIAN of 6720 and 7770 = 7245
Q3	MEDIAN of 9810 and 10600 = 10205

Table 7.16

Note In case 3 the quartile function does not work in Excel because the data is insufficient.

Example 7.17

Table 7.17 reports the age (in years) of children at a fancy dress birthday party.

Male	Female
3	2
3	3
3	3
4	5
5	5
5	10
5	10
10	12

Table 7.17

Draw the box and whisker plot for both datasets and provide appropriate comments.

The results for each descriptor are tabled in Tables 7.18 and 7.19.

Descriptor	Male	Female
Min	3	2
Q1	3	3
Q2	4.5	5
Q3	5	10
Max	10	12
IQR	2	7

Table 7.18

Male	Female
Lower limit = Q1 − 1.5IQR = 3 − 1.5 × 2 = 0	Lower limit = Q1 − 1.5IQR = 3 − 1.5 × 7 = −7.5
Upper limit = Q3 + 1.5IQR = 5 + 1.5 × 2 = 8	Upper limit = Q3 + 1.5IQR = 10 + 1.5 × 7 = 20.5

Table 7.19

Note The quartiles have been calculated with the QUARTILE.EXC function (although for this specific case the QUARTILE.INC function would render the same results); yet, in spite of this, we see some absurd results. For example, the lower limit is zero for males, while the lower and upper limit for females is negative and over 20 years of age. Observe also that the same results would have been obtained with the median approach used in Example 7.15. Hence some box and whisker plots replace the lower and upper limits with the min and maximum values of the dataset.

Student exercises

X7.6 For the following dataset carry out a two data and five data summary exercises; compare and comments on the results of both methods: 29, 30, 67, 45, 67, 38, 19, 28, 41, 56.

X7.7 Reconsider the data in example 7.4. Conduct a five data summary and compare your findings with what is discussed in Example 7.4.

X7.8 Analyse the data provided in Example 7.4 by plotting a box and whisker plot. Then compare the five data summary method with the B & W plot obtained.

7.4 Statistical process control

The control of manufacturing processes is critical for the performance of modern enterprises. Moreover, knowing whether or not a process is under control is mandatory for the overall quality control of the produced goods. The main objective of statistical process control is to establish whether variations in production output quality are due to **assignable causes** or **common causes**, and to evaluate the effects of corrective measures on the quality of produced goods and, also, to take the necessary decisions where needed. By this we mean that:

1. **Assignable causes** are a direct consequence of the state of the manufacturing process and include wear and tear of machinery, defective purchased materials or parts for assembly, operator (human) error, faulty machinery settings, etc.
2. **Common causes** are outside the domain of the manufacturing process and include climate changes—such as variation in humidity, temperature, and sunlight—and defective raw materials, for example. For common causes, adjusting the manufacturing process will not impact on the overall quality of the produced goods.

When assignable causes affect the quality of the produced goods the process is affected and, if excessive, will force the process to be out of control. Statistical process control aims to quantify and monitor quality levels and simplify management decisions. On the other hand, when common causes affect the quality of the produced goods the process is said to be statistically under control and hence the manufacturing process is left alone. Key to statistical process control are statistical procedures that are based on so-called hypothesis testing (see also Chapter 3).

Hypothetical testing in manufacturing considers two possible dimensions namely decisions and state of the manufacturing process as depicted in Figure 7.31.

		State of Manufacturing Process	
		Process in control	Process out of control
Decision	Leave process alone		
	Intervene on process		

Figure 7.31 Overview of process control and decisions

assignable causes also known as 'special cause'. An assignable cause is an identifiable, specific cause of variation in a given process or measurement.

common causes the common cause variation arises from a multitude of small factors that invariably affect any process and will conform to a normal distribution, or a distribution that is closely related to the normal distribution.

The **null hypothesis** H_0 can be true or false and leads (respectively) to establishing if the process is IN CONTROL or OUT OF CONTROL. In terms of decisions the process is either adjusted through some intervention or left alone and the quality level accepted. This brings about 4 possible occurrences and decisions:

1. If the null hypothesis is TRUE then the decision is to leave the process alone since the process is in control. The decision is therefore correct.
2. If the null Hypothesis is FALSE and the decision is to leave the process alone in spite of the fact that the process is out of control this will lead to what is known as a Type TWO error.
3. If the null hypothesis is TRUE and the decision is to adjust the process (which is in control) then this will lead to a Type ONE error.
4. If the null hypothesis is FALSE and the decision is to adjust the process since it is out of control, then the decision is correct.

Figure 7.32 summarizes the occurrences and decisions:

		State of Manufacturing Process	
		Process in control	Process out of control
Decision	Leave process alone	Correct Decision	Type 2 error (implying that the out-of-control process is allowed to continue)
	Intervene on process	Type 1 error (implying the in-control process is adjusted anyway)	Correct Decision

Figure 7.32
Process decision matrix conditions

7.4.1 Control charts

The scope of control charts is to provide a basis and basic graphical tool that summarises the current variation in the output quality of a process such as a manufacturing process. There are various types of control chart depending on the variables that are plotted and the information provided, the simplest of which is known as process sample mean or $\bar{x}$ (or xbar in words) control chart.

This chart is based on the sample mean and sample standard deviation and is depicted in Figure 7.33.

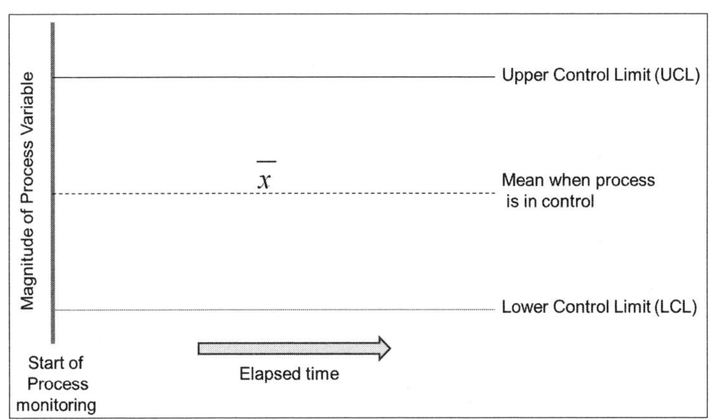

Figure 7.33
$\bar{x}$ Control Chart

null hypothesis the original hypothesis that is being tested.

The key features of the $\bar{x}$ control chart are the centre line that represents the mean value of the variable that measures process quality when it is in control. The vertical axis provides a measure of the magnitude of this variable and also indicates the start of the period of monitoring of the process. The two other horizontal lines represent the LCL and UCL, or lower control limit and upper control limit lines respectively, again when the process is in control. Both the LCL and UCL lines are chosen so that the value of the variable is highly likely to stay within these bounds if the process is in control. If the process is out of control then the value of the variable will lie outside one or both limit lines. Another feature of the $\bar{x}$ control chart is the elapsed time positioned along the x-axis. As time progresses more data will be accumulated, assessed and plotted on the chart which resembles a 'strip' or continuous chart. In practise for processes such as a manufacturing process, samples are taken at regular intervals and the mean values are calculated and then plotted (see Figure 7.35). Other control charts include R chart, P chart, Np chart, C chart, and U chart, which we discuss later in this chapter.

Building a $\bar{x}$ control chart

Example 7.18

The TTT brewing company has recently assessed one of its premium beers that is popular in the 33cl size in normal 'in control' process conditions. The assessment, consisting of 20 different samples each with 5 observations (i.e. fill measures in millilitres), has revealed the following results for this bottle size (see Table 7.20).

	Observations				
Sample ID	1	2	3	4	5
1	335	331	330	329	329
2	338	328	329	333	336
3	333	330	325	330	349
4	341	328	339	328	317
5	340	326	330	333	333
6	332	330	340	323	333
7	336	332	318	329	329
8	346	332	333	333	326
9	330	331	333	331	332
10	333	328	329	330	331
11	333	327	330	327	330
12	323	328	337	337	329
13'	331	329	347	345	327
14	340	325	333	323	325
15	339	320	327	337	327
16	330	321	323	319	335
17	335	332	324	338	336
18	335	330	341	339	337
19	330	323	337	329	330
20	345	333	333	328	329

Table 7.20 TTT Beer Co. bottling assessment results

Figure 7.34 illustrates the Excel solution.

	A	B	C	D	E	F	G	H	I	J
1	Example 7.18									
2					Observations					
3		Sample ID	1	2	3	4	5	Mean	Std Dev	Range
4		1	335	331	330	329	329	330.8	2.2	6
5		2	338	328	329	333	336	332.8	3.9	10
6		3	333	330	325	330	349	333.4	8.2	24
7		4	341	328	339	328	317	330.6	8.7	24
8		5	340	326	330	333	333	332.4	4.6	14
9		6	332	330	340	323	333	331.6	5.5	17
10		7	336	332	318	329	329	328.8	6.0	18
11		8	346	332	333	333	326	334	6.5	20
12		9	330	331	333	331	332	331.4	1.0	3
13		10	333	328	329	330	331	330.2	1.7	5
14		11	333	327	330	327	330	329.4	2.2	6
15		12	323	328	337	337	329	330.8	5.5	14
16		13	331	329	347	345	327	335.8	8.4	20
17		14	340	325	333	323	325	329.2	6.4	17
18		15	339	320	327	337	327	330	7.0	19
19		16	330	321	323	319	335	325.6	6.0	16
20		17	335	332	324	338	336	333	4.9	14
21		18	335	330	341	339	337	336.4	3.8	11
22		19	330	323	337	329	330	329.8	4.4	14
23		20	345	333	333	328	329	333.6	6.1	17
24										
25		Process mean	331.48						Average R	14.45
26		Std Deviation	6.10						Std. Dev of R	5.89
27		Number of observations	100.00							
28										
29		Mean	335.25	328.20	331.90	331.05	331.00			
30		Std. Dev	5.42	3.57	6.77	5.97	6.09			
31										
32		UCL	349.79							
33		LCL	313.17							

Figure 7.34

→ Excel solution

Sample ID Cells B4:B23	Values
Observations Cells C4:C23	Values
Mean Cell H4	Formula: = AVERAGE(C4:G4) Copy down H4:H23
Std Dev Cell I4	Formula: = STDEV.P(C4:G4) Copy down I4:I23
Range Cell J4	Formula: = MAX(C4:G4)-MIN(C4:G4) Copy down J4:J23
Average R Cell J25	Formula: = AVERAGE(J4:J23)
Std. Dev of R Cell J26	Formula: = STDEV.P(J4:J23)
Process Mean Cell C25	Formula: = AVERAGE(C4:G23)
Std Deviation Cell C26	Formula: = STDEV.P(C4:G23)
Number of observations Cell C27	Formula: = COUNT(C4:G23)
Mean Cell C29	Formula: = AVERAGE(C4:C23) Copy across C29:G29
Std. Dev Cell C30	Formula: = STDEV.P(C4:C23) Copy across C30:G30
UCL Cell C32	Formula: = C25+3*C26
LCL Cell C33	Formula: = C25-3*C26

The mean filling capacity is 331 ml or 33.1 cubic centimetres with a standard deviation of 6.1 (see Figure 7.33). The usefulness of the variation of sample mean for a process under control is captured in the standard error of the mean. So for samples of size 'n' we have Equation 7.3 that is used to calculate the standard deviation of the sample mean:

$$\sigma_{\bar{x}} = \frac{\sigma}{\sqrt{n}} \tag{7.3}$$

Since the filling assessment has provided a normal distribution and therefore also $\bar{X}$ is normally distributed (and even more so as 'n' increases - see central limit theorem) it follows that distribution will have a mean μ and a standard deviation σ as illustrated in Figure 7.35:

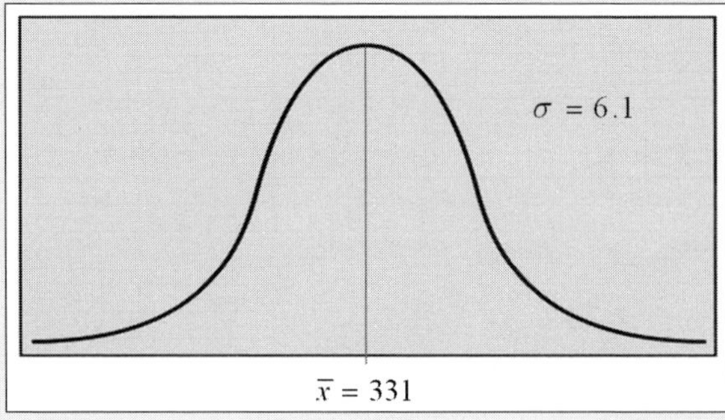

Figure 7.35
Normal distribution of beer bottling samples in cubic centres

The sampling distribution of $\bar{x}$ finds its application in process control, when the upper and lower control limits are added. These are defined as follows:

$$UCL = \bar{x} + 3\sigma \tag{7.4}$$

$$LCL = \bar{x} - 3\sigma \tag{7.5}$$

For beer bottling assessment this results in: UCL = 350 and LCL = 313. So if we were to select another batch of samples for quality control we would check first that the measurements were within 313 to 350ml for acceptance. Clearly this is for a control chart based on $\bar{x}$. The $\bar{x}$ control chart, based on the 20 sample means shown in table 7.19, now becomes as illustrated in Figure 7.36.

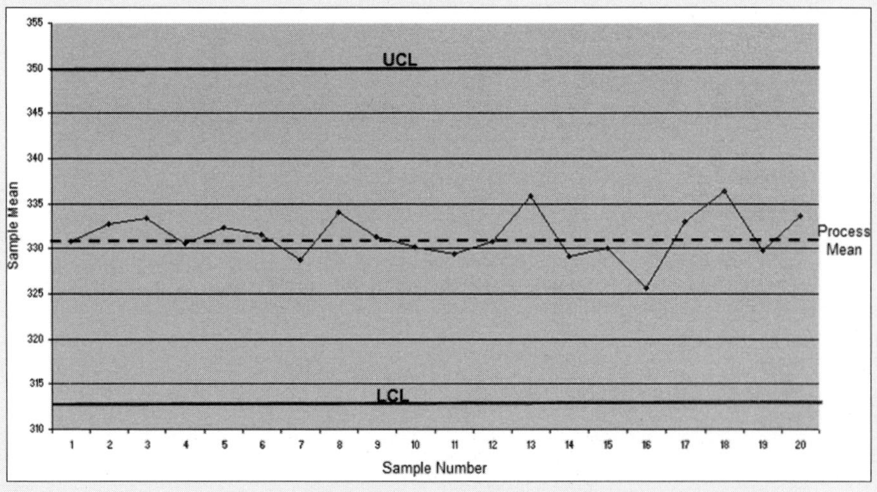

Figure 7.36
Example of xbar plot

⁂ **Interpretation** As can be seen from the graphed result the beer bottling process is clearly under control even though most of the values shown in the table of data are closer to the UCL (see samples 3, 8 and 13). Further, towards the end of the 20 samples (from sample number 15 onwards) the spread of the data is widening, possibly indicating that quality variation is on the increase.

Point estimators

The issue of representing populations through adequate sampling with or without bias, is tackled in sampling through what are called 'point estimators'. These estimators are indicators that show that we are on the right or wrong track in the analysis and are based on sample statistics. Sample statistics are viewed as a collection of features that characterize the sample that will be used to estimate the value of a population parameter. Three sample statistics you have already been exposed to are:

- Sample mean
- Sample standard deviation
- Sample proportion

A sample mean $\bar{x}$ is used as the point estimator for population mean (μ), the sample standard deviation (s) is the point estimator for population standard deviation (σ), and the sample proportion (p) is the point estimator for the population proportion (π). Table 7.21 describes the basic point estimators.

Point estimator	Population equivalent
Sample mean $\bar{x}$	Population mean μ
Sample standard deviation s, that is $s = \sqrt{\frac{\Sigma(x_i - \bar{x})^2}{n-1}}$	Population standard deviation σ
The sample proportion p	Population proportion π.

Table 7.21 Basic point estimators

Example 7.19

The following sample data has been collected during a simple random sample of a population: 87, 175, 178, 192, 167, 156, 178, 189, 182, 183, and 172. Calculate the point estimators for the population mean and population standard deviation.

Point estimator for the population mean is: $\bar{x} = 178.1$.

Point estimator for the population standard deviation is 10.4:

$$s = \sqrt{\frac{\Sigma(x_i - \bar{x})^2}{n-1}} = \sqrt{\frac{1088.91}{11-1}} = 10.4$$

Example 7.20

Doxa, a private market research company, has conducted a 'Doxa' poll based on a sample of 526 adults (females and males). The survey was conducted in the high street to learn if adults thought the banks had learned anything about the financial crisis that escalated from 2008 onwards. The survey provided the following responses (see Table 7.22):

119 adults	The banks had learnt the lesson and had put measures into place to avoid future occurrences
89 adults	The banks had learnt and changed something but not enough
316 adults	The banks had not learnt or changed anything at all

Table 7.22 Doxa poll results summary

Calculate the population proportion point indicators for each of three responses.

The population proportion point indicator is defined as the ratio of the portion of the population with respect to the total population.

$$\text{Point estimator 1: } p = \frac{119}{526} = 0.23$$

$$\text{Point estimator 2: } p = \frac{89}{526} = 0.17$$

$$\text{Point estimator 3: } p = \frac{316}{526} = 0.6$$

7.4.2 When the process mean and standard deviation are unknown

So far we have based our reasoning on known or computable values of the sample mean and relative standard deviation. In practice, samples are taken at regular intervals according to a specific quality control procedure such as at the beginning and end of a shift. Taking, for example, 20 samples with 5 observations each is time consuming or difficult to achieve for each shift. A much quicker way is to exploit the range of values that provides surprisingly good estimates of process variability. Returning to Table 7.17 we see the last column reports the ranges for each sample. We can calculate the **average range** for the 20 samples using Equation (7.6):

$$\bar{R} = \frac{R_1 + R_2 + R_3 \ldots\ldots R_k}{k} \tag{7.6}$$

Where, k is the number of samples.

In our beer bottling example (see Example 7.18) the average range is:

$$\bar{R} = \frac{6 + 10 + 24 \ldots\ldots + 17}{20} = 14.45 \cong 14.5$$

X

average range average range calculated to monitor process variability.

The 'R' chart

This quality control chart is based on the range of the sample observations or samples and, as was discussed in Chapter 2, the measure of range is a measure of dispersion or variability. More specifically the range is used as a measure of the variability of a process and is considered a variable in itself. Hence the average range is used as the process mean. Henceforth the mean and standard deviation of the range is used to plot the R chart, both of which have specific formulae for the 'R' chart. The standard deviation in a 'R' chart is defined by Equation (7.7):

$$\bar{\sigma}_R = \frac{d_3}{d_2}\bar{R} \tag{7.7}$$

The two constants d_3 and d_2 depend on the sample size and are reported in Table 7.23.

Observations in each sample	d_2	d_3	D_3	D_4	A_2	d_3/d_2
2	1.128	0.853	0	3.267	1.88	0.756
3	1.693	0.888	0	2.574	1.023	0.525
4	2.059	0.88	0	2.282	0.729	0.427
5	2.326	0.864	0	2.114	0.577	0.371
6	2.534	0.848	0	2.004	0.483	0.335
7	2.704	0.833	0.076	1.924	0.419	0.308
8	2.847	0.82	0.136	1.864	0.373	0.288
9	2.97	0.808	0.184	1.816	0.337	0.272
10	3.078	0.797	0.223	1.777	0.308	0.259
11	3.173	0.787	0.256	1.774	0.285	0.248
12	3.258	0.778	0.284	1.716	0.266	0.239
13	3.336	0.77	0.308	1.692	0.249	0.231
14	3.407	0.763	0.329	1.671	0.235	0.224
15	3.472	0.756	0.348	1.652	0.223	0.218
16	3.532	0.75	0.364	1.636	0.212	0.212
17	3.588	0.744	0.379	1.621	0.203	0.207
18	3.64	0.739	0.392	1.608	0.194	0.203
19	3.689	0.734	0.404	1.596	0.187	0.199
20	3.735	0.729	0.414	1.586	0.18	0.195
21	3.778	0.724	0.425	1.575	0.173	0.192
22	3.819	0.72	0.434	1.566	0.167	0.189
23	3.858	0.716	0.443	1.557	0.162	0.186
24	3.895	0.712	0.452	1.548	0.157	0.183
25	3.931	0.708	0.459	1.541	0.153	0.180

Table 7.23 Constants for Xbar and R control charts and relative formulae
(printed with permission of ASTM, American Society for Testing and materials, USA)

The upper control limit (UCL) and lower control limit (LCL) in an R chart are defined as:

$$UCL = \bar{R} + 3\bar{\sigma}_R = \bar{R}\left[1 + 3\frac{d_3}{d_2}\right] = \bar{R}D_4 \tag{7.8}$$

$$LCL = \bar{R} - 3\bar{\sigma}_R = \bar{R}\left[1 - 3\frac{d_3}{d_2}\right] = \bar{R}D_3 \tag{7.9}$$

Where, D_3 and D_4 are again constants (see columns 3 and 4 of Table 7.23) and derived as follows:

$$D_4 = 1 + 3\frac{d_3}{d_2} \tag{7.10}$$

$$D_3 = 1 - 3\frac{d_3}{d_2} \tag{7.11}$$

Figure 7.37 illustrates an example of an R plot.

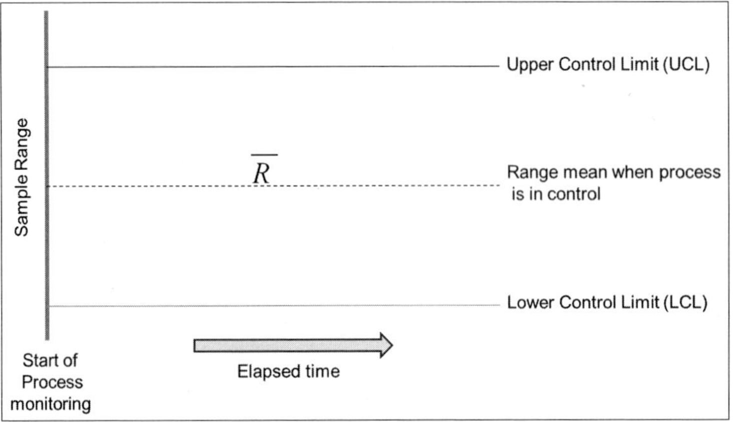

Figure 7.37
Example of R plot

The 'p' chart

In manufacturing, the proportion of defective parts in the population is an indicator of output quality. Similarly, we could view output quality as the proportion of non-defective parts in the population but the former is more popular and perhaps more logical. The control chart that uses the proportion of defective parts or items as a measure of output quality is called the 'p' chart.

In general, in processes even whenever everything is under control we would expect some errors to surface; so, if in a large mail order 1% of the orders requires reprocessing (e.g. wrong or old address, misspelling of customer name or address, wrong goods ordered-delivered, incorrect quantities, etc.). In other words the proportion of errors for the population (π) is 0.01. The UCL and LCL in a p chart are defined as:

$$UCL = \pi + 3\sigma_p \tag{7.12}$$

$$LCL = \pi - 3\sigma_p \tag{7.13}$$

Where σ_p is the standard error of the proportion defined as:

$$\sigma_p = \sqrt{\frac{\pi(1-\pi)}{n}} \tag{7.14}$$

The 'p' chart is used when the sample size varies, when only one defect per unit is possible, and when sample size may change from one period to the next. Examples are defective parts for assembly, defective assembled parts, incorrect meal delivery, incorrect billing. A key feature for this type of chart is to use it as a goal for 'zero defects in a process'. Typically, this implies that a summary of defects is first recorded and reported, as illustrated in Table 7.24.

Latest split of product 'A' defects	
Paint defect	15%
Dented part	3%
Scratched	17%
Incorrect assembly	7%
Poor performance	11%
Packaging	22%
Missing instructions	9%
Other	16%
Total =	100%

Table 7.24 Example of summary of defects for 'p' chart

The defect is then used as the out-of-control parameter and set as a goal.

Example 7.21

A restaurant has assessed typical customer complaints and has decided to improve customer satisfaction by eliminating complaints concerning delivery times for meals or portions of meals (currently standing at 7% of all complaints). The handling of customer orders is changed, since this seems to be the root cause, and for the following seven days the number of complaints monitored. Determine if the change has improved the process for the data in Table 7.25.

Day	Tables served (1 table = 1 customer)	Delivery time complaints
1	111	4
2	134	11
3	178	7
4	78	9
5	98	11
6	178	8
7	210	12

Table 7.25

We note that the case suits the 'p' chart requirements perfectly and the characteristics of the process are defined as follows:

In general we have the ratio of number of occurrences with respect to the total number of samples:

$$\bar{p} = \frac{\sum_{i=1}^{k} p_i}{\sum_{i=1}^{k} n_i} \tag{7.15}$$

Before: 7% or 0.0700

For day 1: $\bar{p} = \frac{\sum_{i=1}^{k} p_i}{k} = \frac{4}{111} = 0.0360$

For all 7 days: $\bar{p} = \frac{\sum_{i=1}^{k} p_i}{\sum_{i=1}^{k} n_i} = \frac{4 + 11 + ... + 12}{111 + 134 + ... + 210} = \frac{62}{987} = 0.0628$

Standard error of proportion:

$$\sigma_p = \sqrt{\frac{\bar{p}(1-\bar{p})}{n}} = \sqrt{\frac{0.0628(1-0.0628)}{987}} = 0.0077$$

$$UCL = \pi + 3\sigma_p = 0.0628 + 3 \times 0.0077 = 0.08599$$

$$LCL = \pi - 3\sigma_p = 0.0628 - 3 \times 0.0077 = 0.03965$$

Note So the limits are approximately four to eight complaints for every one hundred tables served.

The 'np' chart

This type of control chart focuses on the number of defective items in a sample over time (often called 'subgroups') and is traditionally employed in process control. The 'np' chart is essentially based on binary scores (Yes/No, Fail/Pass, Go/No Go, Complete/Incomplete etc.) and is used to determine if a process is stable and predictable, as well as to monitor the effects of process improvements or changes introduced to rectify previous defects or defective items. The defective items may be considered as outliers for which a decision must be made to accept them or not, such as variables with extreme values, goods that do not to conform to specifications, damaged packaging, incomplete survey answers etc. Since batches of samples of the same size are taken over time it follows that the 'np' chart is used to view the trend of non-conforming items over time.

There are two key measures in 'np' charts: the sample size 'n' and the probability of selecting a defective item when the process is under control, that is, the probability 'π'. When the sample size is large enough we may assume that the normal distribution is a good approximation and therefore the following mean and standard deviations hold:

$$\text{Mean in an 'np' chart} = n\pi \tag{7.16}$$

$$\text{Standard deviation in an 'np' chart} = \sqrt{n\pi(1-\pi)} \tag{7.17}$$

These equations are valid providing the following condition is satisfied: $n\pi \geq 5$ and $n(1 - \pi) \geq 5$. Therefore the upper and lower control limits are given by Equations (7.18) and (7.19):

$$UCL = n\pi + 3\sqrt{n\pi(1 - \pi)} \tag{7.18}$$

$$LCL = n\pi - 3\sqrt{n\pi(1 - \pi)} \tag{7.19}$$

Example 7.22

A company specializing in online web surveys has found from a sample of 200 surveys that the probability of incomplete surveys is 0.05 (i.e. 5% probability). Determine the mean and the standard deviation and then the limits for a 'np' control chart. Graphically summarize these results.

We have:

- Mean: $n\pi = 200 \times 0.05 = 10$
- Standard deviation: $\sqrt{n\pi(1 - \pi)} = \sqrt{200 \times 0.05(1 - 0.05)} = \sqrt{10 \times 0.95} = 3.082$

These equations are valid since the following conditions are satisfied: $n\pi \geq 5$ and $n(1 - \pi) \geq 5$. The upper and lower limits for the process are:

$$UCL = n\pi + 3\sqrt{n\pi(1 - \pi)} = 10 + 3 \times 3.082 = 19.25 \cong 19$$

$$LCL = n\pi - 3\sqrt{n\pi(1 - \pi)} = 10 - 3 \times 3.082 = 0.75 \cong 1$$

Note This means that the upper limit would be 19 incorrect surveys and a minimum of 1. Clearly, in the case of surveys like this, LCL values make little sense so circumstances of this type, or when process attribute values are negative, are set to zero on the 'np' chart. In this specific case the company would consider the process out of control if more than 19 surveys are found in future samples of the same size. The results are graphically represented on the 'np' in Figure 7.38.

Figure 7.38 illustrates the 'np' plot for this data problem.

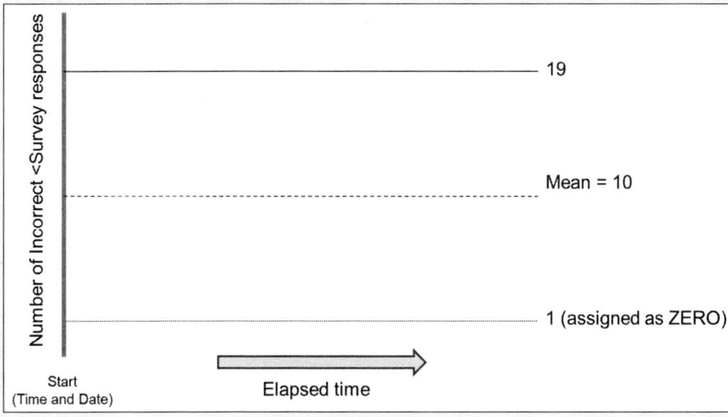

Figure 7.38

Example of 'np' plot

Example 7.23

A manufacturer receives parts that are boxed and packaged by the supplier. The conformity of the parts is regularly checked and it has been decided to add another quality control, in this case to the packaging, because the parts are renowned to suffer from heavy handling and rough transport. Assuming that for every 1000 samples a probability of packaging damage is 0.03, determine the LCL and UCL limits for the 'np' quality chart concerning the packaging. The two conditions are clearly satisfied, indeed we have: $n\pi = 1000 \times 0.03 = 30 \geq 5$ and $n(1-\pi) = 1000(0.97) = 970 \geq 5$. The limits are therefore:

$$UCL = n\pi + 3\sqrt{n\pi(1-\pi)} = 30 + 3 \times \sqrt{30(0.97)} = 30 + 16.18 \cong 46$$

$$LCL = n\pi - 3\sqrt{n\pi(1-\pi)} = 30 - 3 \times \sqrt{30(0.97)} = 30 - 16.18 \cong 14$$

Interpretation We would expect to have between 14 to 36 damaged packages for future sampled supplies of the same size. This implies that for more than 36 cartons or packages we would classify the process out of control and for which the supplier would be flagged. Note that less than 14 packages does not imply the process is out of control rather, in this specific case, handling is better since we have less damaged packages. At this point it would be interesting to conduct the same investigation also on the parts packaged to see if there is a correlation between damaged or undamaged packaging and any defective parts.

The 'c' chart

We observed that 'p' charts plotted proportions of defective items in samples taken from the same process and as such, the attribute being counted indicated whether or not the item was defective. Sometimes we are interested in monitoring how many defects the item has. In modern manufacturing for example, processes are split across factories (e.g. suppliers) or production lines and only when the final product is assembled does one recognize the various defects and consider the product as a non-conforming unit. So a car coming off the production line may have an engine problem, paintwork scratches, missing cigarette lighter, and so forth. Customer complaints form another example. They are usually a collection of unsatisfactory elements that anger the customer, and might include statements like 'the product was delivered late with no working manual and worse didn't work when it was installed and switched ON'. The customer complaint or non-compliance event would be considered an 'occurrence'. In such cases 'c' charts are exploited.

The concept of defects and defective items therefore covers both physical and non-physical aspects. It may also be the case that a defective item, that would normally be discarded as scrap, is reworked or reprocessed, or returned to the supplier or somewhere in the production line or to the interviewee (as in the case of an incomplete enquiry or questionnaire) or even downgraded (think of broken biscuits or foodstuffs that have gone past their 'best before' date). For this reason, when a defective item is considered as being a non-conforming unit within a sample the relative sample (batch) it is seen as an opportunity (indeed it is often referred to as an 'area of opportunity). These 'areas of opportunity' have to be within a sufficiently large enough sample (e.g. over a certain minimum period) to detect such defective items; if they are not within a large sample they would not be an opportunity and be classified as not normal process defects and end up as scrap or be binned. The process of lower and upper limits for 'c' charts are defined as for follows:

$$\text{The upper control limit for 'c' chart: } UCL = \bar{c} + 3\sqrt{\bar{c}} \quad (7.20)$$

$$\text{The lower control limit for 'c' chart: } LCL = \bar{c} - 3\sqrt{\bar{c}} \quad (7.21)$$

$$\text{Where, occurrence proportion indicator for 'c' chart: } \bar{c} = \frac{\sum_{i=1}^{i=k} c_i}{k} \quad (7.22)$$

Where: $\bar{c}$ is the average number of occurrences, k is the number of units sampled, c_i is the number occurrences in unit i.

Example 7.24

A company is assessing customer satisfaction by analysing the number of complaints registered though the customer relationship management (CRM) system. For a period of 24 working days the following complaints has been reported (see Table 7.26).

Day	Number of complaints	Day	Number of complaints
1	5	13	9
2	5	14	0
3	4	15	10
4	10	16	6
5	6	17	2
6	5	18	3
7	4	19	7
8	3	20	9
9	6	21	8
10	6	22	4
11	11	23	9
12	7	24	7

Table 7.26

Determine the UCL and LCL values for the process.

Since we are monitoring defective items that could have a multitude of reasons and such items may be considered for re-processing, the 'c' chart is suggested. To determine the lower and upper limits of the 'c' chart we need to know first the average number of occurrences $\bar{c}$ bearing in mind that, k, is the number of units sampled (i.e. the number of days). Hence we obtain:

$$\bar{c} = \frac{\left(\sum_{i=1}^{k} c_i\right)}{k} = \frac{146}{24} \text{[?]} 6$$

$$LCL = \bar{c} - 3\sqrt{\bar{c}} = 6 - 3\sqrt{6} = 6 - 7.4 = -1.4 \cong 0$$

$$UCL = \bar{c} + 3\sqrt{\bar{c}} = 6 + 7.4 = -13.4 \cong 13$$

Note We have set the LCL to zero since it does not make sense to speak of −1.4 complaints. Similarly, the UCL has been rounded off to 13 complaints.

The 'u' chart

In the case of the 'c' chart we took one item per sample; moreover, the sample size was constant. However, not always do sample sizes remain the same: consignments vary in size for the same time and therefore the number of defective items may change. This circumstance is catered for by the 'u' chart that takes one item per sample but sample has size 't' and consists of n_t items. A quick comparison shows the difference between 'c' and 'u' charts:

Type of chart	Sample size	Item corresponds to	Principal objective
C chart	Fixed (constant)	Number of defects per fixed sample size.	A control chart for the number of defects
U chart	Variable	Number of defects in sample size that may change from sample to sample.	A control chart for the number of defects per item

Table 7.27 Comparison of 'c' versus 'u' type control charts

The control parameters for the 'u' chart are as follows.

The occurrence proportion indicator for 'u' chart:

$$\bar{u} = \frac{\sum_{t=1}^{t=m} T_t}{\sum_{t=1}^{t=m} n_t} \tag{7.23}$$

Where: T_t = total number of defects in all n_t items in sample t, N_t = total number of n_t items in sample t. And the new limits are:

The lower control limit for 'u' chart:

$$LCL = \bar{u} - 3\sqrt{\frac{\bar{u}}{n_t}} \tag{7.24}$$

The upper control limit for 'u' chart:

$$UCL = \bar{u} + 3\sqrt{\frac{\bar{u}}{n_t}} \tag{7.25}$$

Example 7.25

A company has monitored the number of defects for different sample sizes for a product consigned by a supplier daily. Initially the supplier's process is under control but subsequently a process improvement has been introduced by the supplier and the company wishes to know if this process upgrade has effectively changed things for the better. The case is summarized in Table 7.28.

Consignment	Sample Size	Defects	Defects per product	LCL	UCL	Consignment	Sample Size	Defects	Defects per product	LCL	UCL
1	11	0	0.0000	0.0000	0.1075	16	9	0	0.0000	0.0000	0.1176
2	9	0	0.0000	0.0000	0.1176	17	8	0	0.0000	0.0000	0.1240
3	15	0	0.0000	0.0000	0.0936	18	14	0	0.0000	0.0000	0.0965
4	15	0	0.0000	0.0000	0.0936	19	11	1	0.0909	0.0000	0.1075
5	12	0	0.0000	0.0000	0.1034	20	12	0	0.0000	0.0000	0.1034
6	11	0	0.0000	0.0000	0.1075	21	14	0	0.0000	0.0000	0.0965
7	14	0	0.0000	0.0000	0.0965	22	10	0	0.0000	0.0000	0.1121
8	11	0	0.0000	0.0000	0.1075	23	9	0	0.0000	0.0000	0.1176
9	14	0	0.0000	0.0000	0.0965	24	14	0	0.0000	0.0000	0.0965
10	8	0	0.0000	0.0000	0.1240	25	10	0	0.0000	0.0000	0.1121
11	12	1	0.0833	0.0000	0.1034	26	14	0	0.0000	0.0000	0.0965
12	13	0	0.0000	0.0000	0.0997	27	13	1	0.0769	0.0000	0.0997
13	11	0	0.0000	0.0000	0.1075	28	10	0	0.0000	0.0000	0.1121
14	15	1	0.0667	0.0000	0.0936	29	13	0	0.0000	0.0000	0.0997
15	12	0	0.0000	0.0000	0.1034	30	10	0	0.0000	0.0000	0.1121

Table 7.28 Supplier process under control and before process improvements were introduced

This table has been composed as follows:

$$\text{Day 11} \quad \text{Defects per product} = \frac{\text{Number of defects}}{\text{Number of products}} = \frac{1}{12} = 0.0833$$

$$\text{Day 14} \quad \text{Defects per product} = \frac{\text{Number of defects}}{\text{Number of products}} = \frac{1}{14} = 0.0667$$

$$\text{Day 19} \quad \text{Defects per product} = \frac{\text{Number of defects}}{\text{Number of products}} = \frac{1}{11} = 0.0909$$

$$\text{Day 27} \quad \text{Defects per product} = \frac{\text{Number of defects}}{\text{Number of products}} = \frac{1}{13} = 0.0769$$

For all the 30 consignments 354 products have been supplied, four of which were defective. The mean defective products before process improvements were:

$$\bar{u} = \frac{\sum_{t=1}^{m} T_t}{\sum_{t=1}^{m} n_t} = \frac{4}{354} = 0.0113$$

This value represents the center line for the 'u' chart.

❊ **Interpretation** For each sample we may determine the LCL and UCL. Clearly for this case the UCL is automatically set to zero since negative values would be meaningless.

Choosing two random days, for example day 5 and day 25, the values for UCL have determined:

$$\text{Day 5} \quad UCL_{day\,5} = \bar{u}_{day\,5} + 3\sqrt{\frac{\bar{u}}{n_t}} = 0.0113 + 3\sqrt{\frac{0.0113}{12}} = 0.1034$$

$$\text{Day 25} \quad UCL_{day\,25} = \bar{u}_{day\,25} + 3\sqrt{\frac{\bar{u}}{n_t}} = 0.0113 + 3\sqrt{\frac{0.0113}{10}} = 0.1121$$

The UCL values for the other days have been determined in the same way. Following the process upgrade the following results were obtained for the next 20 days (see Table 7.29).

Consignment	Sample Size	Defects	Defects per product	LCL	UCL
31	30	0	0.0000	0.0000	0.0695
32	33	2	0.0606	0.0000	0.0668
33	30	1	0.0333	0.0000	0.0695
34	33	3	0.0909	0.0000	0.0668
35	32	0	0.0000	0.0000	0.0677
36	29	0	0.0000	0.0000	0.0705
37	27	2	0.0741	0.0000	0.0727
38	34	5	9.1471	0.0000	0.0660
39	32	3	0.0938	0.0000	0.0677
40	30	0	0.0000	0.0000	0.0695
41	32	2	0.0625	0.0000	0.0677
42	26	1	0.0385	0.0000	0.0738
43	26	0	0.0000	0.0000	0.0738
44	35	3	0.0857	0.0000	0.0652
45	26	2	0.0769	0.0000	0.0738
46	35	3	0.0857	0.0000	0.0652
47	32	1	0.0313	0.0000	0.0677
48	28	1	0.0357	0.0000	0.0716
49	33	0	0.0000	0.0000	0.0668
50	27	2	0.0741	0.0000	0.0727

Table 7.29 Sample results after process improvements

Note After the upgrade the process was monitored by increasing the sample size from each consignment hence in practise it was likely to find (proportionally) a larger number of defects than before. In order to clarify the quality trend and understand the impact on UCL values a 'u' chart plot would be the next step.

Example 7.26

A sports team has introduced a new training program with the intent to reduce the number of injuries and thus ensure that more players are available for the coach. Determine the LCL and UCL values for both programs and then discuss the results for the data in Table 7.30.

	Sample size	Number of injuries reported
Old programme	54	7
New programme	35	4

Table 7.30 Sports injuries summary table

Old training programme:

$$\frac{\bar{u} = 7}{54} = 0.1296$$

$$LCL = \bar{u} - 3\sqrt{\frac{\bar{u}}{n_t}} = 0.1296 - 3\sqrt{\frac{0.1296}{54}} = -0.0174 = 0$$

$$UCL = \bar{u} + 3\sqrt{\frac{\bar{u}}{n_t}} = 0.1296 + 3\sqrt{\frac{0.1296}{54}} = 0.2766$$

New training programme:

$$\frac{\bar{u} = 4}{35} = 0.1143$$

$$LCL = \bar{u} - 3\sqrt{\frac{\bar{u}}{n_t}} = 0.1143 - 3\sqrt{\frac{0.1143}{35}} = -0.0571 = 0$$

$$UCL = \bar{u} + 3\sqrt{\frac{\bar{u}}{n_t}} = 0.1143 + 3\sqrt{\frac{0.1143}{35}} = 0.2857$$

Note Both programmes have an LCL of zero since it does not make sense to speak of negative injuries. The difference between the programmes is that the new programme has a higher UCL which implies that the programme does not produce better results; however, further data is needed to verify whether or not this is true.

In conclusion we may summarize the various control charts in Table 7.31.

Type of Control Chart	Scope - intended use	Typical application	Key parameters	Remarks
X bar R chart	Continuous process control and when process stability is key.	Ideal for continuous process control and when evaluation of process stability is key	$\bar{x}$ - average $\bar{R}$ - Average range $\overline{\sigma_R}$ - std. dev. of R D_1, D_2, D_3 and D_4 - constants	Based on normal distribution. Particularly suitable when process is repetitive such as pizza deliveries, customer services, monitoring of parts quality etc. Plot the R chart first and if out of control do the xbar chart
P chart	Exploits the proportion of defective parts or items as a measure of output quality with respect to a sample	When events, such as defects, can be classified in binary terms e.g. Yes/No	σ_p - standard error of the proportion. $\bar{p}$ - the average number of occurrences.	Based on binomial distribution. Requires adequate sampling and cannot account for differences in the number of observations from sample to sample
np chart	View the trend of non-conforming items over time in batches of the same size	Analysis of process stability and monitoring of process changes	$n\pi$ - Mean of the batch $\sqrt{n\pi(1-\pi)}$ - std. dev. Of batch	Based on binomial distribution. The np-control chart is used to monitor the conforming fraction in process production but without the classification of errors.
C chart	Charts the number of defects per item and is especially useful when the opportunity is large with respect to the number of defects detected.	Analysis of process quality and when area of opportunity circumstances occur	$\bar{c}$ - the average number of occurrences. k - the number of units sampled.	Based on Poisson distribution. In complaints analysis or where fraction of defects is meaningless the LCL and UCL values are rounded off. Negative LCL values are generally set to zero.
U chart	As per the 'c' chart but also when there may be more than one defect per unit and the sample size varies	Analysis of process quality after process change and when areas of opportunity occur	$\bar{u}$ - mean defects	Based on Poisson distribution. In complaints analysis or where fraction of defects is meaningless the LCL and UCL values are rounded off. Negative LCL values are generally set to zero.

Table 7.31 Summary of control charts

Student exercises

X7.9 Calculate the UCL and LCL for a R quality control plot for the following dataset: 370, 400, 410, 420, 520, 520, 560, 570, 330, 390, 430, 440, 440, 440, 450, 460, 460, 490, 570, 600, 610. The dataset refers to 21 samples or sub-groups with 10 observations each. Each data value provided in the dataset is the average range for the relative 10 observations.

X7.10 Plot the data provided in exercise X7.9 and determine if the process is in or out of control.

X7.11 Figure 7.39 shows a 'p' plot for a product that has gone from launch to full-blown production—from a very small rate of production to a large production output. The production has therefore been ramped up in steps. In the chart, each step represents a sample size that corresponds to each step-up in production: sample size may be considered proportionally constant and representative after the first step. Comment on the graph and provide your conclusions in terms of quality control.

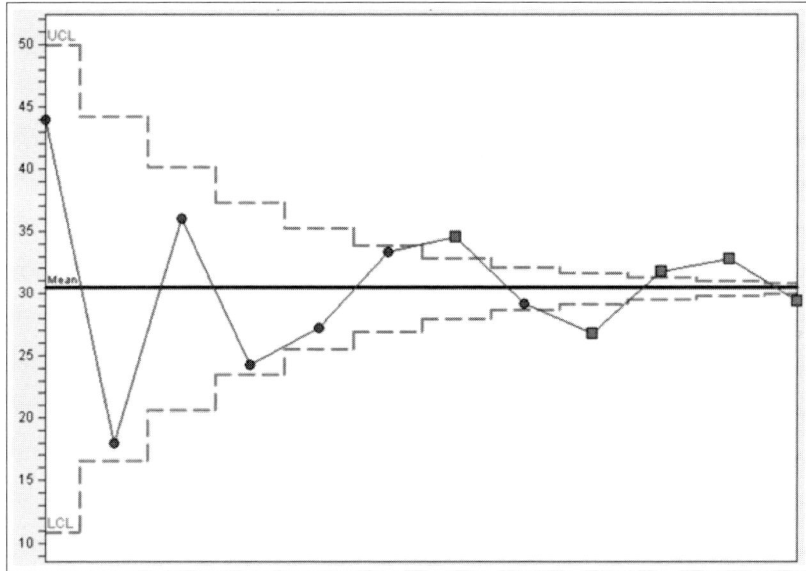

Figure 7.39

X7.12 Figure 7.40 shows an 'np'. Basing your judgement exclusively on the chart shown and assuming the sample size was 100 for all cases, what would be the highest and lowest percantage defects found in the samples? What is the average number of defects found across all samples?

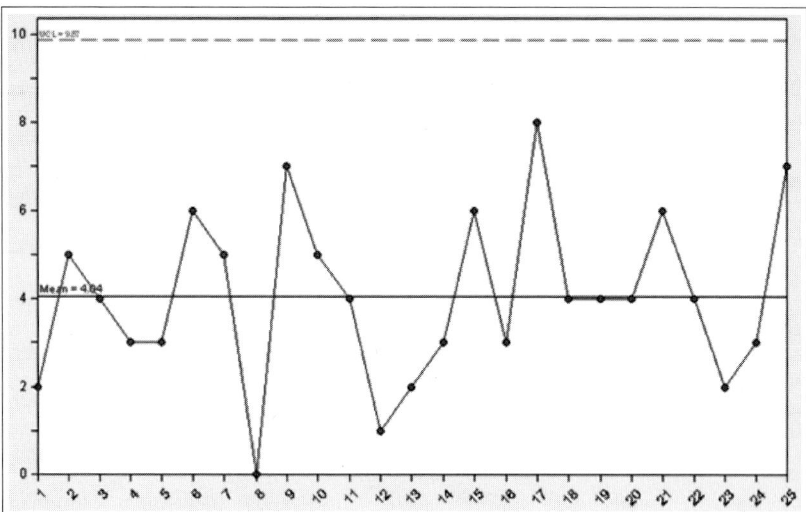

Figure 7.40

X7.13 The number of complaints received by a call centre is shown in Table 7.32.

Day	Number of complaints	Day	Number of complaints
1	45	13	39
2	50	14	40
3	40	15	109
4	100	16	68
5	60	17	21
6	55	18	39
7	54	19	97
8	13	20	69
9	16	21	28
10	96	22	14
11	110	23	19
12	78	24	87

Table 7.32

Determine the UCL and LCL values for a 'c' chart used for this purpose. What is the mean number of complaints expected for the following 24 days?

X7.14 Data transmitted between facilities in a large global corporation is monitored on an hourly basis. It was found that the error rate was 0.01%, which is considered acceptable by the corporation. The dataset in Table 7.33 was collected.

Sample	Number of errors	Sample	Number of errors
1	1	25	1
2	2	26	0
3	0	27	0
4	1	28	0
5	0	29	0
6	1	30	0
7	1	31	1
8	0	32	1
9	0	33	1
10	0	34	0
11	1	35	2
12	2	36	2
13	1	37	0
14	0	38	0
15	0	39	0
16	0	40	1
17	0	41	2
18	1	42	1
19	2	43	4
20	1	44	1
21	3	45	1
22	1	46	0
23	1	47	0
24	1	48	0

Table 7.33

Plot the 'c' chart? Why is the 'c' chart more suitable than the 'u' chart?

X7.15 Reconsider the dataset in exercise X7.14. Is the data transmission process under control? And which sample(s) should be considered as borderline in terms of quality of transmission?

X7.16 Two datasets are being considered for quality control per sample. The first dataset has a fixed sample size while the second has variable sample size. What control charts do you consider to be applicable for the two datasets?

X7.17 The following dataset has been collected concerning the number of defects in freshly picked fruit. Complete Table 7.34.

Sample	Sample Size	Defects recorded	Defects per fruit	LCL	UCL
1	30	0	?	?	?
2	27	2	?	?	?
3	25	1	?	?	?
4	35	3	?	?	?
5	42	0	?	?	?
6	39	1	?	?	?
7	41	2	?	?	?
8	29	3	?	?	?
9	33	5	?	?	?
10	31	2	?	?	?

Table 7.34

7.5 Exploiting sampling results and control charts in decision making

The various control charts introduced and discussed in this chapter are all examples of the transformation of data into information. They are designed to capture and disseminate knowledge; all three are therefore used in decision making. Such decisions vary in degree of structure (i.e. abstractiveness of the data and information), ranging from detailed and highly structured to circumstantial and unstructured. The impact of these decisions may be strategic (long term), tactical (mid-term), or operational (short term).

Most strategic decisions are based on an unstructured and predictive approach (given the uncertainty of the outcome), while operational decisions are fact-based and therefore highly structured. Tactical decisions often lie in between, depending also on the temporal urgency of the decision: the more urgent the decision the more operational it is likely to be and the shorter the time frame for the decision.

This affords the spectrum of management decisions as depicted in Figure 7.41.

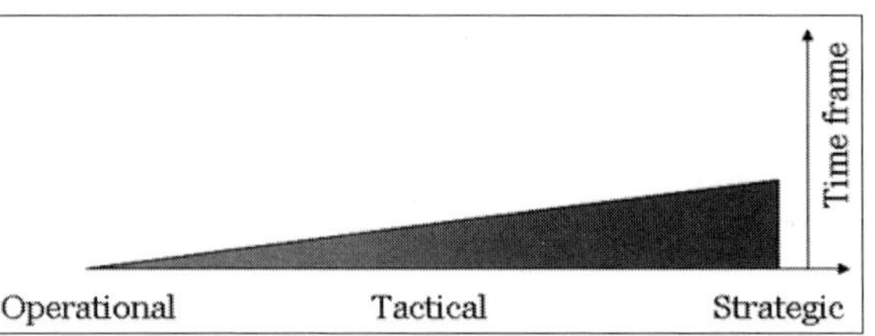

Figure 7.41
Spectrum of management decisions

In practice, therefore, the domain of management decisions (which are usually at three levels: senior, middle, and junior management) often afford a domain (see shaded area in Figure 7.42) that takes into account the level of abstractiveness and decision time

X

abstractiveness availability of appropriate data and information.

structured structured decisions are the decisions which are made under the established situation.

unstructured unstructured decisions are the decisions which are made under the emergent situation.

strategic strategic decisions are the highest level with decisions focusing on general direction and long-term business goals.

tactical tactical decisions support strategic decisions and tend to be medium range, with medium significance, and with moderate consequences.

operational these are everyday decisions used to support tactical decisions. Their impact is immediate, short-term, short range, and usually has a low impact cost to the organization.

spectrum of management decisions explains the three levels of management decision making: operational, tactical, and strategic.

frame. However, the same framework can be used in lower or non-management positions—as on the shop floor, where blue collar workers can be found alongside quality control experts and the line manager. Whatever the situation the objective is to reduce uncertainty, clarify what data, information, and knowledge truly matters and take the most suitable path to exploit all three in decision making.

In addition, decision making can feature competing qualitative and quantitative schools of thought. Those who favour the latter are typically in operational positions in organizations and hence favour tools such as quality control charts. Those who favour the former do this because their mindset is 'planning for the future', understanding the latent needs of the customer, capturing trends and therefore are taking a strategic view. Such people use tools like surveys, questionnaires, interviews to improve their decision making.

In practice, though, decisions will often contemplate both schools of thought and decisions will lie in the shaded area depicted in Figure 7.42.

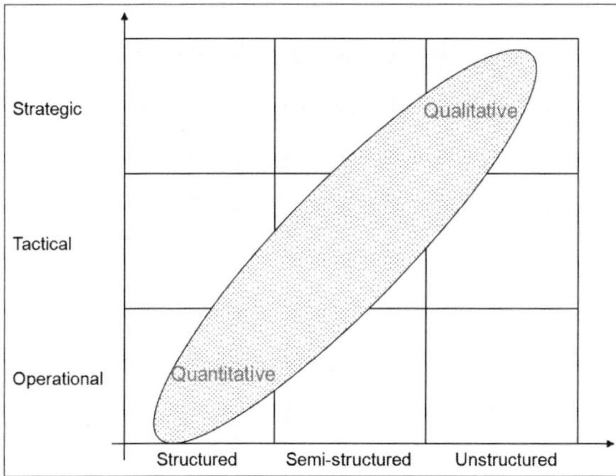

Figure 7.42
Management decisions
(adapted from Vercellis, 2010)

Nevertheless, in the concluding part of this chapter we will focus on the quantitative approach, even though long-term value tends to be more qualitative in nature.

7.5.1 Acceptance and acceptance sampling in quality control

Quality control in manufacturing environments is typically focused on the acceptance of finished products or sub-assemblies or parts that go towards manufacturing finished goods. The same process can be applied to services and indeed anything that has the following key features:

- Known batch size: the size of the batch or lot that is being assessed where the batch or lot is viewed as being representative of the population, production output, goods supplied, etc.
- Reliable acceptance method: the acceptance sampling methodology used to accept or reject the batch of products or sampled service is capable of detecting unacceptable products or services.

- Established criteria and rules: these are the criteria of acceptance and relative rules that qualify products in a quantitative manner.

Figures 7.31 and 7.32 introduced the concept of acceptance or rejection; but here we focus the case of product acceptance and relative acceptance. Product acceptance can be viewed from the market or the producer and decisions depend on which view we take.

Whichever view we take the decision will be based on a hypothesis which leads to the four outcomes depicted in Figure 7.43.

		Batch Condition	
		H_0 True Good quality	H_0 False Poor Quality
Decision	Accept Batch	Correct Decision	Type 2 error (acceptance of poor quality batch)
	Reject Batch	Type 1 error (rejection of good quality batch)	Correct decision

Figure 7.43
Acceptance sampling matrix

In other words, the hypothesis will lead us to make a decision which is either correct or incorrect. In acceptance sampling the two consequences of concern are the type 1 or type 2 errors:

1. A type 1 error has repercussions for the producer (and/or supplier) since a batch would be rejected even though of good quality.
2. A type 2 error has immediate repercussions for the receiver of the product, e.g. trade partner or end-user, and subsequently for the producer too.

7.5.2 The null and alternative hypotheses in acceptance sampling

In acceptance methodology the relative testing requires that we set up two competing hypotheses that are formulated as competing statements. More specifically, acceptance is based on a statistical procedure involving the 'null' hypothesis and the alternative hypothesis. These hypotheses are mutually exclusive and exhaustive. The null hypothesis is much more common because it refers to a statement or condition being tested while the alternative hypothesis takes stage if the former is not proven. So, suppose that for a batch the statement concerns the conformity of the batch versus some measure. In the first case H_0 would refer to a good and acceptable batch quality while in the second case, $H_{1,}$ is a bad and unacceptable batch quality.

Clearly, if H_0 is negated then H_1 is proven (and hence the name alternative hypothesis). Because of the dominance of null hypothesis reasoning the result of acceptance sampling is always given in terms of H_0—thus we reject H_0 in favour of H_1 or do not reject H_0. What is often confusing is that if we conclude 'Do not reject H_0,' this does not necessarily mean that the null hypothesis is true, it only suggests that there is sufficient evidence

X

type 2 error when a survey finds that a result is not significant, though in fact it is.

type 1 error finding a result statistically significant when in fact it is not.

alternative hypothesis in statistical hypothesis testing, the alternative hypothesis and the null hypothesis are the two rival hypotheses which are compared by a statistical hypothesis test.

against H_0 and therefore in favour of H_1. Rejecting the null hypothesis suggests that the alternative hypothesis may be true, in other words the latter is more than likely to be true. The null hypothesis is traditionally assumed to be true unless we find evidence that demonstrates the opposite. If we find that it is unlikely that the null hypothesis holds we assume the alternative hypothesis is more likely to be correct.

In acceptance sampling we are interested in inferring something about the sample with respect to the entire batch. Here we can relate batch also to population or when comparing batches or populations. In the first case the sample will have a certain sample size (n) and a criterion (c) is used to assess the validity i.e. quality of the batch (population) from which the sample is taken. For example, suppose we are sampling a batch of products (n = 50) and the criterion for acceptance is zero defects for the entire sample (c = 0). In this circumstance we have:

- Accept batch if no defects are found.
- Reject batch if one or more defects are found.

In this case we have respectively H_0 = True and H_0 = False;. we have made the correct decision (see the first and third quadrants of Figure 7.43). The problem lies in the second and fourth quadrants of Figure 7.43 and hence acceptance sampling has benefits in assessing the relative risks. For type 1 errors even though we have found a defect it may not be effective to reject all the batch especially if the batch size is large (e.g. 1000 or more products). This is usually considered to be the manufacturer or producers perspective since it implies damage for both these parties. On the other hand for type 2 errors we may accept the batch even though we know that samples have uncovered poor quality. This is usually considered as being the 'consumers' perspective because they might encounter the defect when they buy the product from the batch in question. In practice it is very rare not to accept some defects and conventionally, a minimum probability of defectiveness is judged acceptable. Hence producers view the null hypothesis in acceptance sampling as a way of identifying and assessing risk when accepting poor quality. This circumstance is computed using the binomial probability function.

7.5.3 The binomial probability function for acceptance sampling

To exploit the binomial probability function the following information is needed:

n	the sample size
π	The proportion of defective products or items within the batch or typical batch
x	The number of defective products or items found in the sample
p(x)	The probability of x defective items in the sample

The binomial probability function is expressed in Equation 7.26 as follows:

$$P(X) = \frac{n!}{x!(n-x)!}\pi(1-\pi)^{(n-1)} \tag{7.26}$$

An example will show how this function is used.

Example 7.27

A sample of ten products is taken from a shipping consignment and a defective proportion of 3% is considered to be acceptable for the overall batch, determine the probability that no defective products will be found in the sample.

$$p(x) = \frac{n!}{x!(n-x)!}\pi^x(1-\pi)^{(n-x)} = \frac{10!}{0!(10-0)!}0.03^0(1-0.03)^{(10-0)} = 0.7374$$

The result provided by this equation states that for $\pi = 0.03$ the probability of accepting a poor quality batch is 0.74 (i.e. 74%, which is likely on the spectrum of probability: 1 being certain, 0 (zero) being impossible).

We can equally state in the same conditions that there is 1 – 0.74 = 0.26 or 26% chance that a good quality batch of products is rejected.

Hence the situation is illustrated in Figure 7.44.

	H_0 True Good quality	H_0 False Poor Quality
Accept Batch	Correct Decision	74%
Reject Batch	26%	Correct decision

Figure 7.44

Interpretation We may conclude that the null hypothesis or its alternative can also be used as a decision tool in sampling.

Example 7.28

A male card player claims that he can draw three consecutive aces, repeatedly, and is willing to bet against anyone. Using the null hypothesis prove that this claim is a trick. Assuming that the three cards will be chosen at random and without any trick a possible null hypothesis would be if H_0 is TRUE then the selection process is entirely random and indeed the card player is not a trickster. If H_0 is FALSE then the selection process is not random and some form of trick is being played, implying the card player is a trickster.

Drawing one ace amounts to a probability of about 7% (there are 4 aces in a 52-card pack), which is unlikely but nevertheless possible. If two consecutive aces are drawn then the probability is 0.0769 * 0.0769 = 0.0059 or about 0.6%, this is highly unlikely and already merits serious doubts about the trickster. If three aces are drawn then this amounts to a probability of 0.045%, which is virtually impossible. To really prove that the null hypothesis is FALSE we could ask the trickster to repeat the experiment or add a fourth ace, which amounts to 0.003% or three chances out of a million.

Example 7.29

Let us review Example 7.28 but this time for five different sample sizes 50, 40, 30, 20, 10 and exploit the binomial probability function in Excel 2010 (i.e. BINOM.DIST).

For the case treated in Example 7.28 we have =BINOM.DIST(0,10,0.03,TRUE). Similarly we can complete Table 7.35.

Figure 7.45 illustrates the Excel solution.

Sample size 'n'	Excel function
10	=BINOM.DIST(0,10,0.03,TRUE)
20	=BINOM.DIST(0,20,0.03,TRUE)
30	=BINOM.DIST(0,30,0.03,TRUE)
40	=BINOM.DIST(0,40,0.03,TRUE)
50	=BINOM.DIST(0,50,0.03,TRUE)

Table 7.35

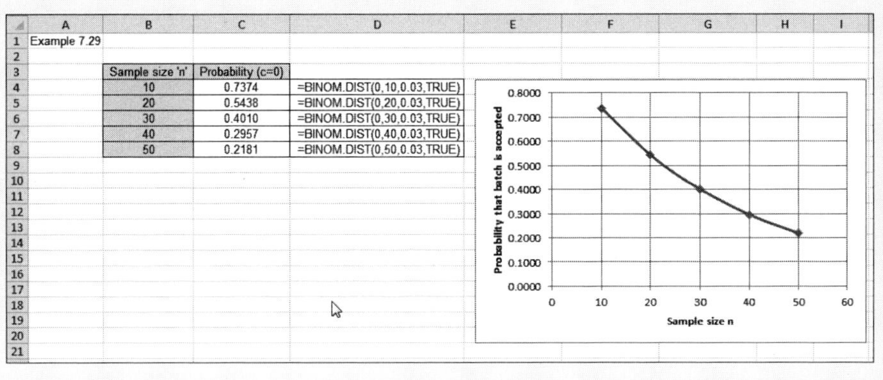

Example 7.29

Sample size 'n'	Probability (c=0)	
10	0.7374	=BINOM.DIST(0,10,0.03,TRUE)
20	0.5438	=BINOM.DIST(0,20,0.03,TRUE)
30	0.4010	=BINOM.DIST(0,30,0.03,TRUE)
40	0.2957	=BINOM.DIST(0,40,0.03,TRUE)
50	0.2181	=BINOM.DIST(0,50,0.03,TRUE)

Figure 7.45

7.5.4 OC–Operating characteristic curve

In Example 7.29 the probability curve for an acceptance sampling case was provided. More specifically, the sample size varied between 10 to 50 while c = 0, the probability of defective products was fixed at 3% and the null hypothesis set to TRUE. The curve was built according to the results provided by the binomial probability (BP) function and is known as the operating characteristic curve or simply OC curve. However, depending on the values associated to the BP function a family of curves can be generated as shown in Figure 7.46.

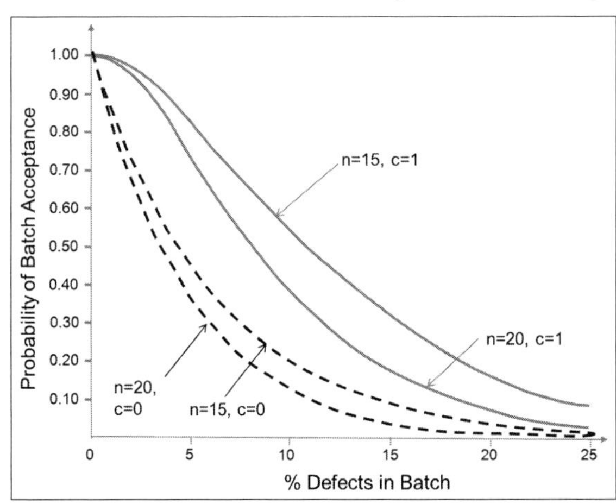

Figure 7.46

Operating characteristic family of curves

operating characteristic curve the OC curve is used in sampling inspection. It plots the probability of accepting a batch of items against the quality level of the batch.

Appendix 2 also provides a set of standard tables built with the BP function in Equation 7.26. In Figure 7.37 two sample sizes (n = 15 or 20) are considered and two reject conditions (c = 0 or 1) are considered for a varying percentage defects in the batch. Example 7.30 will show how to interpret this graph and relate it to the null hypothesis.

Example 7.30

A sample of 15 and 20 products is taken from a shipping consignment and a defective proportion of 5% is considered to be acceptable for the overall batch, determine the probability that no defective products and one product will be found in the sample. We have four possible cases with the probability calculated from Equation (7.26).

Case 1 N = 15 and c = 0 $p(x) = \frac{15!}{0!(15-0)!}0.05^0(1-0.05)^{(15-0)} = 0.4633$

Case 2 N = 20 and c = 0 $p(x) = \frac{20!}{0!(20-0)!}0.05^0(1-0.05)^{(20-0)} = 0.3585$

Case 3 N = 15 and c = 1 $p(x) = \frac{15!}{1!(15-1)!}0.05^1(1-0.05)^{(15-1)} = 0.8290$

Case 4 N = 20 and c = 1 $p(x) = \frac{20!}{1!(20-1)!}0.05^1(1-0.05)^{(20-1)} = 0.7358$

Figure 7.47 illustrates the Excel solution:

	A	B	C	D	E
1					
2	Case ID	n	c	p	Binomial Probability
3	1	15	0	0.05	=BINOM.DIST(C3,B3,D3,TRUE)
4	2	20	0	0.05	=BINOM.DIST(C4,B4,D4,TRUE)
5	3	15	1	0.05	=BINOM.DIST(C5,B5,D5,TRUE)
6	4	20	1	0.05	=BINOM.DIST(C6,B6,D6,TRUE)

Figure 7.47

Figure 7.48 illustrates the operating characteristic curve for the Example 7.30 data.

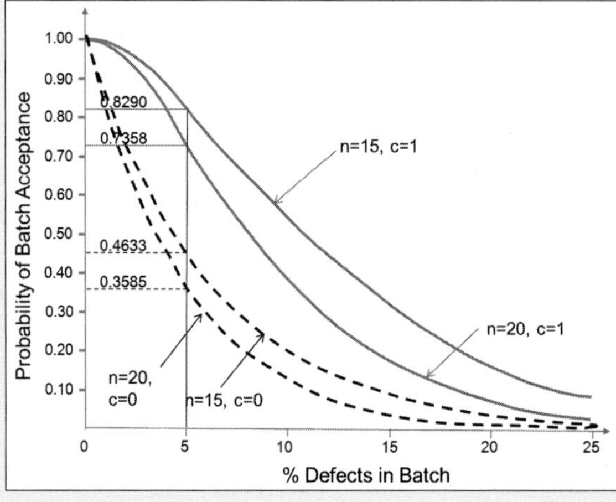

Figure 7.48

❊ **Interpretation** The interpretation of the OC curve or graph is as follows:

1. Type 1 errors are indicated with the Greek letter α and are often referred to as the 'producer's' risk. In this case we discuss the probability that a good batch is rejected and will have p_0 defective products or items.
2. Type 2 errors are indicated with the Greek letter β that are often referred to as the 'customer's or consumer's' risk. In this case we discuss the probability that a poor batch is accepted and will have p_1 defective products or items.

Example 7.31 shows how these are exploited and contextualized.

Example 7.31

A company is evaluating both producer and consumer risks for a certain product and relative process. The conditions are: one dozen samples (n = 12), x = 1 and $\pi = 0.05$ and 0.1 i.e. $p_0 = 0.05$ (5%) and $p_1 = 0.1$ (10%). Discuss the acceptance of both risks under these conditions.

Figure 7.49 is created by making reference to the table provided in appendix 2 and is provided in a dedicated Excel worksheet ('Appendix 2 binomial probabilities):

	A	B	C	D	E	F	G	H	I	J	K	L
1							π					
2	n	x	0.01	0.02	0.03	0.04	0.05	0.06	0.07	0.08	0.09	0.1
33	12	0	0.8864	0.7847	0.6938	0.6127	0.5404	0.4759	0.4186	0.3677	0.3225	0.2824
34		1	0.1074	0.1922	0.2575	0.3064	0.3413	0.3645	0.3781	0.3837	0.3827	0.3766
35		2	0.0060	0.0216	0.0438	0.0702	0.0988	0.1280	0.1565	0.1835	0.2082	0.2301

Figure 7.49

From the above table (see Figure 7.49) excerpt we have: $\alpha = 0.3413$ and therefore the producer's risk is: $1 - 0.3413 = 0.6587$, and $\beta = 0.3766$ and therefore the consumer's risk is 0.3766.

So in these circumstances the company would have to decide if both risks are acceptable, the consumer's risk is probably too high for acceptance. The situation is illustrated in Figure 7.50.

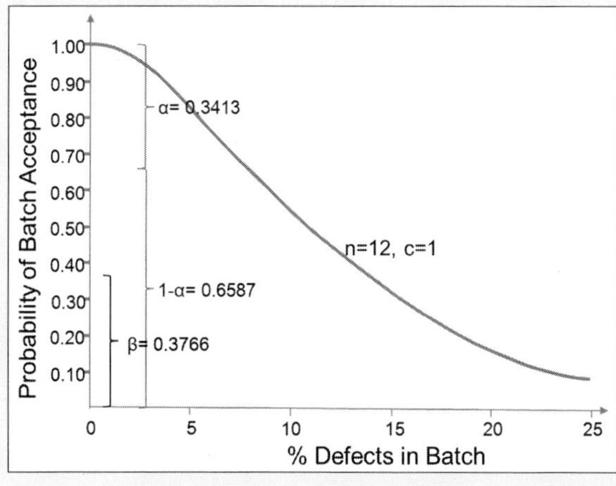

Figure 7.50

(NB. Drawing not to scale)

7.5.5 Acceptance sampling as a process

Let us consider three cases:

1. Either a product batch is received by a manufacturer (as in the case of parts for assembly) or finished products are delivered to a trade partner for the marketplace.
2. A service provider farms out service work to a 'thirds' company who will then implement the work order; e.g. a telephone company requests a 'thirds' company to carry out maintenance work on their behalf. Alternatively, the service provider might measure service performance (e.g. connection speed for internet services) and views the batch as a bundle of services or customers.
3. Surveys are to be processed for final reporting and a batch of surveys is to be processed.

All three cases are to be checked for quality before accepting, releasing and/or processing of the complete batch. For each case a sample is taken and the **acceptance sampling process** started as shown in Figure 7.51.

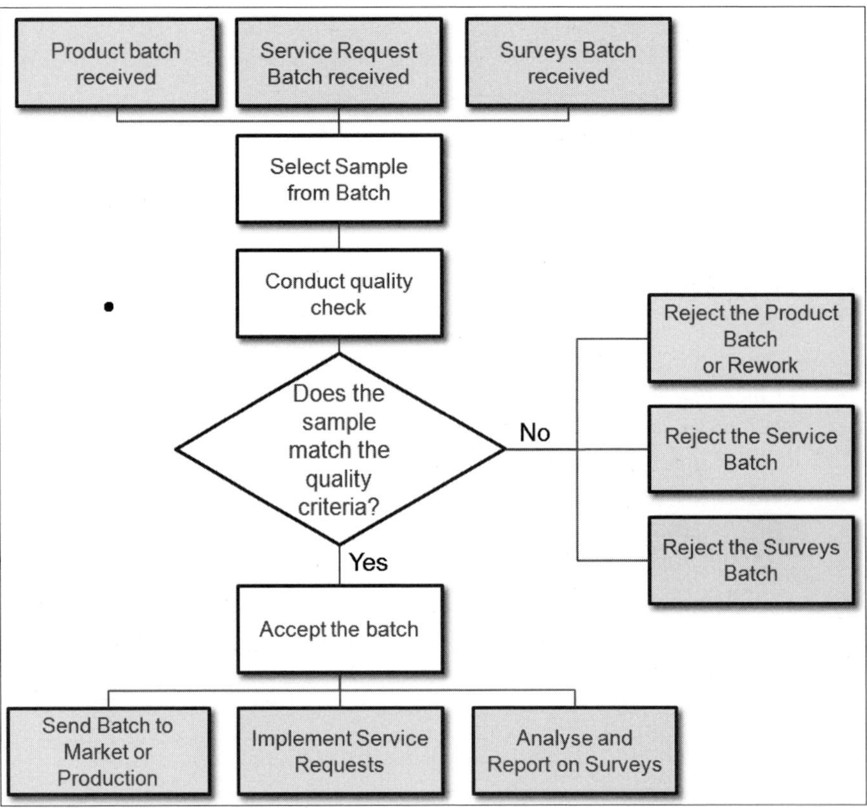

Figure 7.51
Acceptance sampling process

acceptance sampling process acceptance sampling uses statistical sampling to determine whether to accept or reject a production lot of material.

The quality check will require one or more quality variables and the choice of one or more quality control measures (i.e. quality criteria). Table 7.36 reports some possible candidates.

Case	Possible quality variables	Possible quality criteria
Products for production or market	Physical measures such as size, weight, length, etc.	Tolerances on physical measures, etc.
Service performance or requests	Speed, mean time to repair or service, etc.	Tolerances on performance measures, etc.
Surveys	Completeness of surveys	Number of surveys (or parts of) correctly completed

Table 7.36 Acceptance sampling as a process

Student exercises

Please visit the Online Resource Centre which accompanies this textbook for solutions to the student exercises and techniques in practice questions.

X7.18 A sample of 12 products is taken from a shipping consignment and it is known that the defective proportion varies, namely 2, 3, and 5% are considered acceptable for the overall batch. Determine the probability that no defective products will be found in the sample for each of the percentages.

X7.19 Returning to exercise X7.18, consider the case of 5% for the defective proportion. Provide a summary of the null hypothesis for this case (see Figure 7.31 for an example of a possible summary).

X7.20 A repair service company processes customer requests for product service on behalf of a large manufacturer of washing machines. The manufacturer now wants to assess the performance of this service company, what quality variables and criteria would you consider for this assessment?

X7.21 A market research company conducts frequent prospective customer interviews such as focus groups. Each response is collected in a survey document that summarizes what each respondent states or answers. The surveys are then assessed and report sent to the company who requested the market research. If you were the market research company how would you go about checking data quality both from a quality control and quality assurance perspective? Moreover, how would you decide whether or not each survey collected is acceptable?

■ Techniques in practice

TP1 The following dataset covers the price of gasoline in the US between 1976 and 2003. If the price of petrol in January 2004 was 1.592 US$ per gallon would you classify it an outlier with respect to all the months of 2003? Using the five data summary method, determine the five key features of this method for each of the years shown in Table 7.37.

Year	Jan	Feb	Mar	Apr	May	Jun	Jul	Aug	Sep	Oct	Nov	Dec
1976	0.605	0.600	0.594	0.592	0.600	0.616	0.623	0.628	0.630	0.629	0.629	0.626
1977	0.627	0.637	0.643	0.651	0.659	0.665	0.667	0.667	0.666	0.665	0.664	0.665
1978	0.648	0.647	0.647	0.649	0.655	0.663	0.674	0.682	0.688	0.690	0.695	0.705
1979	0.716	0.730	0.755	0.802	0.844	0.901	0.949	0.988	1.020	1.028	1.041	1.065
1980	1.131	1.207	1.252	1.264	1.266	1.269	1.271	1.267	1.257	1.250	1.250	1.258
1981	1.298	1.382	1.417	1.412	1.400	1.391	1.382	1.376	1.376	1.371	1.369	1.365
1982	1.358	1.334	1.284	1.225	1.237	1.309	1.331	1.323	1.307	1.295	1.283	1.260
1983	1.230	1.187	1.152	1.215	1.259	1.277	1.288	1.285	1.274	1.255	1.241	1.231
1984	1.216	1.209	1.210	1.227	1.236	1.229	1.212	1.196	1.203	1.209	1.207	1.193
1985	1.148	1.131	1.159	1.205	1.231	1.241	1.242	1.229	1.216	1.204	1.207	1.208
1986	1.194	1.120	0.981	0.888	0.923	0.955	0.890	0.843	0.860	0.831	0.821	0.823
1987	0.862	0.905	0.912	0.934	0.941	0.958	0.971	0.995	0.990	0.976	0.976	0.961
1988	0.933	0.913	0.904	0.930	0.955	0.955	0.967	0.987	0.974	0.957	0.949	0.930
1989	0.918	0.926	0.940	1.065	1.119	1.114	1.092	1.057	1.029	1.027	0.999	0.980
1990	1.042	1.037	1.023	1.044	1.061	1.088	1.084	1.190	1.294	1.378	1.377	1.354
1991	1.247	1.143	1.082	1.104	1.156	1.160	1.127	1.140	1.143	1.122	1.134	1.123
1992	1.073	1.054	1.058	1.079	1.136	1.179	1.174	1.158	1.158	1.154	1.159	1.136
1993	1.117	1.108	1.098	1.112	1.129	1.130	1.109	1.097	1.085	1.127	1.113	1.070
1994	1.043	1.051	1.045	1.064	1.080	1.106	1.136	1.182	1.177	1.152	1.163	1.143
1995	1.129	1.120	1.115	1.140	1.200	1.226	1.195	1.164	1.148	1.127	1.101	1.101
1996	1.129	1.124	1.162	1.251	1.323	1.299	1.272	1.240	1.234	1.227	1.250	1.260
1997	1.261	1.255	1.235	1.231	1.226	1.229	1.205	1.253	1.277	1.242	1.213	1.177
1998	1.131	1.082	1.041	1.052	1.092	1.094	1.079	1.052	1.033	1.042	1.028	0.986
1999	0.972	0.955	0.991	1.177	1.178	1.148	1.189	1.255	1.280	1.274	1.264	1.298
2000	1.301	1.369	1.541	1.506	1.498	1.617	1.593	1.51	1.582	1.559	1.555	1.489
2001	1.472	1.484	1.447	1.564	1.729	1.64	1.482	1.427	1.531	1.362	1.263	1.131
2002	1.139	1.13	1.241	1.407	1.421	1.404	1.412	1.423	1.422	1.449	1.448	1.394
2003	1.473	1.641	1.748	1.659	1.542	1.514	1.524	1.628	1.728	1.603	1.535	1.494

Table 7.37

TP2 A company manufactures control panels for domestic appliances and a key part of the finishing process is the screen printing of the panels. Recently, due to bad tooling, poorly trained staff, and misaligned tooling, one particular machine is producing too many defective panels. Table 7.38 shows the results of samples taken every 15 minutes for a given day. For this data build the relevant 'p' chart and, assuming p = 0.05, discuss the current status of the process.

Sample	Size	Number of defects	Sample	Size	Number of defects
1	49	6	17	42	1
2	47	2	18	45	4
3	46	2	19	42	3
4	46	0	20	47	1
5	43	1	21	51	7
6	44	3	22	50	7
7	45	2	23	44	3
8	45	0	24	43	5
9	47	1	25	50	10
10	46	2	26	46	8
11	42	2	27	49	8
12	45	1	28	46	3
13	46	3	29	49	10
14	48	6	30	42	12
15	50	6	31	50	12
16	48	6	32	45	9

Table 7.38

■ Summary

In this chapter we have discussed several key concepts and tools in data quality, data summarization, and statistical quality control. First, we focused on understanding the background to data quality and the need to use 'clean' data. This allowed us to examine some basic tools and methods for spotting outliers that otherwise offset and corrupt the subsequent analysis. We then moved onto the exploitation of descriptive statistics in a combined way; this afforded a fresh look at the aggregation of some basic descriptive tools introduced in Chapter 2.

This aggregation not only allowed us to summarize our findings of the analysis but also to tell what the data is already telling us even during the preliminary phase of data mining and analysis. To this end we also provided a new tool called the box and whisker plot that captures and summarizes the dataset, as well as providing a graphical tool to spot and contextualize outliers.

We then moved into the domain of quality control and how basic quality charts and tools help the quality control and assurance worker to make better decisions. This also required an overview of decisions and decision making and provided us with the necessary background to the null and alternative hypotheses in acceptance sampling.

We concluded the chapter by examining acceptance sampling in closer detail and introduced the operating characteristic curve and viewing acceptance sampling also as a process.

Student exercise answers

For all figures listed below, please see the Online Resource Centre.

X7.1 Return to Example 7.4 and set a z-score limit for data acceptance of +/–1.5 then plot the cleaned data. The data values 20, 40, 42 and 45 are outliers with z-scores as indicated in Table X7.1.

Data value	20	40	42	45
z-score	−1.627161	1.51494	1.82915	2.30047

Table X7.1

X7.2 Repeat Example 7.5 but compare the linear function to a second order polynomial plot based on the correlation coefficient. Which of the two plots provides a better result and why? The comparison is summarized in Table X7.2.

Linear	$y = 0.769x + 19.206$	$R^2 = 0.9524$
2nd order polynomial	$y = 0.016x2 + 0.3057x + 21.523$	$R^2 = 0.9738$

Table X7.2

For the given dataset (no outliers removed) the best result is provided by the second order polynomial. This is confirmed by the correlation coefficient which is higher ($R^2 = 0.9738$) for the polynomial.

X7.3 What is the 'deviation of the mean'? Plot the 'deviation of mean' column graph (i.e. deviation for each data value with respect to the mean) for the uncleaned data in Example 7.4. The deviation of the mean is the difference between the mean value of the dataset with respect to each data value. The mean value is 30.36. The dataset and relative plot is therefore as given in Figure X7.3.

Figure X7.3

X7.4 In a normal distributed population 68% are to be considered acceptable for a given trial. What is the limit value for such a case if the mean is 50 and the standard deviation is 10? The upper limit is given when $s = +10$ and we are 1 std. deviation from the mean (i.e. 68%) hence: $x_i = zs + \bar{x} = 1 \times (10) + 50 = 60$, or $x_i = zs + \bar{x} = -1 \times (10) + 50 = 40$. Since the distribution is normal the limit value is defined as $40 \leq x_i \leq 60$.

X7.5 What would be the answer if the limit in exercise X7.4 was now raised to 97%? First we need to translate 97% into the number of std. deviations. By simple inspection we know that it will be more or less between 2 and 3σ, but to determine it exactly we exploit the table for the standard normal curve. The first step is to realize that this table shows only the positive z values hence we convert 97% into have 0.97 and then half its value to get 0.4850. Looking up the table we see $z = 2.17$, and using this value we obtain: $x_i = zs + \bar{x} = -2.17 \times (10) + 50 = 71.7$.

X7.6 For the following dataset carry out a two data and five data summary exercise. Compare and comment on the results of both methods: 29, 30, 67, 45, 67, 38, 19, 28, 41, 56. In the first instance the mean and standard deviation is as given by Table X7.6a.

Mean	42
Standard deviation	15.84

Table X7.6a

In the case of the five data summary we have as given by table X7.6b:

Minimum	19
1st quartile	29.00
Median	39.50
Third quartile	53.25
Maximum	67

Table X7.6b

X7.7 Reconsider the data in Example 7.4. Conduct a five data summary and compare your findings to what is discussed in Example 7.4. Table X7.7 illustrates the five number summary:

Minimum	20
1st quartile	25.75
Median	29.5
3rd quartile	33.5
Maximum	45

Table X7.7

The IQR is 33.5-25.75 i.e. 7.75 and the upper and lower limits for box and whisker plot are:

- Lower limit = $Q_1 - 1.5$ IQR = 25.75 – 7.75 = 18
- Upper limit = $Q_3 + 1.5$ IQR = 33.5 + 7.75 = 41.25

This last result shows that the data value 45 is indeed an outlier and doubts about data value 42 are justified.

X7.8 Analyse the data provided in Example 7.4 by plotting a box and whisker plot. Then compare the five data summary method to the B & W plot obtained.

Figure X7.8

The five data summary method does not have the interquartile measure (which the B & W plot has) so it is difficult to establish if data values 20 and 22 are also outliers. However, the B & W plot provides an immediate indication that such values are acceptable. It is also worth noting that data value 40 is not an outlier for both methods discussed.

X7.9 Calculate the UCL and LCL for a R quality control plot for the following dataset: 370, 400, 410, 420, 520, 520, 560, 570, 330, 390, 430, 440, 440, 440, 450, 460, 460, 490, 570, 600, 610. The dataset refers to 21 samples or sub-groups with 10 observations each. Each data value provided in the dataset is the average range for the relative 10 observations. Referring to table 7.22 the values of D4 and D3 constants are given in Table X7.9.

No. of observations	10
R mean	470.48
D4	1.78
D3	0.80
UCL	836.04
LCL	374.97

Table X7.9

X7.10 Plot the data provided in Exercise X7.9 and determine if the process is in or out of control.

Figure X7.10

From the R chart the process is essentially in control although two of the samples were found to exceed the LCL and the data values appear to be heading towards the UCL.

X7.11 Figure X7.11a shows a 'p' plot for a product that has gone from launch to full-blown production—from a very small rate of production to a large production output. The production has therefore been ramped-up in steps. In the chart each step represents a sample size that corresponds to each step-up in production: sample size may be considered proportionally constant and representative after the first step. Comment on the graph and provide your conclusions in terms of quality.

Figure X7.11a

The graph shows that as production output grows (12 steps are shown in the graph) so the product quality is stabilizing closer to the set mean for the production (approx. 30). Sample sizes are proportionally constant after the first step: this means that as production increases so the sample size increases as well. Quality does not appear to be in control because even though the UCL and LCL values are constantly revised to reflect production and sample size, the sample measurements are outside these bounds. Indeed, up to step 6 the production quality was more or less in control and from step 7 onwards the quality is outside the UCL or LCL bounds (step 8 excluded). This could possibly indicate that the process is incapable of reproducing the requested quality levels for the current production output.

Figure X7.11b

X7.12 Figure X7.12 shows an 'np' plot. Basing your judgement exclusively on the chart shown and asuming the sample size was 100 for all cases, what would be the highest and lowest percantage defects found in the samples? What is the average number of defects found across all samples?

Figure X7.12

The process is clearly in control with a mean of 4 and a UCL value and LCL value equal to 10 and 0 respectively. The highest number of defects occurs at sample 17 with a value of 8 or 8%. The lowest is sample 8 with no defects, that is, 0%.

X7.13 The number of complaints received by a call centre is shown in Table X7.13.

Day	Number of complaints	Day	Number of complaints
1	45	13	39
2	50	14	40
3	40	15	109
4	100	16	68
5	60	17	21
6	55	18	39
7	54	19	97
8	13	20	69
9	16	21	28
10	96	22	14
11	110	23	19
12	78	24	87

Table X7.13

Determine the UCL and LCL values for the process. What is the mean number of complaints expected for the following 24 days? The mean number of complaints is the number of occurrences (1347) divided by the number of days (24)—hence $\bar{c} = 56.1 \cong 56$. Thus the UCL and LCL values are 79 (78.6) and 34 (33.7), respectively.

X7.14 Data transmitted between facilities in a large global corporation is monitored on a hourly basis and it was found that the error rate is 0.01%, which is considered acceptable by the corporation. The following dataset was collected over a 48-day period (Table X7.14):

Sample	Number of errors	Sample	Number of errors	Sample	Number of errors	Sample	Number of errors
1	1	13	1	25	1	37	0
2	2	14	0	26	0	38	0
3	0	15	0	27	0	39	0
4	1	16	0	28	0	40	1
5	0	17	0	29	0	41	2
6	1	18	1	30	0	42	1
7	1	19	2	31	1	43	4
8	0	20	1	32	1	44	1
9	0	21	3	33	1	45	1
10	0	22	1	34	0	46	0
11	1	23	1	35	2	47	0
12	2	24	1	36	2	48	0

Table X7.14

Plot the 'c' chart? Why is the c chart more suitable than the u chart? The occurrence proportion indicator for the 'c' chart, that is, the 'c' bar, is: $\bar{c} = \frac{38}{48} = 0.7917 \cong 1$.

This means that there were a total of 38 errors over the time period of 48 days. Clearly, we only have one fixed sample size for each of the 48 days of the trial or monitoring period. The UCL and LCL are:

$$UCL = \bar{c} + 3\sqrt{0.7917} = 0.7917 + 3\sqrt{0.7917} = 3.46 \cong 4$$

$$LCL = \bar{u} - 3\sqrt{0.7917} \rightarrow 0$$

The chart is:

Figure X7.14

The 'c' chart is used when the areas of opportunity are of constant size while the 'u' chart is used when the areas of opportunity are not of constant size. In this latter case it would be necessary to calculate the UCL and LCL for each subgroup.

X7.15 Reconsider the dataset in exercise X7.14. Is the data transmission process under control? And which sample(s) should be considered as borderline in terms of quality of transmission? The data transmission process is under control and only day 43 was near the UCL (the number of errors = 4). The only other day was No.21 which had 3 errors.

X7.16 Two datasets are being considered for quality control per sample. The first dataset has a fixed sample size while the second has variable sample size. What control charts do you consider to be applicable for the two datasets? The control charts are applied in the following conditions (see Table X7.16):

Fixed sample size: n = 1	C bar chart	You will have only 1 UCl and 1 LCL
Variable sample size: n = varies	U bar chart	You will have most likely different UCL and LCLs for each sample size

Table X7.16

X7.17 The following dataset has been collected concerning the number of defects in freshly picked fruit. Complete Table X7.17a.

Sample	Sample size	Defects recorded	Defects per fruit	LCL	UCL
1	30	0	?	?	?
2	27	2	?	?	?
3	25	1	?	?	?
4	35	3	?	?	?
5	42	0	?	?	?
6	39	1	?	?	?
7	41	2	?	?	?
8	29	3	?	?	?
9	33	5	?	?	?
10	31	2	?	?	?

Table X7.17a

The completed table is:

Sample	Sample size	Defects recorded	Defects per fruit	LCL	UCL
1	30	0	0.00000	−0.07380	0.18826
2	27	2	0.07407	−0.08089	0.19535
3	25	1	0.04000	−0.08631	0.20076
4	35	3	0.08571	−0.06408	0.17854
5	42	0	0.00000	−0.05351	0.16797
6	39	1	0.02564	−0.05769	0.17215
7	41	2	0.04878	−0.05485	0.16931
8	29	3	0.10345	−0.07604	0.19050
9	33	5	0.15152	−0.06770	0.18216
10	31	2	0.06452	−0.07167	0.18613

Total defects	19
Total samples	332
ubar : mean defects	0.057229

Table X7.17b

X7.18 A sample of 12 products is taken from a shipping consignment and it is known that the defective proportion varies, namely 2, 3 and 5% are considered acceptable for the overall batch. Determine the probability that no defective products will be found in the sample for each of the percentages.

Case 1 - 2%

$$p(x) = \frac{n!}{x!(n-x)!}\pi^{x}(1-\pi)^{(n-x)} = \frac{12!}{0!(12-0)!}0.02^{0}(1-0.02)^{(12-0)} = 0.7847$$

The result provided by this equation states that for $\pi = 0.02$ the probability of accepting a poor quality batch is 0.79 (i.e. 79%, which is likely on the spectrum of probability). We can equally state in the same conditions that there is 1 − 0.79 = 0.21 or 21% chance that a good quality batch of products is rejected.

Case 2 - 3%

P(x) = 0.6838 = 0.68 or 68%

Case 3 - 5%

P(x) = 0.5404 = 0.54 or 54%

X7.19 Returning to Exercise X7.18, consider the case of 5% for the defective proportion. Provide a summary of the null hypothesis for this case (see Figure 7.31 for an example of a possible summary). The result provided by this equation states that for $\pi = 0.05$ the probability of accepting a poor quality batch is 0.54 (i.e. 54%, which is almost evens on the spectrum of probability). We can equally state in the same conditions that there is 1 − 0.54 = 0.46 or 46% chance that a good quality batch of products is rejected. The situation is summarized below:

Figure X7.19

X7.20 A repair service company processes customer requests for product service on behalf of a large manufacturer of washing machines. The manufacturer now wants to assess the performance of this service company, what quality variables and criteria would you consider for this assessment? Since we are considering the service and not the product, both the quality variables and criteria need to be in line with the performance of the service. Possible examples are:

- Mean time to repair the washing machine (there may also be a connection with the overall cost of the repair);
- Mean time to answer service call and organize visit to customer's home;
- Customer satisfaction of the service. This could be linked to other details such as 'explanation of the problem', 'suggested recommendations on how to maintain washing machine performance and minimize likelihood of repair', 'technical competency of the service engineer', 'courtesy from service staff' etc.
- Impact on machine performance since repair?
- Follow-up (by service centre) to assess post-repair customer satisfaction;
- Etc.

X7.21 A market research company conducts frequent prospective customer interviews such as focus groups. Each response is collected in a survey document that summarizes what each respondent states or answers. The surveys are then assessed and a report sent to the company who requested the market research.

If you were the market research company's representative how would you go about checking data quality both from a quality control and quality assurance perspective? Moreover, how would you decide if the each survey collected was acceptable or not?

The quality control of surveys such as questionnaires refers to the completeness of the data and not necessarily or, almost certainly not, the correctness. Hence one type of quality control would be to make sure that the name, surname, salary, address, profession, gender, and age of the respondent is recorded. Much will depend on the scope of the survey and the sampling method chosen. However, in all cases, if any questionnaire is found to be incomplete then it is rejected and recorded as unacceptable. In special circumstances parts of the rejected survey may be used. On the other hand, if the questionnaire was complete but parts of it was incorrect (e.g. date of birth was recorded as 1857 instead of 1957, the gender of the respondent was male but 'Mrs' was assigned as his title) the record is wrong and of poor quality. This too may also be judged as being unacceptable and rejected. The type of sampling method may also determine the quality of the survey. For example, if stratified sampling was decided but the identification of the strata is difficult to observe or, worse wrong, then the data collected might be of poor quality or worse, even worthless. A further aspect of surveys concerns the grading of answers. For example, if there is questionnaire question of the type 'How would you rank the new product? – 1 for poor to 5 Excellent' then you may want to consider changing the scale to 1-4 so that 'middle-of-the-road' responses are avoided. Indeed, odd numbered scales (such as 1-Very poor, 2-Poor, 3-Average, 4-Good, 5-Very good) generally tend to attract answers of 3 (i.e. in the middle of the odd scale) while if the scale was even numbered (e.g. 1-Very poor, 2-Poor, 3-Good, 4-Very good) the interviewee would be forced to choose one of the sides of the scale.

To conclude, the reporting phase of the market research is very important. When quality is low the report tends to be more qualitative than quantitative in content. This is because interviewees not only want to express their dissatisfaction in scores and ranking but voice them in writing as well. In general, circumstances like these are not detrimental to findings in the survey but they tend to mask the problem, especially if the expected outcome needs to be more quantitative than qualitative, as when comparing customer satisfaction over periods of time or before and after changes in production processes or product launches.

In this case a multistage survey might be helpful—for example, a first iteration collects qualitative results while the subsequent stages focuses on quantitative measures such as scores and ranking.

TP1 The solution to the problem 'by inspection' was relatively straight forward. However, with larger datasets some form of data elaboration tool is needed. This brought us to consider two approaches both of which are based on the basic statistical functions provided in Excel. The first approach used the minimum, 1st quartile, median, 3rd quartile and maximum functions. The second approach used exclusively the QUARTILE.IINC function for all the 'five data summary' measures. Comparison of the results shows no discrepancies between the two approaches. The dataset used for this exercise was taken from **http://www.wfu.edu/~mccoy/socialjustice/sjcv.pdf** but the original dataset can be found at **http://www.bls.gov/data**. The reader can use this second source to conduct similar assessments. For those interested in understanding what goes on behind the US price index for gasoline prices look-up **http://www.gao.gov/assets/250/246501.pdf** and **http://www.fueleconomy.gov/feg/gasprices/states/index.shtml**.

TP2 The purpose of this exercise was to apply the relevant quality methodologies to a real life case and establish if the process was under control or otherwise. In this specific case even though the process is judged to be under control there is evidence that product quality is getting worse and may well soon exceed the upper limit (UCL). Consequently this process needs additional monitoring effort. Also it is worth noting that Excel provides useful graphing techniques (bar charts, line-graphs etc.) that can be applied in combination to illustrate the quality trend of the process, as is shown in Figure tp7.2b.

Further reading

Textbook resources

1. C. Alexander (1998) *The Handbook of Risk Management and Analysis*, John Wiley & Sons.
2. D. R. Anderson, D. J. Sweeney, T. A. Williams, J. Freeman, and E. Shoesmith (2007) *Statistics for Business and Economics*, Thomson Learning.
3. Anthony, M. and Biggs, N. (2004) *Mathematics for Economics and Finance (Methods and Modelling)*, Cambridge University Press.
4. Blanchard, O. (2003) *Macroeconomics* (3rd edn), Pearson Education.
5. Bradley, T. (2008) *Essential Mathematics for Economics and Business* (3rd edn), Wiley.
6. M. Dodge, and C. Stinson (2011) *Microsoft Excel 2010 Inside Out*, Microsoft Press.

7. R. H. Frank (2003) *Microeconomics and Behaviour* (5th edn), McGraw-Hill.
8. R. Johnson and P. Kuby (2011) *Elementary Statistics*, Cengage Learning.
9. G. Renshaw (2005) *Math for Economics*, Oxford University Press.
10. D. J. Sheskin (2007) *Handbook of Parametric and Non-parametric Statistical Procedures*, CRC Press.
11. J. Soper (2006) *Mathematics for Economics and Business*, Blackwell Publishing.
12. C. Vercellis (2010) *Business Intelligence*, McGraw-Hill.
13. D. Whigham (2007) *Business Data Analysis using Excel*, Oxford University Press.
14. W. L. Winston (2011) *Microsoft Excel 2010: Data Analysis and Business Modeling*, Microsoft Press.

Web resources

1. Engineering Statistics Handbook website:
   http://www.itl.nist.gov/div898/handbook/toolaids/pff/index.htm
2. David Lane, Associate Professor, Departments of Psychology, Statistics, and Management, Rice University. Normal Distribution Applets:
   http://onlinestatbook.com/chapter6/areas_normal.html
3. PQsystems, Software company, Ohio, USA. Quality control in the Health care industry:
   http://www.pqsystems.com/healthcare/HealthcareArticles_p-chart.php
4. UniStat Ltd, London UK, website:
   http://www.unistat.com/quality-control
5. Free Excel spreadsheet datasets:
   http://mathforum.org/workshops/sum96/data.collections/datalibrary/data.set6.html

Formula summary

z-score or index

$$Z_i = \frac{x_i - \bar{x}}{s} \quad (7.1)$$

Average absolute deviation

$$\frac{1}{n}\sum_{i=1}^{n}|x_i - \bar{x}| \quad (7.2)$$

Standard deviation of the sample mean

$$\sigma_{\bar{x}} = \frac{\sigma}{\sqrt{n}} \quad (7.3)$$

UCL equation for xbar chart

$$UCL = \bar{x} + 3\sigma \quad (7.4)$$

LCL equation for xbar chart

$$LCL = \bar{x} - 3\sigma \quad (7.5)$$

Average range

$$\bar{R} = \frac{R_1 + R_2 + R_3 \ldots\ldots R_k}{k} \quad (7.6)$$

Standard deviation in R chart

$$\bar{\sigma}_R = \frac{d_3}{d_2}\bar{R} \quad (7.7)$$

UCL equation for R chart

$$UCL = \bar{R} + 3\bar{\sigma}_R = \bar{R}\left[1 + 3\frac{d_3}{d_2}\right] = \bar{R}D_4 \quad (7.8)$$

LCL equation for R chart

$$LCL = \bar{R} - 3\bar{\sigma}_R = \bar{R}\left[1 - 3\frac{d_3}{d_2}\right] = \bar{R}D_3 \quad (7.9)$$

D_4 equation for R chart

$$D_4 = 1 + 3\frac{d_3}{d_2} \quad (7.10)$$

D_3 equation for R chart

$$D_3 = 1 - 3\frac{d_3}{d_2} \quad (7.11)$$

UCL equation for p chart

$$UCL = \pi + 3\sigma_p \quad (7.12)$$

LCL equation for p chart

$$LCL = \pi - 3\sigma_p \quad (7.13)$$

Standard error of the proportion

$$\sigma_p = \sqrt{\frac{\pi(1 - \pi)}{n}} \quad (7.14)$$

Ratio of number of occurrences

$$\bar{p} = \frac{\sum_{i=1}^{k} p_i}{\sum_{i=1}^{k} n_i} \quad (7.15)$$

Mean in an 'np' chart $= n\pi$ (7.16)

Standard deviation in an 'np' chart $= \sqrt{n\pi(1 - \pi)}$ (7.17)

UCL equation for np chart

$$UCL = n\pi + 3\sqrt{n\pi(1 - \pi)} \quad (7.\ 18)$$

LCL equation for np chart

$$LCL = n\pi - 3\sqrt{n\pi(1-\pi)} \tag{7.19}$$

The upper control limit for 'c' chart:

$$UCL = \bar{c} + 3\sqrt{\bar{c}} \tag{7.20}$$

The lower control limit for 'c' chart:

$$LCL = \bar{c} - 3\sqrt{\bar{c}} \tag{7.21}$$

Occurrence proportion indicator for 'c' chart:

$$\bar{c} = \frac{\sum_{i=1}^{i=k} c_i}{k} \tag{7.22}$$

Occurrence proportion indicator for 'u' chart:

$$\bar{u} = \frac{\sum_{t=1}^{t=m} T_t}{\sum_{t=1}^{t=m} n_t} \tag{7.23}$$

The lower control limit for 'u' chart:

$$LCL = \bar{u} - 3\sqrt{\frac{\bar{u}}{n_t}} \tag{7.24}$$

The upper control limit for 'u' chart:

$$UCL = \bar{u} + 3\sqrt{\frac{\bar{u}}{n_t}} \tag{7.25}$$

Binomial probability function

$$P(X) = \frac{n!}{x!(n-x)!}\pi(1-\pi)^{(n-1)} \tag{7.26}$$

Appendix 7.1

Choosing the right control chart and method

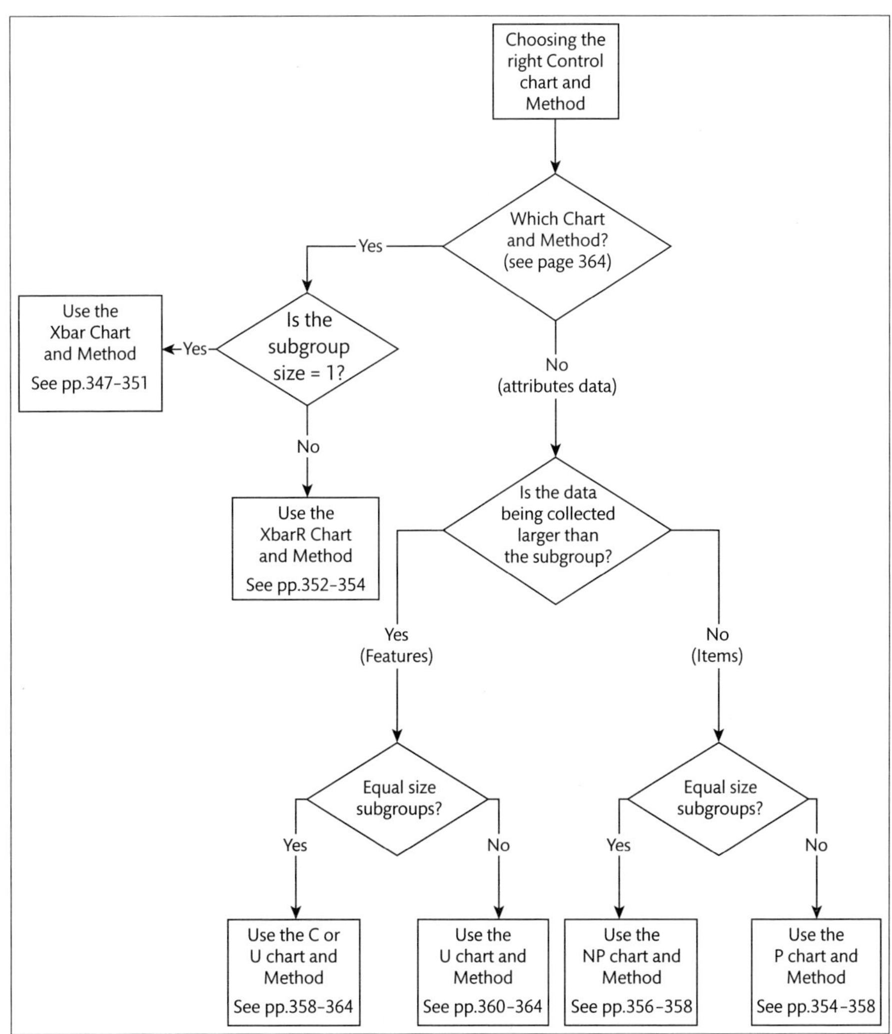

8 Project planning and control

» Overview «

In this chapter we provide the reader with an introduction to the concept of project planning. Techniques that aid management to plan and control projects will be introduced. They will logically connect the various tasks that make up a final project so that we can estimate the shortest project completion time and can then identify which tasks are critical and need to be managed carefully in order to finish the project on time and to cost.

Techniques to study the effect of how uncertain estimation times for the tasks affect the project completion times are introduced. Afterwards we discuss how we can shorten project time by spending money, for example on overtime work or introducing more machines. This is often referred to as crashing a project. We will also introduce Gantt charts and resource histograms, which are used to help control projects and 'smooth' the resource requirements such as people, machines, and beds for a project. This is sometimes referred to as capacity planning.

In real life situations computer software such as Microsoft Project is often used to plan projects and PRINCE2 training methodology is used for project management; but in this chapter we will just discuss the basic techniques of project analysis.

» Learning outcomes «

On completing this chapter you should be able to:

- » Understand the concept of network analysis.
- » Know what is meant by activity, event and dummy activity.
- » Construct network graphs using 'activity on arrow' and 'activity on node' methods.
- » Identify the critical path.
- » Calculate the float and slack time.
- » Calculate the expected time and variance for an activity.
- » Calculate the expected time, variance and standard deviation for project duration.
- » Determine the probability that a project will take more than, or less than, some period of time.
- » Understand the concept of least cost scheduling, or crashing, the network..
- » Use normal and crash costs, normal and crash times, and cost slopes.
- » Crash a simple project using a total enumeration method.
- » Construct a Gantt chart & associated resource histogram for any project.
- » Use these tools to carry out some elementary resource smoothing.
- » Solve problems using the Microsoft Excel spreadsheet.

8.1 Project planning

Any managerial activity can be represented as a project. Such projects normally require a high level of control if they are

- Complex, with many related activities,
- Large, with high capital costs or many facilities or personnel involved,
- Where restrictions may exist and they must be completed within time, cost, or resource limits.

For example:

- developing a new product or service
- marketing a new product or service
- breaking into a new market
- building a new plant or stadium
- installing a new computer system
- planning a training programme
- relocating head office
- Time management.

Once projects exist they have to be controlled and managed so that they can be completed to time and cost. Techniques of project management are also referred to as:

1. **Network analysis**
2. **CPA - critical path analysis**
3. **CPM - critical path method**
4. **PERT - program evaluation & review technique**

What do the example projects above have in common?

Each can be decomposed into constituent parts (or tasks), called project activities. A project can be defined as a collection of related activities.

Three things are important to define an activity:

- Each activity takes time
  An activity is anything that takes time but is not defined by the amount of time. That is, an activity can take 1 day or it can take 100 days. The important part to this simple definition is that once an activity is started it should not be interrupted. If there is an interruption then simply call it two different activities.
- Each activity uses up resources
  An activity is anything that uses resources but is not defined by the amount of those resources. That is, an activity can use 1 person or 100 people. However, the resources stay in place until the end of the activity. If they are variable then simply call them different activities.
- Activities are structured.
  Structure is given by 'Precedence'. That is, some activities have to be completed before others can be started.

X

crashing a project shortening a project time by spending money to reduce critical activities, for example working overtime.

project planning a series of steps or actions to complete the project given the stated activity times and costs.

activities specific jobs or tasks that are components of a project.

network analysis network analysis is an important project management tool used during the planning phase of a project. It demonstrates activities against fixed time frames and helps in controlling the sequence of activities in a project.

critical path analysis (CPA) critical path analysis (and PERT) are powerful tools to help schedule and manage complex projects.

critical path method (CPM) a network-based project scheduling procedure.

Program Evaluation and Review Technique (PERT) a method of Critical Path Analysis that is designed for uncertain activity times.

Example 8.1

A roof cannot be erected unless the foundations have been dug. This means that digging foundations must precede erecting the roof. What about the walls? A roof cannot be erected until the walls have been constructed, but they cannot be constructed until the foundations have been dug.

So it is important to know the order, or precedence, that activities must be completed in, and we refer to the immediately preceding activities.

8.1.1 Precedence tables

The first step for any project is to:

- **List the constituent activities**
- **Arrange them into a precedence table.**

Example 8.2

The project is to build an extension to the recreation centre. Table 8.1 lists the activities and their immediate predecessors, up to the point of starting construction.

Activity	Description	Preceding activity	Time (weeks)
A	Survey site	–	6
B	Develop initial proposal	–	8
C	Obtain approval of Governors	A, B	12
D	Choose architect	C	4
E	Work out budget	C	6
F	Finalize design	D, E	15
G	Agree financing	E	12
H	Hire contractor	F, G	8

Table 8.1

The preceding activity column is the activity, or activities, that must be completed before commencing the new one: for example, C cannot be started until A and B have been completed. Note that a preceding activity of '-' means that no activities precede it; that is, activity A or B can be started at any time—they do not depend upon each other, so A can start and later B can start or vice versa. The advantage of the precedence table is that it begins to structure the project, in that Activity F (for example) will not be done before activities D or E because we must check that those have been finished first. This does not mean that they have to finish at the same time: D may finish now and E may finish next week, but F cannot begin until after they have both been completed. This structure means that, in large projects, activities will not be done out of place.

X

immediately preceding activities the activities that must be completed immediately prior to the start of a given activity.

precedence table table of predecessor tasks.

Very often, people know the beginning and the end point and will start without really knowing how to get to the end (or will start without knowing *if* they can get to the end). But by agreeing a precedence table the project team understand a common project structure before it begins. Even if there are other ways of achieving the project end, the team agrees that the precedence table is the way that they will run this project.

We can allocate times to the various activities. Note that these are estimated times to begin with, but as a project develops the estimates will become more accurate. Let's look at another project that is slightly larger in activity terms, that of purchasing a new car.

Activity	Description	Preceding activity	Duration (days)
A	Decide feasibility of purchase	–	3
B	Find buyer for existing car	A	14
C	Decide on possible models	A	1
D	Investigate models decided upon	C	3
E	Discuss with knowledgeable friends	C	1
F	Get information from dealers	C	2
G	Put all information together	D, E, F	1
H	Narrow down to three options	G	1
I	Test drive all three	H	3
J	Get warranty & finance information	H	2
K	Choose one car	I, J	2
L	Compare dealers & choose one	K	2
M	Decide upon colour etc	L	4
N	Test drive chosen model	L	1
O	Buy new car	B, M, N	3

Table 8.2

Questions

Is activity B a precondition for starting activity I?

Answer

No.

I depends upon H, which depends upon G, which depends upon D, E, and F, which all depend upon C, which depends upon A, which depends upon nothing. So activity B and activity I could (provided that all the precedence had been met) be carried out at the same time. Often this fact is lost in the complexity of the table so the temptation is to do one activity after another to make sure that things are done in order. This is obviously increasing the time before completion.

Is activity A a precondition for starting activity K?

Answer

Yes.

K depends upon I and J, which both depend upon H, which depends upon G, which depends upon D, E, and F, all of which depend upon C, which depends upon A to be completed before it can be begin. Thus, unless A is completed it is pointless thinking about doing K because its preconditions have not been met.

Can activities E and F take place at the same time?

Answer

Yes.

They both depend on C but they do not have to begin at the same time—or they can begin at the same time. All the precedence table says is that they are not dependant on each other.

Precedence tables are a start in structuring the project but they are not always easy to visualize. Very often in complex projects the beginning of the table is physically a long way from the end of the table and mistakes may happen. One cannot always say that activity I can begin before B, which is not a prerequisite for it. Can the complexity be simplified? Yes. A useful visual representation of a project is obtained by drawing a **network diagram**.

8.1.2 Constructing a network diagram

A network diagram is a visual representation of the precedence table.

Two types of network diagram are commonly employed, namely:

1. **Activity on arrow**
2. **Activity on node**.

Initially I will confine our attention to the first type only and later will point out the differences between the two types.

Definitions of the components of network diagrams

Networks have building blocks and rules.

Definition 1: Activity

An activity is represented by an arrow.

For example, the length of the arrow bears no relation to the time that the activity takes

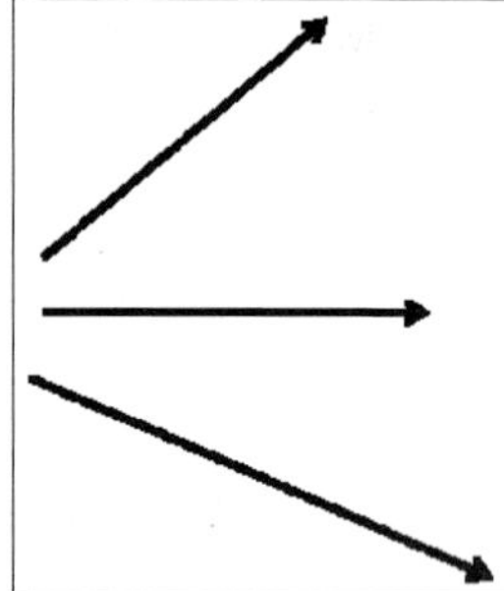

Figure 8.1

Activities are arrows

Arrows should be drawn left to right and never backwards. They can be sloped but can never be vertical. Thus you can imagine moving in time along the arrow, left to right. The arrow signifies direction in that the plain end is the start of the activity and the arrow head is the end of the activity.

X

network diagram a graphic tool for depicting the sequence and relationships between tasks in a project.

activity on arrow a network diagram showing sequence of activities, in which each activity is represented by an arrow, with a circle representing a node or event at each end.

activity on node a network where activities are represented by a box or a node linked by dependencies.

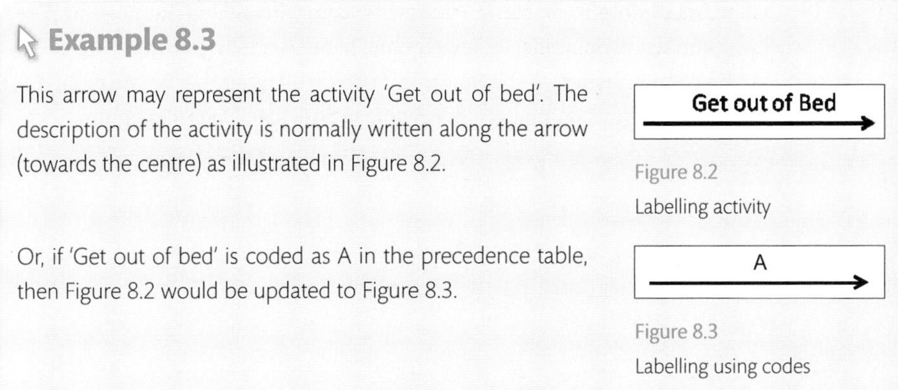

Definition 2: ***Node/Event***

Every activity has a beginning and an end. Diagrammatically these are shown as circles. So:

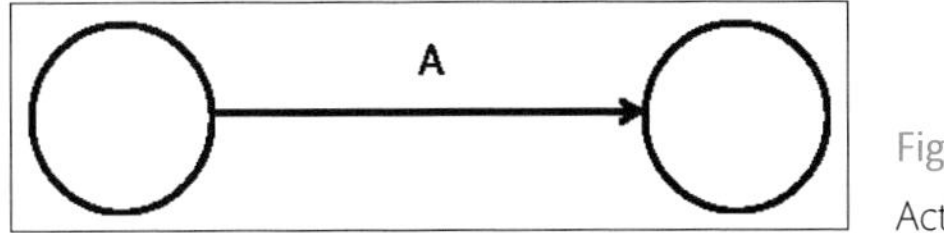

Figure 8.4
Activity with nodes

The circle at the beginning depicts the start of the activity and at the finish depicts the end of the activity. Notice that circles are points in time, while an arrow takes time (and resources).

Definition 3: Network

The network is a logical construction of these elements to represent a precedence table. To form a network arrows and nodes are joined together to form a logical sequence of the activities.

Activity	Preceding activity
A	–
B	A
C	B

Table 8.3

Thus the Precedence Table 8.3 would be drawn as the network in Figure 8.5.

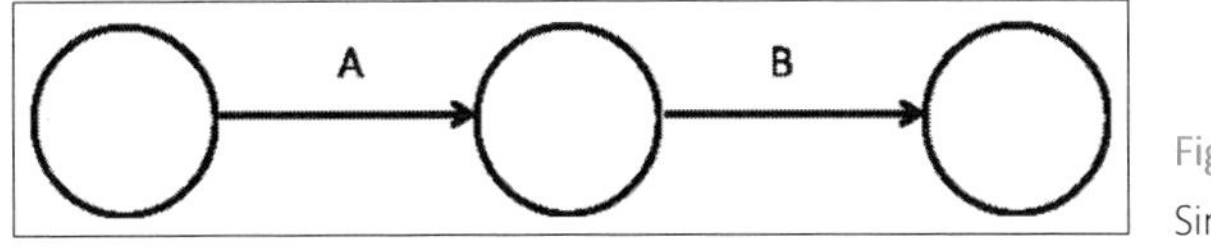

Figure 8.5
Simple network

Note that the end node of A is also the same as the start node of B. This means that when A is complete (at the end) B can begin (not necessarily at the same time – but the project

node an intersection or junction point of an influence diagram or a decision tree.

event an instantaneous occurrence that changes the state of the system in a model.

has to be on the circle before B can start). Imagine walking along the lines, when we are at the end of A, standing on the node, then B can begin, but we do not change nodes.

Lines A and B bear no relation to the duration of the activity. At this point we do not know these anyway, but the diagram does not require it. It is just a logical diagram.

The Precedence Table 8.4 would be drawn as the network in Figure 8.6

Activity	Preceding activity
M	X, Y

Table 8.4

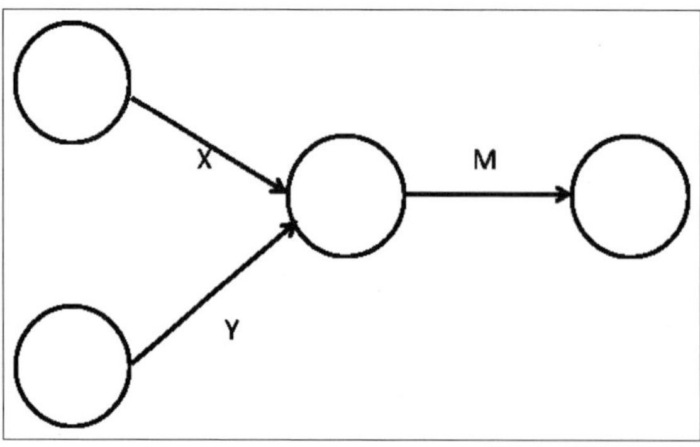

Figure 8.6
Activity depending on two activities

Thus both X and Y must be complete before M can begin. That is, the project has to be at the circle end X, Y before M can start. X could finish now and Y next week but only when both have finished will we be at the node. Sometimes we wait for something to finish before several activities can begin. For example, drawing into a garage allows us to fill up with petrol and clean the windscreen, not necessarily at the same time although they could be (by two different people).

Precedence Table 8.5 would be drawn as the network in Figure 8.7.

Activity	Preceding activity
R	P
Q	P

Table 8.5

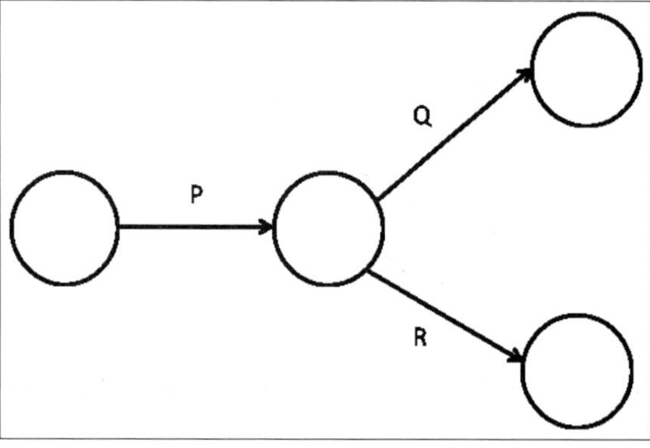

Figure 8.7
Two activities depending on one activity

Rules of Networks

There are very few rules when drawing networks. Networks

1. Must be drawn from left to right.
2. Must have a single starting point.
   This is very important. Any project will start at a point in time—this is represented by the first node. From that node several activities may begin.
3. Must have a single finishing point (node).
   This is even more important. Very often projects are not completed because things are left undone and new projects are undertaken. By having a single end 'node' means that all of the activities left to complete must finish at one node. This node is the end of the project. So it can formally be closed.
4. One arrow (only) per activity.
5. No arrows without associated descriptions (letters).
   However, when using activity on arrow method there is an exception to this - **dummy activities**. See the next section for explanation.
6. Must correctly reflect the precedence table.

Definition 4: Dummy activities

Sometimes we have to use dummy activities. These are drawn as a dashed arrow as in Figure 8.8.

They are activities that do not take any time or resources, but are necessary purely for the logic of the diagram.

A dummy activity may be needed:

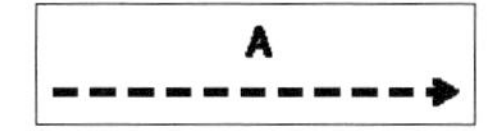

Figure 8.8
A dummy activity

- To prevent two or more activities sharing the same starting and ending events.
  As we shall discover later in this chapter, in order to computerize and time networks it is essential that this is true. Thus:

Activity	Preceding activity
A	–
B	A
C	A
D	B, C

Table 8.6

Could be logically be drawn as

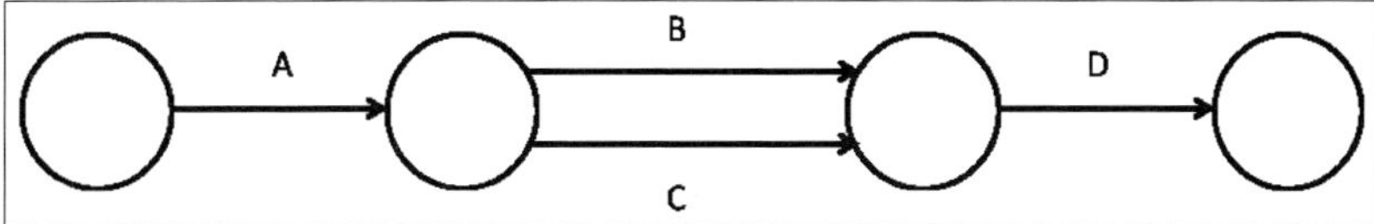

Figure 8.9
Need for dummy activity to separate ends

However B and C share the same nodes at the beginning and at the end. It is better to redraw but introduce a dummy activity.

X
dummy activities a dummy activity is a simulated activity of sorts, one that is of zero duration and is created for the sole purpose of demonstrating a specific relationship and path of action on the arrow diagramming method.

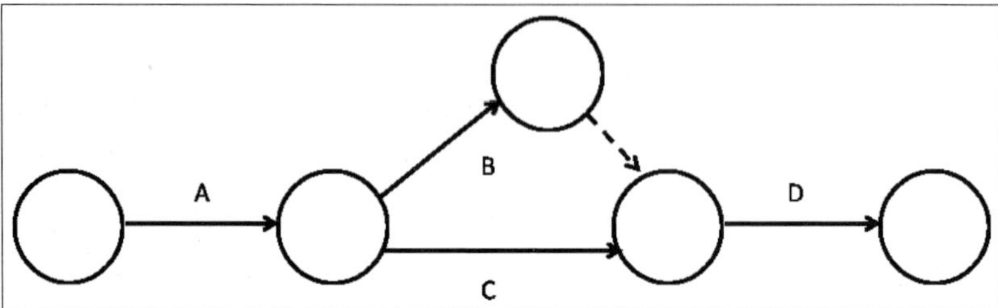

Figure 8.10
Dummy separating ends

Note that D still depends on C and the dummy, but the dummy cannot be done without B being finished. Thus D depends on B and C being completed.

Note that the dummy can be in one of four places start B, end B (as demonstrated), start C or end C. It does not matter, provided that it is there somewhere.

- To maintain network logic; that is, to ensure that the network abides by the precedence table.

  Thus:

Activity	Preceding activity
A	Previous part of network
B	Previous part of network
C	A
D	A, B

Table 8.7

A, B, and C could be logically be drawn as

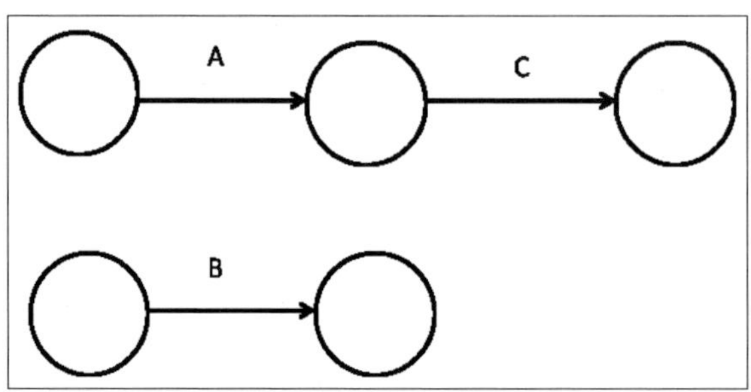

Figure 8.11
Need for a logical dummy

But what about activity D? This depends on A and B but if the start of D is the end of A then how do we connect B? If we drew the arrow for B into the end of A then it would not be correct for C. This is a classic case of the need of a dummy and it is drawn as follows:

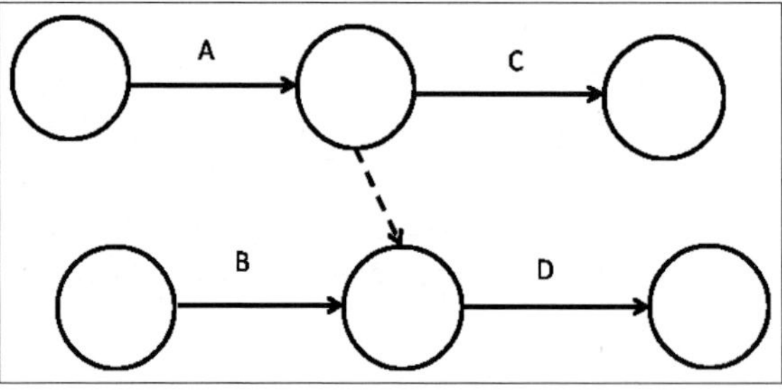

Figure 8.12
Logical dummy

Here D relies upon (cannot start until) B and the dummy are complete, but the dummy has to wait for A before it can be done. Thus D depends upon A and B. C only depends upon A because of the direction of the dummy. You have now been given all of the elements to be able to represent any precedence table in the world. However 'Building the Channel Tunnel' would need a very large sheet of paper. In fact, drawing is just a matter of practice. It may not seem easy but you will improve the more times that it is done. Hints for drawing networks:

- It is best to cover up the precedence table and do only one activity at a time.
- Connect each activity as it occurs without thinking of what happens in the precedence table that follows.
- Be prepared to rub out and redraw constantly.
- Try to connect only with straight lines—but when in rough you may use curved lines.
- Never cross lines.
- Always remember to add the arrow: this represents the end of the activity.
- Read a precedence table as: the first column goes into a node (head), the second column comes out of a node (tail).
- Networks begin with only one node: all the starting activities proceed from that.
- Networks finish with one node so any activities left dangling at the end of the project should be redrawn to enter just the one.
- When finished, check the network against the precedence table. You may find that, after rubbing out and redrawing, an arrow may have gone into the wrong node.
- Remember tail comes out of a node and head (arrow) goes into a node.

Example 8.4

The Precedence Table 8.8 represents the preliminary preparation to build an extension to the recreation centre. Although the times of the activities are given, you may ignore them at the moment.

Activity	Description	Preceding activity	Time (weeks)
A	Survey site	-	6
B	Develop initial proposal	-	8
C	Obtain approval of Governors	A, B	12
D	Choose architect	C	4
E	Work out budget	C	6
F	Finalize design	D, E	15
G	Agree financing	E	12
H	Hire contactor	F, G	8

Table 8.8

Try to draw the network for this project. Figure 8.13 represents this network.

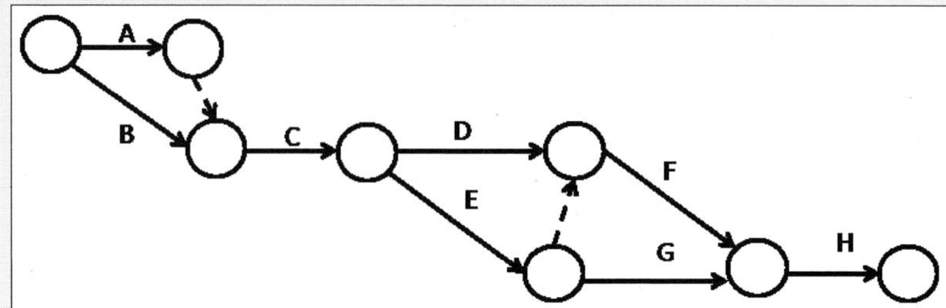

Figure 8.13
Extension to recreation centre network

Note the use of the dummies. The one at A, B is there because of the rule that says that two or more activities cannot start and finish at the same nodes. The dummy at D, E is a logical dummy. A and B come from the same node at the beginning. Remember arrows coming out have to be performed after arrows going in to a node; that is, they depend upon them. The fact that A and B share the same starting node does not mean that they have to begin together, just that they do not depend on any activities before they can start.

Check that it abides by the rules:

- It only has a single starting event and finishing event.
- Everything is moving left to right.
- There is one arrow for each activity.
- There is no arrow without an activity description, unless it is a dummy.
- All activity lines have heads (arrows) and the names are in the centre.
- It conforms to the precedence table.

Cover this network and keep trying to draw it yourself until you are happy. Start the table by drawing A then B then C and so forth, only continuing when your present drawing is correct up until that point. Be prepared to rub out and redraw constantly. If it becomes very complicated then start afresh with a new sheet of paper. Check against the precedence table at the end. Then tidy up the diagram with straight lines, remembering that lines cannot go backwards.

Numbering the nodes

Rather than talking about activities A, B, and so on, network diagrams are usually talked about in terms of node numbers. The nodes are numbered such that the head of an activity (arrow) is a greater number than at the tail. This makes sense in that you can think of the numbers increasing with time, so the end is greater than the beginning. Another advantage is that networks can be numbered as you wish. Usually there are gaps in the initial numbering. This is because, as a project progresses, activities may become more detailed and the network is adapted by having these activities replaced by several arrows (activities), which are more defined. Thus if there are gaps in the numbering then the whole network does not have to be renumbered because these additional activities will fit within the previous gaps. The longer, more complex the project is, the larger the gaps between the initial node numbers.

X
numbering the nodes of a network to identify points in the project, useful for project control as well as identifying the end and start of activities.

Numbering for the recreation centre project is as illustrated in Figure 8.14.

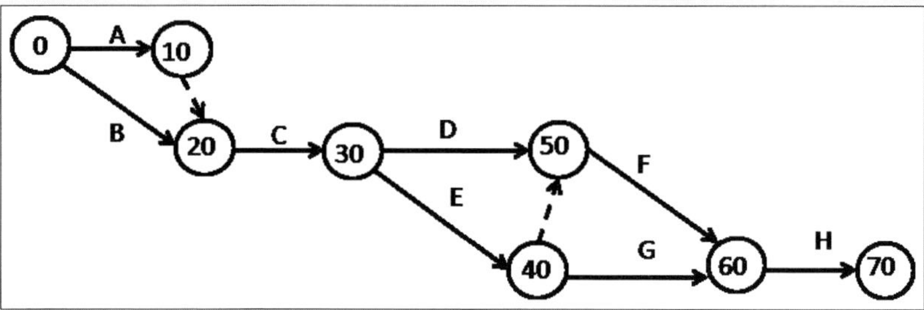

Figure 8.14
Numbering nodes

So instead of saying activity C, it could be described as 20-30. This is the main reason for the necessity to use dummies if there are activities between the same ends: all activities must have different number pairs.

Differences between activity on arrow (AOA) and activity on node (AON)

We have drawn our network with the activity on arrow method. For this the arrow represents the activity and we could visualize the activity being done by movement along the arrow. The other convention of network drawing is activity on node where the node represents the activity and the arrows show the logical flow of activities. Thus the recreation project would be drawn as

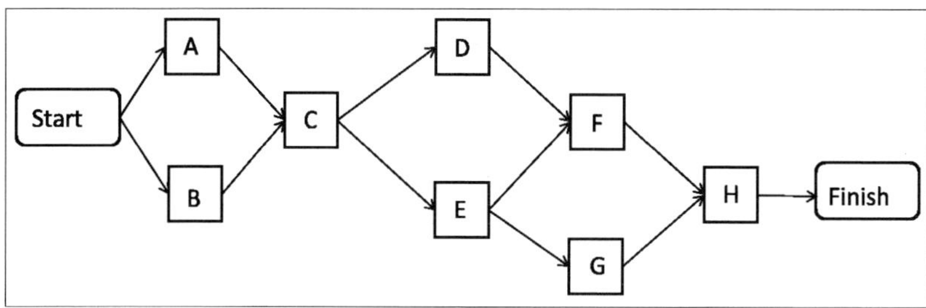

Figure 8.15
Activity on node network for extension to the recreation centre

Note that we use a Start and Finish node otherwise we could have several start and/or Finishes. The strong advantage is that no dummies are required so that it is sometimes easier to draw. The disadvantage is that it is difficult to visualize movement along an activity. Whichever you use you should be consistent in its use and not mix methods. Although I use the Activity on Arrow method, the analyses that follow apply to both methods.

Student exercises

X8.1 Draw the network diagram (no dummies are required) for Precedence Table 8.9.

Activity	Preceding activity
A	-
B	-
C	B
D	A
E	B
F	C

Table 8.9

X8.2 Draw the network diagram (no dummies are required) for Precedence Table 8.10.

Activity	Preceding activity
A	-
B	A
C	A
D	B, E
E	C
F	C
G	F

Table 8.10

X8.3 Draw the network diagram (no dummies are required) for Precedence Table 8.11.

Activity	Preceding activity
A	-
B	-
C	-
D	B
E	A, D
F	C
G	C
H	E, F
I	G

Table 8.11

X8.4 Draw the network diagram (no dummies are required) for Precedence Table 8.12.

Activity	Preceding activity
A	–
B	A
C	A
D	A
E	C, F
F	D
G	B, E
H	D
I	G
J	D
K	H
L	J
M	I, K, L

Table 8.12

X8.5 Draw the network diagram (dummies may be required) for Precedence Table 8.13.

Activity	Preceding activity
A	–
B	–
C	–
D	B, C
E	B
F	A
G	E
H	A
I	D, F
J	H

Table 8.13

X8.6 Draw the network diagram (dummies may be required) for Precedence Table 8.14.

Activity	Preceding activity
A	–
B	–
C	–
D	C
E	B, C
F	C
G	D
H	D
I	E, F
J	I

Table 8.14

X8.7 Draw the network diagram (dummies may be required) for Precedence Table 8.15.

Activity	Preceding activity
A	–
B	–
C	–
D	A, B, C
E	B
F	A
G	D, E, F
H	F
I	E
J	I
K	H

Table 8.15

X8.8 Draw the network diagram (dummies may be required) for Precedence Table 8.16.

Activity	Preceding activity
A	–
B	–
C	–
D	A
E	A
F	C
G	C
H	F
I	B, E, G, H
J	F
K	J

Table 8.16

8.2 Managing and timing a project

We have converted the precedence table into a network and can see (hopefully) that it is easier to visualize the ordering of the activities. Thus in the recreation centre we can see from the network that G can be done at the same time as D – they do not depend upon each other. However the greatest value of a network is that we can time the project from beginning to end. In practice computers will time the projects for us, once we have input the precedence table.

8.2.1 Evaluating a network diagram

Using the recreation centre as an example.

Activity	Description	Preceding activity	Time (weeks)
A	Survey site	–	6
B	Develop initial proposal	–	8
C	Obtain approval of Governors	A, B	12
D	Choose architect	C	4
E	Work out budget	C	6
F	Finalize design	D, E	15
G	Agree financing	E	12
H	Hire contactor	F, G	8

Table 8.17

Note that the activities have been given times for their completion. So Activity A (Survey site) we have estimated will take six weeks, D (Choose architect) will take four weeks. These are deterministic times i.e. we are assuming that they are fixed. In practice times in advance are estimates and they will vary. Maybe one of the activities depends on the weather - if it is good then the time will be short but if it is poor then the time will be longer, so the time we allocate at the moment is the expected time—or the time we would expect on average. Later we will discuss the situation where we are allowed to use a probability distribution for the times.

How do we find the shortest time of the project from start to finish? With a precedence table it is very difficult because we cannot visualize what activities can be operating at the same time. The temptation is to add together all of the activity times. In this case the time of the project would be 6 + 8 + 12 + 4 + 6 + 15 + 12 + 8 = 71 weeks. Can it be shorter?

If we look at the network for the project, but this time add the information about the times of the activities. The activity times are placed next to the letter.

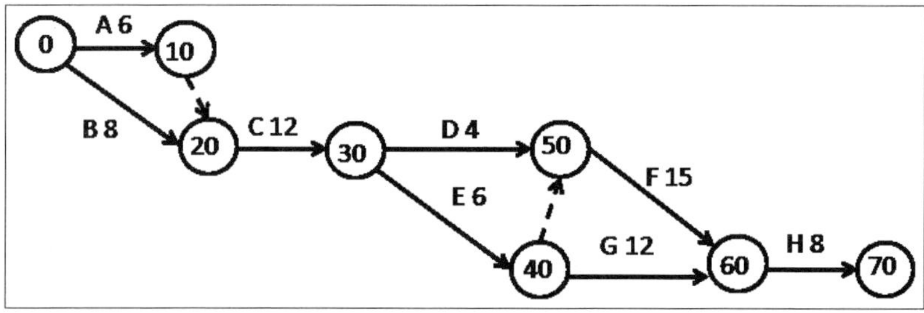

Figure 8.16

Network for extension to the recreation centre with activity times

Now, to get from start to finish of the project (node 0 to node 70) everything has to be completed. In particular every path through the network has to be completed.

expected time the average activity time.

path a sequence of connected nodes that leads from the Start node to the Finish node.

Definition: A path is a connected sequence of activities from start to end of the network.

How many separate paths are there through the network and what are the total times of the activities on that path? There are 6 paths:

A – C – D – F – H time 45 weeks

A – C – E – F – H time 47 weeks

A – C – E – G – H time 44 weeks

B – C – D – F – H time 47 weeks

B – C – E – F – H time 49 weeks

B – C – E – G – H time 46 weeks

All of the activities have to be done so each of these paths must be covered. However the longest path is 49 weeks, B – C – E – F – H, so this must be the time of the project. It cannot be any shorter because if the activities on this path, which all have to be completed, were done as soon as the previous was completed then the overall time is 49 weeks and it cannot be shorter. This is quite an important idea to understand. The shortest time for a project to complete is the time of the path with the longest duration.

So to find how long a project will take to complete all we have to do is find every path through the network, time it and the project time is the longest of these. However, in reality projects may have thousands of paths – building the channel tunnel must have millions of tasks associated with it. To calculate all of the permutations would be impossible. Is there an easier way to time the length of a project?

Fortunately there is. It is a very mechanical way to time a project, no matter how long or how complicated, and we can simply understand it once we have completed the network. For this we need 3 pieces of information

1. The node identifier number
2. The **earliest start time (EST)**. The earliest time that an activity can begin given that everything before has kept to time.
3. The **latest start time (LST)**. The latest time that an activity can begin without delaying project completion.

All of this information is written into the project nodes as in Figure 8.17.

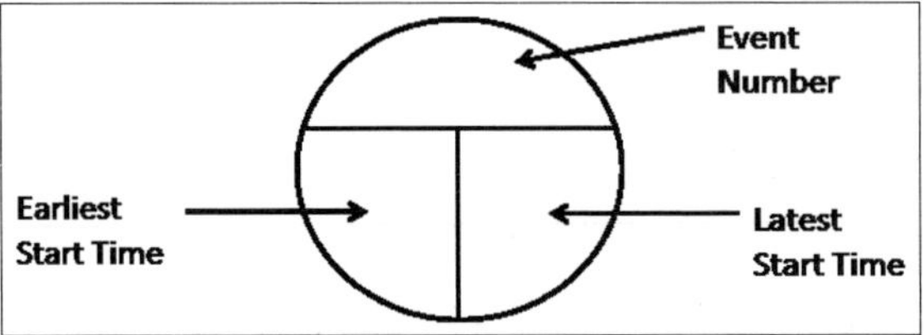

Figure 8.17
Node information

earliest start time (EST) the earliest time an activity may begin.

latest start time (LST) the latest time an activity may begin without increasing the project completion time.

Figure 8.18 shows the Recreation Centre network with nodes ready to be completed with the required information.

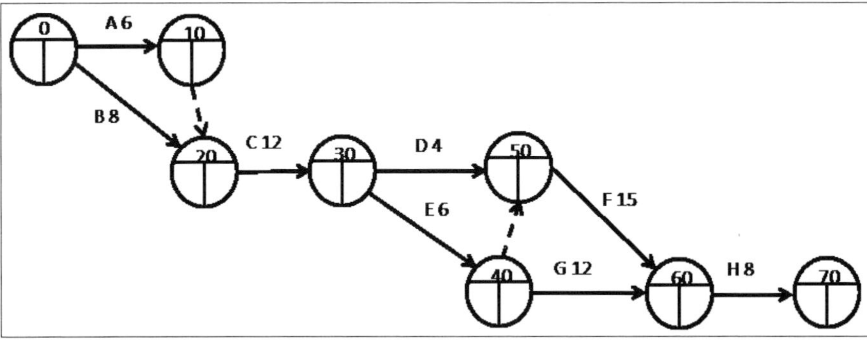

Figure 8.18

Network for extension to the recreation centre with nodes

The EST for each node are completed using a **forward pass**

In Node 0, start the project at time 0. What is the earliest time that the dummy coming out of A can start? It is the EST of A plus the duration. That is 0 + 6. So the EST of node 10 is 6.

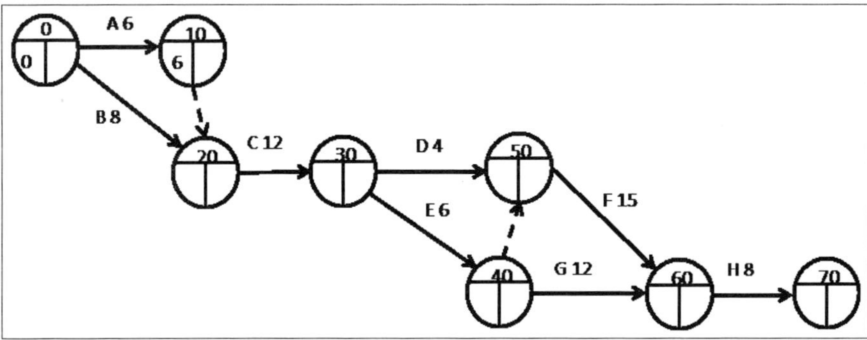

Figure 8.19

Forward pass - node 10

Then what is the earliest time that C can start? C can start when the dummy and B have finished. The dummy can finish at 6 + 0 (time of a dummy is 0), and B can finish 0 + 8 = 8. Therefore the earliest time that C can start is the latest of these ie 8. (Notice that C has to wait until the latest of the activities into it have finished).

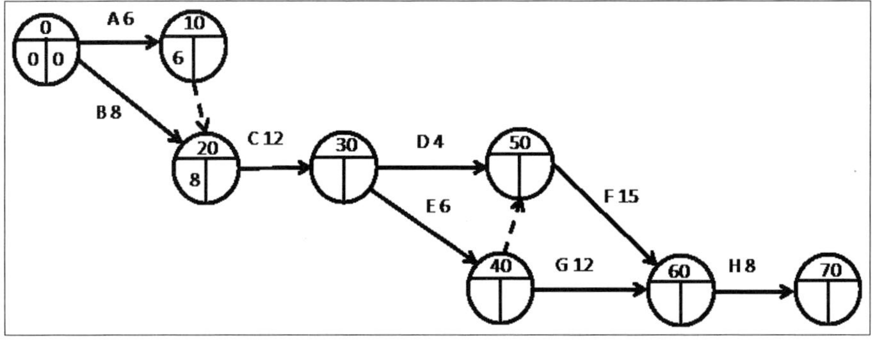

Figure 8.20

Forward pass - node 20

forward pass part of the PERT/CPM procedure that involves moving forward through the project network to determine the earliest start and earliest finish times for each activity.

The rules to use when completing the forward pass are that if one activity enters a node then the EST of that node is the activity EST + duration of activity. If two or more activities enter a node then thc EST of that node is the greater of the EST + duration of each of those activities. Continue all the way through until the end. The beauty of this simple method of timing is that no matter how long or how complicated the network is, we can only do one node at a time. It pulls itself along. Check the network completed for the forward pass is as illustrated in Figure 8.21.

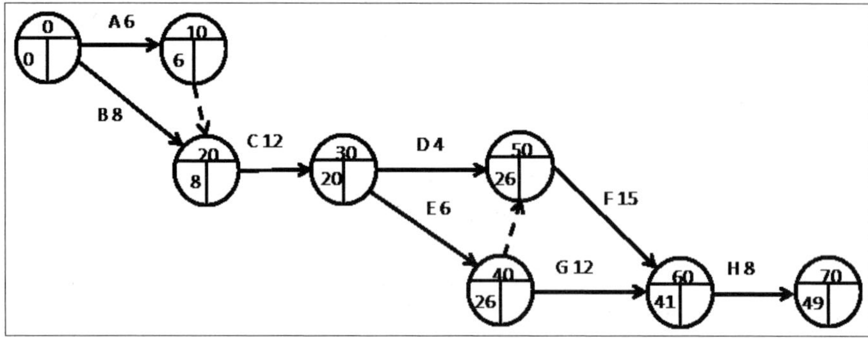

Figure 8.21
Forward pass - complete network

This tells us that if all the activities take the estimated duration, and they all begin as soon as they can, then the time for the project will be 49 weeks. Note that this is the earliest time that the project can finish. Now we would like to find the LSTs, that is, the latest time that an activity can start without delaying project completion, or the latest possible time that a preceding activity can finish without increasing project duration of 49 weeks.

The LSTs for each node are completed using a backward pass. For this we complete the LST section of the nodes. Node 70 starts at 49 weeks (it cannot be finished earlier - and why finish later?):

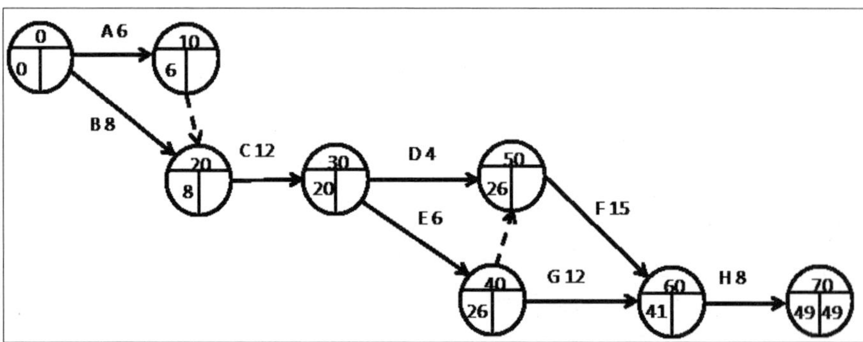

Figure 8.22
Backward pass - end node 70

backward pass part of the PERT/CPM procedure that involves moving backwards through the network to determine the latest start and latest finish times for each activity.

On a backwards pass we reverse the operations of the forward pass. That is LST at the start of an activity = LST at the end of the activity - duration. So at the beginning of H LST = 49 – 8 = 41, at the beginning of F LST = 41 – 15 = 26:

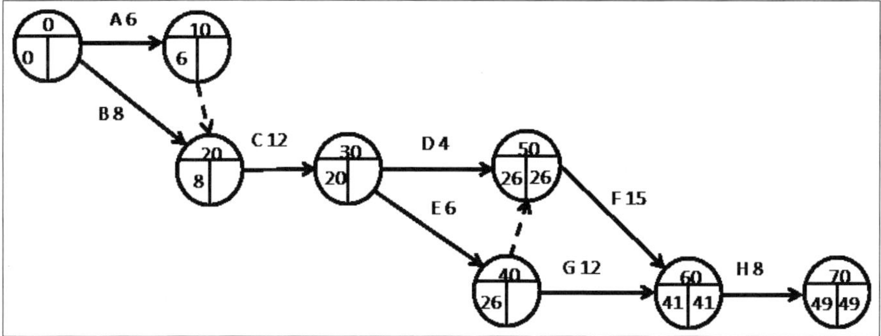

Figure 8.23

Backward pass - node 50 and 60

If 2 or more activities leave a node then the LST to enter is the smallest of the calculations (LST - duration) for them. The reasoning is a little more complicated backwards but if we take node 40, then 2 activities leave it - the dummy and G. The latest time the dummy could start to finish at 26 is 26 – 0 = 26. The latest time that G could start to finish at 41 is 41 – 12 = 29. Thus the time to enter in node 40 is the smallest of these i.e. 26. An activity must have left this node by week 26 otherwise the project will be late. NB G can leave up until 29 and still be on time but the dummy must have left be 26 in order for F to leave on time.

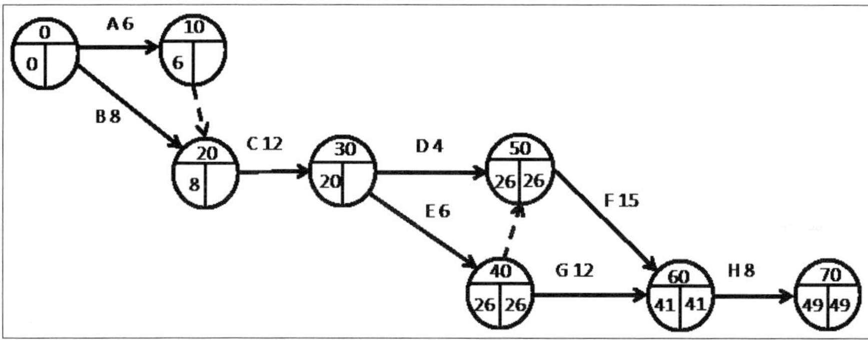

Figure 8.24

Backward pass - node 40

Check that the rest of the LST s are completed as follows

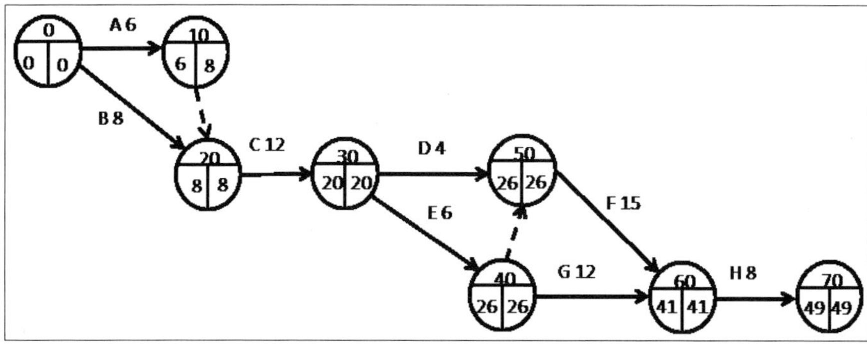

Figure 8.25

Backward pass - complete network

We have finished back at 0. Don't be tempted to put 0 into the node because it should follow from the rules. If it doesn't then something has gone wrong. In order to finish the project at the earliest possible time, by week 49, the project must start at time 0. No earlier and no later. You may remember the 6 paths through the project:

A – C – D – F – H time 45 weeks

A – C – E – F – H time 47 weeks

A – C – E – G – H time 44 weeks

B – C – D – F – H time 47 weeks

B – C – E – F – H time 49 weeks

B – C – E – G – H time 46 weeks

Because completion of the project requires that all paths through the network are completed, and the longest path, B – C – E – F – H, will take 49 weeks, then the project time calculated above is correct.

However the beauty of the system is that it is entirely mechanical - even a computer can do it (and does).

B – C – E – F – H is called the critical path since it is the longest. To reiterate, the critical path is the shortest time for the project and it is the path with the longest duration. A delay to any activity on the critical path will necessarily delay completion of the project. Hence activities that are on the critical path must be given the highest degree of control for the project to finish on time. Critical activities can be deduced from the network diagram because EST = LST on the start and end nodes of the activity. Also the time difference between the nodes is the same as the duration of the activity.

What about the activities that are not on the critical path?

Activity A can start at 0 but does not have to finish until 8 weeks, which is the LST at node 10, but it only takes 6 weeks duration. So it has a slack time of 8 – 6 = 2 weeks. This time is called float time. Thus Total float is a measure of the *maximum delay* possible for any activity, given that there is to be no delay regarding the project as a whole. Float time is time that can be used to delay the start of the activity to two weeks or, maybe, spread the activity out to take eight weeks without pushing forward the end time, hence not delaying the project time.

critical path method (CPM) a network-based project scheduling procedure.

Total float slack time or float time of an activity.

float the amount of time available for a task to slip before it results in a delay of the project end date. It is the difference between the task's early and late start dates.

earliest finish time (EFT) the earliest time an activity may be completed.

latest finish time (LFT) the latest time an activity may be completed without increasing the project completion time.

Diagrammatically if we look at activity X.

X is drawn between nodes i and j and has duration d_{ij}, as in Figure 8.26.

Figure 8.26
Node algebra

Float of activity X is $LST_j - EST_i - d_{ij}$

Notice that critical path activities have a Float of 0, ie they have no spare time. Note that the EST at node j is often referred to as the early finish time (EFT) and LST at node j would be the latest finish time (LFT). Then the formula for float time would read $LFT_j - EST_i - d_{ij}$.

So, Float of activity X is $LFT_j - EST_i - d_{ij}$. If we use this formula on the activities of the Recreation Centre then:

Activity	EST start node	LFT end node	Duration	Float
A	0	8	6	2
B	0	8	8	0
C	8	20	12	0
D	20	26	4	2
E	20	26	6	0
F	26	41	15	0
G	26	41	12	3
H	41	49	8	0

Table 8.18

The critical path activities, B, C, E, F, and H, have Floats of 0, but the other activities A, D, and G have Floats of 2, 2 and 3 weeks respectively. As we shall see in a later section, the use of floats is very important to controlling a project. Note that nodes are useful for project management in that milestone meetings can be set at certain times which coincide with node times. Thus we know what activities can be expected to be completed and what are to begin.

Example 8.5

Draw the network diagram, determine the earliest and latest start times for each event and, hence, find the critical path, and shortest completion time, for the following project. (All times are in weeks.) What are the floats?

Activity	Preceding activity	Normal time
A	–	4
B	–	2
C	–	3
D	A	5
E	B	3
F	B	4
G	A, C	6
H	A, C, E	3
I	D, G	4
J	H, F	7

Table 8.19

Answer

The network diagram is as follows. Try to draw it remembering the rules and hints.

X

normal time the project time under normal conditions.

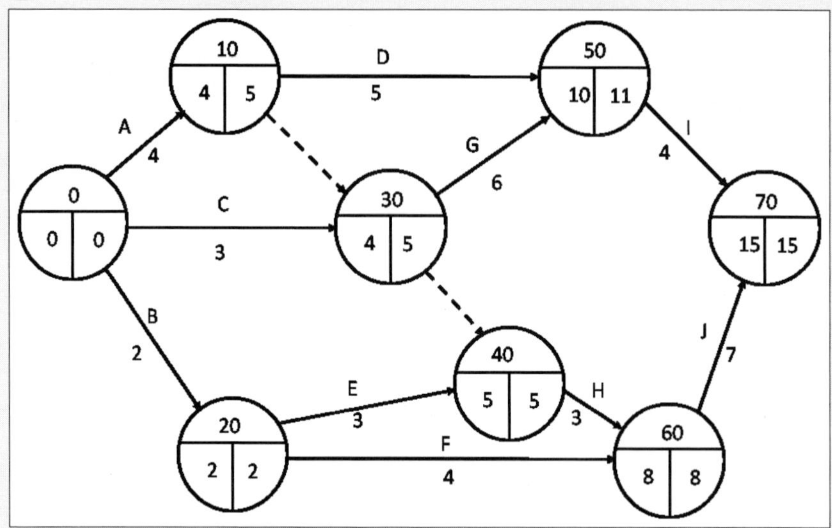

Figure 8.27

Network diagram for Example 8.5

To find which activities are on the critical path, the EST = LST at the beginning node, and the ending node of the activity, and the difference between the node times is the same as the duration of the activity:

A is unequal at end

B 2 − 0 − 2 = 0 .... **Critical**

C is unequal at end

D is unequal at both ends

E 5 − 2 − 3 = 0 .... **Critical**

F equal at ends but difference is not equal to the duration.

G unequal at ends

H 8 − 5 − 3 = 0 .... **Critical**

I unequal at beginning

J 15 − 8 − 7 = 0 .... **Critical**

So the critical path is B - E - H - J and the minimum time of the project is 15 weeks. Note there is always at least one critical path and very often, more than one. All the other activities must have float. Remember the equation is LFT - EST - duration:

Activity	EST start node	LFT end node	Duration	Float (weeks)
A	0	5	4	1
C	0	5	3	2
D	4	11	5	2
F	2	8	4	2
G	4	11	6	1
I	10	15	4	1

Table 8.20

Student exercises

X8.9 Draw the network diagram, determine the earliest and latest start times for each event and, hence, find the critical path, and shortest completion time, for the following project. (All times are in weeks.) What are the floats?

Activity	Preceding activity	Normal time
A	–	2
B	–	3
C	–	15
D	A, B	4
E	A	4
F	E, H	6
G	E, H	1
H	D	2
I	D	4
J	I, G	2
K	I, G	3

Table 8.21

X8.10 Draw the network diagram, determine the earliest and latest start times for each event and, hence, find the critical path, and shortest completion time, for the following project. (All times are in weeks.) What are the floats?

Activity	Preceding activity	Normal time
A	–	4
B	–	3
C	–	5
D	A, B, F	6
E	A, F	2
F	C	7
G	C	4
H	D	4
I	G	7
J	D	2
K	D, E, G	3
L	I	1

Table 8.22

X8.11 Draw the network diagram, determine the earliest and latest start times for each event and, hence, find the critical path, and shortest completion time, for the following project. (All times are in weeks.) What are the floats?

Activity	Preceding activity	Normal time
A	–	3
B	–	3
C	–	2
D	C	2
E	C	2
F	A, D	1
G	B, C	3
H	B, C	5
I	E, F	2
J	H, I	2
K	A, D	3
L	G	2
M	E, F, K	3

Table 8.23

8.3 Uncertain activity times

In the projects that we've examined to this point it's been assumed that activity duration times are estimated with certainty. However, there's no reason why this should necessarily be the case. So for project management to have a secure foundation uncertainty has to be allowed for. This is the basis of a technique, developed in the USA, called PERT (programme evaluation & review technique).

For this we make a more realistic assumption about the activity times i.e. that they are variable. For each activity we estimate a most likely time (probably the time that you put in before), an optimistic time (if everything goes as well as it can) and a pessimistic time (even if disasters happen). The actual time of the activity is a random variable that follows a probability distribution; that is, we do not know the time of the actual activity until after it has happened, but we have some idea of the probability of the activity being completed within a certain time. The name of this particular distribution is the beta distribution. Unlike the normal distribution it is a family of curves based upon two parameters. The shape of an example beta distribution is in Figure 8.28. You do not need to know how it is calculated because we do not actually use the activity distribution. However given three estimates you can see that the probabilities of taking times between the optimistic and pessimistic estimates follow the shape of the function between the two limits.

X

uncertain activity times degree of uncertainty within the completion time for certain activities.

optimistic time an activity time estimate based on the assumption that the activity will progress in an ideal manner.

pessimistic time an activity time estimate based on the assumption that the most unfavourable conditions apply.

beta distribution the Beta distribution models events which are constrained to take place within an interval defined by a minimum and maximum value.

normal distribution the normal distribution is a good approximation to the beta distribution in the centre of the distribution and is easy to work with, so it is often used as an approximation.

expected value in a mixed strategy game, a value computed by multiplying each payoff by its probability and summing. It can be interpreted as the long-run average payoff for the mixed strategy.

variance the difference between estimated cost, duration, or effort and the actual result of performance. In addition, it can be the difference between the initial or baseline product scope and the actual product delivered.

standard deviation a measure of the data spread, equal to the square root of variance.

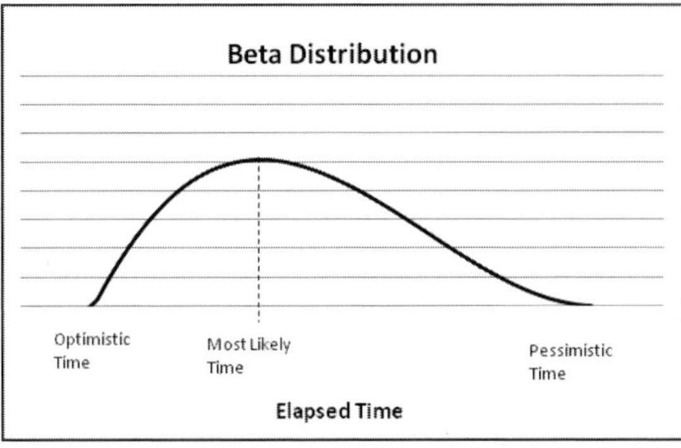

Figure 8.28
Shape of beta distribution

For a beta distribution it has been found that a good estimate for the mean (expected value) of the activity time is given by:

$$\left(\frac{\text{Optimistic Time} + 4(\text{Most Likely Time}) + \text{Pessimistic Time}}{6}\right) \tag{8.1}$$

And a good estimate of the variance of the activity is:

$$\left(\frac{\text{Pessimistic Time-Optimistic Time}}{6}\right)^2 \tag{8.2}$$

From Chapter 3 it can be seen that a distribution can be defined by the expected value and the standard deviation (i.e. √variance), so these two values help define this shape. The individual activity distributions are 'summed' to make a distribution of time for each path through the network. Thus, for each path we can determine a probability distribution of times. An example will be used to explain the process.

Example 8.6

Activity	Preceding activity	Optimistic time	Most likely time	Pessimistic time
A	-	2	3	4
B	-	2	5	8
C	-	7	8	12
D	B	6	7	9
E	A	3	10	12
F	A	11	12	13
G	C, D	2	4	8
H	E	4	7	10
I	F, G	5	9	19
J	H	3	5	15

Table 8.24

First we draw the network diagram.

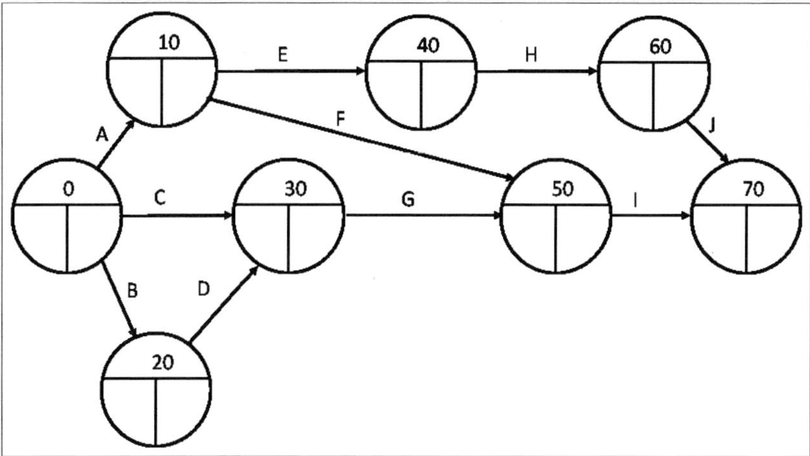

Figure 8.29

Network for Example 8.6

Calculating the mean and variance for each activity using the above formulae we obtain the following:

Activity	Preceding Activity	Optimistic Time	Most Likely Time	Pessimistic Time	Expected Value	Variance	Formula in Column G	Formula in Column H
A	-	2	3	4	3.00	0.11	=(D7+4*E7+F7)/6	=((F7-D7)/6)^2
B	-	2	5	8	5.00	1.00	=(D8+4*E8+F8)/6	=((F8-D8)/6)^3
C	-	7	8	12	8.50	0.69	=(D9+4*E9+F9)/6	=((F9-D9)/6)^2
D	B	6	7	9	7.17	0.25	=(D10+4*E10+F10)/6	=((F10-D10)/6)^2
E	A	3	10	12	9.17	2.25	=(D11+4*E11+F11)/6	=((F11-D11)/6)^2
F	A	11	12	13	12.00	0.11	=(D12+4*E12+F12)/6	=((F12-D12)/6)^2
G	C, D	2	4	8	4.33	1.00	=(D13+4*E13+F13)/6	=((F13-D13)/6)^2
H	E	4	7	10	7.00	1.00	=(D14+4*E14+F14)/6	=((F14-D14)/6)^2
I	F, G	5	9	19	10.00	5.44	=(D15+4*E15+F15)/6	=((F15-D15)/6)^2
J	H	3	5	15	6.33	4.00	=(D16+4*E16+F16)/6	=((F16-D16)/6)^2

Figure 8.30

Expected value and variance for activities of Example 8.6

→ **Excel solution**

Expected Value Cell I7	Formula: = (D7+4*E7+F7)/6 Copy down I7:I16
Variance Cell J7	Formula: = (F7-D7)/6)^2 Copy down J7:J16

Adding the expected activity times to the network we obtain:

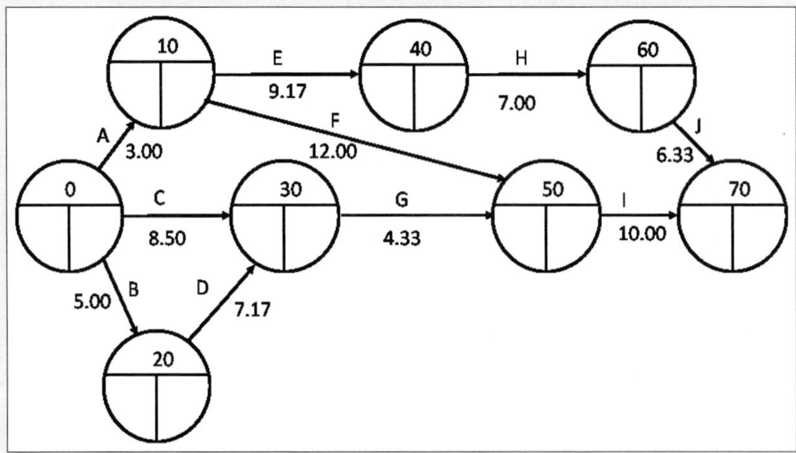

Figure 8.31

Network for Example 8.6 with expected activity times

Unlike timing of the previous networks we cannot use the forward and backward pass to achieve the network times using uncertain activity times, because of the dispersion around the mean. Instead we have to determine all the possible paths through the network and time them separately. The possible paths through this network are as follows:

A - E - H - J

A - F - I

C - G - I

B - D - G - I

Now we need to find the length of each of these paths, but they are probability distributions. Without giving the proof we can use two results for this.

1. The expected time for a path is given by the sum of the expected times for its component activities.
2. The variance for a path is given by the sum of the variances for its component activities. (NB this is why we use variance rather than standard deviation, because we can sum variances but not standard deviations.) Note that we are making the assumption that the activities are independent. We can then take the square root of the summed variance to give the standard deviation of the path.

X

expected activity time the time that an activity is expected to take, an average from pessimistic, optimistic and most likely times.

Path	Expected Value	Variance	Standard Deviation
A - E - H - J	25.50	7.36	2.71
A - F - I	25.00	5.67	2.38
C - G - I	22.83	7.14	2.67
B - D - G - I	26.50	7.69	2.77

Table 8.25

Now another simplifying assumption is that the distribution of the path (the sum of the activity distributions) is a normal distribution. This follows from the central limit theorem mentioned in Chapter 3, provided that there are enough tasks in the paths. Let's assume that there are.

So we can consider that the time of each path follows N $(25.5, 2.71^2)$, N $(25.0, 2.38^2)$, N $(22.83, 2.67^2)$ and N $(26.5, 2.77^2)$. This, of course, means that the length of the project can only be determined with a probability: we can never be exact. At this point revise your understanding of probability and normal curves from Chapter 3. We can now ask questions such as:

1. What is the probability that the project will be completed in 25 weeks?
2. What is the probability that the project time exceeds 28 weeks?

Example 8.7

Taking the first question, 'What's the probability that the project will be completed in 25 weeks?': because the paths may overlap (due to the probability distribution) we need to find the probability of each path being longer than 25 weeks. To establish this we'll make use of the multiplication rule of probability. Start by determining the probability that each path taken separately completes within 25 weeks.

(i) · Path A - E - H - J follows a normal distribution $N(25.5, 2.71^2)$

The Excel solution is illustrated in Figure 8.32.

	A	B	C	D
1				
2				
3		Normal Distribution		
4				
5		Mean μ =	25.5	
6		Standard Deviation σ =	2.71	
7				
8		X =	25	
9				
10		(P <= 25.0) =	0.4268	=NORM.DIST(C8, C5, C6, TRUE)

Figure 8.32
Path A - E - H - J, $P(X \leq 25.0)$

From Excel, the NORM.DIST () function can be used to calculate $P(X \leq 25.0) = 0.4268$.

multiplication rule of probability the multiplication rule is a result used to determine the probability that two events, A and B, both occur.

→ Excel solution

Mean Cell C5	Value
Standard deviation Cell C6	Value
X = Cell C8	Value
P(X <= 25) = Cell C10	Function: = NORM.DIST(C8,C5,C6,TRUE)

Interpretation We observe that the probability that Path A - E - H - J is less than or equal to 25 weeks is 0.4268 or 42.7%.

Or we could use the normal tables (available via the Online Resource Centre): Prob ($X \le 25.0$) = Prob ($Z \le (25.0 - 25.5)/2.71$) = Prob ($Z \le -0.18$) = Prob ($Z \ge 0.18$) = 0.4286.

Note The Excel method and tables will not be the same answer because the tables only use Z to 2 decimal places. The NORM.DIST answer is more accurate.

(ii) Path A - F - I follows a normal distribution N (25.0, 2.38^2)

The Excel solution is illustrated in Figure 8.33.

	A	B	C	D
1				
2				
3		Normal Distribution		
4				
5		Mean μ =	25	
6		Standard Deviation σ =	2.38	
7				
8		X =	25	
9				
10		(P <= 25.0) =	0.5000	=NORM.DIST(C8, C5, C6, TRUE)

Figure 8.33
Path A - F - I, $P(X \le 25.0)$

From Excel, the NORM.DIST () function can be used to calculate $P(X \le 25.0) = 0.5000$.

→ Excel solution

Mean Cell C5	Value
Standard deviation Cell C6	Value
X = Cell C8	Value
P(X <= 25) = Cell C10	Function: = NORM.DIST(C8,C5,C6,TRUE)

Interpretation We observe that the probability that Path A - F - I is less than or equal to 25 weeks is 0.50000 or 50.0%.

Or using the normal tables: Prob $(X \leq 25.0)$ = Prob $(Z \leq (25.0 - 25.0)/2.38)$ = Prob $(Z \leq 0)$ = 1 – Prob $(Z \geq 0) = 1 - 0.50 = 0.5000$.

Note The Excel method and tables will not be the same answer because the tables only use Z to 2 decimal places. The NORM.DIST answer is more accurate.

(iii) Path C - G - I follows a normal distribution $N(22.83, 2.67^2)$

The Excel solution is illustrated in Figure 8.34.

	A	B	C	D
1				
2				
3		Normal Distribution		
4				
5		Mean μ =	22.83	
6		Standard Deviation σ =	2.67	
7				
8		X =	25	
9				
10		(P <= 25.0) =	0.7918	=NORM.DIST(C8, C5, C6, TRUE)

Figure 8.34
Path C - G - I, $P(X \leq 25.0)$

From Excel, the NORM.DIST () function can be used to calculate $P(X \leq 25.0) = 0.7918$.

→ Excel solution

Mean Cell C5	Value
Standard deviation Cell C6	Value
X = Cell C8	Value
P(X <= 25) = Cell C10	Function: = NORM.DIST(C8,C5,C6,TRUE)

Interpretation We observe that the probability that Path C - G - I is less than or equal to 25 weeks is 0.7918 or 79.2%.

Or using the normal tables: Prob $(X \leq 25.0)$ = Prob $(Z \leq (25.0 - 22.83)/2.67)$ = Prob $(Z \leq 0.81)$ = 1 – Prob $(Z \geq 0.81) = 1 - 0.2090 = 0.7909$.

Note The Excel method and tables will not be the same answer because the tables only use Z to 2 dp. The NORM.DIST answer is more accurate.

(iv) And lastly, Path B - D - G - I follows a normal distribution N (26.5, 2.77^2).

The Excel solution is illustrated in Figure 8.35.

	A	B	C	D
1				
2				
3		Normal Distribution		
4				
5		Mean μ =	26.5	
6		Standard Deviation σ =	2.77	
7				
8		X =	25	
9				
10		(P <= 25.0) =	0.2941	=NORM.DIST(C8, C5, C6, TRUE)

Figure 8.35
Path B - D - G - I, P(X ≤ 25.0)

From Excel, the NORM.DIST () function can be used to calculate P(X ≤ 25.0) = 0.2941.

→ Excel solution

Mean Cell C5 — Value
Standard deviation Cell C6 — Value
X = Cell C8 — Value
P(X <= 25) = Cell C10 — Function: = NORM.DIST(C8,C5,C6,TRUE)

Interpretation We observe that the probability that Path B - D - G - I is less than or equal to 25 weeks is 0.2941 or 29.4%.

Or using the normal tables: Prob (X ≤ 25.0) = Prob (Z ≤ (25.0 – 26.5)/2.77) = Prob (Z ≤ –0.54) = Prob (Z ≥ 0.54) = 0.2946

Note The Excel method and tables will not be the same answer because the tables only use Z to 2 decimal places. The NORM.DIST answer is more accurate.

Therefore, the probability that each Path is below 25 weeks:

Path	Probability ≤ 25 weeks
A - E - H - J	0.4268
A - F - I	0.5000
C - G - I	0.7918
B - D - G - I	0.2941

Table 8.26

The project will finish when all paths are complete, that is, A - E - H - J, A - F - I, C - G - I and B - D - G - I are complete. To make matters simpler let's assume that each path is independent of the others. (We know that they are not because of overlapping activities - but the error is not too large for examples.)

Multiplication rule of probability

For two (or more) independent events (say X & Y): Probability (X & Y both occur) = Pr(X) * Pr(Y).

So in this context:

Probability (project completes in 25 weeks)
= Probability (all paths complete in 25 weeks)
= 0.4268 * 0.5000 * 0.7918 * 0.2941 = 0.05

So the probability that project finishes in less than 25 weeks = 0.050.

Interpretation There is only a 5%, or 1 in 20, chance of finishing the project within 25 weeks.

Example 8.8

For the second question, 'What's the probability that the project time exceeds 28 weeks?', we use the fact that a project is completed when all paths through it are completed. Or, the project time will exceed 28 weeks if at least one of the paths exceeds 28 weeks. The combinations of this happening could be huge. For example:

- No of ways that 1 path ≥ 28 weeks = 4 ways
- No of ways that 2 paths ≥ 28 weeks = 6 ways
- No of ways that 3 paths ≥ 28 weeks = 4 ways
- No of ways that 4 paths ≥ 28 weeks = 1 way

So there are 15 ways that the project time could exceed 28 weeks. To enumerate the chances of each of these combinations being true would be time consuming. However, we can use the complement rule of probability to simplify the problem.

The Prob (project time ≥ 28 weeks) = 1 – Prob (project time ≤ 28 weeks) = 1 – Prob (all paths ≤ 28 weeks). So we need to calculate the probability that each path completes within 28 weeks.

(i) Path A - E - H - J follows a normal distribution $N(25.5, 2.71^2)$

The Excel solution is illustrated in Figure 8.36.

	A	B	C	D
1				
2				
3		Normal Distribution		
4				
5		Mean μ =	25.5	
6		Standard Deviation σ =	2.71	
7				
8		X =	28	
9				
10		(P <= 28.0) =	0.8219	=NORM.DIST(C8, C5, C6, TRUE)

Figure 8.36
Path A - E - H - J, P(X ≤ 28.0)

From Excel, the NORM.DIST () function can be used to calculate P(X ≤ 28.0) = 0.8219.

→ Excel solution

Mean	Cell C5	Value
Standard deviation	Cell C6	Value
X =	Cell C8	Value
P(X <= 28) =	Cell C10	Function: = NORM.DIST(C8,C5,C6,TRUE)

Interpretation We observe that the probability that Path A - E - H - J is less than or equal to 28 weeks is 0.8219 or 82.2%.

Or, using the normal tables: Prob(X ≤ 28.0) = Prob(Z ≤ (28.0 – 25.5)/2.71) = Prob(Z ≤ 0.92) = 1 – Prob(Z ≥ 0.92) = 1 – 0.1788 = 0.8212.

Note The Excel method and tables will not be the same answer because the tables only use Z to 2 dp. The NORM.DIST answer is more accurate.

(ii) Path A - F - I follows a normal distribution N(25.0, 2.38^2)

The Excel solution is illustrated in Figure 8.37.

	A	B	C	D
1				
2				
3		Normal Distribution		
4				
5		Mean μ =	25	
6		Standard Deviation σ =	2.38	
7				
8		X =	28	
9				
10		(P <= 28.0) =	0.8963	=NORM.DIST(C8, C5, C6, TRUE)

Figure 8.37
Path A - F - I, P(X ≤ 28.0)

From Excel, the NORM.DIST () function can be used to calculate P(X ≤ 28.0) = 0.8963.

→ Excel solution

Mean Cell C5	Value
Standard deviation Cell C6	Value
X = Cell C8	Value
P(X <= 28) = Cell C10	Function: = NORMDIST(C8,C5,C6,TRUE)

❊ **Interpretation** We observe that the probability that Path A - F - I is less than or equal to 28 weeks is 0.8963 or 89.6%.

Or using the normal tables: Prob(X ≤ 28.0) = Prob(Z ≤ (28.0 – 25.0)/2.38) = Prob(Z ≤ 1.26) = 1 – Prob(Z ≥ 1.26) = 1 – 0.1038 = 0.8962.

Note The Excel method and tables will not be the same answer because the tables only use Z to 2 dp. The NORM.DIST answer is more accurate.

(iii) Path C - G - I follows a normal distribution N(22.83, 2.67^2)

The Excel solution is illustrated in Figure 8.38.

	A	B	C	D
1				
2				
3		Normal Distribution		
4				
5		Mean μ =	22.83	
6		Standard Deviation σ =	2.67	
7				
8		X =	28	
9				
10		(P <= 28.0) =	0.9736	=NORM.DIST(C8, C5, C6, TRUE)

Figure 8.38
Path A - G - I, P(X ≤ 28.0)

From Excel, the NORM.DIST () function can be used to calculate P(X ≤ 28.0) = 0.9736.

➜ Excel solution

Mean Cell C5	Value
Standard deviation Cell C6	Value
X = Cell C8	Value
P(X <= 28) = Cell C10	Function: = NORM.DIST(C8,C5,C6,TRUE)

❊ **Interpretation** We observe that the probability that Path C - G - I is less than or equal to 28 cms is 0.9736 or 97.4%.

Or using the normal tables: Prob(X ≤ 28.0) = Prob(Z ≤ (28.0 – 22.83)/2.67) = Prob(Z ≤ 1.94) = 1 – Prob(Z ≥ 1.94) = 1 – 0.0262 = 0.9738.

Note The Excel method and tables will not be the same answer because the tables only use Z to 2 dp. The NORM.DIST answer is more accurate.

(iv) And lastly, Path B - D - G - I follows a normal distribution $N(26.5, 2.77^2)$.

The Excel solution is illustrated in Figure 8.39.

	A	B	C	D
1				
2				
3		Normal Distribution		
4				
5		Mean μ =	26.5	
6		Standard Deviation σ =	2.77	
7				
8		X =	28	
9				
10		(P <= 28.0) =	0.7059	=NORM.DIST(C8, C5, C6, TRUE)

Figure 8.39
Path B - D - G - I, $P(X \leq 28.0)$

From Excel, the NORM.DIST () function can be used to calculate $P(X \leq 28.0) = 0.7059$.

→ Excel solution

Mean Cell C5 — Value
Standard deviation Cell C6 — Value
X = Cell C8 — Value
P(X <= 28) = Cell C10 — Function: = NORM.DIST(C8,C5,C6,TRUE)

Excel 2010 has a new function that allows for the calculation of the normal cumulative distribution: NORM.DIST.

Interpretation We observe that the probability that Path B - D - G - I is less than or equal to 25 cms is 0.7059 or 70.6%.

Or using the normal tables: $Prob(X \leq 28.0) = Prob(Z \leq (28.0 - 26.5)/2.77) = Prob(Z \leq 0.54) = 1 - Prob(Z \geq 0.54) = 1 - 0.2946 = 0.7054$.

Note The Excel method and tables will not be the same answer because the tables only use Z to 2 dp. The NORM.DIST answer is more accurate.

Therefore the probability that each path completes within 28 weeks:

Path	Probability ≤ 28 weeks
A - E - H - J	0.8219
A - F - I	0.8963
C - G - I	0.9736
B - D - G - I	0.7059

Table 8.27

So we assume that they are independent paths (obviously this is not true because they share activities but the arithmetic is simplified while the principle stays the same). By the multiplication rule the probability that all paths complete within 28 weeks is 0.8219 * 0.8963 * 0.9736 * 0.7059 = 0.505.

Therefore the probability that the project will exceed 28 weeks is 1 – 0.505 (Complement Rule) which is 0.495.

Interpretation There is nearly a 50%, or 1 in 2, chance of the project taking longer than 28 weeks to finish.

Student exercises

X8.12 See the project listed below. All times are in weeks.

Activity	Preceding activity	Optimistic time	Most likely time	Pessimistic time
A	-	7	9	11
B	A	2	5	14
C	A	1	3	5
D	-	3	3	3
E	D	2	5	8
F	D	7	8	9
G	B	2	4	12
H	C, F	1	4	13
I	H	2	5	8

Table 8.28

(a) Draw the network for this project.

(b) Determine the mean time and variance for each activity.

(c) Determine the mean time and standard deviation for each path through the network.

(d) What is the probability that the project will take longer than 19 weeks?

(e) What is the probability that the project will be completed within 24 weeks?

8.4 Controlling a project

How can we adjust the time of activities? For example what happens if projects are beginning to run late? We can do two things:

1. We can spend money on the activities to try and reduce the time of them. That is hire/buy more machines, pay for overtime working, pay for more labour. This is called **crashing a network**.
2. We can reallocate the network so that the present resources can be utilized to bring late activities back into time. This is called **resource allocation**.

8.4.1 Crashing a network

There is no reason why we should necessarily suppose that project activity times should have fixed durations. Poor managerial control can obviously cause activity times to be increased. On the other hand reducing activity times may be a possibility. Usually activity cost is related to the time of the activity. The shorter the activity the more it will cost to do it. So a rough 'model' of the cost function could be

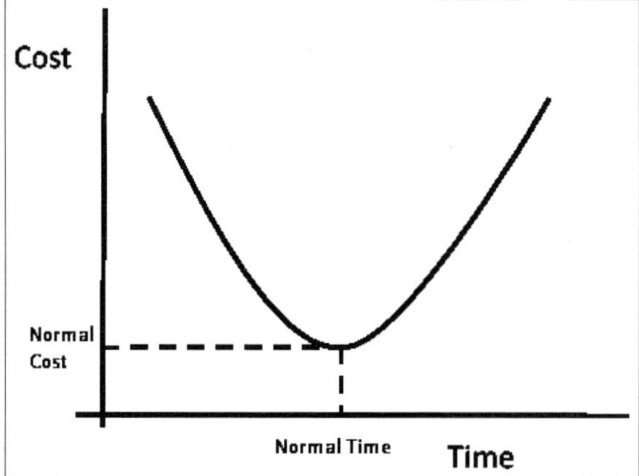

Figure 8.40
Activity cost function

Normal cost is the minimum cost for an activity and the Normal time is the corresponding time.

crashing a network the shortening of activity times by adding resources and hence usually increasing cost.

resource allocation resources allocated to complete the tasks in a project.

activity cost function a methodology that measures the cost of activities, resources, and cost objects.

normal cost the project cost under normal conditions.

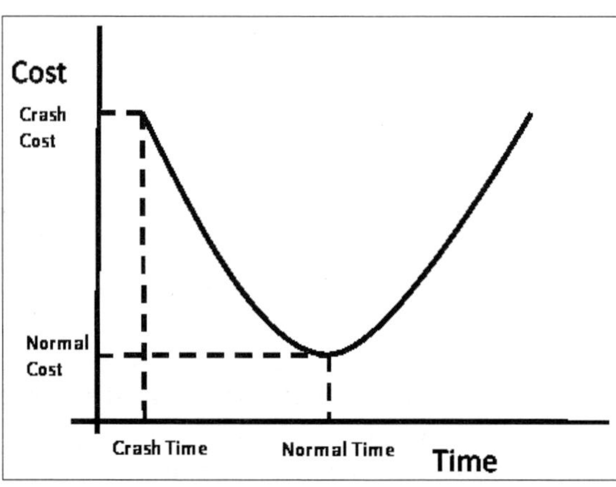

Figure 8.41
Activity cost function indicating normal and crash points

Crash time is the shortest time for the activity and the **crash cost** is the corresponding cost.

So suppose that the normal cost is €500 and normal time is ten weeks and the crash time is 5 weeks but crash cost is €1500. But we would be able to have weeks in between and not just these limits. Without further information as to the individual weekly costs let us assume that the cost function is linear between these extremes. Thus:

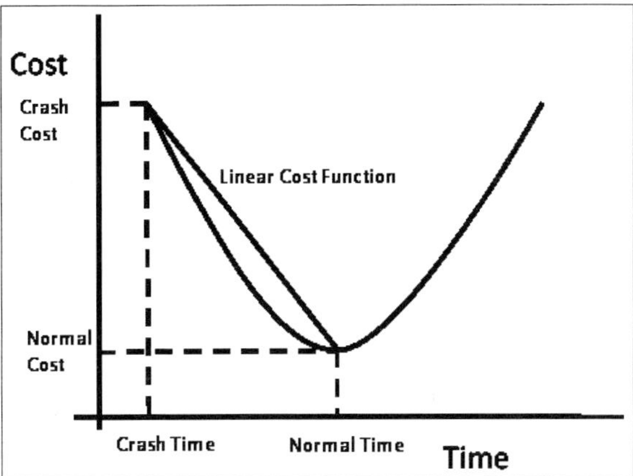

Figure 8.42
Linear cost function approximation of activity cost function

So, the crash cost per week is the gradient of this line, that is:

$$\frac{(\text{Crash Cost} - \text{Normal Cost})}{(\text{Normal Time} - \text{Crash Time})}$$

So in this example crash cost per week = (1500 – 500) / (15 – 10) = 1000/5 = €200 per week. Let us assume that we can only have whole time units. So the table below lists the possibilities for the time duration for this activity. The process is referred to as crashing.

Weeks for activity	Cost (€)
10	500
9	700
8	900
7	1100
6	1300
5	1500

Table 8.29

For each activity we will have crash tables similar to the above (which is not always easy to find in practice). Our objective is to find the minimum time within which a project can be completed. In achieving this minimum time we wish to minimize cost.

crash time time to crash a project.
crash cost cost of crashing a project.

Example 8.9

Consider the following project.

Activity	Preceding activity	Normal time (weeks)	Normal cost (euros)	Crash time (weeks)	Crash cost (euros)
A	–	10	800	6	1200
B	–	8	1000	4	1600
C	A	2	200	1	300
D	–	7	600	5	900
E	A, B	5	500	3	900
F	C	2	100	2	100

Table 8.30

First, draw the network and time the network; hence find the normal time for the project and the critical path.

Check that the following is correct:

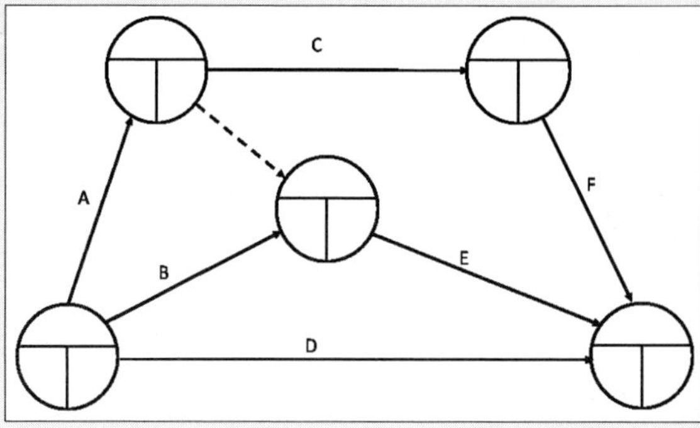

Figure 8.43
Network of Table 8.30

Put in the node numbers and durations. Then use forward and backward pass to obtain the following

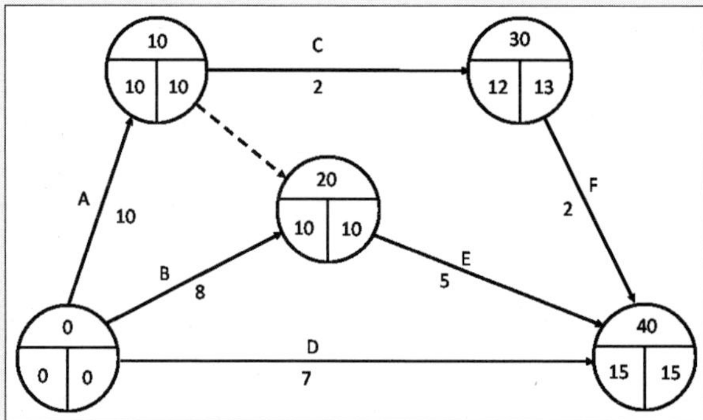

Figure 8.44
Timed network of Table 8.30

- Normal time of project is 15 weeks
- Critical path is A – E
- Normal cost (sum of all costs) €3200

What are the distinct paths through the project and how long do they take?

Path	Duration (weeks)
A – C – F	14
A – E	15
B – E	13
D	7

Table 8.31

Why are these important? At the moment the critical path is A – E. If we decreased A – E by spending money on it then one of the other paths may become critical (e.g. A – C – F). If it does then it is pointless reducing A – E further because the project time is the longest path (the other path e.g. A – C – F) which may or may not have activities in common with A – E.

We can now start work on crashing this project. Remember that we seek the minimum time for completing the project, at minimum cost.

There are three approaches that can be used.

1. Crashing a network can be set up as a linear programming problem.
2. A network can be crashed using a heuristic method. It's a method that is known to give a 'good', but not necessarily 'best', solution to a problem.
3. A total enumeration, of all the paths through a network, can be used to crash a project.

In this chapter we will consider only method 3. It's suitable only for small projects, but will give a good introduction to what is entailed.

To enumerate all the paths we must:

1. Keep track of the reduced time.
2. Keep track of the increased cost to achieve that time.
3. Keep track of the critical path in case it changes during crashing (it nearly always does.).
4. Keep track of the number of weeks we can reduce an activity by and the new amounts by which they can be reduced.

First, lay out the spreadsheet identifying the possible paths as columns and the rows as activities. The cell of a particular activity/path contains the activity duration. I will first demonstrate the tables rather than showing the screen print.

	Path			
Activity	[1]	[2]	[3]	[4]
A	10	10		
B			8	
C	2			
D				7
E		5	5	
F	2			

Table 8.32

total enumeration tracking and evaluating all paths in a project during crashing.

crashing the shortening of activity times by adding resources and hence usually increasing cost.

So Path [1] is A - C - F, Path [2] is A - E, Path [3] is B - E and Path [4] is D.

For each activity we now calculate the number of weeks that it can be crashed by and how much it costs to crash per week, assuming a linear relationship as above.

For example, activity A normal time = 10 weeks, crashed time = 6 weeks, so crash time = 4 weeks.

Normal cost is €800, crash cost = €1200 so crash cost per week = (€1200 – €800)/4 = €100. Note that this is (normal time - crash time)/(crash cost - normal cost).

Insert two additional columns on the spreadsheet to record these and we add an extra row with the duration of each path.

	Path					
Activity	[1]	[2]	[3]	[4]	Cost per week €	Crash time available (weeks)
A	10	10			100	4
B			8		150	4
C	2				100	1
D				7	150	2
E		5	5		200	2
F	2				–	–
Duration	14	15	13	7		

Table 8.33

Note that activity F has a dash for crash time. This is not unusual it just means that F cannot be reduced - whatever the cost. Path [2] (A - E) is the longest path hence it is the critical path which controls the project time.

Now to reduce the project time we only look at activities on the critical path (or paths). If they cannot be reduced then no matter how much we spend on other activities the project time remains the same - so it is wasted expenditure. In this case we only look at A or E at this point. We look for the cheapest of those activities on the critical path. It is pointless spending a lot of money when the same effect can be achieved more cheaply. Importantly, we only crash as far as the next longest path. If we find that we cannot reduce the next path then it is pointless reducing this one below it.

In our case we can reduce A by 4 weeks (€100 each week) and E by 2 weeks (€200 each week) but the next longest path is [1] (A - C - F) which is 14 weeks. At the moment do not look what is in path [1] but only crash path [2] by 1 week (ie not below 14 weeks.). A is the cheaper so knock 1 week off A.

We now produce step 2:

Activity	Path [1]	[2]	[3]	[4]	Cost per week €	Crash time available (weeks)
A	10	10			100	4
B			8		150	4
C	2				100	1
D				7	150	2
E		5	5		200	2
F	2				–	–
Duration	14	15	13	7		
A(1)	–1	–1			100	

Table 8.34

The first column of the new row keeps information as to what we have done (reduced A by 1 week).

The next four columns record the reduction under the columns which are affected. (i.e. all those that involve A). The Cost per week column has the extra crash cost (€100). If we add this row to the previous row we obtain:

	A	B	C	D	E	F	G	H	I
2	**Activity**	**[1]**	**[2]**	**[3]**	**[4]**	**Cost per Week €**	**Crash Time Available (weeks)**	**Formula in Column B (C, D and E similar)**	**Formula in Column G**
3	A	10	10			100	4		
4	B			8		150	4		
5	C	2				100	1		
6	D				7	150	2		
7	E		5	5		200	2		
8	F	2				-	-		
9	Duration	14	15	13	7			=SUM(B3:B8)	
10	A(1)	-1	-1			100			
11	Duration	13	14	13	7		100	=SUM(B9:B10)	=G9+F10

Figure 8.45
Crashing example 8.9 by A(1)

Notice that the final figure under crash time available keeps the accumulated crash cost, which at the moment is €100.

→ Excel solution

Row 9

Time for Path[1] Cell B9 Function = SUM(B3:B8)

Row 10

Reduced activities Cell A10 Value

Reduced Times Cell B10:E10 Values

Crash cost of reduction Cell F9 Values

Row 11

Time for Path[1] Cell B11 Function = SUM(B9:B10)

Path[2] : [4] Copy across B11: E11

Accumulated Cost Cell G11 Formula: = G9+F10

Path [2] is still the longest and we can reduce A or E but only as far as 13. So crash A by 1 week again (only 2 weeks of A left now.) to obtain the following:

	A	B	C	D	E	F	G	H	I
1		Path							
2	Activity	[1]	[2]	[3]	[4]	Cost per Week €	Crash Time Available (weeks)	Formula in Column B (C, D and E similar)	Formula in Column G
3	A	10	10			100	4		
4	B			8		150	4		
5	C	2				100	1		
6	D				7	150	2		
7	E		5	5		200	2		
8	F	2				-	-		
9	Duration	14	15	13	7			=SUM(B3:B8)	
10	A(1)	-1	-1			100			
11	Duration	13	14	13	7		100	=SUM(B9:B10)	=G9+F10
12	A(1)	-1	-1			100			
13	Duration	12	13	13	7		200	=SUM(B11:B12)	=G11+F12

Figure 8.46

Crashing example 8.9 by A(1) again

→ Excel solution

Row 12

Reduced activities Cell A12 Value

Reduced Times Cell B12:E12 Values

Crash cost of reduction Cell F11 Value

Row 13 Cell A12: G12 Copy A11:G11

Every step below enter equivalent to Row 12 then copy Row 13

Note Although we are reducing the time left to crash at every step the values G3:G7 do not change. It is best to keep a note of how much time is left to crash as you go along; e.g., at this stage, A has 2 weeks left and all the other activities are unchanged.

We now have a project with two critical paths [2] A – E and [3] B – E. If we are to reduce further then we need to make sure that we can reduce something in each, otherwise it is not worth proceeding. In this example E is in common so we can reduce E by 1 week (remember only to the next longest which is [1]).

Reverting back to the table rather than the screenshot, we have:

	Path					
Activity	[1]	[2]	[3]	[4]	Cost per week €	Crash time available (weeks)
A	10	10			100	4
B			8		150	4
C	2				100	1
D				7	150	2
E		5	5		200	2
F	2				–	–
Duration	14	15	13	7		
A(1)	–1	–1			100	
Duration	13	14	13	7		100
A(1)	–1	–1			100	
Duration	12	13	13	7		200
E(1)		–1	–1		200	
Duration	12	12	12	7		400

Table 8.35

We now have three paths that are critical ([1], [2] and [3]). We have 2 weeks of A left, 4 weeks of B, 1 week of C, 2 weeks of D and 1 week of E. We can now reduce the 3 paths to week 7 (path [4]) if possible, but what combination? It is obvious that we will need more than 1 activity because we have nothing in common to the three paths. A and B would be €250 per week or C and E would be €300 per week. So reduce A and B as far as we can (only 2 weeks because of A). We obtain:

	Path					
Activity	[1]	[2]	[3]	[4]	Cost per week €	Crash time available (weeks)
A	10	10			100	4
B			8		150	4
C	2				100	1
D				7	150	2
E		5	5		200	2
F	2				–	–
Duration	14	15	13	7		
A(1)	−1	−1			100	
Duration	13	14	13	7		100
A(1)	−1	−1			100	
Duration	12	13	13	7		200
E(1)		−1	−1		200	
Duration	12	12	12	7		400
A(2), B(2)	−2	−2	−2		500	
Duration	10	10	10	7		900

Table 8.36

We still have three paths but we have used all of the 4 weeks crashing of A so we now reduce by C and E but only by 1 week because both cannot be crashed by anymore. We obtain:

	Path					
Activity	[1]	[2]	[3]	[4]	Cost per week €	Crash time available (weeks)
A	10	10			100	4
B			8		150	4
C	2				100	1
D				7	150	2
E		5	5		200	2
F	2				–	–
Duration	14	15	13	7		
A(1)	−1	−1			100	
Duration	13	14	13	7		100
A(1)	−1	−1			100	
Duration	12	13	13	7		200
E(1)		−1	−1		200	
Duration	12	12	12	7		400
A(2), B(2)	−2	−2	−2		500	
Duration	10	10	10	7		900
C(1), E(1))	−1	−1	−1		300	
Duration	9	9	9	7		1200

Table 8.37

Now we still have three paths critical [1], [2], and [3]. But to reduce those would need a combination of A, B, C, and E to be crashed. A, C, and E have used all of their crash time so we cannot reduce all of the paths any further, so we have reached the end.

The shortest project time could be 9 weeks at a cost of €3200 + €1200 = €4400.

Note Notice that B still has 2 weeks to crash and D has 2 weeks. Reducing activity B and/or D would not reduce the project time hence would be wasted expenditure.

As a project manager we would recommend the whole variety of solutions to management; management could vary the length between 9 and 15 weeks, with costs varying between €4400 and €3200.

There is another further modification to this problem before we have to leave it because it is becoming too complex. Usually a project will entail fixed costs—an obvious example is the site office to be found on any large construction site. These management costs are additional to activity costs and will be incurred throughout the life of the project. We'll make the assumption that these costs occur at a constant fixed rate. How will this affect the crashing problem?

In the previous example assume that, in addition to the activity costs, we have a fixed cost of €200 per week. Thus the normal cost becomes €3200 + 15 * €200 = €6200. But when crashing the project we can crash in weeks, and as long as the increased activity cost is less than the fixed cost that we are saving due to less weeks, then we will actually save money. If the increase in activity costs is greater than the saving in fixed costs then the overall cost will begin to increase.

So, using the previous Excel template, now, include the fixed cost reduction (€200 per week for every week saved) next to the variable cost increase due to crashing, and then add another column, net cost change, where we can keep track of the accumulated changes.

Note Because we are now keeping track of three costs at each step, crash cost, fixed cost saving, and accumulated cost, where they are kept in the spreadsheet is a matter of personal choice. We could keep the template as before but remember to reduce the weekly cost as we proceed. I use the following:

	L	M	N	O	P	Q	R	S	T	U	V
1			Path								
2		Activity	[1]	[2]	[3]	[4]	Cost per Week €	Crash Time Available (weeks)	Net cost change €	Formula in Column N (P, Q and R similar)	Formula in Column T
3		A	10	10			100	4			
4		B			8		150	4			
5		C	2				100	1			
6		D				7	150	2			
7		E		5	5		200	2			
8		F	2				-	-			
9		Duration	14	15	13	7				=SUM(N3:N8)	
10		A(1)	-1	-1			100	-200			
11		Duration	13	14	13	7			-100	=SUM(N9:N10)	=T9+R10+S10
12		A(1)	-1	-1			100	-200			
13		Duration	12	13	13	7			-200	=SUM(N11:N12)	=T11+R12+S12

Figure 8.47

Crashing Example 8.9 with fixed cost

fixed costs the portion of the total cost that does not depend on the volume; this cost remains the same no matter how much is produced.

→ Excel solution

Row 9
Time for Path[1] Cell N9 — Function = SUM(N3:N8)
Row 10
Reduced activities Cell M10 — Value
Reduced Times Cell N10:Q10 — Values
Crash cost of reduction Cell R10 — Values
Fixed cost reduction Cell S10 — Value (-)
Row 11
Time for Path[1] Cell N11 — Function = SUM(N9:N10)
Path[2] : [4] — Copy across N11 to Q11
Accumulated Cost Cell T11 — T9+R10+S10
Row 12 — Copy and repeat Row 10
Row 13 — Copy and repeat Row 11

Every step below enter equivalent to Row 12 then copy Row 13

Continuing with the table rather than screenshots we finish with Table 8.38.

	Path						
Activity	[1]	[2]	[3]	[4]	Cost per week €	Crash time available (weeks)	Net cost change €
A	10	10			100	4	
B			8		150	4	
C	2				100	1	
D				7	150	2	
E		5	5		200	2	
F	2				–	–	
Duration	14	15	13	7			
A(1)	–1	–1			100	–200	
Duration	13	14	13	7			–100
A(1)	–1	–1			100	–200	
Duration	12	13	13	7			–200
E(1)		–1	–1		200	–200	
Duration	12	12	12	7			–200
A(2), B(2)	–2	–2	–2		500	–400	
Duration	10	10	10	7			–100
C(1), E(1)	–1	–1	–1		300	–200	
Duration	9	9	9	7			0

Table 8.38

From this we can see that the effect of a fixed cost is actually to reduce the overall cost where the crash cost (+) is cheaper than the fixed cost (–). So we can actually reach a cheapest plan and shortest plan, which are usually different.

So here the original critical path is [2] A – E, time = 15 weeks, cost €6200.

The cheapest (shortest as well) critical paths are [1], A – C – F, [2], A – E, and [3], B – E, time 12 weeks, cost €6200 – €200 = €6000.

The overall shortest critical paths [1], A – C – F, [2], A – E, and [3], B – E, time 9 weeks, cost €6200 + €0 = €6200.

Without other information, management must make the choice.

Student exercises

X8.13 For the project below all times are in weeks and costs in £s.

Activity	Preceding activity	Normal time (weeks)	Normal cost (£s)	Crash time (weeks)	Crash cost (£s)
A	–	4	450	3	500
B	–	5	490	3	800
C	A	7	720	5	920
D	A, B	7	810	4	960
E	C, D	4	80	3	470
F	A, B	9	980	6	1,205
G	A, B	6	540	5	635
H	C, D, G	6	570	4	890
I	E	1	230	1	230

Table 8.39

(a) Draw the network assuming normal times. Determine the project's normal time and normal cost.

(b) Determine its minimum completion time and the associated cost.

X8.14 A project consists of eight activities as shown below. Times are in weeks and costs in £s.

Activity	Preceding activity	Normal time (weeks)	Normal cost £	Crash time (weeks)	Crash cost £
A	–	5	300	3	600
B	A	3	450	2	550
C	A	4	200	1	800
D	B, C	2	250	2	250
E	C	6	300	4	500
F	E	3	80	2	160
G	D	7	500	3	900
H	D, F	2	100	1	150

Table 8.40

In addition there are fixed costs of £150 per week.

(a) Draw the network and find the normal time and normal cost of this project.

(b) Find the minimum cost of the project and the associated duration.

(c) Find the project's minimum duration and the associated cost.

8.4.2 Resource histogram

Activities use up resources as well as time, so the other way that we can control projects is to reallocate resources, using a Gantt chart, and thus reduce activity time because of more resources allocated to it. A Gantt chart is a different, more easily understood, way of representing activity times from the network. It is primarily used for controlling the project once it begins. Again this is only an introduction, but we'll explain with an example.

Example 8.10

A project consists of eight activities, as detailed below. Assume that time is in weeks. Also suppose that resources are the numbers of staff required for the completion of each activity. Further suppose that all staff can be allocated to *any* of the eight activities.

Activity	Preceding activity	Time	Resources
A	–	6	5
B	–	3	4
C	–	5	6
D	A	4	3
E	D	3	5
F	A, B	8	6
G	C	6	2
H	F, G	4	4

Table 8.41

So, for example, C takes 5 weeks and requires six members of staff. Remember that this is an initial situation, in reality complexity means that some staff will spread over several activities at the same time. As usual draw the network to give the logical structure of the activities. Check the network in Figure 8.48. It is best to cover it and try to redraw. Remember to check the final network against the precedence table.

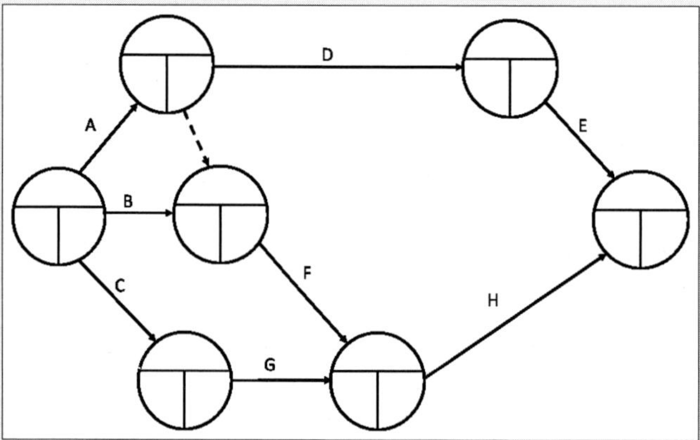

Figure 8.48

Network of Example 8.10

X

resource histogram a block diagram representing the sum of the activity resources at a particular point in time.

Gantt chart a bar chart that depicts a schedule of activities and milestones. Generally activities are listed along the left side of the chart and the time line along the top or bottom. The activities are shown as horizontal bars of a length equivalent to the duration of the activity. Gantt charts may be annotated with dependency relationships and other schedule-related information.

After numbering the nodes and timing the network, using forward and backward pass, you should achieve:

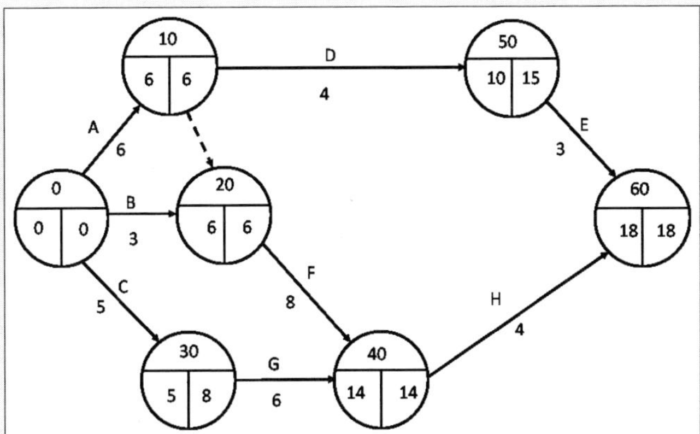

Figure 8.49
Timed network of Example 8.10

The critical path is A - F - H (through the dummy), and the time to completion is 18 weeks.

It is important to find the float times for the Gantt chart. Remember they are LFT - EST - duration, so the float table is shown in Table 8.42.

Activity	EST start node	LFT end node	Duration	Float
B	0	6	3	3
C	0	8	5	3
D	6	15	4	5
E	10	18	3	5
G	5	14	6	3

Table 8.42

Remember that this is the slack time available for an activity and does not affect the duration of the project. A network, or a list of activity times and floats, do not enable you to easily control a project. What we need is a chart to indicate what activities are operating, when and if they are late. This is achieved by translating the network and the floats into a Gantt chart.

This is best drawn and demonstrated via a spreadsheet. First, allocate the columns of the spreadsheet to represent units of time (weeks in this case). It is best to reduce the width of the columns to 3 in order to obtain the grid effect. We know that the project should be finished in 18 weeks, so this is our maximum at the moment.

	A	B	C	D	E	F	G	H	I	J	K	L	M	N	O	P	Q	R	S	T	U	V
1																						
2																						
3																						
4																						
5																						
6																						
7																						
8																						
9																						
10		1	2	3	4	5	6	7	8	9	10	11	12	13	14	15	16	17	18			
11																						
12																						

Figure 8.50

Grid for Gantt chart of Example 8.10

The critical path activities are recorded along the top of the chart. The length of the line represents the duration. Remember that A takes 6 weeks, F takes 8 weeks, and H takes 4 weeks.

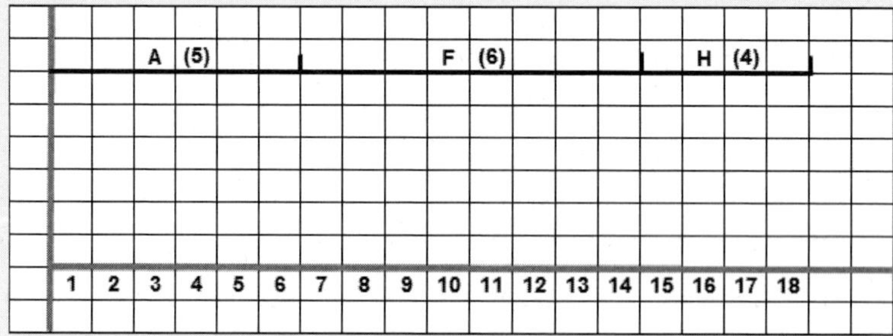

Figure 8.51

Gantt chart of Example 8.10 showing critical path activities

The numbers in brackets are the number of the resource used for that activity thus A is 5 staff, F is 6 staff, and H is 4 staff. Thus we can see from across the room what activity should be running and what should be finished if we are looking at, say, week 10.

All other activities are again drawn as a solid line representing the duration, but the time they start will be at the EST (because they have float they could have a difference). The float time is drawn as a dashed line. They are drawn on separate lines one for each activity. These activities could be imagined to move along the dashed lines if they are to use their float.

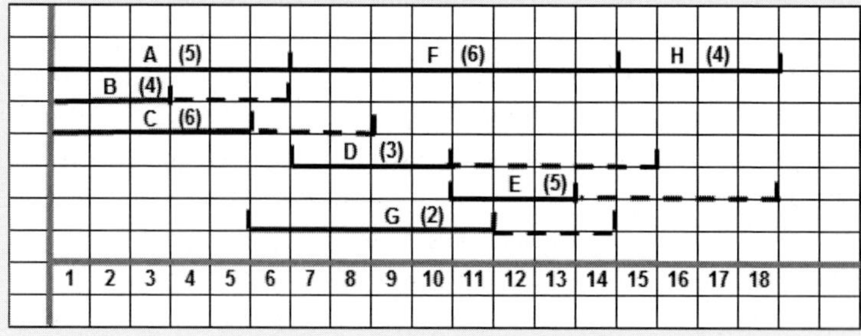

Figure 8.52

Full Gantt chart of Example 8.10

From this Gantt chart we can see what activities should be running on any particular week, what should be finished and what are about to start. To see the resources being used at any particular week we extend below the Gantt chart to make a resource histogram (Figure 8.53). This is a block chart which is the sum of the resources used on a particular week. Thus week 1 will be A5, B4, C6 = 15, week 7 will be F6, D3, and G2 = 11. The row below the Gantt chart is the sum of the resources for a particular week. These are then translated into the block diagram below that.

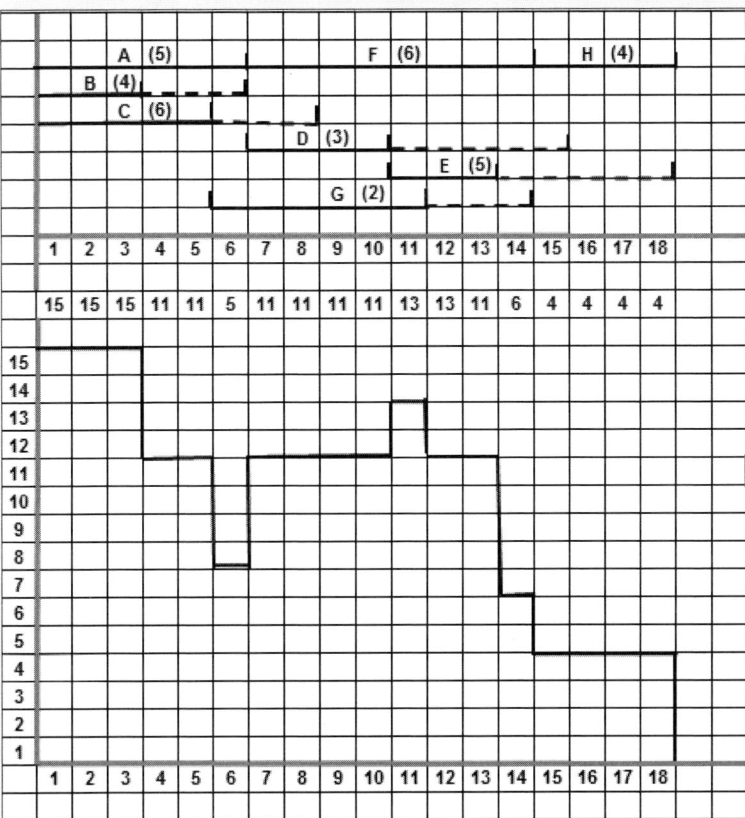

Figure 8.53

Resource histogram of Example 10

It's quite usual for a project to exhibit considerable resource usage fluctuations. So the issue arises, can the resource usage be smoothed out? The answer is yes, provided the activities are not on the critical path and dependent upon their float. Peak usage is in weeks 1–3 (when 15 staff are needed) and to a lesser degree in week 11 (when 13 staff are required). From the Gantt chart we can see that Activity C has 3 weeks float and so its start can be delayed by 3 weeks, by which time B is finished. This reduces staff in weeks 1–3 to just 9. However it makes the situation worse in weeks 7 and 8. Showing this on the diagram below, where the resources are accumulated on the line below the weeks rather than the full resource histogram.

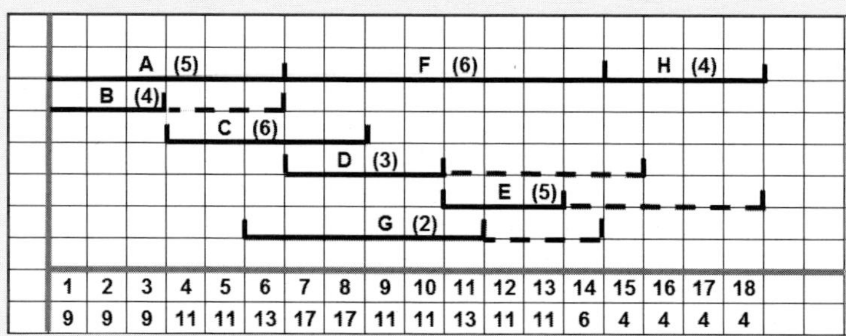

Figure 8.54

Amended Gantt chart and resources of Example 8.10

Weeks 7 and 8 can be reduced by moving D and/or G. Note that if D is moved then E should move with it. The fact that these are dependant can be shown on the Gantt chart by putting the node number at the beginning and end of an activity (although sometimes it can get a bit messy.) 50 would be at the end of D and beginning of E which will act as a reminder that they should move together. If we move E to the latest start time.

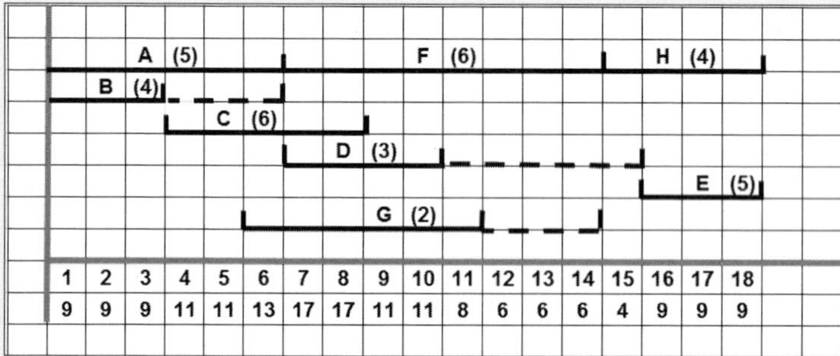

Figure 8.55

Amended Gantt chart and resources of Example 8.10

Then D and G can be moved to start at week 9, so not using all of their Float but reducing resources and still allowing for lateness later.

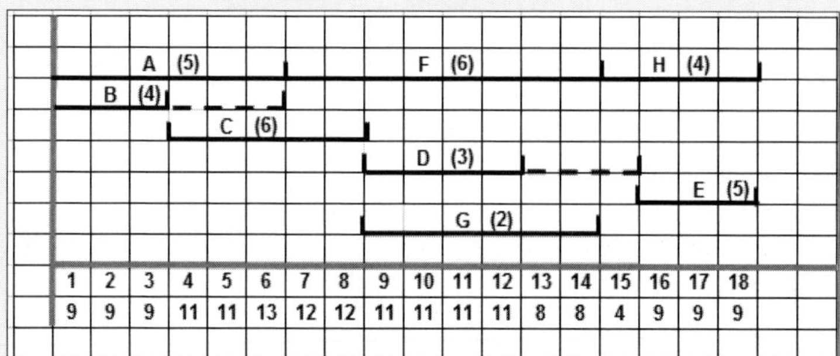

Figure 8.56

Smoothed Gantt chart and resources of Example 8.10

This has reduced the maximum weekly staff requirement from 15 to 12. Note that D and G could be moved further if required.

Student exercises

Please visit the Online Resource Centre which accompanies this textbook for figures solutions in Excel to the student exercises and Techniques in Practice.

X8.15 See the project listed below. In addition to the time duration for each activity, the number of staff required is listed. Staff are multifunctional and are able to work on any activity.

Activity	Preceding activity	Duration (days)	Number of staff required
A	–	4	9
B	–	2	6
C	–	3	3
D	A, B, C	2	4
E	A, B, C	2	7
F	A	4	11
G	A, C	7	7
H	D, G	4	3
I	D, G	5	4
J	E, I	6	2

Table 8.43

(a) Draw the network and identify the critical path and earliest finish time.

(b) On the assumption that all activities start at their earliest time, construct a Gantt chart and resource histogram for this project.

(c) By rescheduling activities, what is the minimum number of staff required to complete the project within the time that you determined in (a)?

Techniques in practice

TP8.1 You are a consultant in Charles Stodge Associates Ltd, a large management consultancy organization.

A syndicate of Welsh business people have been formed to provide a challenge for the Transatlantic Cup. It is your responsibility, on behalf of Charles Stodge Associates, to plan the project.

Welsh Challenge

The project can start on 1 March 2012, but the two yachts *must* be at the start venue by 1 March 2014. As a necessary first step you have broken down the project into separate activities. The table below identifies these activities, the order in which they must be enacted, their durations and costs. For simplicity a week is to be taken to be 5 days and there are 50 weeks in a year (all bank holidays accounted for).

Activity	Description	Preceding activity	Time (weeks)	Cost (£000s)
A	Engage design team	–	10	10
B	Design prototype	A	20	1000
C	Design sails	A	15	45
D	Build scale model and test	B	12	144
E	Have sails made	C	30	600
F	Modify hull design	D	10	10
G	Have electronic equipment Designed and made	–	16	1008
H	Design and build deck equipment	B	10	900
I	Build prototype	F, G, H	20	1000
J	Crew selection	–	40	80
K	Sea trials and crew training	E, I, J	10	250
L	Design and build Second boat	F, G, H	20	1000
M	Extensive sea trials of both boats	K, L	10	500
N	Analysis of boats performance	M	6	12
O	Purchase additional equipment	N	10	900
P	Ship boat to starting venue	N	4	200

Table TP8.1a

In addition, there is a weekly overhead charge of £10,000. The duration of some activities can be reduced at increased cost by working overtime. These are identified below:

Activity	Normal time (weeks)	Crash time (weeks)	Normal cost (£000s)	Crash cost (£000s)
D	12	6	144	200
E	30	20	600	1000
F	10	9	10	12
G	16	12	1008	1500
H	10	7	900	1800
I	20	15	1000	2000
L	20	15	1000	2000
N	6	5	12	14
O	10	9	900	950

Table TP8.1b

The syndicate would like to keep expenditure below £9m but would be prepared to increase this if it was essential.

1. Draw the network and establish the normal duration and cost of the project, and identification of the critical path.
2. Calculate the total float table.

3. Some activities may be subject to alteration. Consider, separately, the likely effects on the timing of the project of the following (do not consider the cost implications.):
    (a) The syndicate would like to book berth facilities for sea trials and crew training (Activity K), from week 70. Should the booking be changed?
    (b) Design prototype (Activity B) may be delayed by 4 weeks.
    (c) Design sails (Activity C) may be delayed by 8 weeks.
    (d) Ship boat to starting venue (Activity P) may be affected by storm and take 7 weeks, instead of 4.

Assuming the project will be timetabled as originally scheduled:

4. Determine the minimum cost of the project and the associated duration.
5. Determine the minimum duration and expected cost.
6. What is the duration of the project if the syndicate insisted in keeping to the original £9m expenditure? What is the associated expected project cost?

TP8.2 Charles Stodge Associates are retained by a client to plan for a restoration project. A stage of this project must be completed as in Precedence Table TP8.2a. What is the probability that this stage will take longer than 30 weeks, and what is the probability that the stage can be completed in 25 weeks?

Activity	Preceding activity	Optimistic time	Most likely time	Pessimistic time
A	-	2	5	8
B	-	3	3	3
C	-	2	4	12
D	A	4	5	12
E	A	2	7	24
F	C	3	6	9
G	B, E	1	4	13
H	F	2	5	14
I	D, G	7	8	9

Table TP8.2a

(a) Draw the network for this project.
(b) Determine the mean time and variance for each activity.
(c) Determine the mean time and standard deviation for each path through the network.
(d) What is the probability that the project will take longer than 30 weeks?
(e) What is the probability that the project will be completed within 25 weeks?

TP8.3 Charles Stodge Associates represent a client with a people resource problem. As a temporary measure they wish to smooth the resources for a particular project in order to be able to reallocate the staff saved elsewhere. The project is listed below. In addition to the time duration for each activity, the number of staff required is listed. Staff are multifunctional and are able to work on any activity.

Activity	Preceding activity	Duration (days)	Number of staff required
A	–	5	7
B	–	8	4
C	–	4	3
D	A	10	2
E	C	12	2
F	A, B, E	7	6
G	B, E	4	4
H	B, E	10	3
I	D, F, K	15	3
J	I, G, H	3	5
K	B, E	5	1

Table TP8.3a

(a) Draw the network and identify the critical path and earliest finish time.

(b) On the assumption that all activities start at their earliest time, construct a Gantt chart and resource histogram for this project.

(c) By rescheduling activities, what is the minimum number of staff required to complete the project within the time that you determined in (a)?

■ Summary

This chapter has introduced several techniques that allow management to control projects. In particular, we first focused on describing the logic of a project by representing it as a set of related tasks to be completed. The project was then represented as a precedence table and then a network. There are two ways of representing the network–'activity on arrow' and 'activity on node'. Throughout the chapter 'activity on arrow' was used. From the network we constructed a set of rules to time the project, that is to say how long it would take given that everything proceeded as planned. A critical path through the project was identified. This is a set of tasks such that as one finishes the next has to begin without a break in time. These set of tasks control the project time and have to be managed very carefully. Along the way we learnt some techniques of controlling projects; for example, milestone meetings at certain node or event times. We can see from these meetings what activities are late, on time or early according to the initial project plan. In order to visualize progress of the project we introduced the Gantt chart. This is the network represented in a more visual form for ease of control. If tasks are not critical they have spare time associated with them i.e. they could start later or earlier and the project overall time would not be affected. This spare time is called float or slack time.

Two techniques of controlling critical paths were introduced: crashing and resource allocation. Crashing is where money is spent on a task (working overtime, more machines, more staff, etc.) to reduce the activity time. From this we can recommend to management ways of completing projects earlier if money is spent on it, or, possibly more likely, reducing times of projects that are beginning to run late. Resource allocation is a way that the project manager or team can control the allocation of resources (men, machines, etc.) between parallel tasks. Thus tasks can be extended in time or started earlier or later than originally planned but at the same time money may be saved by 'smoothing' resource usage in the project. This is an introduction to capacity planning.

Initially project planning (CPA/CPM – critical path analysis/method) uses 'normal' fixed times as estimates for the future tasks, which can be amended as the project progresses and a new network analysis produced. In reality, activity times are not exact and many activity times are estimated at the start of the project; for example, optimistic time, most likely time, and pessimistic time. To analyse these, techniques of uncertain activity times were introduced that allow the project manager to estimate the probability of completing a project within a certain time rather than saying how long the project would take.

Project management in practice is a combination of all of the above techniques and computer software such as Microsoft Project is used for the necessary complex computations and presentations. There are various methodologies, such as PRINCE2, which train the skills of project management.

Student exercise answers

For all figures listed below, please see the Online Resource Centre.

X8.1 **Figure X8.1**

X8.2 **Figure X8.2**

X8.3 **Figure X8.3**

X8.4 **Figure X8.4**

X8.5 **Figure X8.5**

X8.6 **Figure X8.6**

X8.7 **Figure X8.7**

X8.8 **Figure X8.8**

X8.9 **Figure X8.9**

There are two critical paths: B – D – H – F and C. Float Table:

Figure X8.9a

Figure X8.9b

X8.10 The critical path is: C – F – D – H. Float Table:

Figure X8.10a

Figure X8.10b

X8.11 There are two critical paths: C – D – K – M and B – H – J. Float Table:

Figure X8.11a

Figure X8.11b

X8.12 You should check your solution against that given below.

(a) **Figure X8.12a**

(b) Time and variance for each activity

Figure X8.12b

X

capacity planning is the process of determining the production capacity needed by an organization to meet changing demands for its products.

critical path analysis critical path analysis (and PERT) are powerful tools to help schedule and manage complex projects.

most likely time the most likely activity time under normal conditions.

Microsoft Project computer software to plan and control projects.

(c) Expected time, variance and standard deviation for each path

Path	Expected value	Variance	Standard deviation
A - B - G	20	7.22	2.69
A - C - H - I	22	5.88	2.42
D - F - H - I	21	5.11	2.26
D - E	8	1.00	1.00

Table X8.12

(d) Probability project time exceeds 19 weeks

$$\Pr(\text{project time} \geq 19) = 1 - \Pr(\text{project time} \leq 19).$$

(i) Path A - B - G

The Excel solution is illustrated

Figure X8.12c

From Excel, the NORM.DIST () function can be used to calculate $P(X \leq 19.0) = 0.3550$.

Or we could use the normal tables from the Online Resource Centre.

$$\Pr(\text{path A-B-G} \leq 19) = \Pr(Z \leq [(19 - 20) / 2.69]) = \Pr(Z \leq -0.37)$$
$$= \Pr(Z \geq 0.37) = 0.3557$$

(ii) Path A - C - H - I

The Excel solution is illustrated

Figure X8.12d

From Excel, the NORM.DIST () function can be used to calculate $P(X \leq 19.0) = 0.1075$.

Or we could use the normal tables.

$$\Pr(\text{path A - C - H - I} \leq 19) = \Pr(Z \leq [(19 - 22) / 2.42]) = \Pr(Z \leq -1.24)$$
$$= \Pr(Z \geq 1.24) = 0.1075$$

(iii) Path D - F - H - I

The Excel solution is illustrated

Figure X8.12e

From Excel, the NORM.DIST () function can be used to calculate $P(X \leq 19.0) = 0.1881$.

Or, using the normal tables:

$$\Pr(\text{path D - F - H - I} \leq 19) = \Pr(Z \leq [(19 - 21) / 2.26]) = \Pr(Z \leq -0.88)$$
$$= \Pr(Z \geq 0.88) = 0.1881$$

(iv) Path D - E

The Excel solution is illustrated

Figure X8.12f

From Excel, the NORM.DIST () function can be used to calculate $P(X \leq 19.0) = 1.0000$.

It is a certainty that path D-E will complete within 19 weeks.

Then, by using the multiplication rule:

$$\begin{aligned}\text{Pr(project completes in 19 weeks)} &= 0.3550 * 0.1075 * 0.1881 * 1.0000 \\ &= 0.0072\end{aligned}$$

So the probability that the project exceeds 19 weeks = 1 – 0.0072 = 0.9928.

That is a 99% chance.

(e) Probability project completed within 24 weeks

(i) Path A - B - G

The Excel solution is illustrated

Figure X8.12g

From Excel, the NORM.DIST () function can be used to calculate $P(X \leq 24.0) = 0.9315$.

Or we could use the normal tables.

$$\begin{aligned}\text{Pr(path A-B-G} \leq 24) &= \Pr(Z \leq [(24 - 20) / 2.69]) = \Pr(Z \leq 1.49) \\ &= 0.9319\end{aligned}$$

(ii) Path A - C - H - I

The Excel solution is illustrated

Figure X8.12h

From Excel, the NORM.DIST () function can be used to calculate $P(X \leq 24.0) = 0.7957$

Or, using the normal tables.

$$\begin{aligned}\text{Pr(Path A-C-H-I} \leq 24) &= \Pr(Z \leq [(24 - 22) / 2.42) = \Pr(Z \leq 0.83) \\ &= 1 - \text{Prob}(Z \geq 0.83) = 1 - 0.2033 = 0.7967\end{aligned}$$

(iii) Path D - F - H - I

The Excel solution is illustrated

Figure X8.12i

From Excel, the NORM.DIST () function can be used to calculate $P(X \leq 24.0) = 0.9078$.

Or we could use the normal tables.

$$\begin{aligned}\text{Pr(Path D-F-H-I} \leq 24) &= \Pr(Z \leq [(24 - 21) / 2.26) = \Pr(Z \leq 1.33) \\ &= 1 - \text{Prob}(Z \geq 1.33) = 1 - 0.0918 = 0.9082\end{aligned}$$

(iv) Path D - E

It is a certainty that path D–E completes in 24 weeks.

So, using the multiplication rule, the probability that the project completes within 24 weeks is given by: 0.9315 * 0.7957 * 0.9078 * 1.0000 = 0.6729.

That is a near enough 70% chance.

X8.13 You should check your solution against that given below.

Figure X8.13

Normal time of project is 18 weeks

Critical path is B – D – H

Normal cost (sum of all costs) £4,870

Below is a crashing table to establish the minimum time for the project (at minimum extra cost).

Minimum time: 12 weeks, associated cost: £4,870 + £1,465 = £6,335

	Path											
Activity	A-C-E-I	A-C-H	A-D-E-I	A-D-H	A-G-H	A-F	B-D-E-I	B-D-H	B-G-H	B-F	Crash cost per week	Crash time available
A	4	4	4	4	4	4					50	1
B							5	5	5	5	155	2
C	7	7									100	2
D			7	7			7	7			50	3
E	4		4				4				390	1
F						9				9	75	3
G					6				6		95	1
H		6		6	6			6	6		160	2
I	1		1				1				-	-
Duration	16	17	16	17	16	13	17	18	17	14		
D(1)			–1	–1			–1	–1			50	
Duration	16	17	15	16	16	13	16	17	17	14		50
H(1)		–1		–1	–1			–1	–1		160	
Duration	16	16	15	15	15	13	16	16	16	14		210
A(1), D(1), G(1)	–1	–1	–2	–2	–2	–1	–1	–1	–1		195	
Duration	15	15	13	13	13	12	15	15	15	14		405
B(1), C(1)	–1	–1					–1	–1	–1	–1	255	
Duration	14	14	13	13	13	12	14	14	14	13		660
B(1), C(1)	–1	–1					–1	–1	–1	–1	255	
Duration	13	13	13	13	13	12	13	13	13	12		915
E(1), H(1)	–1	–1	–1	–1	–1		–1	–1	–1		550	
Duration	12	12	12	12	12	12	12	12	12	12		1465

Table X8.13

Note: 1 week of D and 3 weeks of F have not been crashed. Doing so would be a waste of money.

X8.14 You should check your solution against that given below.

Figure X8.14

Normal time = 20 weeks.

Critical path is A - C - E - F - H

Normal cost = activity costs + fixed costs = 2180 + 20(150) = £5180.

(i) Minimum cost

	Path							
Activity	A-B-D-G	A-B-D-H	A-C-D-G	A-C-D-H	A-C-E-F-H	Crash cost per week	Crash time available	Net cost change £
A	5	5	5	5	5	150	2	
B	3	3				100	1	
C			4	4	4	200	3	
D	2	2	2	2		-	-	
E					6	100	2	
F					3	80	1	
G	7		7			100	4	
H		2		2	2	50	1	
Duration	17	12	18	13	20			
F(1),H(1)		–1		–1	–2	130	–300	
Duration	17	11	18	12	18			–170
A(2)	–2	–2	–2	–2	–2	300	–300	
Duration	15	9	16	10	16			–170

Table X8.14a

So the minimum cost = 5180 – 170 = £5010. The associated duration is 16 weeks.

(ii) Minimum time

	Path							
Activity	A-B-D-G	A-B-D-H	A-C-D-G	A-C-D-H	A-C-E-F-H	Crash cost per week	Crash time available	Net cost change £
A	5	5	5	5	5	150	2	
B	3	3				100	1	
C			4	4	4	200	3	
D	2	2	2	2		–	–	
E					6	100	2	
F					3	80	1	
G	7		7			100	4	
H		2		2	2	50	1	
Duration	17	12	18	13	20			
F(1),H(1)		–1		–1	–2	130	–300	
Duration	17	11	18	12	18			–170
A(2)	–2	–2	–2	–2	–2	300	–300	
Duration	15	9	16	10	16			–170
C(1)			–1	–1	–1	200	–150	
Duration	15	9	15	9	15			–120
G(2), E(2)	–2		–2		–2	400	–300	
Duration	13	9	13	9	13			–20
G(2), C(2)	–2		–4	–2	–2	600	–300	
Duration	11	9	9	7	11			280

Table X8.14b

So the minimum time is 11 weeks. The associated cost is 5180 + 280 = £5460.

X8.15 (a) **Figure X8.15a**

Critical path: A-G-I-J, earliest finish time: 22 days.

Float table:

Activity	EST start node	LFT end node	Duration	Float
A	0	4	4	0
B	0	9	2	7
C	0	4	3	1
D	4	11	2	5
E	4	16	2	10
F	4	22	4	14
G	4	11	7	0
H	11	22	4	7
I	11	16	5	0
J	16	22	6	0

Table X8.15

(b) Gantt chart and resource histogram

Figure X8.15b

(c) The minimum number of staff required to complete the project within 22 days is 13: below shows one possible rescheduling of activities.

Figure X8.15c

TP8.1 1. Draw the network and establish the normal duration and cost of the project, and identification of the critical path.

Figure TP8.1a

Normal duration = 108 weeks

Critical path = ABDFIKMNO

Normal cost activities £7,659,000 + overheads 108 * £10,000 = £8,739,000

2. Total float table

Activity	EST start node	LFT end node	Duration	Float (weeks)
A	0	10	10	0
B	10	30	20	0
C	10	42	15	17
D	30	42	12	0
E	25	72	30	17
F	42	52	10	0
G	0	52	16	36
H	30	52	10	12
I	52	72	20	0
J	0	72	40	32
K	72	82	10	0
L	52	82	20	10
M	82	92	10	0
N	92	98	6	0
O	98	108	10	0
P	98	108	4	6

Table TP8.1c

3. Some activities may be subject to alteration. Consider, separately, the likely effects on the timing of the project of the following (do not consider the cost implications.):
   (a) Activity K begins at week 72; so booking should be put forward by 2 weeks.
   (b) Activity B is on the critical path; hence delay project by 4 weeks.
   (c) Activity C has Float of 17 weeks, with no overall effect, but the float will be reduced from following activity (E).
   (d) No effect on overall project time.

   Assuming the project will be timetabled as originally scheduled:

4. We must keep track of the paths in the network to determine the critical ones during crashing, and we must only crash the critical paths.

   There are 16 paths through the network.

Path	Duration
ABHLMNO	87
ABHIKMNO	96
ABDFLMNO	98
ABDFIKMNO	108
ACEKMNO	91
GLMNO	62
GIKMNO	72
JKMNO	76
ABHLMNP	81
ABHIKMNP	90
ABDFLMNP	92
ABDFIKMNP	102
ACEKMNP	85
GLMNP	56
GIKMNP	66
JKMNP	70

Table TP8.1d

We can enumerate this using every individual path; however, note that a path involving P can never be critical. P is parallel to O, P is 4 weeks, O is 10 weeks and can only be crashed to 9 weeks. Also, the critical path ABDFIKMNO can be reduced by a maximum of 13 weeks; therefore any path below 95 weeks would never become critical.

So we only need to crash

Path	Duration
ABHIKMNO	96
ABDFLMNO	98
ABDFIKMNO	108

Table TP8.1e

Crash table:

Figure TP8.1b

So, the minimum cost of the project is at line 26; that is, normal cost activities £8,739,000 – £20,000 = £8,719,000. Associated duration is 100 weeks.

5. The minimum duration is 94 weeks but the cost is £8,739,000 + £970,000 = £9,709,000.
   Minimum duration below £9,000,000 is 99 weeks which means that the boats could be at the starting venue 1 week early. Expected cost is £8,739,000 + £20,000 = £8,759,000.

TP8.2 (a) **Figure TP8.2a**

(b) **Figure TP8.2b**

(c)

Path	Mean	Variance	Std Dev
A-D-I	19.00	2.89	1.70
A-E-G-I	27.00	18.56	4.31
B-G-I	16.00	4.11	2.03
C-F-H	17.00	7.78	2.79

Table TP8.2b

(d) Probability project time exceeds 30 weeks

$$\Pr(\text{project time} \geq 30) = 1 - \Pr(\text{project time} \leq 30).$$

(i) Path A - D - I

The Excel solution is illustrated

Figure TP8.2c

From Excel, the NORM.DIST () function can be used to calculate $P(X \leq 30.0) = 1.0000$.

It is a certainty that path A - D - I will complete within 30 weeks.

Or we could use the normal tables.

$$\Pr(\text{path A - D - I} \leq 30) = \Pr(Z \leq [(30 - 19) / 1.7]) = \Pr(Z \leq 6.47)$$
$$= 1 - \Pr(Z \geq 6.47) = 1.0000$$

(ii) Path A - E - G - I

The Excel solution is illustrated

Figure TP8.2d

From Excel, the NORM.DIST () function can be used to calculate $P(X \leq 30.0) = 0.7568$

Or we could use the normal tables.

$$\Pr(\text{path A - E - G - I} \leq 30) = \Pr(Z \leq [(30 - 27) / 4.31]) = \Pr(Z \leq 0.70)$$
$$= 1 - \Pr(Z \geq 0.70) = 1 - 0.2420 = 0.7580$$

(iii) Path B - G - I

The Excel solution is illustrated

Figure TP8.2e

From Excel, the NORM.DIST () function can be used to calculate $P(X \leq 30.0) = 1.0000$.

It is a certainty that path B - G - I will complete within 30 weeks.

Or using the normal tables

$$\Pr(\text{path B - G - I} \leq 30) = \Pr(Z \leq [(30 - 16) / 2.03]) = \Pr(Z \leq 6.90)$$
$$= 1.0000$$

(iv) Path C - F - H

The Excel solution is illustrated

Figure TP8.2f

From Excel, the NORM.DIST () function can be used to calculate $P(X \leq 30.0) = 1.0000$.

It is a certainty that path C - F - H will complete within 30 weeks.

Or using the normal tables

$$\Pr(\text{path C - F - H} \leq 30) = \Pr(Z \leq [(30 - 17) / 2.79]) = \Pr(Z \leq 4.66)$$
$$= 1.0000$$

Then, by using the multiplication rule:

$$\Pr(\text{project completes in 30 weeks}) = 1.0000 * 0.7568 * 1.0000 * 1.0000$$
$$= 0.7568.$$

So the probability that the project exceeds 30 weeks = 1 – 0.7568 = 0.2432. That is a 24% chance.

(e) Probability project completed within 25 weeks

(i) Path A - D - I

The Excel solution is illustrated

Figure TP8.2g

From Excel, the NORM.DIST () function can be used to calculate $P(X \leq 25.0) = 0.9998$.

Or we could use the normal tables.

$$\Pr(\text{path A - D - I} \leq 25) = \Pr(Z \leq [(25 - 19) / 1.7]) = \Pr(Z \leq 3.53)$$
$$= 1 - \Pr(Z > 3.53) = 1 - 0.0002 = 0.9998$$

(ii) Path A - E - G - I

The Excel solution is illustrated

Figure TP8.2h

From Excel, the NORM.DIST () function can be used to calculate $P(X \leq 25.0) = 0.3213$.

Or using the normal tables

$$\Pr(\text{Path A - E - G - I} \leq 25) = \Pr(Z \leq [(25 - 27) / 4.31) = \Pr(Z \leq -0.46)$$
$$= \text{Prob}(Z \geq 0.46) = 0.3228$$

(iii) Path B - G - I

The Excel solution is illustrated

Figure TP8.2i

From Excel, the NORM.DIST () function can be used to calculate $P(X \leq 25.0) = 1.0000$.

It is a certainty that path B - G - I will complete within 25 weeks.

Or we could use the normal tables.

$$\Pr(\text{Path B - G - I} \leq 25) = \Pr(Z \leq [(25 - 16) / 2.03) = \Pr(Z \leq 4.43) = 1.0000$$

(iv) Path C - F - H

The Excel solution is illustrated

Figure TP8.2j

From Excel, the NORM.DIST () function can be used to calculate $P(X \leq 25.0) = 0.9979$.

Or we could use the normal tables.

$$\Pr(\text{Path C - F - H} \leq 25) = \Pr(Z \leq [(25 - 17) / 2.79) = \Pr(Z \leq 2.87)$$
$$= 1 - \text{Prob}(Z \geq 2.87) = 1 - 0.0021 = 0.9979$$

So using the multiplication rule, the probability that the project completes within 25 weeks is given by: 0.9998 * 0.3213 * 1.0000 * 0.9979 = 0.3206.

That is a near enough 32% chance.

TP8.3 **Figure TP8.3a**

Critical path C-E-F-I-J

Earliest finish time 41 days

Float Table

Activity	EST start node	LFT end node	Duration	Float
A	0	13	5	8
B	0	16	8	8
C	0	4	4	0
D	5	23	10	8
E	4	16	12	0
F	16	23	7	0
G	16	38	4	18
H	16	38	10	12
I	23	38	15	0
J	38	41	3	0
K	16	23	5	2

Table TP8.3b

Gantt chart

Figure TP8.3b

The maximum number of staff required is 14 in weeks 1-4 and 17-20.

(c) To complete the project within 41 days a minimum of 9 staff are required. One schedule possible schedule is as below.

Figure TP8.3c

Further reading

Textbook resources

1. D. R. Anderson, D. J. Sweeney, T. A. Williams, and K. Martin (2008) *An Introduction to Management Science: Quantitative Approaches to Decision Making* (12th edn), Thomson Learning.
2. F. Hillier, M. Hillier, K. Schemedders, and M. Stephens (2008) *Introduction to Management Science: A Modeling and Case Studies Approach with Spreadsheets* (3rd edn), McGraw Hill.
3. S. J. Mantel and J. R. Meredith (2000) *Project Management: A Managerial Approach* (4th edn), John Wiley & Sons.
4. C. Morris (2008) *Quantitative Approaches in Business Studies* (7th edn), Prentice Hall.
5. B. Render, R. Stair, M. Hanna (2012) *Quantitative Analysis for Management* (11th edn), Pearson Education.

Web resources

1. http://www.apm.org.uk
2. http://www.prince2.com

Formula summary

Expected Activity Time

$$\left(\frac{\text{Optimistic Time} + 4(\text{Most Likely Time}) + \text{Pessimistic Time}}{6}\right) \qquad (8.1)$$

Variance of Activity Time

$$\left(\frac{\text{Pessimistic Time-Optimistic Time}}{6}\right)^2 \qquad (8.2)$$

Part IV

Decision Making in Finance

Decision making in business

9

» Overview «

In this chapter we provide the reader with an introduction to the concept of decision making techniques within business.

» Learning outcomes «

On completing this chapter you should be able to:

» Understand the concept of decision making under certainty, uncertainty, risk, and utility.

» Use a payoff table to make a decision.

» Apply various decision rules, including maximin, maximax, minimax regret and the Hurwicz rule.

» Define and apply the expected value criterion for decision making.

» Compute the value of perfect information.

» Incorporate a degree of uncertainty into the decision making process via the calculation of the return-to-risk ratio.

» Know what is meant by a decision tree and use to solve problems.

» Incorporate Bayes' Theorem into a decision tree.

» Undertake sensitivity analysis on a decision tree.

» Incorporate the decision maker's attitude to risk via the calculation of a utility function.

» Solve problems using the Microsoft Excel spreadsheet.

9.1 Introduction to decision making

In this section and subsequent sections of this chapter we will use the ideas discussed in earlier sections on probability to apply to the concept of decision making. Making decisions is a key component in managing organizations or even in your own personal life.

For an organization, decision making may involve deciding on whether it is a good idea to invest resources in the development of a major new computer project. At a personal level, decision making could mean having to decide whether or not to take out building and contents insurance for a property with no mortgage. All decision models have common characteristics as outlined below:

1. **States of nature** - the decision maker should develop a decision model with mutually exclusive and exhaustive list of all possible future events.
2. **Decision alternatives** - the decision maker develops a finite number of alternative decisions available when the decision model is developed.
3. **Payoff table** - the decision maker should construct a payoff table if the monetary costs are known for each alternative event within the decision model. In most cases this model will be dependent upon a series of conditional probabilities given that any course of action will be dependent upon a number of consecutive alternatives events. In the case where monetary value is not known then we decide based on a concept of **utility**.

Example 9.1

Consider the situation where a house owner who needs to decide whether or not to take building and contents insurance on a property with no mortgage. The owner can decide from alternative decisions:

1. Purchase building and contents insurance
2. Do not purchase building and contents insurance

At this point the following two events can occur:

1. Owner spills paint on the new stair carpet
2. Owner does not spill paint on the new stair carpet

Figure 9.1 illustrates a diagrammatic representation of these alternatives (purchase insurance, do not purchase insurance) and the two possible events (spill, do not spill). If we know the costs of each potential outcome, this decision tree can then be used to make a decision.

1. Insure, spill.
2. Insure, do not spill.
3. Do not insure, spill.
4. Do not insure, do not spill.

X

states of nature the decision maker should develop a decision model with mutually exclusive and exhaustive list of all possible future events.

decision alternatives the decision maker develops a finite number of alternative decisions available when the decision model is developed.

payoff table (or matrix) table that shows the outcomes for each combination of alternatives and events in a decision.

utility a measure that shows the real value of money to a decision maker.

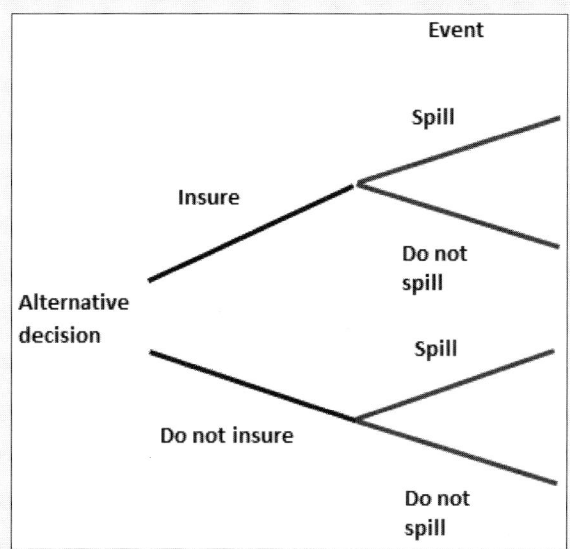

Figure 9.1

If we assume that the cost of insurance is €1500 and the cost of replacing the carpet after a paint spill is €900 then we can create a payoff table (or payoff matrix), as illustrated in Table 9.1.

		States of nature	
		Spill paint	Do not spill paint
Decision Alternative	Insure	€1500	€1500
	Do not insure	€900	€0

Table 9.1 Payoff table

We observe from this example that the cost of insurance is greater than the cost of replacing the carpet. In this case, we would not pay for the insurance but the insurance covers the building and cost of contents within the building and therefore we would make a decision on this basis together with all other information at the disposal of the home owner (including quotes from other insurance companies). In general, managers will use the following key steps when making a decision:

1. Define the problem - correctly identify the problem to the decision maker.
2. Gather information - information gathering aims to identify relevant facts related to the decision problem.
3. Identify action alternatives - use step 1 and 2 to confirm problem solution alternatives.
4. Evaluate the alternative - compare the advantages and disadvantages of each alternative action and select the best alternative.
5. Implement the chosen alternative - based upon the problem and alternatives construct a course of action that will require managerial tasks to be performed, e.g. sales, marketing, and finance.

X

payoff table (or matrix) table that shows the outcomes for each combination of alternatives and events in a decision.

Together with these five key steps we can evaluate the alternative scenarios by using decision criterion that will be dependent upon the degree of certainty (or uncertainty) associated with each of the possible outcomes identified within the payoff table (or decision tree). This degree of uncertainty can be classified as follows:

1. **Decision making with certainty.**
2. Decision making with uncertainty.
3. Decision making with risk.

Figure 9.2 illustrates the types of decision making environments.

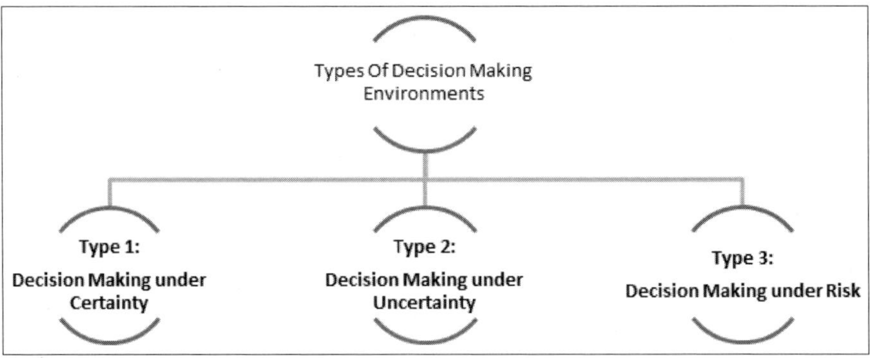

Figure 9.2

Student exercises

X9.1 Describe the five main steps in making a decision.

9.2 Type 1: Decision making with certainty

The decision maker knows for sure (that is, with certainty) the outcome or consequence of every decision alternative. If we know from a given starting point what will be the final outcome of the decision making then we would choose the alternative with the most attractive payoff (values are deterministic). This is called decision making with certainty.

Example 9.2

For example, if we invest in a bank savings account we would be guaranteed a savings rate of P% and the interest earned would be known. In many situations, making a decision can be quite difficult even if you know all the factors and outcomes.

X

certainty the decision maker knows for sure (that is, with certainty) the outcome or consequence of every decision alternative.

uncertainty (or strict uncertainty) situation in which we can list possible events for a decision, but cannot give them probabilities.

decision making with certainty the decision maker knows for sure (that is, with certainty) the outcome or consequence of every decision alternative.

deterministic describing a situation of certainty.

Example 9.3

For example, is it best to pay a fair salary to your employees and what do we mean by a fair salary? Is it best to give medical doctors a 5% increase in salary or do you focus on increasing nurses salaries by 20% given the perceived low level of nurse salaries compared to doctor salaries. This implies that when making decisions involving certainty we still have a subjective element to the decision making.

Although this case appears straightforward, the problem of calculating the payoff for each alternative action, or at least of identifying an action that would result in an outcome which was satisfactory, may not be trivial. Methods of operational research may be required to solve this type of problem. In some cases outcomes may be characterized by several attributes which are not directly comparable.

For example, when choosing between different computer systems for a department, considerations such as speed, price, reliability, memory size, and portability may all be important factors. Somehow, a set of weights for the different types of attribute has to be found, so that a single figure for the overall utility of an action can be calculated.

Student exercises

X9.2 Which alternative investment would you choose if presented with the investments outlined in Table 9.2?

	Investment	Profit
Alternative	A	150
	B	200
	C	139
	D	180
	E	200

Table 9.2

X9.3 Describe what we mean by making a decision under certainty and illustrate with a practical example.

9.3 Type 2: Decision making with uncertainty

In many situations we will not have information at all about various outcomes or states of nature. The uncertainty evident in making decisions can also include not being able to provide an estimate of the probability that a given event will occur. This defines decision making under uncertainty where the chance of an event (or events) occurring in the decision making process is unknown or difficult to assess. This is called probabilistic or stochastic decision making, when uncertainty is measured by probabilities. If the decision maker does not know with certainty which state of nature will occur, then he/she is said to be making a decision under uncertainty. For example, a manufacturing firm may sell a particular product where the level of sales may be unpredictable due to the large number of factors that will affect the level of sales—this could include price, product reputation, manufacturer reputation, warranty, and quality of service that potential customers have obtained from this manufacturer. To make decisions with uncertainty we can apply a range of decision criteria for decision making under uncertainty as follows:

Type 1 The maximax criterion: the maximax criterion indicates that the decision maker should choose the alternative which maximizes the maximum value of the outcome. This optimistic approach implies that the decision maker should assume the best of all possible worlds.

Type 2 Wald's maximin criterion or 'best of worst': the maximin criterion suggests that the decision maker should choose the alternative that maximizes the minimum payoff he can get. This pessimistic approach implies that the decision maker should expect the worst to happen.

Type 3 Hurwicz criterion of realism: the Hurwicz criterion rule is a weighted average method that is a compromise between the optimistic and pessimistic decisions.

Type 4 The Savage minimax regret approach: the regret of an outcome is the difference between the value of that outcome and the maximum value of all the possible outcomes, in the light of the particular chance event that actually occurred. The decision maker should choose the alternative that minimizes the maximum regret he could suffer.

Type 5 Laplace insufficient reason criterion: if the probabilities of several chance events are unknown, they should be assumed equal, and the different actions should be judged according to their payoffs averaged over all the states of nature. The Laplace equally likely criterion finds the decision alternative with the highest average payoff.

X

decision making under uncertainty the chance of an event (or events) occurring in the decision making process is unknown or difficult to assess.

probabilistic (or stochastic) containing uncertainty that is measured by probabilities.

decision criteria simple rules that recommend an alternative for decisions with uncertainty.

optimistic approach would be used by an optimistic decision maker where the largest possible payoff is chosen (maximax criterion rule).

pessimistic (or conservative approach approach) would be used by a pessimistic decision maker to minimize payoff for each decision and then select the maximum of these minimum payoffs (Wald's maximin criterion rule).

Hurwicz criterion rule is a weighted average method that is a compromise between the optimistic and pessimistic decisions.

Savage minimax regret the regret of an outcome is the difference between the value of that outcome and the maximum value of all the possible outcomes, in the light of the particular chance event that actually occurred. The decision maker should choose the alternative that minimizes the maximum regret he could suffer.

Laplace equally likely criterion finds the decision alternative with the highest average payoff.

Example 9.4

To illustrate each criterion approach let us consider the standard problem of a decision maker exploring the possibility of building a new factory in France for UK Pro Ltd. Based on the research conducted the analyst has identified three alternative factory types that could be built (large factory, average factory, and small factory) with estimated profits based upon the state of the national economy (strong economy, stable economy, weak economy). The current accepted date available is as presented in Table 9.3.

Investment choice (alternatives)	Profits in €1000s (states of nature)		
	Strong economy	Stable economy	Weak economy
Large factory	200	50	–120
Average factory	90	120	–30
Small factory	40	30	20

Table 9.3 UK profits on potential investments

Based upon this information, use each criterion method to decide what decision to make; that is, which factory to build. What is important here is to realize that no probability information is provided concerning the probability of each event (or outcome) occurring. Therefore, we will use the six uncertainty criterion methods described above to make the required decision.

Type 1 Optimistic approach (maximax criterion)

The optimistic approach would be used by an optimistic decision maker where the largest possible payoff is chosen (**maximax criterion rule**). If the payoff table was in terms of costs, the decision with the lowest cost would be chosen (**minimin criterion rule**). The steps in the solution process are as follows:

Step 1 Calculate the maximum possible payoff for each alternative.

Step 2 From these maximum payoff values choose the largest maximum.

Example 9.5

The Excel solution is illustrated in Figure 9.3.

	A	B	C	D	E	F	G	H
1	Example 9.5							
2								
3								
4		Investment choice (alternatives)	Profits in €1000's					
5			(states of nature)					
6			Strong economy	Stable economy	Weak economy	Maximum profit	Excel formula	Largest maximum profit
7		Large factory	200	50	-120	200	=MAX(C7:E7)	Yes
8		Average factory	90	120	-30	120		
9		Small factory	40	30	20	40	=MAX(C9:E9)	

Figure 9.3

→ Excel solution

Data values Cell C7:E9 Values

Max profit Cell F7 Formula: = MAX(C7:E7)

Copy down from F7:F9

maximax criterion rule the optimistic decision maker chooses the largest possible payoff.

minimin criterion rule the optimistic decision maker chooses the lowest cost.

❊ **Interpretation** From Figure 9.3, we observe that the largest maximax profit is €200,000, corresponding to building a large factory.

Note

1. The minimin criterion rule is applicable when the payoff matrix consists of negative cash flows (costs, losses) where the optimistic decision maker would be attracted by minimizing the level of costs or losses.
2. It should be observed from the table that this criterion rule uses the numbers 200, 50, and −120. The implication is that only three out of nine pieces of information are used in making this decision. Therefore, two-thirds of the available numbers are not used in making a decision.

Type 2 Conservative approach (maximin criterion)

The conservative approach (or pessimistic approach) would be used by a conservative decision maker. For each decision the minimum payoff is listed and then the decision corresponding to the maximum of these minimum payoffs is selected (**Wald's maximin criterion rule**). (Hence, the minimum possible payoff is maximized.) If the payoff was in terms of costs, the maximum costs would be determined for each decision and then the decision corresponding to the minimum of these maximum costs is selected (hence, the maximum possible cost is minimized). The steps in the solution process are as follows:

Step 1 Calculate the minimum possible payoff for each alternative (worst possible outcome for each alternative decision).

Step 2 From these minimum payoff values choose the largest maximum minimum payoff.

X

conservative approach (or pessimistic approach) would be used by a conservative decision maker to minimize payoff for each decision and then selecting the maximum of these minimum payoffs (Wald's maximin criterion rule).

Wald's maximin criterion rule would be used by a conservative (or pessimistic) decision maker to minimize payoff for each decision and then select the maximum of these minimum payoffs.

Example 9.6

The Excel solution is illustrated in Figure 9.4.

	A	B	C	D	E	F	G	H
1	Example 9.6							
2								
3								
4		Investment choice (alternatives)	Profits in €1000's					
5			(states of nature)					
6			Strong economy	Stable economy	Weak economy	Minimum profit	Excel formula	Largest minimum profit
7		Large factory	200	50	-120	-120	=MIN(C7:E7)	
8		Average factory	90	120	-30	-30		
9		Small factory	40	30	20	20	=MIN(C9:E9)	Yes

Figure 9.4

→ **Excel solution**

Data values Cell C7:E9 — Values

Max profit Cell F7 — Formula: = MIN(C7:E7)

Copy down from F7:F9

Interpretation From Figure 9.4, we observe that the largest minimum profit is €20,000, corresponding to building a small factory.

Note

1. The minimax criterion rule applies when the payoff matrix measures negative flow (e.g. costs, losses).
2. Again, like the Maximax rule, this criterion does not consider most of the data with two-thirds of the available numbers are not used in making a decision.

Type 3 Hurwicz criterion of realism

The Hurwicz criterion rule is a weighted average method that is a compromise between the optimistic and pessimistic decisions. The method consists of computing a weighted average for every alternative with the aid of a coefficient of realism, α (Greek letter alpha), which lies between zero and one ($0 \le \alpha \le 1$). This method incorporates a degree of optimism and conservatism by assigning a certain weight to optimism and the balance to conservatism. The steps in the solution process are as follows:

Step 1 Select coefficient of realism, α.

Step 2 For every alternative compute its Hurwicz weighted average, H.

Step 3 Choose the alternative with the best Hurwicz weighted average as the chosen decision.

For positive cash flow payoffs (e.g. profits, income)

$$H = \alpha\,(\text{column maximum}) + (1 - \alpha)\,(\text{column minimum}) \quad (9.1)$$

Choose maximum H for positive-cash flows.
For negative cash flow payoffs (e.g. costs, losses)

$$H = \alpha\,(\text{column minimum}) + (1 - \alpha)\,(\text{column maximum}) \quad (9.2)$$

Choose minimum H for negative-cash flows.

X

minimax criterion rule states that the decision maker should ignore all possible events except the one most likely to occur, and should select the course of action that produces the best possible result (maximum gain or minimum loss) in the given circumstances

Note When the value of α is close to 1 the decision maker is optimistic about the future, and when α is close to 0 the decision maker is pessimistic about the future.

Example 9.7

The company decide that a level of optimism can be set at 65% for this project ($\alpha = 0.65$) then we can calculate the value of H for each alternative as follows (given positive-cash flow):

$$H = \alpha\,(\text{column maximum}) + (1 - \alpha)\,(\text{column minimum})$$

For large factory

$$H = \alpha\,(\text{column maximum}) + (1 - \alpha)\,(\text{column minimum})$$

$$H = 0.65^*(200) + (1 - 0.65)^*(-120)$$

$$H = 88$$

For average factory

$$H = \alpha\,(\text{column maximum}) + (1 - \alpha)\,(\text{column minimum})$$

$$H = 0.65^*(120) + (1 - 0.65)^*(-30)$$

$$H = 67.5$$

For small factory

$$H = \alpha\,(\text{column maximum}) + (1 - \alpha)\,(\text{column minimum})$$

$$H = 0.65^*(40) + (1 - 0.65)^*(20)$$

$$H = 33$$

The Excel solution is illustrated in Figure 9.5.

	A	B	C	D	E	F	G	H
1	Example 9.7							
2								
3		alpha =	0.65					
4								
5		Investment choice (alternatives)	Profits in €1000's					
6			(states of nature)					
7			Strong economy	Stable economy	Weak economy	H	Excel formula	Maximum H
8		Large factory	200	50	-120	88	=$C$3*MAX(C8:E8)+(1-$C$3)*MIN(C8:E8)	Yes
9		Average factory	90	120	-30	67.5		
10		Small factory	40	30	20	33	=$C$3*MAX(C10:E10)+(1-$C$3)*MIN(C10:E10)	

Figure 9.5

→ Excel solution

Alpha = Cell C3	Value
Data values Cell C8:E10	Values
H Cell F8	Formula: = $C$3*MAX(C8:E8)+(1-$C$3)*MIN(C8:E8)
	Copy down from F8:F10

Interpretation From Figure 9.5, we observe that the maximum Hurwicz statistic is €88,000, which corresponds to building a large factory.

Note

1. The decision that we conclude from this method is dependent upon the value of realism (α) that we have chosen. In the example above we choose to be optimistic with alpha (α) value of 65%. But what if we decided to be more pessimistic with α value of 23%?
2. Again, this method uses two-thirds of the available data and therefore ignores one-third of the available data in making a decision. This problem will grow as the number of states of nature increases; e.g. for 10 states we would have 80% of the data not being used within the decision making.

Type 4 The Savage minimax regret approach

The Savage minimax regret approach requires the construction of a regret table or an opportunity loss table. This is done by calculating for each state of nature the difference between each payoff and the largest payoff for that state of nature. Then, using this regret table, the maximum regret for each possible decision is listed. The decision chosen is the one corresponding to the minimum of the maximum regrets.

Step 1 For each alternative, find the maximum opportunity loss (or 'regret').

Step 2 Choose the option with the smallest maximum loss.

For positive cash flow payoffs (e.g. profits, income)

$$\text{OL} = \text{maximum payoff in that state} - \text{reward payoff in that cell} \tag{9.3}$$

For negative cash flow payoffs (e.g. costs, losses)

$$\text{OL} = \text{reward payoff in that cell} - \text{minimum payoff in the state} \tag{9.4}$$

Example 9.8

Consider the original problem presented in Example 9.4 which represents a positive cash flow (given it is a profit). Regret is defined as the opportunity loss to the decision maker if alternative 1 is chosen and the state of nature occurs. For example, for the three investment alternatives then the opportunity loss for a strong economy would be calculated as follows:

- Large factory, opportunity loss = maximum payoff in that state – reward payoff in that cell = 200 – 200 = 0.
- Average factory OL = 200 – 90 = 110.
- Small factory OL = 200 – 40 = 160.

The Excel solution is illustrated in Figure 9.6 for the opportunity loss table.

	A	B	C	D	E	F	G	H	I	J	K	L
1	Example 9.8											
2												
3												
4			Profits in €1000's					Opportunity Loss in €1000's				
5		Investment choice (alternatives)	(states of nature)				Investment choice (alternatives)	(states of nature)				
6			Strong economy	Stable economy	Weak economy			Strong economy	Stable economy	Weak economy	Maximum opportunity Loss	Smallest maximum loss
7		Large factory	200	50	-120		Large factory	0	70	140	140	
8		Average factory	90	120	-30		Average factory	110	0	50	110	Yes
9		Small factory	40	30	20		Small factory	160	90	0	160	

Figure 9.6

➜ Excel solution

Data values Cells C7:E9	Values
Opportunity loss calculations:	
OL Cell H7	Formula: = MAX(C$7:C$9)-C7
	Copy down and across from H7:J9
Maximum OL Cell K7	Formula: = MAX(H7:J7)
	Copy down from K7:K9

Interpretation From Figure 9.6, we observe that the smallest maximum loss is €110,000, corresponding to building a average factory.

Note This method is considered a better decision making criterion than maximax, maximin, and Hurwicz given it uses more of the data values within the calculation process for the opportunity losses compared to the other methods.

Type 5 Laplace insufficient reason criterion

The Laplace equally likely criterion finds the decision alternative with the highest average payoff. The steps in the solution process are as follows:

Step 1 Calculate the average payoff for each alternative.

Step 2 Choose the alternative with maximum average payoff.

Example 9.9

Consider the original problem presented in Example 9.4 which represents a positive cash flow and calculate the average for each alternative. For example, for the large factory alternative the average value = (200 + 50 + −120)/3 = 130/3 = 43.33'. Complete the other average calculations as illustrated in Figure 9.7.

The Excel solution is illustrated in Figure 9.7.

	A	B	C	D	E	F	G	H
1	Example 9.9							
2								
3								
4		Investment choice (alternatives)	Profits in €1000's					
5			(states of nature)					
6			Strong economy	Stable economy	Weak economy	Average profit	Excel formula	Largest average profit
7		Large factory	200	50	-120	43.3333	=AVERAGE(C7:E7)	
8		Average factory	90	120	-30	60.0000		Yes
9		Small factory	40	30	20	30.0000	=AVERAGE(C9:E9)	

Figure 9.7

→ Excel solution

Data values Cells C7:E9 — Values

Average profit Cell F7 — Formula: = AVERAGE(C7:E7)

Copy down from F7:F9

Interpretation From Figure 9.7, we choose to build the average factory where largest average profit of €60,000 is achieved.

Note The Laplace method assumes that the states of nature (S1, S2, and S3) above are uniformly distributed given that the method assumes that each state is equally likely to occur. When using this technique it is advisable that you have sufficient evidence to show that this indeed is likely to be a correct assumption. If not then use one of the previous methods or if you have probability estimates then use the expected value method described next. The strength of this method is that the method uses all the available information in the calculation process.

expected value the mean of a probability distribution is called the expected value and can be found by multiplying each payoff value by its associated probability.

Student exercises

X9.4 What do we mean by decision making under uncertainty?

X9.5 Describe the key methods that can be used to make a decision under uncertainty.

X9.6 Which of the uncertainty methods uses all the information for each alternative within the calculation?

X9.7 Table 9.4 represents the potential growth rates associated with 3 possible investments: invest in bonds, stocks, or deposits.

		States of nature			
		Growth	Medium growth	No growth	Low growth
Alternatives	Bonds	16	9	5	−5
	Stocks	11	10	4	−1
	Deposits	9	6	9	8

Table 9.4

(a) What decision would you make if you were optimistic and applied the maximax criterion?

(b) What decision would you make if you were pessimistic and applied the maximin criterion?

(c) Which method would you use if you were not neither optimistic nor too pessimistic? Apply this method to this problem with a coefficient of optimism $\alpha = 0.7$.

X9.8 The decision maker in X9.7 decides to repeat the calculation but this time the decision making criteria will be dependent upon minimizing regrets. What would the decision maker decide?

X9.9 From your answers to X9.7 and X9.8 comment on which investment opportunity the decision maker should make.

X9.10 A decision maker has been provided with data that are cost estimates for 5 alternative projects (Table 9.5) which are dependent upon five possible states of the national economy (states of nature 1–5). Use Wald, Savage and Laplace decision making criteria to comment upon which alternative project should be chosen.

		States of nature				
		1	2	3	4	5
Alternatives	A	120	90	156	86	65
	B	67	100	153	95	132
	C	121	99	56	156	113
	D	53	87	48	112	86
	E	64	123	111	165	143

Table 9.5

9.4 Type 3: Decision making with risk

Risk implies a degree of uncertainty and an inability to fully control the outcomes or consequences of such an action. The role of the manager would be to either eliminate risk or reduce the size of the risk within a project and would involve a risk assessment to be undertaken which would identify the project variables and the level risk to be attached to each project variable. The **decision making process with risk** is as follows:

1. The problem is defined and all likely alternatives are identified.
2. All possible outcomes for each likely alternative are identified.
3. Outcomes are discussed based on their monetary payoffs or net gain in reference to assets or time.
4. The uncertainties are allocated a probability of occurrence.
5. The quality of the optimal strategy depends upon the quality of the judgments made by the decision maker in identifying the alternatives/outcomes and allocating appropriate probabilities to the associated uncertainties.
6. The decision maker should undertake **sensitivity analysis** to check how sensitive the answer is to the allocated probabilities.

The decision making process can now be stated in terms of a series of calculations:

1. Allocate a value of probability to each state of nature – this probability is called subjective probability if it is estimated from the decision maker's experience.
2. For each alternative/state of nature state the associated payoff (profit or loss) value.
3. Calculate the expected monetary value (EMV), or expected opportunity loss (EOL), for each alternative.
4. Your decision will be based on either maximizing expected payoff when dealing with profits or minimizing expected payoff when dealing with costs.

9.4.1 Calculating the expected monetary value, EMV

The mean of a probability distribution is called the expected value and can be found by multiplying each payoff value by its associated probability as given by Equation (9.5):

$$EMV(A_j) = \sum_{i=1}^{N} A_{ji} \times P(S_i) \tag{9.5}$$

Where N = number of states of nature, $P(S_i)$ = the probability of the state of nature, and A_{ji} = the payoff value corresponding to decision A_j and state of nature S_i.

Example 9.10

Reconsider the payoff table given in Example 9.4 where the probability of each alternative is known ($P_1 = 0.1$, $P_2 = 0.6$, and $P_3 = 0.3$), as illustrated in Figure 9.8. The expected monetary value is calculated for each alternative using Equation (9.5). For example, for the large factory the expected monetary value would be as follows:

X

decision making process with risk implies a degree of uncertainty and an inability to fully control the outcomes or consequences of such an action.

sensitivity analysis the study of how changes in the coefficients of a linear programming problem affect the optimal solution.

EMV (large factory) = 200*0.1 + 50*0.6 + (−120)*0.3 = 14

Repeat for the other two alternatives to obtain the final table as illustrated in Figure 9.8: The Excel solution is as illustrated in Figure 9.8.

	A	B	C	D	E	F	G	H
1	Example 9.10							
2								
3		P1 =	0.1					
4		P2 =	0.6					
5		P3 =	0.3					
6								
7		Investment choice (alternatives)	Profits in €1000's					
8			(states of nature)					
9			Strong economy	Stable economy	Weak economy	EMV	Excel formula	Maximum EMV
10			$P_1 = 0.1$	$P_2 = 0.6$	$P_3 = 0.3$			
11		Large factory	200	50	-120	14	=\$C\$3*C11+\$C\$4*D11+\$C\$5*E11	
12		Average factory	90	120	-30	72		Yes
13		Small factory	40	30	20	28	=\$C\$3*C13+\$C\$4*D13+\$C\$5*E13	

Figure 9.8

➜ Excel solution

P1 = Cell C3	Value
P2 = Cell C4	Value
P3 = Cell C5	Value
Data values Cells C11:E13	Values
EMV Cell F11	Formula: = \$C\$3*C11+\$C\$4*D11+\$C\$5*E11
	Copy down from F11:F13

❊ Interpretation From Figure 9.8, we observe that the maximum expected profit is €72,000, corresponding to building an average factory.

9.4.2 Calculating the expected opportunity loss, EOL

In this case we are looking to minimize the **expected loss** by choosing the alternative loss with the smallest expected loss. This can be achieved by calculating the opportunity loss associated with each value and multiplying by the associated probability, as illustrated in Figure (9.9), but with the payoff values now replaced by their corresponding opportunity losses. For example, for the large factory the expected opportunity loss would be as follows:

expected loss in this case we are looking to minimize the expected loss by choosing the alternative loss with the smallest expected loss.

$$\text{EOL (large factory)} = 0.1 * 0 + 0.6 * 70 + 0.3 * 140 = 84$$

Example 9.11

The Excel solution is illustrated in Figure 9.9 for the opportunity loss table.

	A	B	C	D	E	F	G	H	I	J	K	L	M	N
1	Example 9.11													
2														
3		P1 =	0.1											
4		P2 =	0.6											
5		P3 =	0.3											
6														
7		Investment choice (alternatives)	Profits in €1000's						Investment choice (alternatives)	Opportunity Loss in €1000's				
8			(states of nature)							(states of nature)				
9			Strong economy	Stable economy	Weak economy	EMV	Maximum EMV			Strong economy	Stable economy	Weak economy	EOL	Minimum EOL
10			$P_1 = 0.1$	$P_2 = 0.6$	$P_3 = 0.3$					$P_1 = 0.1$	$P_2 = 0.6$	$P_3 = 0.3$		
11		Large factory	200	50	-120	14			Large factory	0	70	140	84	
12		Average factory	90	120	-30	72	Yes		Average factory	110	0	50	26	Yes
13		Small factory	40	30	20	28			Small factory	160	90	0	70	

Figure 9.9

→ Excel solution

P1 = Cell C3	Value
P2 = Cell C4	Value
P3 = Cell C5	Value
Data values Cells C11:E13	Values
EMV Cell F11	Formula: = \$C\$3*C11+\$C\$4*D11+\$C\$5*E11 Copy down from F11:F13

Opportunity loss calculations:

OL Cell J11	Formula: = MAX(C\$11:C\$13)-C11 Copy down and across from J11:L13
EOL Cell M11	Formula: = \$C\$3*J11+\$C\$4*K11+\$C\$5*L11 Copy down from M11:M13

Interpretation From Figure 9.9, we observe that the smallest expected loss is €26,000, corresponding to building an average factory.

Note It should be noted that the expected monetary value and expected opportunity loss both provide the analyst with the same decision.

9.4.3 Expected value of perfect information

Suppose we could obtain 100% reliable information about the nature of the outcome. There is an a priori belief of 0.1, 0.6, and 0.3 of a strong, stable, and weak economy. Thus, there is a 10%, 60%, and 30% chance that perfect information would tell us that the economy would be strong, stable, and weak respectively.

The expected monetary value of perfect information

Therefore, the **expected monetary value of perfect information** (EVPI) is the expected profit when in possession of perfect information minus the best expected payoff we could obtain without any extra information: EVPI = Expected profit under certainty (EPUC) – expected value without information (EV):

$$EVPI = EPUC - EV \quad (9.6)$$

The solution process consists of the following steps:

Step 1 Calculate the best decision for each nature of state.

Step 2 Calculate the expected value under certainty, EPUC.

Step 3 Calculate the best expected value, EV.

Step 4 Calculate the expected value of perfect information, EVPI.

Example 9.12

The Excel solution is illustrated in Figure 9.10.

	A	B	C	D	E	F	G	H
1	Example 9.12							
2								
3		P1 =	0.1					
4		P2 =	0.6					
5		P3 =	0.3					
6								
7		Investment choice (alternatives)	Profits in €1000's (states of nature)					
8								
9			Strong economy	Stable economy	Weak economy			
10			$P_1 = 0.1$	$P_2 = 0.6$	$P_3 = 0.3$	EMV	Excel formula	Maximum EMV
11		Large factory	200	50	-120	14	=C11*$C$3+D11*$C$4+E11*$C$5	
12		Average factory	90	120	-30	72		Yes
13		Small factory	40	30	20	28	=C13*$C$3+D13*$C$4+E13*$C$5	
14		Best decision	200	120	20			
15			=MAX(C11:C13)		=MAX(E11:E13)			
16								
17		EPUC =	98	=C3*C14+C4*D14+C5*E14				
18		EV =	72	=MAX(F11:F13)				
19		EVPI =	26	=C17-C18				

Figure 9.10

→ Excel solution

P1 = Cell C3 Value
P2 = Cell C4 Value
P3 = Cell C5 Value
Data values Cells C11:E13 Values
EMV Cell F11 Formula: = C11*$C$3+D11*$C$4+E11*$C$5
Copy down from F11:F13

X
expected monetary value of perfect information the expected value of information that would tell the decision maker exactly which state of nature is going to occur (i.e. perfect information).

Best decision Cell C14	Formula: = MAX(C11:C13)
	Copy across from C14:E14
EPUC = C17	Formula: = C3*C14+C4*D14+C5*E14
EV = C18	Formula: = MAX(F11:F13)
EVPI = C19	Formula: = C17-C18

❊ **Interpretation** From Figure 9.10, the expected value of perfect information is €26,000, which represents the value of information which is 100% reliable.

Step 1 Calculate the best decision for each nature of state. For example, the best decision for the strong economy would give a profit of €200,000. A completed table is presented in Figure 9.10.

Step 2 Calculate the expected profit under certainty, EPUC. This the expected value of the best decision for each state of nature multiplied by the known probability of that state of nature:

$$EPUC = 200 * 0.1 + 120 * 0.6 + 20 * 0.3 = 98$$

Step 3 Calculate the expected value without information, EV. This is represented by maximizing the expected value, EV. For this example, this is when we chose the average factory with an EV = 72.

$$EV = 72$$

Step 4 Calculate the expected value of perfect information, EVPI.

$$EVPI = EVUC - EV = 98 - 72 = 26.$$

The expected value of perfect information is €26,000 which represents the value of information which is 100% reliable, or, to put it another way, it represents the maximum amount that you should be willing to pay for perfect information. This implies that it would never be worthwhile obtaining information that cost more than this, but remember that perfect information is probably unobtainable, and the recommendation would be that you never pay the expected value of perfect information. The EVPI provides an upper bound on the expected value of any sample data collected.

Expected opportunity loss of perfect information

This calculation can be repeated when you are dealing with expected opportunity loss. For Example 9.11, the best expected loss and expected loss of perfect information can be calculated as illustrated in the following example.

Example 9.13

The Excel solution is illustrated in Figure 9.11.

	A	B	C	D	E	F	G	H	I	J	K	L	M	N
1	Example 9.13													
2														
3		P1 =	0.1											
4		P2 =	0.6											
5		P3 =	0.3											
6														
7		Investment choice (alternatives)	Profits in €1000's						Investment choice (alternatives)	Opportunity Loss in €1000's				
8			(states of nature)							(states of nature)				
9			Strong economy	Stable economy	Weak economy	EMV	Maximum EMV			Strong economy	Stable economy	Weak economy	EOL	Minimum EOL
10			$P_1 = 0.1$	$P_2 = 0.6$	$P_3 = 0.3$					$P_1 = 0.1$	$P_2 = 0.6$	$P_3 = 0.3$		
11		Large factory	200	50	-120	14			Large factory	0	70	140	84	
12		Average factory	90	120	-30	72	Yes		Average factory	110	0	50	26	Yes
13		Small factory	40	30	20	28			Small factory	160	90	0	70	
14									Best decision	0	0	0		
15										=MIN(J11:J13)		=MIN(L11:L13)		
16														
17									ELUC =	0	=C3*J14+C4*K14+C5*L14			
18									EV =	26	=MIN(M11:M13)			
19									EVPI =	26	=J18-J17			

Figure 9.11

→ Excel solution

P1 = Cell C3	Value
P2 = Cell C4	Value
P3 = Cell C5	Value
Data values Cells C11:E13	Values
EMV Cell F11	Formula: = $C$3*C11+$C$4*D11+$C$5*E11
	Copy down from F11:F13

Opportunity loss calculations:

OL Cell J11	Formula: = MAX(C$11:C$13)-C11
	Copy down and across from J11:L13
EOL Cell M11	Formula: = $C$3*J11+$C$4*K11+$C$5*L11
	Copy down from M11:M13
Best decision Cell J14	Formula: = MIN(J11:J13)
	Copy formula across from J14:L14
ELUC = Cell J17	Formula: = C3*J14+C4*K14+C5*L14
EV = Cell J18	Formula: = MIN(M11:M13)
EVPI = Cell J19	Formula: = J18-J17

Interpretation The expected value of perfect information is €26,000. This represents the value of information that is 100% reliable, which is consistent with the expected monetary value method.

Note The expected value of perfect information (EVPI) will always equal the expected opportunity loss (EOL).

9.4.4 Return-to-risk ratio

The expected monetary value method provides an average value of the monetary value (or loss) and does not tell us anything about the degree of dispersion between the data sets or allow a method to compare the variability of different data sets. To calculate the standard deviation for a probability distribution we can use Equation (9.7):

$$\sigma_j = \sqrt{\sum_{i=1}^{N} (X_i - E(X_i))^2 \times P(X_i)} \tag{9.7}$$

Where: σ_j = standard deviation for each alternative, $(X_i - E(X_i))$ is the difference between each value and its corresponding expected value for each alternative, and $P(X_i)$ is the corresponding probability for each alternative. Given that we are comparing alternative data scenarios with different average values then we should use Equation (9.8) to calculate the relative risk associated with each alternative:

$$CV_j = \left(\frac{\sigma_j}{EMV_j}\right) \times 100\% \tag{9.8}$$

If we have large differences in variability then we should not use the EMV (or EOL) method in making a decision but we can make use of the **return-to-risk ratio** (Equation 9.9):

$$RTRR_j = \frac{EMV_j}{\sigma_j} \tag{9.9}$$

Where: EMV_j = expected monetary value for each alternative, σ_j = standard deviation for each alternative. The decision would be to choose the largest value of the return-to-risk ratio.

Example 9.14

The Excel solution is illustrated in Figure 9.12.

	A	B	C	D	E	F	G	H
1	Example 9.14							
2								
3		P1 =	0.1					
4		P2 =	0.6					
5		P3 =	0.3					
6								
7			Profits in €1000's					
8		Investment	(states of nature)					
9		choice (alternatives)	Strong economy	Stable economy	Weak economy	EMV	Variance, σ^2	Standard deviation, σ
10			$P_1 = 0.1$	$P_2 = 0.6$	$P_3 = 0.3$			
11		Large factory	200	50	-120	14	9624.0000	98.1020
12		Average factory	90	120	-30	72	4536.0000	67.3498
13		Small factory	40	30	20	28	36.0000	6.0000
14								
15						CV large =	700.7284839	=(H11/F11)*100
16						CV average =	93.54143467	=(H12/F12)*100
17						CV small =	21.42857143	=(H13/F13)*100
18								
19						RTRR large =	0.142708627	=F11/H11
20						RTRR average =	1.069044968	=F12/H12
21						RTRR small =	4.666666667	=F13/H13

Figure 9.12

X

return-to-risk ratio the observed average return divided by the standard deviation of returns. This is the simplest measure of return to risk trade-off and can be used to compare portfolio returns.

→ Excel solution

P1 = Cell C3	Value
P2 = Cell C4	Value
P3 = Cell C5	Value
Data values Cells C11:E13	Values
EMV Cell F11	Formula: = C11*$C$3+D11*$C$4+E11*$C$5
	Copy down from F11:F13
Variance Cell G11	Formula:
	= $C$3*(C11-F11)^2+$C$4*(D11-F11)^2+$C$5*(E11-F11)^2
	Copy down from G11:G13
Standard deviation Cell H11	Formula: = SQRT(G11)
	Copy down from H11:H13
CV large = Cell G15	Formula: = (H11/F11)*100
CV average = Cell G16	Formula: = (H12/F12)*100
CV small = Cell G17	Formula: = (H13/F13)*100
RTRR large = Cell G19	Formula: = F11/H11
RTRR average = Cell G20	Formula: = F12/H12
RTRR small = Cell G21	Formula: = F13/H13

✻ Interpretation From Figure 9.12, we observe that there is a great more variation with the large and average factories than with the small factory. Furthermore, given the large differences in variability we calculated the return-to-risk ratio, which shows that the small factory as a return-to-risk ratio of 4.7%, which is a great deal higher than the other two alternatives. Thus, relative to the measure of dispersion within each alternative data set, the expected return is higher for the small factory than the other two alternatives.

Student exercises

X9.11 Explain what we mean by decision making with risk.

X9.12 Describe the method used in making a decision.

X9.13 You are considering putting money into one of two investments, A and B. The net profits for identical periods and probabilities of success for investments A and B are given in Table 9.6.

	Probability of return	
Net profits	A	B
8000	0.0	0.1
9000	0.3	0.2
10,000	0.4	0.4
11,000	0.3	0.2
12,000	0.0	0.1

Table 9.6

(a) Which investment yields a higher net profit?

(b) Can you make a decision on which investment is better, given this extra information?

X9.14 Wicked investments are an investment club of 25 members who invest in stocks and shares. The club has a decision to make in terms of the purchase of three new investments, and to help with decision making the club have agreed on the possible returns over the next six months for each of the three alternative investments A, B, and C (Table 9.7).

Investment choice (alternatives)	Change in stock market investments (€1000s) (states of nature)		
	Increase	No change	Decreasing
A	210	43	–58
B	123	58	4
C	2	8	63

Table 9.7 Change in stock market for three investments

(a) Use the maximax, maximin, and minimax regret criterion rules to decide on which investment to choose.

(b) Further information has now been made available by the club where the chance of the stock market increasing, not changing, and decreasing is 33%, 20%, and 47% respectively: (i) calculate the expected monetary value, (ii) calculate the expected monetary value assuming perfect information.

9.5 Using decision trees

9.5.1 Decision trees

In the previous sections we explored the application of a payoff table to help the decision maker to make decisions. In general, decisions will usually be dependent upon a number of decisions that have to be made before we make a final decision. The decision tree is a method that can be used to visualize the problem and the possible solution. For example, you might decide that you wish to purchase a computer but you have five alternative computer shops that you may purchase from. As soon as you have decided where to shop from, you then decide on a computer model, specification, software, and so on. Obviously, this list can continue with decisions representing your choices and possible alternative choices.

The decision tree consists of not only branches with probabilities attached to each branch as in probability tree diagrams but also includes decision branches that allow alternative choices within the decision making process. A decision tree shows a decision problem, beginning with the initial decision and ending with all possible outcomes and payoffs. When constructing decision trees we employ three rules, as follows:

1. The symbol ■ represents a **decision node**.
2. The symbol ○ represents a state of nature (event) node.
3. Branches emanating from a decision node reflect the alternative decisions possible at that point.

Figure 9.13 represents a pictorial representation of a standard tree diagram with the decision node, decision branches, probability nodes, and probability branches identified. The solution process consists of the following steps:

1. Calculate the EMV at each probability node.
2. Select the maximum EMV for the decision node.

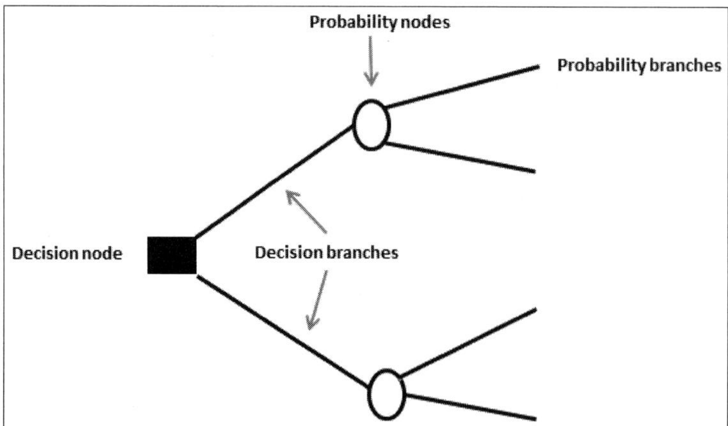

Figure 9.13

Example 9.15

Reconsider Example 9.12. The Excel solution is illustrated in Figure 9.14 for the opportunity loss table.

	A	B	C	D	E	F	G	H	I	J	K	L	M	N
1	Example 9.15													
2														
3										Payoff		P strong =	0.1	
4							EMVs					P stable=	0.6	
5								0.1	Strong	200		P weak =	0.3	
6							14							
7							A	0.6	Stable	50		Pay large, strong =	200	
8												Pay stable =	50	
9							0.3		Weak	-120		Pay weak =	-120	
10					Large									
11								0.1	Strong	90		Pay average, strong =	90	
12				72	Average		72					Pay average, stable =	120	
13			Decision	■			B	0.6		120		Pay average, weak =	-30	
14			node:						Stable					
15							0.3		Weak	-30		Pay small, strong =	40	
16												Pay small, stable =	30	
17								0.1	Strong	40		Pay small, weak =	20	
18					Small		28							
19								0.6				EMV node A =	14	=M3*M7+M4*M8+M5*M9
20							C		Stable	30		EMV chance node B =	72	=M3*M11+M4*M12+M5*M13
21												EMV chance node C =	28	=M3*M15+M4*M16+M5*M17
22							0.3		Weak	20				
23												EMV decision node =	72	=MAX(M19:M21)
24							States of nature							

Figure 9.14

decision node points in a decision tree where decisions are made.

→ Excel solution

P strong = Cell M3 Value
P stable = Cell M4 Value
P weak = Cell M5 Value
Pay large, strong = Cell M7 Value
Pay stable = Cell M8 Value
Pay weak = Cell M9 Value
Pay average, strong = Cell M11 Value
Pay average, stable = Cell M12 Value
Pay average, weak = Cell M13 Value
Pay small, strong = Cell M15 Value
Pay small, stable = Cell M16 Value
Pay small, weak = Cell M17 Value
EMV node A = Cell M19 Formula: = M3*M7+M4*M8+M5*M9
EMV chance node B = Cell M20 Formula: = M3*M11+M4*M12+M5*M13
EMV chance node C = Cell M21 Formula: = M3*M15+M4*M16+M5*M17
EMV decision node = Cell M23 Formula: = MAX(M19:M21)

Copy these values into the decision tree cells as illustrated in Figure 9.15.

Interpretation From the decision tree we observe that the largest expected monetary value is €72,000.

Example 9.16

Consider the problem of a geothermal company drilling for a supply of hot water that could be used to generate electricity. According to the company the chance of hitting a viable source of hot water is estimated to be 45% with the drilling costs of €84 million and envisaged revenue of €220 million. The company estimate that the cost of test drilling to be €10 million with historical records suggesting that the chances of a viable field being 55%. However, based on historical data the chance that these tests are reliable given that they are correct is 80%. An alternative is for the company to sell its drilling option with alternative scenarios as follows: (a) test indicates hot water, selling price €55 million, (b) tests do not indicate hot water, selling price €7 million, and (c) no tests carried out, selling price €23 million.

The Excel solution showing the initial and calculated probability values is illustrated in Figure 9.15.

	A	B	C	D
1	Example 9.16			
2				
3				
4		Revenue =	220	
5		P(HW/Drill) =	0.45	
6		Drill cost =	-84	
7		P(NHW/Drill) =	0.55	=1-C5
8		Payoff HW given drill =	136	=C4+C6
9		Payoff HHW given drill =	-84	=C6
10				
11		Test drill cost =	-10	
12		P(Viable field) =	0.55	
13		P(Not viable field) =	0.45	=1-C12
14		P(Test reliable/correct) =	0.6	
15				
16		Payoff test says HW =	55	
17		Payoff test says NHW =	7	
18		Payoff no test =	23	
19		Payoff HW/Drill/Viable/Test =	126	=C4+C6+C11
20		Payoff NHW/Drill/Viable/Test =	-94	=C6+C11
21		Payoff Sell/Viable/Test =	45	=C16+C11
22		Payoff HW/Drill/not viable/test =	126	=C4+C6+C11
23		Payoff NHW/Drill/not viable/test =	-94	=C6+C11
24		Payoff Sell/Not viable/Test =	-3	=C17+C11
25				
26				
27		Calculate EMVs:	EMV	
28		Prob node A =	15	=M5*K6+M9*K10
29		Prob node C =	60	=T7*R8+T13*R13
30		Prob node D =	-28	=T16*R16+T20*R20
31		Decision node 2 =	60	=MAX(Q10,P14)
32		Decision node 3 =	-3	=MAX(Q16,P20)
33		Prob node B =	31.65	=M13*K14+M17*K18
34		Decision node 1 =	31.65	=MAX(J7,J14,I21)

Figure 9.15

The Excel decision tree solution with initial values and calculated values is illustrated in Figure 9.16.

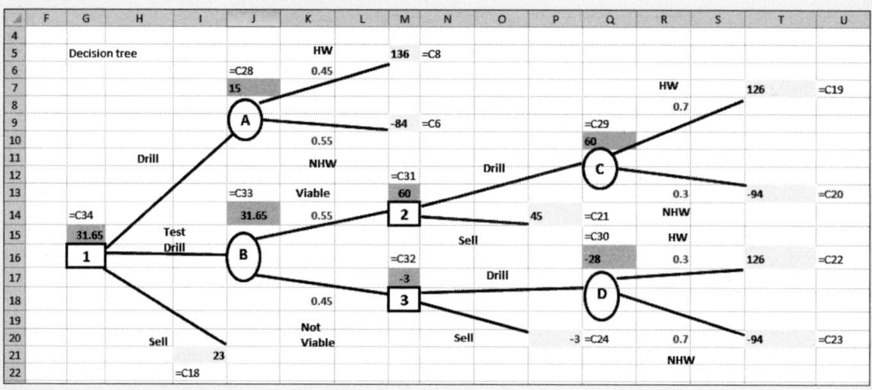

Figure 9.16

> **Interpretation** The best decision is to choose the largest expected monetary value of €31.65 million, which corresponds to test drill first.

9.5.2 Decision trees and Bayes' theorem

In the previous example we were given the prior probabilities which could then be used to calculate the conditional probabilities. In this section we will explore the use of **decision trees** when we need to apply **Bayes' theorem** in updating prior probabilities given access to new information.

Example 9.17

Hydropod Ltd has developed a new hydrogen fuel cell for the growing demand for electric cars. The company is a new technology group from a leading university that has had success in the past with this type of technology but as limited experience of marketing its products. Based on past experience the company have provided the following information with three options for the company:

Marketing by company

The company has estimated that based on past experience that the probability that sales will be high is 50%. If a high profit occurs then the profit is estimated at £23 million, but if sales are low then the estimated profit reduces to a loss of £3 million.

Employ a marketing company to check on the possibility of high sales

From past experience Hydropod Ltd know that this particular company has a prediction success rate of 82% when sales are high, but this reduces to a 73% prediction success rate when sales are low.

Sell rights for £5 million.

Construct a decision tree, calculate probabilities and expected monetary value, and make a decision.

The Excel solutions are illustrated in Figures 9.17–9.22.

	A	B	C	D
1	Example 9.17 - decision tree with Bayes's theorem			
2				
3				
4		Marketing by company		
5		P(High sales) =	0.5	
6		P(low sales) =	0.5	=1-C5
7		Payoff with high profit =	23	
8		Payoff with low profit =	-3	
9				
10		Employ marketing company		
11		P(prediction success rate says high/high sales) =	0.82	
12		P(prediction success rate says high/low sales) =	0.18	=1-C11
13		P(prediction success rate says low/low sales) =	0.73	
14		P(prediction success rate says low/high sales) =	0.27	=1-C13
15				
16		Sell rights		
17		Payoff =	5	
18				
19		EMV at probability node A =	10.00000	=O7*Q6+O11*Q10
20		EMV at decision node 2 =	10.00000	=MAX(N8,N13)

Figure 9.17

decision tree diagram that represents a series of alternatives and events by the branches of a tree.

Bayes' theorem Bayes' theorem is a result that allows new information to be used to update the conditional probability of an event.

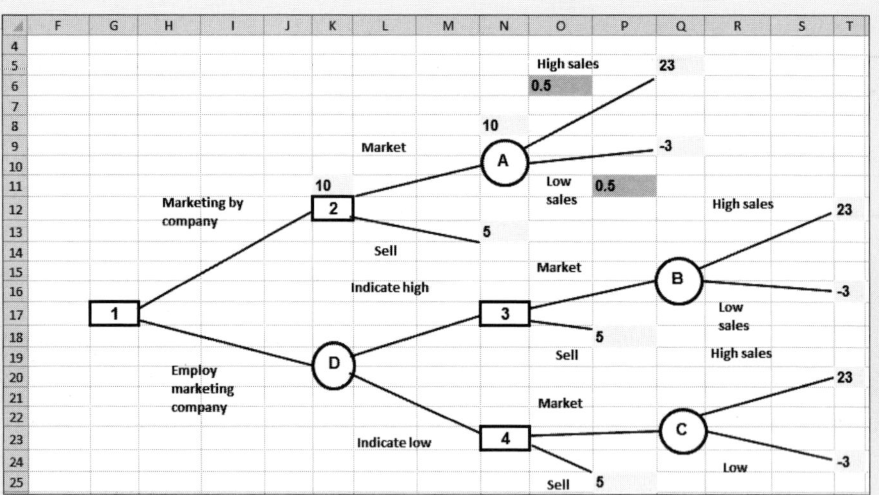

Figure 9.18

	A	B	C	D
30				
31		Require probabilties at probability nodes B, C, D		
32		These values are conditional on the success rate for the marketing company		
33				
34		P(MR company indicates high sales) =	0.54500	=L31+L41
35		P(MR company indicates low sales) =	0.45500	=L35+L45
36		P(High sales/MR indicates high sales) =	0.75229	=L31/C34
37		P(High sales/MR indicates low sales) =	0.19780	=L35/C35
38		P(Low sales/MR indicates high sales) =	0.24771	=L41/C34
39		P(Low sales/MR indicates low sales) =	0.80220	=L45/C35

Figure 9.19

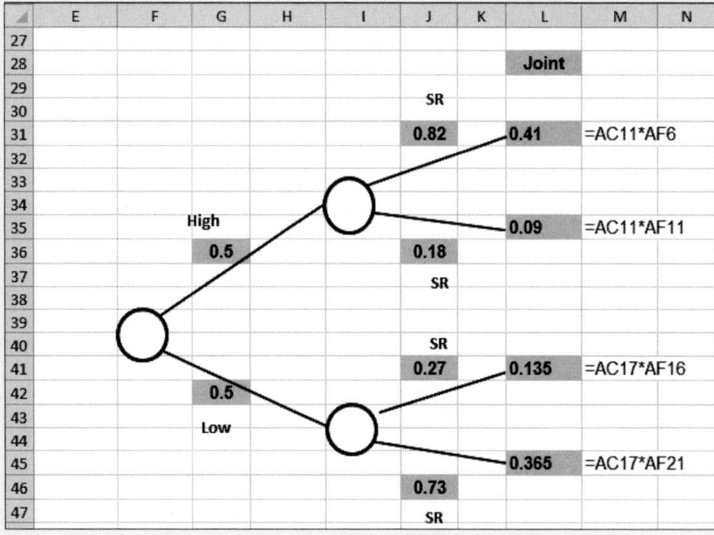

Figure 9.20

	A	B	C	D
51		Add these posterior probabilities to the tree diagram - completed		
52				
53		Then calculate EMVs at chance (B, C, then D) and decision nodes (3, 4 then 1):		
54				
55		EMV at chance node B =	16.55963	=T58*R59+T62*S63
56		EMV at decision node 3 =	16.55963	=MAX(Q60,P64)
57				
58		EMV at chance node C =	2.14286	=T66*R66+T70*R70
59		EMV at decision node 4 =	5.00000	=MAX(Q67,P71)
60				
61		EMV at chance node D =	11.30000	=N62*L63+N68*L68
62				
63		EMV at decision node 1 =	11.30000	=MAX(K57,K64)

Figure 9.21

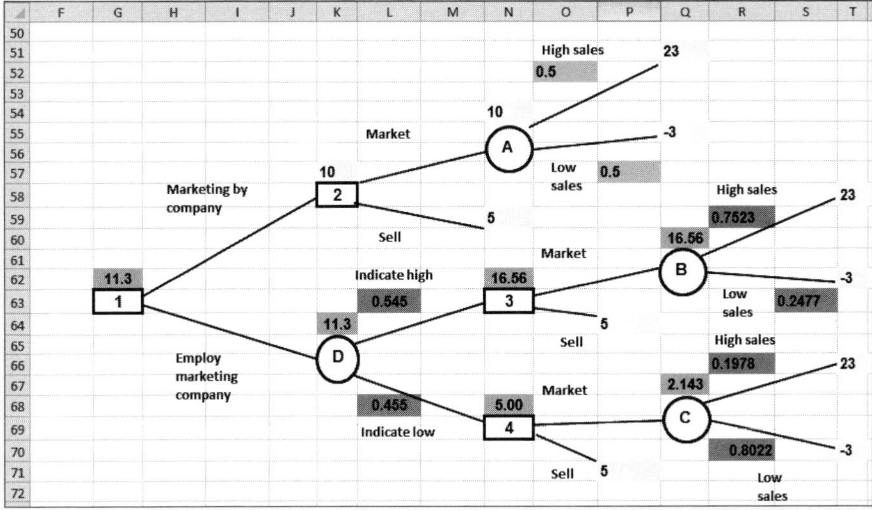

Figure 9.22

❋ **Interpretation** It should be noted that we are not given any information about the cost of the market research. It can be observed from Figure 9.22 that the maximum cost of market research is = 1.3 (= K64 – K57), which represents the expected value of imperfect information (EVII) as it takes into account the fact that the market research is not completely reliable. Therefore, should not pay more than £1.3 million for the market research to be conducted by the MR company. The best decision is to commission the MR company and only market if the research suggests the sales are high. Otherwise, sell the rights to make £5 million.

9.5.3 Undertake sensitivity analysis on a decision tree

In Examples 9.15 and 9.16 we solved decision making problems where the value of each probability is known. The question to be asked is how sensitive the decision is to the value of the probabilities given that these probability values are likely to be guesses of the true value at a moment in time. If we modify the probability values by a small amount and the decision changes then we say that the decision is sensitive to the probability value. Conversely, if a large change in probability is required then we say the decision is now sensitive to the probability value and we say that the decision is robust to the value of probability. To illustrate let us re-examine Examples 9.16 and 9.17.

Example 9.18

Reconsider Example 9.16. In this example the decision was to choose to test drill with an expected monetary value of €31.65 million. According to the information in Figures 9.15 and 9.16, the decision is quite close between choosing to drill with an expected monetary value = €35 million and to test drill with an expected monetary value of €31.65 million. The question we need to ask is if these two values are equal ($EMV_B = EMV_A$) then we would potentially be neutral between the two choices. Given that the input parameter for EMV_B is the probability of hitting a viable source of water (currently 45%) then what would this value need to be for $EMV_B = EMV_A$ (given other values constant).

This problem can be solved in Excel via the use of Goal Seek in What-If Analysis on Cell C12 in Figure 9.23.

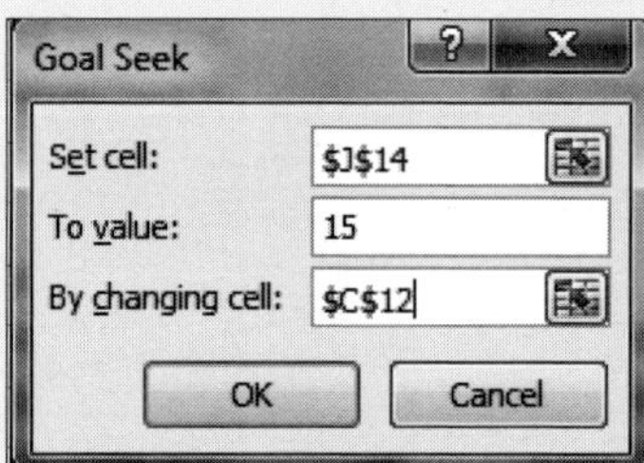

Figure 9.23

DATA > What-If Analysis > Goal Seek. . . .

Goal Seek . . . screenshot is illustrated in Figure 9.23.

→ Excel solution using Figures 9.15 and 9.16

Set Cell J14 (currently = 31.65)

To value = 15 (corresponds to the value in J7)

By changing cell C12 (currently 0.55)

Click OK

From Excel, the value of the probability of a viable field is calculated to be 0.2857 . . .

Interpretation By applying Goal Seek we have shown that we would be indifferent between choosing drill or test drill when the probability of a viable field is 29%.

Example 9.19

Reconsider Example 9.17. In this example the decision was to choose to pay no more than £1.3 million for the market research company to market the product. According to the information in Figures 9.17–9.22, the decision is quite close between choosing to market with an expected monetary value = €10 million and to employ a marketing research company to undertake the market research with an expected monetary value of €11.30 million.

The question we need to ask is if these two values are equal ($EMV_D = EMV_2$) then we would potentially be neutral between the two choices. Given that the input parameter for EMV_D is the probability of the marketing success of the marketing company (currently 82%) then what would this value need to be for $EMV_D = EMV_2$ (given other values constant).

This problem can be solved in Excel via the use of Goal Seek in What-If Analysis on Cell C11 in Figure 9.24.

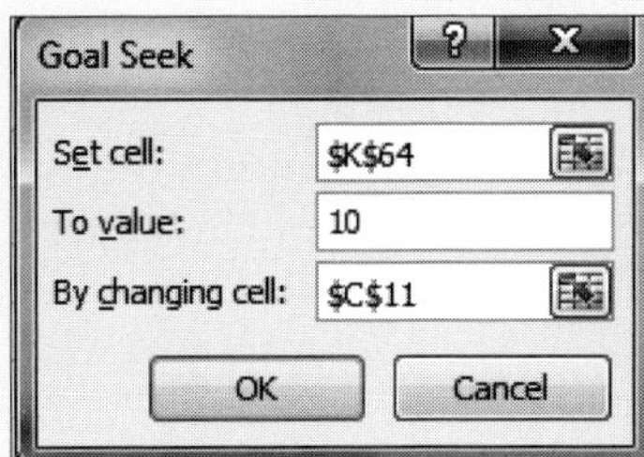

Figure 9.24

DATA > What-If Analysis > Goal Seek. . . .

Goal Seek . . . screenshot is illustrated in Figure 9.24.

→ Excel solution using Figures 9.17–9.22

Set Cell K64 (currently = 11.3)

To value = 10 (corresponds to the value in K57)

By changing cell C11 (currently 0.82)

Click OK

From Excel, the value of the probability of a marketing research company is reliable is calculated to be 0.67555.....

Interpretation By applying Goal Seek we have shown that we would be indifferent between choosing the company undertakes the market research or employ a marketing research company when the probability of a the marketing research company being reliable is 68%.

Student exercises

X9.15 A company manufactures a product which can be sold either direct to the customer via its e-commerce website or via a retailer. The company has business intelligence which shows that if it sells direct to its customers the level of profit is £100 compared with £70 if it sells via a retailer. The associated sale probabilities of selling the product are 0.6 for direct and 0.8 via the retailer. If a sale is not made then the losses on each unsold product are £30 for selling direct and £50 for selling via the retailer: (a) construct a decision tree, (b) calculate the expected value for each alternative, and (c) decide which sales route should be recommended to the company.

X9.16 The manager of a national firm manufacturing solar PV panels has to decide whether to build either a large or small manufacturing plant to meet the tremendous growth in demand. A key decision factor is the level of demand with a 85% chance of a high demand if a large plant is built and a 50% chance of a high demand if a small plant is built. The company can expand after two years if it decides to build a small plant with the lifetime of the plant estimated to be ten years. To help to make a decision, the final income and cost estimates have been estimated (Table 9.8).

Capital costs (£m)	
Build large plant	4
Build small plant	2
Cost of expanding small plant	3

Annual revenue estimates (£m)	
Large plant with high demand	1.5
Large plant with low demand	0.3
Small plant with high demand	0.9
Small plant with low demand	0.7

Table 9.8

Calculate the project expected values and comment on what choice the manager should make if he assumes that there is no requirement to borrow to complete the project.

9.6 Making a decision using the concept of utility

In the previous sections we explored the use of expected monetary value (or opportunity loss) in making decisions; but this method does not take into account the decision maker's attitude to risk. For example, would we accept £200,000 now from an investor for an investment portfolio or wait six months where the value of the investment is dependent upon a range of decisions which are subject to a degree of uncertainty and risk.

A second problem with the expected monetary value method is that the method assumes a linear relationship between the value of money and its risk value to the decision maker. Figure 9.25 illustrates the relationship between monetary value and the decision makers risk value which we call the utility.

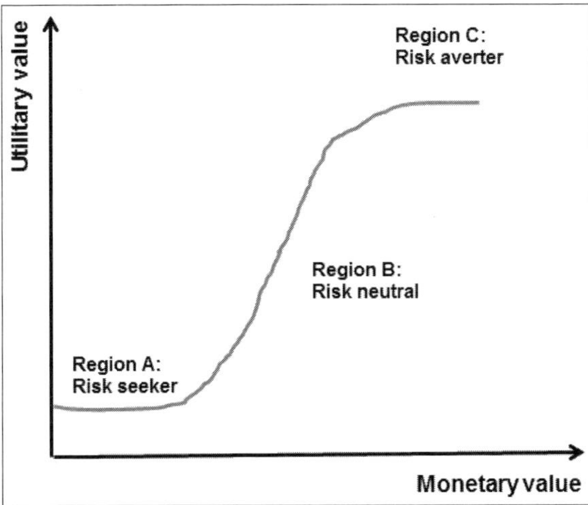

Figure 9.25

Relationship between the value of money and utility.

We note that the utility value is not a linear function of the monetary value and we can observe from this figure that we can identify 3 key regions: A, B, and C.

Region A: risk seeker This region shows that the value of utility is greater for larger monetary values and shows that this decision maker is prepared to take increased risks to make larger profits.

Region B: risk neutral This region shows a linear relationship between utility and monetary value. This implies that for every extra unit of currency provided the change in utility would be constant. A different way of looking at this is to say that inputting a unit increase in resources would give the same increase in utility which represents the level of risk. This is the assumption behind the expected monetary value method described in the earlier sections.

Region C: risk averter This region shows that after an initial increase from utility from B to C the value of utility gradually decreases as the monetary value increases. The implication is that any extra money invested will not produce the same rates of return as seen in regions A and B. This implies that the decision maker would be cautious at investing any more funds within this investment.

The concept of utility provides a framework for the evaluation of alternative choices made by individuals and organizations by providing a measure of satisfaction that each choice provides to the decision maker.

X

risk seeker implies that the decision maker is prepared to take increased risks to make larger profits.

risk neutral implies that for every extra unit of currency provided the change in utility would be constant.

risk averter implies that the decision maker would be cautious of investing any more funds within this investment.

Example 9.20

To illustrate the utility method reconsider Example 9.10 as illustrated in Figure 9.26.

	A	B	C	D	E
1	Example 9.20				
2					
3		P1 =	0.1		
4		P2 =	0.6		
5		P3 =	0.3		
6					
7					
8		Investment choice (alternatives)	Profits in €1000's		
9			(states of nature)		
10			Strong economy	Stable economy	Weak economy
11		Large factory	200	50	-120
12		Average factory	90	120	-30
13		Small factory	40	30	20

Figure 9.26

When using the expected monetary value method we found the maximum monetary value is given when we select the average factory with an expected value of €72,000. The issue now is to integrate the decision maker's attitude to risk within the calculation and use this to make a conclusion.

To illustrate the calculation of a utility function consider the problem where an investment choice is to be made as follows: (1) accept €120,000 now or (2) enter a game where the chance of winning €200,000 is 60% but with a 40% chance of losing €120,000. The decision maker was then asked at what probability value they would be indifferent between accepting the €120,000 now and entering the game of chance.

This was repeated for different a range of win values with corresponding probability values when they would be indifferent as illustrated in Table 9.9.

Win (€000)	Probability
120	0.8
90	0.7
40	0.6

Table 9.9 Win versus probability

The next stage is now to calculate the utility function as illustrated in stages 1–3:

Stage 1 Calculate given utility values

The largest payoff of €200,000 is given a utility of 1 and the smallest value - €120,000 is given a utility of 0. From the information given we can now calculate the utility values for payoff values €120,000, €90,000, and €40,000 as follows:

U(120,000) = 0.8*U(200,000) + 0.2*U(–120,000) = 0.8*1 + 0.2*0 = 0.8

U(90,000) = 0.75*U(200,000) + 0.25*U(–120,000) = 0.75*1 + 0.25*0 = 0.75

U(40,000) = 0.6*U(200,000) + 0.4*U(–120,000) = 0.6*1 + 0.4*0 = 0.6

The Excel solution is illustrated in Figure 9.27.

	G	H	I	J
3		Utilities:		
4		Max value =	200	=MAX(C11:E13)
5		min value =	-120	=MIN(C11:E13)
6		Umax =	1	=IF(I4=I4,1,0)
7		Umin =	0	=IF(I5=I5,0,1)
8				
9		U(120)?		
10		p =	0.8	
11		q =	0.2	=1-I10
12		U(120) =	0.8	=I10*I6+I11*I7
13		U(90)?		
14		p =	0.75	
15		q =	0.25	=1-I14
16		U(90) =	0.75	=I14*I6+I15*I7
17		U(40)?		
18		p =	0.6	
19		q =	0.4	=1-I18
20		U(40) =	0.6	=I18*I6+I19*I7
21				
22		Utility summary table		
23				
24		Value	Utility	
25		200	1.00	=I6
26		120	0.80	=I12
27		90	0.75	=I16
28		40	0.60	=I20
29		-120	0.00	=I7

Figure 9.27

❊ **Interpretation** Utility values are U(200,000) = 1, U(–120,000) = 0, U(120,000) = 0.8, U(90,000) = 0.75, and U(40,000) = 0.6.

Stage 2 Estimate unknown utility values from graph using linear interpolation

From stage 1 we note that we now need to calculate the utilities for payoff values of €50,000, €30,000, €20,000 and –€30,000. This can be achieved by plotting the known utilities and payoff values given in stage 1 and using the graph to read off the unknown values as illustrated in Figure 9.28.

Figure 9.28 Plot of known utility values against payoffs. From Figure 9.29 we can estimate the unknown values.

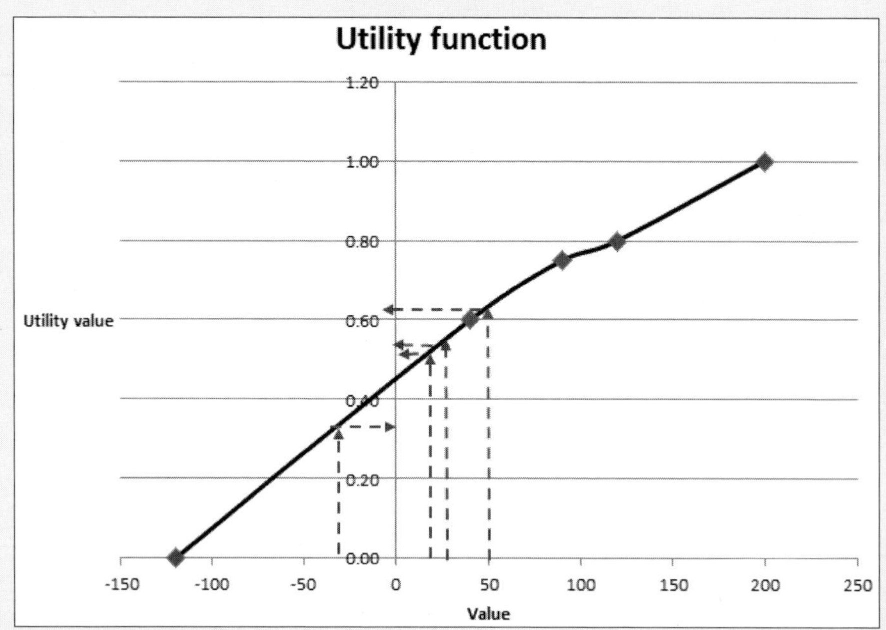

Figure 9.28

	G	H	I	J
30				
31		Unknown utilities		
32		U(50) =	0.61	approx
33		U(30) =	0.53	approx
34		U(20) =	0.5	approx
35		U(- 30) =	0.36	approx

Figure 9.29

Interpretation Graph estimates utility values are: U(50) = 0.61 U(30) = 0.53, U(20) = 0.5, U(−30) = 0.36.

Stage 3 Replace payoff values with utility values and calculate the expected utility values

Figure 9.30 includes the utility values replacing payoff values and the calculation of the expected monetary values for each alternative investment. For example, expected utility value for the large factory = 0.1*1 + 0.6*0.61 + 0.3*0 = 0.47.

The Excel solution is illustrated in Figure 9.30.

	G	H	I	J	K	L	M	N	O
36									
37		Replace payoff values with utility values and re-calculate emv's							
38									
39									
40		Investment choice (alternatives)	Profits in €1000's						
41			(states of nature)						
42			Strong economy	Stable economy	Weak economy	EMV			
43		Large factory	1	0.61	0	0.466	=$C$3*I43+$C$4*J43+$C$5*K43		
44		Average factory	0.75	0.80	0.36	0.663			
45		Small factory	0.60	0.53	0.5	0.528	=$C$3*I45+$C$4*J45+$C$5*K45		

Figure 9.30

Interpretation The best expected utility value is given by the average factory choice to build. This agrees with the expected monetary value decision.

Note It can be very difficult to assign a utility function to a problem given that decision makers will have different ideas about what probability value to assign to risk scenarios with the added problem that these probability estimates can be heavily influenced by both internal and external influences on the decision maker.

Student exercises

Please visit the Online Resource Centre which accompanies this textbook for solutions to the student exercises and techniques in practice questions.

X9.17 Reconsider X9.14. To aid the decision making process the club regularly assess the members attitude to risk with members voting at each meeting for a group attitude to risk. The perceived group attitude to risk for this investment is as follows: (i) indifferent between a profit of €123,000 now and a lottery that would give me a 0.6 probability of a €210,000 return and a 0.4 probability of a loss of €58,000, and (ii) indifferent between a profit of €43,000 now and a lottery that would give me a 0.45 probability of a €210,000 profit and a 0.55 probability of a loss of €58,000. (i) Construct the utility graph and comment on the clubs attitude to risk, (ii) estimate the utilities for profits of €63,000, €58,000, €8000, €4000, and €2000. What is the best decision for the club?

Techniques in practice

TP1 Coco S.A. has decided to stock a new in-house magazine called 'How to play the financial markets'. They have no previous experience of how well this magazine will sell but plan to stock up to ten copies for sale to employees and consider all sales outcomes to be equally likely; that is, up to ten copies to be sold. Coco S.A. inform you that they will take your advice on how many copies to order but that you should minimize the maximum regret possible from the decision. What do you advise when informed that 'How to play the financial markets' is bought at 40p, sold at 60p with no refund for unsold copies?

TP2 Bakers Ltd is due to purchase a new generator for one of its factories with a choice of ordering 20 spare sets of windings. Spare windings are required to replace burnt-out windings due to overloading of the system at infrequent intervals. The company thinks that the most likely number of burn-outs will be 10 with 0 and 20 equally least likely within the life of the generator. Advise the company on how many spare sets of windings to order with the generator and base your advice on the calculation of expected monetary value of each possible decision. The winding costs are:

	Bought with generator (€)	Bought later (€)
(a)	1000	8000
(b)	2000	8000
(c)	4000	8000

Table 9.10

TP3 Skodel Ltd has a central accounting department. Batches of invoices are sent to the department for checking and processing. 90% of the batches are satisfactory, containing only 1% incorrect invoices. The remaining 10% are, however, unsatisfactory, and contain 5% incorrect invoices.

(a) What is the probability that a new batch arriving in the department will be unsatisfactory?

(b) One invoice is taken from the batch. It is incorrect. With this new information, what is the probability that the batch is unsatisfactory?

(c) A second invoice is taken and is also incorrect. With these two pieces of information, what is the probability that the batch is unsatisfactory?

Summary

In this chapter we have explored the concept of quantitative decision making in business.

Student exercise answers

For all figures listed below, please see the Online Resource Centre.

X9.1 Define the problem, gather information, identify action alternatives, evaluate the alternative, and implement the chosen alternative.

X9.2 Choose alternative B and E which have the maximum profit of €200.

X9.3 We know what the final outcome will be – in this case we would choose the best payoff offered by the scenario.

X9.4 With decision making under uncertainty we may have a series of alternative events but we are unlikely to know which alternative events are more likely.

X9.5 Describe the five types outlined in section 9.3.

X9.5 The Laplace method is the only uncertainty method to use all the available alternative information.

X9.6 Laplace criterion method uses all alternative outcomes.

X9.7 (a) Maximax = 16: corresponds to choosing bonds, (b) maximin = 6% corresponds to choosing deposits, and (c) Hurwicz's H = 9.7% corresponds to choosing bonds.

X9.8 Applying Savage's method gives the smallest maximum growth of 7% corresponding to choosing deposits.

X9.9 Choose the Laplace solution – recommend choose deposits.

X9.10 All methods would select alternative project D (Wald's minimax criterion = 112, Savage's minimax regret criterion = 26, and Laplace's insufficient reason criterion = 77.2).

X9.11 The alternative events can be provided with an associated probability of occurrence.

X9.12 Calculate the expected value associated with each alternative event and choose the maximum profit or minimum loss.

X9.13 (a) E(A) = E(B) = £10,000, (b) A yields a better profit profile – variance lower for A compared to B – reduces overall risk.

X9.14 (a) (i) Maximax rule says alternative A with €210,000, (ii) Maximin rule says alternative B with €4000, (iii) Minimax regret criterion says alternative B with maximin opportunity loss of €87,000; (b) (i) EMV = €54,070, (ii) EVPI = €56,440.

X9.15 Therefore, EV B > EV C (48 > 46), choose B.

X9.16 Build the small plant. The expected value of building the small plant is £9.8m > expected value of building the large plant £9.2m.

X9.17 (i) utility graph (see below), (ii) Estimates from utility graph: U(63,000) = 0.50, U(58,000) = 0.50, U(8000) = 0.30, U(4000) = 0.28, and U(2000) = 0.26. Best decision is to accept alternative B with utility expected value $EV_B = 0.43$ (although this is a borderline decision given utility $EV_A = 0.42$ and $EV_C = 0.3808$).

Figure X9.17d

Utility function for X9.17

TP1 Minimax analysis of regret table shows that the best action (or decision) by Coco GmbH is to stock 3 copies of the in-house magazine.

TP2 Find: Case A: Minimum expected cost is €16,600 with n = 15, Case B: Minimum expected cost is €30,480 with n = 13, Case C: Minimum expected cost is €53,200 with n = 10. Advise manager that case A would be least expensive in total costs (b = 1000, a = 8000), when 15 windings are bought at onset with generators.

TP3 (a) 0.1, (b) 0.357, (c) 0.74. So the probability that this particular batch is unsatisfactory has changed from 0.10 with historical data only, to 0.36 with one piece of additional information, and to 0.74 with two pieces of additional information.

Further reading

Textbook resources

1. G. Davis and B. Pecar (2010) *Business Statistics Using Excel*, Oxford University Press.
2. D. Whigham (2007), *Business Data Analysis using Excel*, Oxford University Press.
3. J. K. Lindsey, *Introduction to Applied Statistics: A Modelling Approach* (2nd edn), Oxford University Press.
4. D. Anderson, D. Sweeney, and T. Williams (2011) *Essentials of Statistics for Business and Economics* (6th edn), Cengage Learning.
5. D. Levine, D. Stephan, T. C. Krehbie, and M. Berenson (2011) *Statistics for Managers using MS Excel* (6th edn). Pearson.
6. S. Albright, W. Winston, and C. Zappe (2009) *Data Analysis and Decision Making* (3rd edn), Cengage Learning.

Web resources

1. StatSoft Electronic Textbook **http://www.statsoft.com/textbook/stathome.html** (accessed 24th May 2012).
2. HyperStat Online Statistics Textbook **http://davidmlane.com/hyperstat/index.html** (accessed 24th May 2012).
3. Decision analysis society **http://www.informs.org/Community/DAS** (accessed 24th May 2012).
4. Dr Arsham's statistics site **http://home.ubalt.edu/ntsbarsh/Business-stat/opre504.htm** (accessed 24th May 2012).
5. The ISI glossary of statistical terms provides definitions in a number of different languages **http://isi.cbs.nl/glossary/index.htm** (accessed 24th May 2012).

Formula summary

$$H = \alpha\,(\text{column maximum}) + (1 - \alpha)\,(\text{column minimum}) \qquad (9.1)$$

$$H = \alpha\,(\text{column minimum}) + (1 - \alpha)\,(\text{column maximum}) \qquad (9.2)$$

$$OL = \text{maximum payoff in that state} - \text{reward payoff in that cell} \qquad (9.3)$$

$$OL = \text{reward payoff in that cell} - \text{minimum payoff in the state} \qquad (9.4)$$

$$EMV(A_j) = \sum_{i=1}^{N} A_{ji} \times P(S_i) \qquad (9.5)$$

$$EVPI = EPUC - EV \qquad (9.6)$$

$$\sigma_j = \sqrt{\sum_{i=1}^{N} (X_i - E(X_i))^2 \times P(X_i)} \qquad (9.7)$$

$$CV_j = \left(\frac{\sigma_j}{EMV_j}\right) \times 100\% \qquad (9.8)$$

$$RTRR_j = \frac{EMV_j}{\sigma_j} \qquad (9.9)$$

Decision making in finance

10

» Overview «

This chapter explores key concepts in financial mathematics, namely compound interest, depreciation, future value, sinking funds, annuities, present value, trust funds, loan repayments, present value of an ordinary annuity, net present value, perpetual annuity, internal rate of return, modified internal rate of return, and mortgage repayments. Microsoft Excel contains a range of financial functions that provide solutions to these financial problems.

» Learning outcomes «

On completing this chapter you should be able to:

- » Understand the key terms used within financial mathematics.
- » Solve simple and compound interest problems.
- » Solve problems involving depreciation.
- » Calculate the value of an investment when a sum is added on a regular basis.
- » Calculate the future value of an ordinary annuity (sinking funds).
- » Understand the concept of present value and discounting.
- » Calculate the amount invested to be able to withdraw a sum on a regular basis until the amount is zero (trust funds and loan repayments or present value of an ordinary annuity).
- » Calculate the net present value of a series of cash flows.
- » Calculate the present value of an annuity and perpetuity.
- » Calculate the internal rate of return (IRR) for a series of cash flows.
- » Calculate the modified internal rate of return (MIRR) where negative and positive cash flows have different interest rates.
- » Calculate the cost of a mortgage.
- » Solve problems using the Microsoft Excel spreadsheet.

X

compound interest interest paid on both the principal and the interest previously earned.

depreciation amount by which a business reduces the value of its assets.

future value value of an investment after a period of time.

sinking fund (see future value of an ordinary annuity) a fund that receives regular payments so that a specified sum is available at some point in the future.

trust fund (see present value of an ordinary annuity) is the value of a stream of expected or promised future payments that have been discounted to a single equivalent value today.

annuity amount invested to give a fixed income over some period.

internal rate of return discount rate that gives a net present value of zero.

rate interest rate per annum.

future value of an ordinary annuity (see sinking fund) a fund that receives regular payments so that a specified sum is available at some point in the future.

discounting value of $(1 + r)^{-n}$ when discounting to present value.

interest amount paid to lenders as reward for using their money.

10.1 Simple interest

Do you remember Equation (10.1)?

$$SI = \frac{PRT}{100} \tag{10.1}$$

There can hardly be an adult alive today who did not meet this formula at school. It tells us how much simple interest (SI) we would earn if we deposited a principal of £P in a bank for time T years, and if the bank paid an interest rate at R% per annum.

Example 10.1

If the bank paid 8% per annum on deposits, a deposit of £250 left in the bank for four years would earn:

$$SI = \frac{250 * 8 * 4}{100} = £80$$

Before we examine the implications of this calculation it will be convenient to modify it somewhat. Rather than expressing the rate as a percentage, let us instead express it as a proportion, r. To do this, we divide the percentage rate by 100. So, for example, if R = 8% then r = 8/100 = 0.08. Our equation for calculating interest now becomes:

$$SI = PTr \tag{10.2}$$

From now on, we shall use r as the rate of interest. Of course, this does not affect the result of the calculation: SI = 250*4*0.08 = £80. Whichever way we express the rate of interest, we still predict that £250 deposited for four years at 8% per annum would earn us £80. But is this figure correct? We would earn £80 only if we withdrew the interest of £20 each year. Over the four years we would have earned what is called simple interest. The value of this investment earning simple interest is called a future value (FV) and is given by Equation (10.3).

$$FV = P + SI \tag{10.3}$$

Figure 10.1 illustrates the Excel solution.

	A	B	C	D	E	F	G
1	Example 10.1 Simple interest example						
2							
3		Initial data			Excel calculations		
4							
5		Deposit P =	£250.00				
6		Time T =	4				
7		Rate R =	8		r =	0.08	=C7/100
8					Simple interest (SI) =	£80.00	=C5*C6*C7/100
9					SI =	£80.00	=C5*C6*F7
10					Future value (FV) =	£330.00	=C5+F8

Figure 10.1

simple interest interest paid on only the initial deposit, but not on interest already earned.

time time period of the investment/loan in years.

→ Excel solution

P = Cell C5	Values
T = Cell C6	Values
R = Cell C7	Values
r = Cell F7	Formula: = C7/100
SI = Cell F8	Formula: = C5*C6*C7/100
SI = Cell F9	Formula: = C5*C6*F7
FV = Cell F10	Formula: = C5+F8

Interpretation From Excel, the future value of the investment after four years which earned simple interest at 8% is £330. The simple interest earned is £20 per year with a total interest earned of £80 over the four years.

Note The number representing deposit in cell C5 is formatted as currency (£s).

Student exercises

X10.1 Find the interest on the amount of £1000 at the following annual simple interest rates: (a) 4.5% for one year, (b) 5.25% for two years, (c) 3.5% for six months, and (d) 5% for ten months.

X10.2 At what rate of simple interest will: (a) £2000 amount to £2110 in one year, and (b) £720 amount to £744 in 10 months?

X10.3 What sum invested today at 5% simple interest will amount to £1000 in eight months' time?

10.2 Compound interest and depreciation

But suppose we did not withdraw our interest from the bank. If we do not, then the interest on deposit would itself earn interest. We would then be earning what is called **compound interest**.

compound interest arises when interest is added to the principal, so that, from that moment on, the interest that has been added also earns interest.

Example 10.2

Let us now compare the two methods of earning interest on a year-by-year basis where the initial deposit is £250 at an interest rate of 8% per annum, as illustrated in Table 10.1.

Year	Simple interest		Compound interest	
	Future value (£)	Interest earned (£)	Future value (£)	Interest earned (£)
0	250		250	
1	270	250 * 0.08 = 20	270	250 * 0.08 = 20
2	290	250 * 0.08 = 20	291.60	270 * 0.08 = 21.60
3	310	250 * 0.08 = 20	324.93	291.60 * 0.08 = 23.33
4	330	250 * 0.08 = 20	340.12	314.93 * 0.08 = 25.19
Total interest earned		80		90.12

Table 10.1 Comparison between simple and compound interest

So we see that there is a considerable difference between the two methods, as illustrated in Figure 10.2.

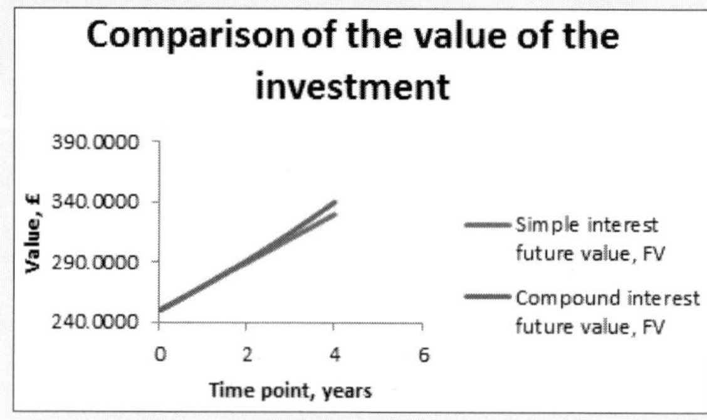

Figure 10.2

Compound interest is the method that is invariably used in the business world.

Figure 10.3 illustrates the effect of time on the growth rates of investments, which are invested using simple compared to compound interest.

We observe from Figure 10.3 the large difference between the future value based on simple interest (£1250) and compound interest (£11,725) after 50 years.

If we are going to calculate compound interest on a year-to-year basis, the calculation will be tedious to say the least. What we require is a formula for compound interest, and to obtain this we shall use our example, though this time from a slightly different angle. We shall calculate the value of the deposit at the end of each year if £P is invested at an interest rate r and left for n years.

Value of deposit at end of year = value of deposit at beginning of year plus interest earned during the year.

Value of deposit at end of first year = deposit + interest = $P + rP = P(1 + r)$

Value of deposit at end of second year = $P(1 + r) + rP(1 + r) = (1 + r)(P + rP) = (1 + r) \times P(1 + r) = P(1 + r)^2$

Value of deposit at end of third year = $P(1 + r)^2 + rP(1 + r)^2 = (1 + r)^2(P + rP) = P(1 + r)^3$

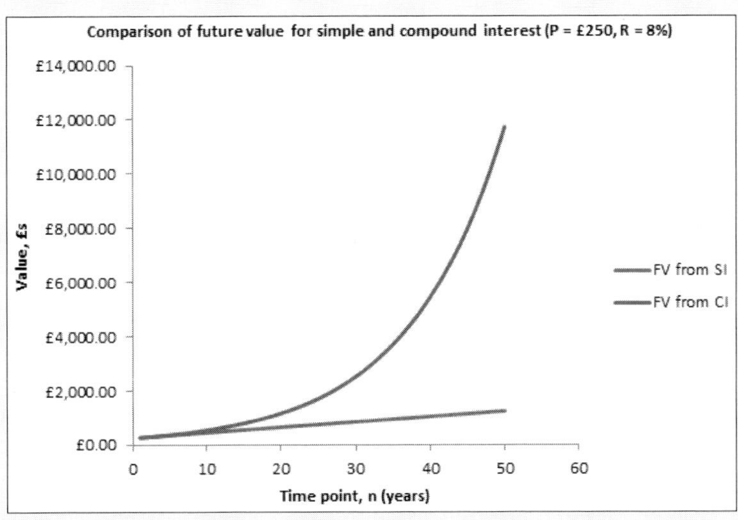

Figure 10.3

From this we can observe a pattern that allows Equation (10.4) to be written to allow the reader to calculate the future value of an investment with compound interest:

$$FV = P(1 + r)^n \tag{10.4}$$

→ Excel command to calculate future value = FV(RATE, NPER, PMT, PV, TYPE)

Note In the Excel formula for FV the terms represent the following:

1. RATE is the interest rate per period.
2. NPER is the total number of payment periods in an annuity.
3. PMT is the payment made each period; it cannot change over the life of the annuity. Typically, PMT contains principal and interest but no other fees or taxes. If PMT is omitted, you must include the PV argument.
4. PV is the present value, or the lump-sum amount that a series of future payments is worth right now. If PV is omitted, it is assumed to be 0 (zero), and you must include the PMT argument.
5. Type is the number 0 or 1 and indicates when payments are due. If type is omitted, it is assumed to be 0. Set type equal to if payments are due: 0 at the end of the period and 1 at the beginning of the period.

And the total compound interest earned would be

$$I = P(1 + r)^n - P \tag{10.5}$$

➜ Excel command to calculate the interest payment for a given period for an investment based on periodic, constant payments and a constant interest rate = IPMT(RATE, PER, NPER, PV, FV, TYPE)

Note In the Excel formula for IPMT we have a new term called PER, which represents the period for which you want to find the interest and must be in the range 1 to NPER.

The Excel solutions are given in Figures 10.4 and 10.5 for the Example 10.2 data problem.

	A	B	C	D	E	F	G	H
1	Example 10.2 Compound interest example							
2								
3		Deposit P =	£250.00					
4		Rate R =	8					
5								
6		r =	0.08					
7								
8		Using Equation (10.3) to calculate the future value when interest compounded.						
9								
10		Time Point, T	Compound interest future value, FV		Interest, I		Interest at the end of each period	
11		1	270.0000	=\$C\$3*(1+\$C\$6)^B11	20.0000	=C11-\$C\$3	20.0000	=E11
12		2	291.6000		41.6000		21.6000	=E12-E11
13		3	314.9280		64.9280		23.3280	
14		4	340.1222	=\$C\$3*(1+\$C\$6)^B14	90.1222	=C14-\$C\$3	25.1942	=E14-E13

Figure 10.4

Calculating future value using Equation (10.4).

	A	B	C	D	E	F	G	H
17		Using Excel functions to calculate the future value and compound interest.						
18								
19		Time Point, T	Compound interest future value, S		Interest, I		Interest at the end of each period	
20		1	270.0000	=FV(\$C\$6,B20,0,-\$C\$3,1)	20.0000	=C20-\$C\$3	20.0000	=IPMT(\$C\$6,B20,4,-\$C\$3,\$C\$23,0)
21		2	291.6000		41.6000		21.6000	
22		3	314.9280		64.9280		23.3280	
23		4	340.1222	=FV(\$C\$6,B23,0,-\$C\$3,1)	90.1222	=C23-\$C\$3	25.1942	=IPMT(\$C\$6,B23,4,-\$C\$3,\$C\$23,0)

Figure 10.5

Calculating future value using Excel functions FV() and IMPT().

➜ Excel solution

P = Cell C3	Value
R = Cell C4	Value
r = Cell C6	Formula: = C4/100
T = Cells B11:B14	Values

Using Equation (10.4) to calculate the future values when interest compounded

FV = Cell C11	Formula: = \$C\$3*(1+\$C\$6)^B11
	Copy down C11:C14
I = Cell E11	Formula: = C11-\$C\$3
	Copy down E11:E14

Interest per period = Cell G11 Formula: = E11

Cell G12 Formula: = E12-E11

Copy down G12:G14

Using Excel function FV to calculate future value when interest compounded

FV = Cell C20 Formula: = FV($C$6, B20, 0, - $C$3, 1)

Copy down C20:C23

I = Cell E20 Formula: = C20-$C$3

Copy down E20:E23

i = Cell G20 Formula: = IPMT($C$6, B20, 4, - $C$3 ,$C$23, 0)

Copy down G20:G23

Interpretation From Excel, the future value of £250 over four years compounded at 8% will be worth £340.12. The interest earned would be I = FV – P = £90.12 to the nearest penny. At this point, a few words of warning would be appropriate. Compound interest mounts up very quickly, and yields surprisingly large sums. For this example we have £100 invested at 8% per annum for 20 years and we would earn interest of $I = 100(1.08)^{20} - 100 = £366.10$.

The equation we have derived can also be used to calculate the rate of interest or the number of years required for an investment to grow.

Note Accessing Excel dialog menu for future value (FV): Select Formulas > Select Insert Function > Select Financial > Select FV function (see Figure 10.6).

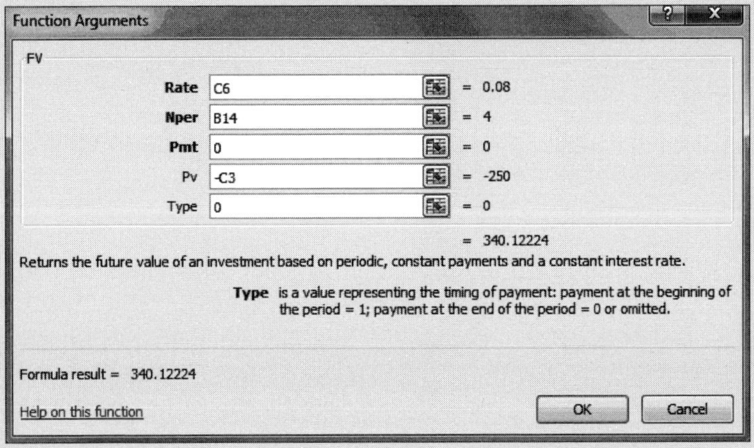

Function Arguments

FV

Rate	C6	= 0.08
Nper	B14	= 4
Pmt	0	= 0
Pv	-C3	= -250
Type	0	= 0

= 340.12224

Returns the future value of an investment based on periodic, constant payments and a constant interest rate.

Type is a value representing the timing of payment: payment at the beginning of the period = 1; payment at the end of the period = 0 or omitted.

Formula result = 340.12224

Help on this function

OK Cancel

Figure 10.6

Accessing Excel dialog menu that returns the interest payment for a given period for an investment based on periodic, constant payments and a constant interest rate (IPMT): Select Formulas > Select Insert Function > Select Financial > Select IPMT function (see Figure 10.7).

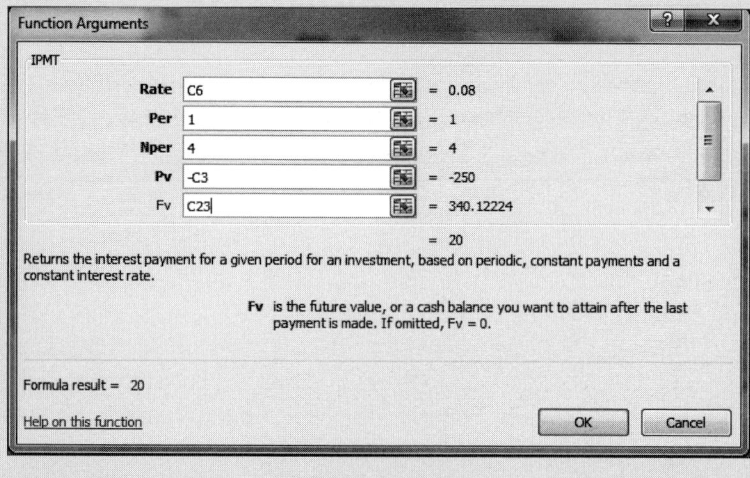

Figure 10.7

Note

1. Notice that the Excel formula in cells C11:C14 have $ signs on the cell references e.g. in cell C11 we have =$C$3*(1+$C$6)^B11. This use of the absolute copying feature of Excel is to allow the equation to be used to calculate the future value at time points n = 1, 2, 3, and 4.
2. Using Equation (10.4) gives $FV = 250*(1.08)^4 = £340.12$
3. Using Excel function FV gives =FV(8%, 4, 0, - 250, 1) = £340.12
4. The present value P is negative in the Excel FV function since we are depositing £250.

In Example 10.2, the interest rate was given as 8% per annum that would be paid once at the end of the year. This interest rate is called the nominal interest rate. If we repeated Example 10.2, but this time we added the interest every six months, then equation 10.5 can be used to calculate the future value of this investment after six months and after the first year. Table 10.2 illustrates the calculation of the compound interest and future values after six months and one year where the interest rate for each time period, $r = 0.08/2 = 0.04$.

Time point (years)	Balance at start of time period	Interest to be added	Balance at end of time period
0	250		
0.5	250	250 * 0.04 = 10	250 + 10 = 260
1	260	260 * 0.04 = 10.4	260 + 10.4 = 270.4

Table 10.2 Calculation of compound interest and future value

We observe that at the end of the first year the future value is £270.40 (with total interest paid of 270.40 – £250 = £20.40). Compare the one interest payment at the end of the year where the future value was £270 (with interest of £270 – £250 = £20). From this we can calculate the percentage increases for each of the investments:

- One interest period per year: percentage increase = [(270 – 250)/250]*100% = 8%.
- Two equal interest periods per year: percentage increase = [(270.40 – 250)/250]*100% = 8.16%.

This tells us that if the interest is paid twice a year then the interest rate would be 8.16% and not 8% (the nominal interest rate). This is called the effective annual interest rate (EAIR) and can be calculated using Equation (10.6):

$$EAIR = \left(1 + \frac{r}{f}\right)^f - 1 \qquad (10.6)$$

Where r = nominal interest rate, f = number of times interest is added per year. If we have one interest period then we can show from Equation (10.6) that the effective annual interest rate is equal to the nominal interest rate (EAIR = r).

Example 10.3

A sum of money is deposited now at 10% per annum. How long will it take for the sum to double? Suppose that the sum invested is £1000, then after n years we require the sum to be £2000. Figure 10.8 illustrates the Excel solution (pv is negative in the Excel NPER function given that we deposit this amount).

C9 =NPER(C3,C4,-C5,C6,C7)

	A	B	C	D
1	Example 10.3 Calculating time for investment, n			
2				
3		rate, r =	0.1	
4		pmt =	0	
5		pv =	1000	
6		fv =	2000	
7		type =	1	
8				
9		n =	7.272541	=NPER(C3,C4,-C5,C6,C7)

Figure 10.8

effective annual interest rate is the interest rate on a loan or financial product restated from the nominal interest rate as an interest rate with annual compound interest payable in arrears.

→ Excel solution

Rate, r = Cell C3	Value
PMT = Cell C4	Value
PV = Cell C5	Value
FV = Cell C6	Value
TYPE = Cell C7	Value
n = Cell C9	Formula: = NPER(C3, C4, – C5, C6, C7)

Interpretation From Excel, the sum will double after 7.27 years if the interest rate was 10% per annum.

Note

$$FV = 2P \quad \text{and} \quad FV = P(1 + r)^n$$

Therefore, $P(1 + r)^n = 2P$

To solve this equation we apply the laws of logarithms (using base 10 but you can use any base number) as follows:

$$LOG_{10}(P(1 + r)^n) = LOG_{10}(2P)$$

$$LOG_{10}(P) + LOG_{10}(1 + r)^n = LOG_{10}(2) + LOG_{10}(P)$$

Simplifying gives: $n * LOG_{10}(1.1) = LOG_{10}(2)$

$$n = LOG_{10}(2)/LOG_{10}(1.1)$$

$$n = 7.27 \text{ years to two decimal places}$$

Sum will double in 7.27 years.

Example 10.4

£100 is invested now, and we are prepared to leave it on deposit for 15 years. What rate of interest would it be necessary if the sum invested is to grow to £750?

Figure 10.9 illustrates the Excel solution (pv is negative in the Excel RATE function given that we deposit this amount).

C9 =RATE(C3,C4,-C5,C6,C7)

	A	B	C	D
1	Example 10.4 Calculating discount rate, r			
2				
3		nper =	15	
4		pmt =	0	
5		pv =	100	
6		fv =	750	
7		type =	1	
8				
9		r =	0.143767	=RATE(C3,C4,-C5,C6,C7)

Figure 10.9

➜ Excel solution

NPER = Cell C3 Value
PMT = Cell C4 Value
PV = Cell C5 Value
FV = Cell C6 Value
TYPE = Cell C7 Value
r = Cell C9 Formula: = RATE(C3, C4, - C5, C6, C7)

Interpretation From Excel, the annual interest rate is 14.38% for the initial sum of £100 to grow to £750 in 15 years.

Note

This problem can be solved by rearranging Equation (10.4) to make r the subject of the equation:

$$FV = P(1 + r)^n$$

$$750 = 100(1 + r)^{15}$$

$$7.5 = (1 + r)^{15}$$

To make r the subject of the equation we take logarithms and apply the laws of logarithms:

$$LOG_{10}(7.5) = LOG_{10}(1 + r)^{15}$$

$$LOG_{10}(7.5) = 15 * LOG_{10}(1 + r)$$

Using your calculator or Excel function LOG_{10}, we find $LOG_{10}(7.5) = 0.875061263$.

$$0.875061263 = 15 * LOG_{10}(1 + r)$$

$$0.0583 = LOG_{10}(1 + r)$$

$$10^{0.0583} = (1 + r)$$

$$r = 0.1437$$

Now we could use the formula to find the sum we must deposit to achieve a specified sum in the future.

Example 10.5

We require £10,000 in 15 years' time and we deposit money at 12% per annum. How much must we invest now (called the present value) to achieve this sum?

Figure 10.10 illustrates the Excel solution.

	A	B	C	D
1	Example 10.5 Calculating principal value, pv			
2				
3		rate, r =	0.12	
4		nper =	15	
5		pmt =	0	
6		fv =	10000	
7		type =	1	
8				
9		pv =	-£1,826.96	=PV(C3,C4,C5,C6,C7)

C9 =PV(C3,C4,C5,C6,C7)

Figure 10.10

➜ Excel solution

Rate, r = Cell C3 Value
NPER = Cell C4 Value
PMT = Cell C5 Value
FV = Cell C6 Value
TYPE = Cell C7 Value
PV = Cell C9 Formula: = PV(C3, C4, C5, C6, C7)

Interpretation From Excel, the present value of £1826.96 would be needed to be deposited now to achieve £10,000 in 15 years' time with an interest rate of 12% per annum (P is negative since we are depositing £1827).

Note

$FV = 10{,}000$ and $FV = P(1 + r)^n$

$P(1.12)^{15} = 10{,}000$

$P(5.4736) = 10{,}000$

$P = 10{,}000/5.4736 = £1826.95$

When interest is added N times per year then Equation (10.4) needs to be modified to allow the future value to be calculated as given by Equation (10.7):

$$FV = P(1 + j/f)^{fm} \quad (10.7)$$

Example 10.6

An investment quotes an interest rate of 12% per annum nominally, but in fact interest is compounded at 4% three times per year. How much will an investment of £1200 be worth after six years with payment at end of year?

Let j = nominal interest rate (annual rate) = 12% = 0.12

m = number of years of transaction = 6

f = frequency of conversion i.e. annually $f = 1$, monthly $f = 12$

$\therefore \quad f = 3$

r = rate of interest per period = $j/f = 0.12/3 = 0.04$

N = number of interest periods = $f*m = 3*6 = 18$

P = present value = 1200

FV = value of investment after time m

Figure 10.11 illustrates the Excel solution.

	A	B	C	D
1	Example 10.6 Calculating the future value, fv			
2				
3		Nominal interest rate rate, j =	0.12	
4		Number of years of transaction, m =	6	
5		Frequency of conversion, f =	3	
6		Rate of interest per period, r =	0.04	=C3/C5
7		Number of interest periods, n =	18	=C5*C4
8		Present value, PV =	£1,200.00	
9				
10		Future value, FV =	£2,430.98	=FV(C6,C7,0,-C8,0)

Figure 10.11

→ Excel solution

j = Cell C3	Value
m = Cell C4	Value
f = Cell C5	Value
r = Cell C6	Formula: = C3/C5
n = Cell C7	Formula: = C5*C4
PV = Cell C8	Value
FV = Cell C9	Formula: = FV(C6, C7, 0,- C8, 0)

❊ Interpretation

From Excel, the future value after six years is £2430.98 when interest is payable at 4% three times per year with an initial deposit of £1200.

Note Substituting the values into Equation (10.6) gives: $FV = P(1 + j/f)^{fn} = 1200*(1.04)^{18} = 2430.98$

A further application of the concept of compound interest is the idea of **depreciation**, where the value of an item decreases over time usually at a constant rate of reduction.

Example 10.7

A manufacturing company buys a piece of capital equipment for £1,750,000. Its value is assumed to depreciate at a constant rate of 8% per annum. What will the equipment's value be when it is scheduled to be scrapped after five years?

Figure 10.12 illustrates the Excel solution.

C7 f_x =FV(-C4,C5,0,-C3,0)

	A	B	C	D
1	Example 10.7 Depreciation			
2				
3		PV =	£1,750,000.00	
4		r =	0.08	
5		n =	5	
6				
7		FV =	£1,153,392.67	=FV(-C4,C5,0,-C3,0)

Figure 10.12

The rate in the Excel function FV is negative given that the present value is depreciating.

→ Excel solution

PV = Cell C3 Value
r = Cell C4 Value
n = Cell C5 Value
FV = Cell C7 Formula: = FV(- C4, C5, 0, - C3, 0)

Interpretation From Excel, the equipment's scrap value is £1,153,392.67.

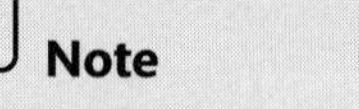

Note

$$FV = P(1 + r)^n = 1{,}750{,}000*(1 - 0.08)^5 = 1{,}153{,}392.67$$

depreciation refers to the decrease in the value of assets.

Student exercises

X10.4 What sum would be available in seven years' time if £3250 is invested now with a compound interest rate of 11% per annum (use Equation (10.4) and Excel FV function)?

X10.5 What compound annual interest rate would cause £3,265 to grow to £5,776 in six years' time (use Equation (10.4) and Excel RATE function)?

X10.6 Find the effective rate of interest which is equivalent to the following nominal rates (use Equation (10.6) and Excel function EFFECT):

(a) 16% compounded half-annually.

(b) 16% compounded quarterly.

(c) 16% compounded monthly.

(d) 16% compounded daily (1 year = 365 days).

X10.7 Find the nominal rate, j, compounded monthly equivalent to 16% compounded semi-annually.

X10.8 At what nominal rate compounded monthly will £2000 amount to £4650 in six years' time (use Equation (10.4) and Excel RATE function)?

10.3 Increasing the sum invested

So far, we have examined how an initial deposit would grow if it earned compound interest. But suppose we added to the amount deposited at the end of each year (called **increasing the sum invested**). Specifically, suppose we deposited £1000 on the first of January of a certain year, and decided to deposit £100 at the end of each year. If interest is compounded at 10% per annum, then we can use Equation (10.3) to deduce the value of the investment after n years:

sum on deposit at the end of the first year is

$1000(1 + 0.1) + 100$

sum on deposit at the end of the second year is

$1000(1 + 0.1)^2 + 100(1 + 0.1) + 100$

sum on deposit at the end of the nth year is

$1000(1 + 0.1)^n + 100(1 + 0.1)^{n-1} + 100(1 + 0.1)^{n-2} + \ldots\ldots.. + 100$

If we generalize the quantities, then we can derive a formula to solve problems like this swiftly and efficiently. If we let P be the initial deposit, r the interest rate and a the amount that we deposit at the end of each year, then after n years the sum available would be: $FV = P(1 + r)^n + a(1 + r)^{n-1} + a(1 + r)^{n-2} + \ldots\ldots\ldots + a$. Now it can be shown that this expression is equivalent to:

$$FV = P(1 + r)^n + \frac{a(1 + r)^n - a}{r} \qquad (10.8)$$

X

increasing the sum invested adding to the amount deposited at the end of each year to increase the sum invested.

We can use this equation to calculate the sum left on deposit if we withdraw fixed amounts from the bank each year.

Example 10.8

So if we deposit £1000, and add £100 to our deposit at the end of each year, and if interest is compounded at 10% p.a. then the sum available after four years is given by Equation (10.8). Figure 10.13 illustrates the Excel solution.

	A	B	C	D
1	Example 10.8 Increasing the Sum Invested			
2				
3		Deposit PV =	£1,000	
4		Extra payments, a =	£100.00	
5		Rate r =	0.1	
6				
7				
8		Time Point	Future Value	
9		T	FV	
10		1	£1,200.00	=FV($C$5,B10,-$C$4,-$C$3,0)
11		2	£1,420.00	
12		3	£1,662.00	
13		4	£1,928.20	=FV($C$5,B13,-$C$4,-$C$3,0)

Figure 10.13

Excel solution

Deposit PV = Cell C3	Value
Extra payment = Cell C4	Value
Rate r = Cell C5	Value
Time point, T Cells B10:B13	Values
Future value, FV Cell C10	Formula: = FV($C$5, B10, –$C$4, –$C$3, 0)
	Copy down C10:C13

Interpretation From Excel, the future value of the investment is £1928.20 after four years.

Note PV and PMT are negative since we are making payments.

$$FV = 1000(1 + 0.1)^4 + \frac{100(1 + 0.1)^4 - 100}{0.1} = £1928.20$$

Example 10.9

Suppose we deposit £20,000 at the beginning of a year at 5% per annum compounded. We withdraw £2,000 at the end of each year. What would be the sum available after four years?

Figure 10.14 illustrates the Excel solution.

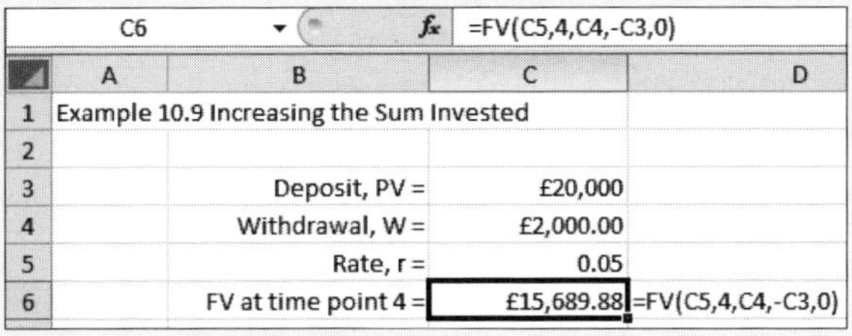

C6 =FV(C5,4,C4,-C3,0)

	A	B	C	D
1	Example 10.9 Increasing the Sum Invested			
2				
3		Deposit, PV =	£20,000	
4		Withdrawal, W =	£2,000.00	
5		Rate, r =	0.05	
6		FV at time point 4 =	£15,689.88	=FV(C5,4,C4,-C3,0)

Figure 10.14

Excel solution

PV = Cell C3 Value
W = Cell C4 Value
r = Cell C5 Value
FV = Cell C6 Formula: = FV(C5, 4, C4, -C3, 0)

Interpretation From Excel, the future value is £15,689.88 which would be available in four years' time when £20,000 is deposited at the beginning at 5% per annum and £2000 is withdrawn at the end of each year.

Note Here we have P = £20,000, a = –£2,000 (withdraw, ∴ negative), R = 5% (∴ r = 0.05), and n = 4:

$$FV = P(1+r)^n + \frac{a(1+r)^n - a}{r} = 20{,}000(1.05)^4 + \frac{((-2000)\times(1.05)^4 - (-2000))}{0.05} = £15{,}689.88$$

Equation (10.8) assumes that a constant is added (or withdrawn) from the deposit, and if this amount varies then you must not use the Equation (10.8). Instead you must use Equation (10.9):

$$FV = P(1+r)^n + a_1(1+r)^{n-1} + a_2(1+r)^{n-2} + \dots\dots\dots + a^n \qquad (10.9)$$

Where, a_1 is the sum added after 1 year, a_2 the sum after 2 years, and so on.

Example 10.10

Suppose we have £20,000 deposited at the beginning of a certain year at 9% per annum compounded. At the end of the first year we add £1000 to the deposit, at the end of the second year we add £2000 and at the end of the third year we add £3000. How much would we have on deposit after four years?

Figure 10.15 illustrates the Excel solution.

	A	B	C	D	E
1	Example 10.10 Increasing the sum invested				
2					
3		r =	0.09		
4		n =	4		
5					
6		Time	Deposit	FV	
7		0	20000	28231.6322	=C7*(1+$C$3)^($C$4-B7)
8		1	1000	1295.029	
9		2	2000	2376.2	
10		3	3000	3270	
11		4	0	0	=C11*(1+$C$3)^($C$4-B11)
12					
13			FV =	35172.8612	=SUM(D7:D11)

Figure 10.15

→ Excel solution

r = Cell C3	Value
n = Cell C4	Value
Time Cells B7:B11	Values
Deposit Cells C7:C11	Values
FV Cells D7	Formula: = C7*(1+$C$3)^($C$4-B7)
	Copy formula down from D7:D11
FV = Cell D13	Formula: = SUM(D7:D11)

Interpretation From Excel, future value of the investment is £35,172.86 after four years.

Note From Equation (10.7): In this case, P = 20,000, $a_1 = 1000$, $a_2 = 2000$, $a_3 = 3000$, $a_4 = 0$.

$$FV = P(1 + r)^4 + a_1(1 + R)^3 + a_2(1 + r)^2 + a_3(1 + r)^1 + a_4(1 + r)^0$$

$$FV = P(1 + r)^4 + a_1(1 + R)^3 + a_2(1 + r)^2 + a_3(1 + r)^1 + a_4$$

$$FV = 20{,}000(1.09)^4 + 1000(1.09)^3 + 2000(1.09)^2 + 3000(1.09)^1 + 0$$

$$FV = 20{,}000(1.4116) + 1000(1.2950) + 2000(1.1881) + 3000(1.09)$$

$$FV = 28{,}232 + 1295 + 2376.20 + 3270$$

$$FV = £35{,}173 \text{ to the nearest £}$$

If we wish to withdraw varying annual amounts, then we would use Equation (10.9) with negative values for a.

Example 10.11

If the deposits in the above example became withdrawals (a_1, a_2, a_3 all negative), then the amount on deposit after four years would be:

$$FV = 20{,}000(1.09)^4 - 1000(1.09)^3 - 2000(1.09)^2 - 3000(1.09) - 0$$

$$FV = 28{,}231.63 - 1295.03 - 2376.20 - 3270$$

FV = £21,290.40 to the nearest penny.

After four years the deposit is worth £21,290.

Student exercises

X10.9 Suppose £9500 is invested on the first of January of a certain year at 12% compound and £800 is withdrawn at the end of each year. Use the Excel function FV to calculate the amount remaining after 12 years?

X10.10 Suppose £7500 is invested on the 1st of January at 9% compound. Withdrawals are: £1000 at the end of the first year, £1200 at the end of the second year and £2000 at the end of the third year. How much would then remain after three years?

X10.11 Find the future value of this investment that involves a series of unequal cash flows (called a terminal value) with an initial outlay of £80,000 (Table 10.3).

The annual interest rate available for deposits is 6%.

Year	Cash flow (£)
1	30,000
2	0
3	80,000

Table 10.3

X10.12 Find the future value of this investment that involves a series of unequal cash flows (called a terminal value) with an initial outlay of £100,000 (Table 10.4).

The annual interest rate available for deposits is 8%.

Year	Cash flow (£)
1	10,000
2	20,000
3	30,000
4	50,000

Table 10.4

10.4 Sinking funds or future value of an ordinary annuity

A common form of investment made by investors is an annuity. The investor can purchase the annuity either by a single payment or a series of payments over the lifetime of

X

sinking fund is a sum set apart periodically from the income of a government or a business and allowed to accumulate in order ultimately to pay off a debt.

the investment. The investor will then receive regular payments each year, either until the investor's death or for a guaranteed minimum number of years. A further example would be when a company wishes to set aside a sum of money at the end of each year to replace an asset. We can use Equation (10.8) to solve this problem:

$$FV = P(1+r)^n + \frac{a(1+r)^n - a}{r}$$

The problem involves a zero initial investment, P = 0.0. Substituting P = 0 into Equation (10.8) gives Equation (10.10):

$$FV = \frac{a(1+r)^n - a}{r} \qquad (10.10)$$

If we now make 'a' the subject of this formula, we will have an expression telling us how much we must set aside at the end of each year to achieve a specified future value of an ordinary annuity (or sinking fund) formula (final payment at start of year n):

$$a = \frac{rFV}{(1+r)^n - 1} \qquad (10.11)$$

Example 10.12

Suppose a machine is expected to last 8 years and its replacement price is estimated at £5000. What annual provision must be made to ensure sufficient funds are available if money can be invested at 8% per annum with payment at the end of the year? Figure 10.16 illustrates the Excel solution.

C7 | fx =PMT(C5,C3,0,C4,0)

	A	B	C	D
1	Example 10.12 Sinking Funds			
2				
3		n =	8	
4		FV=	£5,000	
5		r =	0.08	
6				
7		a =	-£470.07	=PMT(C5,C3,0,C4,0)

Figure 10.16

→ Excel solution

n = Cell C3 Value
FV = Cell C4 Value
r = Cell C5 Value
a = Cell C7 Formula: = PMT(C5,C3,0,C4,0)

Interpretation From Excel, £470.07 deposited at the end of the year would be sufficient to yield the required future value.

Note Using Equation (10.11):

$$a = \frac{0.08 * 5000}{(1.08)^8 - 1} = \frac{400}{1.85093021 \ldots - 1} = £470.07$$

Spreadsheet command to calculate the payments, a
= PMT(RATE, NPER, PV, FV, TYPE) = PMT(0.8, 8, 0, –5000, 0) = £470.07

Spreadsheet command to calculate the Future Value, FV
= FV(RATE, NPER, PMT, PV, TYPE) = FV(0.8, 8 , –470.09, 0, 0) = £5000

Spreadsheet command to calculate the annual rate, R
= RATE(NPER, PMT, PV, FV, TYPE) = RATE(8, –470.09, 0, 5000, 0) = 8%

Spreadsheet command to calculate the present value, P
= PV(RATE, NPER, PMT, FV, TYPE) = PV(0.8, 8, –470.09, 5000, 0) = 0

Now suppose (as is more likely) the firm wishes to start the fund now and add to it at annual intervals, then Equation (10.9)) cannot be used to calculate the future value. We will have to use the expression

$$FV = a(1+r)^n + a(1+r)^{n-1} + a(1+r)^{n-2} + \ldots\ldots\ldots + a(1+r)$$

Now it can be shown that this expression is equal to

$$FV = a\frac{(1+r)^{n+1} - (1+r)}{r} \tag{10.12}$$

Rearrange Equation (10.12) to make 'a' the subject:

$$a = \frac{rFV}{(1+r)^{n+1} - (1+r)} \tag{10.13}$$

Example 10.13

Repeat the above example, this time assuming that the sum is invested at the beginning of each year. Figure 10.17 illustrates the Excel solution.

C8 f_x =PMT(C5,C3,0,C4,1)

	A	B	C	D
1	Example 10.13 Sinking Funds			
2				
3		n =	8	
4		FV=	£5,000	
5		r =	0.08	
6				
7		a =	£435.25	=C5*C4/((1+C5)^(C3+1)-(1+C5))
8		a =	-£435.25	=PMT(C5,C3,0,C4,1)

Figure 10.17

→ Excel solution

n = Cell C3	Value
FV = Cell C4	Value
r = Cell C5	Value
Formula a = Cell C7	Formula: = C5*C4/((1+C5)^(C3+1)-(1+C5))
Excel a = Cell C8	Formula: = PMT(C5, C3, 0, C4, 1)

Interpretation From Excel, £435 deposited at the beginning of the year would be sufficient to yield the required future value.

Note Using Equation (10.13):

$$a = \frac{0.08 * 5000}{(1.08)^9 - (1.08)} = £435.25 \text{ to the nearest penny}$$

Spreadsheet command to calculate the payment, a
= PMT(RATE, NPER, PV, FV, TYPE) = PMT(8%, 8, 0, 5000, 1) = −£435.25
('a' negative since you will have to deposit)

Spreadsheet command to calculate the Future Value, FV
= FV(RATE, NPER, PMT, PV, TYPE) = FV(8%, 8, −435.25, 0, 1) = £5000

Spreadsheet command to calculate the annual rate, R
= RATE(NPER, PMT, PV, FV, TYPE) = RATE(8, −435.25, 0, 5000, 1) = 8%

Spreadsheet command to calculate the present value, P
= PV(RATE, NPER, PMT, FV, TYPE) = PV(8%, 8, −435.25, 5000, 1) = 0

Student exercises

X10.13 A machine costing £12,500 now will need replacing in six years' time.

(a) Use the Excel FV function to estimate the replacement price if the rate of inflation is 11% per annum.

(b) Use the PMT Excel function to calculate how much must be set aside: (i) at the end of each year, (ii) at the beginning of each year to replace the machine, if money can be invested at 9% per annum.

10.5 The concept of present value

Suppose you were offered the choice of receiving £1000 now or £1000 in 12 months' time. Which would you choose? It is almost certain that you would take the money now, even if you had a cast iron guarantee of receiving the money in the future. It would appear that we have strong preference for holding cash now against receiving cash in the future: economists call this preference 'liquidity preference'. One reason for this universally held preference has to do with inflation—after all, if prices are rising, £1000 will buy less in one year's time than it will now, and so it will have less value than it has now.

During inflation it would make more sense to take the £1000 now. But even if we had stable prices, we would still almost certainly choose to take the money now. Why? The great advantage of taking the money now is that it can be invested, earn interest, and grow. Our £1000 invested now at 10% would grow to £1000*(1.1) = £1100 in one year's time and to £1000*$(1.1)^2$ = £1210 in two years' time. Given stable prices we should be indifferent between £1000 now, £1100 in one year's time and £1210 in two years' time. In other words, £1000 receivable today has the same value as £1100 receivable in one year and £1210 receivable in two years. So we can now see why we would prefer the £1000 now: if £1000 now is worth £1100 in one year's time, it follows that £1000 in one year's time has a present value of less than £1000.

We have introduced a very important concept—that of **present value**—and this concept needs defining carefully. The present value of a sum of money receivable in the future is the sum you would be prepared to accept now, rather than have to wait for it. We use the interest earning capacity of money to enable us to calculate the present value. As £1000 invested at 10% p.a. would grow to £1100 in one year's time we would say that £1100 in one year's time has a present value of £1000. We reduce or discount the value of a sum receivable in the future to find its present value, and the discount factor that we use to do this is the current rate of interest. For this reason, finding the present value is called discounting, which is simply the reverse of compounding.

How can we do this? Equation (10.3) can be used to calculate how a sum invested now would grow under compound interest to a future value of $FV = P(1 + r)^n$. If FV is the sum receivable in the future, then P must be its present value:

$$P = \frac{FV}{(1+r)^n} = FV(1+R)^{-n} \qquad (10.14)$$

The quantity $(1 + r)^{-n}$ is the discounting factor reducing the value of the future value (or sum).

Example 10.14

What is the present value of £1000 receivable in 2 years if money can be invested at 10% per annum compounded?

Figure 10.18 illustrates the Excel solution.

C7 | f_x =PV(C5,C4,0,C3,0)

	A	B	C	D
1	Example 10.14 Present Value			
2				
3		FV =	£1,000	
4		n =	2	
5		r =	0.1	
6				
7		PV =	-£826.45	=PV(C5,C4,0,C3,0)

Figure 10.18

present value is the current worth of a future sum of money or stream of cash flows given a specified rate of return.

→ Excel solution

FV = Cell C3 Value
n = Cell C4 Value
r = Cell C5 Value
PV = Cell C7 Formula: = PV(C5, C4, 0, C3, 0)

Interpretation From Excel, £1000 receivable in two years' time has a present value of £826.45 now at the current interest rate it would grow to £1000 in two years' time. It should be indifferent between receiving £1000 in two years' time and £826.40 now.

Note The present value is negative given that we will make a payment of £826.45. Using Equation (10.14) to solve this problem gives: $P = 1000*(1.1)^{-2} = 1000*0.826446281......$ = £826.45.

Student exercises

X10.14 Use the Excel PV function to calculate the present value of £100 received in two years' time if the interest rate is 12% per annum.

X10.15 Use the Excel function PV to calculate the greatest sum of money if the interest rate is 14% per annum: (a) £1500 received in three years' time, or (b) £2000 received in five years' time.

X10.16 Use the Excel function PV to calculate the present value of £2000 at 10% per annum for one year, two years, and three years.

10.6 Trust funds and loan repayments or present value of an ordinary annuity

Let us suppose that we deposit a certain sum of money now, and from this we wish to withdraw at the end of each year a fixed amount. We will continue to withdraw until nothing is left on deposit. In equation (10.5):

$$FV = P(1 + r)^n + \frac{a(1 + r)^n - a}{r}$$

The terminal future value FV would be zero, and because we are withdrawing 'a' would be negative. Therefore, Equation (10.8) can be written as follows:

$$P(1+r)^n - \frac{a(1+r)^n - a}{r} = 0$$

Simplifying this equation gives:

$$P = a\frac{1-(1+r)^{-n}}{r} \tag{10.15}$$

$$a = \frac{rP}{1-(1+r)^{-n}} \tag{10.16}$$

Equation (10.15) represents the **present value of an ordinary annuity** (or **trust fund**) and Equation (10.16) represents the amount of the withdrawal at the end of the year (or time period).

Example 10.15

You have decided to set up a trust fund for your son. You require the fund to pay him £2000 per year for the next ten years. How much will this fund cost you if money can be invested at 10% per annum compounded with payment at the end of the year?

This problem involves finding P, the initial investment, so Equation (10.15) is the one required. Figure 10.19 illustrates the Excel solution.

C7 fx =PV(C5,C4,C3,0,0)

	A	B	C	D
1	Example 10.15 Trust Funds			
2				
3		a =	£2,000	
4		n =	10	
5		r =	0.1	
6				
7		PV =	-£12,289.13	=PV(C5,C4,C3,0,0)

Figure 10.19

→ Excel solution

a = Cell C3 Value
n = Cell C4 Value
r = Cell C5 Value
PV = Cell C7 Formula: = PV(C5, C4, C3, 0, 0)

Interpretation From Excel, you will need to pay in £12,289.13 now for him to receive £2000 per year for the next ten years if we assume money can be invested at 10% per annum.

X

present value of an ordinary annuity is the value of a stream of expected or promised future payments that have been discounted to a single equivalent value today.

trust fund is an arrangement that allows individuals to create sustained benefits for another individual or entity.

Note The present value is negative given that we will make a payment of £12,289.13. Using Equation (10.15) to solve this problem gives:

$$P = 2000\frac{1-(1.1)^{-10}}{0.1} = £12{,}289$$

Spreadsheet command to calculate the Present Value, P
= PV(RATE, NPER, PMT, FV, TYPE) = PV(10%, 10, 2000, 0, 0) = –£12,289

Spreadsheet command to calculate the payment value, a
= PMT(RATE, NPER, PV, FV, TYPE) = PMT(10%, 10, –12,289.13, 0, 0) = £2000

Spreadsheet command to calculate the future value, FV
= FV(RATE, NPER, PMT, PV, TYPE) = FV(10%, 10, 2000, –12,289.13, 0) = –£0.01 (if you increase the accuracy of the value of PMT then your value will reduce to zero)

Spreadsheet command to calculate the % rate, R
= RATE(NPER, PMT, PV, FV, TYPE) = RATE(10, 2000, –12,289.13, 0, 0) = 10%

Example 10.16

Suppose you borrow £3000 at 14% per annum compounded, and you wish to repay this loan in ten annual instalments. How much must you repay each year at the end of the year?

If you think carefully about this problem, you will realize that it is equivalent to asking how much can be withdrawn at the end of each year if £3000 is invested now at 14% per annum. Equation (10.16) is the equation to use to solve this problem. Figure 10.20 illustrates the Excel solution.

	A	B	C	D
1	Example 10.16 Trust Funds			
2				
3		PV =	£3,000	
4		n =	10	
5		r =	0.14	
6				
7		a =	-£575.14	=PMT(C5,C4,+C3,0,0)

Figure 10.20

→ Excel solution

PV = Cell C3	Value
n = Cell C4	Value
r = Cell C5	Value
a = Cell C7	Formula: = PMT(C5, C4, +C3, 0, 0)

❋ **Interpretation** From Excel, you will need to pay ten equal instalments of £575.14.

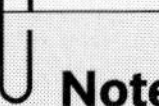

Note

$$\text{Repay, } a = \frac{0.14 * 3000}{1 - (1.14)^{-10}} = £575.14 \text{ to the nearest penny}$$

Example 10.17

A company borrows £1,250,000 from the bank at an interest rate of 8.5% per annum over 10 years. What is the annual repayment?

Figure 10.21 illustrates the Excel solution.

C7 | f_x =PMT(C4,C5,C3,0,0)

	A	B	C	D
1	Example 10.17 Loans			
2				
3		PV =	£1,250,000.00	
4		r =	0.085	
5		n =	10	
6				
7		a =	-£190,509.63	=PMT(C4,C5,C3,0,0)

Figure 10.21

➜ Excel solution

PV = Cell C3	Value
r = Cell C4	Value
n = Cell C5	Value
a = Cell C7	Formula: = PMT(C4,C5,C3,0,0)

❋ **Interpretation** From Excel, you will need to pay ten equal instalments of £190,509.63.

Student exercises

X10.17 Use the Excel function PV to calculate how much must be invested now to yield an income of £5000 per year, paid at the end of each year for eight years, if money can be invested at 9% per annum.

X10.18 Use the Excel function PMT to find the annual repayment necessary to pay off a £6500 loan in 12 years' time when interest is charged at 18% per annum.

X10.19 Use the Excel PMT function to calculate the value of an annuity that can be purchased for £20,000 now and continuing for ten years at an annual interest rate of 5%.

X10.20 Calculate the value of an annuity that can be purchased if £15,000 was invested now at an annual interest rate of 8% with the annuity due to commence in five years' time and run for ten years, with payment at the start of the year.

10.7 The present value and net present value of a stream of earnings

The present value of a stream of earnings in the future is the amount you would pay now to provide the sum at a future date. The net present value (NPV) of a project or investment is the total of the present values of all the monetary inflows and outflows from the project or investment.

Example 10.18

Let us suppose that we have been promised £2000 in one year, £3000 in two years' time, £4000 in three years' time and £3000 in four years' time. Equation (10.17) represents the present value of a series of payments:

$$PV = \sum_{i=1}^{n} \frac{\text{values}}{(1 + \text{rate})^i} \tag{10.17}$$

Where values represent the net cash flow occurring at end of period i, rate is the discount rate used to discount the cash flow, and n is the time period of the project. It is convenient to perform this calculation in a tabular form (Table 10.5).

Year	Earning	Discount factor $(1.12)^{-n}$	Present value
1	2000	0.8930	1785.71
2	3000	0.7972	2391.58
3	4000	0.7118	2847.12
4	3000	0.6355	1906.55
			8930.97

Table 10.5

X

present value of a stream of earnings is the current worth of a future sum of money or stream of cash flows given a specified rate of return.

net present value is the difference between the present value of cash inflows and the present value of cash outflows.

discount rate value of r when discounting to present value.

If the current rate of interest is 12%, then the present value would be:

$$PV = \frac{2000}{(1+0.12)} + \frac{3000}{(1+0.12)^2} + \frac{4000}{(1+0.12)^3} + \frac{3000}{(1+0.12)^4} = £8930.97$$

So the stream of earnings has a present value of £8930.97. In other words, if we deposited £8930.97 now at 12% per annum then we could draw £2000 at the end of the first year, £3000 at the end of the second year, £4000 at the end of the third year and £3000 at the end of the fourth year. We can now modify this problem to include an initial investment of £10,000 and ask whether this investment is worthwhile. Given that we have made an investment we will need to calculate the net present value (NPV) which represents the present value of a series of future cash flows minus the initial investment required to obtain the future cash flows. Therefore, Equation (10.18) represents the net present value:

$$NPV = -\text{initial investment} + \text{present value of stream of earnings} \tag{10.18}$$

We observe from this definition that the NPV represents the increase in wealth that you get if you make the investment. The question then becomes would we pay £10000 for this investment given that we receive a present value of £8930.97.

Figure 10.22 illustrates the Excel solution.

F14 | f_x =-F3+NPV(C4,C7:C10)

	A	B	C	D	E	F	G
1	Example 10.18Present Value of a Stream of Earnings						
2							
3		R =	12%		Investment =	£10,000.00	
4		r =	0.12				
5							
6		Year	Earning	Discount Factor $(1.12)^{-n}$		Present Value	
7		1	£2,000	0.892857143	=(1+$C$4)^(-B7)	£1,785.71	=C7*D7
8		2	£3,000	0.797193878		£2,391.58	
9		3	£4,000	0.711780248		£2,847.12	
10		4	£3,000	0.635518078	=(1+$C$4)^(-B10)	£1,906.55	=C10*D10
11							
12					PV equation =	£8,930.97	=SUM(F7:F10)
13					NPV =	-£1,069.03	=-F3+SUM(F7:F10)
14					NPV =	-£1,069.03	=-F3+NPV(C4,C7:C10)

Figure 10.22

→ Excel solution

R = Cell C3	Value
r = Cell C4	Formula: = C3
Investment = Cell F3	Value
Year Cells B7:B10	Values
Earning Cells C7:C10	Values
Discount Factor Cell D7	Formula: = (1+$C$4)^(-B7) Copy down D7:D10
Present value Cell F7	Formula: = C7*D7 Copy down F7:F10
PV equation = Cell F12	Formula: = SUM (F7:F10)
NPV = Cell F12	Formula: = - F3 + SUM (F7:F10)
NPV = Cell F14	Formula: = - F3 + NPV (C4, C7:C10)

Interpretation From Excel, we find the present value = £8930.97 (using Equation 10.17) and the net present value is –£1069.03 (= –10,000 + 8930.97, using Equation 10.18). From this calculation we would conclude that this would be a bad investment given that we would pay £1069.03 more than we would receive from the investment.

Note The NPV function in Excel has some limitations:

1. Excel's NPV function calculates the present value of future cash flows and is different to the finance definition of NPV which includes the initial cash flow (see Equation (10.18)).
2. NPV can only be used to calculate NPV for a series of cash flows that are periodic.
3. If you have a cash flow problem with dates then you can use the Excel XNPV function to calculate the net present value.

Example 10.19

A customer is interested in buying a new caravan in two years that costs £23,000. The customer can deposit an amount of money today with the same amount deposited at the end of year 1. The saving account chosen can earn 8% per annum. How much will the customer need to deposit now and at the end of year 1?

This problem can be solved using Excel and Excel Solver as illustrated in Figure 10.23.

	A	B	C	D	E	F	G	H
1	Example 10.19 Accumulating a future value using a saving plan							
2								
3		Deposit =	£6,500.00					
4		Interest rate =	8.00%					
5		Cost of caravan =	£23,000.00					
6								
7		Year	Deposit or withdrawal		Total at start of year		Total at end of year with interest	
8		0	£6,500.00	=C3	£6,500.00	=C8	£7,020.00	=E8+E8*$C$4
9		1	£6,500.00	=C3	£13,520.00	=E8+G8	£14,601.60	=E9+E9*$C$4
10		2	-£23,000.00	=-C5	-£8,398.40	=C10+G9	-£9,070.27	=E10+E10*$C$4
11								
12		NPV =	-£7,200.27	=C3+NPV(C4,C9:C10)				

Figure 10.23

→ Excel solution

Deposit = Cell C3 Value
Interest rate = Cell C4 Value
Cost of caravan = Cell C5 Value
Year Cells B8:B10 Values
Deposit or withdrawal Cell C8 Formula: = C3
Cell C9 Formula: = C3
Cell C10 Formula: = –C5

Total at start of year	Cell E8	Formula: = C8
	Cell E9	Formula: = E8+G8
	Cell E10	Formula: = C10+G9
Total at end of year	Cell G8	Formula: = E8+E8*$C$4
	Cell G9	Formula: = E9+E9*$C$4
	Cell G10	Formula: = E10+E10*$C$4
NPV = Cell C12		Formula: = E8+NPV(C4,C9:C10)

Interpretation From Excel, if we deposit initially £6500 at the beginning of the year and at the end of year 1 we find that the net present value is –£7200.27. If we deposit initially £12,000 at the beginning and end of year 1 we find the npv is +£3,392.32. We want the value of the deposits to meet the cost of the caravan.

This means that we need to calculate the value of the deposit such that NPV = 0. This calculation can be achieved by using the Excel solver as follows:

Step 1 Make sure that the solver is available via Excel add-ins

Step 2 Select Data > Solver

Step 3 Enter the required information as illustrated in Figure 10.24.

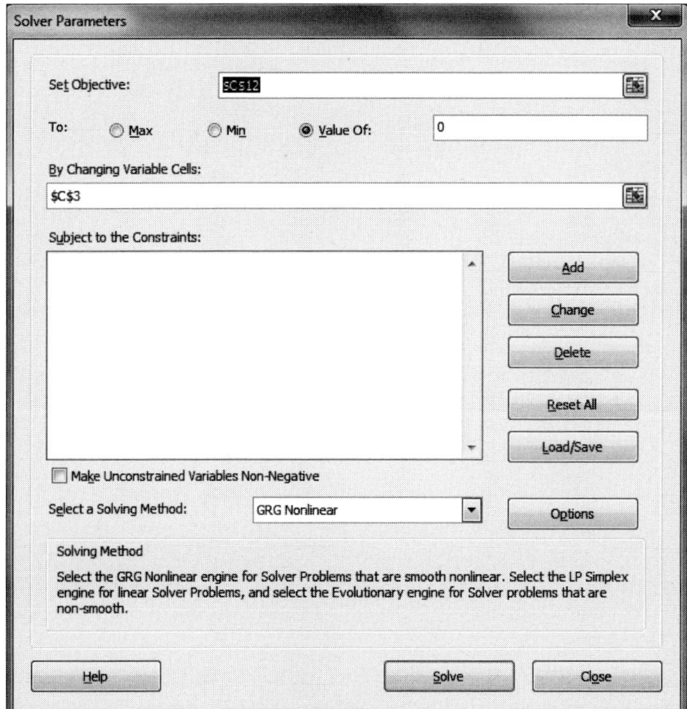

Figure 10.24

This problem can be solved using Excel and Excel Solver as illustrated in Figure 10.25.

C12 f_x =E8+NPV(C4,C9:C10)

	A	B	C	D	E	F	G	H
1	Example 10.19 Accumulating a future value using a saving plan using Excel Solver							
2								
3		Deposit =	£10,238.60					
4		Interest rate =	8.00%					
5		Cost of caravan =	£23,000.00					
6								
7		Year	Deposit or withdrawal		Total at start of year		Total at end of year	
8		0	£10,238.60	=C3	£10,238.60	=C8	£11,057.69	=E8+E8*$C$4
9		1	£10,238.60	=C3	£21,296.30	=E8+G8	£23,000.00	=E9+E9*$C$4
10		2	-£23,000.00	=-C5	£0.00	=C10+G9	£0.00	=E10+E10*$C$4
11								
12		NPV =	£0.00	=E8+NPV(C4,C9:C10)				

Figure 10.25

Interpretation From Excel, the deposit of £10,238.60 will allow the £23,000 required for the caravan to be achieved.

Suppose we now consider an annuity that pays a stream of earnings indefinitely (such an asset is called a perpetual annuity). How would we find the present value of such an asset? We observe from Equation (10.14) that as the value of n increases towards infinity then the term $(1 + r)^{-n}$ reduces in size towards zero and Equation (10.15) simplifies to Equation (10.19):

$$P = \frac{a}{r} \tag{10.19}$$

Example 10.20

An annuity yields £1200 per year for ever. What is its present value if the current rate of interest is 20% p.a.?

$$P = \frac{1200}{0.2} = £6000$$

It is easy to see that the present value must be £6000, for if £6000 was invested at 20% p.a. then the simple interest earned would be £1200 per year. So we could withdraw £1200 per year and leave the capital intact.

Note The NPV can be used to make a decision regarding whether or not to make an investment as follows:

1. Undertake a project investment if project net present value (NPV) is > 0 (a positive number).
2. If you have more than one project then choose the project with the largest positive net present value.

An alternative is to use the internal rate of return (IRR) to make a decision on whether to make an investment (see Section 10.8).

perpetual annuity is an annuity that has no end, or a stream of cash payments that continues forever.

Student exercises

X10.21 Calculate the value of a present value of an annuity given a discount rate of 14% per annum, which yields: (a) £650 per year for 8 years, (b) £650 per year in perpetuity?

X10.22 The replacement cost of a machine is estimated to be £150,000 and its estimated running costs over its life of 5 years are as illustrated in Table 10.6:

Assume all running costs are paid at the end of each year, and that money can be invested at 12% per annum compound.

Year	Runnings costs
1	1250
2	2250
3	3000
4	3100
5	3200

Table 10.6

(a) How much must be set aside to cover running costs?

(b) How much must be set aside to cover running costs and replace the machine?

X10.23 Two investments are available to an individual: (a) investment A requires an initial outlay of £20,000, and (b) investment B requires an initial outlay of £24,000. The returns are as illustrated in Table 10.7.

Which investment is best, assuming an average interest rate of 13%?

	A	B
Year 1	6000	7000
Year 2	8500	8500
Year 3	14,000	17,000
Year 4	10,000	12,000

Table 10.7

10.8 Internal rate of return and investment decisions

The internal rate of return (IRR) of a series of cash flows is the discount rate that sets the net present value of the cash flows equal to zero.

Example 10.21

To aid understanding of the internal rate of return (IRR) consider how we calculated the net present value (NPV) in Example 10.18 with an initial investment of £10,000:

$$NPV = -10{,}000 + \frac{2000}{(1+r)} + \frac{3000}{(1+r)^2} + \frac{4000}{(1+r)^3} + \frac{3000}{(1+r)^4} = -£1069.03$$

With the internal rate of return we would like to know at what discount rate, r, would the net present value (NPV) become exactly zero. In general, we can write the expression as follows:

$$-10{,}000 + \frac{2000}{(1+r)} + \frac{3000}{(1+r)^2} + \frac{4000}{(1+r)^3} + \frac{3000}{(1+r)^4} = 0$$

X

Internal rate of return is a rate of return used in capital budgeting to measure and compare the profitability of investments - also called the discounted cash flow rate of return or the rate of return.

In this case we need to solve this equation for r given that the equation is non-linear in the unknown variable, r.

Figure 10.26 represents a graph of the variation of NPV against different values of the discount rate, r.

As we can see the NPV value becomes zero between a discount rate of r = 6% and r = 8%, where the NPV changes from a positive number to a negative value.

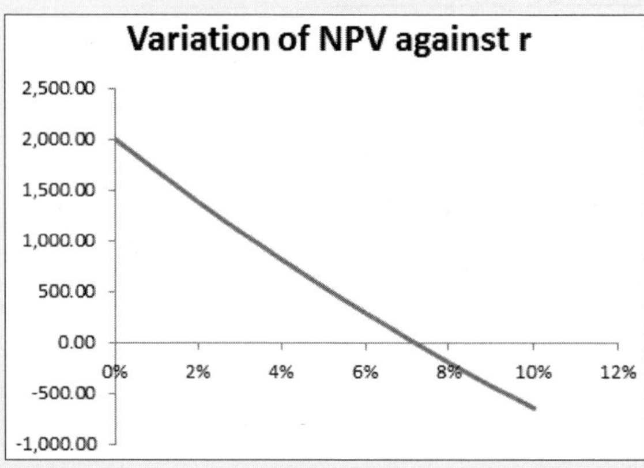

Figure 10.26

Figure 10.27 illustrates the Excel solution to create this graph.

	A	B	C	D	E	F
1	Example 10.21 Internal rate of return (IRR)					
2						
3		Interest rate, r =	0.12			
4						
5		Year	Payment	Discount rate, r	NPV	
6		0	-10000	0%	2,000.00	=NPV(D6,$C$7:$C$10)+$C$6
7		1	2000	1%	1,686.39	
8		2	3000	2%	1,385.12	
9		3	4000	3%	1,095.56	
10		4	3000	4%	817.14	
11				5%	549.31	
12				6%	291.54	
13				7%	43.35	
14				8%	-195.71	
15				9%	-426.09	
16				10%	-648.18	=NPV(D16,$C$7:$C$10)+$C$6

Figure 10.27

→ Excel solution

r = Cell C3	Value
Year Cells B6:B10	Values
Payment Cells C6:C10	Values
Discount rate Cells D6:D16	Values
NPV Cell E6	Formula: = NPV(D6,$C$7:$C$10)+$C$6
	Copy formula E6:E16

Fortunately, we can use Excel to calculate the internal rate of return (IRR).

Figure 10.28 illustrates the Excel solution.

D15 | f_x | =IRR(C6:C10)

	A	B	C	D	E
1	Example 10.21 Internal rate of return (IRR)				
2					
3		Interest rate, r =	0.12		
4					
5		Year	Payment	Present value	
6		0	-10000	-10000	=C6
7		1	2000	1785.714286	=C7/(1+$C$3)^B7
8		2	3000	2391.581633	
9		3	4000	2847.120991	
10		4	3000	1906.554235	=C10/(1+$C$3)^B10
11					
12					
13			NPV equation =	-£1,069.03	=D6+SUM(D7:D10)
14			Excel NPV =	-£1,069.03	=D6+NPV($C$3,C7:C10)
15			IRR =	0.07178595	=IRR(C6:C10)

Figure 10.28

→ Excel solution

r = Cell C3	Value
Year Cells B6:B10	Values
Payment Cells C6:C10	Values
Present value Cells D6	Formula: = C6
Cells D7	Formula: = C7/(1+$C$3)^B7
	Copy formula down D7:D10
NPV equation = Cell D13	Formula: = D6+SUM(D7:D10)
Excel NPV = Cell D14	Formula: = D6 + NPV($C$3, C7:C10)
IRR = Cell D15	Formula: = IRR(C6:C10)

Interpretation From Excel, the IRR is 7.18%. The IRR represents the value of the discount rate when NPV = 0. The IRR is often used to make investment decisions. For example, we may be offered an opportunity to invest in a product with an IRR of 7.18% or place the money into a savings account with a local bank earning 4.56%. In this case we would not place the money into the bank account earning 4.56% but we would invest in the product described above earning 7.18%.

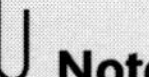

Note

1. The IRR can be used to make a decision regarding whether or not to make an investment as follows: undertake an investment if project IRR > interest rate available from an alternative investment.
2. If you were comparing two investments then you would calculate the IRR for both investments and choose the investment with the higher IRR.

While the IRR assumes the cash flows from a project are reinvested at the IRR, the **modified internal rate of return** (MIRR) assumes that positive cash flows are re-invested at the firm's cost of capital, and the initial outlays are financed at the firm's financing cost. Rather than using the IRR we can use the MIRR to account for both interest rates.

Example 10.22

For example, consider a five-year project with an initial outlay of £120,000 and associated cost of capital of 10% will return £39,000 in year 1, £30,000 in year 2, £21,000 in year 3, £37,000 in year 4, and £46,000 in year 5. To find the IRR of the project so that the NPV = 0 we solve the equation:

$$-120{,}000 + \frac{39{,}000}{(1+r)^1} + \frac{30{,}000}{(1+r)^2} + \frac{21{,}000}{(1+r)^3} + \frac{37{,}000}{(1+r)^4} + \frac{46{,}000}{(1+r)^5} = 0$$

This problem can be solved using the IRR Excel function. Now, if we assume that the negative cash flows cost a finance rate of 10% and the positive cash flows are reinvested at 12% then we can calculate an MIRR to represent the interest rate using Equation (10.20):

$$\text{MIRR} = \sqrt[n]{\frac{-\text{FV(positive cash flows, re - investment rate)}}{\text{PV(negative cash flows, finance rate)}}} - 1 \qquad (10.20)$$

Figure 10.29 illustrates the Excel solution.

C15 | f_x =MIRR(C7:C12,C3,C4)

	A	B	C	D	E
1	Example 10.22 Modified internal rate of return for a series of periodic cash flows, MIRR.				
2					
3		Finance rate, Frate =	0.1		
4		Reinvest rate, RErate =	0.12		
5					
6		Years	Payment		
7		0	-120000		
8		1	39000		
9		2	30000		
10		3	21000		
11		4	37000		
12		5	46000		
13					
14		IRR =	0.130735539	=IRR(C7:C12)	
15		MIRR =	0.12609413	=MIRR(C7:C12,C3,C4)	

Figure 10.29

→ Excel solution

Finance rate Frate = Cell C3	Value
Reinvest rate RErate = Cell C4	Value
Year Cells B7:B12	Values
Payment Cells C7:C12	Values
IRR = Cell C14	Formula: = IRR (C7:C12)
MIRR = Cell C15	Formula: = MIRR (C7:C12, C3, C4)

X

modified internal rate of return is a modification of the internal rate of return which is a financial measure of an investment's attractiveness.

Interpretation From Excel, IRR = 13% and MIRR = 12.61%. You can see here that the 12.61% MIRR is lower than the IRR of 13%. In this case, the IRR gives a too optimistic picture of the potential of the project, while the MIRR gives a more realistic evaluation of the project.

Note If you were comparing two investments then you would calculate the MIRR for both investments and choose the investment with the higher MIRR.

The **compound annual growth rate** (CAGR) describes the rate at which an investment or expenditure would have grown if it grew during a period of time at a steady rate. Thus, if the cost of electricity was €5000 in 2004 and three years later was €10,000, then its spending grew 100%. This is the growth for the three years but what is the growth per year? Excel allows the calculation of the CAGR by making use of the Rate and XIRR functions.

Example 10.23

Consider the problem of calculating what constant growth rate results in sales figures growing from €18,718 to €35,678 during a five-year period illustrated in Table 10.8. To calculate this value we will use the Rate function in Excel.

Period	1	2	3	4	5
Sales (€)	18,718	22,861	28,142	30,218	35,678

Table 10.8

Using the Excel RATE function gives the following solution (see Figure 10.30).

Rate = RATE(NPER, PMT, PV, FV, TYPE, GUESS)

Rate = RATE(4, 0, - C5, C9, 0)

Each sales value is deemed to be the sales value at the end of the period (type = 0).

C12 =RATE(4,0,-C5,C9,0)

	A	B	C	D
1	Example 10.23 Calculate a compound annual growth rate (CAGR)			
2				
3				
4		Period	Sales	
5		1	€ 18,718.00	
6		2	€ 22,861.00	
7		3	€ 28,142.00	
8		4	€ 30,218.00	
9		5	€ 35,678.00	
10				
11				
12		CAGR =	0.17499296	=RATE(4,0,-C5,C9,0)

Figure 10.30

Compound Annual Growth Rate (CAGR) the year-over-year growth rate of an investment over a specified period of time.

→ Excel solution

Period Cells B5:B9	Values
Sales Cells C5:C9	Values
CAGR = Cell C12	Formula: = RATE(4, 0, - C5, C9, 0)

Interpretation The compound annual growth rate of 17.5% will result in €18,718 growing to €35,678 during the 5 year period.

Example 10.24

Consider the problem of calculating the compound annual growth rate that consists of an initial expenditure of €4500 and results in a series of interest payments on the dates specified in Table 10.9.

Date	21 Feb. 2008	5 Apr. 2008	22 Aug. 2008	1 Oct. 2008	1 Feb. 2009
Payment (€)	−4500	3200	2250	4850	1750

Table 10.9

The CAGR can be calculated for this problem using the Excel function XIRR.

CAGR = XIRR(values, dates, guess)

CAGR = XIRR(B6:B10, C6:C10)

C12 | f_x =XIRR(B6:B10,C6:C10)

	A	B	C	D
1	Example 10.24 Calculate a compound annual growth rate (CAGR)			
2				
3				
4		Sales (€)	Date	
5				
6		-4,500.00	21/02/2008	
7		3,200.00	05/04/2008	
8		2,250.00	22/06/2008	
9		4,850.00	01/10/2008	
10		1,750.00	01/02/2009	
11				
12		CAGR =	11.7135	=XIRR(B6:B10,C6:C10)
13		PV =	6933.9789	=XNPV(C12/100,B6:B10,C6:C10)

Figure 10.31

From Figure 10.31 we have the compound annual growth rate of 11.7%.

→ Excel solution

Sales Cells B6:B10	Values
Date Cells C6:C10	Values
CAGR = Cell C12	Formula: = XIRR(B6:B10, C6:C10)
PV = Cell C13	Formula: = XNPV(C12/100, B6:B10, C6:C10)

Interpretation Compound annual growth rate is 11.7% with the present value of the schedule of cash flows equal to €6933.98.

Note

1. The Rate function cannot be used for this problem since it requires regular investment (or expenditure) periods for payments.
2. The XIRR function requires that at least one value must be positive and one negative value.

Student exercises

X10.24 Find the IRR of the following cash flows: an investment of £2,226,000 to produce £500,000 annually in arrears for five years.

X10.25 An investment opportunity is available which requires a single cash outlay of £850. Cash inflows of £388 will then arise at a 12-month interval for three years commencing in one year. Bank overdraft finance is available at 8% per annum. Estimate the internal rate of return for this project and comment on whether you would go ahead with the investment opportunity. Would your answer change if the finance rate changed to 20% given that the cash flows did not change?

10.9 Calculating the cost of a mortgage

Most people will be familiar with the concept of a mortgage, where a property can be purchased by buying a financial product from a financial services company. If we borrow £P over m months at an interest rate, r, and then the mortgage is repaid at a constant monthly rate of £a, paid at the end of the month with the value given by Equation (10.21):

$$a = \frac{Pr(1+r)^n}{(1+r)^n - 1} \tag{10.21}$$

mortgage is a loan secured on the purchase of a property.

Example 10.25

In this example we will assume that your mortgage application has been agreed for £200,000 to be repaid over eight years at 12% interest per annum. The mortgage agreement assumes that the payment will be made at the end of the year. How much will this yearly payment be at the end of the year and the effective interest rate?

Figure 10.32 illustrates the Excel solution.

C23 =(1+C4/1)^1-1

	A	B	C	D
1	Example 10.25 Calculation of mortgage payments			
2				
3		Amount borrowed, P =	£200,000.00	
4		Interest rate, r =	0.12	
5		Mortgage term, n =	8	
6				
7		Annual payment, a =	-£40,260.57	=PMT(C4,C5,C3,0,0)
8				
9				
10		Year	Mortgage cash flow	
11		0	£200,000.00	=C3
12		1	-£40,260.57	=$C$7
13		2	-£40,260.57	
14		3	-£40,260.57	
15		4	-£40,260.57	
16		5	-£40,260.57	
17		6	-£40,260.57	
18		7	-£40,260.57	
19		8	-£40,260.57	=$C$7
20				
21		IRR =	0.120	=IRR(C11:C19)
22		Monthly IRR using Excel Rate function =	0.120	=RATE(C5,-C7,-C3,0,0)
23		Effective annual interest rate, eair =	0.120	=(1+C4/1)^1-1

Figure 10.32

→ Excel solution

P = Cell C3	Value
r = Cell C4	Value
n = Cell C5	Value
a = Cell C7	Formula: = PMT(C4, C5, C3, 0, 0)
Year Cells B11:B19	Values
Mortgage cash flow Cell C11	Formula: = C3
Cell C12	Formula: = $C$7
	Copy formula down C12:C19
IRR = Cell C21	Formula: = IRR(C11:C19)
IRR Excel = Cell C22	Formula: = RATE(C5, - C7, - C3, 0, 0)
EAIR = Cell C23	Formula: = (1+C4/1)^1 - 1

Interpretation From Excel, the amount to pay back at the end of each year will be £40,260.57 with an effective annual interest rate of 12%. The effective annual interest rate (EAIR, see Cell C23) for this mortgage is simply the annual internal rate of return of its payments (see Cells C21 and C22) given that the mortgage consists of annual payments.

Note

$$\text{From Equation (10.21): } a = \frac{Pr(1+r)^n}{(1+r)^n - 1} = \frac{200{,}000 * 0.12 * (1.12)^8}{(1.12)^8 - 1} = 40{,}260.57$$

Example 10.26

Repeat example but calculate the payments per month if the mortgage is paid over one year and calculate the monthly interest rate and effective annual interest rate.

Figure 10.33 illustrates the Excel solution.

	A	B	C	D
1	Example 10.26 Calculation of mortgage payments			
2				
3		Amount borrowed, P =	£200,000.00	
4		Interest rate, r =	0.12	
5		Mortgage term, n =	1	
6				
7		Number of payments =	12	
8		Monthly payment, a =	-£17,769.76	=PMT(C4/C7,C5*C7,C3,0,0)
9				
10		Month	Monthly payment	
11		0	£200,000.00	=C3
12		1	-£17,769.76	=$C$8
13		2	-£17,769.76	
14		3	-£17,769.76	
15		4	-£17,769.76	
16		5	-£17,769.76	
17		6	-£17,769.76	
18		7	-£17,769.76	
19		8	-£17,769.76	
20		9	-£17,769.76	
21		10	-£17,769.76	
22		11	-£17,769.76	
23		12	-£17,769.76	=$C$8
24				
25		Monthly IRR USING Excel IRR function =	0.0100	=IRR(C11:C23)
26		Monthly IRR using Excel Rate function =	0.0100	=RATE(C5*C7,C8,C3,0,0)
27				
28		EAIR =	0.1268	=((1+C4/C7)^C7)-1
29		EAIR using Excel EFFECT function =	0.1268	=EFFECT(C4,B23)

Figure 10.33

→ Excel solution

P = Cell C3	Value
r = Cell C4	Value
n = Cell C5	Value
Number of payments = Cell C7	Value
a = Cell C8	Formula: = PMT(C4/C7, C5*C7, C3, 0, 0)
Month Cells B11:B23	Values
Mortgage cash flow Cell C11	Formula: = C3
Cell C12	Formula: = $C$8
	Copy formula down C12:C23
Monthly IRR Excel IRR = Cell C25	Formula: = IRR(C11:C23)
Monthly IRR Excel Rate = Cell C26	Formula: = RATE(C5*C7, C8, C3, 0, 0)
EAIR = Cell C28	Formula: = ((1+C4/C7)^C7) - 1
EAIR using Excel EFFECT = Cell C29	Formula: = EFFECT(C4, B23)

❊ Interpretation From Excel, the amount to pay back will be £17,769.76 per month with a monthly internal rate of return of 1% and an effective annual interest rate of 12.68%.%

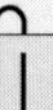

Note

1. The monthly interest rate = R/f = 12%/12 = 1%, which agrees with the IRR calculation.
2. If the IRR = 1%, then the annualized interest rate = $(1 + 12\%/12)^{12} - 1 = 12.68\%$, which agrees with the EAIR calculation in Excel in Cells C28 and C29.

Example 10.27

Repeat Example 10.26 but calculate the payments per month if the mortgage is paid over 30 years. Calculate the monthly interest rate and effective annual interest rate.

Figure 10.34 illustrates the Excel solution.

	A	B	C	D
1	Example 10.27 Calculation of mortgage payments			
2				
3		Amount borrowed, P =	£200,000.00	
4		Interest rate, r =	0.12	
5		Mortgage term, n =	30	
6				
7		Annual payment, a =	-£2,057.23	=PMT(C4/B22,C5*B22,C3,0,0)
8				
9		Month	Monthly payment	
10		0	£200,000.00	=C3
11		1	-£2,057.23	=$C$7
12		2	-£2,057.23	
13		3	-£2,057.23	
14		4	-£2,057.23	
15		5	-£2,057.23	
16		6	-£2,057.23	
17		7	-£2,057.23	
18		8	-£2,057.23	
19		9	-£2,057.23	
20		10	-£2,057.23	
21		11	-£2,057.23	
22		12	-£2,057.23	=$C$7
23				
24		Monthly interest rate =	0.0100	=RATE(C5*B22,C7,C3,0,0)
25		EAIR =	0.1268	=((1+C4/B22)^B22)-1
26		EAIR =	0.1268	=EFFECT(C4,B22)

Figure 10.34

→ Excel solution

P = Cell C3	Value
r = Cell C4	Value
n = Cell C5	Value
a = Cell C7	Formula: = PMT(C4/B22, C5*B22, C3, 0, 0)
Month Cells B10:B22	Values
Mortgage cash flow Cell C10	Formula: = C3
Cell C11	Formula: = $C$7
	Copy formula down C11:C22
IRR Excel = Cell C24	Formula: = RATE(C5*B22, C7, C3, 0, 0)
EAIR = Cell C25	Formula: = ((1+C4/B22)^B22) – 1
EAIR = Cell C26	Formula: = EFFECT(C4, B22)

Interpretation From Excel, the amount to pay back will be £2057.23 per month over 30 years with a monthly interest rate of 1% and an effective annual interest rate of 12.68%.

Student exercises

Please visit the Online Resource Centre which accompanies this textbook for figures solutions in Excel to the student exercises and Techniques in Practice.

X10.26 Use the Excel function PMT to calculate the annual repayments on a mortgage of £40,000 over five years at 12% per annum.

X10.27 An investor wishes to set up a company and needs to obtain finance of £30,000. Calculate the annual payment in each of the following situations:

(a) He takes out an immediate mortgage of £30,000, repayable in six equal annual repayments, the first payment to be made one year after receiving the mortgage with an annual interest rate of 15%.

(b) The investor takes out an identical mortgage as in part (a) but, due to unforeseen circumstances, is unable to pay the third instalment. It is decided that the investor should re-arrange the payments so that he completes the repayment at the end of the six years as originally agreed, by making three equal annual payments commencing when the fourth instalment is due. The rate of interest is set at 15%.

Techniques in practice

TP1 Coco S.A. has appointed a financial manager to provide advice to members of staff via the HR department. One key issue for staff is saving for their children's university education. The financial manager has been asked to provide a series of case studies that will provide staff with estimates of what they would need to save to pay off university course fees. The example provided by the finance manager is as follows:

- Student name
- Agreed annual deposit on each birthday from the 10th to 17th birthday = £4000
- Estimated interest rate = 8% per annum
- Agreed annual withdrawal of £20,000 on the student's 18th to 21st birthday to pay for university education.

(a) Is the £4000 per year sufficient to pay for the costs of the university education?

(b) If not, what deposit would be required to achieve the cost of the university education?

TP2 Bakers Ltd is considering buying a piece of machinery that costs £15,000. If the machine is purchased by taking a five-year loan at 9% per annum, which will be paid off in five equal annual installments, calculate the size of each installment to the nearest £.

TP3 Skodel Ltd has arranged via a bank for a £50,000 mortgage to be paid over 15 years at a rate of interest of 10% per annum. The loan is to be repaid by 15 equal installments, the first being due at the end of each year. Calculate: (a) the annual installments, (b) the amount outstanding after two complete years, and (c) the revised annual installment if the rate of interest changes to 13% after two complete years.

Summary

In this chapter we have explored a range of methods that can be used to calculate the time value of investments using the Excel spreadsheet to undertake the required calculations.

Student exercise answers

For all figures listed below, please see the Online Resource Centre.

X10.1 (a) £45, (b) £105, (c) £17.50, (d) £41.67.

X10.2 At what rate of simple interest will: (a) 5.5%, (b) 4%

X10.3 P = £963.86

X10.4 £6747.52

X10.5 9.97%

X10.6 (a) 16.64%, (b) 16.99%, (c) 17.23%, (d) 17.35%.

X10.7 15.49%

X10.8 15.1%

X10.9 £17,705.27

X10.10 £5216.62

X10.11 £18,426.72 (project accepted)

X10.12 −£17,723.78 (project rejected)

X10.13 (a) 23,380.18, (b) £3107.69 and £2851.09.

X10.14 £79.72

X10.15 (a) £1012.46, (b) £1038.74. Therefore, (b) is the greater sum.

X10.16 (a) £1818.18 invested now to yield £2000 in one year's time, (b) £1652.89 invested now to yield £2000 in two years' time, (c) £1502.63 invested now to yield £2000 in three years' time.

X10.17 £27,674.10

X10.18 £1356.08

X10.19 £2590.09

X10.20 £3041.29

X10.21 (a) £3015.26, (b) £4642.86

X10.22 (a) £8830.97, (b) £93,945

X10.23 Investment A increases wealth by £7802.37, investment B increases wealth by £7993.11, Choose investment B.

X10.24 IRR = 4%

X10.25 (a) Given IRR > finance rate (17.5% > 8%) then invest, (b) For the same cash flows, the IRR < finance rate (17.5% < 20%) then do not invest.

X10.26 Repayment = £11,096

X10.27 (a) Repayment = £7928, (b) £11,399

TP1 (a) Will run out of money between 19th and 20th birthdays with a level of debt at the end of the university career at £34,817. The net present value is negative and therefore plan underfunded. (b) Using Excel Solver deposit equal £6227.78.

TP2 Instalment at end of year £3856.39

TP3 (a) £6573.69, (b) £46,695.25, (c) £7627.69.

Further reading

Text book resources

S. Benninga (2006) *Principles of Finance with Excel*, Oxford University Press.

Formula summary

$$SI = \frac{PRT}{100} \quad (10.1)$$

$$SI = PTr \quad (10.2)$$

$$FV = P + SI \quad (10.3)$$

$$FV = P(1 + r)^n \quad (10.4)$$

$$I = P(1 + r)^n - P \quad (10.5)$$

$$EAIR = \left(1 + \frac{r}{f}\right)^f - 1 \quad (10.6)$$

$$FV = P(1 + j/f)^{fm} \quad (10.7)$$

$$FV = P(1 + r)^n + \frac{a(1 + r)^n - a}{r} \quad (10.8)$$

$$FV = P(1 + r)^n + a_1(1 + r)^{n-1} + a_2(1 + r)^{n-2} + \dots\dots\dots + a^n \quad (10.9)$$

$$FV = \frac{a(1 + r)^n - a}{r} \quad (10.10)$$

$$a = \frac{rFV}{(1 + r)^n - 1} \quad (10.11)$$

$$FV = a\frac{(1 + r)^{n+1} - (1 + r)}{r} \quad (10.12)$$

$$a = \frac{rFV}{(1 + r)^{n+1} - (1 + r)} \quad (10.13)$$

$$P = \frac{FV}{(1 + r)^n} = FV(1 + R)^{-n} \tag{10.14}$$

$$P = a\frac{1 - (1 + r)^{-n}}{r} \tag{10.15}$$

$$a = \frac{rP}{1 - (1 + r)^{-n}} \tag{10.16}$$

$$PV = \sum_{i=1}^{n} \frac{\text{values}}{(1 + \text{rate})^i} \tag{10.17}$$

$$NPV = -\text{initial investment} + \text{present value of stream of earnings} \tag{10.18}$$

$$P = \frac{a}{r} \tag{10.19}$$

$$MIRR = \sqrt[n]{\frac{-FV(\text{positive cash flows, re - investment rate})}{PV(\text{negative cash flows, finance rate})}} - 1 \tag{10.20}$$

$$a = \frac{Pr(1 + r)^n}{(1 + r)^n - 1} \tag{10.21}$$

11 Monte Carlo simulation using Excel

» Overview «

There are many things that faster computers have made possible in recent years. For scientists, engineers, statisticians, managers, investors, and others, computers have made it possible to create models that simulate reality and aid in making predictions. One of the methods for simulating real systems is the ability to take into account randomness by investigating hundreds of thousands of different scenarios. The results are then compiled and used to make decisions. This is called the Monte Carlo simulation method. Monte Carlo simulation is often used in business for risk and decision analysis, to help make decisions given uncertainties in market trends, fluctuations, and other uncertain factors. In the science and engineering communities, Monte Carlo simulation is often used for uncertainty analysis, optimization, and reliability-based design. In manufacturing, Monte Carlo methods are used to help allocate tolerances in order to reduce cost. In finance, Monte Carlo methods are used to construct probabilistic financial models, evaluate portfolios, and undertake personal finance planning.

» Learning outcomes «

On completing this chapter you should be able to:

- » Define simulation and know why it is used.
- » Understand what is meant by a model and how models are developed.
- » Generate samples.
- » Describe Monte Carlo simulation.
- » Describe the typical variables used in simulation.
- » Develop a simulation model.
- » Discuss the advantages and disadvantages of simulation.
- » Provide examples of Monte Carlo simulation software.
- » Solve problems using the Microsoft Excel spreadsheet.

X

Monte Carlo simulation method is a computerized mathematical technique that allows people to account for risk in quantitative analysis and decision making.

11.1 Introduction to simulation and probability distributions

This chapter will guide you through the process of performing a Monte Carlo simulation using Microsoft Excel. Although Excel will not always be the best software to run a scientific simulation, the basics are easily explained with just a few simple examples. If you frequently use Excel for modelling, whether for engineering design or financial analysis, we strongly recommend one of the Excel add-ins listed in section 11.3.

Simulation is an exceptionally versatile technique. Simulation is used under two conditions: (a) when experimentation is not possible, and (b) when the analytical solution is unknown or uncertain. It can be used in various applications such as:

- Design and operation of queuing systems.
- Managing inventory systems.
- Estimating probability of completing a project by a given deadline.
- Design and operation of manufacturing systems.
- Design and operation of distributed systems.
- Financial risk analysis.
- Minimizing hospital waiting lists.
- Minimizing ambulance response times.

The Monte Carlo method is just one of many methods for analysing uncertainty propagation, where the goal is to determine how random variation, lack of knowledge, or error affects the sensitivity, performance, or reliability of the system that is being modelled.

Monte Carlo simulation is categorized as a sampling method because the inputs are randomly generated from probability distributions to simulate the process of sampling from an actual population. So, we try to choose a distribution for the inputs that most closely matches data we already have, or best represents our current state of knowledge. Monte Carlo simulation randomly samples inputs to produce many thousands of possible outcomes, rather than a few discrete scenarios as produced, for example, by deterministic modelling using single-point estimates. Monte Carlo results can also give probabilities for different possible outcomes.

Consider the simple example of tossing a coin. If we toss a fair coin then we would expect 50% of the coins to land 'heads' and 50% to land 'tails'. Furthermore, we could calculate exactly the probability of two heads from seven tosses of a fair coin by applying the binomial theorem to calculate the value of $P(X = 2)$. If we wanted to know the probability of getting at least 12 'heads' from 500 tosses of a fair coin then the calculation process can still be solved exactly but the calculation process is more time consuming. Monte Carlo simulation can be used to simulate at least 12 'heads' from 500 tosses of the fair coin as easily as calculating two 'heads' from seven tosses of the coin.

Figure 11.1 illustrates the key steps in applying simulation to model physical relationships.

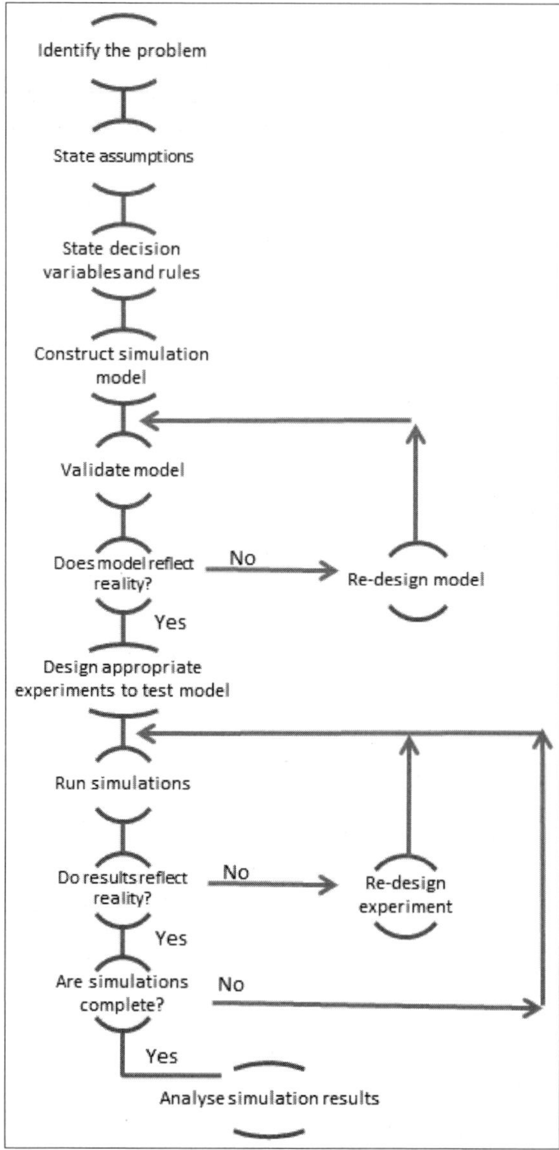

Figure 11.1

Computer simulation has to do with using computer models to imitate real life or make predictions. When you create a model with a spreadsheet like Excel, you have a certain number of input parameters and a few equations that use those inputs to give you a set of outputs (or response variables). This type of model is called a **deterministic model**, meaning that you get the same results no matter how many times you recalculate. Figure 11.2 illustrates a model which maps a set of input variables to a set of output variables.

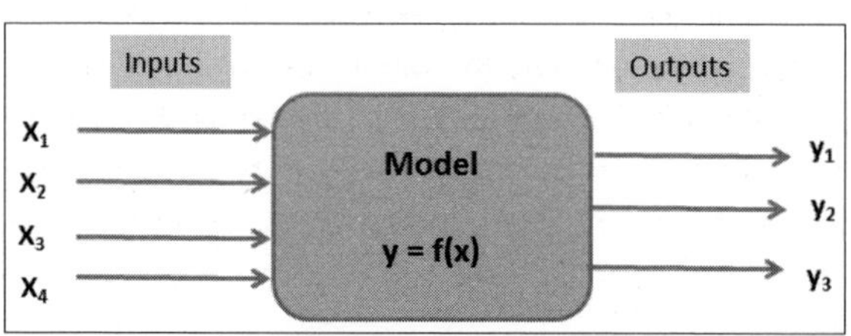

Figure 11.2

deterministic model a deterministic model will give the same result output(s) based upon the same input(s).

Example 11.1

An example of a deterministic model is the calculation to determine the future value of a £1000 investment over five years with an annual interest rate of 7%, compounded monthly. Equation (10.7) enables the calculation of the future value:

$$FV = P\left(1 + \frac{j}{f}\right)^{fm}$$

Where, the inputs are the initial investment (P = \$1000), annual interest rate (j = 7% = 0.07), the compounding period (f = 12 months), and the number of years (m = 5). The Excel solution to this problem is illustrated in Figure 11.3:

	A	B	C	D
1	Example 11.1			
2				
3		Present value, P =	1000	
4		Nominal rate, j =	0.07	
5		Periods/Year, m =	12	
6		Years, n=	5	
7		Future value, FV =	£1,417.63	=FV(C4/C5,C5*C6,0,-C3,0)
8		Future value, FV =	£1,417.63	=1000*(1+C4/C5)^(C5*C6)

Figure 11.3

Excel solution

Present value, P = Cell C3	Value
Nominal rate, j = Cell C4	Value
Periods/Year, m = Cell C5	Value
Years, n = Cell C6	Value
Future value, FV = Cell C7	Excel Formula: = FV(C4/C5,C5*C6,0,-C3,0)
Future value, FV = Cell C8	Manual Formula: = 1000*(1+C4/C5)^(C5*C6)

Interpretation From Excel we observe that the future value is £1417.63.

Note The future value has been calculated using the Excel function FV and the definition of the future value of a compounded investment as given by Equation (10.7).

One of the purposes of a model such as this is to make predictions and or try **what-if analysis**. You can change the inputs and recalculate the model and you'll get a new answer. You might even want to plot a graph of the future value (FV) versus years (n). In some cases, you may have a fixed interest rate, but what do you do if the interest rate is allowed to change? For this simple equation, you might only care to know a worst/best case scenario, where you calculate the future value based upon the lowest and highest interest rates that you might expect.

X

what-if analysis you can use several different sets of values in one or more formulas to explore all the various results.

Example 11.2

In this example, we have an assembly of four parts that make up a cardboard box, with three boxes fitted into the larger box, as illustrated in Figure 11.4.

From Figure 11.4, we would conclude that if D is less than A + B + C, we would have a hard time putting the internal boxes inside the larger box.

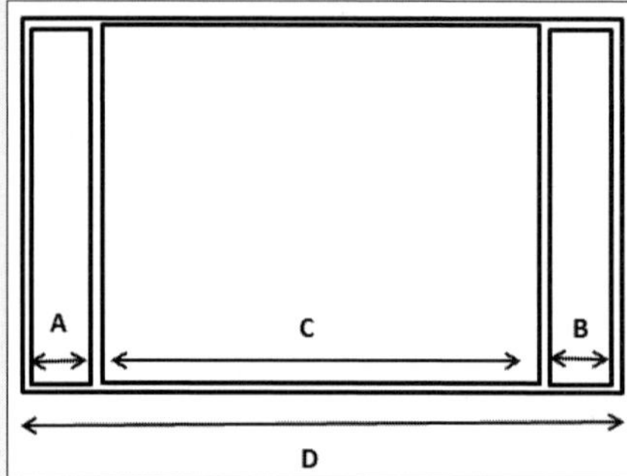

Figure 11.4

The manufacturer is required to complete thousands of these completed boxes per day but has noted that no two parts are going to be exactly the same size. But, if we have an idea of the range of sizes for each part, then we can simulate the selection and assembly of the parts mathematically.

In Example 11.2, the deterministic model is D = A + B + C. If D > 0, the model will operate efficiently, but the values of A, B, and C do not have fixed values—they can vary with known minimum and maximum values of A (1.95, 2.05), B (1.95, 2.05), and C (29.5, 35), as illustrated in Figure 11.5.

	A	B	C	D
1	Example 11.2			
2				
3				
4				
5		Part	MIN	MAX
6		A	1.95	2.05
7		B	1.95	2.05
8		C	29.5	30.5
9		D =	33.4	34.6

Figure 11.5

→ Excel solution

Part Cells B6:B9	Values
Min Cells C6:C8	Values
Max Cells D6:D8	Values
Dmin = Cells C9	Formula: = SUM(C6:C8)
Dmax = Cells D9	Formula: = SUM(D6:D8)

Interpretation From the Excel solution, we observe that the tolerance D ranges from a minimum value of 33.4 to a maximum value of 34.6.

Given that the values of A, B, and C are not fixed, the value of D will vary. To solve this problem we can use the Monte Carlo method with a uniform distribution adopted to generate the random numbers. The Monte Carlo simulation is a method for iteratively evaluating a deterministic model using sets of random numbers as inputs. By using random inputs, you are essentially turning the deterministic model into a stochastic model.

In Chapter 5, we introduced the concept of optimization via a detailed discussion of linear programming. This concept of linear programming is a classic deterministic method that attempts to optimize an objective function (e.g. maximize profit or minimize costs) that depends upon a series of decision variables which will be constrained within a particular set of positive integer values. Furthermore, in Chapter 5 we explored the use of the Excel Solver in solving numerical problems. Monte Carlo Simulation is an alternative approach to linear programming, assuming that the conditions can be matched.

11.1.1 Probability distributions and generating random numbers using Excel

Monte Carlo simulation allows a person to model all potential combination of scenarios for the uncertain variables. After specification of the uncertain variables characteristics the Monte Carlo simulation generates random numbers, which reflects the chosen characteristics. In Monte Carlo simulations the uncertain variable characteristics are defined in terms of probability distribution such as the uniform distribution, normal distribution, or triangular distribution. One of the requirements of almost any simulation model is some facility for generating random numbers. Microsoft Excel provides two uniform random number generators in the form of functions: RAND () and RANDBETWEEN (a, b). However, other theoretical distributions, such as the normal distribution, are encountered more frequently than the uniform distribution. In many cases, an empirical distribution is used. In this chapter, we will discuss procedures for generating random numbers from empirical and frequently used theoretical distributions.

11.1.2 Key characteristics of probability distributions

When deciding which probability distribution to use it is worthwhile noting the following key characteristics of probability distributions:

- Is the variable being measured discrete or continuous? A variable is discrete if it can take a finite number of possible values. For example, the number of red cars passing a given spot per hour within a specified 24-hour time period. Examples of discrete distributions are: discrete, binomial, Poisson. A variable is continuous if it is possible to have any value within a specified range. For example, the weight of a group of students could take any value between 65 and 100 kilograms. Examples of continuous distributions include normal and triangular distributions. It should be noted that in certain cases we can use continuous distributions to model variables that are discrete when the gap between allowable variables is insignificant. For example, project costs are discrete with pounds and pennies or euros and cents. Further examples of continuous event simulations include flight simulations, marine simulations where it is important to reflect changing values as a continuous function, and discrete event simulations

X

uniform distribution all values within the range are deemed to have the same constant probability density, where that density changes to zero at the minimum and maximum values.

stochastic model (or probabilistic) containing uncertainty that is measured by probabilities.

normal distribution the normal distribution is a good approximation to the beta distribution in the centre of the distribution and is easy to work with, so it is often used as an approximation.

triangular distribution is often used when the minimum, maximum, and the most likely values are known.

such as turning the kettle on, water has boiled but not the temperature of the water which would be represented by a continuous function.

- Is the variable distribution symmetric or skewed? Choose a distribution shape that mirrors what is likely to happen in reality. For example, if you plan to measure student performance on an examination then you would expect few students to achieve low marks and a large proportion of the students achieving higher marks, suggesting a left-skewed distribution with mean < median (value of skewness negative). Or, if you timed how long it takes for customers to queue at a service station kiosk you would find that most customers took less than three minutes to complete payment with very few customers completing in more than three minutes, suggesting a right skewed distribution with mean > median (value of skewness positive). Finally, you may decide to measure the time taken to complete a project where we would expect the variable distribution to be symmetric around the mean time for similar projects (value of skewness = 0).
- Is the variable distribution bounded or unbounded? A distribution that lies between two determined values is said to be a bounded distribution. Examples of bounded distributions include uniform (lies between minimum and maximum), triangular (lies between minimum and maximum), and binomial (lies between 0 and n). A distribution that can extend from minus to plus infinity is called an unbounded distribution. Examples include the normal distribution. A distribution that is bounded at one end of the distribution is called partially bounded. Examples include Chi squared (lies > 0) and **Poisson distributions** (lies between 0 and > 0).

Note Roger Myerson provides a free add-in called Simtools that adds up to Excel 32 statistical functions. The add-in can be downloaded from **http://home.uchicago.edu/~rmyerson/addins.htm; usage** is free for students and staff in an academic institution.

This section provides an introduction to generating random numbers in Excel for the following distributions:

1. Discrete or empirical,
2. Uniform,
3. Triangular,
4. Normal,
5. Binomial,
6. Poisson.

Poisson distribution
Poisson distributions model a range of discrete random data variables.

11.1.3 Discrete or empirical distribution

Using the inverse transformation method for a general discrete distribution is essentially a table lookup. To generate random numbers from an empirical distribution, we can use either the LOOKUP, VLOOKUP, or HLOOKUP functions provided by Excel. The vector form of LOOKUP function is discussed here. The syntax of the vector form is:

= LOOKUP (lookup_value, lookup_vector, result_vector)

Note For the LOOKUP function to work, the values in the lookup vector must ALWAYS be in ascending order.

LOOKUP compares the lookup_value to each cell in the lookup_vector until it finds a cell larger than the lookup_value. It then moves up one cell and returns the content of the corresponding cell in the result_vector as the answer.

Example 11.3

For example, assume the relative frequency of sales in unit per month for laser printers is as shown in Table 11.1.

It has been decided to generate monthly sales figures for six months from the empirical distribution provided in Table 11.1 using Monte Carlo simulation. To solve this problem we apply the following two steps:

Unit sales per month	Relative frequency
350	0.1
450	0.1
550	0.5
650	0.3

Table 11.1 Unit sales of laser printers

1. Convert table 11.1 into a cumulative relative frequency table, as illustrated in Figure 11.6.
2. The final step is to insert the following Excel formula: =LOOKUP(RAND(),$G$5:$G$8, $E$5:$E$8) in Cell K5 as illustrated in Figure 11.7. Finally, copy the formula down from K5:K10.

	A	B	C	D	E	F	G	H
1	Example 11.3							
2								
3								
4		Unit Sales Per Month	Relative Frequency		Unit sales per month (BIN)		Cumulative relative frequency	
5		350	0.1		350	=B5	0	
6		450	0.1		450		0.1	=G5+C5
7		550	0.5		550		0.2	
8		650	0.3		650	=B8	0.7	=G7+C7

Figure 11.6

	I	J	K	L
3				
4		Month	Sales	
5		1	550	=LOOKUP(RAND(),$G$5:$G$8, $E$5:$E$8)
6		2	550	
7		3	550	
8		4	450	
9		5	650	
10		6	550	=LOOKUP(RAND(),$G$5:$G$8, $E$5:$E$8)

Figure 11.7

➜ Excel solution

Unit sales per month	Cells B5:B8	Values
Relative frequency	Cells C5:C8	Values
Unit sales per month (BIN)	Cell E5	Formula: = B5 Copy formula down B5:B8
Cumulative frequency		
	Cell G5	Value
	Cell G6	Formula: = G5+C5 Copy down from G6:G8
Month	Cell J5:J10	Values
Sales	Cell K5	Formula: = LOOKUP(RAND(),$G$5:$G$8, $E$5:$E$8) Copy down from K5:K8

❊ Interpretation From the Excel solution, the possible solutions for the sales figures for the six months are 550, 550, 550, 450, 650, and 550 respectively.

Notes

1. Copying and pasting data values only
   When your model is complete and you are ready to analyse the data it can be helpful to 'freeze' the results by copying the data values only either to spare space on the current worksheet or to a new worksheet.
2. Stopping recalculation when using the RAND() or RANDBETWEEN() functions in Excel
   A different method is to stop recalculation during data entry by setting the calculation mode to manual: select File > Options > Formulas > Calculation Options from the menu bar and choose Manual option and de-select 'recalculate workbook before saving'. Remember this will affect all worksheets in the workbook. This will keep your workbooks from updating automatically. To force recalculation manually press the F9 keyboard key. When you have finished with this type of analysis, e.g. using the RAND () function, remember to reset the Calculation Option back to Automatic.

11.1.4 Uniform distribution

The uniform distribution is used as a very approximate model where there is very little or no available data.

It is rarely a good approximation of the perceived uncertainty given that all values within the range are deemed to have the same constant probability density, where that density changes to zero at the minimum and maximum values as illustrated in Figure 11.8. Distribution defined by the minimum and maximum values (a, b).

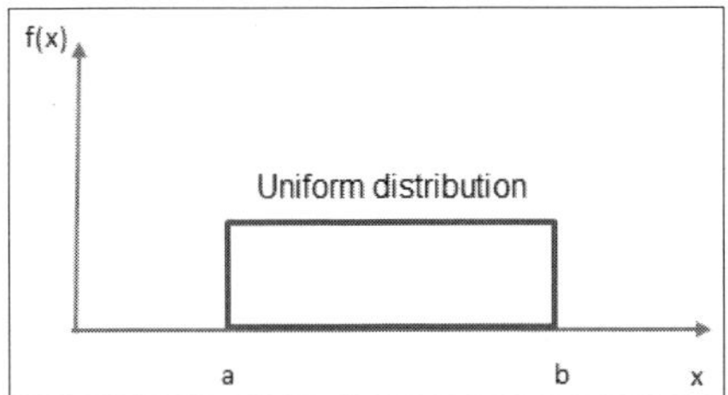

Figure 11.8

The characteristics of a uniform distribution are as follows:

1. Continuous.
2. Symmetric.
3. Bounded in both directions.
4. Variable can be positive or negative.

Uniform (min, max)

$$f(x) = \frac{1}{\max - \min} \quad (11.1)$$

$$\text{Mean} = \frac{\max + \min}{2} \quad (11.2)$$

$$\text{Variance} = \frac{(\max - \min)^2}{12} \quad (11.3)$$

To generate a random number from a uniform distribution we use the Excel function RAND, where the RAND function returns numbers from the interval (0, 1). If you need to generate numbers from another interval you should use the following formula: = a + (b – a) * RAND (), where the random number generated would be equal or greater than 'a' but less than 'b'.

= a + (b – a) * RAND ()

The Excel RANDBETWEEN (minimum, maximum) function returns a random integer number between a minimum and maximum value:

= RANDBETWEEN (minimum, maximum)

Note For the uniform distribution no unique mode exists.

Uniform distribution (min, max) all values within the range are deemed to have the same constant probability density, where that density changes to zero at the minimum and maximum values.

Example 11.4

Consider the tossing of a fair coin where the probability of a 'head' and 'tail' are equal at 0.5.

(a) Use Monte Carlo simulation to simulate 100 and 1000 tosses of the fair coin. Compare the average number of 'heads' and 'tails' with the expected number of 'heads' and 'tails'.

(b) Calculate the exact probability of seven 'heads' from ten tosses of the fair coin. Use your results from 1000 simulations to estimate this value. Do the results agree? If not, why not? What would happen if we increased the number of simulations to the accuracy of your result?

(a) Use the Excel RANDBETWEEN () function to undertake 100 and 1000 simulations of tossing a fair coin. From these simulations estimate the average number of 'head'. In simulation we represent the number 1 with 'heads' and 0 with 'tails'. The Excel solution to part (a) is illustrated in Figure 11.9.

	A	B	C	D	E
1	Example 11.4 (a)				
2					
3		Monte Carlo simulation of tossing a fair coin			
4					
5		100 simulations, average =	0.5400	=AVERAGE(C9:C108)	
6		1000 simulations, average =	0.5000	=AVERAGE(E9:E1008)	
7					
8		Simulation number	Results (100 tosses)	Simulation number	Results (1000 tosses)
9		1	0	1	0
10		2	1	2	0
11		3	0	3	0
12		4	0	4	1

Figure 11.9

→ Excel solution

100 simulations, average = Cell C5 Formula: = AVERAGE(C9:C108)
1000 simulations, average = Cell C6 Formula: = AVERAGE(E9:E1008)
Simulation number Cells B9:B108 Values
Results (100 tosses) Cell C9 Formula: = RANDBETWEEN(0,1)
Copy down from C9:C108
Simulation number Cells D9:D1008 Values
Results (100 tosses) Cell E9 Formula: = RANDBETWEEN(0,1)
Copy down from E9:E1008

Interpretation From Excel, the average number of 'heads' is 0.5400 for 100 simulations and 0.5000 for 1000 simulations. From these results we can observe that the 1000 simulation result is in closer agreement with the theoretical value of 0.5.

Notes

1. To check that the simulation average gives a closer approximation to the theoretical value as the number of simulations increases then calculate the measure of spread for each set of results and note that this spread decreases as the number of simulations increases; e.g. check for 100, 1000, 20,000 simulations.
2. If we have one toss of the coin where we have two possible outcomes (heads or tails), this is an example of a Bernoulli distribution.
3. Press the F9 keyboard key to recalculate if you have stopped automatic recalculation.

(b) The Excel solution to part (a) is illustrated in Figure 11.10.

	A	B	C	D	E	F	G	H	I	J	K	L	M	N
1	Example 11.4 (b)													
2														
3		Exact value:												
4		P(X = 7 from 10 tosses) =	0.1171875	=BINOM.DIST(7,10,0.5,FALSE)										
5														
6		Simulation results:												
7														
8		Number of iterations =	1000	=COUNT(N14:N1013)										
9		Number of iterations with 7 heads =	118	=COUNTIF(N13:N1013,7)										
10		P(X = 7 from 10 tosses) =	0.118	=C9/C8										
11														
12			Toss number:											
13		Simulation number	1	2	3	4	5	6	7	8	9	10		Number of heads
14		1	1	1	1	1	0	0	0	0	1	1		6
15		2	0	1	0	0	1	0	0	1	0	0		3
16		3	0	0	0	1	0	1	0	1	0	1		4
17		4	1	1	1	1	1	0	1	1	1	1		9

Figure 11.10

→ Excel solution

Exact value:

P(X = 7 from 10 tosses) = Cell C4	Formula: = BINOM.DIST(7,10,0.5,FALSE)
Simulation results:	
Number of iterations = Cell C8	Formula: = COUNT(N14:N1013)
Number of iterations with 7 heads = Cell C9	Formula: = COUNTIF(N13:N1013,7)
P(X = 7 from 10 tosses) = Cell C10	Formula: = C9/C8
Simulation number Cells B14:B1013	Values
Toss number Cells C13:L13	Values
Random value Cell C14	Formula: = RANDBETWEEN(0,1) Copy across and down from C14:L1013
Number of heads Cell N14	Formula: = SUM(C14:L14) Copy down from N14:N1013

Interpretation From Excel, the exact value for the probability that we have seven 'heads' from ten tosses of the coin is 0.117 with the value from 1000 simulations equal to 0.118.

Note

1. In part (b), we calculated the probability of seven 'heads' from ten tosses of a fair coin and found that the exact value of 11.7% was close to the value from the 1000 simulations of 11.8%. This technique could be extended to solving other probability values; e.g. if we would like to know the probability of at least four 'heads' then we would modify the Excel equation 'Number of iterations with seven heads = COUNTIF (N13:N1013, 7)' to 'Number of iterations with at least 4 heads = COUNTIF (N13:N1013,'>3')'.
2. Press the F9 keyboard key to re-calculate if you have stopped automatic recalculation.

11.1.5 Triangular distribution

The **triangular distribution** is often used when we know the minimum, maximum and the most likely value. This distribution is illustrated in Figure 11.11. Distribution defined by the minimum, most likely and maximum values (a, b, c).

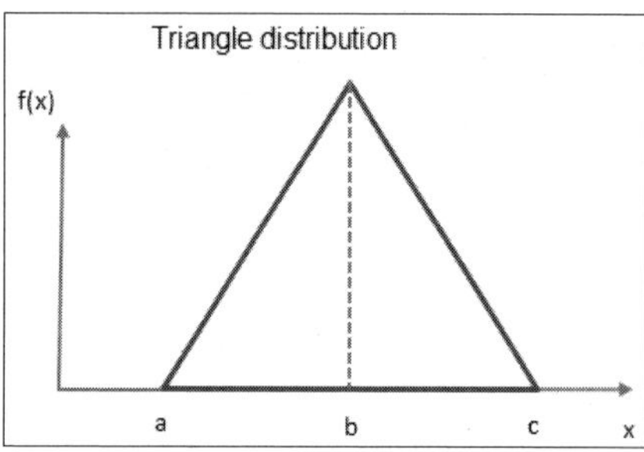

Figure 11.11
Triangular distribution

The characteristics of a triangular distribution are as follows:

1. Continuous.
2. Can be symmetric or skewed.
3. Bounded in both directions.
4. Variable can be positive or negative.

Triang (min, most likely, max)

$$f(x) = \frac{2(x-a)}{(b-a)(c-a)} \text{ if } a \le x \le b \tag{11.4}$$

$$f(x) = \frac{2(c-a)}{(c-a)(c-b)} \text{ if } b \le x \le c \tag{11.5}$$

$$\text{Mean} = \frac{a+b+c}{3} \tag{11.6}$$

$$\text{Variance} = \frac{a^2+b^2+c^2-ab-ac-bc}{18} \tag{11.7}$$

To generate a random number from a triangular distribution the Excel function is:

= IF(r <= (b – a)/(c – a), a + SQRT (r * (c – a) * (b – a)), c – SQRT ((1 – r) * (c – a) * (c – b)))

triangular distribution is a continuous probability distribution with lower limit a, upper limit c and mode b, where a ≤ b ≤ c.

triang (min, most likely, max) is often used when the minimum, maximum, and the most likely values are known.

Where r can be generated by the RAND () function. Storing the value from the RAND () function in the variable r is important because the RAND () function returns a new value each time it is called.

Note For the triangular distribution the mode = b.

Example 11.5

Consider the problem of estimating the profit from the sales of a new product. The model inputs are as follows: the competitor's sales price for a competing product, the new product sales price, the market size, and the manufacturing cost. The outputs to be calculated are as follows:

- The % market share—which depends on the new product sales price and our competitor's sales price via the following linear equation: % market share = 0.4 – 0.05*new product sales price + 0.05*competitors sales price.
- The total sales—which depends on the market size, market share, and our new product sales price via the following linear equation: total sales = market size * % market share * new product sales price.
- The total profit—which depends on the market size, % market share, our new product sales price, and the manufacturing cost via the following linear equation: total profit = market size * % market share * (new product sales price – manufacturing cost).

Given the following data values we wish to construct simulation model to calculate the outputs when the input variables are represented by a triangular distribution with the parameters given as follows:

	Competitor's sales price	New product sales price	Market size	Manufacturing cost
Minimum	19	19	800,000	13
Mode	21	20	1,000,000	15
Maximum	23	23	1,200,000	17

Table 11.2 Data table

(a) Construct the simulation model and run for 1000 simulations.

(b) Calculate the minimum, maximum, average, and standard deviation for the total profit.

The Excel solutions to part (a)–(b) are illustrated in Figures 11.12–11.14.

	A	B	C	D
1	Example 11.5			
2				
3		Inputs:		
4		Competitors sales price =	£21.00	
5		New product sales price =	£20.00	
6		Market size =	1000000	
7		Manufacturing cost =	£15.00	
8				
9		Outputs:		
10		% market share =	0.45	=0.4-0.05*C5+0.05*C4
11		Total sales =	9000000	=C6*C10*C5
12		Total profit =	£2,250,000.00	=C6*C10*(C5-C7)

Figure 11.12

	G	H	I	J	K	L	M	N	O
14									
15		Min, a =	19	19	800000	13			
16		Mode, b =	21	20	1000000	15			
17		Max, c =	23	23	1200000	17			
18									
19	Simulation	r	Competitors sales price (£)	New product sales prices (£)	Market size	Manufacturing cost (£)	% market share	Total sales	Total profit (£)
20	1	0.976185948	£22.56	£22.47	1156352.272	£16.56	0.404904801	10518595.56	£2,783,345.73
21	2	0.258012055	£20.44	£20.02	943669.6363	£14.44	0.421031461	7952675.829	£2,216,765.50
22	3	0.140573496	£20.06	£19.75	906046.5919	£14.06	0.415530164	7435619.639	£2,141,999.20

Figure 11.13

	B	C	D	E
19		% market share	Total sales	Total profit
20	Number of simulations =	1000	1000	1000
21	Min =	0.400513132	6135685.999	£1,929,938.25
22	Max =	0.423606798	10985321.38	£2,867,807.62
23	Mean =	0.416676833	8620639.311	£2,357,888.38
24	Median =	0.417906004	8661662.114	£2,340,282.82
25	Stdev =	0.005748669	1016893.82	£197,660.27

Figure 11.14

→ Excel solution

Inputs:

Competitors sales price = Cell C4 Value
New product sales price = Cell C5 Value
Market size = Cell C6 Value
Manufacturing cost = Cell C7 Value

Outputs:

% market share = Cell C10 Formula: = 0.4-0.05*C5+0.05*C4
Total sales = Cell C11 Formula: = C6*C10*C5
Total profit = Cell C12 Formula: = C6*C10*(C5-C7)

Competitors' sales price

Min, a = Cell I15 Value
Mode, b = Cell I16 Formula: = C4
Max, c = Cell I17 Value

New product sales price

Min, a = Cell J15 Value
Mode, b = Cell J16 Formula: = C5
Max, c = Cell J17 Value

Market size

Min, a = Cell K15 Value
Mode, b = Cell K16 Formula: = C6
Max, c = Cell K17 Value

Manufacturing cost

Min, a = Cell L15 Value
Mode, b = Cell L16 Formula: = C7
Max, c = Cell L17 Value

Simulation

r Cell H20 Formula: = RAND()
Copy formula down H20:H1019

Competitors' sales price = Cell I20	Formula: = IF($H20<=(I$16-I$15)/(I$17-I$15),I$15+ SQRT($H20*(I$17-I$15)*(I$16-I$15)),I$17-SQRT((1-$H20)*(I$17-I$15)*(I$17-I$16)))
	Copy formula down I20:I1019
New product sales price = Cell J20	Formula: = IF($H20<=(J$16-J$15)/(J$17-J$15),J$15+ SQRT($H20*(J$17-J$15)*(J$16-J$15)),J$17-SQRT((1-$H20)*(J$17-J$15)*(J$17-J$16)))
	Copy formula down J20:J1019
Market size = Cell K20	Formula: = IF($H20<=(K$16-K$15)/(K$17-K$15),K$15+ SQRT($H20*(K$17-K$15)*(K$16-K$15)),K$17-SQRT((1-$H20)*(K$17-K$15)*(K$17-K$16)))
	Copy formula down K20:K1019
Manufacturing cost = Cell L20	Formula: = IF($H20<=(L$16-L$15)/(L$17-L$15),L$15+ SQRT($H20*(L$17-L$15)*(L$16-L$15)),L$17-SQRT((1-$H20)*(L$17-L$15)*(L$17-L$16)))
	Copy formula down L20:L1019
% market share = Cell M20	Formula: = 0.4-0.05*J20+0.05*I20
	Copy formula down M20:M1019
Total sales = Cell N20	Formula: = K20*M20*J20
	Copy formula down N20:N1019
Total profit = Cell O20	Formula: = K20*M20*(J20-L20)
	Copy formula down O20:O1019

% market share

Number of simulations = Cell C20	Formula: = COUNT(M20:M1019)
Min = Cell C21	Formula: = MIN(M20:M1019)
Max = Cell C22	Formula: = MAX(M20:M1019)
Mean = Cell C23	Formula: = AVERAGE(M20:M1019)
Median = Cell C24	Formula: = MEDIAN(M20:M1019)
Stdev = Cell C25	Formula: = STDEV.S(M20:M1019)
	Copy formulae across from C20:C25 to E20:E25

Interpretation From Excel, the minimum, maximum, and mean total profit from 1000 simulations is £1,929,938.25; £2,867,807.62; and £2,357,888.38 respectively.

Note Press the F9 keyboard key to re-calculate if you have stopped automatic recalculation.

11.1.6 Normal distribution

The normal distribution (or Gaussian distribution) occurs in a wide variety of applications due to the central limit theorem. The distribution is observed within a range of naturally occurring variables and is used extensively within the statistical and financial analysis of data.

Figure 11.15 illustrates the shape of the normal distribution. Note that the value of x goes from minus infinity to plus infinity ($-\infty \rightarrow \infty$).

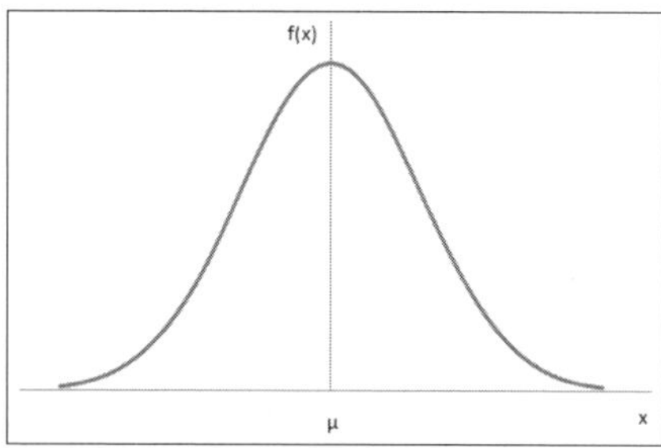

Figure 11.15
Normal distribution

The characteristics of a normal distribution are as follows:

1. Continuous.
2. Symmetric (bell-shaped).
3. Unbounded in both directions.
4. Variable can be positive or negative.

The normal probability density function is given by Equation (11.8).

$$f(x) = \frac{1}{\sigma\sqrt{2\pi}} e\left[-\frac{(x-\mu)^2}{2\sigma^2}\right] \quad (11.8)$$

$$\text{Mean} = \mu \quad (11.9)$$

$$\text{Variance} = \sigma^2 \quad (11.10)$$

The Excel NORM.INV function calculates the inverse of the cumulative normal distribution function for a supplied value of x, a supplied distribution mean and standard deviation: =NORM.INV (probability, mean, standard deviation). To generate a random number from a normal distribution the Excel function is:

=NORM.INV (RAND (), μ, σ)

If $\mu = 0$ and $\sigma = 1$, then =NORM.INV (RAND (), 0, 1) essentially returns a random Z-value from a normal distribution, ~N(0, 1).

Note For the normal distribution the mean = median = mode.

Once the distribution characteristics are defined in terms of probability distribution then the Monte Carlo simulation produces in iteration random values for each variable. It also produces thousands of interaction with different combinations of scenarios. As well, the simulation calculates the corresponding outcome. After all iterations are completed the simulation produces the probability distribution of outcomes and depicts in a graphical manner.

Example 11.6

In this example we want to simulate 400 trials or iterations for a normal random variable with a mean of 40,000 and a standard deviation of 10,000.

Solution

The Excel solution is illustrated in Figure 11.16.

	A	B	C	D	E	F	G
1	Example 11.6						
2							
3		Mean =	40000				
4		Standard deviation =	10000				
5							
6		Simulation results:			Simulation	RAND()	Normal.INV
7					1	0.22065861	32300.29221
8		N =	400	=COUNT(E7:E406)	2	0.94203767	55721.11614
9		Mean =	40661.7999	=AVERAGE(G7:G406)	3	0.88091289	51795.62623
10		Standard deviation =	9908.54341	=STDEV.S(G7:G406)	4	0.30127106	34792.51694

Figure 11.16

→ Excel solution

Mean = Cell C3	Value
Standard deviation = Cell C4	Value
Simulation Cells E7:E406	Values
RAND() Cell F7	Formula: = RAND()
	Copy down from F7:F406
Normal.INV Cell G7	Formula: = NORM.INV(F7,$C$3,$C$4)
	Copy down from G7:G406

Simulation results:

N = Cell C8	Formula: = COUNT(E7:E406)
Mean = Cell C9	Formula: = AVERAGE(G7:G406)
Standard deviation = Cell C10	Formula: = STDEV.S(G7:G406)

Interpretation From Excel, the formula NORM.INV (RAND (), mean, sigma) generates 400 different trial values from a normal distribution with a simulation mean of 40,661.80 and a standard deviation of 9,908.54.

Note

(a) Essentially, for a random number x, the formula NORM.INV (p, mu, sigma) generates the pth percentile of a normal random variable with a mean mu (μ) and a standard deviation sigma (σ). For example, the random number 0.94 in cell F8 generates in cell G8 approximately the 94th percentile (= 55,721) of a normal distribution with a mean of 40,661.80 and a standard deviation of 9,908.54.

(b) Press the F9 keyboard key to recalculate if you have stopped automatic recalculation.

11.1.7 Binomial distribution

The binomial equation to calculate the probability of 'x' successes from 'n' attempts is given by the probability density function, equation (11.11):

$$P(X = x) = \binom{n}{x} p^x q^{n-x} \tag{11.11}$$

$$\text{Mean} = np \tag{11.12}$$

$$\text{Variance} = np(1 - p) \tag{11.13}$$

The characteristics of a **binomial distribution** are as follows:

1. Discrete.
2. Can be symmetric or skewed.
3. Variable bounded below by 0 and above by n.
4. Variable can be zero or positive (not negative).

To generate a random number from a binomial distribution with parameters 'n' and 'x', we can generate n standard uniform numbers and the number of these standard random numbers that are less than or equal to 'x' is the binomially distributed random number generated. This procedure is useful when the value of n is not large. To generate a random number from a binomial distribution the Excel function is: =IF (RAND () <= x, 1, 0) + IF (RAND () <= x, 1, 0) + IF (RAND () <= x, 1, 0) +.....+ IF (RAND () <= x, 1, 0). In this method the function (RAND () <= x, 1, 0) appears n times. For large values of n, the normal approximation to the binomial distribution may be used.

The Excel BINOM.INV function returns the inverse of the cumulative binomial distribution i.e. for a given number of independent trials, the function returns the smallest value (number of successes) for which the cumulative binomial distribution is greater than or equal to a given probability: BINOM.INV (trials, probability, alpha). However, this function is simply a new version of the CRITBINOM function that is available in earlier versions of Excel: CRITBINOM (trials, probability, alpha). To generate a random number of successes from a binomial distribution the Excel function is:

binomial distribution a binomial distribution can be used to model a range of discrete random data variables.

=BINOM.INV (n, p, RAND ())

=CRITBINOM (n, p, RAND ())

BINOM.INV (n, p, RAND ()) and CRITBINOM (n, p, RAND ()) both simulate a random draw from a binomial probability distribution with n trials and a probability of success p.

Example 11.7

For example, we wish to randomly sample from a Binomial distribution with n = 4 and p = 0.4. Figure 11.17 illustrates the Excel solution to randomly select a binomial number between 1 and n.

	A	B	C	D
1	Example 11.7			
2				
3		Probability of success, p =	0.4	
4		Number of trials, n=	4	
5				
6		Generate random number =	0.736386	=RAND()
7				
8		Random binomial number using BINOM.INV() =	2	=BINOM.INV(C4,C3,C6)
9				
10		Random binomial number using CRITBINOM() =	2	=CRITBINOM(C4,C3,C6)

Figure 11.17

→ Excel solution

p = Cell C3 Value

Number of terms, N = Cell C4 Value

Generate random number = Cell C6 Formula: = RAND ().

Random binomial number using BINOM.INV() = Cell C10

Formula: = BINOM.INV(C4,C3,C6)

Random binomial number using CRITBINOM() = Cell C8

Formula:=CRITBINOM(C4,C3,C6)

Interpretation From the Excel solution, we observe that the random binomial number generated is 2 using the two different methods.

Note Press the F9 keyboard key to re-calculate if you have stopped automatic recalculation.

11.1.8 Poisson distribution

The Poisson equation to calculate the number of events occurring within a given interval is given by the probability density function given by equation (11.12):

$$P(X = x) = \frac{\lambda e^{-\lambda}}{x!} \tag{11.14}$$

$$\text{Mean} = \lambda \tag{11.15}$$

$$\text{Variance} = \lambda \tag{11.16}$$

The characteristics of a Poisson distribution are as follows:

1. Discrete.
2. Can be symmetric or skewed.
3. Variable bounded below by 0 but unbounded in positive direction.
4. Variable can be zero or positive (non-negative).

To generate a random number from a Poisson distribution cannot be coded in a single expression. However, we may use the POISSON function to construct a cumulative distribution table. Then the LOOKUP function can be used to access the table to generate the Poisson random numbers in our spreadsheet simulation model. The Excel formula for the Poisson distribution is:

= POISSON(x, mean, cumulative)

If cumulative is TRUE, POISSON returns the cumulative probability that $0 \leq X \leq x$; if FALSE, it returns the probability that $X = x$.

Example 11.8

For example, we wish to randomly sample from a Poisson distribution with mean value of 3. Figure 11.18 illustrates the Excel solution to randomly select a Poisson number between 0 and n.

	A	B	C	D	E	F
1	Example 11.8					
2						
3		Mean =	3			
4		n =	16	=COUNT(B7:B23)-1		
5						
6		Number of events	Poisson PDF		Poisson CDF	
7		0	0.0498	=POISSON(B7,$C$3,FALSE)	0.0498	=POISSON.DIST(B7,$C$3,TRUE)
8		1	0.1494		0.1991	
9		2	0.2240		0.4232	
10		3	0.2240		0.6472	
11		4	0.1680		0.8153	
12		5	0.1008		0.9161	
13		6	0.0504		0.9665	
14		7	0.0216		0.9881	
15		8	0.0081		0.9962	
16		9	0.0027		0.9989	
17		10	0.0008		0.9997	
18		11	0.0002		0.9999	
19		12	0.0001		1.0000	
20		13	0.0000		1.0000	
21		14	0.0000		1.0000	
22		15	0.0000		1.0000	
23		16	0.0000	=POISSON(B23,$C$3,FALSE)	1.0000	=POISSON.DIST(B23,$C$3,TRUE)
24						
25		Poisson random number generated from 0 to n =	2	=LOOKUP(RAND(),E7:E23,B7:B23)		

Figure 11.18

→ Excel solution

Mean = Cell C3	Value
n = Cell C4	Formula: = COUNT(B7:B23)-1
Number of events Cell B7:B23	Values
Poisson PDF	
Cell C7	Formula: = POISSON(B7, $C$3, false) Copy formula down from C7:C23
Poisson CDF	
Cell E7	Formula: = POISSON(B7, $C$3, true) Copy formula down from E7:E23
Poisson random number generated from 0 to n	
Cell C25	Formula: = LOOKUP(RAND(),E7:E23,B7:B23)

Interpretation From the Excel solution, we observe that the random Poisson number generated is 2.

Note Press the F9 keyboard key to re-calculate if you have stopped automatic recalculation.

Student exercises

X11.1 Use the Excel RAND (), COUNT () and COUNTIF () functions to generate 50 random numbers: (a) calculate the proportion of 50 random numbers smaller than 0.5, (b) calculate the proportion of 50 random numbers greater than 0.5?

X11.2 Repeat X11.1 with 500 simulations.

X11.3 Modify your Excel functions in X11.2 to calculate the proportion of numbers which are less than 0.3. What proportion of random number would lie between 0.25 and 0.47?

X11.4 Generate 500 random numbers from a uniform distribution using the Excel RANDBETWEEN () function, where the minimum value is 220 and a maximum value is 420: (a) use Equation (11.2) to calculate the mean value and estimate the mean value from the generated random numbers (do the answers agree and if not, why not), (b) use equation (11.3) to calculate the variance for this uniform distribution and compare with the variance calculated from the 500 random numbers (do the numbers agree and if not, why not), (c) calculate the probability that a number generated is > 380, and (d) calculate the probability that a random number lies between 440 and 460 (explain why this result is what you could have stated without undertaking the Excel calculation).

X11.5 Generate 400 random numbers from a triangular distribution with minimum, most likely, maximum equal to 150, 180, 220 respectively: (a) use Equation (11.6) to calculate the mean value and estimate the mean from the 400 random numbers (do the answers agree and if not, why not), (b) calculate the probability that the random value from this distribution is greater than 202, (c) what is the probability that the value lies between 175 and 192?

X11.6 Generate 400 random numbers from a normal distribution with population mean of 230 and standard deviation of 24. Use the generated random numbers to calculate the following probabilities: (a) $P(X \geq 230)$, (b) $P(X < 189)$, and (c) $P(X > 294)$. In Chapter 3, we provided an empirical rule for the normal distribution regarding the proportion of values within 1, 2, and 3 standard deviations of the population mean; (d) use the generated random values to check on the number within 1, 2, and 3 standard deviations of the mean and compare with the theoretical values from Chapter 3.

X11.7 A company is considering developing a new product for the UK market where the cost of developing the project is uncertain. Based upon previous projects the following scenarios are considered possible: (i) development cost distribution symmetric with minimum and maximum values of £1,250,000 and £1,850,000 respectively, or (ii) the distribution is normally distributed with mean equal to £1,550,000 and standard deviation £100,000. Use both scenarios to calculate: (a) the expected value, (b) the simulation model equation, and (c) undertake 1000 simulations to estimate the average development cost for both scenarios.

X11.8 A company is planning to undertake a major investment in a product that it only sells overseas. To help with the decision making process the company would like appropriate analysis performed to estimate the potential profit for this product over a given time interval. The profit is related to revenue and cost by the equation profit = revenue – cost. The revenue and cost can be considered random variables with the revenue being normally distributed with mean = £450,000 and standard deviation = £85,000, and the cost being uniformly distributed with a minimum and maximum value of £100,000 and £200,000 respectively.

11.2 Introduction to Monte Carlo simulation

11.2.1 Creating a Monte Carlo simulation model

Monte Carlo methods involve running sampling experiments whose aim is to estimate the distribution of an output variable which is dependent upon several input random variables. For example, the future value of an investment may be required over the next ten years where the future value may be dependent upon several unknown variables. In this case the unknown variables are modelled using a particular probability distribution and the output variable is calculated for a set of input variables. This calculation is then repeated for different sets of input variables to create a set of output variable solutions or scenarios (also called a trial or iteration). This set of output solutions forms the distribution of possible values which then allows the calculation of the most likely output value.

The Monte Carlo method is often used when the model is complex, nonlinear, or involves more than just a couple of uncertain parameters. A simulation can typically involve thousands of evaluations of the model, a task which in the past was only practical using super computers but is now possible with modern home and business computers. The Monte Carlo method consists of the following five steps:

1. Create a parametric model.
2. Generate a random set of inputs (X_1, X_2, ..., X_n).
3. Evaluate the results (Y_1, Y_2, ..., Y_n).
4. Repeat step 1–3 for each iteration i = 1 to n.
5. Analyse the results using descriptive statistics.

Advantages of simulation:

- Relatively straightforward.
- Can be used to solve large, complex problems.
- Allows 'what-if' analysis.

Disadvantages of simulation:

- Requires generation of all conditions and constraints.
- Each model is unique.
- Does not generate an optimal solution.

When to use Monte Carlo simulation methods:

- where an analytical solution either does not exist or is too complicated,
- where there are lots of uncertainties.

Do not use Monte Carlo simulation methods:

- that might require extraordinary long computer time—it is not worth it.
- where an analytical solution exists and is simple. In this case it is easier to use the analytical solution to solve the problem.

Example 11.9

Reconsider Example 11.1 but this time the value of the nominal interest rate is not known exactly but it is known that it can vary from 0.058 to 0.082. Use Monte Carlo simulation to calculate the future value using 100 iterations. In this example we are told that the value of the nominal interest rate can vary from a minimum value of 0.058 to a maximum value of 0.082. If we assume that all values of the nominal rate within this range have the same probability of occurrence then we can use the uniform distribution and the Excel RAND () function to simulate as illustrated in Figures 11.19–11.20 by undertaking 100 simulations.

	A	B	C	D	E	F
1	Example 11.9					
2						
3		Present value, P =	1000			
4		Nominal rate, j =	0.07			
5		Periods/Year, m =	12			
6		Years, n=	5			
7		Future value, FV =	£1,417.63	=FV(C4/C5,C5*C6,0,-C3,0)		
8		Future value, FV =	£1,417.63	=1000*(1+C4/C5)^(C5*C6)		
9						
10		Min r =	0.058			
11		Max r =	0.082			
12						
13		Simulation	r		FV	
14		1	0.0673	=$C$10+RAND()*($C$11-$C$10)	£1,399.02	=FV($C14/$C$5,$C$5*$C$6,0,-$C$3,0)
15		2	0.0788		£1,481.34	
16		3	0.0673		£1,398.38	

Figure 11.19

	G	H	I	J
13		Summary statistics		
14				
15		n =	100	=COUNT(B14:B113)
16				
17		min r =	0.05822686052	=MIN(C14:C113)
18		max r =	0.08157862594	=MAX(C14:C113)
19		Mean r =	0.06964965091	=AVERAGE(C14:C113)
20				
21		Mean FV =	£1,415.97	=AVERAGE(E14:E113)

Figure 11.20

→ Excel solution

Present value, P = Cell C3	Value
Nominal rate, j = Cell C4	Value
Periods/Year, m = Cell C5	Value
Years, n = Cell C6	Value
Future value, FV = Cell C7	Formula: = FV(C4/C5,C5*C6,0,-C3,0)
Future value, FV = Cell C8	Formula: = 1000*(1+C4/C5)^(C5*C6)
Min r = Cell C10	Value
Max r = Cell C11	Value
Simulation Cells B14:B113	Values
r Cell C14	Formula: = $C$10+RAND()*($C$11-$C$10) Copy down from C14:C113
FV Cell E14	Formula: = FV($C14/$C$5,$C$5*$C$6,0,-$C$3,0) Copy down from E14:E113

Summary statistics

n = Cell I15	Formula: = COUNT(B14:B113)
Min r = Cell I17	Formula: = MIN(C14:C113)
Max r = Cell I18	Formula: = MAX(C14:C113)
Mean r = Cell I19	Formula: = AVERAGE(C14:C113)
Mean FV = Cell I21	Formula: = AVERAGE(E14:E113)

✻ Interpretation From the Excel solution, we observe that the average nominal rate is 6.96% with a future value of £1,415.97.

Note Press the F9 keyboard key to recalculate if you have stopped automatic recalculation.

Example 11.10

Now we have seen how to apply Monte Carlo Simulation, let us reconsider Example 11.2.

	A	B	C	D	E	F
1	Example 11.10					
2						
3		Assuming uniform distribution				
4						
5		Part	MIN	MAX	Random value	Random formulas
6		A	1.95	2.05	1.9520	=C6+RAND()*(D6-C6)
7		B	1.95	2.05	2.0240	
8		C	29.5	30.5	30.3270	
9		D =	33.4	34.6	34.2661	=C9+RAND()*(D9-C9)
10				Error = D - (A + B + C) =	-0.0369	=E9-(E6+E7+E8)
11						
12				Re-calculate		
13						
14		Save as Excel macro enabled workbook (.xlsm) to allow re-calculate button to work.				

Figure 11.21

→ Excel solution

Part Cells B6:B9	Values
Min Cells C6:C8	Values
Max Cells D6:D8	Values
Dmin = Cells C9	Formula: = SUM(C6:C8)
Dmax = Cells D9	Formula: = SUM(D6:D8)
Random value = Cell E6	Formula: = C6+RAND()*(D6-C6)
	Copy down from E6:E9
Error = Cell E10	Formula: = E9-(E6+E7+E8)

Interpretation From the Excel solution, we observe that the tolerance error (= D – A – B – C) = –0.0369. In this simulation, we find that the dimension combination of A, B, and C parts will be too small to fit into the dimension of D.

Each time you press the recalculate button you are simulating the creation of an assembly from a random set of parts for A, B, and C. For each simulation undertaken the value of the error will either be negative or positive. For positive errors, the combination of parts A, B, and C will fit within the dimensions of D. For the hinge to operate efficiently, you would require D to be positive ($D > 0$) and in practice the value of D would be greater than a particular tolerance value. Confirm by pressing F9 that the value of the error can either be positive or negative.

Note If you would like to create the recalculate button in your spreadsheet, you can find the instructions how to do this here:

1. Insert a shape into the worksheet (Insert>Shape) and choose rectangle shape.
2. Input appropriate text (re-calculate) into the rectangular shape and format.
3. Right click on rectangular shape and choose Assign Macro.
4. Click on the name of the shape and click on edit.
5. Add the following code (ActiveSheet.Calculate) to this macro as illustrated in Figure 11.22.

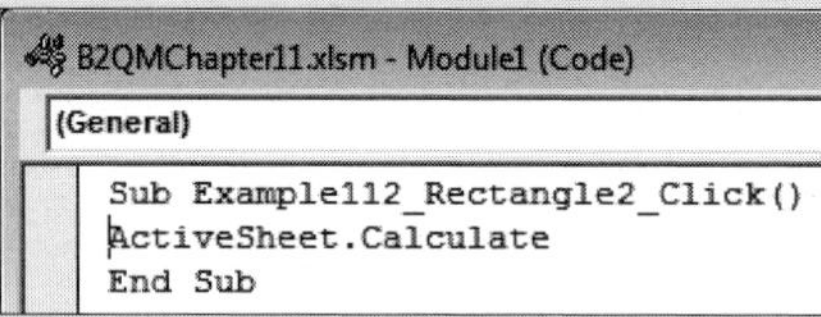

Figure 11.22

Select File > Close and return to Microsoft Excel

6. Save Excel file. Save as Excel macro enabled workbook (.xlsm) to allow recalculate button to work.

This example demonstrates almost all the steps in a Monte Carlo simulation. The deterministic model is simply D – (A + B + C). We are using the uniform distributions to generate the values for each input. All we need to do now is press the recalculate button a few thousand times, record all the results, create a histogram to visualize the data, and calculate the probability that the parts cannot be assembled.

Example 11.11

New Gadgets Ltd has developed a new gadget which will be sold by a leading UK supermarket chain. The company undertake Monte Carlo simulation for all new gadgets to estimate the market profitability per month based upon the uncertainty associated with the variables that define the profit equation; e.g. profit per month = revenue per month - costs per month.

1. Create the model

Given that we are calculating the profit then the relationship between profit and the two uncertain variables revenue (R) and costs (C) is as follows:

$$\text{Profit (P)} = \text{revenue} - \text{costs} = R - C \qquad (11.17)$$

It is very important when you build simulation models that you attempt to write the independent variables (R, C) such that the new equations provide greater detail.

For example, the revenue term (R) can be broken down into independent variables as follows:

Assume that revenue term (R) is dependent upon the number of sales (N) multiplied by the profit per sale (PS):

$$R = N * PS \tag{11.18}$$

The profit per sale takes into account the sale price and other costs such as manufacturing costs. Based upon past experience the company have estimated that the profit per sale will vary between £48 and £54. After further research it has been identified that New Gadgets Ltd generates sales through purchasing leads. The number of sales per month (N) is the number of leads per month (NLM) multiplied by the percentage of leads that result in sales (PLS). Equation (11.18) can now be written as follows:

$$R = NLM * PLS * PS \tag{11.19}$$

Similarly, the cost term (C) in Equation (11.17) can be broken down into independent variables as follows:

The costs can be considered to be a combination of a fixed cost (FC) plus the total cost of the leads (TCL):

$$C = FC + TCL \tag{11.20}$$

The total cost of the leads is the NLM multiplied by the cost per lead (CL):

$$TCL = NLM * CL \tag{11.21}$$

Therefore, substituting Equation (11.21) into Equation (11.20) gives:

$$C = FC + NLM*CL \tag{11.22}$$

Based upon past experience the company have estimated that the NLM will vary between 1560 and 1660 and the cost per lead (CL) will vary between £0.30 and £0.70.

Finally, we can combine Equations (11.17)–(11.22) to give the final model relationship between profit, revenue and costs:

$$P = NLM * PLS * PS - (F + NLM * CL) \tag{11.23}$$

Equation (11.23) describes how the profit (P) changes as the other variables NLM, PLS, PS, NLM and CL vary with the fixed cost F assumed to be equal to £1000. Assume the PLS varies with minimum 3% and maximum 6%.

Note It should be noted that the two terms for revenue and costs in Equation (11.23) are not independent given that they both contain the variable NLM. It is very important that the equations for revenue and costs are broken down such that the two terms are independent but given that we cannot do this then we will assume in the Monte Carlo simulation that they are independent. Due to this dependence between revenue and costs, due to the term NLM, we will have a measure of correlation between the two variables. Note that this is beyond the scope of this introductory chapter on Monte Carlo simulation.

2. Generate random numbers and undertake model simulations

Variable	Min	Max	Distribution
NLM	1560	1660	Uniform
CL	£0.30	£0.70	Uniform
PLS	3%	6%	Uniform
PS	£48	£54	Uniform
FC	£1000	£1000	

Table 11.3 Description of uncertain variable inputs

In this section we need to generate the random number for the uncertain variables as stated in table 11.3.

For this example, we're going to use a uniform distribution to represent the four uncertain parameters NLM, CL, PLS, and PS. The table above uses the minimum and maximum to indicate the uncertainty in NLM, CL, PLS, and PS with the Excel RAND () formula used to generate the random numbers for each variable: = min + RAND () * (max-min). In this example we will develop the Monte Carlo Excel spreadsheet and run for 5000 simulations.

Input initial values in to Excel, as illustrated in Figure 11.23.

	A	B	C	D	E	F
1	Example 11.11					
2						
3	Sales Forecast Model					
4						
5		Input Values				
6						
7			Minimum	Maximum	Initial values	Stochastic
8		Leads per month, NLM =	1560	1660	1610	1655.79
9		Cost per lead, CL =	£0.30	£0.70	£0.50	£0.43
10		Conversion rate, PLS =	0.03	0.06	0.05	0.03
11		Profit per sale, PS =	£48.00	£54.00	£51.00	£49.30
12		Fixed cost per month, FC =			£1,000.00	
13						
14		Results with one simulation				
15						
16			Deterministic	Stochastic		
17		Monthly revenue =	£3,694.95	£2,677.73		
18		Monthly costs =	£1,805.00	£1,717.74		
19		Projected monthly profit =	£1,889.95	£959.99		

Figure 11.23

→ Excel solution

NLM min = Cell C8	Value
NLM max = Cell D8	Value
NLM initial = Cell E8	Formula: = (C8+D8)/2
NLM stochastic = Cell F8	Formula: = C8+RAND()*(D8-C8)
CL min = Cell C9	Value
CL max = Cell D9	Value
CL initial = Cell E9	Formula: = (C9+D9)/2
CL stochastic = Cell F9	Formula: = C9+RAND()*(D9-C9)
PLS min = Cell C10	Value
PLS max = Cell D10	Value
PLS initial = Cell E10	Formula: = (C10+D10)/2
PLS stochastic = Cell F10	Formula: = C10+RAND()*(D10-C10)

PS min = Cell C11	Value
PS max = Cell D11	Value
PS initial = Cell E11	Formula: = (C11+D11)/2
PS stochastic = Cell F11	Formula: = C11+RAND()*(D11-C11)
FC = Cell E12	Value
Monthly revenue (deterministic) = Cell C17	Formula: = E8*E10*E11
Monthly revenue (scholastic) = Cell C17	Formula: = F8*F10*F11
Monthly costs (deterministic) = Cell C18	Formula: = E12+E8*E9
Monthly costs (scholastic) = Cell D18	Formula: = E12+F8*F9
Monthly profit (deterministic) = Cell D19	Formula: = C17-C18
Monthly profit (scholastic) = Cell D19	Formula: = D17-D18

❊ Interpretation From Excel, the projected monthly profit is £1889.95 using the deterministic model (where the initial values are given by (min + max)/2) and £959.99 using the stochastic model with one Monte Carlo simulation.

Set up the worksheet to run 5000 simulations, as illustrated in Figure 11.24.

	H	I	J	K	L	M	N
27	Simulation	NLM (rand)	CL (rand)	PLS (rand)	PS (rand)	FC (const)	Profit (Monte Carlo simulations)
28	1	1618.9227	0.5909	0.0302	49.0447	1000.0000	438.4109
29	2	1643.2083	0.4204	0.0321	53.9858	1000.0000	1156.5110
30	3	1639.2168	0.4413	0.0577	52.1367	1000.0000	3207.4301

Figure 11.24

→ Excel solution

Simulation Cell H28:H5027	Values
NLM (rand) Cell I28	Formula: = \$C\$8 + RAND () * (\$D\$8 – \$C\$8)
	Copy down from I28:I5027
CL (rand) Cell J28	Formula: = \$C\$9 + RAND () * (\$D\$9 – \$C\$9)
	Copy down from J28:J5027
PLS (rand) Cell K28	Formula: = \$C\$10 + RAND () * (\$D\$10 – \$C\$10)
	Copy down from K28:K5027
PS (rand) Cell L28	Formula: = \$C\$11 + RAND () * (\$D\$11 – \$C\$11)
	Copy down from L28:L5027
FC (const) Cell M28	Formula: = \$E\$12
	Copy down from M28:M5027
Profit (Monte Carlo simulations) Cell H28	Formula: = I28*K28*L28-(M28+I28*J28)
	Copy down from H28:H5027

❊ Interpretation From Excel, we have generated 5000 simulations of the projected profit.

3. Calculate sample statistics using the 5000 simulated sample points, as illustrated in Figure 11.25

	B	C
27	Results of Monte Carlo Simulation with 5000 simulations	
28		
29	Summary Statistics	
30		
31	Sample Size (*n*):	5000.00
32	Sample mean =	1907.80
33	Sample standard deviation =	755.41
34	Sample mean standard error =	10.68
35	Minimum =	250.23
36	Q1 =	1285.83
37	Median =	1902.16
38	Q3 =	2526.19
39	Maximum =	3666.91
40	Skew =	0.02
41	Critical skew =	0.07
42	Kurtosis =	-0.99
43	Critical Kurtosis =	0.14

Figure 11.25

→ Excel solution

Sample size = Cell C31 Formula: = COUNT(H28:H5047)
Sample mean = Cell C32 Formula: = AVERAGE(N28:N5027)
Sample standard deviation = Cell C33 Formula: = STDEV.S(N28:N5027)
Sample mean standard error = Cell C34 Formula: = C33/SQRT(C31)
Minimum = Cell C35 Formula: = MIN(N28:N5027)
Q1 = Cell C36 Formula: = QUARTILE.INC(N28:N5027,1)
Median = Cell C37 Formula: = QUARTILE.INC(N28:N5027,2)
Q3 = Cell C38 Formula: = QUARTILE.INC(N28:N5027,3)
Maximum = Cell C39 Formula: = MAX(N28:N5027)
Skew = Cell C40 Formula: = SKEW(N28:N5027)
Critical skew = Cell C41 Formula: = 2*SQRT(6/C31)
Kurtosis = Cell C42 Formula: = KURT(N28:N5027)
Critical kurtosis = Cell C43 Formula: = 2*SQRT(24/C31)

❋ Interpretation From the Excel solution, we observe that the sample summary statistics for the 5000 simulations is as follows: mean = £1907.80 and standard deviation = £755.41. The skewness statistic (= 0.02) suggests that the simulated distribution is not significantly skewed (0.02 < critical skewness value = 0.07). This suggested symmetry in the simulated distribution can be visualized by constructing the simulated distribution histogram (see Figure 11.28). Remember that these results can change as you repeat the simulation exercise by pressing F9 to recalculate values.

Note

1. If the distribution is significantly skewed then it is normal to report the median statistic with the mean value.
2. Press the F9 keyboard key to recalculate if you have stopped automatic recalculation.

4. Calculate confidence intervals for the true population mean (μ), as illustrated in Figure 11.26

The sample mean is just an estimate of the true population mean. How accurate is the estimate? You can see by repeating the simulation (using F9 in this Excel example) that the mean is not the same for each simulation. If you repeated the Monte Carlo simulation and recorded the sample mean each time, the distribution of the sample mean would end up following a normal distribution (based upon the Central Limit Theorem). The standard error is a good estimate of the standard deviation of this distribution, assuming that the sample is sufficiently large (n >= 30). Finally, you can use Excel to estimate a confidence interval for this population mean, as illustrated in Figure 11.26.

	B	C
45	95% Central Interval	
46		
47	Alpha (a):	0.05
48	% Interval:	0.95
49	Q(0.025):	599.47
50	Q(0.975):	3241.42

Figure 11.26

→ Excel solution

Alpha = Cell C47 Value
% interval = Cell C48 Formula: = 1-C47
Q(0.025) = Cell C49 Formula: = PERCENTILE.INC(N28:N5027,0.025)
Q(0.975) = Cell C50 Formula: = PERCENTILE.INC(N28:N5027,0.975)

Interpretation From Excel, we can be 95% confident that the true mean of the population falls somewhere between £599.47 and £3241.42.

Note It should be noted that the population has been artificially created and depends upon the model assumptions, model developed, and the input distributions. In this example, we assumed that the input variables NLM, CL, PLS, and PS were uniform distributions with particular minimum and maximum values.

5. Create appropriate graphical representations for the simulation values

The final step in the analysis is to create a frequency histogram and cumulative probability distribution for the 5000 profit simulations, as illustrated in Figures 11.27 and 11.28.

	P	Q	R	S
27	Histogram Plot			
28				
29	Sample min =	250.23		
30	Sample max =	3666.91		
31				
32	Bin min =	-200		
33	Bin max =	4000		
34	Number of bins =	40		
35				
36	Bins	Count	Scaled	Total
37	-200	0	0.0000000	0.0000000
38	-95	0	0.0000000	0.0000000

Figure 11.27

→ Excel solution

Sample min = Cell Q29	Formula: = C35
Sample max = Cell Q30	Formula: = C39
Bin min = Cell Q32	Value
Bin max = Cell Q33	Value
Number of bins = Cell Q34	Value
Bins Cell P37	Formula: = Q32
Cell P38	Formula: = ($Q$33-$Q$32)/$Q$34+P37
	Copy down P38:P77
Count Cells Q37:Q77	Array formula: {=FREQUENCY(N28:N5027,P37:P77)}
Scaled Cell R37	Formula: = (Q37/$C$31)/($P$38-$P$37)
	Copy down R37:R77
Total Cell S37	Formula: = SUM($Q$37:Q37)/$C$31
	Copy down S37:S77

Note Adding an array formula to cells Q37:Q77

1. Highlight cells Q37:Q77
2. Type the formula = FREQUENCY (N28:N5027, P37:P77) into the highlighted region.
3. To enter formula and convert to an array formula press Ctrl, Shift, and Enter keys on the keyboard at the same time.

Remember to repeat this procedure each time you add a new array formula or edit a current array formula. If you do this properly, Excel will display the formula enclosed in curly brackets { }. You do not type in the curly brackets, Excel will display them automatically.

Plotting count versus bin for the histogram and total versus bin for the cumulative probability gives Figure 11.28.

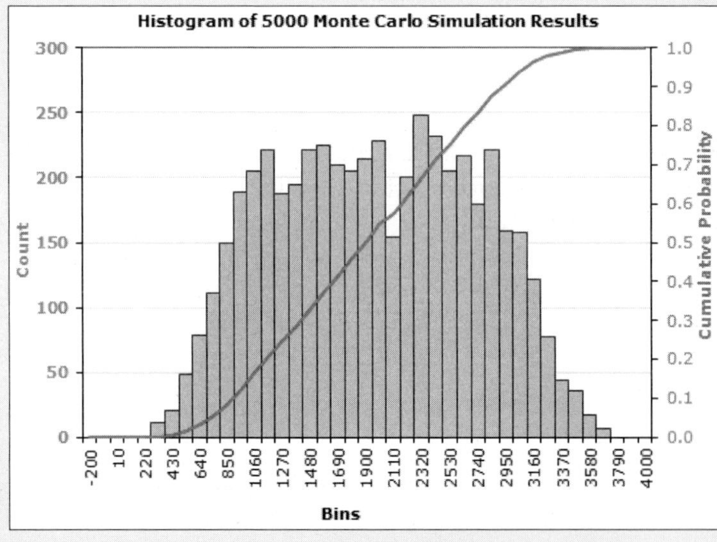

Figure 11.28

From the histogram in Figure 11.28 we note:

- It appears that the profit is always positive.
- The uncertainty is quite large.
- The distribution looks like a normal distribution.
- From the histogram there does not appear to be any extreme values (or outliers).

6. Use of Excel functions to calculate probabilities as illustrated in Figure 11.29

For example, what percentage of the results were less than £700?

This question is answered using the percent rank function: = PERCENTRANK.INC (array, x), where the array is the data range and x is £700. If x matches one of the values in the array, this function is equivalent to the Excel formula: = (RANK(x)-1)/(N-1), where N is the number of data points. If x does not match one of the values, then the PERCENTRANK.INC function interpolates.

	B	C
52	P(x < 700)	
53		
54	x =	700.00
55	Pr(x < 700) =	0.04

Figure 11.29

→ Excel solution

x = Cell C54	Value
P(x < 700) = Cell C55	Formula: = PERCENTRANK.INC(N28:N5027,C57,4)

Interpretation The probability of x < 700 is 4%.

11.2.2 Calculating minimum sample size

There are numerous situations where the leading criterion for using a simulation is the level of confidence that we are interested to achieve. In this section we will discuss a method to estimate the number of simulations (or samples) required for the output statistic to be accurate to within $\pm\delta$ with confidence α. Monte Carlo simulation estimates the true mean (μ) of the output distribution by summing the simulation values and dividing by the number of simulations:

$$\hat{\mu} = \frac{\sum_{i=1}^{n} x_i}{n} \tag{11.23}$$

If Monte Carlo simulation is employed then each X_i is an independent sample from the same distribution and the distribution of the estimate of the true mean ($\hat{\mu}$), is given by Equation (11.24):

$$\hat{\mu} = \text{Normal}\left(\mu, \frac{\sigma}{\sqrt{n}}\right) \tag{11.24}$$

Where σ is the true standard deviation of the model's output. Equation (11.24) can be modified to make the true mean (μ) the subject of the equation by using a statistical principle called the pivotal method as illustrated by Equation (11.25):

$$\mu = \text{Normal}\left(\hat{\mu}, \frac{\sigma}{\sqrt{n}}\right) \tag{11.25}$$

Figure 11.30 illustrates the cumulative form of the normal distribution where the chosen level of confidence (α) we specify to estimate the mean is translated into a relationship between δ, σ, and n (in Figure 11.30 we have plotted the CDF with $\mu = 0$, $\sigma = 2$, $n = 100$).

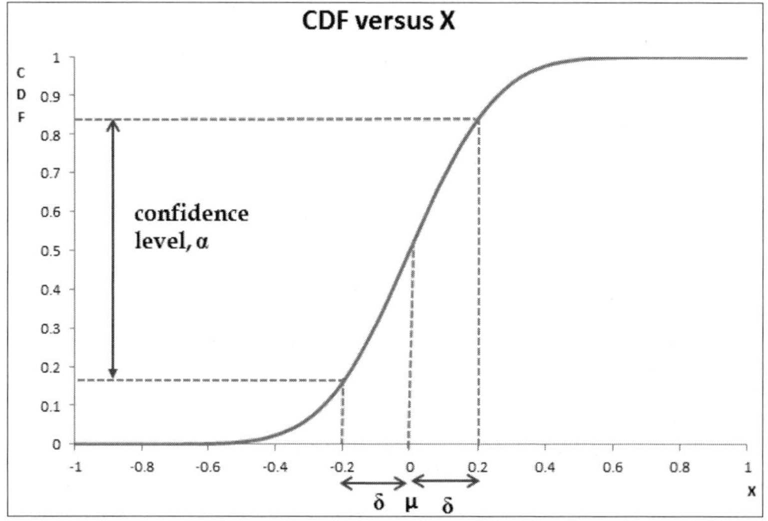

Figure 11.30

From Figure 11.30, we can rewrite Equation (11.25) in terms of δ, σ, n, and the cumulative density function (CDF) as illustrated by Equation (11.26):

$$\delta = \frac{\sigma}{\sqrt{n}} \Phi^{-1}\left(\frac{1+\alpha}{2}\right) \tag{11.26}$$

Where $\Phi^{-1}(x)$ is the inverse of the standard normal cumulative distribution function where mean = 0, and standard deviation = 1. If we now re-arrange Equation (11.26) to make 'n' the subject of the equation as illustrated in Equation (11.27):

$$n = \left(\frac{\sigma \times \Phi^{-1}\left(\frac{1+\alpha}{2}\right)}{\delta}\right)^2 \tag{11.27}$$

Example 11.12

Calculate the minimum number of simulations for a 90% confidence interval for the population mean given that we wish to have an accuracy of ±2. The population standard deviation has been estimated from the first 100 simulations and found to be equal to 23.

	A	B	C	D
1	Example 11.12			
2				
3		Confidence interval, α=	0.9	
4		(1+α)/2 =	0.95	=(1+C3)/2
5		Inverse standard normal distribution function, $\Phi^{-1}(x)$ =	1.644853627	=NORM.INV(C4,0,1)
6				
7		Accuracy, δ =	2	
8		Estimate population standard deviation, σ =	23	
9		Estimate of sample size, n =	357.8081218	=(C8*C5/C7)^2
10		Estimate of minimum sample size, n =	358	=INT(C9)+1

Figure 11.31

→ Excel solution

Confidence interval, α = Cell C3	Value
(1+α)/2 = Cell C4	Formula: = (1+C3)/2
Inverse standard normal distribution function, Φ-1(x) = Cell C5	Formula: = NORM.INV(C4,0,1)
Accuracy, δ = Cell C7	Value
Estimate population standard deviation, σ = Cell C8	Value
Estimate of sample size, n = Cell C9	Formula: = (C8*C5/C7)^2
Estimate of minimum sample size, n = Cell C10	Formula: = INT(C9)+1

Interpretation Minimum sample size of 358 simulations to achieve an accuracy of ±2 with confidence 90%.

11.2.3 Savage's 'flaw of averages'

A common cause of bad models is an error called the flaw of averages, which may be stated as follows: plans based on average assumptions are wrong on average. Savage describes a set of common avoidable mistakes in assessing risk in the face of uncertainty and which help to explain why conventional methods of gauging the future are so wrong so often. Savage introduced the concept of uncertainty versus risk, where two people might look at the same uncertainty but, with different risk attitudes, will perceive very different risks. The concept behind the flaw of averages is to realize that an uncertain number is a not a single number, but a shape (a 'distribution') with a range of possibilities. If you start doing calculations with uncertain numbers, then the average output is almost certainly not the calculation done with average. The average (or expected) profit is very likely less than the profit associated with average demand. The solution to the 'flaw of averages' is to embrace uncertainty and take advantage of the cheap and ubiquitous computing power that surrounds us. Monte Carlo simulation can allow us to play with thousands of scenarios and quickly and easily see how the decisions we take can affect the distribution of the outcomes we care about.

Example 11.13

To illustrate why this is important consider the following problem that compares the output solution for a deterministic problem that uses a best guess with a simulation model that incorporates uncertainty explicitly using Monte Carlo simulation.

Problem

A local bookshop is considering placing an order for a book that sells for £18.50 but costs the bookshop £14.50 per copy. The decision date for the order is on 1 June with all unsold copies being returned to the publisher with a refund per copy of £4.53. Based upon previous experience the bookshop expects that the average number of copies sold by 1 June will be expected to be 100.

Deterministic solution

In this case we will assume that the bookshop will order to the average demand of 100 copies. Figure 11.32 illustrates the Excel solution for the deterministic model.

	A	B	C	D
1	Example 11.13 Flaw of averages			
2				
3		Input cost data:		
4		Unit cost =	£14.50	
5		Unit price =	£18.50	
6		Unit refund =	£4.53	
7				
8		Decision variable:		
9		Order quantity =	100	
10				
11	Deterministic model			
12				
13		Uncertain quantity:		
14		Demand (average) =	100	=C9
15				
16		Profit model:		
17				
18		Revenue =	£1,850.00	=C5*MIN(C14,C9)
19		Cost =	£1,450.00	=C4*C9
20		Refund =	£0.00	=C6*MAX(C9-C14,0)
21		Profit =	£400.00	=C18-C19+C20

Figure 11.32

→ Excel solution

Unit cost = Cell C4 Value
Unit price = Cell C5 Value
Unit refund = Cell C6 Value
Order quantity= Cell C9 Value
Demand (average) = Cell C14 Formula: = C9
Revenue = Cell C18 Formula: = C5*MIN(C14,C9)
Cost = Cell C19 Formula: = C4*C9
Refund = Cell C20 Formula: = C6*MAX(C9-C14,0)
Profit = Cell C21 Formula: = C18-C19+C20

Interpretation The deterministic model suggests that if the bookshop orders the average number of copies of 100 on 1 June then the average expected profit will be £400.

Monte Carlo simulation solution

In the deterministic model, the order size equates to the average demand of 100 copies which is the expected value and is subject to uncertainty. To model the uncertainty in the average demand we replace the 100 (see cell C14) with a probability distribution. If we assume that this is a normal distribution and an estimate of the variables standard deviation is provided (say 15) then we can use the following simulated variable equation to estimate the average demand: =(NORM.INV(RAND(), C27,C28). Figure 11.33 illustrates the Excel solution for the simulation model with one simulation.

	A	B	C	D
23	Simulation model			
24				
25		Uncertain quantity (assumed normal, mu=100, sigma=15):		
26				
27		mu =	£100.00	
28		sigma =	£15.00	
29		demand (average) =	79	=ROUND(NORM.INV(RAND(),C27,C28),0)
30				
31				
32		Profit model:		
33				
34		revenue =	£1,461.50	=C5*MIN(C29,C9)
35		Cost =	£1,450.00	=C4*C9
36		Refund =	£95.13	=C6*MAX(C9-C29,0)
37		Profit =	£106.63	=C34-C35+C36

Figure 11.33

→ Excel solution

Mu = Cell C27	Value
Sigma = Cell C28	Value
Demand (average) = Cell C29	Formula: = ROUND(NORM.INV(RAND(),C27,C28),0)
Revenue = Cell C34	Formula: = C5*MIN(C29,C9)
Cost = Cell C35	Formula: = C4*C9
Refund = Cell C36	Formula: = C6*MAX(C9-C29,0)
Profit = Cell C37	Formula: = C34-C35+C36

Interpretation From Excel, conducting one simulation results in an expected profit of £106.63 with an expected demand of 79 copies of the book.

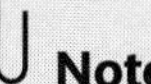

Note

1. The ROUND function is used to output the calculated value to zero decimal place.
2. Press the F9 keyboard key to re-calculate if you have stopped automatic recalculation.

If we pressed the F9 key on the computer keyboard these values in cells C29, C34-C37 would change, given that the Excel function RAND() changes values in the Excel formula in cell C29. We know that when the average demand equals 100 the deterministic expected profit is £400, and when the simulated average demand is 79 the expected profit is now £106.63. What happens to the expected profit if we undertake 1000 simulations? Figures 11.34 and 11.35 illustrate the Excel solution for 1000 simulations, with only six simulations illustrated in the screenshot.

	G	H	I	J	K	L
32	Simulation	Demand (random)	Revenue	Cost	Refund	Profit
33	1	105	£1,850.00	£1,450.00	£0.00	£400.00
34	2	107	£1,850.00	£1,450.00	£0.00	£400.00
35	3	107	£1,850.00	£1,450.00	£0.00	£400.00
36	4	103	£1,850.00	£1,450.00	£0.00	£400.00
37	5	89	£1,646.50	£1,450.00	£49.83	£246.33
38	6	96	£1,776.00	£1,450.00	£18.12	£344.12

Figure 11.34

	A	B	C	D
39	1000 simulations			
40				
41		min =	-£424.23	=MIN(L33:L1032)
42		max =	£400.00	=MAX(L33:L1032)
43		mean =	£314.57	=AVERAGE(L33:L1032)

Figure 11.35

→ Excel solution

Simulation Cell G33:G1032	Values
Demand (random) Cell H33	Formula: = ROUND(NORM.INV(RAND(),$C$27,$C$28),0) Copy formula down H33:H1032
Revenue Cell I33	Formula: = $C$5*MIN(H33,$C$9) Copy formula down I33:I1032
Cost Cell J33	Formula: = $C$4*$C$9 Copy formula down J33:J1032
Refund Cell K33	Formula: = $C$6*MAX($C$9-H33,0) Copy formula down K33:K1032
Profit Cell L33	Formula: = I33-J33+K33 Copy formula down L33:L1032
Min = Cell C41	Formula: = MIN(L33:L1032)
Max = Cell C42	Formula: = MAX(L33:L1032)
Mean = Cell C43	Formula: = AVERAGE(L33:L1032)

Interpretation From Excel, the expected mean value from the 1000 Monte Carlo simulations is £314.57. Furthermore, the simulated value is a great deal less than the deterministic value and illustrates the reason why the flaw of averages is an important concept in modelling with uncertainty.

Student exercises

Please visit the Online Resource Centre which accompanies this textbook for solutions to the student exercises and techniques in practice questions.

X11.9 XXX Appliance Repair Company Ltd is in the business of dispatching service personnel to repair two types of appliances. About 70% of the customers calling XXX want service of appliance type 1 and the remainder are for type 2. An analysis of the dispatch logs and the service records show the following:

(a) The travel time for the technicians to get to/from customer locations is normal with mean of 30 minutes and standard deviation of 5 minutes.

(b) The time to repair appliance 1 can be 20, 25, 30, or 35 minutes, with associated probabilities 0.1, 0.4, 0.3, and 0.2 respectively. For appliance 2 the repair time is 15, 30, or 60 minutes with probability 0.2, 0.3, and 0.5 respectively.

Use 500 Monte Carlo simulations to provide an estimate of the probability that the total travel time is less than 58 minutes.

X11.10 (a) Reconsider X11.9 where further research shows that the service time for appliance 2 are 20, 30, 40, 50 and 60 minutes with probabilities of 0.1, 0.2, 0.2, 0.2, and 0.3 respectively. Modify the X11.9 Excel solution to accommodate these changes. In general, how does this total time change compared with your answer to X11.9?

(b) Suppose that the service time for appliance 1 is uniform between 20 and 40 minutes. How will the service time formula in Excel change?

(c) State the equation you would use if you were required to calculate the number of simulations required to provide a 95% confidence interval (Hint: assume distribution normal).

X11.11 A production line turns out about 50 trucks per day; fluctuations occur for many reasons. Finished trucks are transported by train at the end of the day. If the train capacity is only 51 what will be the average number of trucks waiting to be shipped and what will be the average number of empty spaces on the train?

(a) Devise a model to calculate these values, if the daily production values are known as follows: 49, 49, 51, 49, 50, 51, 54, and 48.

(b) Replace the daily production values with 200 simulations using the RAND () function and the probability distribution as in Table 11.4.

Production per day	Probability
45	0.03
46	0.05
47	0.07
48	0.10
49	0.15
50	0.20
51	0.15
52	0.10
53	0.07
54	0.05
55	0.03
Total =	1.00

Table 11.4

Hint:

i. Trucks waiting = trucks left overnight + day's production.

ii. If trucks waiting ≥ 51, then the empty spaces = 0, and trucks left overnight = trucks waiting - 51.

iii. If trucks waiting < 51, then empty spaces = 51 - trucks waiting, and trucks left overnight = 0.

X11.12 King Kong restaurant stocks a popular brand of Chinese cake. Previous experience indicates that the daily demand for the next ten days is as follows: 25, 25, 35, 35, 35, 35, 35, 45, 25, and 25. Assuming the restaurant bakes 30 cakes per day, create an Excel solution table to calculate over ten days: (a) the number of available cakes per day, (b) the number of cakes spare at the end of the day after shipment, (c) the number of cakes that we are short to meet demand, and (d) the average daily cake demand over the ten days. (Assume that the use by date for each cake > 10 days.)

X11.13 Reconsider X11.12. After further research the daily demand is deemed to be unknown but the following probability distribution data (Table 11.5) has been collected from King Kong restaurant:

Daily demand	Probability
0	0.01
15	0.15
25	0.20
35	0.50
45	0.12
50	0.02

Table 11.5

Modify the X11.12 Excel solution to simulate demand for ten days and state the average daily cake demand over the ten days.

X11.14 A production line produces a packet which contains six products with a 10% probability of a product being defective: (a) calculate the expected probability that a packet contains no defective products, and (b) use Monte Carlo simulation to undertake ten simulations and compare your result with part (a).

X11.15 Repeat X11.14 but solve using the Excel function CRITBINOM.

X11.16 A bakery keeps stock of a popular brand of cake. Previous experience shows the demand pattern for the item with associated probabilities, as given in Table 11.6.

Daily demand	0	10	20	30	40	50
Probability	0.01	0.20	0.15	0.50	0.12	0.02

Table 11.6

(a) Use the following sequence of random numbers to simulate the demand for the next ten days: 40, 19, 87, 83, 73, 84, 29, 9, 2, and 20.

(b) Estimate the daily average demand for the cakes on the basis of the simulated data.

X11.17 Repeat X11.16 but simulate demand using the Excel RANDBETWEEN function.

X11.18 A bookshop wishes to carry a particular book in stock. Demand is probabilistic and replenishment of stock takes two days (i.e. if an order is placed on 1 March it will be delivered at the end of the day on 3 March). The probabilities of demand are given in Table 11.7.

Daily demand	0	1	2	3	4
Probability	0.05	0.10	0.30	0.45	0.10

Table 11.7

Each time an order is placed, the store incurs an ordering cost of £10 per order. The store also incurs a carrying cost of £0.50 per book per day. The inventory carrying cost is calculated on the basis of stock at the end of the day. The manager of the bookshop wishes to compare two options for his inventory decision:

A. Order five books when the inventory at the beginning of the day plus orders outstanding is less than eight books.

B. Order eight books when the inventory at the beginning of the day plus orders outstanding is less than eight books.

Currently (beginning of day 1) the store has a stock of eight books plus six books ordered two days ago and expected to arrive next day. Using Monte Carlo simulation for ten cycles, recommend which option the manager should choose (in this exercise use the following random numbers to simulate daily demand: 89, 34, 78, 63, 61, 81, 39, 16, 13, and 73).

X11.19 Repeat X11.18 but with the random numbers generated using the Excel RANBETWEEN function.

X11.20 In this exercise use Monte Carlo simulation with 10,000 simulations to model the following scenario that provide three steps that a motorist takes in travelling to work:

(a) Drive 2 miles on an A road, with a 90% probability that you will be able to average 65 miles per hour the whole distance, but with a 10% probability that a traffic jam will result in an average speed of 20 miles per hour.

(b) The motorist comes to a traffic light at the end of the A road that is red for 90 seconds, then green for 30 seconds.

(c) The motorist drives two more miles with the following probability distributions: 70% probability of travelling at 30 miles per hour, 10% probability of travelling at 20 miles per hour, 10% of the time of travelling at 40 miles per hour, and 10% of the time that the motorist will be slowed down by a traffic jam to complete the final two miles at 30 miles per hour.

From the simulation results answer the following two questions:

(a) How much time would the motorist need for a 75% confidence of arriving on time?

(b) How much time would the motorist need for a 99.5% confidence of arriving on time?

Hint: Convert all variables to time: seconds.

Scenario 1 model: Segment 1 = IF (RAND () < 0.9, 111, 360)

Scenario 2 model: Traffic light = MAX (0, (RAND ()*120)-30)

Scenario 3 model: Segment 2 = VLOOKUP (RAND(), LOOKUP TABLE, 2)

X11.21 Core Mining Ltd mine for gold in a number of locations in Australia. Table 11.8 provides conversion factors and estimates of variables which can be used to calculate the expected profit.

Amount of gold mined (t)	1,000,000
Gold grade (g/t Au)	1.68
Gold price (U$/oz Au)	1200
Exchange rate (A$/U$)	0.92
Mine unit cost ($/t)	40
Process unit cost ($/t)	25

Table 11.8

(a) Setup an Excel model to calculate total cost ($), total revenue ($), and total profit ($) for data problem given in Table X11.8. What is the average profit? (The conversion factor to convert ounces to grams is 1 ounce = 31.10419907 grams.)

(b) Modify the Excel model to conduct 1000 Monte Carlo simulations of your model where the exchange rate is allowed to vary as a normal distribution with mean 0.92 and standard deviation 0.02. What is the average profit? (Hint: Use the Excel function NORM.INV(RAND(), 0.92, 0.02) which will generate a random exchange rate with a distribution normal with mean = 0.93 A$/U$ and a spread of approximately 6 cents each way e.g. there will be a 99.7% probability of the exchange rate between 0.86 → 0.98 A$/U$.)

X11.22 Use Monte Carlo simulation with 1000 and 10,000 simulations to provide an estimate of π.

X11.23 Use Monte Carlo simulation with 500 and 10,000 simulations to provide an estimate of the probability $P(0 \leq Z \leq 1)$ in the standardized normal distribution.

11.3 Monte Carlo simulation software

The popularity of Monte Carlo methods has led to a number of good commercial tools. Table 11.9 provides a list of software products which work directly with Excel as add-ins including software cost estimates (June 2011) and web addresses for further product information.

Commercial software packages	Web address (accessed 25th May 2012)
@Risk	http://www.palisade.com/risk
Oracle Crystal Ball	http://www.oracle.com/us/products/middleware/bus-int/crystalball/index-066566.html
Risk Solver Pro for Excel	http://www.solver.com/platform/risk-solver-pro.htm
Risk Analyzer	http://www.add-ins.com/analyzer
RiskAmp	http://www.riskamp.com
Witness	http://www.lanner.com

Table 11.9

Free or open source software packages	Web address (accessed 25th May 2012)
Fairmat	http://www.fairmat.com
ModelRisk 4 Standard	http://www.vosesoftware.com
MonteCarlito 1.10	http://www.montecarlito.com
SimulAr	http://www.simularsoft.com.ar

Table 11.9 *(cont'd)*

Techniques in practice

TP1 Bakers Ltd keeps stock of a popular brand of cake. Previous experience shows the demand pattern for the item with associated probabilities, as given in Table 11.10.

Daily demand	0	20	40	60	70	80
Probability	0.05	0.15	0.20	0.45	0.10	0.05

Table 11.10

(a) Use the Excel RANDBETWEEN function to simulate the demand for the next ten days.

(b) Estimate the daily average demand for the cakes on the basis of the simulated data.

TP2 Coco S.A. supplies a range of computer hardware and software to 2000 schools within a large municipal region of Spain. The company is concerned at the time taken to respond to complaints from the contract schools. The latest data collected by the company suggests that the time to respond to complaints can be modeled using either of the following two scenarios: (a) uniform distribution with minimum and maximum values of 2 and 16 respectively, and (b) normal distribution with mean and standard deviation of 8 and 2 respectively. In both cases undertake 1000 simulations and provide an estimate of the average time to react to customer complaints.

TP3 Skodel Ltd is producing a new low calorie lager where the design mean is 43 calories per 100 ml with a standard deviation of 8 calories per 100 ml. Use this information to undertake 5000 simulations. Calculate the average calorific value from the 5000 simulations.

Summary

This chapter provided an introduction to the concept of Monte Carlo simulation which allows uncertainty to be explicitly built into the model. Furthermore, the application of Excel is utilized to perform the required numerical calculations to solve a range of business problems.

Student exercise answers

For all figures listed below, please see the Online Resource Centre.

X11.1 (a) 0.46, (b) 0.54 (both answers will be variable due to RAND () function).

X11.2 (a) 0.54, (b) 0.46 (both answers will be variable due to RAND () function).

X11.3 (a) 0.31, (b) 0.28 (both answers will be variable due to RAND () function).

X11.4 (a) 321.5120, (b) variance from Equation (11.3) = 3333.33′, variance from simulation = 3402.4427, (c) P (X ≥ 320) = 0.4940, (d) P (X ≥ 380) = 0.2120, € P (440 ≤ X ≤ 460) = 0.0000 (all answers will be variable due to RAND () function, except the variance value from Equation (11.3)).

X11.5 (a) mean from Equation (11.6) = 183.33′, mean from simulation = 182.8096, (b) P (X > 202) = 0.1050, (c) P (175 ≤ X ≤ 192) = 0.3875 0000 (all answers will be variable due to RAND () function, except the mean value from Equation (11.6)).

X11.6 (a) P (X ≥ 230) = 0.5, (b) P (X < 189) = 0.0225, (c) P (X > 294) = 0.0050, (d) P (206 ≤ X ≤ 254) for values of k = 1, 2, 3 are 0.7200, 0.9700, and 1.0000 respectively (the theoretical values would be approximately 0.68, 0.95, 0.98).

X11.7 (a) Expected value for both distributions = £1,550,000, (b) uniform model: = min + (max − min)*RAND(), normal model = NORM.INV (RAND(), mu, sigma), (c) uniform distribution average = £1,546,057.42 and normal distribution average = £1,548,189.40. (All answers will be variable due to RAND () function, except for parts (a), and (b)).

X11.8 Average profit = £194,958.43 (answer will be variable due to RAND () function).

X11.9 P (X < 58) = 0.356 (answer will be variable due to RAND () function).

X11.10 (a) P (X < 58) = 0.3525 (answer will be variable due to RAND () function), (b) Old formula: =IF(K5=1,VLOOKUP(RAND(),$C$6:$D$10,2),VLOOKUP(RAND(),$G$6:$H$11,2)) & new formula: '=IF(K5=1,Q26+(Q27-Q26)*RAND(),VLOOKUP(RAND(),$G$6:$H$11,2)), (c) 95% confidence interval for μ = simulation average ± 1.96*simulation sample standard deviation/square root of number of simulations.

X11.11 (a) Average number of trucks waiting to be shipped and the average number of empty spaces on the train will be 50.13 and 0.88 respectively, (b) Average number of trucks waiting to be shipped and the average number of empty spaces on the train will be 50.05 and 0.96 respectively (answers will be variable due to RAND () function).

X11.12 The average daily cake demand over the ten days = 32.

X11.13 The average daily cake demand over the ten days = 31 (answer will be variable due to RAND () function).

X11.14 (a) P (X = 0) = 0.53, and (b) P (X = 0) using 10 simulations = 0.40 (answer will be variable due to RAND () function).

X11.15 (a) P (X = 0) = 0.53, and (b) P (X = 0) using 10 simulations = 0.53 (answer will be variable due to RAND () function).

X11.16 Expected daily demand = 22.

X11.17 Expected daily demand = 28 (answer will be variable due to RANDBETWEEN () function).

X11.18 Since option B has a lower cost (£52.50) than option A (£59.50), then the manager should choose option B.

X11.19 Since option B has a lower cost than option A, then the manager should choose option B (answer will be variable due to RANDBETWEEN () function).

X11.20 75% and 99.5% confidence interval is 7.85 and 36.43 respectively (answers will be variable due to RAND () function).

X11.21 (a) Average profit = £5,450,434.78, (b) average profit = £5,449,372.95 (answer will be variable due to RAND () function).

X11.22 The value of π from 1000 and 10,000 simulations is 3.176 and 3.1384 respectively with a correct value of π to 15 decimal places = 3.14159 26535 89793 (answer will be variable due to RAND () function).

X11.23 The value of $P(0 \leq Z \leq 1)$ from 500 and 10,000 simulations is 0.332 and 0.3437 with a correct value of 0.3413 to 4 decimal places.

TP1 Expected daily demand = 56 (answer will be variable due to RANDBETWEEN () function).

TP2 Uniform distribution and normal distribution average times are 8.9 and 7.9 days (answers will be variable due to RAND () and NORM.INV functions).

TP3 Average calorific value from the 5000 simulations is 43.03 95 (answer will be variable due to RAND () function).

■ Further reading

Each chapter to include identified further reading resources that can be accessed by students. This list will include traditional textbooks and online resources in statistics and the application of the Excel spreadsheet.

Textbook resources

1. S. C. Albright, C. J. Zappe, and W. L. Winston (2011) *Data Analysis, Optimization, and Simulation Modelling* (4th edn), Cengage Learning.
2. J. R. Evans (2010) *Statistics, Data Analysis, and Decision Modelling* (4th edn), Pearson.
3. George S. Fishman (2003) *Monte Carlo: Concepts, Algorithms, and Applications*, Springer.
4. S. L. Savage (2000) *The Flaw of Averages: Why We Underestimate Risk in the Face of Uncertainty*, Wiley.
5. D. Vose (1996) *Quantitative Risk Analysis: A Guide to Monte Carlo Simulation Modelling*, Wiley.
6. D. Vose (2007) *Risk Analysis: A Quantitative Guide* (3rd edn), Wiley.

Web resources

1. **http://office.microsoft.com/en-us/excel-help/statistical-functions-HP005203066.aspx (accessed 25 May 2012).**
2. ExcelFunctions.net **http://www.excelfunctions.net (accessed 25 May 2012).**

Formula summary

$$f(x) = \frac{1}{\max - \min} \tag{11.1}$$

$$\text{Mean} = \frac{\max + \min}{2} \tag{11.2}$$

$$\text{Variance} = \frac{(\max - \min)^2}{12} \tag{11.3}$$

$$f(x) = \frac{2(x-a)}{(b-a)(c-a)} \text{ if } a \le x \le b \tag{11.4}$$

$$f(x) = \frac{2(c-a)}{(c-a)(c-b)} \text{ if } b \le x \le c \tag{11.5}$$

$$\text{Mean} = \frac{a+b+c}{3} \tag{11.6}$$

$$\text{Variance} = \frac{a^2+b^2+c^2-ab-ac-bc}{18} \tag{11.7}$$

$$f(x) = \frac{1}{\sigma\sqrt{2\pi}} e\left[-\frac{(x-\mu)^2}{2\sigma^2}\right] \tag{11.8}$$

$$\text{Mean} = \mu \tag{11.9}$$

$$\text{Variance} = \sigma^2 \tag{11.10}$$

$$P(X = x) = \binom{n}{x} p^x q^{n-x} \tag{11.11}$$

$$\text{Mean} = np \tag{11.12}$$

$$\text{Variance} = npq \tag{11.13}$$

$$P(X = x) = \frac{\lambda e^{-\lambda}}{x!} \tag{11.14}$$

$$\text{Mean} = \lambda \tag{11.15}$$

$$\text{Variance} = \lambda \tag{11.16}$$

$$\text{Profit per month (P)} = \text{revenue per month} - \text{costs per month} = R - C \tag{11.17}$$

$$R = N * PS \tag{11.18}$$

$$R = NLM * PLS * PS \tag{11.19}$$

$$C = FC + TCL \tag{11.20}$$

$$TCL = NLM * CL \tag{11.21}$$

$$C = FC + NLM * CL \tag{11.22}$$

$$P = NLM * PLS * PS - (FC + NLM * CL) \tag{11.23}$$

$$\hat{\mu} = \frac{\sum_{i=1}^{n} X_i}{n} \tag{11.24}$$

$$\hat{\mu} = \text{Normal}\left(\mu, \frac{\sigma}{\sqrt{n}}\right) \tag{11.25}$$

$$\mu = \text{Normal}\left(\hat{\mu}, \frac{\sigma}{\sqrt{n}}\right) \tag{11.26}$$

$$\delta = \frac{\sigma}{\sqrt{n}} \Phi^{-1}\left(\frac{1+\alpha}{2}\right) \tag{11.27}$$

$$n = \left(\frac{\sigma \times \Phi^{-1}\left(\frac{1+\alpha}{2}\right)}{\delta}\right)^2 \tag{11.28}$$

Glossary of key terms

a priori probability method assumes that you already know what the probability should be from a theoretical understanding of the experiment being conducted.

Abstractiveness availability of appropriate data and information.

Acceptance sampling acceptance sampling is used by industries worldwide for assuring the quality of incoming and outgoing goods.

Acceptance sampling process acceptance sampling uses statistical sampling to determine whether to accept or reject a production lot of material.

Accuracy it is the difference between the average, or mean, of a number of readings and the true, or target, value.

Activities specific jobs or tasks that are components of a project.

Activity cost function a methodology that measures the cost of activities, resources, and cost objects.

Activity on arrow a network diagram showing sequence of activities, in which each activity is represented by an arrow, with a circle representing a node or event at each end.

Activity on node a network where activities are represented by a box or a node linked by dependencies.

Addition law the addition rule is a result used to determine the probability that event A or event B occurs or both occur.

Additive model A model from the classical decomposition method that assumes that the components are related in an additive way.

Aggregate price indices monitors the way that price changes over time.

Algebra use of symbols to represent variables and describe the relationships between them.

Allocating resources apportioning shared resources, e.g. men, machines, time, finance, among the users of those resources, usually in a measured economic fashion to reduce cost for example.

Alpha, α Alpha refers to the probability that the true population parameter lies outside the confidence interval. In a time series context, i.e. exponential smoothing, alpha is the smoothing constant.

Alternative hypothesis a hypothesis that is true when we reject the null hypothesis.

Annuity amount invested to give a fixed income over some period.

Answer report a report obtainable from using Solver indicating the solution variables and their values.

Arithmetic calculations with numbers.

Arithmetic mean the average of a set of numbers.

ARMINA Auto Regressive Integrated Moving Average. A type of the stochastic model that describes the time series by using both the auto regressive and the moving average component.

Assignable causes also known as 'special cause'. An assignable cause is an identifiable, specific cause of variation in a given process or measurement.

Autocorrelation Correlation between the time series with itself, but where the observations are shifted by a certain number of periods. The series of these autocorrelation coefficients for every time shift produces the autocorrelation function.

Average range average range calculated to monitor process variability.

Axes rectangular scales for drawing graphs.

Backward pass part of the PERT/CPM procedure that involves moving backwards through the network to determine the latest start and latest finish times for each activity.

Bar chart a diagram that represents the frequency of observations in a class by the length of bar.

Base period the fixed point of reference for an index.

Bayes' theorem Bayes' theorem is a result that allows new information to be used to update the conditional probability of an event.

Beta distribution the Beta distribution models events which are constrained to take place within an interval defined by a minimum and maximum value.

Beta, β Beta refers to the probability that a false population parameter lies inside the confidence interval.

Biased a systematic error in a sample.

Binomial distribution a binomial distribution can be used to model a range of discrete random data variables.

Binomial probability distribution is the discrete probability distribution of the number of successes in a sequence of n independent yes/no experiments, each of which yields success with probability p.

Binomial probability function the binomial distribution is a type of discrete probability distribution. It shows the probability of achieving 'd' successes in a sample of 'n' taken from an 'infinite' population where the probability of a success is 'p'.

Box and whisker plot is a way of summarizing a set of data measured on an interval scale.

Capacity planning is the process of determining the production capacity needed by an organization to meet changing demands for its products.

Category a set of data is said to be categorical if the values or observations belonging to it can be sorted according to category.

Central Limit Theorem states that whenever a random sample of size n is taken from any distribution with mean μ and variance σ^2, then the sample mean will be approximately normally distributed with mean μ and variance σ^2. The larger the value of the sample size n, the better the approximation to the normal.

Central tendency measures the location of the middle or the centre of a distribution.

Changing cell in a Solver model, one or more cells that feed into a target cell whose value is to be determined by the Solver. Changing cells will always be numerical values and will never contain formulae.

Chart used to refer to any form of graphical display.

Cherbyshev's theorem is an empirical rule that enables us to identify outliers.

Chi-squared distribution with k degrees of freedom is the distribution of a sum of the squares of k independent standard normal random variables. It is useful because, under reasonable assumptions, easily calculated quantities can be proven to have distributions that approximate to the chi-squared distribution if the null hypothesis is true.

Class range or entry in a frequency distribution.

Classical decomposition method approach to forecasting that decomposes a time series into constituent components (trend, cyclical, seasonal, and random component), makes estimates of every component and then recomposes the time series and extrapolates the values into the future.

Coefficient of correlation a value that indicates the strengths of relationship between two variables.

Coefficient of variation measures the spread of a set of data as a proportion of its mean. It is often expressed as a percentage.

Coefficient of determination the ration of the explained and the total variance. It provides a measure of how well the model describes the data set.

Coefficients of objective the variable multipliers in the objective function.

Common causes the common cause variation arises from a multitude of small factors that invariably affect any process and will conform to a normal distribution, or a distribution that is closely related to the normal distribution.

Common logarithms logarithm to the base 10.

Compound Annual Growth Rate (CAGR) the year-over-year growth rate of an investment over a specified period of time.

Compound interest arises when interest is added to the principal, so that, from that moment on, the interest that has been added also earns interest.

Conditional probability allows event probability values to be updated when new information is made available.

Confidence interval a confidence interval specifies a range of values within which the unknown population parameter may lie, e.g. mean.

Confidence level the confidence level is the probability value $(1 - \alpha)$ associated with a confidence interval.

Conservative approach (or pessimistic approach) would be used by a conservative decision maker to minimize payoff for each decision and then selecting the maximum of these minimum payoffs (Wald's maximin criterion rule).

Constraints restrictions or limitations imposed on a problem.

Constraints limitations upon the values that can be adopted by a target cell and/or changing cells that reflect the logical requirements of the model.

Continuous probability distribution if a random variable is a continuous variable, its probability distribution is called a continuous probability distribution.

Continuous quality improvement (CQI) the ongoing betterment of products, services, or processes through incremental and breakthrough enhancements.

Continuous variable a set of data is said to be continuous if the values belong to a continuous interval of real values.

Contribution the value of each variables contribution within the linear programming objective function and constraints.

Control chart control charts are used to monitor the output of a process. They generally monitor the process mean, the process variation, or a combination of both.

Convex polyhedron geometrically, the linear constraints define a convex polyhedron, which is called the feasible region.

Coordinate geometry values of x and y that define a point on Cartesian axes.

Crash cost cost of crashing a project.

Crash time time to crash a project.

Crashing the shortening of activity times by adding resources and hence usually increasing cost.

Crashing a network the shortening of activity times by adding resources and hence usually increasing cost.

Crashing a project shortening a project time by spending money to reduce critical activities, for example, working overtime.

Critical path the longest path in a project network.

Critical path activities the activities on the critical path.

Critical path analysis critical path analysis (and PERT) are powerful tools to help schedule and manage complex projects.

Critical path method (CPM) a network-based project scheduling procedure.

Critical test statistic the critical value for a hypothesis test is a limit at which the value of the sample test statistic is judged to be such that the null hypothesis may be rejected.

Cumulative frequency distribution the cumulative frequency for a value x is the total number of scores that are less than or equal to x.

Curve a curved line that visualises a non-linear function.

Cyclical component one of the components from the classical time series analysis that will define the long-term regularities (more than a year) of the movements of the time series.

Cyclical variations variations around the trend line that take place over a larger number of years.

Data collection the gathering of facts that can then be used to make decisions.

Data presentation the method used to present findings in numerical and graphical form.

Decimal fraction part of the whole described by a number following a decimal point, such as 0.2, 0.34.

Decision alternatives the decision maker develops a finite number of alternative decisions available when the decision model is developed.

Decision criteria simple rules that recommend an alternative for decisions with uncertainty.

Decision making make decisions based upon the data and information available.

Decision making process with risk implies a degree of uncertainty and an inability to fully control the outcomes or consequences of such an action.

Decision making under uncertainty the chance of an event (or events) occurring in the decision making process is unknown or difficult to assess.

Decision making with certainty the decision maker knows for sure (that is, with certainty) the outcome or consequence of every decision alternative.

Decision node points in a decision tree where decisions are made.

Decision tree diagram that represents a series of alternatives and events by the branches of a tree.

Decision variables a controllable set of inputs for a linear programming model.

Definite integral evaluation of the indefinite integral at two points to find the difference.

Degrees of freedom refers to the number of independent observations in a sample minus the number of population parameters that must be estimated from sample data.

Depreciation refers to the decrease in the value of assets.

Deseasonalized values of the variable from which any seasonal influences have been removed.

Deterministic describing a situation of certainty.

Deterministic model a deterministic model will give the same result output(s) based upon the same input(s).

Deviation a difference between the actual values in the series and the trend that approximates the time series.

Differentiation algebraic process to calculate the instantaneous rate of change of one variable.

Directed numbers the numbers which have a direction and a size are called directed numbers.

Directional test implies a direction for the implied hypothesis (one tailed test).

Discount rate value of r when discounting to present value.

Discounting value of $(1 + r)^{-n}$ when discounting to present value.

Discrete data where the values or observations belonging to it are distinct and separate.

Discrete probability distribution if a random variable is a discrete variable, its probability distribution is called a discrete probability distribution.

Dual price the improvement in the value of the optimal solution per unit increase in a constraint right-hand side value.

Dummy activities a dummy activity is a simulated activity of sorts, one that is of zero duration and is created for the sole purpose of demonstrating a specific relationship and path of action on the arrow diagramming method.

Earliest start time (EST) the earliest time an activity may begin.

Earliest finish time (EFT) the earliest time an activity may be completed.

Effective annual interest rate is the interest rate on a loan or financial product restated from the nominal interest rate as an interest rate with annual compound interest payable in arrears.

Empirical probability method whereby the value of a probability is based on measurement.

EOQ the optimal level of an inventory item that should be ordered periodically so that all relevant costs are minimized.

Equation algebraic formula that shows the relationship between variables, saying that the value of one expression equals the value of the second expression.

Equation of the line equation of the line representing the equation y = mx + c.

Error a difference between the active and predicted value (in the context of time series).

Estimate an estimate is an indication of the value of an unknown quantity based on observed data.

Event an instantaneous occurrence that changes the state of the system in a model.

Excel solver is an Excel add in that can solve for the values of one or more unknowns in a spreadsheet model.

Expected activity time the time that an activity is expected to take, an average from pessimistic, optimistic and most likely times.

Expected loss in this case we are looking to minimize the expected loss by choosing the alternative loss with the smallest expected loss.

Expected monetary value of perfect information the expected value of information that would tell the decision maker exactly which state of nature is going to occur (i.e. perfect information).

Expected time the average activity time.

Expected value in a mixed strategy game, a value computed by multiplying each payoff by its probability and summing. It can be interpreted as the long-run average payoff for the mixed strategy.

Expected value the mean of a probability distribution is called the expected value and can be found by multiplying each payoff value by its associated probability.

Explained variations also called the regression sum of squares (SSR). This is the portion of the variations between the actual and modelled data that can be explained by the model. Together with SSE, this produces the Total Sum of Squares (SST), or the total variations from the model.

Exponential smoothing method forecasting method that uses a constant (or several constants in some cases) to predict the future values by 'smoothing' the past values in the series. The effect of this constant decreases exponentially as the older observations are taken into calculation.

Ex-post forecasts the forecasts that are approximating the past (actual) values of the variable, as opposed to the true future forecasts. The ex-post forecasts are also called the fitted values.

F distribution a continuous statistical distribution which arises in the testing of whether two observed samples have the same variance.

Factor a coefficient or the value that indicates the rate of change of variable (multiplier).

Feasible region the set of all feasible solutions.

Feasible solution a decision alternative or solution that satisfies all constraints.

Finite population population with a fixed number of items.

Finite population correction factor it is common practice to use finite population correction factors in estimating variances when sampling from a finite population.

First derivative of y on x result of differentiating a function of the form y = f(x).

Five data summary consists of using also the minimum and maximum values together with the quartiles to summarize data.

Five-number summary a 5-number summary is especially useful when we have so many data that it is sufficient to present a summary of the data rather than the whole data set. It consists of 5 values: the most extreme values in the data set (maximum and minimum values), the lower and upper quartiles, and the median.

Fixed costs the portion of the total cost that does not depend on the volume; this cost remains the same no matter how much is produced.

Float the amount of time available for a task to slip before it results in a delay of the project end date. It is the difference between the task's early and late start dates.

Forecasting errors a series of differences between every actual and its corresponding forecasted value in the time series.

Forecasting horizon a number of future observations that are to be extrapolated.

Forecasting a method of predicting the future value of a variable, usually represented as the time series values.

Formulation formulating the linear programming equations based upon the information provided.

Forward pass part of the PERT/CPM procedure that involves moving forward through the project network to determine the earliest start and earliest finish times for each activity.

Four data summary the four data summary exploits a measure of dispersion together with quartiles that can also represent skewness.

Fraction part of the whole expressed as the ratio of a numerator over a denominator.

Frequency distribution diagram showing the number of observations in each class.

Function (as per P152) in this context a subprogram or a mini routine that converts a formula or an algorithm into a single value, or an array of values.

Future value value of an investment after a period of time.

Future value of an ordinary annuity (see sinking fund) a fund that receives regular payments so that a specified sum is available at some point in the future.

Gantt chart a bar chart that depicts a schedule of activities and milestones. Generally activities are listed along the left side of the chart and the time line along the top or bottom. The activities are shown as horizontal bars of a length equivalent to the duration of the activity. Gantt charts may be annotated with dependency relationships and other schedule-related information.

General addition law the addition rule is a result used to determine the probability that event A or event B occurs or both occur.

Goal programming a linear programming approach to multicriteria decision problems whereby the objective function is designed to minimize the deviations from goals.

Gradient a measure of how steeply a function is changing (dy/dx).

Gradient of the line gradient of the line of the form $y = mx + c$.

Graph used to refer to any form of graphical display.

Graphical method a method for solving linear programming problems with two decision variables on a two-dimensional graph.

Grouped data raw data already divided into classes.

Grouped frequency distribution data arranged in intervals to show the frequency with which the possible values of a variable occur.

Histogram frequency distribution for continuous data.

Holding costs the cost of holding a given level of inventory of a period of the production run. It is assumed to depend upon the average stock level, the purchase cost of the item, and a percentage of this cost representing the opportunity cost of the funds tied up.

Homoscedasicity also called homogeneity or uniformity of variance. Implies that the variance is finite, i.e. the variance around the regression line is constant for all values of the predictor.

Hurwicz criterion rule is a weighted average method that is a compromise between the optimistic and pessimistic decisions.

Hypothesis test procedure a series of steps to determine whether to accept or reject a null hypothesis, based on sample data.

Immediately preceding activities the activities that must be completed immediately prior to the start of a given activity.

Increasing the sum invested adding to the amount deposited at the end of each year to increase the sum invested.

Indefinite integral the reverse of differentiation.

Independent events are events that do not influence each other.

Index or index number a number that compares the value of a variable at any point in time with its value in a base period.

Infeasible solution a decision alternative or solution that does not satisfy one or more constraints.

Infeasible solution a solution for which at least one constraint is violated.

Instantaneous gradient gradient of a curve at a single point.

Integer programming a linear programme with the additional requirement that one or more of the variables must be integer.

Integration the reverse of differentiation.

Intercept a point at which the function crosses vertical y-axis.

Interest amount paid to lenders as reward for using their money.

Internal rate of return is a rate of return used in capital budgeting to measure and compare the profitability of investments - also called the discounted cash flow rate of return or the rate of return.

Interquartile range (IQR) the inter-quartile range is a measure of the spread of or dispersion within a data set.

Interval an interval scale is a scale of measurement where the distance between any two adjacent units of measurement (or 'intervals') is the same but the zero point is arbitrary.

Interval estimate is a range of values within which, we believe, the true population parameter lies with high probability.

Inventories items such as raw materials, components, finished, and semi-finished goods that are essential inputs in the process of manufacturing the firm's end products.

Inventory replacement is the rate at which the required amount of new inventory can be bearded to existing stock.

Irregular variations any variations around the trend line that are neither cyclical nor seasonal. Also used as another expression for errors or residuals.

Kurtosis is a measure of the 'peakedness' of the distribution.

Laplace equally likely criterion finds the decision alternative with the highest average payoff.

Laspeyres' index base-weighted index.

Latest finish time (LFT) the latest time an activity may be completed without increasing the project completion time.

Latest start time (LST) the latest time an activity may begin without increasing the project completion time.

Lead time the length of time between placing an inventory order and receipt of the delivery from the supplier. A lead time of zero implies immediate delivery, although this may either be in full or in batches.

Least squares method a method used to estimate parameters that will enable the fitting of a curve to a series of historical data. The criterion is that the sum of all squared differences between the fitted and actual data has to be the minimum value.

Limits report a report obtainable from using Solver. Range over which decision variables can change without breaking constraints while keeping one fixed.

Linear programming a mathematical model with a linear objective function, a set of linear constraints, and non-negative variables.

Linear regression a method that models relationships between a response variable and a predictor, or explanatory variable. This relationship has to be linear, i.e. described by a linear model.

Linear relationship a relationship between two variables of the form $y = ax + c$, giving a straight line graph.

Logarithm the value of n when a number is represented in the logarithmic format $b^n = x$.

Mathematical programming (MP) a family of techniques to optimize objectives when the resources are constrained.

Maximax criterion rule the optimistic decision maker chooses the largest possible payoff.

Maximizing the greatest value in the domain of a variable is its maximum.

Mean the average of a set of numbers.

Mean error the mean value of all the differences between the actual and forecasted values in the time series.

Mean square error the mean value of all the squared differences between the actual and forecasted values in the time series.

Measure of dispersion (or spread) showing how widely data is dispersed about its centre.

Measure of location showing the typical value for a set of data values.

Median the middle value of a set of numbers.

Microsoft Project computer software to plan and control projects.

Minimum criterion rule the optimistic decision maker chooses the lowest cost.

Minimizing the smallest value in the domain of a variable is its minimum.

Mode the most frequent value in a set of numbers.

Model an abstraction of reality i.e. as implified method of representing reality.

Modified internal rate of return is a modification of the internal rate of return which is a financial measure of an investment's attractiveness.

Monte Carlo simulation method is a computerized mathematical technique that allows people to account for risk in quantitative analysis and decision making.

Mortgage is a loan secured on the purchase of a property.

Most likely time the most likely activity time under normal conditions.

Moving averages a series of averages calculated for a rolling, or a moving, number of periods. Every subsequent interval excludes the first observation from the previous interval and includes the next observation following the previous period.

Multiplication rule of probability the multiplication rule is a result used to determine the probability that two events, A and B, both occur.

Multiplicative model a model from the classical decomposition method that assumes that the components are related in a multiplicative way.

Mutually exclusive events where only one can happen, but not both.

Natural logarithms logarithm to the base e.

Net present value is the difference between the present value of cash inflows and the present value of cash outflows.

Network analysis network analysis is an important project management tool used during the planning phase of a project. It demonstrates activities against fixed time frames and helps in controlling the sequence of activities in a project.

Network diagram a graphic tool for depicting the sequence and relationships between tasks in a project.

Node an intersection or junction point of an influence diagram or a decision tree.

Nominal data data for which there is no useful quantitative measure.

Non-linear programming an optimization problem that contains at least one non-linear term in the objective function, or a constraint.

Non-linear regression a method that models a relationship between a response variable and a predictor, or explanatory variable. This relationship has to be non-linear, i.e. described by a non-linear model.

Non-linear relationship a relationship between y and x that is not of the form $y = mx + c$ but depends upon the power of x, e.g. $y = x^2 + 4$.

Non-negativity constraints a set of constraints that requires all variables to be non-negative.

Non-parametric tests (also called distribution-free tests) are often used in face of their parametric counterparts when certain assumptions about the underlying population are questionable.

Normal cost the project cost under normal conditions.

Normal distribution is a continuous probability distribution that has a bell-shaped probability density function.

Normal probability plot graphical technique to assess whether the data is normally distributed.

Normal time the project time under normal conditions.

Null hypothesis the original hypothesis that is being tested.

Numbering the nodes of a network to identify points in the project, useful for project control as well as identifying the end and start of activities.

Number of combinations number of ways of selecting r items from n, when the order of selection does not matter.

Objectives what we are trying to achieve or optimise towards, e.g. maximizing profit.

Objective function a mathematical expression that describes the problem's objective.

One sample test is a statistical hypothesis test which uses one sample from the population.

One sample t-test a one sample t-test is a hypothesis test for answering questions about the mean where the data are a random sample of independent observations from an underlying normal distribution $N(\mu, \sigma^2)$, where σ^2 is unknown.

One-tail test a one tailed test is a statistical hypothesis test in which the values for which we can reject the null hypothesis, H_0, are located entirely in one tail of the probability distribution.

Operating characteristic curve the OC curve is used in sampling inspection. It plots the probability of accepting a batch of items against the quality level of the batch.

Operational these are everyday decisions used to support tactical decisions. Their impact is immediate, short-term, short range, and usually has a low impact cost to the organization.

Optimal solution a best feasible solution according to the objective function.

Optimizing the specific decision-variable value(s) that provide the 'best' output for the model.

Optimistic approach would be used by an optimistic decision maker where the largest possible payoff is chosen (maximax criterion rule).

Optimistic time an activity time estimate based on the assumption that the activity will progress in an ideal manner.

Ordering costs the cost of ordering a delivery of inventory from the supplier.

Ordinal data data that cannot be precisely measured, but that can be ranked or ordered.

Origin the point where x and y Cartesian axes cross.

Outcome the result of an experiment.

Outlier in statistics, an outlier is an observation that is numerically distant from the rest of the data.

Output cells the cells in a spreadsheet that provide output that depends on the changing cells.

Paasche index current-weighted index.

Parameter a single value (quantity) used to multiple a variable in an equation.

Parametric any statistic computed by procedures that assume the data were drawn from a particular distribution.

Parametric test hypothesis test that concerns the value of a parameter.

Pareto analysis a statistical method of identifying the extent to which the majority of stoppages in production can be attributed to stockouts in relatively few items.

Path a sequence of connected nodes that leads from the Start node to the Finish node.

Pattern a recurring and predictable sequence of values that look identical or similar.

Payoff table (or matrix) table that shows the outcomes for each combination of alternatives and events in a decision.

Percentage fraction expressed as a part of 100.

Percentile are values that divide a sample of data into one hundred groups containing (as far as possible) equal numbers of observations.

Permissable region a region inside the confidence interval that implies that certain values are not a result of random variations.

Permutation number of ways of selecting r items from n, when the order of selection is important.

Perpetual annuity is an annuity that has no end, or a stream of cash payments that continues forever.

Pessimistic (or conservative approach approach) would be used by a pessimistic decision maker to minimize payoff for each decision and then select the maximum of these minimum payoffs (Wald's maximin criterion rule).

Pessimistic time an activity time estimate based on the assumption that the most unfavourable conditions apply.

Pie chart diagram that represents the frequency of the observations in a class by the area of a circle.

Point estimate a point estimate (or estimator) is any quantity calculated from the sample data that is used to provide information about the population.

Point estimators in statistics, point estimation involves the use of sample data to calculate a single value which is to serve as a 'best guess' of an unknown population parameter.

Poisson distribution Poisson distributions model a range of discrete random data variables.

Poisson probability distribution is a discrete probability distribution that expresses the probability of a given number of events occurring in a fixed interval of time and/or space if these events occur with a known average rate and independently of the time since the last event.

Polynomial equations containing a variable raised to some power.

Population is any entire collection of people, animals, plants or things from which we may collect data.

Population mean (μ) mean value when taking into account the entire population of data values.

Population standard deviation (σ) standard deviation value when taking into account the entire population of data values.

Posterior probability is the new probability value based upon the original conditions and the new information identified.

Power value of n when a number is represented as x^n (x to the power n).

Precedence table table of predecessor tasks.

Precision is a measure of how close an estimator is expected to be to the true value of a parameter.

Predecessor task a task (or activity) that must be started or finished before another task or milestone can be performed.

Prediction interval an interval that will, given a certainty level or level of confidence, define the upper and lower value of the forecast within which the actual value is likely to fluctuate.

Present value is the current worth of a future sum of money or stream of cash flows given a specified rate of return.

Present value of a stream of earnings is the current worth of a future sum of money or stream of cash flows given a specified rate of return.

Present value of an ordinary annuity (see **trust fund**) is the value of a stream of expected or promised future payments that have been discounted to a single equivalent value today.

Primary data is data collected by the user.

Principal amount originally borrowed for a loan.

Prior probability is the original probability value before new information is identified.

Probabilistic (or stochastic) containing uncertainty that is measured by probabilities.

Probabilistic demand a situation in which the estimated demand for the end product, and therefore the inventory item, is subject to random variation rather than being known for certain.

Probability provides a number value to the likely occurrence of a particular event.

Probability distribution a description of the relative frequency of observations.

Probability sampling the concept of probability sampling assumes some form of random selection of the data and it is assumed that such data, even though random, represents the population.

Probability value (p-value) of a statistical hypothesis test is the probability of getting a value of the test statistic as extreme as or more extreme than that observed by chance alone, if the null hypothesis H_0 is true.

Process control is the manipulation of the conditions of a process to bring about a desired change in the output characteristics of the process.

Program Evaluation and Review Technique (PERT) a method of Critical Path Analysis that is designed for uncertain activity times.

Project planning a series of steps or actions to complete the project given the stated activity times and costs.

P-value the p-value is the probability of getting a value of the test statistic as extreme as or more extreme than that observed by chance alone, if the null hypothesis is true.

Quadratic equation equation with the general form $y = ax^2 + bx + c$.

Qualitative variable variables can be classified as descriptive or categorical.

Quality assurance having confidence that a service provides a quality service.

Quality control actions or methods that are used to ensure the quality of a product or service.

Quantitative variable variables can be classified using numbers.

Quartile quartiles are values that divide a sample of data into four groups containing (as far as possible) equal numbers of observations.

Quartile range difference in value between the third and first quartiles.

Questionnaire set of questions used to collect data.

R chart is a type of control chart used to monitor variable data when samples are collected at regular intervals from a business process.

Random a property that implies impossibility to predict precisely the future value. The general shape of a random time series is that without a trend and any regularity. This is the shape and the property that a series of errors should have after fitting a forecasting model to a time series and subtracting the corresponding values.

Random experiment is a sampling technique where we select a group of subjects (a sample) for study from a larger group (a population). Each individual is chosen entirely by chance and each member of the population has a known, but possibly non-equal, chance of being included in the sample. By using random sampling, the likelihood of bias is reduced.

Range difference between largest and smallest values in a data set.

Rate interest rate per annum.

Ratio ratio data are continuous data where both differences and ratios are interpretable and have a natural zero.

Raw data raw facts that are processed to give information.

Redundant constraint a constraint that does not affect the feasible region.

Region of rejection the range of values that leads to rejection of the null hypothesis.

Regression a generic name for a method that describes and predicts movements of one variable with another related variable.

Relative frequency relative frequency is another term for proportion; it is the value calculated by dividing the number of times an event occurs by the total number of times an experiment is carried out.

Re-order stock level the level of current inventory that triggers an order for more stock.

Re-order time the time at which an order for more inventory must be placed. This will depend upon the usage rate, the lead time, the replenishment rate, and the initial amount of stock that was received.

Replenishment rate the rate at which inventory that has been ordered is delivered by the supplier. This may be in full or in lots or batches over a period of time.

Residuals the same as errors, i.e. the differences between the actual and predicted values. Also used for unexplained variations after fitting a regression model.

Resource allocation resources allocated to complete the tasks in a project.

Resource histogram a block diagram representing the sum of the activity resources at a particular point in time.

Return-to-risk ratio the observed average return divided by the standard deviation of returns. This is the simplest measure of return to risk trade-off and can be used to compare portfolio returns.

Risk averter implies that the decision maker would be cautious of investing any more funds within this investment.

Risk neutral implies that for every extra unit of currency provided the change in utility would be constant.

Risk seeker implies that the decision maker is prepared to take increased risks to make larger profits.

Safety stock the amount of inventory held in excess of the EOQ to prevent random variations in the level of demand, causing a stockout.

Sample a group of units collected from a larger group (the population).

Sample from a normal population collection of a sample from a normal population.

Sample mean an estimator available for estimating the population mean.

Sample proportion is the ratio of the number elements in the sample to the complete sample size.

Sample space an exhaustive list of all the possible outcomes of an experiment.

Sample standard deviation is a measure of the spread of or dispersion within a set of sample data.

Sample variance is a measure of the spread of or dispersion within a set of sample data.

Sampling distribution the sampling distribution describes probabilities associated with a statistic when a random sample is drawn from a population.

Sampling distribution of the mean distribution of the mean of samples from the population.

Sampling error sampling error refers to the error that results from taking one sample rather than taking a census of the entire population.

Sampling frame a list of every member of the population.

Sampling is without replacement sample item not replaced.

Savage minimax regret the regret of an outcome is the difference between the value of that outcome and the maximum value of all the possible outcomes, in the light of the particular chance event that actually occurred. The decision maker should choose the alternative that minimizes the maximum regret he could suffer.

Scatter plot graph of a set of points (x, y).

Seasonal component one of the components from the classical time series analysis that will define the short-term regularities (less than a year) of the movements of the time series.

Seasonal indices are the values that indicate by how much a time series deviates from the trend in every seasonal period. As the deviation is typically multiplied by 100, the values are called indices.

Seasonal variations variations around the trend line that take place within one year.

Second derivative of y on x the result of differentiating the first derivative (d^2y/dx^2).

Secondary data is data collected by someone other than the user.

Semi-interquartile range half the interquartile range.

Sensitivity the size of a response value to changes of one of the input values.

Sensitivity analysis the study of how changes in the coefficients of a linear programming problem affect the optimal solution.

Sensitivity Report a report obtainable from using Solver indicating the ranges over which solution variables may hold true. For example, the sensitivity values of a linear programme.

Serial correlation same as autocorrelation, i.e. a relationship between a variable and itself over different time intervals. The use 'serial correlation' is mainly used in regression analysis to describe a relationship of errors over different time intervals.

Shadow price is the change in the objective function value that would arise if the constraint level is adjusted by 1 without changing the optimal constraint.

Significance a percentage that indicates if some event is random or a result of some pattern. Most frequently used levels of significance are 1%, 5% and 10%. They are the thresholds indicating the probability beyond which an event or relationship is random (due to chance).

Significance level, α the significance level of a statistical hypothesis test is a fixed probability of wrongly rejecting the null hypothesis, H_0, if it is in fact true.

Sinking fund is a sum apart periodically from the income of a government or a business and allowed to accumulate in order, ultimately, to pay off a debt.

Simple equations equations containing but one unknown quantity, and that quantity only in the first degree.

Simple index is a number that expresses the relative change in price, quantity, or value from one period to another.

Simple interest interest paid on only the initial deposit, but not on interest already earned.

Simple random sample is a basic sampling technique where we select a group of subjects (a sample) for study from a larger group (a population). Each individual is chosen entirely by chance and each member of the population has an equal chance of being included in the sample. Every possible sample of a given size has the same chance of selection; i.e. each member of the population is equally likely to be chosen at any stage in the sampling process.

Simple tables a table consisting of an ordered arrangement of rows and columns that allow data and information to be accessible in a visual form.

Simplex method an algebraic procedure for solving linear programming problems. The simplex method uses elementary row operations to iterate from one basic feasible solution (extreme point) to another until the optimal solution is reached.

Sinking fund (see **future value of an ordinary annuity**) a fund that receives regular payments so that a specified sum is available at some point in the future.

Skewness skewness is defined as asymmetry in the distribution of the data values.

Slack the length of time an activity can be delayed without affecting the project completion time.

Smoothing constant alpha a constant used in exponential smoothing to predict the future values by 'smoothing' or 'discounting' the influence that all the past values in the series have on this future value. The influence decreases exponentially the further in the past we go.

Solver a software package for solving certain types of mathematical models, such as linear programming models.

Spectrum of management decisions explains the three levels of management decision making: operational, tactical, and strategic.

Spread the distance an observation is from the mean.

Square of a number is that number multiplied by itself.

Square root of a number the square root of n ($\sqrt{n}$) is the number that is multiplied by itself to give n.

Standard deviation a measure of the data spread, equal to the square root of variance.

Standard error standard deviation of the actual values around the regression line. Calculated by dividing the error sum of squares (unexplained variations) by the degrees of freedom.

Standard error of the mean (SEM) standard deviation of the sampling error of the mean.

Standard form (or scientific notation) a number written in the form A * 10^n.

Standard normal distribution is a normal distribution with zero mean and unit standard deviation.

Stated limits the lower and upper limits of a class interval.

States of nature the decision maker should develop a decision model with mutually exclusive and exhaustive list of all possible future events.

Statistic a statistic is a quantity that is calculated from a sample of data.

Statistical inference concerns the problem of inferring properties of an unknown distribution from data generated by that distribution.

Statistical process control statistical process control involves using statistical methods to monitor processes.

Stochastic model (or probabilistic) containing uncertainty that is measured by probabilities.

Stockout a situtation in which there is no stock left and output still to be produced.

Straight line graph a plot of y against x for y = 2x + 3 will result in a straight line when the line is plotted through the coordinate points (x, y).

Strategic strategic decisions are the highest level with decisions focusing on general direction and long-term business goals.

Structured structured decisions are the decisions which are made under the established situation.

Student's t distribution is a family of continuous probability distributions that arises when estimating the mean of a normally distributed population in situations where the sample size is small and population standard deviation is unknown.

Student's t test is any statistical hypothesis test in which the test statistic follows a Student's t distribution if the null hypothesis is supported.

Subjective probability a subjective probability describes an individual's personal judgement about how likely a particular event is to occur.

Symmetrical a data set is symmetrical when the data values are distributed in the same way above and below the middle value.

T value a calculated value that will be compared with the critical t-value from study t-distribution to decide if a hypothesis will be accepted or rejected.

Tactical tactical decisions support strategic decisions and tend to be medium range, with medium significance, and with moderate consequences.

Target cell a cell in a worksheet that is to be minimized, maximized or made equal to a defined value by the Solver on the basis of one or more defined changing cells in the same or another linked worksheet. It must always contain a formula that is linked to the changing cells.

Target cell value is the value that the target cell is required to adopt. This can be a maximum, minimum or specified value.

Three data summary the mean, median, and mode are all measures of central tendency since all three provide an understanding of where the majority of the data hang out and tend to centralize.

Time time period of the investment/loan in years.

Time series a set of data points (x, y) where variable x represents the time point.

Total enumeration tracking and evaluating all paths in a project during crashing.

Total float slack time or float time of an activity.

Transportation problem a network flow problem that often involves minimizing the cost of shipping goods from a set of origins to a set of destinations; it can be formulated and solved as a linear programme by including a variable for each arc and a constraint for each node.

Tree diagram is a useful visual aid to help map out alternative outcomes of an experiment and associated probabilities.

Trend either a component in the classical time series, or a generic expression for the general direction and the shape of the time series movements.

Trend component the trend component is the long term movements in the mean.

Triang is often used when the minimum, maximum, and the most likely values are known.

Triangular distribution is a continuous probability distribution with lower limit a, upper limit c and mode b, where $a \le b \le c$.

Trust fund (see **present value of an ordinary annuity**) is an arrangement that allows individuals to create sustained benefits for another individual or entity.

Turning points maxima and minima on a graph.

Two data summary the mean is the most common indicator of central tendency while the standard deviation is a popular and normalized measure of dispersion.

Two sample test is a statistical hypothesis test which uses two samples from the population.

Two-tail tests a two tailed test is a statistical hypothesis test in which the values for which we can reject the null hypothesis, H_0, are located in both tails of the probability distribution.

Type 1 error finding a result statistically significant when in fact it is not.

Type I error, α a type I error occurs when the null hypothesis is rejected when it is in fact true; that is, H_0 is wrongly rejected.

Type 2 error when a survey finds that a result is not significant, though in fact it is.

Type II error, β a type II error occurs when the null hypothesis H_0 is not rejected when it is in fact false.

Typical seasonal index a single value for every seasonal period that represents all corresponding seasonal periods.

UK consumer price index (CPI) the consumer price index is the official measure of inflation of consumer prices of the United Kingdom published monthly by the Office for National Statistics. The CPI calculates the average price increase as a percentage for a basket of 600 different goods and services with the CPI using the geometric mean of prices to aggregate items at the lowest levels, instead of the arithmetic mean as used by the RPI. This means that the CPI will generally be lower than the RPI.

UK retail consumer price index (RPI) is a separate measure of inflation published monthly by the Office for National Statistics. The RPI uses the arithmetic mean and in general will be higher than the CPI.

Unbiased when the mean of the sampling distribution of a statistic is equal to a population parameter, that statistic is said to be an unbiased estimator of the parameter.

Uncertain activity times degree of uncertainty within the completion time for certain activities.

Uncertainty (or strict uncertainty) situation in which we can list possible events for a decision, but cannot give them probabilities.

Unexplained variations also called the Residual (Error) Sum of Squares (SSE). This is the portion of the variations between the actual and modelled data that cannot be explained by the model. Together with SSR, this produces the Total Sum of Squares (SST), or the total variations from the model.

Uniform distribution all values within the range are deemed to have the same constant probability density, where that density changes to zero at the minimum and maximum values.

Unstructured unstructured decisions are the decisions which are made under the emergent situation.

Usage rate the periodic rate at which inventory is used up by the production process.

Utility a measure that shows the real value of money to a decision maker.

Variable a variable is a symbol that can take on any of a specified set of values.

Variance the difference between estimated cost, duration, or effort and the actual result of performance. In addition, it can be the difference between the initial or baseline product scope and the actual product delivered.

Variation a difference between the regression line values and the actual time series values that the regression line approximates.

Venn diagrams a diagram that represents probabilities as circles that may or may not overlap.

Vertex the point or corner of a feasible region where two or more points intersect on the feasible region.

Wald's maximin criterion rule would be used by a conservative (or pessimistic) decision maker to minimize payoff for each decision and then select the maximum of these minimum payoffs.

Weighted index a price index that takes into account both prices and the importance of items.

What-if analysis you can use several different sets of values in one or more formulas to explore all the various results.

Y-intercept point on the y-axis that a linear equation ($y = mx + c$) crosses the $x = 0$ axis.

Zero float a condition where there is no excess time between activities. An activity with zero float is considered a critical activity.

Z-score in statistics, a standard score indicates how many standard deviations an observation is above or below the mean value.

Index

D

E

F

N

Q

R

S

T

U